Infrastructure to 2030

Volume 2

MAPPING POLICY FOR ELECTRICITY, WATER AND TRANSPORT

ORGANISATION FOR ECONOMIC CO-OPERATION AND DEVELOPMENT

ORGANISATION FOR ECONOMIC CO-OPERATION AND DEVELOPMENT

The OECD is a unique forum where the governments of 30 democracies work together to address the economic, social and environmental challenges of globalisation. The OECD is also at the forefront of efforts to understand and to help governments respond to new developments and concerns, such as corporate governance, the information economy and the challenges of an ageing population. The Organisation provides a setting where governments can compare policy experiences, seek answers to common problems, identify good practice and work to co-ordinate domestic and international policies.

The OECD member countries are: Australia, Austria, Belgium, Canada, the Czech Republic, Denmark, Finland, France, Germany, Greece, Hungary, Iceland, Ireland, Italy, Japan, Korea, Luxembourg, Mexico, the Netherlands, New Zealand, Norway, Poland, Portugal, the Slovak Republic, Spain, Sweden, Switzerland, Turkey, the United Kingdom and the United States. The Commission of the European Communities takes part in the work of the OECD.

OECD Publishing disseminates widely the results of the Organisation's statistics gathering and research on economic, social and environmental issues, as well as the conventions, guidelines and standards agreed by its members.

This work is published on the responsibility of the Secretary-General of the OECD. The opinions expressed and arguments employed herein do not necessarily reflect the official views of the Organisation or of the governments of its member countries.

Also available in French under the title:

Les infrastructures à l'horizon 2030

Volume 2

ÉLECTRICITÉ, EAU ET TRANSPORTS : QUELLES POLITIQUES ?

Cover photo credits: Getty Images/Digital Vision (for wastewater treatment plant, electricity pylons, freight train) and Ron Garnett, AirScapes International (for The Confederation Bridge, Canada).

Foreword

This publication is the final report on the two-year OECD Futures Project "Global Infrastructure Needs: Prospects and Implications for Public and Private Actors". It presents the main findings and policy recommendations from the project, as well as expert papers that assess the future viability of current business models in electricity, water, rail, road and urban public transport infrastructure sectors.

Following an extensive international consultation process with government departments and agencies, corporations and research institutes, the global infrastructure needs project was carried out over 2005-07 with the purpose of taking stock of the long-term opportunities and challenges facing infrastructures world wide, and to propose a set of policy recommendations to OECD governments that aim to enhance infrastructures' contribution to economic and social development in the years to come. The project had a time horizon out to 2020-30 and covered electricity, surface transport, water and telecommunications. The focus was on OECD countries, with the so-called BRICs (Brazil, Russian Federation, India, China) included in some of the analysis.

The project was funded by voluntary contributions from governments, public agencies and corporations, who were represented on the Steering Group. The Steering Group advised the OECD Project Team on the content and direction of the project. (The reader will find a list of the Group's members at the end of the book.) Countries represented were Canada, Denmark, France, Mexico, the Netherlands, Norway, Portugal, Spain, Sweden, Switzerland and the United Kingdom. The Steering Group met four times between June 2005 and December 2006. An interim report was published in 2006 as an OECD book under the title Infrastructure to 2030: Telecom, Land Transport, Water and Electricity, *reflecting the findings from the first stages of the project and establishing a broad picture of trends and developments likely to impact on infrastructures and infrastructure investment over the next few decades.*

All the chapters in this volume have benefited from expert advice and comment from the Steering Group. The conclusions and policy recommendations contained here build on a wide range of research, discussions and exchanges of views conducted within the project. These include primarily the papers written by the OECD International Futures Programme Secretariat and outside consultants; materials supplied by participants in the Steering Group and OECD specialists from other Directorates involved in the project; the rich discussions conducted during the Steering Group meetings; and detailed written comments provided by Steering Group members. The recommendations are addressed primarily to policy makers in OECD countries, and also to those in the larger non-OECD economies. However, many of the conclusions and recommendations have implications for decision makers in the private sector.

The project was led by the OECD's International Futures Programme, a forward-looking multidisciplinary unit which provides the OECD Secretary-General and the Organisation with early warning on emerging policy issues. It does this by identifying major developments and analysing key long-term concerns to help governments map strategy. Its role is also to promote horizontal, cross-Directorate themes in the OECD. Hence, the work was conducted in co-operation with several OECD Directorates and Agencies, notably: The European Council of Ministers of Transport (ECMT) and the Joint Transport Research Centre (JTRC); the Environment Directorate; the Directorate for Science, Technology and Industry; the Statistics Directorate; and the International Energy Agency (IEA). The project has benefited substantially from inputs and comments from colleagues in those parts of the house. A list of contributing experts, both in-house and outside, involved in the project appears at the end of the book.

Barrie Stevens directed the work of the authors and the preparation of the two publications in this project. Pierre-Alain Schieb was initiator and co-ordinator of the project. Michael Oborne was Chairman of the project's Steering Group. Anita Gibson, Manon Picard, Emilie Goux and Concetta Miano provided technical support over the course of the project; and Belinda Hopkinson, the editing for this volume.

Our thanks are extended to all those who contributed to the project over the course of the two years.

Paris, June 2007

Table of Contents

List of boxes

List of tables

List of figures

ISBN 978-92-64-03131-9
Infrastructure to 2030 – Vol. 2
Mapping Policy for Electricity, Water and Transport

Executive Summary

Infrastructures are not an end in themselves. Rather, they are a means for ensuring the delivery of goods and services that promote prosperity and growth and contribute to quality of life, including the social well-being, health and safety of citizens, and the quality of their environments. The longer-term future performance of OECD economies, and indeed of the global economy, will depend to an important extent on the availability of adequate infrastructures to sustain growth and social development. Through to 2030, annual infrastructure investment requirements for electricity, road and rail transport, telecommunications and water are likely to average around 3.5% of world gross domestic product (GDP).

A large share of investments will be undertaken in the developing world, where countries such as China, India and Brazil will be spending billions of dollars on infrastructures to underpin their booming economies and satisfy the growing aspirations of their populations.

However, despite their significantly lower economic growth rates over the next few decades, OECD countries too will be required to invest heavily to maintain, upgrade or replace existing (and often ageing) infrastructures, and to preserve their international competitiveness. For OECD countries as a whole, investment requirements in electricity transmission and distribution are expected to more than double through to 2025/30, in road construction almost to double, and to increase by almost 50% in the water supply and treatment sector.

The purpose of the OECD International Futures Programme project on "Global Infrastructure Needs: Prospects and Implications for Public and Private Actors" was to take stock of the long-term opportunities and challenges facing infrastructures world wide and to propose a set of policy recommendations to OECD governments that aim to enhance infrastructures' contribution to economic and social development in the years to come. The project had a time horizon to 2020-30 and covered electricity, surface transport (road, rail and urban public transport), water and telecommunications.

Infrastructure investment gap

In OECD countries, traditional sources of public finance alone will not suffice to meet future infrastructure needs, which are huge and growing. This book addresses key questions:

- Where will new sources of finance come from and what role will the private sector play?
- Will the financial, organisational, institutional and regulatory arrangements (the "business models") currently in place be able to respond adequately to the complex challenges they face, and are they sustainable over the longer term?

Bridging the infrastructure investment gap will demand innovative approaches, both to finding additional finance, and to using infrastructures more efficiently and more intelligently through new technologies, demand management strategies, regulatory changes and improved planning.

Long-term challenges

In particular for OECD countries, infrastructure investment will be challenged by a range of fundamental long-term trends. These include:

- Demographic developments – ageing populations, population growth or decline, urbanisation trends, and population movements to rural and coastal areas.
- Increasing constraints on public finances due to ageing populations, security concerns, etc.
- Environmental factors, such as climate change and rising quality standards.
- Technological progress especially, but not only, in information and communication technology.
- Trends towards decentralisation, and growing local public involvement.
- The expanding role of the private sector.
- The growing importance of maintenance, upgrading and rehabilitation of existing infrastructures.

At present, governments are not well placed to meet these growing, increasingly complex challenges. The traditional sources of finance, *i.e.* government budgets, will come under significant pressure over the coming decades in most OECD countries – due to ageing populations, growing demands for social expenditures, security, etc. – and so too will their financing through general and local taxation, as electorates become increasingly reluctant to pay higher taxes. Moreover, looking across the full range of economic, social and environmental forces affecting the infrastructure sectors addressed in this project, nowhere does the current public policy, regulatory and planning framework appear adequate to tackle the multiple challenges facing infrastructure development over the next 25 years.

Failure to make significant progress towards bridging the infrastructure gap could prove costly in terms of congestion, unreliable supply lines, blunted competitiveness, and growing environmental problems, with all the implications for living standards and quality of life.

Infrastructures will also need to work more efficiently. Ways of squeezing more efficiencies out of the system include investment in new technologies, and demand management strategies to better control traffic flows through road, rail, electricity and water systems. In the BRICs and most developing countries, by contrast, the lion's share of investment is likely to go on new construction as governments strive to expand inadequate networks.

Where will the financing come from?

Looking across the globe, a not insignificant part of infrastructure is already in private hands. This is especially true of telecommunications and, to a lesser degree, of power generation and railways; and it is to be expected that private money will continue to flow to these activities. More problematic is the area of publicly owned and operated infrastructures, because it is here that pressures on budgets and tax-raising capacity are already starting to be felt.

Evidence suggests that in the advanced countries, public capital investment has accounted for a steadily declining proportion of total government expenditure. For the OECD area as a whole, government spending on gross fixed capital formation as a share of total general government outlays fell from 9.5% in 1990 through 8% in the mid-1990s, to approximately 7% in 2005.

At the same time, social expenditures have increased their share noticeably. Between 1980 and 2003, they rose on average from about 16% to 21% of GDP. The two key drivers of increases in social spending have been expenditures on health and on the retired population. Both are expected to expand considerably in the coming decades, outpacing the growth of government budgets and that of GDP by a substantial margin. Projections suggest that for the OECD area as a whole, spending on public health and long-term care could increase from the current level of 6.7% of GDP to between 10.1% and 12.8% by 2050, while pensions could rise on average by around three to four percentage points of GDP over the same period.

These mounting pressures will probably only be offset in small part by lower spending on education for the young, and child or family benefits. Moreover, scarcer labour is expected to put pressure on governments to increase investment in all forms of education, including lifelong learning. Accordingly, the scope for public investment in infrastructure within government budgets will be increasingly constrained.

What are the options for the public sector to bridge the infrastructure gap?

Despite growing pressures on public budgets, general and local taxes will continue to provide the single most important source of financing in many cases. However, in most OECD countries and some BRICs, ageing populations are likely to lead to shrinking wage bills, thereby reducing tax receipts. To some extent, the severity of the effect will depend on such factors as the evolution of labour market participation rates, immigration, productivity, and the balance between consumption-based and income-based tax revenues. Some compensation may be forthcoming in the guise of increased tax receipts from accumulated pension assets, but the offset effect is likely to be limited to generally no more than one percentage point of GDP.

In other words, public budgets fed by taxes will not suffice to bridge the infrastructure gap. What is required is greater recourse to private sector finance, together with greater diversification of public sector revenue sources.

Private sector finance, as noted above, has traditionally had a strong presence in some infrastructure sectors in some countries. In recent years, as the share of government investment in infrastructures has declined, that of the private sector has increased. Privatisations (*i.e.* the sale of state-owned assets) have been an important driver. Since the 1980s more than USD 1 trillion of assets has been privatised in OECD countries. Infrastructures have consistently been on centre stage. Averaged out over the 1990-2006 period, almost two-thirds of all privatisations in the OECD area have concerned utilities, transport, telecommunications and oil facilities.

Elsewhere, too, privatisation activity has been vigorous. Over roughly the same period, some USD 400 billion of state-owned assets were sold in non-OECD countries, of which about half were accounted for by infrastructures.

New business models with private sector participation, notably variants of public-private partnership models (PPPs) that are being increasingly used particularly in OECD countries, offer further scope for unlocking private sector capital and expertise. So too do the huge pools of private sector capital managed by pension funds and insurance companies. Infrastructures, with their low-risk and steady-return profile, are of considerable potential interest to such funds. Alone in the OECD area, pension funds today amount to some USD 18 trillion, up from USD 13 trillion in 2001.

Diversifying the sources of public sector finance includes:

- Making more and better use of user fees.
- Creating mechanisms for securing long-term financing for infrastructures (*e.g.* long-term infrastructure funds).
- Exploring the possibilities offered by land value capture.
- Promoting innovative variations on traditional financing mechanisms.

Expanding access to additional private and public sector sources of finance will make a significant contribution to bridging the infrastructure gap. However, it will not suffice on its own. The challenges facing governments are simply too diverse and complex. In the coming years, policy makers will in addition need to:

- Improve efficiency in the construction and operation of infrastructures.
- Increase efficiency levels in the use of infrastructures through better management of demand.
- Ensure infrastructures are reliable and resilient.
- Enhance the design and capacity of infrastructures to meet future environmental and security challenges.
- Strengthen life-cycle management of infrastructure assets as the focus of investment turns increasingly to maintenance, upgrading and refurbishment of existing facilities and networks.
- Raise the effectiveness of infrastructure development both in meeting multiple objectives – economic, social, environmental, etc. – and in allocating resources to create maximum value.

In rising to meet these challenges, governments will need to complement the search for fresh sources of capital with a wide array of other measures. These must include *inter alia*: regulatory changes to encourage the emergence of new business models and the development and integration of new technologies; the promotion of more competition in procurement and operation; legal and administrative changes to speed up planning, procurement and implementation; application of new technologies and new schemes to enhance efficient use of infrastructures and better manage demand; closer international co-operation; improved security; and the underpinning of infrastructure design, financing and funding with long-term strategic planning.

Finally, the planning, financing and management of infrastructures will need to be supported by better basic tools. Information, data collection, research and analysis need strengthening. Accounting for improved asset management should be used more widely, as should rigorous evaluation methods for stronger evidence-based policy making. Greater use can be made of online tools for communication and dialogue. And there is ample scope in education and training institutions for greater efforts to develop the interdisciplinary skills and knowledge that will be required to tackle the opportunities and problems raised by infrastructures in the years ahead.

ISBN 978-92-64-03131-9
Infrastructure to 2030 – Vol. 2
Mapping Policy for Electricity, Water and Transport

Chapter 1

Infrastructure to 2030: Main Findings and Policy Recommendations

by

Barrie Stevens *and* Pierre-Alain Schieb*

The longer-term future performance of OECD economies, and of the global economy, will depend to an important extent on the availability of adequate infrastructures to sustain growth and social development. This is a huge challenge for governments and businesses around the globe. Traditional sources of public finance alone will not suffice to meet future infrastructure investment needs. Where will the financing come from? What can governments do to respond to the complex challenges they face? The OECD International Futures Programme completed a two-year project on "Global Infrastructure Needs: Prospects and Implications for Public and Private Actors" which took stock of the challenges and opportunities facing OECD countries and some of the larger developing countries to 2030 in electricity, water, surface transport (rail freight and road), and telecommunications. The main findings and policy recommendations from this project are presented, along with case studies.

* Barrie Stevens is Deputy Director and Pierre-Alain Schieb is Counsellor and Head of Futures Projects at the OECD International Futures Programme (IFP). The IFP is part of the OECD Advisory Unit on Multidisciplinary Issues to the Secretary-General.

1. Introduction and overview of the main findings and policy recommendations

Building on the analysis and findings of the work conducted throughout the duration of the OECD project on global infrastructure needs to 2030, this chapter is intended to provide OECD governments, but also decision makers elsewhere in the public and private sectors, with recommendations about what steps should be taken to improve the capacity for meeting future infrastructure needs, including measures that could be taken by governments collectively and individually to create a more favourable policy and regulatory framework.

The central message of this chapter is that a gap is opening up in OECD countries between the infrastructure investments required for the future, and the capacity of the public sector to meet those requirements from traditional sources. Bridging the gap will demand innovative approaches, both to finding additional finance, and to using infrastructures more efficiently and more intelligently through new technologies, demand management strategies, regulatory changes and improved planning.

Infrastructures are not an end in themselves. Rather, they are a means for ensuring the delivery of goods and services that promote prosperity and growth and contribute to quality of life, including the social well-being, health and safety of citizens, and the quality of their environments. In the past, infrastructures have provided significant social and economic benefits. Looking to the future, they will continue to play a vital role in economic and social development, not least because the networked economy is becoming increasingly important, and society ever more dependent on the smooth running of a growing range of infrastructure services. Moreover, the various infrastructure systems themselves are interacting ever more closely with one another, engendering interdependencies and complementarities, as well as heightened vulnerability, and thereby posing new policy challenges such as interoperability and reliability.

The infrastructure requirements of OECD countries and the larger non-OECD countries, such as China, India and Brazil, are growing. To a large extent, this has to do with economic growth and the drive for improved economic performance and competitiveness. Central projections for the next two decades or so suggest that the world economy is set to grow on average at close to 3% per annum to 2030, with developing countries' performance outstripping that of the developed countries by a wide margin (4% per annum *versus* 2.4% per annum) (World Bank, 2007). The two-way street – along which economic growth encourages demand for infrastructure, and infrastructure generates economic growth – is set to get much busier in the years to come. Moreover, globalisation and the emergence of new markets and new players are helping lengthen supply chains and exacerbate congestion around key ports, airports and transit corridors.

However, infrastructure needs will also be shaped by an array of other factors. These include:

- Demographic developments – ageing populations, population growth or decline, urbanisation trends, and population movements to rural and coastal areas.
- Increasing constraints on public finances due to ageing populations, security concerns, etc.
- Environmental factors, such as climate change and rising quality standards.
- Technological progress especially, but not only, in information and communication technology.
- Trends towards decentralisation, and growing local public involvement.
- The expanding role of the private sector.
- The growing importance of maintenance, upgrading and rehabilitation of existing infrastructures.

At present, governments are not well placed to meet these growing, increasingly complex infrastructure needs. The traditional sources of finance, *i.e.* government budgets, will come under significant pressure over the coming decades in most OECD countries – due to ageing populations, growing demands for social expenditures, security, etc. – and so too will their financing through general and local taxation, as electorates become increasingly reluctant to pay higher taxes. Moreover, looking across the full range of economic, social and environmental forces affecting the infrastructure sectors addressed in this project,[1] nowhere does the current public policy, regulatory and planning framework appear adequate to tackle the multiple challenges facing infrastructure development over the next 25 years.

Failure to make significant progress towards bridging the infrastructure gap could prove costly in terms of congestion, unreliable supply lines, blunted competitiveness, and growing environmental problems, with all the implications for living standards and quality of life.

What orders of magnitude of infrastructure investment are likely to be needed through to 2030? Rough estimates from the OECD Infrastructure Project suggest that annual investment requirements for telecommunications, road, rail, electricity (transmission and distribution) and water taken together are likely to total around an average of 2.5% of world GDP. If electricity generation and other energy-related infrastructure investments in oil, gas and coal are included (as the

IEA does in its *Investment Outlook*), the annual share rises to around 3.5%.[2] Clearly, the figure would rise further if one were to include other infrastructures not covered by this project, *e.g.* ports, airports and storage facilities.

How are these investments likely to be allocated? Globally, a large share will be used for new additional infrastructure, but much will also be accounted for by maintenance, replacement and upgrading. The shares vary across regions. In OECD countries, infrastructure networks and systems are, broadly speaking, in place, and the scope for adding new infrastructure is limited. Consequently, a larger effort will need to be directed towards maintenance and upgrading of existing infrastructures and to getting infrastructures. For OECD countries as a whole, investment requirements in electricity transmission and distribution are expected to more than double through to 2025/30, in road construction almost to double, and to increase by almost 50% in the water supply and treatment sector. Rail infrastructure requirements are likely to increase by one-third by 2020 (see Figure 1.1).

Infrastructures will also need to work more efficiently. Ways of squeezing more efficiencies out of the system include investment in new technologies, and demand management strategies to better control traffic flows through road, rail, electricity and water systems. In the BRICs and most developing countries, by contrast, the lion's share of investment is likely to go on new construction as governments strive to expand inadequate networks.

Where will the financing come from? Looking across the globe, a not insignificant part of infrastructure is already in private hands – this is especially true of telecommunications and, to a lesser degree, of power generation and railways – and it is to be expected that private money will continue to flow to these activities. More problematic is the area of publicly owned and operated infrastructures, because it is here that pressures on budgets and tax-raising capacity are already starting to be felt.

Evidence suggests that in the advanced countries, public capital investment has accounted for a steadily declining proportion of total government expenditure. As Figure 1.2 shows, for the OECD area as a whole, government spending on gross fixed capital formation as a share of total general government outlays fell from 9.5% in 1990 through 8% in the mid-1990s, to approximately 7% in 2005.

At the same time, social expenditures have increased their share noticeably. Between 1980 and 2003, they rose on average from about 16% to 21% of GDP. Experiences differ across OECD countries, but on average public spending-to-GDP ratios increased most significantly in the early 1980s, and then again in the beginning of the millennium when average ratios rose by 1% of GDP between 2000 and 2003.

The two key drivers of increases in social spending have been expenditures on health and on the retired population.[3] Both are expected to expand

Figure 1.1. **Average annual infrastructure investment requirements in OECD countries to 2025/30**

In billions USD

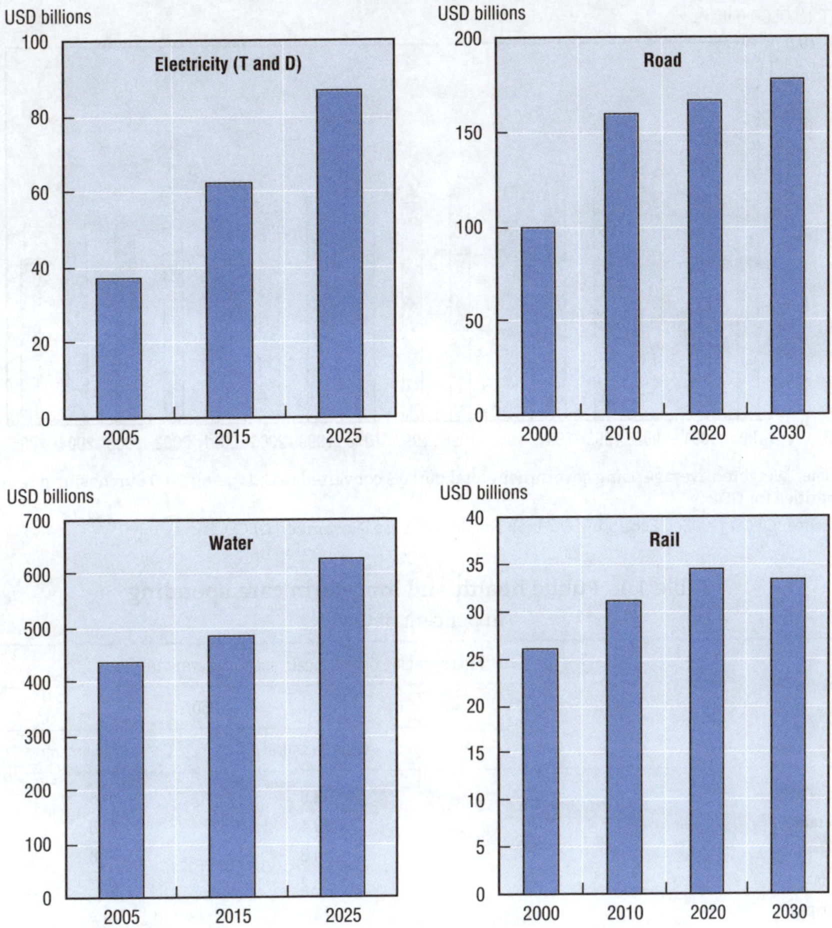

Note: Estimates for electricity are transmission and distribution (T&D) only.

Source: OECD (2006a), *Infrastructure to 2030: Telecom, Land Transport, Water and Electricity*, OECD, Paris; estimates drawn from data in Table 3.6 (electricity), p. 167; Table 4.5 (road), p. 195; Table 4.6 (rail), p. 199; Table 5.16 (water), pp. 313-314.

considerably in the coming decades, outpacing the growth of government budgets and that of GDP by a substantial margin. Projections in Table 1.1 suggest that for the OECD area as a whole, spending on public health and long-term care could increase from the current level of 6.7% of GDP to between 10.1% and 12.8% by 2050, while pensions could rise on average by around 3 to 4 percentage points of GDP over the same period.[4]

These mounting pressures will probably only be offset in small part by lower spending on education for the young, and child or family benefits. Moreover,

Figure 1.2. **General government gross fixed capital formation (GFCF), as percentage of total government outlays, 1990-2005**

Average for all OECD countries

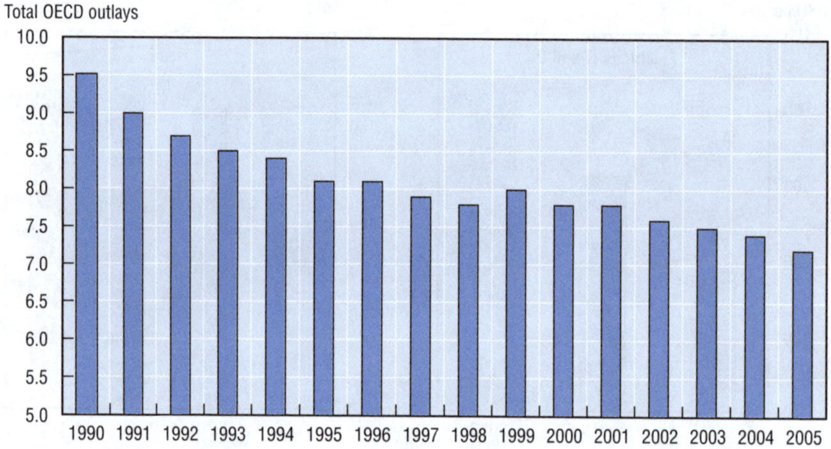

Note: Weighted average using government total outlays converted to USD using 2000 purchasing power parities for GDP.

Source: OECD (2006c), Economic Outlook No. 80 database, November, OECD, Paris.

Table 1.1. **Public health and long-term care spending**

In per cent of GDP

	Total spending on healthcare and long-term care		
	2005	2050	
		Cost-pressure[1]	Cost-containment[2]
Canada	7.3	13.5	10.8
France	8.1	13.4	10.8
Germany	8.8	14.3	11.8
Italy	6.6	13.2	10.7
Japan	6.9	13.4	10.9
United Kingdom	6.1	12.7	10.0
United States	6.3	12.4	9.7
OECD average	**6.7**	**12.8**	**10.1**

1. The "cost pressure" scenario assumes no policy action.
2. The "cost-containment scenario" embodies the assumed effects of policies curbing expenditure growth.

Source: OECD (2006d), *Projecting OECD Health and Long-Term Care Expenditures: What Are the Main Drivers?*, Economics Department Working Papers, No. 477, ECO/WKP(2006)5, OECD, Paris.

scarcer labour is expected to put pressure on governments to increase investment in all forms of education, including lifelong learning.[5] Accordingly, the scope for public investment in infrastructure within government budgets will be increasingly constrained.

What are the options for the public sector to bridge the infrastructure gap? Despite growing pressures on public budgets, general and local taxes will continue to provide the single most important source of financing in many cases. However, in most OECD countries and some BRICs, ageing populations are likely to lead to shrinking wage bills, thereby reducing tax receipts. To some extent, the severity of the effect will depend on such factors as the evolution of labour market participation rates, immigration, productivity, and the balance between consumption-based and income-based tax revenues. Some compensation may be forthcoming in the guise of increased tax receipts from accumulated pension assets, but the offset effect is likely to be limited to generally no more than one percentage point of GDP.[6]

In other words, public budgets fed by taxes will not suffice to bridge the infrastructure gap. What is required is greater recourse to private sector finance, together with greater diversification of public sector revenue sources.

Private sector finance, as noted above, has traditionally had a strong presence in some infrastructure sectors in some countries. In recent years, as the share of government investment in infrastructures has declined, that of the private sector has increased. Privatisations (*i.e.* the sale of state-owned assets) have been an important driver. Since the 1980s more than USD 1 trillion of assets have been privatised in OECD countries. Infrastructures have consistently been on centre stage. Averaged out over the 1990-2006 period, almost two-thirds of all privatisations in the OECD area have concerned utilities, transport, telecommunications and oil facilities (see Figure 1.3).

Elsewhere, too, privatisation activity has been vigorous. Over roughly the same period, some USD 400 billion of state-owned assets were sold in non-OECD countries, of which about half were accounted for by infrastructures.

Figure 1.3. **Value of privatisation infrastructure transactions, 1990-2006**

As a percentage of the total value of privatisation transactions

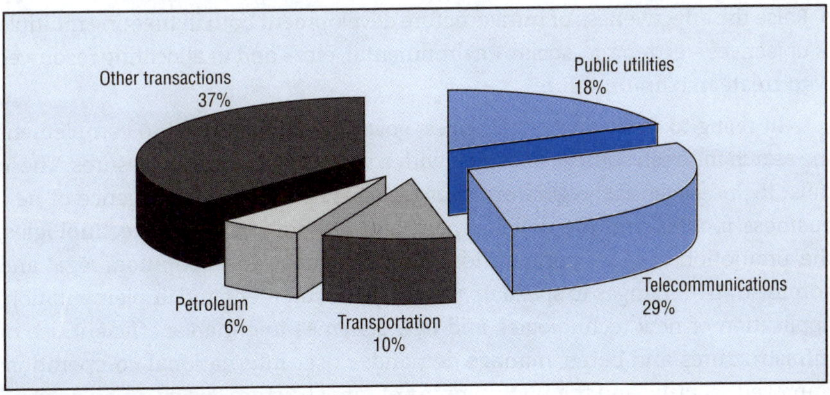

Source: OECD (2002), *Financial Market Trends*, No. 82, June, OECD, Paris; and The Privatization Barometer, *www.privatizationbarometer.net*.

New business models with private sector participation, notably variants of public-private partnership models (PPPs) that are being increasingly used particularly in OECD countries, offer further scope for unlocking private sector capital and expertise. So too do the huge pools of private sector capital managed by pension funds and insurance companies. Infrastructures, with their low-risk and steady-return profile, are of considerable potential interest to such funds. Alone in the OECD area, pension funds today amount to some USD 18 trillion, up from USD 13 trillion in 2001.

Diversifying the sources of public sector finance includes making more and better use of user fees, creating mechanisms for securing long-term financing for infrastructures (*e.g.* long-term infrastructure funds), exploring the possibilities offered by land value capture, and promoting innovative variations on traditional financing mechanisms.

Expanding access to additional private and public sector sources of finance will make a significant contribution to bridging the infrastructure gap. However, it will not suffice on its own. The challenges facing governments are simply too diverse and complex. In the coming years, policy makers will in addition need to:

- Improve efficiency in the construction and operation of infrastructures.
- Increase efficiency levels in the use of infrastructures through better management of demand.
- Ensure infrastructures are reliable and resilient.
- Enhance the design and capacity of infrastructures to meet future environmental and security challenges.
- Strengthen life-cycle management of infrastructure assets as the focus of investment turns increasingly to maintenance, upgrading and refurbishment of existing facilities and networks.
- Raise the effectiveness of infrastructure development both in meeting multiple objectives – economic, social, environmental, etc. – and in allocating resources to create maximum value.

In rising to meet these challenges, governments will need to complement the search for fresh sources of capital with a wide array of other measures. These must include *inter alia*: regulatory changes to encourage the emergence of new business models and the development and integration of new technologies; the promotion of more competition in procurement and operation; legal and administrative changes to speed up planning, procurement and implementation; application of new technologies and new schemes to enhance efficient use of infrastructures and better manage demand; closer international co-operation; improved security; and the underpinning of infrastructure design, financing and funding with long-term strategic planning.

Finally, the planning, financing and management of infrastructures will need to be supported by better basic tools. Information, data collection, research and analysis need strengthening. Accounting for improved asset management should be used more widely, as should rigorous evaluation methods for stronger evidence-based policy making. Greater use can be made of online tools for communication and dialogue. And there is ample scope in education and training institutions for greater efforts to develop the interdisciplinary skills and knowledge that will be required to tackle the opportunities and problems raised by infrastructures in the years ahead.

2. The principal policy recommendations in brief

Emerging from research, discussions and exchanges of views conducted during the two-year Infrastructure to 2030 Project, seventeen policy recommendations to enhance governments' capacity to meet future infrastructure needs have been developed. Box 1.1 presents these policy

Box 1.1. The principal policy recommendations in brief

1. Innovative approaches to finance

1. Encourage public-private partnerships (PPPs) as a means of raising additional financing for infrastructure investment and diversifying business models.
2. Encourage the investment of pension funds and other large institutional investors in infrastructures.
3. Make greater use of user charges for funding infrastructures. They should be designed to signal prices, reflect real costs and contribute to demand management.
4. Diversify and expand traditional revenue-raising sources.
5. Explore the funding possibilities offered by land value capture.

2. Improving the regulatory and institutional framework conditions

6. Examine the legal and regulatory framework conditions with a view to encouraging the emergence of fresh sources of capital and new business models for the construction, maintenance and operation of infrastructures.
7. Encourage the emergence of new players and new business models through the creation and promotion of frameworks that stimulate the development of effective competition either in or for the market.
8. Place greater emphasis on the issue of reliability of infrastructure functioning.
9. Strengthen the framework for standards, as a tool both for encouraging new operational models and for improving interoperability.
10. Explore the potential for new institutional arrangements that may provide more effective and efficient financing, funding and/or delivery of infrastructure.

Box 1.1. **The principal policy recommendations in brief** *(cont.)*

3. Strengthening governance and strategic planning

11. Support the development of long-term, co-ordinated approaches to infrastructure development.
12. Reduce the vulnerability of long-term infrastructure planning and implementation to short-term thinking and priority setting.
13. Ensure the involvement of a broader range of stakeholders in the process of needs assessment, prioritisation, design, planning and delivery of infrastructures.
14. Step up efforts to reduce the length and complexity of the planning-to-implementation process.
15. Strengthen international co-operation to improve the efficiency, reliability and security of flows of goods, services and information across transborder infrastructures.

4. Developing and integrating technology

16. Support the use of technologies both to improve efficiency in infrastructure and to enhance demand management.

5. Expanding and improving the toolkit

17. Strengthen public capacity to inform decision making, improve analysis, monitor performance, and develop the requisite interdisciplinary skills to address infrastructure issues.

recommendations in a summary fashion. Each of the recommendations is developed fully in the next section.

3. The policy recommendations in detail

The recommendations have been grouped together under five headings that emphasise the cross-sectoral, integrative approach of the Infrastructure to 2030 Project: 1) Innovative approaches to finance; 2) Improving the regulatory and institutional framework; 3) Strengthening governance and strategic planning; 4) Developing and integrating technology; and 5) Expanding and improving the toolkit. Each principal recommendation has three or four component parts: an explanation of the broader context of the recommendation and why the recommendation is being made; a section setting out as concretely as possible how the recommendation might be implemented; and examples and best practice illustrations from a range of OECD and non-OECD countries.

3.1. *Innovative approaches to finance*

Governments have an essential role to play in the provision of infrastructures, and public budgets are a major – indeed, often the principal – source of finance. But as the introduction to these policy recommendations has made clear, the challenges facing the development of infrastructures over the next couple of decades are considerable. Future infrastructure requirements are massive even in OECD countries, where much of the investment will be needed in maintenance and upgrading, and also in replacement, as many infrastructure systems approach the costly stages of their life-cycle and some component parts reach the end of their serviceable life. Pressures will increase with globalisation, economic growth, changing urban settlement patterns, and increasing environmental and security burdens. Traditional sources for financing (*i.e.* providing the upfront capital) and funding (repaying or recovering the initial capital cost) infrastructures are through debt, public budgets and national and local taxes; but these will all come under mounting strain as competition for limited public resources increases as a result of such trends as ageing populations, and growing security and environmental concerns. Similarly, traditional delivery of infrastructure and related services though the public sector is challenged with more and more difficulties in the face of rapid social, economic, political and technical changes identified elsewhere in this chapter. The search is on for greater diversity and much needed innovation in all these fields.

For both diversity and innovation, it is essential to look across regional and national borders to benefit from experience elsewhere with different techniques and approaches applied to different areas of infrastructure. In so doing, it is important to realise that there is virtually nothing truly new in the world in terms of financing, funding or provision of infrastructures – innovation is very much a relative concept. What is a traditional way of doing things in one country may be a highly innovative approach for another country, and *vice versa*. The temporal dimension is also important: what was an innovation ten years ago may now have become traditional.

The work conducted in this project suggests that there are two main avenues to be explored in the search for additional, more innovative sources of finance. One is engaging the private sector through such channels as contracting out, partial or full privatisation, and encouraging investments by pension funds and insurance companies. However, much if not most infrastructure is likely to remain in public hands, and public budgets will continue to play an essential role. Hence, the other avenue that has to be explored is that of diversifying and expanding the public sector's traditional sources of revenue.

Engaging the private sector

The private sector is already heavily involved in the provision and operation of infrastructure, either for historical reasons (*e.g.* railways and power generation in the US) or following the wave of privatisations that has swept mainly the industrialised countries of the world over the last 25 years or so. In OECD countries alone, some USD 1 trillion of state-owned assets have been sold in recent decades. Out of total privatisations of around USD 900 billion since 1990, more than 550 billion (63%) have been accounted for by infrastructures, notably utilities, transport and telecommunications.[7] (During the same period, over USD 400 billion of state-owned assets were privatised in developing countries, of which 50% were infrastructures.)

Potentially, considerable scope remains for further privatisations of existing state-owned assets. For example, even in the US with its already large share of privately owned infrastructures, it is estimated that around USD 3 trillion of infrastructures (transportation, power, highways and streets) are in public hands (Löwik and Hobbs, 2006). Despite significant privatisations in past years, in 2005 the French state still had listed companies worth around EUR 45 billion in its portfolio, and non-listed companies (railways, post office network, etc.) in the region of EUR 100 billion.[8] And Germany is currently gearing up for further sales of state-owned businesses, notably with the planned partial floatation of Deutsche Bahn shares, which is expected to generate about EUR 7 billion. In non-OECD countries, too, significant infrastructure assets remain in public ownership.

The extent to which privatisation potential will actually translate into asset sales will of course depend on a number of factors, for example, political developments, general economic conditions, the appetite of the general public for share offerings, and not least the level of maturity of the market for infrastructure.

But it will also depend importantly on the willingness and capacity of institutional investors, such as pension funds and insurance companies, to invest their very considerable resources in infrastructures. Moreover, with respect to new infrastructure and maintenance and upgrading of existing infrastructures, it will be crucial to tap into the vast capital and expertise of the private sector through various forms of public-private partnerships. Both of these – PPPs and institutional funds – offer substantial scope for expanding the financial resources available for investment in infrastructures.

The main function of the state is to conceive the development of infrastructures and related services, and to ensure they are effectively and efficiently provided to users. This does not necessarily imply that government should itself develop the infrastructure and deliver the service. But it does need to assume its responsibilities in making trade-offs among various policy objectives; defining the policy and regulatory environment for the construction

Recommendation 1: Encourage public-private partnerships (PPPs) as a means of raising additional finance for infrastructure investment and diversifying business models.

and operation of the facility; preserving social justice; making certain the process is transparent; and, last but not least, ensuring that decisions on the financing of the project are founded on criteria of affordability and efficiency, so that ultimately it increases the benefits to society for the same or less money. In this context, greater private sector participation in infrastructure is not a retreat of the state but rather a redefinition of its role.

The involvement of the private sector in the building, operation and maintenance of infrastructures can take on many different forms – from the more traditional procurement process and concessions to more complex partnership arrangements in which the different segments of the process (design, planning, finance, construction, operation, maintenance) are redistributed between the public and private parties involved.

Unlike the term itself, public-private partnerships have existed for decades in some OECD countries, generally in the form of risk-sharing concession structures. In recent years, they have taken on increasingly diverse forms. For reasons of history as well as public policy, public-private partnerships are more widely developed in some countries than in others. The UK, Ireland, Spain, Portugal, the Netherlands, some of the Nordic countries and Australia have perhaps acquired the most extensive experience with PPPs, and interest is picking up significantly in Canada, France and a number of other countries. This suggests that there is further scope for development of PPPs across the OECD area (see Figure 1.4).

PPPs appear to be best suited to larger projects where access can be controlled. Hence, successful ventures of this kind are mainly to be found in the provision of urban public transport, water systems, toll motorways, and so on. In addition to providing fresh sources of capital and expertise, PPPs strengthen focus on core competence. In countries with considerable experience with various forms of public-private partnerships, it has been found that PPPs generally lead to a reduction of construction costs, faster delivery of the infrastructure, and lower operating costs. The British experience is a case in point. (See Box 1.2.)

However, the primary benefit of PPPs flows from their capacity for ensuring that the many different risks inherent in major infrastructure projects are borne by the parties best suited to handle those risks. This in turn

Figure 1.4. **Variations in infrastructure market maturity across global markets**

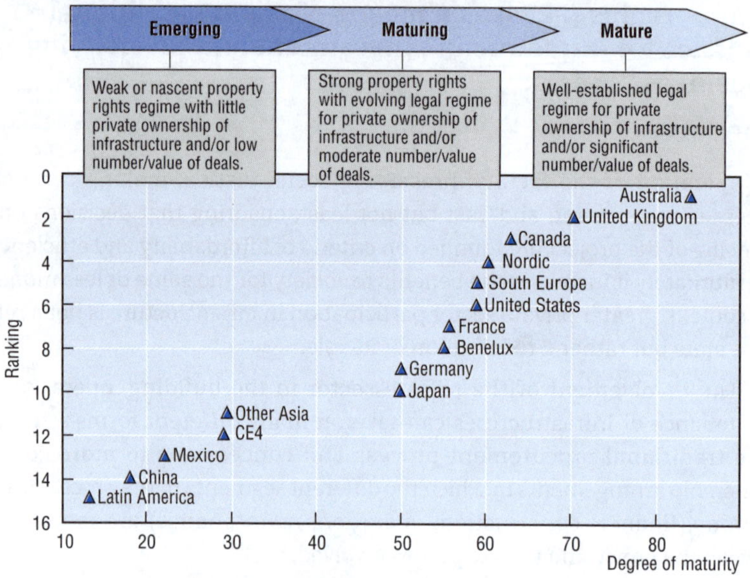

Note: This figure, developed by RREEF Infrastructure, ranks countries by maturity based on country risk (including legal and regulatory risk along with political, economical and financial risk) together with the value of completed deals in the last 24 months as a percentage of GDP (reflecting a country's experience with private involvement in infrastructure projects). CE4 are Poland, Hungary, the Czech Republic and the Slovak Republic.

Source: Löwik and Hobbs (2006) of RREEF Infrastructure, using data and analysis from IMF (April 2006), Thomson Financial (11 April 2006), Euromoney (March 2006).

creates the appropriate disciplines and incentives for the private sector, so that value for money is generated through more effective risk management. Risks that the government typically transfers to the private sector through such vehicles are: meeting required standards of delivery; cost overruns during construction; timely completion of the facility; risk of industrial action; and certain market risks. These risks can, in turn, be reallocated among the different private sector parties best placed to manage them. The risks usually retained by the public sector are: whether the facility or service meets public demand and expectations; the possibility of a change in public sector requirements in the future; and general inflation risk.[9]

Also, PPPs allow more competition to be introduced into the public sector, a competitive environment generally being more beneficial to innovation in infrastructure design, construction and facility management when compared with the public sector. Finally, PPP arrangements can be used to encourage a life-cycle approach to planning and budgeting through the use of long-term contracts that embrace maintenance costs, asset replacement costs and asset management plans.

Box 1.2. **The British experience with PFI**

Since the mid-1990s, the UK has had extensive experience with the use of Private Finance Initiative (PFI) as a form of procurement for the delivery of a broad range of public services. More than 500 PFI projects are currently operational. The departments most active in this regard (in terms of total capital investment in PFI projects) include the Department of Health (GBP 6 billion), the Department of Education and Skills (GBP 4.1 billion), the Department of Transport (GBP 4.7 billion) and the Ministry of Defence (GBP 4.5 billion).

The choice between PFI and other forms of procurement is made only on the basis of value for money. The value-for-money benefits of PFI flow from the long-term focus it brings on whole-life costs, the private sector's risk management expertise incentivised by having private finance at risk, and the certainty for public services it provides of specified outputs being delivered at the cost contracted for.

On the basis of the experience acquired to date, the UK government sees PFI continuing to play a small but important role in the overall objective of delivering modernised public services. Its use is likely to continue to comprise around 10-15% of total investment in public services. The total PFI deal pipeline over the next five years is around 200 projects worth GBP 26 billion in capital value, one of the largest comparable programmes in the world.

The evaluation of the more than 500 operational projects conducted so far confirms the benefits of PFI. This research concludes that:

- Users are satisfied with the services provided by PFI projects, with 79% of projects reporting that service standards are delivered always or almost always.
- Public authorities are reporting good overall performance and high levels of satisfaction against the contracted levels of service. Authorities report that the overall performance of 96% of projects is at least satisfactory, and that in 89% of projects, services are being provided in line with the contract or better.
- The services contracted for are appropriate, with 83% of projects reporting that their contracts always or almost always accurately specify the services required, with this result getting better the more recent the contract.
- The incentivisation within PFI contracts is working. While payment deductions have been low reflecting the general levels of high performance, almost all projects report satisfactory levels of service after a deduction has been applied, and 72% report good or very good performance.

The evaluation also suggests that improvements can be made to strengthen PFI further. This includes efforts to reform the assessment of value for money, improve delivery in PFI procurement and ensure efficiency and flexibility in private finance. The HM Treasury report released in March 2006 documents the measures the government is taking to support authorities in getting consistent high performance from the operational phase of their projects, bolster public sector PFI procurement professionalism, and make sure authorities understand the long-term trade-offs about flexibility and value for money when designing projects.

Source: HM Treasury (2006), *PFI: Strengthening Long-term Partnerships*, March, HM Treasury, London.

Among the potential stumbling blocks to the successful implementation of PPPs is, first, that the cost of capital to the private sector may be higher than to the public sector. However, this is often offset by lower overall project costs and the greater probability that the facility will be completed within the agreed budgetary and time limits. In addition, the contractual arrangements may prove extremely complex, leading some governments to reject PPP projects under a certain size because of the high transaction costs involved. Finally, PPPs are not well suited to all types of infrastructure, notably information technology (IT) ventures. They would appear to be most suitable when applied to transportation, water and sewerage, urban regeneration, and projects with high annual maintenance costs. Recent examples of successful PPPs are the Confederation Bridge in Canada (see Box 1.3), and the Millau Viaduct in France.

The Millau Viaduct in France, which opened in 2006, is the tallest bridge in the world. It offers the fastest and cheapest link from Paris to the Mediterranean. All the risks (construction, financing, operation, maintenance, ownership over the concession period), except the conception of the work, were assumed by the private partner (Eiffage). The full cost of construction (EUR 320 million) was borne by Eiffage, which obtained a 78-year concession. The overpass will then be returned to the state. The concessionaire guarantees that the bridge will remain operational for at least 120 years, and that toll increases shall not exceed the rate of inflation. The PPP is clearly a win-win solution. The state gains substantially: the bridge was constructed without public funding; most of the risks were transferred to the private sector; and the state will eventually take possession of the facility. The concessionaire also gains: the expected internal rate of return (calculated by the École Nationale des Ponts et Chaussées) ranges from 9.2% to 17.3% (Andrieu, 2007).

However, shifting some of the key risks from the public sector to the private sector can come at a high cost to the latter. For example, the London Underground PPP, signed in 2003 with two infrastructure companies for the maintenance and renewal of London Underground trains, stations, tracks and signalling, has demonstrated some genuine achievements, but has also fallen short of a number of maintenance and renewal contract targets. As a result, the two companies are facing penalties of a combined total of more than GBP 4 million. And the Cross City Tunnel in Sydney, Australia, is now facing bankruptcy. It is currently thought to be worth little more than one-third of its original construction cost (AUD 900 million), and the creditor banks are looking at losses of around AUD 570 million.

Box 1.3. **Creative financing and funding of infrastructures – the Confederation Bridge, Canada**

The Confederation Bridge over the Northumberland Straits, one of Canada's most ambitious construction undertakings ever, is a good example of a creative mix of financing and funding in a PPP. In 1987, the government of Canada issued a proposal call challenging the private sector to devise an environmentally, technically and financially sound alternative to the ferry system that existed at the time between Prince Edward Island and New Brunswick. The finalist would be paid by the federal government an inflation-indexed sum equal to the avoided cost of the existing ferry service. This amount, to be paid annually throughout the 35-year concession period, was to be inclusive of the right to own and charge tolls for the use of the facility. Therefore, market risk for the operator is considerably mitigated. The government was obliged to pay this inflation-indexed amount; otherwise the project would not have been financially feasible for the private sector.

After an extensive process, Strait Crossing Development Inc. was named as the developer charged with designing, building, financing and operating the Confederation Bridge. The 12.9 kilometre two-lane structure was completed in 1997 in time, with rumours about cost overruns which were borne by the private consortium. Its subsidiary company, Strait Crossing Bridge Limited, privately manages, maintains and operates the bridge until 2032, after which such operations will be transferred to the government of Canada. The duration of the concession is 35 years, a time period selected as most appropriate and attractive for the economic life of the project to investors (in terms of long-term and guaranteed rate of return). With respect to other concessions, the government recognised the developer's long-term commitment to the region and the vested interest in maintaining and enhancing use of the bridge.

Based on the performance within the Regional Benefits Agreement, the government agreed to negotiate further concessions and rights adjacent to the bridge landfall for any developments or activities. The government agreed not to construct another facility or service that might compete with the bridge service throughout the concession period, and has guaranteed to cease the existing marine Atlantic service by the time that the bridge is in operation.

Real rate bonds have been issued, secured against guaranteed government annual payments; as well as toll revenue bonds, pledged against bridge toll revenue. Within the existing economic and financial model and the Toll Agreement, the concessionaire is obligated to provide a toll structure, based on the revenues of the 1992 ferry operations. This implies that the bridge and toll rate are to be established at the ferry service rate. Annual toll rate increases will not be permitted to exceed 75% of inflation. The Concession Agreement does not deal with maximum or minimum profit figures for Strait Crossing, although the government has guaranteed that the revenue will not fall below the level previously generated by the ferry in 1992, subject to an inflationary index. Strait Crossing is obligated to a long-term maintenance plan which will uphold the integrity of the structure and turn it over to the government of Canada in perfect condition on the transfer date in 2032.

Source: Virtuosity Consulting (2005); the Confederation Bridge website *www.confederationbridge.com*; Center for Design Informatics (1996); Transport Canada website *www.tc.gc.ca/pol/en/Report/brochure/confederation_bridge.htm*.

Recommendation 2: Encourage the investment of pension funds and other large institutional investors in infrastructures.

Relatively new and very promising sources of fresh capital for infrastructure are pension funds, insurance companies and similar large institutional investors. They are attracted by the long-term, stable returns offered by investments in water and power utilities, natural gas networks, tolled motorways, ports and airports, to name but a few. For some institutions in some countries, shares already account for a large proportion of the pension funds – over 40% in the case of Finland, the Netherlands, the United Kingdom and United States. But some pension funds are following a global trend now by moving away from volatile stock markets into the more secure equity offered by infrastructures.

As Figures 1.5 and 1.6 show, some OECD countries have accumulated very considerable consolidated pension and life insurance assets, representing very large proportions of GDP in some cases.

Figure 1.5. **Consolidated pension and life insurance assets in selected OECD countries, 2005**

In per cent of GDP

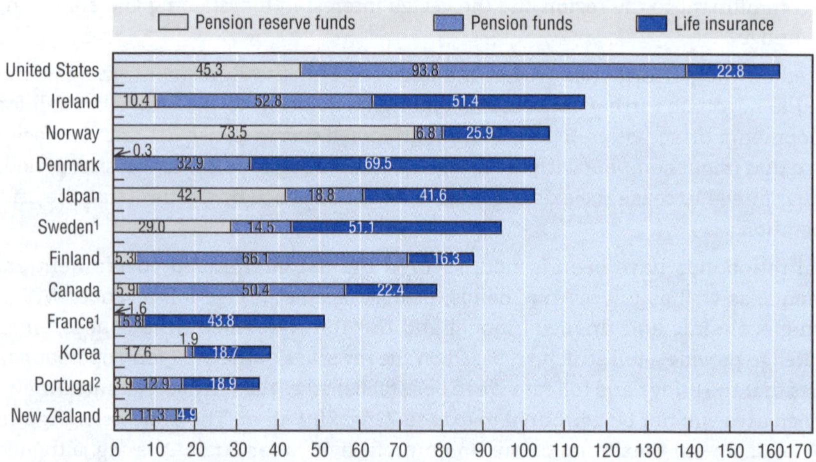

Note: For the purposes of this chart, unallocated pension insurance contracts are excluded from pension funds' assets and counted under life insurance.

1. Pension reserve fund data are 2004 data.
2. Life insurance data are 2003 data.

Source: OECD (2006e), "Pensions Markets in Focus", Issue 3, October. Data drawn from OECD Global Pension Statistics, Insurance Statistics and other administrative sources.

Alone, pension funds have increased considerably in recent years. In the OECD area, total pension fund assets amounted to USD 17.9 trillion in 2005, up from USD 13 trillion in 2001. This represents more than 87% of OECD area GDP. Outside the OECD area, a number of countries have also succeeded in building up substantial pension fund assets, *e.g.* Chile, Singapore, Malaysia and South Africa.

Figure 1.6. **Pension funds in OECD countries, 2005**

In per cent of GDP

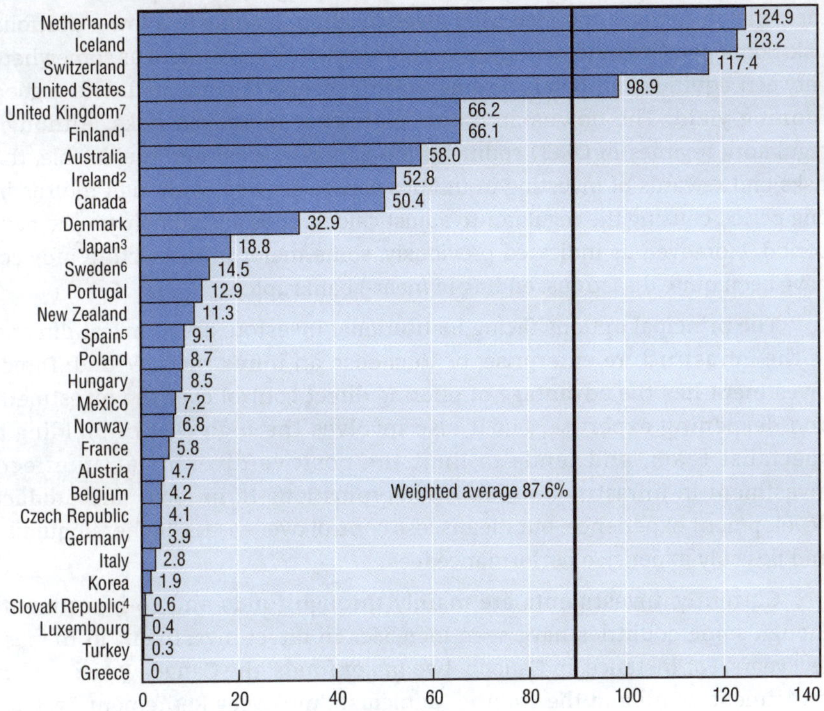

Note: Weighted total averages using weights of pension fund assets.

1. Data for 2004 and 2005 include the statutory pension funds.
2. *Source:* Irish Association of Pension Funds.
3. Data do not include Mutual Aid Trusts; 2004 and 2005 data are estimates.
4. 2004 pension assets data are 2003.
5. Data for 2004 and 2005 include Mutual Funds.
6. Includes assets from the premium pension system for 2004 and 2005. 2005 data are estimates.
7. 2005 pension assets data are staff estimates; 2002 pension assets data are 2001.

Source: OECD (2006e), "Pensions Markets in Focus", Issue 3, October, OECD, Paris. Data drawn from OECD, Global Pension Statistics.

At the moment, only a small proportion of pension funds is allocated to infrastructures. For example, ABP, the world's second largest pension fund at around EUR 200 billion, has been investing in infrastructure assets, but on a modest scale so far – just under 1% of total funds. However, levels are higher in countries where pension funds have been quicker off the mark, *e.g.* Australia and Canada. And ABP has declared its intention to increase the amount of investment in infrastructures in 2007 by a substantial margin (bfinance, 2006). Indeed, across the OECD as whole, even if only 1% of total pension funds were allocated in this way, around USD 180 billion would be available for investment in infrastructures. (This does not include the substantial resources at the disposal of pension reserve funds and life insurance funds.)

One of the attractive features of such a strategy from the point of view of the pension funds is the increased diversification, leading to a lower portfolio risk. Some pension fund managers see infrastructure investment as somewhere between equities and bonds – some growth prospects combined with a good running yield. The downside is the somewhat increased risks. Although regulatory regimes in OECD countries are generally clear and predictable, the risks and rewards of investing in utilities can be skewed, with high returns in one period causing the regulator to adjust calculations accordingly for the next period. Moreover, as indicated previously, some major infrastructure projects have been quite disastrous, ending in (near-) bankruptcy.

The principal options facing institutional investors are to invest directly in the infrastructure enterprise, or to choose an infrastructure fund. Direct investment has the advantage of offering direct control over the investment and deepening expertise, but it also involves the high cost of building a specialist team, and tends to limit the positive diversification effect. Investment in infrastructure funds underpins long-term focus and product development experience, but means less control over assets, higher illiquidity and possibly expensive performance fees.

Currently, investments are mainly through funds and co-investment, though some countries have seen increases in direct investment in the last few years. For instance, in Canada, two major funds, the Canada Pension Plan Investment Board and the Ontario Municipal Employees Retirement System, recently struck billion-dollar deals to acquire stakes *inter alia* in the British water company AWG Plc.

Successful expansion of pension and similar funds into infrastructures in the future will depend to a large extent on regulatory changes to pension fund regimes. These should aim to encourage greater uptake of infrastructure equity while ensuring that appropriate mechanisms are in place to manage risks and that those risks are assumed by those most able to do so. (See Section 3.2 of this chapter on improving the regulatory and institutional framework.)

Diversifying and expanding the sources of revenue for public finances

The introduction to this chapter suggests that, for most OECD countries, ageing populations and stabilising or shrinking workforces will create an increasingly difficult context for raising additional revenues through income tax, while at local level, the efforts of many municipalities to raise local taxes are also meeting with resistance from electorates. The onus therefore needs to be on attempts to diversify the sources of revenue for public capital investment. A number of paths are open to decision makers. They range from making more use of charging for the use of infrastructure services, to exploring the potential for earmarked consumption taxes, and reaping the rewards of land development more effectively.

Recommendation 3: Make greater use of user charges for funding infrastructures. They should be designed to signal prices, reflect real costs and contribute to demand management.

User fees offer a sustainable solution to help meet the growing demands on infrastructure investment. Moreover, globalisation and the emergence of dynamic non-OECD economies will place a rising premium on competitiveness and overall economic efficiency, much of which will need to come through the efficient delivery and operation of infrastructures. It is user fees rather than tax-based solutions which are better suited to achieving those objectives – providing greater incentives for efficiency gains, attracting more private-sector capital and expertise, and offering better tools for managing demand and addressing congestion. Designed appropriately, and supplemented by carefully crafted subsidies where necessary, they can also offset negative redistributive effects, thereby making for more equitable outcomes. However, it has to be recognised that for most public sector infrastructure taxation will remain the mainstay of funding, at least for the foreseeable future. User fees will therefore increasingly need to be deployed as an important complement to tax-based funding. Moreover, their introduction will require careful case-by-case examination of the specific features of the infrastructure to which they may be applied, so as to ensure that the economic costs (including the transaction costs, which can be quite high) and the social costs of moving to user fees do not outweigh the benefits. To the extent that user fees are employed on a larger scale, it may also become necessary to review them within the overall fiscal context, especially where they are perceived to be adding to the overall tax burden of citizens.

Design user fees to signal prices and reflect costs... Across a wide spectrum of infrastructures (with the notable exception of telecommunications) and throughout the OECD area and the developing world, many user fees are not employed as a price signalling device. Indeed, most user fees do not nearly capture the full cost of providing services. This is perhaps most obviously the case in road transport where free access at the point of demand frequently leads to congestion. But in other sectors, too, charges seldom cover costs. In urban public transport systems, the fares are rarely sufficient to meet operating costs. In the water sector, chronic underinvestment is in large part due to keeping rates too low for far too long, and also the price of water tends to vary among users (residential, industrial, agricultural), suggesting gross misallocations of water resources. The situation in the OECD area (though not everywhere) is significantly better in the electricity sector, but in many non-OECD countries generators are often forced to provide electricity at tariffs that are too low to produce revenues sufficient to maintain the network. The Indian Electricity Board is a striking case in point.

Hence, a first step is to aim to recuperate at least the operating costs through a system of marginal cost pricing, structuring charges in such a way that they reflect marginal costs as clearly as possible. Where appropriate, a mark-up can be applied to reflect congestion costs. Thereafter, a further mark-up can be added to bring cost recovery closer or even all the way to cover full costs.

One of the most promising innovations is currently taking place in road tolling, where developments in remote sensing technology and satellite Global Positioning System (GPS) are increasing potential capabilities to track the distances travelled by each and every vehicle. This could open the way to road network pricing at a highly sophisticated level. Individual drivers could be directly charged on the basis of what they drive, where they drive, how often and how much they drive. This in turn could lead to a single revenue source replacing, partially or eventually perhaps even fully, the patchwork of taxes and fees currently predominant in all countries.

The technological feasibility of such a national road pricing scheme is not considered the most significant obstacle to its realisation. Rather, it is finding an appropriate, accountable and acceptable method for overseeing and administering the funds such a system would generate. The issues range from technical enforcement, privacy and equity concerns, to problems of revenue neutrality (between urban and rural communities) and governance (notably the affects on local government finance, and the balance of power between local and national administrations). But in reality, and looking to the longer-term future, there seems to be little alternative to this form of user charging in some form sooner or later, if the mounting congestion is to be tackled effectively.

... and to help manage demand for infrastructure services. The two key interrelated areas in which user fees can be applied to improve reliability and throughput of infrastructure services are in providing incentives for greater efficiency and tackling congestion. The first of these has been addressed above. The second, congestion, is common to all the infrastructures addressed in this project.

After telecommunications, electricity is the infrastructure sector where demand management by pricing is perhaps at its most advanced, but not in all OECD countries. Experience in market design in Britain, North America, the Nordic region and Australia suggests that allowing for the possibility of demand responses to spot-price signals on wholesale markets, typically among large industrial consumers, can help reduce the need for peak capacity and reduce loads at congested nodes on the network. Overall, the potential contribution of demand responses in setting prices has not been fully exploited in any liberalised electricity market.

In water supply and wastewater treatment, there is scope for effective demand management in reducing water consumption and peak demand, and increasing water recycling. Similarly, on toll motorways, there is still much potential for differential charging to manage peak traffic flows, as for example practised on some stretches in France.

One of the most critical and visible areas of congestion is transport on trunk roads as well as on urban roads and untolled urban expressways where, as noted above, the heart of the problem is that roads are generally free at the point of consumption. Perhaps among the most promising innovations in this area is the advent of cordon pricing and zone pricing around or in conurbations, as practised for example in London, Melbourne, Singapore and some cities in Scandinavia. Their main objective is to reduce congestion in the urban area. However, to the extent that they can be designed to generate revenues which can be used to fund other infrastructures – for example, the improvement and expansion of public urban transport – they also open the door to the possibility of much more imaginative schemes. These could involve a move away from the funding of individual, separate means of transport, towards a global, integrated system of urban transport pricing in which the concept of mobility within the urban area plays the central role and all users of (more or less) all modes of transport participate in its funding.

Where subsidies are necessary for reasons of social equity, they should not undermine the long-term sustainability of the infrastructure. As noted elsewhere in this chapter, infrastructures are at the interface of public and private goods, with some – such as telecommunications, electricity and rail freight – being closer to the private good category, and others – such as water and urban public transport – closer to public goods. All, however, have a strong element of public interest. The difficulty resides in disentangling which segments are mainly private and which mainly public, because this in turn determines such questions as: to what extent commercial criteria should be applied to their construction and operation; to what extent taxpayers' money should be involved; how large the subsidy should be; how far user-charging can be extended, and so on.

User charges are equitable in the sense that they can be designed to ensure that those who consume infrastructure and services also pay for what they use. However, user charges may disadvantage certain population groups (*e.g.* those on lower incomes, residents in rural areas, or groups targeted for policy support of one kind or another, such as rail passengers). Hence, an important argument for subsidising infrastructures and their operation is that it redistributes income – in the form of goods and services. However, such subsidisation "in kind" is seldom as efficient and effective as direct money transfer and can lead to significant distortions in resource allocation.

Infrastructure services often have a strong social dimension that needs to be reflected in the business model for their delivery and in public policy. However, the way it is taken into account should not undermine the long-term sustainability of the infrastructure. This implies that, to the extent possible, social obligations should not be met through cross-subsidies or by keeping rates significantly below cost, as illustrated in all the infrastructures covered by this project.

In the rail freight sector, cross-subsidy obligations in favour of passenger travel have been a heavy burden on operators throughout the world, from Europe and North America (where the situation has improved since deregulation and privatisation of freight) to India and Russia, in some cases being the root cause of steady declines in rail freight traffic. Enforcement of separate accounting for social and commercial services would go a long way to rendering transparent the levels of cross-subsidy and building support for their removal, and replacement with other instruments, where appropriate.

In water supply and wastewater treatment, the question of how to provide services to the poor is of critical importance, even in OECD countries. It affects the pricing structure of utilities and their plans to achieve full cost recovery. There are numerous successful strategies to ensure that water is provided to the less fortunate without unduly distorting price structures. These include rising block tariffs, free basic amounts of water, rebates and voucher systems. Similarly in urban public transport, redistribution "in kind" towards the less well-off members of the community could be at least partially replaced by travel allowances, mobility vouchers and similar schemes.

From a long-term perspective, therefore, direct user fees tend to offer the more sustainable solutions to infrastructure funding. However, for political or cost reasons, their introduction may be difficult, slow or impractical. In such circumstances, it may be preferable to seek second-best solutions. These are principally to be found in dedicated or earmarked taxes such as fuel tax, vehicle registration fees or local improvement taxes.

Recommendation 4: Diversify and expand traditional revenue-raising sources.

Notwithstanding the trend to an ever more difficult context for taxation as a channel for infrastructure funds, and the need to look for other sources elsewhere, there still remains some scope in OECD countries for exploring new ways of raising tax-based revenues. At the national level, earmarked taxes such as vehicle licence fees and fuel taxes are quite widespread, and some countries (such as the United States) have succeeded quite well in using these to support sufficient growth in highway spending and capacity, for example. At the local level, European, Asian and North American authorities have shown that municipal sources of taxation can be diversified into such areas as general sales taxes, selective sales and excise taxes, parking and local fuel taxes, etc. While not the mainstay of infrastructure financing, they can make a significant difference at the margin.

Moreover, some countries earmark a share of taxation revenue to service debt incurred in building or delivering a major infrastructure. (In the UK, Australia and New Zealand these are also termed "hypothecated" taxes.) A recent successful example is the introduction of a dedicated water tax in Montreal, Canada. At the municipal level, it could involve devising guidelines for ensuring that key sources of tax revenue, *e.g.* property taxes, keep pace with incomes or economic growth more generally, although in some OECD countries there are signs of growing resistance to rising property tax levels. Where close identification of local inhabitants with an infrastructure project is sought, community bonds may provide a new avenue. And in the area of water treatment facilities, solid waste disposal, and even power plants, there is increasing recourse in some countries to leaseback arrangements as a means of alleviating debt burdens.

There is also room for innovation in the traditional financing instruments available to public authorities, namely bonds. In many countries, local governments use general obligation bonds which are supported by the general revenues derived from the municipality. A promising variation is revenue bonds which are tied to a revenue stream from a specific asset. They are particularly useful where the beneficiaries of the project are identifiable, *i.e.* those that use the service, pay for it. However, care needs to be taken in choosing appropriate projects. If creditors perceive the risks involved in the infrastructure facility to be greater than those associated with general municipal revenues, then the bonds may be more expensive to the municipality because of the ensuing risk markup.

Revenue-based bonds are particularly suitable for projects involving substantial and stable revenue streams flowing from the use of the infrastructure. Toll bridges are a case in point (see for example Box 1.3 on the Confederation Bridge, Canada), but there are other interesting, innovative examples, for instance in rail freight transport. In the US, the funding of the Alameda Corridor Project in Southern California, for example, has the railways repaying public sector raised debt through a charge per container hauled. Experts believe that if the railways had had to raise private borrowing up front, the project would never have got off the ground.

Box 1.4. **The Alameda Corridor Project, US**

The origins of the Alameda Corridor Project date to 1981, when the Southern California Association of governments established a Ports Advisory Committee to deal with concerns about growing traffic at the area's ports. The specific task of the project was to alleviate the highway and rail congestion that growing traffic through the ports would create. The initial focus of the analysis was highway access to the ports, and a number of purely highway projects were identified and have been implemented over the last two decades.

By 1984, however, attention began to focus on the need to reduce potential rail congestion. It became clear that improved rail access could also act to relieve road and highway congestion, with corresponding environmental benefits in reduced air pollution emissions. A number of alternatives were considered, ranging from relatively minor upgrading of rail lines, up to a comprehensive project to consolidate all of the local rail lines of two Class I railroads – the Burlington Northern Santa Fe (BNSF) and the Union Pacific (UP) – and relocate the major access lines to the ports into an exclusive right of way that would be put into a trench below ground level. By 1989, the Alameda Corridor Transportation Authority (ACTA) had been created; and after six years of discussion and planning, the project was set at USD 2.4 billion, involving a 32-kilometre double track, signalled main line of which 16 kilometres would be in a depressed trench, and the remainder on the surface. It consolidated four local rail lines and included a series of bridges, rail flyovers and street improvements that act to separate rail freight from road traffic and from local passenger trains. The result is a much improved rail connection between the two ports and the main interstate rail network, with much reduced impact on the road system.

Financing included a combination of grants and loans. The grants included USD 394 million from the two ports, USD 347 million from local government, and USD 123 million from various state and federal sources. The loans included USD 400 million from the US Department of Transportation (DOT), and USD 1.161 billion in bonds that were to be paid back by revenues generated by charges to be paid by the railroads for each loaded container (USD 15/TEU), empty container (USD 4/TEU) and USD 8 for each loaded rail car carrying bulk freight to or from the ports. These charges

Box 1.4. **The Alameda Corridor Project, US** *(cont.)*

are subject to yearly increases for inflation and stood at USD 16.75, USD 4.47 and USD 8.93 respectively in early 2006. Significantly, the port authorities agreed to guarantee the revenue bonds in the event that usage fees fall short of the levels required to pay off the bonds.

Rail traffic on the project facilities has grown rapidly, from 10 259 trains in 2002 (9 months of operations) to an estimated 19 000 trains in 2006 (an average of 51 trains per day). Traffic in 2006 on the corridor was expected to amount to nearly 300 000 TEU, and total usage fees to approach USD 70 million with another USD 3.5 million in maintenance charges paid by the railroads. Over the same period, the initial lenders, including the US DOT, have been paid back, essentially by issuing a new series of revenue-backed bonds that amount to a total of USD 1.8 billion in 2006.

The project has been successful in meeting the congestion and environmental impact objectives. Whether the project is financially (as opposed to economically) successful remains to be seen. In fiscal year 2005, the ACTA had an operating income of USD 32 million, including depreciation of USD 24 million. But, it also had a non-operating loss of USD 98 million, including interest expense of USD 107 million and amortisation charges of USD 4 million. Rail companies report that they are unable to charge the container rates on which the investment was planned because of price competition from trucking. Based on this performance, there is a significant possibility that either the ports or local authorities will have to pay some of the revenue bond obligation. Whether this is poor financial performance or merely a reasonable balance of the public and private benefits cannot be resolved at this point.

The rail parts of the Alameda Corridor Project did not fit any established state or federal funding framework. The response was therefore *ad hoc*, involving laborious negotiations amongst a series of local, regional, state and federal authorities as well as the private railroads over an extended period of time (more than 20 years). The project was ultimately successful, in the sense that it serves the purpose of adding port interface capacity and reducing congestion, but it took a long time to plan and execute, and it furnishes no clear precedent for similar projects in the future.

Source: Thompson, Louis S. (2007), "Key Trends and Implications for Policy Change in Long-Term Rail Freight Traffic and Infrastructure", in *Infrastructure to 2030 (Volume 2): Mapping Policy for Electricity, Water and Transport*, OECD, Paris.

Recommendation 5: Explore the funding possibilities offered by land value capture.

More attention has been brought to bear recently on the potential of land value tax, whereby a proportion of the increased value that accrues to landowners benefiting from new or improved infrastructure in the proximity is captured and used to fund the infrastructure provided. Successfully conceived and implemented, it shows interesting possibilities for integrated financial, land-use and infrastructure planning. Where infrastructures are being put in place in already densely populated, built-up areas, land value capture is of course limited. But where relatively undeveloped areas benefit from new infrastructures, it has considerably more potential. An interesting recent illustration is the Copenhagen metro in Denmark.

Box 1.5. **Integrating land value capture, land use and new infrastructure – the Copenhagen metro, Denmark**

The Copenhagen metro, scheduled for completion in 2007, is one of Scandinavia's most ambitious transport infrastructure projects. The Ørestad Development Corporation (ODC) was established with the dual task to build the metro in Copenhagen and to develop the Ørestad area. It is owned 45% by the government and 55% by the municipality of Copenhagen. The area to be developed is about 600 metres wide and 5 kilometres long, and is situated about 2 kilometres from the city centre of Copenhagen. The project is characterised by a close interconnection of infrastructure, land use development and financing. By putting infrastructure in place, this facilitated the sale of land to private investors to help finance the metro system.

The ODC has carried out the following actions:

- Took over the Ørestad land covering around 310 hectares from the owners, *i.e.* the municipality of Copenhagen and the Danish government.
- Raised loans on commercial market terms, but with joint liability with the Danish government and the municipality of Copenhagen.
- Designed, built and initiated the operation of the new Copenhagen metro. At the same time, the corporation continued the planning and construction of other infrastructure projects.
- Sold/sells the land to developers and investors. The corporation used/uses the surplus from the proceeds of the sales to repay the loans.

Box 1.5. **Integrating land value capture, land use and new infrastructure – the Copenhagen metro, Denmark**

The ODC refrained from establishing a full permanent technical organisation of its own and decided to outsource as many tasks as possible to external consultants and advisors. The two main contractors in constructing the system are Ansaldo Trasporti, which holds the contract for the entire transport system and the first five years of operation, and COMET consortium, which was charged with building and constructing the metro. The total cost of the project – building the metro and preparing the Ørestad area for development – is estimated at EUR 1.7 billion (DKK 12 billion). The cost should be met by selling the land (50%), direct payments from the owners not contributing land themselves (10%), in lieu payments of real estate taxes (10%), and operation profit from the metro (30%).

It is estimated that the metro will be free of debt 30 years after completion. Two stages of the metro are up and running (with passenger numbers of 37 million in 2006, an increase of 2% over 2005). The actual passenger numbers have been lower than originally forecast due to a longer time for adjustment to the new transport system, but an increase is still expected. In 2007, a third stage to the Copenhagen airport is to be finished. The metro struggled with a few technical difficulties in the initial stages which resulted in delays and cancelled services. The situation has subsequently improved, with 98% of services running on time in 2005 and 2006.

In 2000, the Danish National Audit Office published a report criticising the ODC for not providing adequate control and proper management information on the project's progress, impacting on the project's delay and cost calculations. The four years envisaged for the huge civil works under the Copenhagen city centre and the system development, plus system certification, manufacture and approval, turned out to be a timeframe impossible to stick to. Initially, the total cost of the metro was estimated at EUR 1.3 billion (DKK 9.7 billion), but due to changes and adjustments the budget has increased by about 26% to a total cost of approximately EUR 1.6 billion (DKK 12 billion).

In Ørestad, a total of 3.1 million square metres (floorage) can be built upon. Ørestad is still under development and therefore it is difficult to entirely assess the success of the project. However, there are a number of positive signs. By the end of 2006, sales of approximately 1 601 000 square metres (floorage) have been realised corresponding to 52% of the overall site. The overall sales as of 31 December 2006 amount to approximately DKK 4 650 million (in current prices). The average price per square metre has been increasing over the years and is expected to increase further.

The result for the year 2006 is estimated to be a profit of approx. DKK 1 700 million. The repayment of the debt of DKK 17.1 billion began in 2006, and ODC is expected to be debt free in the year 2038.

Box 1.5. **Integrating land value capture, land use and new infrastructure – the Copenhagen metro, Denmark** *(cont.)*

Significant investment has been attracted from the public and private sectors, with Copenhagen University, the IT University and Denmark's Radio (main public service broadcaster in Denmark) all relocating to the town. Major private companies attracted to the town include Ferring Pharmaceuticals, Atkins, Accenture, Dell, Hi3G Denmark, Masterfoods, Svenska Handelsbanken, and Biogen. Moreover, a 146 000 square metre shopping centre (Field's) was opened in March 2004.

The Ørestad model of financing new major infrastructure projects has also been used in the fourth stage of the Copenhagen metro: The City Circle Line. The City Circle Line will include 17 stations, two of which are extensions of already existing stations. The overall expenditure of the City Circle Line will come to approximately DKK 15 billion (EUR 2 billion) and will be financed by city of Copenhagen (DKK 4.8 billion), city of Frederiksberg (DKK 0.8 billion), the national government (DKK 4 billion) and revenue from passenger fees, etc. (DKK 5.4 billion). The governmental financial contribution consists of the value of the company Copenhagen Port which implies that a new city district of 400 000 to 600 000 square metres is to be developed in Nordhavnen along with connecting infrastructure. The legal framework is expected to be established in 2006/07.

Source: Ørestad Development Co-operation (2004) and website *www.orestadsselkabet.dk*; European Commission's Urban Transport Benchmarking Initiative (2004), Metro Copenhagen (2002).

3.2. Improving the regulatory and institutional framework

Encouraging diversity and innovation in approaches to the building and operation of infrastructures will require some scrutiny of the laws and regulations that may be hindering the emergence of new business models for their financing, funding and management. Among the areas concerned here are finance, competition, standards, technology, and institutional arrangements.

Recommendation 6: Examine the legal and regulatory framework conditions with a view to encouraging the emergence of fresh sources of capital and new business models for the construction, maintenance and operation of infrastructures.

Engaging the private sector in infrastructure development has clearly been easier for some governments than others, as indicated by the relatively widespread presence of private sector money in countries such as the US, the UK and Australia, and the slower progress it has made in others, such as Mexico and some central European countries. The obstacles can be major. For example, in some countries private participation in certain infrastructure sectors (such as water) is only possible through a change to the constitution. But many obstacles are not quite as insurmountable, and it is often a case of ensuring that the legal framework is flexible enough to attract private investors and ensure sufficient project volume to make large investors' opportunity costs worthwhile. An interesting case in point is the German F Model for road construction which foresees the possibility of assigning the building, operation and financing of trunk roads to private partners. However, the law on which the model is based restricts those possibilities to bridges, tunnels and mountain-pass crossings, thereby considerably reducing the number of projects. Such investors may also need some protection against risks they cannot influence (*e.g.* in the form of compensation for revenue shortfalls beyond their control). Investors value as few delays as possible in the award of tenders; and they require transparent, stable criteria for the award of tenders and a legally reliable framework. What is also required is the continuing commitment by governments to open international procurement and competition among infrastructure companies.

Enabling greater participation of pension funds and life assurance funds in infrastructures will in some countries necessitate review of the regulatory regimes governing pension asset allocations. By way of illustration, in general, Anglo-Saxon countries adopt the prudent person rule (PPR) in pension fund investment which requires only that funds be invested "prudently" rather than limited according to category. Furthermore, there are few restrictions on investment in specific assets. In many other countries, however, different quantitative restrictions have traditionally been applied, normally stipulating upper limits on investment in specific asset classes, including equity.[10]

Similarly, there are differences among countries in the regulations governing the use of bonds. Whereas in Canada municipalities use general obligation bonds, across the border in the US municipalities are permitted to use both general obligation and revenue bonds. North America has on the whole been quite entrepreneurial in the use of less traditional forms of debt issue. Together with Australia, Canada and the US have moved towards more widespread use of tax-exempt bonds. The interest proceeds accruing to the bondholder are exempted from local or general forms of taxation, making the bonds more attractive to certain, in some cases new, groups of investors. Along with other countries, the US has shown itself at the forefront of innovative thinking in such areas as surface transport. For example, within the last decade a total of some 38 states have established Infrastructure Banks in the wake of major regulatory changes which allowed states to capitalise a proportion of the transportation infrastructure grants they receive from the federal government.

The US has also been active in extending tax revenue sharing schemes from more traditional to newer uses. This has been the case in the US with GARVEEs (Great Anticipation Revenue Vehicle debt-financing instruments) whereby future federal-aid grants are pledged as repayment mechanisms for both principal and interest. Originally employed for financing small projects such as hospitals and schools, they are now increasingly applied to much larger local and national infrastructure projects. The US has also seen interesting moves to link regulatory changes to new forms of finance with a view to stimulating greater diversification in approaches to the delivery of infrastructure services. An example is the introduction of the Drinking Water Revolving Fund, which helps states meet specific federal requirements under the Safe Drinking Water Act by making available a large number and variety of grants. These endeavour to ensure that as wide a range of business models as possible (traditional centralised plants, non-traditional on-site facilities) has access to the capital needed to finance investments, such as the installation of new facilities to improve the quality of drinking water, as well as the maintenance necessary to sustain ageing infrastructure.

Recommendation 7: Encourage the emergence of new players and new business models through the creation and promotion of frameworks that stimulate the development of effective competition either in or for the market.

The work conducted within this project has established that across all infrastructure sectors, the public monolith model suffers from public failures which impair not only its economic performance but also its ability to innovate. Given the need for greater diversity and innovation in addressing the many challenges facing infrastructures in the coming decades, it follows that governments should explore ways and means of enlarging the scope for some degree of competition and private sector participation that will facilitate the emergence of new entrants and new business models.

The key is to find ways of employing private skills, techniques and resources for the delivery of infrastructure. One option is to retain state ownership of the infrastructure asset but introduce – under competitive conditions – private expertise into downstream activities such as construction, operation and maintenance, through procurement, concessions and similar arrangements. In all such cases, the quality of the tendering process in ensuring effective competition is crucial. A second option is to encourage the partial or full privatisation of state-owned infrastructure assets and subsequently introduce competition *in* the market. But this may not be possible (for example because of very considerable economies of scale), nor preferable (because the state operator is doing as good a job as a private operator could do), nor politically feasible (*e.g.* overwhelming public opposition). In such cases, a third option is to generate the conditions for competition *for* the market.

Where infrastructure assets remain in state ownership, it is important to make use of business models that build on the comparative advantages offered by private sector skills and resources. From the design and construction of the project through to the delivery of services, be it through procurement, concession, leasing or other solutions, the basis for the selection of the private sector partner needs to be competitive.

Where public failure is particularly severe and private ownership offers substantial economic and innovation benefits, it is important to explore the possibilities for expanding the scope for privatisation of assets. In telecommunications, privatisation has already run its course in most OECD and larger non-OECD countries. In OECD countries, a substantial shift has taken place in this direction in the electricity sector and rail freight, both of which provide services that are perhaps closest to being a private good. Progress in this direction has been very much slower in urban public transport and water, where economies of scale and social factors play a major role. In road transport, while the scope for privatisation of assets is acknowledged to be more limited, there have been some interesting recent examples in France and the US of transfers of tolled motorways to the private sector.

Where markets are competitive or at least contestable, governments should increase efforts to lower barriers to new entrants, without compromising regulatory oversight. Such barriers are lowest in information and communication technology (ICT) which has benefited from almost thirty years of privatisation and regulatory reform. The key is to ensure that fair competition and a level playing field continue to prevail for the new infrastructure technologies that are coming on-stream. Future investments, for example in all-IP (all-Internet Protocol) next generation networks, should be made in the same competitive spirit as that which telecommunications deregulation has followed over the last decade. Similarly with mobile communications – the key technology – new alternative wireless technology (AWT) entrants to the mobile market need to be encouraged to ensure competition against entrenched incumbents. This would mean endorsing an "open commons" for spectrum for new ATWs, with many large unlicensed bands.

Encouraging more new entrants in electricity means first of all that barriers to electricity generation and restraints on transmission capacity need to be loosened. This needs to be complemented by smooth, rapid and transparent procedures for approving construction of new power plants. Moreover, governments should encourage independent market monitoring units to detect anti-competitive behaviour and practices. Also, wholesale markets should, where practical, be designed competitively and coupled with possibilities for large industrial consumers to respond quickly to spot-price signals, thereby restricting the scope for market abuse by dominant generators.

In the water sector, much could be done to assist new players by promoting technology-neutral standards that afford providers with greater flexibility to innovate, *e.g.* through on-site water and wastewater facilities. Indeed, it is not inconceivable that a more proactive stance could be taken by regulators, such as requiring new large generators of water to provide on-site wastewater systems as is the case in parts of India. And in urban public transport, a strong case can be made for mandatory tendering of certain services, and for widening the scope for potential new suppliers (*e.g.* of minicabs and minibuses) with a view to creating a more innovative multimodal public transport supply.

In particular, governments should encourage, where practical, third-party access/common carriage. Third-party access or common carriage is the use of a capital-intensive network by a third party to supply services. Now common currency in telecommunications, it has applications in electricity and freight rail, but is still quite rare in the water sector. However, it is an effective instrument for increasing competition at the supply end or at the demand end.

In the electricity sector, one option available to governments in shaping competition conditions *ex ante* is to require the dominant generators to sell the rights of their capacity to other generators or new entrants to the market under long-term contracts. France, Belgium, the Netherlands and Denmark have adopted this technique. The contracts are called virtual power plants (VPPs), and experience suggests that they have on the whole enhanced competition. With respect to rail freight, efforts are already underway in Europe to promote competition through the encouragement of more effective access to the network by competing rail freight companies. In the water sector, common carriage is furthest along in the few countries which have substantial privatised assets: England and Wales, and Australia. Although it will probably be a further 10-20 years before common carriage gains significant momentum internationally, it does have the potential to make an important impact on the water sector since it could usher in new public and private competition in abstraction, treatment of water and retailing. New business models could include desalination plants entering water directly into the water network, new players focused on generating efficiency gains as hitherto unexploited sources of water, and parallel licensing arrangements with small and informal water vendors.

Where competition *in* the market is not practicable, strengthen competition *for* the market. This is largely a question of benchmarking and appears to have most potential in the two infrastructure sectors in which, for the reasons mentioned above, competition in the market is not very practical and therefore relatively rare – in urban public transport and in water. In urban transport, competitive tendering for concessions is still not a common phenomenon. National and international performance benchmarks, conducted and publicised at regular intervals (on a par, for example, with schools and hospitals), can significantly enhance the capacity to evaluate urban transport policy. In the water sector, governments should encourage operators to develop standardised performance measurements to be used by customers and senior management to evaluate the performance of utilities. These can be published periodically in the form, for example, of performance scorecards. (See Box 1.6.)

Finally, at the international level, governments can do much to improve competitive conditions by ensuring a more level playing field for investors bidding for infrastructure contracts. Going beyond national borders to attract international investment for major infrastructure works can generate considerable benefits in the form of more vigorous competition for contracts, fresh sources of capital, skills and experience, and innovative work practices. For the policy makers involved, however, the challenges are considerable. This has much to do with the nature of the projects themselves. Infrastructures tend to be highly complex in their planning, design and delivery; they have long economic lives, and more often than not find themselves at the interface between public and private interest; and bringing in international investors may add a further layer of complicated business relations.

In such cases, clear principles and guidelines on the full and proper participation of international investors in infrastructure projects can facilitate the policy makers' role significantly. Among the key principles set out in the recently approved "OECD Principles for Private Sector Participation in Infrastructure"[11] are:

There should be full disclosure of all project-relevant information between public authorities and the private investors, including the state of pre-existing infrastructure, performance standards and penalties in the case of non-compliance. The principle of due diligence must be upheld.

The awarding of infrastructure contracts or concessions should be designed to guarantee procedural fairness, non-discrimination and transparency.

In addition, there are of course other OECD instruments and guidelines which have an important role in shaping the international rules of the game in infrastructure investment.[12]

Box 1.6. Water utility performance indicators – an example

Organizational development

- Employee health and safety accident frequency and severity index.
- Training hours per employee.
- Customer accounts per employee.
- Water delivered per employee.
- Wastewater processed per employee.

Customer relations

- Customer service complaints.
- Technical water quality complaints.
- Disruptions of water service.
- Residential cost of water or sewer services.
- Customer service cost per account.
- Billing accuracy.

Business management

- Debt ratio.
- System renewal/replacement rate.
- Return on assets.

Water operations

- Drinking water compliance rate.
- Distribution system water loss.
- Water distribution system integrity.
- Operations and maintenance cost ratios.
- Planned maintenance ratio.

Wastewater operations

- Sewer overflow rate.
- Collection system integrity.
- Wastewater treatment effectiveness rate.
- Operations and maintenance cost ratios.
- Planned maintenance ratios.

Source: Crotty, P. (2004), *Selection and Definition of Performance Indicators for Water and Wastewater Utilities*, American Water Works Association and American Water Works Association Research Foundation, Denver, Colorado.

Recommendation 8: Place greater emphasis on the issue of reliability of infrastructure functioning.

This project has highlighted the vital role that infrastructures play in modern societies and how their proper functioning shapes economic performance and competitiveness in crucial ways. Reliability of infrastructure services – from "keeping the lights on" to keeping goods, people and information moving – has become paramount and will remain so in the future. However, the studies in this project have also argued that in the coming decades the threats to infrastructures are set to rise. They will become increasingly vulnerable not only to growing congestion, disruption from technical accidents and extreme weather events, but also to terrorism and other malicious acts. The effects are likely to be all the more serious as the interdependencies among infrastructures continue to tighten. Moreover, the commercial pressures weighing on reserve margins are unlikely to diminish. The reliability of infrastructures needs to be placed firmly on the policy agenda.

An array of measures is available. They include expanding capacity and stepping up maintenance and upgrading of networks; demand management to relieve congestion at choke points; providing for increased security at key plants; and supporting research and development (R&D) on reliability and security issues with a view to strengthening the contribution that technology can make. These issues are addressed later in these policy recommendations.

This section focuses on the improvements that could be made to the regulatory and institutional framework which could help improve reliability and security:

- Develop a strategic framework which enables governments and stakeholders to evaluate and better balance different policy aims, including more effective trade-offs between economic objectives on the one hand and the provision of adequate levels of system redundancy, reserve supplies and back-up on the other.
- Establish mechanisms to identify and monitor risks and vulnerabilities.
- Conduct systematic risk management reviews of arrangements for planning and operating critical infrastructures, in particular with respect to co-operation and policy making across traditional administrative and sectoral boundaries.
- Introduce and/or strengthen independent monitoring of compliance with mandatory requirements and adherence to existing security standards.
- Reduce dependence of critical infrastructure operation on open access ICT and on inadequately secured public telecommunications networks.

Box 1.7. **Regulating for reliability: the case of electricity**

Particularly in the electricity sector, there is a question of creating and preserving sufficient capacity to be able to withstand shocks and provide continuous reliable service. In principle, competitive electricity markets can provide incentives for timely and effective investments, as long as the market is well designed and the regulatory framework appropriate. There are growing concerns however about the adequacy of generation and transmission investment in liberalised markets – notably in Europe, the United States and parts of Asia. Reserve capacity margins are falling in several countries as a result of a downturn in investment in recent years. In most cases, market reforms were introduced at a time of overcapacity, so the initial focus was on reducing operating costs. The focus is now shifting to the adequacy of incentives to invest in new capacity and streamlining regulatory procedures for authorising new investment in generating plant and high-voltage transmission lines.

Governments and regulators have a variety of avenues to choose from through which they should work towards ensuring adequate reserves:

a) ***Reduce uncertainty.*** Minimising regulatory uncertainty helps to encourage timely and adequate investment. Some degree of uncertainty is inevitable, but policy makers and regulators can help reduce it by improving access to market information, refraining from *ad hoc* interventions in the way markets operate (*e.g.* price capping), and establishing transparent procedures for licensing. Similarly, on the environmental front, they need to set up a legal and market framework that ensures environmental objectives are met flexibly and at least cost. (One such approach is to cap and trade emission allowances – see US system for sulphur dioxide emissions, and the EU Emission Trading Scheme for CO_2).

b) ***Enhance incentive regulation with reliability criteria.*** Incentive regulation has helped lower operating costs, but has not provided sufficient incentive for efficient maintenance and investment in new capacity. Great Britain, Norway and Sweden have recently reformed their regulations to incorporate quality and reliability criteria, with penalties (reduced revenues) if the utilities' performance fall short of established benchmarks. Also, California appears to be progressing towards a more sustainable balance between market forces and effective regulation. The authorities there are requiring "resource adequacy" plans from utilities that directly serve consumers, requiring the utilities to demonstrate that they can meet their load requirements for one year into the future, with the strong possibility that a four-year requirement will be put in place before end-2007. It is left to the utility to find its own equilibrium between self-generated power and power purchased from other producers.

Box 1.7. **Regulating for reliability: the case of electricity** *(cont.)*

c) ***Improve demand response.*** Rapid demand response by customers contributes to the balance of the system and improves system security, as well as enhancing the efficiency and economy of balancing arrangements. Demand response can also be used in network areas where congestion is most frequent and the network security most vulnerable.

d) ***Direct intervention.*** Given increasing doubts that markets alone will be able to provide sufficient incentive, policy makers and regulators need to consider alternative mechanisms for remunerating reserve capacity. These could include capacity payments, or capacity obligations buttressed by a competitive market mechanism for trading capacity.

e) ***Organisational solutions.*** Policy makers in many countries are actively encouraging the development and deployment of distributed generation because of the economic, environmental, and also energy security benefits it brings. In particular, it can enhance the reliability of electric power systems by reducing dependency on centralised systems and helping overcome local bottlenecks (provided it does not require a need for extra reserve capacity to deal with operating variability, *e.g.* wind power).

f) ***Give more visibility to the need for renewal and upgrading of networks.*** Especially in OECD countries, the investment requirements for renewing and refurbishing transmission and distribution networks need to be given particular attention because of the vital role that their quality plays in the provision of high-quality power to business and households.

g) ***Recourse to international networks.*** Strengthening transmission interconnections across borders offers policy makers further options for improving access to capacity reserves and thereby achieving greater supply reliability. An efficient use of existing interconnections can be achieved by using interconnector pricing ("market coupling", already being used in the Nordic, Australian and some US markets). Moreover, there may be substantial scope for trading reserves across borders.

- Support the creation of institutions that promote voluntary standards and best professional design practice.

Recent illustrations of such moves to improve reliability and security can be found in the US and Norway. In 2006, the North American Electric Reliability Council – a self-regulatory industry body – took on new powers to develop and enforce mandatory reliability standards, including the imposition of fines on utilities that fail to meet those standards. Also in 2006, both the OECD and the national public accounting office were invited to conduct (in separate exercises) independent reviews of the efficacy of the arrangements in place to manage serious breaches of Norway's information system.

Recommendation 9: Strengthen the framework for standards, as a tool both for encouraging new operational models and for improving interoperability.

Standards are clearly important for the smooth, secure and reliable functioning of all infrastructure systems. But they also play a role in hampering or promoting diversity in the technical, organisational and management solutions used to deliver the service through the infrastructure.

The water sector is a case in point where it is vital that regulations leave new technological possibilities open rather than foreclosing them. The regulatory system in OECD countries is typically "hardwired" to regulate piped water supply and water-borne sewage treatment in centralised systems using a set of accepted technologies. New actors attempting to provide on-site treatment of waste and fresh water may be limited because regulations require new and existing properties to connect to underground systems of water supply and waste disposal. There may also be no method to disconnect from the existing system or be served by a non-conventional entity. Hence, standards for water and waste treatment need to state quantitative and qualitative objectives to achieve public health goals, rather than stipulating the type of technology that should be employed. Technology neutral standards afford providers in the water sector with greater flexibility and capability to innovate to meet needs.

Standards are also key to interoperability of systems across borders and therefore to the efficiency and reliability of international flows of goods and services through infrastructure networks. In the rail sector, interoperability of systems is a major issue on European and other transnational rail systems, and the question of standards will require particular attention in the coming years. In particular, disparities in signalling systems and lack of qualifications for crews working across boundaries need to be addressed. Also, with respect to reliability of service, much could be gained from setting intergovernmental standards on security, quality assurance and so on, in order to cope better with the challenges which the railway system will increasingly have to contemplate – higher timetable density, tighter safety margins, and long-distance trans-frontier transport of dangerous goods, etc. Similarly, in cross-border power transmission, benefits could be gleaned from the regular monitoring of compliance with reliability standards. And in the field of water and wastewater management, there would seem to be substantial benefits to be gained in some areas from the formulation and implementation of water standards, as seen with the EU's water directives.

Recommendation 10: Explore the potential for new institutional arrangements that may provide more effective and efficient financing, funding and/or delivery of infrastructure.

In road transport, urban public transport, water and some areas of power generation and transmission, the role of the private sector has emerged as that of a contractor to central, regional and local government. Contracting roles can now include everything from planning, consulting and scientific analysis, through to reconstruction, maintenance and operational services. In a number of countries, it is at this practical level where organisational change has been greatest – public authorities have moved from being employers of large direct labour organisations to being clients for services delivered by the private sector.

But the network character of the infrastructures remains; indeed, it has grown in significance, making the integrative management of networks increasingly challenging. In a number of countries a re-think of the institutional arrangements for such network management is underway in the light of current and future changes in the different roles assumed by public and private sector actors alike. The organisation of national roads administration is a case in point. The UK for example has opted for an arm's-length agency in the form of the Highways Agency, reducing political vulnerability and separating responsibility for road scheme promotion from the assessment and decision-making process. This separation is reflected also in the arrangements in Sweden. Austria has created a publicly owned, limited-responsibility company to manage its motorways and expressways. It has wide ranging responsibilities including *inter alia* financing, design, construction, operation, maintenance and toll collection. And in Portugal, the formerly state-owned highway monopoly operator was completely privatised between 1997 and 2001. Subsequently, the move from shadow tolls to real tolls has picked up momentum. (See Box 1.8.)

Thus, looking across the OECD area, there is a rich and diverse set of models which are used for addressing these tasks and which, cultural and political differences notwithstanding, offer pointers to new ways of handling the challenges facing more traditional, public sector management of networks.

Box 1.8. **Private operation of motorways, shadow tolls and real tolls in Portugal**

Portugal has a strong track record of alternative models of financing and operating its motorways. Tolled motorways in Portugal go back to the 1960s and 1970s, when they were operated by a state-owned monopoly, BRISA. The monopoly was privatised in four stages between 1997 and 2001 via the stock market. On the basis of 30-year concession contracts, BRISA's main role is the construction, operation and maintenance of motorways, as well as the right to levy tolls until 2032. There are eight other, smaller private operators of Portugal's motorway network. Some motorways are untolled, so-called SCUTs, and are funded through shadow tolls paid by the government.

Portugal's 2 750 kilometres of motorways are about two-thirds tolled and one-third untolled. Most of the untolled roads have been financed with shadow tolls – government payments to the private enterprise financiers and constructors of the road based on traffic. Shadow tolls are a way to have the private sector provide the initial financing, which is attractive. But the government still has to come up with the money to pay off the shadow toll concessionaire year by year, so it can get into a situation little different from a government which simply borrows and builds the road itself, and then has to service the debt and carry out maintenance. In 2006, the government announced the introduction of tolls in three of the six existing SCUTs. The initial schedule for this to materialise was targeted at the end of 2007, although some delays are to be expected.

In 2004, the minister for public works at that time indicated that by 2008 the cost to the state budget would be USD 800 million, which the government considered an "unbearable weight" on the state budget. Moreoever, by 2007 SCUT payments would have increased to 0.4% of Portuguese GDP. Hence, the outgoing government announced it would stop paying shadow tolls under long-term concession agreements and move instead toward payment of real tolls by users.

A leading analyst of toll roads for Standard and Poors in London has pointed out that even without tolls the SCUTS have been forecast to have light traffic, and that traffic projections (which would have to be further reduced under real tolling) lie below the levels of demand usually associated with "standalone" toll road projects, that is, projects that can meet their debt-service obligations through toll revenues alone.

In 2003, toll collection was reintroduced on the 34-kilometre A9-CREL highway, which represented the return to the original operating model in line with BRISA's main concession model. The motorway started as a tolled motorway when it was inaugurated in September 1995; however, in December of that same year, the government decided to abolish tolls against paying BRISA a compensation for changes in the operation conditions of a relevant part of the concession. In 2002, BRISA and the Portuguese government concluded an agreement providing for the reintroduction of tolls on the A9-CREL, against BRISA's payment to the state of approximately EUR 290 million.

Source: Tollroadsnews (2004); BRISA (2003); EIB (2005).

3.3. Strengthening governance and strategic planning

There is a persuasive set of arguments for governments to develop a strategic, co-ordinated approach to infrastructures. First, infrastructures serve different economic, social and environmental purposes. A framework is required within which the trade-offs among the various, sometimes competing, policy objectives can be effectively and democratically arbitrated. Second, it is vital to consider infrastructure as a system and a series of systems, rather than as distinct sectors, taking into account to the extent possible the interdependencies and synergies among them. This is becoming increasingly important as infrastructure systems continue to converge, critical vulnerabilities and the significance of reliability become more evident, and the mix of potential positive spin-offs from different infrastructures ever more difficult to harness. Third, and related to the previous point, the financing of different infrastructures is increasingly interdependent. And finally, with the spread of regulatory reform and privatisation in OECD and non-OECD countries in recent years, the complexity of the financing, funding and provision of infrastructure has risen in tandem with the multiplication of players involved – different levels of government, business, associations, and so on.

That it should be government that establishes the strategic policy framework is also clear. In the rapidly changing environment characterised above, what has emerged is not so much less government as different government. Whether infrastructures remain largely in the hands of the public authorities, or whether key operations are handed off to business, or whether infrastructure assets are privatised and regulated with public oversight, the sheer importance of infrastructures to modern economic and social life means that it is the state that bears the ultimate responsibility for the smooth, reliable running of a nation's infrastructure systems.

Recommendation 11: Support the development of long-term, co-ordinated approaches to infrastructure development.

There are two interrelated processes involved in fostering such a strategic, comprehensive approach to infrastructure: the development of national, long-term policy frameworks for key individual infrastructure sectors; and improved integration of the different levels of government in the design, planning and delivery of infrastructures.

Develop national long-term policy frameworks. Within individual infrastructure sectors, strategic policy frameworks are not uncommon. Many if not most OECD countries develop at some juncture longer-term plans for road and rail transport. Such comprehensive plans for energy in liberalised markets, for water management, or the role that IT might play (both as an infrastructure in its own right and as a facilitating technology) are less common.

To the extent that they do not already exist, governments should support the development of national long-term strategic policy frameworks for individual key infrastructure sectors.

It is in the transport sector that one more readily finds examples of long-term strategic planning. For example, England, France, Germany, the Netherlands and Spain and Switzerland, to name but a few, all use national transport infrastructure plans with a time horizon of between 10 and 20 years. Similarly comprehensive efforts should be undertaken in other sectors such as water and power. Regular *ex post* evaluation of past planning and implementation cycles (as practiced by France and the UK in transport infrastructure, for example) can allow for gradual improvement of planning systems. However, few countries have developed an overarching economic approach to such long-term planning. An interesting step in the right direction is the recent Eddington Transport Study.

Box 1.9. **The Eddington Transport Study – an economic approach to long-term strategic policy frameworks for transport in the UK**

In December 2006, the UK government released the Eddington Transport Study, which sets out the evidence to inform a more comprehensive understanding of transport's role in supporting the productivity of the UK economy and its sustainable growth. Its scope includes all road and rail transport, airports and sea ports. After examining the overall relationship between transport and the economy, the study examines the underlying economic drivers through which transport impacts on economic performance, and concludes by identifying a series of principles that should guide the development of transport policies to support sustainable development of the UK economy over the next 15-30 years.

Long-term transparent framework. In setting out the lessons for future transport strategy, the study establishes the importance of developing a long-term transparent framework. Few countries adopt an overarching economic approach to designing transport policy. That is, transport policy is rarely treated as an instrument of economic policy, and appraisals of transport interventions fail to recognise fully the contribution that transport polices or schemes can make to economic success. Indeed, at both national and local levels, the economic consequences of transport interventions are often considered only: *i)* once the transport problem has become extreme; *ii)* to justify a favoured transport solution; or *iii)* on the basis that competitor countries have introduced a particular technology or level of service.

Box 1.9. **The Eddington Transport Study – an economic approach to long-term strategic policy frameworks for transport in the UK** *(cont.)*

A transport strategy needs to be sufficiently forward looking to anticipate (as far as possible), and deal proactively with, some very long-term, far-reaching issues. A clear vision of the future of the UK economy is essential to help define the future problems and transport needs. These challenges include:

- The strong growth in transport demand forecast as a consequence of economic success, which without action is expected to lead to increased congestion, alongside growing expectations concerning the quality of infrastructure and transport services.
- Transport's role in responding to the challenges and opportunities of the knowledge economy and globalisation, which will continue to shape the economic geography of the UK. Change is happening faster than has historically been the case.
- Transport's key role in responding to the global challenge of climate change, as well as to more local impacts, such as air quality and biodiversity.
- Responding to new technological advances, both general purpose technologies, for example the use of the Internet and real-time information influencing demand for transport and its provision, and more transport-specific technology.
- Demographic, social, environmental and scientific trends, and their implications for transport policy objectives and pressures.

A further challenge is that transport lead times are often long (years and often decades), and decisions can involve significant investments in some very long-lived assets, many of which, such as railway lines and airports, are quite inflexible once they are established.

Taken together this suggests that a long-term strategic outlook for transport policy in the UK must extend over a 20 to 30-year time horizon. This would allow early identification of issues to be addressed, including where transport may contribute to productivity and to other government objectives, as well as consideration of the full range of appropriate policy options. It would also allow sufficient time for preparatory action by the government, and others affected by decisions, and the securing of funding for agreed priorities.

This strategic outlook could include, or be supported by, medium-term strategies for achieving particular strategic transport objectives, analysing the problem to be solved and setting out the range of policy options that could be pursued, and identifying those that were likely to be most effective. However, transport policy must be responsive to the changing shape of the economy. Logically, this can involve changing course, and even stopping doing some things, as well as doing more.

Box 1.9. **The Eddington Transport Study – an economic approach to long-term strategic policy frameworks for transport in the UK** *(cont.)*

Governments need to be sufficiently forward looking in order to commit to implementing such long-term strategies, which will not necessarily come to fruition for many years. Furthermore, government decisions on transport can also have significant impacts on related private sector operations, investment and location decisions. As a result, providing certainty about near-term actions and transparency about long-term strategy can increase the impact that transport improvements have on economic success and environmental goals.

Hence, accompanying the long-term strategic outlook and medium-term strategies should be a short to medium-term 5 to 10-year statement of commitment that clarifies the policies to be implemented over this period of time.

Approach to the development of strategy. Although governments globally are responding to their citizens' demand for transport, this Eddington study attempts to provide a more sophisticated understanding of this relationship – being smarter about where the UK might want to invest to get the best returns, whilst reflecting environmental, social and other government objectives. It suggests four key principles that should inform a transport strategy aimed at identifying and funding those policies which most cost-effectively deliver government's objectives:

1. Start with a clear articulation of the policy objectives and the transport outcomes required to deliver these objectives, focusing where relevant on the "whole journey" rather than particular stages or modes in a journey.
2. Consider the full range of policy options for meeting the policy objectives, including different modal options, and policies for making more efficient use of existing capacity, as well as small and larger scale capacity enhancements and packages of policy measures.
3. Prioritise limited public resources on those policies which most cost-effectively deliver government's objectives, taking account of the full social, environmental and economic costs and benefits of policy options.
4. Ensure the evidence base can support this process, providing information on the needs of users, current and anticipated use and performance of the network, supporting option generation through modelling and appraisal of options, and evaluating impacts to inform future decision making.

Source: Eddington, Sir Rod (2006), *The Eddington Transport Study, Main Report: Transport's Role in Sustaining the UK's Productivity and Competitiveness*, December, HM Treasury and UK Department of Transport, London.

Where elements of long-range planning are already in place, governments can usefully step up efforts to develop strategic policy frameworks that integrate several key infrastructure systems. Such frameworks need to take a holistic approach to the task by *inter alia*:

- Providing a longer-term view of the development of the country or the region and its territorial "cohesion".
- Taking stock of the nation's infrastructure assets.
- Spelling out relationships between infrastructure and economic growth, as well as to other key objectives (social, technological, environmental sustainability, security, etc.).
- Offering a view of the trade-offs among the different policy objectives.
- Identifying current and future policy settings for infrastructure.

Examples of such approaches at national level are rare. However, first attempts in this direction are being made in New Zealand with its Infrastructure Policy Framework (based on an Infrastructure Stocktake Programme initiated in 2003 by the Ministry of Economic Development). Canada saw the creation in 2002 of Infrastructure Canada, a central agency tasked with formulating overall federal strategy for infrastructure development, administering programmes for financing infrastructures, and assuming the federal government's role *vis-à-vis* cities and municipalities. Noteworthy are also the endeavours of India to tackle urban infrastructure regeneration through a national strategy.

Box 1.10. **Strategic planning of urban infrastructures for an expanding population in India**

Not only is India expected to become the most populous country in the world during the third decade of this century, but also its urbanisation level is set rise quite dramatically – from the estimated current level of 27.8% in 2001 to 55% by 2025. Urban populations are expected to reach the 800 million mark by 2025 and 1 274 million by 2050. Urbanisation and economic growth in developing regions are strongly correlated. Urban centres' contribution to GDP increased from 30% in 1950-51 to 60% in 1990-91.

The future strategies of the country focus on achieving high GDP growth. This in turn will require considerable improvement of the urban infrastructure, which hitherto has been the subject of neglect and low priority in the national development plans. The issues and concerns related to inadequate resources for development of urban infrastructure following the pursuance of a closed and regulated economy have plagued the development of infrastructure in urban areas, not least that for transport. As a consequence of this, urban areas are extremely poorly served with urban public transport systems. Failure to develop

Box 1.10. **Strategic planning of urban infrastructures for an expanding population in India** *(cont.)*

these, coupled with low road space allocations and rising trends of motorisation to maintain a reasonable level of mobility for economic survival means that cities are faced with multiple problems related to congestion, safety and degradation.

Recognising the need and importance of urban settlements in the economic revival of the Indian economy, a number of programmes have been set in motion to revive the otherwise degraded urban settlements using different financial instruments. Mumbai, the financial capital of the country, has developed an urban transport vision directed towards making it a world class city and is currently receiving massive assistance from the World Bank. The city of Delhi is currently resurrecting its transport infrastructure by developing a high capacity mass transit system with financial assistance from the Japan Bank for International Co-operation (JBIC). The Mumbai and Delhi airports have been placed under public-private partnerships for modernisation, maintenance, operation and development. Also, plans are afoot to develop and upgrade the public transport systems and urban road systems in other metropolitan cities, such as Hyderabad, Bangalore, Chennai, Kolkata, Cochin, Ahmedabad and Chandigarh, pursuing different financial models and partnerships.

The central government has recently drawn up a reform-driven, fast track national urban renewal mission known as JNNURM (Jawaharal Nehru National Urban Renewal Mission) for the integrated and planned development of cities with focus on efficiency in urban infrastructure, infrastructure services delivery mechanisms, community participation and accountability. The main thrust of the sub-mission on urban infrastructure and governance will be on major infrastructure projects related to water supply, sanitation, sewerage, solid waste management, road network and urban transport, and redevelopment of inner city areas, with a view to upgrading infrastructure and shifting industrial and commercial establishments to conforming areas. Notwithstanding the paucity of resources and the administrative constraints, 63 cities and towns will be covered by this intensive urban infrastructure improvement programme.

Source: Sharma, A.K. (2006), "Country Report on India's Transport Infrastructure: Visions, Plans and Programme", paper prepared for the Infrastructure to 2030 Project, OECD IFP, Paris.

Improve integration of the different levels of government in the design, planning and delivery of infrastructures. The analysis conducted in this project has shown that there are forces at work which in the coming years will require policy makers to take a perspective on infrastructure which cuts through the different levels of government – municipal, regional and national. The first among these forces will be the search for greater efficiency in the operation of infrastructures, as governments seek to exploit economies of scale and scope to boost competitiveness and overall economic performance. The second will be the growing realisation that the reliability of infrastructures depends to a large extent on their geographical interconnectedness, necessitating closer interaction among local, regional and national authorities in the design and implementation of projects. There will also be a growing need to respond effectively and coherently at all levels of government to the impact of climate change and other environmental challenges, not least through the application of national funding schemes and national or even supranational standards of quality and safety. And finally, as the security of critical infrastructures moves up the policy agenda, central governments are likely to see themselves increasingly assuming the responsibility for helping ensure the protection of key installations and networks at all administrative and jurisdictional levels.

At least three avenues can lead to much improved integration of different levels of government in the design planning and delivery of infrastructures.

First, policy makers can expand the scope for pooling and networking of infrastructure resources across administrative and jurisdictional boundaries.

In several infrastructure sectors, especially water supplies, water treatment, electricity generation, gas, and urban public transport, such pooling and network widening can serve several objectives at once: greater efficiency, greater diversity of sourcing, and added security. Water for example is typically managed at municipal level, but watersheds and river basins often straddle several administrative boundaries. Watershed management is much better suited to water resource planning, security, demand management, infrastructure development and financing. Similarly, significant benefits can be garnered from banding together several municipal water systems, enabling expertise to be shared and the number of water sources to be multiplied, thus guarding better against supply failure. Governments may need to encourage greater openness to the idea of shared water services, support the establishment of formal supramunicipal structures for managing regional systems, and require the preparation of plans for watershed protection. They will also need to develop cost-sharing schemes with authorities at local and regional levels when it comes to addressing broader nationwide challenges such as climate change and security. Canada, France, the UK and US, to name but a few countries, have considerable experience already in this field, but the practice is not widespread throughout the OECD area or in the larger developing countries covered in this project. (See Box 1.11.)

Second, governments can take the lead in fostering active co-operation and constructive interaction among national government, regional and local governments in infrastructure planning and operation.

Interaction among different levels of government needs to go beyond mere co-ordination. This can be achieved through a variety of means, for example, the

Box 1.11. **The management of water systems in France**

In the French system, the state is basically responsible for setting and enforcing the rules and meeting social objectives, while municipalities have main responsibility for the development and management of water and water treatment facilities.

State. More specifically, the state is responsible for the water police (authorisation of water withdrawal and rejection of used water) and guarantees the safety and security of water provision. It controls the legality of contracts and public markets, enforces technical standards and audits budgets.

The state also ensures solidarity between users at two levels: *a)* At the level of the water basin, a public water agency collects a fee on the withdrawal of water and the disposal of used waters, which is used to finance investment in water treatment facilities in the water basin; and *b)* At the national level, a special fund for the development of water systems (le Fond National pour le Développement des Adductions d'Eau or FNDAE) collects a fee on each cubic metre of water distributed in France, which is used for assisting small rural communities to upgrade their water and water treatment facilities throughout the country.

Municipalities. The municipalities assume full responsibility for the development and management of water and water treatment facilities. They may do it on their own or may chose to join force with other municipalities. Currently, for 36 763 municipalities in France, there are 15 244 water systems and 11 992 water treatment facilities, suggesting that economies of scale may not be very significant in the sector.

Regarding the development and management of the facilities, the municipalities or groupings of municipalities may either develop and manage the facilities themselves or choose to delegate this responsibility to a private operator. Such delegation is the most common solution (75% of all water distribution facilities and more than 35% of water treatment facilities). This contractual approach guarantees levels of performance, clearly establishes the responsibilities of each party and provides for an equitable allocation of risks. On balance, it has proved its worth over more than a century. The large number of systems under public and private management also provides ample scope for benchmarking.

The application of the general principle that "water should pay for water" guarantees that water prices are set so as to ensure that budgets are balanced, although some forms of cross-subsidies across users exist. Despite this rigorous financial approach to water management, the cost of water to users in France remains reasonable (equivalent to about the price of two litres of petrol per cubic metre of water).

Source: Andrieu, Michel (2007), "A Cross-Sectoral Synthesis on the Long-Term Outlook for Infrastructure Business Models", in *Infrastructure to 2030 (Volume 2): Mapping Policy for Electricity, Water and Transport*, OECD, Paris.

establishment of trilateral agreements between federal government, regions and cities with their particularly complex problems; direct engagement of local governments in the identification of national and regional infrastructure priorities; design of infrastructure projects that are delivered by partnerships of two or more levels of government. An illustrative example from North America is Infrastructure Canada's Municipal Rural Infrastructure Fund which works in partnership with provincial and territorial governments, and the integrated community sustainability plans (ICSP) which need to be submitted as a pre-condition for securing federal funds for certain schemes. In Europe, an interesting approach is that of the recently decided infrastructure fund in Switzerland (see Box 1.12). Out of this new fund, CHF 5.5 billion is reserved for local transport infrastructure projects in urban areas. However, local municipalities need to fulfil some pre-requirements in order to obtain financial assistance from the fund. In particular, they must present a comprehensive long-term infrastructure plan, including all transport modes and land-use planning, to the federal transport ministry. Money from the fund will only be allocated to infrastructure projects after approval of this plan by the federal transport ministry.

Thirdly, policy makers can improve channels of communication for national-level objectives and standards.

This is especially relevant for ensuring coherent and consistent approaches to such key issues as environmental targets (*e.g.* reducing air pollution or groundwater pollution); safety, quality and technical standards; and designing and implementing measures to enhance the security of critical infrastructure installations. Mechanisms need to be developed to allow lower levels of government to tap into funds at national level to finance local infrastructure projects.

Recommendation 12: Reduce the vulnerability of long-term infrastructure planning and implementation to short-term thinking and priority setting.

Precisely because of the overwhelming presence of the state in the domain of infrastructure – whether as owner, operator, regulator or client – infrastructure can and does fall victim to the "short-termism" that characterises much of the public sector decision-making process. In land transport, water supply networks and treatment facilities, power generation plants and transmission connections, systems have long economic lives – well over 30 years in some cases – and require lengthy capital planning and budgeting cycles frequently of 10 to 20 years. This contrasts strongly with what are roughly 7-year business cycles, 4 to 5-year political cycles and 1 to 3-year budgetary cycles. All too often in times of short-term crisis, long-term plans for infrastructure investment are sacrificed in the name of short-term expediency to meet other, more pressing political matters and policy agenda goals. (This is, in fact, an "agency" problem: how to align the interests of the politician elected for just a few years with the much longer-term national interest that should accommodate the needs also of unborn generations.)

This sits awkwardly with the pressures building up on infrastructures over the next two decades or so in OECD countries in particular: ageing public capital stock with some systems close to the end of their natural life cycle; lack of previous investment and maintenance in several sectors; continuing urban sprawl; growing congestion in cities and on key transport and power supply corridors, to name but a few. What has often been ignored is that long-term investment is required to maintain public infrastructure and boost nation's productive capital. What is needed for the coming decades is sustained and steady investment and rehabilitation. The challenge is to find ways and means of framing long-term strategies, securing long-term sources of finance and shielding them as effectively as possible from short-term political exigencies.

There are two key ingredients that can be helpful in setting infrastructure investment in a longer-term, more stable framework.

The first, as seen earlier, is putting in place a long-term strategic framework for decision making.

The very presence of a long-term strategic plan for infrastructures, even if imperfect and not effectively enforced, can be of considerable benefit in terms of orientating decision makers' views to the future and imbuing a sense of vision and long-term purpose. Not surprisingly, perhaps, empirical evidence from a number of countries in several areas of infrastructure seems to indicate that existence of long-term planning tends to be associated with lower volatility of infrastructure funding over time. Ten to twenty-year strategic plans that set out government commitments and identify infrastructure projects in the pipeline can also play a crucial role in attracting private capital, since they create greater transparency and increased certainty for the private sector.

The second is establishing long-term infrastructure funds.

Going beyond such strategic planning, some countries have taken concrete steps to create a stronger link between the long-term nature of infrastructure and the equally long-term nature of the financing requirements, while at the same time endeavouring to shield the decision-making processes from unduly disruptive short-term political intervention. Canada for example has a CAD 6 billion Strategic Infrastructure Fund directed to projects of major federal and regional significance. It attaches special conditions to the attribution of funding (*e.g.* requirement for mass transit projects to explore demand management strategies, or water projects to address issues of metering and pricing). In 1998, Switzerland created a long-term infrastructure fund for rail in the order of CHF 30 billion; and in autumn 2006, parliament decided on the creation of a CHF 21 billion fund for long-term investment in urban transport, the motorway network and main roads in peripheral regions.

Box 1.12. **Securing adequate and stable levels of long-term investment in surface transport infrastructure – the Swiss infrastructure funds**

In 1998, the Swiss population agreed by referendum to a comprehensive modernisation and extension of the railway system. It involved four programmes aimed at improvements to the railway network with better connections among main cities, the construction of two new transalpine tunnels, integration of eastern and western Switzerland into the European high-speed network, and substantial noise abatement measures.

The fund has a total envelope of CHF 30.5 billion (equivalent to about 9% of 1995 GDP) provided through partially earmarked heavy goods vehicle (HGV) fees, value-added taxes and excise duties. The Swiss parliament decides on the projects within in each of the four programmes, and it releases the money annually from the fund.

In autumn 2006, the Swiss parliament decided on the creation of a road transport infrastructure fund which will secure total investments of CHF 20.8 billion (equivalent to about 5% of GDP at current prices) over a period of 20 years, starting in 2008. The fund is to be used for improving urban traffic flows, the national motorway network, and main roads in mountain areas and peripheral regions. The fund has several objectives, including to: facilitate the planning and consolidation of investment finance; guarantee long-term investment finance; provide new finance for urban traffic; establish priorities in the use of limited resources by planning transport and land use in a co-ordinated fashion. The underlying rationale is that infrastructures should only be extended when the full potential of existing infrastructures has been utilised.

The revenues for the fund will be drawn from earmarked vehicle fuel taxes and from annual motorway user charges. An initial deposit of CHF 2.6 billion will be made available up front in order to provide sufficient liquidity to the fund. Thereafter, the Swiss parliament will determine the level of financing by deciding each year, in the context of the budget, the share of revenues (taxes and charges) to be paid into the fund – around CHF 900 million on the basis of current planning, or about 25% of total earmarked revenues. The sum of CHF 8.5 billion is foreseen for completion of the national trunk road network; CHF 5.5 billion for extensions of the existing motorway network, aiming to reduce congestion problems; and CHF 6 billion for the federal government's contribution to the improvement of public and private urban traffic infrastructures, including road, rail, regional express rail networks, and "soft" mobility schemes. The remaining CHF 800 million will be

Box 1.12. Securing adequate and stable levels of long-term investment in surface transport infrastructure – the Swiss infrastructure funds (cont.)

used for main roads in mountain areas and peripheral regions. This money will be released from the fund in 4-year periods.

Both the overall financial outlook and simulations conducted to estimate flows of revenues over the 20-year period indicate that the means will be sufficient to secure the infrastructure fund, as well as other financing needs, in particular for infrastructure operation and maintenance. As things currently stand, it should not be necessary to raise the rates of vehicle fuel tax.

Though long-term in its conception, the infrastructure fund is in fact a provisional measure. It will be dissolved at the end of the 20-year period, unless the federal council (government) decides to extend it – which it can do for a maximum of 5 years. It is also limited in scope to the CHF 20.8 billion foreseen in the legislation.

The key advantages of the funds are that they permit bundling of several infrastructure projects within long-term programmes; allow for flexibility and adjustments through time subsequent to debate in parliament once every election term; tie their revenue streams to earmarked fees and taxes; provide for continuous supplies of funds to individual projects, avoiding the frequently experienced problems of stop-and-go in planning and execution; and are subject to a strong controlling and reporting mechanism, including parliament.

Source: Based on Albrecht, Christian (2006), "Infrastructure Funds in Switzerland: How They Contribute to Reducing the Gap Between Short-Term Thinking in Politics and the Need for Long-Term Infrastructure Planning", paper prepared for the Infrastructure to 2030 Project, OECD IFP, Paris; and Swiss Federal Council (2005), "Message about the Infrastructure Funds for Urban Agglomeration Traffic and the Network of National Roads", 2 December, Bern.

Experience with these funds suggests that it is useful to follow a number of basic principles:

- Ensure the projects and programmes to be financed through the fund are clearly defined and well accepted.
- Finance the fund through tied revenue streams to secure the long-term credits.
- Place time limits on the fund and limit the amount of total funding.
- Avoid using the money for permanent, ongoing duties such as infrastructure maintenance.
- Ensure proper reporting and control mechanisms are in place to guarantee the effectiveness and transparency of the funds.

Recommendation 13: Ensure the involvement of a broader range of stakeholders in the process of needs assessment, prioritisation, design, planning and delivery of infrastructures.

The analysis conducted in this project suggests two interrelated conclusions: that in OECD countries, but also in other parts of the world, the pressures for greater participation of stakeholders in the various stages of infrastructure development are gaining in strength; and that, conducted in the appropriate fashion, such stakeholder involvement can on balance be of significant benefit to the success and sustainability of infrastructure projects.

The forces pushing in this direction are many and varied. First, by their very nature, infrastructures embody both public and private benefits, with the latter moving increasingly to the fore as the role of the private sector in infrastructure provision expands. Second, in the wake of shifting patterns of urban and rural settlement, infrastructure projects are affecting many more assets, especially in already densely inhabited residential areas. Thirdly, in recent years there have been signs that public confidence is waning in the ability of public administrations to deliver on their own the services that citizens want. Fourthly, modern information technologies ensure that citizens can be mobilised more quickly, numerously and effectively than ever before. Fifthly, the principle of partial or full cost recovery is set to gain momentum, tightening the links between users and their infrastructures. And finally, experience suggests that by involving the full range of perspectives of the community members who will be impacted by the project, consensus generally (but not always) tends to emerge around reasonable outcomes that lay the groundwork for successful implementation.

It is argued, however, that wide stakeholder involvement can be time-consuming, tie the hands of government, reduce flexibility in negotiations, make it difficult to achieve significant policy reform, and preclude significant changes in policy direction that might be resisted by citizens. These arguments have to be weighed not only against past experience in a specific regional or national context, but also against the opportunities offered by new tools and different experiences elsewhere.

With an eye to growing demands for greater participation of citizens and professional groups in the future, public authorities can capitalise on the knowledge base and competences of stakeholders in two ways: by adjusting the style and substance of their approach; and by widening their access to different private and professional groups in timely fashion.

Devise new approaches for moving from traditional forms of citizen consultation towards citizen engagement in infrastructure planning. Traditionally, citizens have had relatively little direct involvement in infrastructure planning. When it has taken place, it has generally tended to be in the form of consultation or public hearings in which government and its experts inform the public and seek public views on governmental plans. In North American and European experience, a particularly problematic issue for many citizens involved in deliberative exercises is the lack of direct, observable and substantial policy impact of their participation. What is emerging in many OECD countries is a stronger move to citizen engagement by which citizens act as partners with the public authorities in developing plans. Experience suggests that to be effective, the processes to facilitate citizen engagement need to be: inclusive and representative; provide for genuine deliberation; allow access to accurate information; and offer the prospect of effectively influencing outcomes and achieving clear results.

The range of new tools and mechanisms for achieving more effective citizen engagement around infrastructure development is wide, diverse and expanding. They include facilitated town meetings, polls to measure public opinion about deliberation outcomes, large-scale online dialogue, citizen juries, national issues fora and community-wide study circles. In particular, recent years have seen online communication and dialogue with stakeholders and the general public grow in importance and effectiveness.

In addition to facilitating the planning and implementation process, successful participation of this kind can help to create a stronger sense of identity or ownership of the project. With stakeholders and citizens in general informed and knowledgeable about the importance and benefits to themselves and/or to society as a whole, the task of gaining public support for the construction of new projects, disruptive maintenance work on existing projects, the introduction or raising of earmarked taxes or user fees, etc. can be made much easier. Experience from the water sector demonstrates that public awareness of the water and wastewater system, the state of its assets, and the need for repair and upgrade, is critical for the success of the utility (public or private) to meet its investment needs and, where relevant, to gain public acceptance of increases in overall water prices. Similarly, with road transport charging schemes, experience suggests that careful consideration needs to be given to explaining to the general public how the revenues are to be used (*e.g.* earmarked for specific local improvements or national purposes), if public acceptance of the scheme is to be assured. Moreover, ensuring open access to documents, information and contracts instils public trust and inspires public confidence. Transparency in contractual negotiations also ensures that decisions are sustained from one government to the next, and public access to information ensures that government and potential private sector partners are accountable for agreed-upon outcomes.

Widen the range of stakeholders by engaging non-traditional actors and involve all stakeholders from an early stage onwards. The general public aside, OECD governments increasingly need to consider making more use of other knowledge bases and sources of expertise in society more broadly. In addition to NGOs (for whose inclusion in the infrastructure consultation process governments are developing increasingly structured processes), there is a wealth of competence, experience and potential support on which to draw in the form of universities, professional groupings (*e.g.* civil engineering societies), civic associations led by business executives (though in the US currently less engaged in urban development than previously), foundations, industrial associations, chambers of commerce, consumer observatories, etc., as well as that of the stakeholders directly or indirectly affected – local businesses, residential and commercial land developers.

Box 1.13. **Public involvement in infrastructure planning in France**

In France, formal procedures for consultation and collaboration are now included in the technical instructions regarding the preparation of road, rail and power generation and transmission infrastructure projects. Since 2002, legislation provides for a public debate to be organised as early as possible on the timeliness, objectives and main characteristics of the project and the specifications for subsequent studies.

Under the terms of the legislation, provision must be made for the public to participate in all the later stages of project development, from the initiation of the preliminary design studies until completion of the public enquiry. The public must also be kept fully informed during the construction stage until the final entry into service of the infrastructure.

An independent administrative authority, the National Commission for Public Debate (CNDP) is charged with the task of ensuring that these principles are respected, and of organising the relevant procedures. In particular, according to the scale of the project and its overall impact in all areas, the Commission determines whether the public debate should be organised by the Commission itself, a special commission, or the owner acting under the supervision of the Commission.

The entire system is a clear advance towards "participatory" democracy. At the same time, it poses an additional challenge to the owners of works whose collaboration must, without hesitation, be open to and both available and prepared for this additional debate.

One of the prerequisites of success will also be to reconcile the desire to organise the public debate at the earliest date possible with the need to inform that debate with a sufficiently detailed project assessment, in order to be able to discuss the forecast cost and expected benefits in full knowledge of the relevant facts. A fair balance must also be struck between this form of "participatory" democracy and the traditional organisation of "representative" democracy, in that the role, prerogatives and eminent responsibilities of those elected to office by universal suffrage must be properly respected.

Source: OECD and ECMT (2005), *National Systems of Transport Infrastructure Planning*, Round Table 128, OECD, Paris.

Public outreach can play an important role in the priorities that governments set for infrastructure. It can also often be a pre-condition for the emergence of new models for tackling old problems. The case of new "mobility managers" in the Netherlands is an instructive example involving a pilot project in the Hague city region that brings together public road managers, public transport companies, all the relevant public authorities, local interest groups, employers' associations, etc. to develop a co-ordinated approach to mobility.

Public authorities should ensure that a full range of general public representatives (press, advocacy groups, residents' groups), as well as direct and indirect stakeholders, participate early on in the strategy design process and should provide for their active involvement throughout implementation and monitoring. Such early involvement can be crucial in gaining broad support for projects.

Recommendation 14: Step up efforts to reduce the length and complexity of the planning-to-implementation process.

Substantial delays and unduly complicated processes from the planning stage to completion are not an uncommon feature of infrastructure development both in OECD and non-OECD countries. A quite frequent occurrence in the fields of road and rail transport and power transmission lines, they are happening increasingly also in such areas as the siting of radio masts. A variety of causes can be identified ranging *inter alia* from lengthy but necessary steps to protect the public interest, to poor planning, unnecessarily complex tendering procedures, cost overruns, and disputes among the parties involved. To the extent that the projects are politically sound and offer clear net economic, social and/or environmental benefits, such delays can have serious consequences not only because of the mounting costs they provoke but also because they may jeopardise the very project itself, with all the attendant risks for the future of the regional or national economy, environment, network security, and the quality of life of local populations.

The analysis in this project suggests that there are four steps involved in making progress on this issue: involve all interests early in the process (but not at each and every stage of the project's life); accelerate the planning process; simplify procurement; and speed up the legal procedures.

Involve all stakeholders in a timely but efficient manner. The conundrum facing the public authorities is that they need to respond to the growing expectations of citizens to have their views heard on major infrastructure projects, while at the same time endeavouring to ensure that the consultation process (including in particular the public inquiry) is conducted in an effective and expedient fashion. As noted earlier, consultation of all relevant stakeholders early in the process is vital if major problems and delays are to be avoided in later phases of the venture. The case of the Betuwe Line in the Netherlands highlights the severity of the costs that may be incurred if consultation is neither timely nor adequate.

Box 1.14. **The Betuwe Line in the Netherlands – determining the public and commercial objectives**

International trade has always been especially important to the Netherlands: 20% of the Dutch GDP is attributed to activities in the Port of Rotterdam and to Schiphol Airport. As a result, port access issues have a high priority in transport planning in the country, and landside port capacity issues are critical in a country that has among the highest population densities in the world.

Rotterdam, in addition to being one of the world's larger general cargo ports, is the largest container port outside Asia. The Rotterdam container traffic, at over 8 million TEU, would amount to around 11 000 trucks per day – a serious challenge to the Dutch highway system, and a potentially significant creator of noise and pollution. It is important that as much of the container traffic as possible be shifted to rail and water (Rhine River) for inland movement.

The efficiency of the port is not just important to the Netherlands, because Rotterdam, along with Hamburg, is a major interface point for Europe in world trade. For example, 57% of all European distribution centers for US companies are located in the Netherlands, making Rotterdam a key link in transatlantic trade.

In 1990, the Dutch government announced its intention to proceed with a project to construct a new rail link from the Rotterdam area to a connection with the German railway network in order to speed up the connection of Rotterdam with inland, rail-based trade, to relieve the congestion on the existing railway (NS) lines that were already carrying large volumes of passenger trains (the Dutch rail system has higher traffic density and a higher percentage of passenger traffic than any other EU15 railway), and to relieve congestion on the Dutch highways. This decision was apparently based on extensive studies in various fields. However, to this day, there is much criticism over the validity of these studies.

Subsequent planning studies led to a commitment to upgrade an existing 40-kilometre rail line in the port area (from Maasvlakte to Kijfhoek, near Rotterdam), and to connect it with a new, 120-kilometre line to Zevenaar where it connects with the German network. The overall project is called the Betuwe Line. The upgraded section has been used as an internal railway to integrate the Port of Rotterdam and to improve the existing linkages. The second section should complete the high capacity (up to 10 trains per hour each way), all-freight link with the German network.

Box 1.14. **The Betuwe Line in the Netherlands – determining the public and commercial objectives** *(cont.)*

The project has had a troubled history in a number of ways. The completion date has stretched from 2004 to 2007, and the cost in constant terms has doubled since the early planning stage from EUR 2.3 billion to around EUR 4.6 billion during the realisation phase. About 60% of the escalation is due to scope additions, and 40% is due to cost escalation. The majority of the cost increases was instigated by parliament as a result of environmental and safety issues. The early traffic estimates (and the financial and economic viability of the project) have been called into question.

After a long period of decline since the 1960s, rail freight traffic has increased since 1994. However, the future demand picture specifically for the Betuwe Line is uncertain, particularly because of problems concerning the choice of infrastructure charges.

The government's plans for the institutional management of the Betuwe Line have also evolved, partly in line with the evolution of the structure of the national railway. Originally planned to be part of the national rail infrastructure, the government gave serious consideration in the mid to late 1990s to setting the project up as a PPP before building the line. This idea was abandoned on grounds of "risk and policy uncertainties" (the Netherlands Court of Audit suggests). Under pressure from parliament, the operation (and therefore the infrastructure charges) of the line must be sufficiently profitable to cover the cost of administration and maintenance. This is in strong contrast with the existing network. On the other hand, infrastructure charges have to compete with transport charges of the other modes. In order to achieve this, the government has asked the national infrastructure agency (ProRail) to manage the facility for the first few years after completion until the actual traffic flows and operating costs can be determined. Current estimates are that the line will need public support over and above the funds generated from access charges (set at marginal cost), through 2011, after which no further government support to operations is expected. ProRail has announced the proposed 2007 access charges for the line, which include a discount from the national charge structure in order to promote traffic on the line.

After 2011, the government will start a tender procedure for the operation of the Betuwe Line. It is interesting also that the predominant freight operator on the line is Railion, a subsidiary of the Deutsche Bahn holding company, though there are 7 other licensed operators, including Rail4Chem. Railion is the only significant rail freight carrier serving both of the two largest EU container ports – Hamburg and Rotterdam – putting much of the traffic on the Betuwe Line under the control of a company that might feel conflicting pressures between promoters of traffic through the two ports.

The analysis of the project by the court of audit highlights the similarity of the Betuwe Line to a number of other major public rail infrastructure projects. On the positive side, the Dutch government has been quite aggressive in determining the public objectives in improved access to the Port of Rotterdam, and has been willing to have a clear distinction between commercial and public objectives, accompanied by public support for the public

Box 1.14. **The Betuwe Line in the Netherlands – determining the public and commercial objectives** *(cont.)*

goals. On the negative side, the essential scope of the project appears to have been committed on the basis of weak forecasts. Because the real performance and structure of the line were not pinned down until recently, the institutional structure – especially the role of the private sector – could not be committed. In addition, the goal of keeping the infrastructure charges low in order to promote traffic conflicted with the stated goal of promoting private sector investment. Finally, because of the enormous size of the project (it is the second largest public works project in Holland's history after the Delta Works), the management team was not initially up to the challenge. Several years, and several reorganisations, were necessary before the project was brought under control.

It is not at all uncommon for projects like this to be over budget and behind schedule. Flyvbjerg, Bruzelius and Rothengatter argue in *Megaprojects and Risk: An Anatomy of Ambition* (2003) that these kinds of short falls are endemic to public megaprojects. For the Betuwe Line, two other factors play a role. Firstly, the plans of past governments to discourage freight transport by road by pricing measures have largely not materialised. Secondly, the Betuwe Line currently will end at the Dutch-German border. Although a covenant has been signed between the Dutch and German governments to extend the line, no concrete building action has taken place yet in Germany.

Source: Based on Thompson, Louis S. (2007), "Key Trends and Implications for Policy Change in Long-Term Rail Freight Traffic and Infrastructure", in *Infrastructure to 2030 (Volume 2): Mapping Policy for Electricity, Water and Transport*, OECD, Paris.

The consultation process itself can be streamlined in various ways. Careful preparation of the process by the project promoters, for example, can go a long way towards reducing the risk of disputes among administrators, environmental groups, community representatives and so on. Also new process mechanisms for use in inquiries may warrant consideration. In the UK, for instance, one of the most significant reforms that has recently been introduced is the possibility of different inquiry inspectors holding concurrent rather than consecutive sessions of the same inquiry, and reporting to a lead inspector. Moreover, judicious use of timetabling for the proceedings, plus greater emphasis on written submissions, as opposed to oral evidence at inquiries, can help render the process more effective.

Speed up the planning process. There is, to begin with, a very basic but important need to clarify procedures, obtain approvals and secure rights of way at an early stage. Thereafter, however, delays may still result because of the complexity of the administrative processes and the number and variety of levels of government and administrations involved. Some countries have made recent moves to simplify such arrangements by redistributing decision-making powers. In France, for example, in the area of motorway construction (which is plagued by very long intervals – 14 to15 years – between the initiation of design studies and the commissioning of major motorway sections), the government has introduced steps to speed up the process. It is doing this by devolving decision making powers to *préfets* and simplifying and shortening procedures for discussion both among individual administrations and between administrations and the local territorial authorities concerned. And in the Netherlands, the new Spatial Planning Act will increase the decision-making powers of both the national government and the provinces with respect to large, spatially extensive infrastructure projects, thereby reducing the capacity of municipalities to delay decisions.

Devise procedures that simplify and accelerate the procurement process. As governments increasingly involve the private sector in the design, implementation and delivery of infrastructures, they need to ensure that mechanisms are in place to protect the public interest and oversee the process, while endeavouring to simplify and shorten the process itself where it is unduly prone to delays. Clearly, every country has to operate in its own specific political, economic and cultural context; yet some general principles for policy makers for bringing such improvements about do seem to apply. For example:

- Prepare a thorough feasibility study, which lays the basis for well-drafted requests for proposals and for effective subsequent evaluation of the proposals submitted by bidders.
- Restrict the number of bidders to a reasonable figure through pre-selection (see case studies in Boxes 1.15 and 1.16).
- Draw up standard concession agreements wherever possible. For example, for the upgrading of some twelve possible motorway sections of more than 500 kilometres in length, the German transport ministry commissioned a group of experts to draw up a standard concession agreement for application in 2005/06.
- Contract with a single private sector entity, such as through a PPP consortium, to reduce the need for the public authorities and agencies to manage relations with multiple private contractors.

Two case studies offer concrete illustrations of how procedures from bidding to financial closure can be speeded up substantially: the Dutch high speed train project HSL-Zuid, and recent changes to the legislation governing procurement procedures in Spain (see Boxes 1.15 and 1.16).

Explore ways of accelerating legal procedures. Some OECD countries are experimenting with innovative approaches to accelerate particularly tedious and prolonged procedures. The Netherlands introduced a special act in 2003

Box 1.15. **HSL-ZUID – fast-track processing of contract bids in high-speed rail in the Netherlands**

The Netherlands' HSL-ZUID infrastructure project was innovative in a number of respects. It was decided to divide the overall PPP project into three distinct and separate key contractual elements: civil construction of substructure (through classic public procurement); infrastructure/superstructure (bid by the private sector on a PPP design); and supply and operation of trains (bid by the private sector on an independent train operator arrangement, fully funded by the successful bidder).

Among its key procedural features was the design of a particularly streamlined process for the stages of "best and final offer" through to financial close. The two shortlisted bidders were required to submit detailed and committed proposals under which the commercial and financial elements had to:

- Confirm that both the bidder and its bankers had completed all due diligence and investigation.
- Submit a detailed financial term sheet in final form.
- Make all comments and changes to the draft implementation agreement before submission of the best and final offer.
- Provide heads of agreement signed by all relevant parties covering all key contractual agreements (*e.g.* construction and maintenance arrangements).
- Accept that any proposed changes to the documents and bid submission after "best and final offer" by either the bidder or his bankers could cause immediate disqualification.
- Submit very strong letters of commitment (pre-agreed with HSL and its advisors) from their equity participants and lead bankers with respect to the full amount of funding.

The purpose of this strategy was to ensure full competitive pressures were upheld. This reduced the usual time delays between letter of intent and financial closure, often as a consequence of renegotiation.

Source: Siemens Financial Services (2003), *Project Finance Yearbook 2002/2003*, Siemens Financial Services GmbH, Munich.

which makes it possible to process a specific set of highway projects (34 in all) under one single, relatively short procedure, saving up to two years in the planning stage. The projects focus on the most heavily congested locations in the country. The special act is a provisional piece of legislation and will expire on completion of the projects.

Box 1.16. **Non-negotiated proposals in the procurement process in Spain**

Legislation in Spain facilitates the speeding up of the procurement process by offering the possibility to avoid the negotiated procedure. The information submitted in the bids is expected to be adequate enough to determine not only qualified bidders, as no separate pre-qualification stage is made use of, but also the ranking of the bids.

The technical and financial proposals must be presented at the same time. During the normal evaluation procedure, the bidders are not allowed to examine each other's offers. The request for proposal sets out the project and the draft contract in great detail, as provided for in the existing legislation. The framework for the allocation of risks is given *ex ante*, as is much of the tariff regime. In Spain, it is not necessary to prepare a detailed design of the project before the bidding process is initiated; a preliminary design is sufficient. This approach to procurement is thus structured in such a way as to make it possible to "price" the bid based on the request for proposals, thereby eliminating the need for negotiations.

The Spanish track record for speed of contracting is exceptional, as also witnessed by the number of deals concluded. In general, the total period until closure is about 8 months. Some additional features of the Spanish process that contribute to reducing transaction costs and streamlining procedures are that: *i)* during tender evaluation bidders are able to review each others' offers, thus ensuring full transparency and early elimination of potential conflicts; and that *ii)* financial closure does not have to be reached at the time of the conclusion of the project agreement. Instead, the successful bidder has to pay a 4% bid bond (on the total investment amount) to ensure commitment to the agreement.

Source: Based on OECD and ECMT (2007), *Transport Infrastructure Investment: Options for Efficiency*, OECD, Paris, forthcoming.

A recent study of 15 major Dutch infrastructure projects (Van der Krabben *et al.*, 2007) concluded that a range of factors determine a successful decision-making process. In addition to many of the points raised above, the study also underlines the significance of the presence of private sector parties in the project, the innovativeness of the contractual arrangements, and the key facilitating role played by the potential benefits of real estate development that may be associated with the venture.

As globalisation continues apace, markets expand, and supply chains lengthen across the world, the capacity of economies to handle increasing volumes of international movements will grow in importance. Without decisive action to facilitate cross-border infrastructure connections, opportunities for trade and economic expansion will be missed, and the incidence of congestion

Table 1.2. **Success factors *versus* bottlenecks in infrastructure decision making**

Success factors for infrastructure decision making	Bottlenecks in infrastructure decision making
• Relatively low procedural complexity. • Strong entrepreneurial attitude of local government. • (Early) involvement of market parties; innovative contracting models, based on risk-taking by private partners. • Leading role in project planning for market consortium. • Optimal project scope: positive balance of costs and benefits for different groups of actors and interest groups involved (after completion of the project). • Combination of infrastructure and real estate development makes sure that projects not only cost money, but will also generate income. • Innovative (temporary) legislation may contribute in certain cases to success of decision-making.	• Decision-making processes and budgeting problems on the national level. • Provinces' lack of decision (low degree of decisiveness on the regional level). • Inadequate co-operation between municipalities (in case of regional projects). • Problems with co-operation and/or contracting between public and private actors involved in the project. • Overly centralised approach neglecting support from public, decentralised authorities and market parties. • No or insufficient involvement of market parties (in the case of "traditional" line infrastructure projects). • Inappropriate project scope (problems with tuning of decision-making; missing opportunities for capturing value). • Ambitions too high causing overly high costs. • Incomplete public debate on necessity and added value of the project.

Source: Van der Krabben, Erwin, Bas Zonnenberg, and Rob van der Heijden (2007), "Understanding the Implementation of Infrastructure Projects: Speed of Decision-Making Processes, Participation and Complexity Levels of Dutch Infrastructure Projects", paper prepared for the Infrastructure to 2030 Project, OECD IFP, Paris.

Recommendation 15: Strengthen international co-operation to improve the efficiency, reliability and security of flows of goods, services and information across transborder infrastructures.

at key crossing points will grow in severity. Especially in the international arena, reliability and efficiency of supply will remain crucial to successful national and regional economic performance.

In all infrastructure sectors, perhaps most notably in electricity, rail, water and telecommunications, there is considerable scope for international action.

Recent blackouts in parts of Europe and North America highlight the importance of adequate and reliable transmission capacity. In terms of creating the right conditions for more capacity, regional pooling of resources offers considerable potential, as demonstrated by the establishment of Nord Pool. The transmission system operators (TSO) in Denmark, Finland, Norway and Sweden have equipped Nord Pool with a monopoly over all available transmission capacity among the countries (and their respective price zones) for day-ahead trade. Elsewhere in Europe, the power exchanges of France, Belgium and the Netherlands have agreed on a mechanism for trading transmission capacity.

And the Norwegian (Statnett) and Netherlands (TenneT) TSOs are currently embarked on the construction of an interconnector which will also permit trading of transmission capacity.

Box 1.17. **Network congestion management and pricing in the Nordic market**

The prices of power and capacity in the Nordic market are determined on a zonal basis. Norway and Denmark are both made up of two zones; and Sweden and Finland, one each. The network owners are responsible for making good network losses by buying power in the market and recovering the cost through the zonal pricing system. The transmission system operators in each country grant Nord Pool, the market operator for the entire Nordic region jointly owned by the system operators, a monopoly over all available transmission capacity between price zones for day-ahead trade. Thus, Nord Pool collects all the congestion rent – differences in market prices between each zone. Transmission capacity is firm and can be taken fully into account in the day-ahead settlement of spot prices. The system operators are responsible for managing any deviations between the transmission capacity made available for trade and the actual physical transmission capacity, normally through out-of-merit-order dispatch. Nord Pool then distributes the congestion rents to system operators under an established formula. The Nordic system operators are bound by the EU regulation on cross-border trade in electricity (EC, 2003). The regulation allows congestion rents to be used to guarantee actual availability of allocated capacity through out-of-merit-order dispatch or to pay for network investment. Otherwise they must be set against their allowed costs used to determine their return on assets and network tariffs. Nord Pool also offers a financial product, known as a "contract for differences", that allows market players to hedge price differences between zones.

In Sweden, load is concentrated in the south, while production – largely based on hydropower – is centred in the north. The national system operator, Svenska Kraftnät, manages congestion within Sweden, typically by using out-of-merit-order dispatch or by restricting the transmission capacity available for trade across borders at short notice (less than 24 hours). This has led to pressure from large electricity consumers in Norway and Denmark to introduce locational signals, to deter the practice of curbing cross-border capacity which they see as discriminating against them in favour of Swedish consumers. In 2003, the Association of Energy Retail Consumers, an association of Denmark's largest industrial consumers, sent a formal complaint to the European Commission. Danish Energy, an industry association, did likewise in 2006. Neither case has yet been resolved. In 2004, the Swedish regulator published a report showing that all the Nordic system operators shift internal congestion to their national borders to a certain degree.

Source: International Energy Agency (IEA) (2005), *Lessons from Liberalised Electricity Markets*, OECD/IEA, Paris; and Morgan, Trevor (2007), "Assessing the Long-Term Outlook for Business Models in Electricity Infrastructure and Services", in *Infrastructure to 2030 (Volume 2): Mapping Policy for Electricity, Water and Transport*, OECD, Paris.

In terms of improving reliability, the blackouts referred to above have demonstrated the importance not just of routine co-ordination and co-operation among systems operators, but also the full implementation of bilateral agreements. Indeed, given the growing need for safe operation and control in closer-to-real-time mode based on adequate data acquisition and binding rules, including contingency procedures, there would seem to be further scope for improvement in co-ordination among TSOs.

Rail freight, notably in Europe, is still handicapped by a patchwork of inconsistent access charge regimes and by lack of interoperability, both of which act to hinder the flow of rail freight traffic across national boundaries. Progress, though difficult, is very necessary. Simplification of access charges is what is required, rather than harmonisation of regimes and prices. And on the interoperability issue, as well as on a range of other issues such as timetabling, co-ordinated elimination of bottlenecks, etc., there are – in parallel with the TEN Programme – several examples of successful international co-operation to build on. The Rotterdam-Genoa rail freight corridor is one such case.

Box 1.18. **Efforts of the international group to improve the quality of rail transport in Corridor A (IQ-C)**

The European Union has recognised the need to improve the quality of rail transport in the main European corridors. The EC has decided to focus on the six main rail freight transport corridors in order to introduce a new European train steering and control system (ETCS) as soon as possible, as well as operational measures for improving the quality of rail transport.

The Rotterdam-Genoa rail freight corridor, known as Corridor A, is continuing to develop rapidly. In January 2003, a memorandum of understanding was signed by the ministers of the four corridor countries (Italy, Germany, the Netherlands and Switzerland) to improve framework conditions for the development of rail freight services. This scheme includes a range of quality improving measures, which focus on actions not only from infrastructure managers, but also measures that have to be implemented by the ministries.

The International Group for Improving the Quality of Rail Transport in the North-South Corridor (IQ-C) has reached a good level of co-operation and has brought about some remarkable results. However, considerable efforts are still necessary in order to further improve the quality and punctuality standards in transalpine rail freight transport.

Box 1.18. **Efforts of the international group to improve the quality of rail transport in Corridor A (IQ-C)** *(cont.)*

In March 2006, the ministers signed a "Letter of Intent" with the aim to complete the ETCS infrastructure on Corridor A by 2015. The infrastructure managers on that corridor have developed quality improving actions, such as, common deadlines for the planning and allocation process for timetabling; development of customer relationships; establishment of common and harmonised operations management processes; further development of infrastructure; and international co-ordinated bottleneck elimination. Great efforts have been made to improve punctuality and analysis of the causes of delays. Measures to simplify customs procedures were established, and progress is being made regarding countries' mutual recognition of locomotives and engine-drivers. The solution for a simplified customs procedure in the North-South Corridor has recently been extended. The regulatory bodies along Corridor A have established a platform for successful co-operation.

In May 2006, the ministries agreed upon a new Action Plan 2006-10 to focus and amend the actions of the memorandum of understanding. In addition to the above mentioned activities, it includes some other actions, especially focused on improving punctuality, ETCS implementation and terminal issues.

The market of international rail freight services is performing strongly: combined transport on the corridor has increased by more than 10% each year since 2003; and the total market share of transalpine rail freight increased in Corridor A (Rotterdam-Milan) to 65% in 2006. Nevertheless, great potential still remains. The quality improvement scheme, established by the ministers of Italy, Germany, the Netherlands and Switzerland is affecting results due to the network created amongst relevant stakeholders. The close monitoring of volumes, punctuality and costs shall be continued from 2006 onward and shall be made available to all interested stakeholders.

Source: Communicated by the Swiss Federal Office of Transport (2006). For further information, see the document "IQ-C Action Plan for Rail Freight Corridor Rotterdam-Genoa" on the European Commission Directorate for Energy and Transport website at *http://ec.europa.eu/transport/rail/market/doc/action-plan-rdam-genoa.pdf*.

In the water sector, a growing recognition of the multidimensional nature of the issues at stake is gradually imposing the necessity of a more holistic approach to the management of resources everywhere. This is reflected not least in the growing necessity to manage water at the water basin level, irrespective of administrative boundaries. In some cases, where the water basin straddles the territories of several countries, policy makers will need to join forces across borders to achieve more efficient management of the common resource. The Mexican-US agreement on water co-operation is an interesting example of how such agreements can evolve over time to take into account changes in climate.

Box 1.19. **International agreements on water between the US and Mexico – adapting to climate change conditions**

Mexico has a long history of water agreements with the United States. In 1889, a special International Boundary and Water Commission (IBWC) was established to manage the boundary water treaties between the United States and Mexico, and settle differences that may arise out of those treaties. The IBWC is an international body composed of the US Section and the Mexican Section, each headed by an engineer-commissioner appointed by his or her respective president.

The two governments, through the IBWC, jointly administer the terms of the 1944 Water Treaty relating to the Colorado River, which provides that: *a)* a guaranteed annual quantity (1 850 million cubic metres) of water is allocated to Mexico; as well as *b)* any other quantities arriving at the Mexican points of diversion, with certain conditions stipulated in the 1944 Treaty.

The procedure is as follows. Mexico, before the first of each calendar year, presents through the IBWC an annual schedule of requested deliveries by month, within the treaty annual allotment and specified rates. Mexico also submits a weekly schedule of deliveries by day, within the monthly amounts scheduled. Mexico's requests are transmitted by the US Section to the Bureau of Reclamation, which makes the releases as necessary from the US storage works on the Colorado River to fulfil the delivery schedule. The deliveries to Mexico are jointly monitored by the IBWC to ensure compliance with the Treaty allotment and schedules.

The 1944 Treaty provides an example of how international water treaties might evolve over time depending on climate conditions. New strategies and programmes of the IBWC have been developed in response to emerging circumstances and necessities. For example, additional provisions for protection from floods were added later to the original agreement and proved necessary. A possible reform of the 1944 Treaty is now being discussed by the governments of Mexico and the US in order to deal with issues that did not exist in 1944 (*e.g.* drought). In 2002, both governments signed the agreement regarding water conservation to address water scarcity resulting from population growth and droughts.

Source: Levina, Ellina (2006), "Domestic Policy Frameworks for Adaptation to Climate Change in the Water Sector. Part II: Non-Annex I Countries: Lessons Learned from Mexico, India, Argentina and Zimbabwe", COM/ENV/EPOC/IEA/SLT(2006)11, Environment Directorate and International Energy Agency, OECD, Paris.

In the field of ICT, on which all the infrastructure systems depend to a high degree for their smooth running, international co-operation will be vital on a wide array of issues. For example, current Internet governance arrangements are in need of improvement with respect to Internet stability, security, cybercrime, data protection, and so on. And there are also calls for network operators and telecommunications interconnection facility operators to review their procedures governing emergency power sources.

3.4. Developing and integrating technology

So far, this chapter has concentrated on governance, organisation, regulation and market mechanisms as means for addressing the growing demands on infrastructure. However, technology is also a key tool at the policy maker's disposal. In all the infrastructure sectors considered in this project, it has considerable potential, albeit in varying degrees. In ICT, technology is considered to hold out the promise of particularly far-reaching change, firstly because it is in itself the most innovative and rapidly changing infrastructure sector, and secondly, because it is the foundation and driver of much innovation in all the other infrastructure sectors. Hence, the development of new mobile technologies, the widespread adoption of Voice over Internet Protocol (VoIP), further progress in fibre optic, greater data processing capabilities, the introduction of location-based services, radio frequency identification (RFID), and more sophisticated satellite communications, all are expected to make a palpable difference in the search for efficiency and improved demand management in infrastructures – be it in the control of electricity networks, remote metering of water use, road capacity utilisation, or better public transport logistics. But other technologies also have significant potential in this respect: biotechnology in water treatment, fuel technologies in land transport, carbon sequestration in power generation, and nanotechnology applications in almost all the forementioned sectors.

Much, but not all of the potential in these technologies will and should be achieved without direct government involvement. But given the vital and growing importance of infrastructures in economy and society, it is incumbent on policy makers to play a supportive role.

Recommendation 16: Support the use of technologies both to improve efficiency in infrastructure, and to enhance demand management.

Governments should in general support fundamental research that has the potential to stimulate innovation and diversity in addressing the challenges facing infrastructures, and that is so broad that individual investors are unlikely to capture the full benefits and therefore underinvest in it. In addition, however, a strong case can be made for governments actively to encourage progress in those areas of technological research and development that are likely to generate benefits associated with the public-good aspects of infrastructure in which governments have particular responsibility, *i.e.* overall reliability of infrastructure systems, security, environment, and the social dimension. In doing so, attention needs to be paid not only to new technologies but also to the more effective application and integration of technologies into existing infrastructure networks.

Actively support efforts to improve the overall reliability of infrastructure systems. Several examples stand out:

- Intelligent transport systems and capacity improvement programmes that keep road network at maximum capacity in peak periods during the day.
- New systems of road tolling and road network pricing which hold out much potential for traffic management and congestion relief; they are becoming increasingly feasible (technologically at least) with the strengthening and greater sophistication and accuracy of satellite communication and navigation systems (Galileo).
- Development of cross-border electrical transmission interconnection.
- Development of microbial fuel cells for energy production from wastewater, as well as on-site water and wastewater treatment facilities.
- Intelligent ICT-driven public transport management schemes.
- Enhanced signalling and improved freight rail cargo capacity.
- Use of geographic information systems (GIS) codes to facilitate life-cycle management of infrastructure assets.

Actively support efforts to harness technologies in the interest of reducing infrastructures' environmental footprint.

- Research into the possibilities of ICT to reduce demands on land transport through telework, e-commerce, tele-education, telemedicine, etc., notably in the light of many cities' efforts to greatly increase high-capacity Internet connections.
- Development of distributed generation facilities, where appropriate, in connection with the deployment of alternative energy sources.
- Research into alternative fuels for public transport vehicles.
- Development of standardised methods for testing the performance of new technologies in water treatment and wastewater recycling, and cheaper and more efficient wireless technologies for remote reading of water meters.

The development of mobile telephony in Sweden is an interesting illustration of the role that regulation can place in lowering the environmental impact of new technologies. When 3G operators proved reluctant to collaborate with a view to reducing the number of mobile communications masts necessary for the rollout, the government introduced legislation making provision for the national Post and Telecom Agency to enforce co-operation on mast-sharing.

Box 1.20. **The problems of 3G rollout in Sweden**

In Europe, Sweden is the country with the highest third generation (3G) coverage, and according to a recent survey from the Swedish National Post and Telecom Agency, approximately 97% of Sweden's 9.1 million citizens are currently able to use 3G services, a figure that is expected to reach 100% over the next two years. With a total of 9.3 million cell phone user accounts, this number is higher than Sweden's entire population.

3G or UMTS (Universal Mobile Telecommunications System) is the third generation mobile telephony system and provides the opportunity for more rapid information transmission to and from mobile telephones and other mobile terminals than with second generation (2G, for example, GSM or global system for mobile communications). The system allows for making ordinary voice calls, but also sending and receiving graphics, still pictures and moving images and more advanced information services, such as, for example, positioning-based services.

The EU member states had committed themselves in 1998 to facilitate the introduction of 3G services in their respective countries no later than 1 January 2002. The Swedish government and parliament entrusted the National Post and Telecom Agency (PTS) with granting licences for radio use and to implement the allocation of the 3G licences in Sweden. In a so-called beauty contest, the applications were assessed along the lines of financial capacity, technical and commercial feasibility and access to appropriate expertise and experience. An in-depth review of the applications retained examined the extent and speed at which they could offer coverage by the end of 2003, 2006 and 2009, with coverage defined on the basis of three factors: proportion of population, territorial coverage and distribution throughout Sweden.

Of the ten applications received on the closing date, 1 September 2000, four were successful and granted a license by PTS up to 31 December 2015. The successful candidates were Europolitan (now Telenor), Hi3G (3), Orange and Tele2. All had committed to covering at least 8 860 000 people by the end of 2003. An appeal against the allocation decision filed by the unsuccessful candidates Telia, Telenordia and ReachOut Mobile, which were not granted 3G licences, was rejected.

PTS considered the application of Telia technically unfeasible and therefore did not grant it a licence; however, Telia and Tele2 indicated after some time that they would share Tele2's licence. Similarly, Europolitan (now Telenor) and Hi3G decided to collaborate on the rollout and to build parts of their network together. Such collaboration was approved by PTS as being in accordance with the Telecommunications Act. The 3G licence conditions allow up to 70% of the network to be jointly owned and built. Moreover, masts can be shared up to 100%. Despite the fact that co-operation in rolling out the network can be beneficial not only for keeping down the costs and also in terms of protecting the environment, operators have been hesitant to collaborate on mast sharing. A report by Chalmers University of Technology revealed that operator collaboration on rollout could result in cost savings up to SEK five billion. A new law, which makes it easier for PTS to force collaboration on mast sharing, entered into force on 1 July 2006.

Box 1.20. **The problems of 3G rollout in Sweden** *(cont.)*

Orange, revealing its intention to withdraw from the Swedish market, requested permission to transfer its licences to another company within the same group. PTS rejected this, as it considered the aim to be selling the licences to this new company. Also rejected was a subsequent request to transfer the licences to Tele2/Telia on the grounds that not doing so would impair competition. Orange's 3G licences were finally revoked. To address the needs of the three network operators coping with increasing traffic and to introduce an evolved version of 3G (HSPA), PTS allocated the frequency space that was made available when Orange's licence was revoked to the three current 3G licence holders.

PTS rejected several applications for amended licence conditions and extension of the rollout period. This was done on the grounds, for instance, that operators should have known that the municipalities' processing of building permit applications for the 3G network would take significantly longer than the processing of building permits for the GSM network, as the new system involved significantly more building permits. Moreover, PTS considered that the operators should have been aware of the armed forces' role in network development.

After all 3G operators were given the opportunity to demonstrate whether they could assure the continued rollout of 3G with other technologies – without this having adverse effects for the consumer – PTS decided in 2005 that the 3G operators should continue to use the same technology as previously in the networks, UMTS (universal mobile telecommunications system). PTS reasoned that it was impossible to cross UMTS with other technologies without this having adverse effects for the consumer.

By the end of 2003, the rollout of the network should have been finished. At that time, however, even though from an international perspective Sweden had very high 3G coverage, operators had in fact only achieved between 67.5 and 74% of the promised population coverage. PTS notified the operators to implement measures to rectify the inadequacies in coverage no later than end of 2004, and a new check undertaken confirmed that operators had then achieved 84% to 86% of the population coverage. Since small changes were made in the license conditions, when those new conditions entered into force on 1 July 2006, PTS once again had to notify the operators to implement measures to rectify the inadequacies in coverage. This was to be completed no later than 1 December 2006 (Telia/Tele2) and 1 June 2007 (Telenor and 3). Telia/Tele2 informed PTS on 1 December 2006 that their UMTS network then covered more than 8 860 000 people and that the promised population coverage had thus been achieved.

An analysis of the 3G licensees raises worries about their future profitability. There is a lack of profitability due the fact that average revenue per user will not increase much more, while the operator's costs will do so in the future. Profitability differs markedly between incumbents and greenfield operators, with the result that the Swedish market will be faced with restructuring and repositioning.

Source: Based on Post and Telestyrelsen (2005), "3G Rollout Report", PTS-ER-2006:26, 23 June, PTS, Stockholm; and Björkdahl, Joakim and Erik Bohlin (2002), "Financial Analysis of the Swedish 3G Market", paper presented at First International Conference on Mobile Business (mBusiness-2002), 8-9 July, Athens.

Devote more political attention and, where appropriate, more funding to research and development in technologies that offer greater protection to critical infrastructures. As security issues move up the policy agenda in the coming years, and infrastructures intermesh yet further with one another, more support will be needed to develop innovative solutions to protect telecommunications, the Internet, gas and electricity networks, water distribution systems and so on.

Play a more active role in stimulating thinking in society about the desired shape and role of infrastructures in the future and the contribution that technologies could make to achieving appropriate outcomes. It is part of governments' political responsibilities to reflect on the longer-term economic and social development of the country and engage its citizens in that process. Technology foresight exercises can be useful in this regard, but often fail to take sufficiently into account the role of infrastructures in the development of the economy and in society more broadly. There are however interesting examples of projects, such as those in the UK, which have tried to rectify this shortcoming.

Box 1.21. **The Foresight Project on Intelligent Infrastructure Systems in the UK**

In September 2004, the UK government launched a Foresight Project on Intelligent Infrastructure Systems (IIS) in order to explore how science and technology may be applied over the next 50 years to the design and implementation of intelligent infrastructure systems that are robust, sustainable and safe.

It was felt that just as science and technology have given us the freedom to move, they will play a key role in helping us to respond to the new challenges of global warming, limited supply of oil, as well as increasing congestion on roads and rail.

In order to achieve this overall goal, intelligence needs to be built at four levels. First, the need to move should be minimised through intelligent urban design, efficient integration and management of public transport, and local provision of production and services. Second, the system needs to be able to provide information to support the decisions of individuals and service providers, with sensors and data mining capability. Third, the infrastructure should be able to process the vast amounts of information collected to adapt in real time to provide the most effective services. Fourth, the system should promote an intelligent use of infrastructure where people modify their behaviour to achieve a more sustainable outcome.

Box 1.21. **The Foresight Project on Intelligent Infrastructure Systems in the UK** *(cont.)*

Several studies were commissioned to explore the potential for building such intelligence in transport infrastructure. The main conclusions reached were that advances in science and technology could provide us with the necessary technology.

However, while technology can indeed improve the efficiency of infrastructure, a key issue is how to use the technologies to ensure that we not only improve efficiency, but also deliver sustainable and robust solutions. This will very much depend on the way the infrastructure will be used, which in turn is influenced by the psychology and economics of travel.

In this overall context, technology can be used to increase the choices open to users individually and collectively. Technology allows users to choose more effectively between face-to-face and virtual communications, as well as between different modes of transport. Technology also increases the feasibility and attractiveness of local production (local manufacturing or even home manufacturing), reducing the need to move goods. Laboratory-on-a-chip technology could offer a similar capability for the local production of medicines.

In addition, technology offers opportunities for behavioural change first by providing more timely and more pertinent information to travellers so that they can choose the optimal route and mode of transport. Moreover, technology allows charging users for the real cost of travel more effectively, including environmental costs.

Hence, IIS have a great potential over the long run. They could contribute to economic growth, reduced energy use, enhanced social cohesion (*e.g.* for caring for vulnerable members of society) and long-term sustainability (*e.g.* through the use of technology that supports closed-loop production).

Source: UK Office of Science and Technology, Foresight Directorate (2006), *Intelligent Infrastructure Futures (Project Overview)*, Department of Trade and Industry, London.

3.5. *Expanding and improving the toolkit*

Essential for meeting future infrastructure requirements – beyond improving finance, regulation, governance and planning – is a solid basis of information, data, research and analysis. Without that, the regulatory and oversight functions of effective governance cannot be conducted properly, the competition framework cannot be adequately monitored, the distributive or redistributive impacts of major infrastructure projects cannot be calculated and communicated persuasively, assets cannot be properly valued and managed, and so on.

Recommendation 17: Strengthen public capacity to inform decision making, improve analysis, monitor performance, and develop the requisite interdisciplinary skills to address infrastructure issues.

The analysis has shown that all the infrastructure sectors in this project suffer in one way or another from insufficient data, analysis and assessment. Freight rail in Europe, for example, cannot rid itself of cross-subsidisation because *inter alia* data to calculate the marginal cost of infrastructure is not available, and there is no separate accounting for social and commercial services. In urban transport, urban data – especially on urban travel and land use – remain sparse and poor in quality; data are not collected in a consistent way among cities, and collection methods are vulnerable to frequent modification. On electricity markets, all the information necessary to enable market participants and regulators to understand market conditions is not always made available. The ability of authorities to plan and manage in an integrative fashion the maintenance, repair, replacement and new construction of water facilities and networks, trunk roads and motorways, etc. is heavily constrained by the lack of information on assets – their amount, their value, their depreciation, and so on. Poor data, poor accounting, and poor assessment and evaluation tools make for poor decisions.

Thus, with a view to strengthening the evidence-base for policy and decision making on infrastructure, there is a clear need to improve information, data collection and research; enhance the use of accounting as an effective tool for planning, transparency and asset management; encourage greater use of rigorous evaluation methods; make greater use of online tools for communication and dialogue; and develop new interdisciplinary approaches to education and training.

Strengthen information and data collection, and research and analysis. One way in which governments can help make progress in this area is by strengthening formal mandatory requirements to provide information and data on certain key activities. Generally speaking, private and public actors will only collect and publish fundamental data on their activities if they are obliged to do so. Hence, authorities must devise a clear set of rules and requirements governing the collection and disclosure of information. In electricity, for example, access to basic market prices is perhaps the most important condition. In parts of the US, and in British, Nordic and Australian wholesale markets, day-ahead prices have to be made public through operators' websites; and in the Nordic and Australian markets, all spot market-sensitive information, such as unplanned outages, plant reconnections, changes in schedules for planned outages, must be disclosed immediately. Another way is to encourage the introduction of indicators. This is spreading, for example, among water utilities in the United States, where various associations are promoting the gathering and publication of data on such matters as organisational development, customer relations, business management, water and wastewater operations.

Similarly, greater efforts are required to improve the analysis of data and indicators, for instance to better understand the productivity impacts of infrastructure at the macro- and micro-levels, and to move towards more optimal investments in terms of sector, region and timeframes.

Hence, strengthening research and analysis is a key instrument in the improvement of decision making and performance monitoring. As the work on this project has shown, this is equally true of the need to foster more multidisciplinary research on infrastructure (*e.g.* business, engineering, geography, political economy, etc.).

Improve accounting methods and asset management. In the private sector, the condition of assets and their valuation are carefully measured and monitored, and included in accounting statements. In the public sector, however, most countries do not demand such accounting from their public sector entities (municipal utilities, etc.). Consequently, public planners and policy makers have little knowledge of the facilities, their condition or utilisation, making it nearly impossible to make efficient decisions on resource allocation. Given the growing problem of ageing infrastructures, mounting maintenance and upgrading costs, and the lack of reliable data, there is quite widespread interest in establishing some form of accrual accounting for the public sector. To be a useful strategic management tool, a comprehensive range of specific data on assets would have to be gleaned: an inventory of infrastructure assets, their condition and age, their replacement value, the types of spending required, an expenditure timeline, and an assessment of the future costs that would need to be incurred in order to preserve and service infrastructure assets at target levels. An illustration of the kind of work already available in this area is that of the Government Finance Officers Association of US and Canada (*www.gfoa.org*). The utility of such asset management data and techniques would of course be considerably enhanced through improvements to existing statistical standards relating for example to the definition of capital assets, and comparability across national statistical systems and agencies.

Improve and widen the use of cost-benefit and similar methods for project assessment. There is quite broad agreement in most planning circles that the basic evaluation method for taking decisions on infrastructure projects should be cost-benefit analysis. However, cost-benefit analysis is not applied everywhere, nor on all projects, nor with equal rigour. Moreover, it suffers from well-known weaknesses: the difficulty of incorporating non-monetary effects such as pollution, lower accident rates, time savings, etc.; the problem of political and economic trade-offs on such matters as distributional objectives; or the thorny question of how to integrate wider economic impacts in the form of modified settlement patterns or changes to industrial structures and regional specialisation. In all these cases, experiments are underway in OECD countries which warrant further exploration. These include the use of qualitative multicriteria analyses to complement standard cost-benefit analysis; formal requirements to include special sections in planning documentation on disadvantaged groups (*e.g.* in France and Germany), and sophisticated *ex ante* evaluation methods which go well beyond standard cost-benefit analysis (see *e.g.* pilot studies in UK or the sustainability indicator method to evaluate road transport infrastructure projects in Switzerland [NISTRA, 2003]).

Make greater use of online tools for communication and dialogue. Informing and communicating with stakeholders, and particularly those contributing in one way or another (taxation, user fees, etc.) to the financing and funding of the infrastructure project, is crucial if they are to buy into the policy objectives. In addition to the more traditional tools and platforms described earlier, the high rates of computer utilisation in OECD economies and in the more advanced developing countries, coupled with rapidly increasing Internet capacity especially in urban areas, have opened up new possibilities. In particular, recent years have seen online communication and dialogue with stakeholders and the general public grow in importance and effectiveness. See for example the Swedish schemes for the Öresund fixed link (*www.oresundsbron.com*), and the City Tunnel project (*www.citytunneln.se*), as well as US and Canadian schemes (*www.imaginechicago.org* and *www.imaginecalgary.ca*).

Develop new interdisciplinary approaches to education and training. This project has regularly highlighted the growing interdependence of infrastructure systems and the increasing complexity of their planning, implementation and operation in the context of changing economic, social and environmental circumstances. This suggests that the skill profiles of the professionals who will be engaged in infrastructure projects in the coming years will need to adapt accordingly. It is therefore essential to foster the development of new university curricula for engineering students which cover for instance non-traditional issues such as infrastructure and climate adaptation, sustainable infrastructures, financing and demand management strategies. Such new multidisciplinary programmes will need to be designed to view infrastructures from a systematic, holistic perspective that leads to a better understanding of their interaction both with one another and with their immediate environment and the diverse range of stakeholders involved. It is afterall the next generation of students in diverse fields of study who will be expected, as professionals, to rise to the challenges posed by infrastructure development to 2030 and beyond.

Notes

1. Surface transport (road, rail and urban public transport), telecommunications, electricity transmission and distribution, and water.
2. Total cumulative infrastructure requirements in the five sectors through to 2030 would amount to about USD 53 trillion. Adding in electricity generation would raise the figure to around USD 65 trillion, and other energy-related infrastructure investments would take it up to more than USD 70 trillion. These are estimated orders of magnitude of infrastructure needs, and may not of course necessarily translate into effective demand. The point of departure for OECD authors' projections was the 2003 World Bank Policy Research Working Paper 3102, "Investing in Infrastructure: What is Needed from 2000 to 2010?" by Marianne Fay and Tito Yepes. The projection period is 2005-10. The methodology for forecasting infrastructure capital stock and new construction (additions plus maintenance) is based on the elasticity between infrastructure capital stock and GDP per capita. Growth in the latter results in forecasts for capital stock, which can then be transformed into a forecast for new construction. The same model is used for all infrastructure sectors. The estimates produced by OECD authors differ from those provided by Fay and Yepes in a number of ways. First and foremost, different methodological approaches have been employed, and the projection period is much longer, namely to 2030. But even for the medium-term estimates to 2010, there are considerable differences. These can, however, be explained by different assumptions about economic growth rates (*i.e.* the OECD estimates are based on more recent World Bank projections for the world economy than those used by Fay and Yepes), by the use of different base years for the USD values (*i.e.* 1995 constant USD in Fay and Yepes *versus* 2005 constant USD in OECD), as well as by differences in sectoral coverage (*e.g.* in contrast to the Fay and Yepes study, the OECD estimates cover major European rail projects such as TEN-T; electricity transmission and distribution only; and include renewal and upgrading in telecommunications). Adjusting for these differences makes the results of the World Bank and OECD studies quite consistent with one another. Where there does appear to be an irreconcilable difference between the Fay and Yepes study and OECD estimates is in water infrastructures. The authors of the OECD report on water examined a large number of recent independent studies (*e.g.* Offwat in UK, EPA in US, OECD for Central and Eastern Europe) in OECD countries and middle-income countries (*e.g.* BRICs and Central and Eastern Europe) all of which point to considerably higher annual investment requirements – for example, equivalent to around 0.75% of GDP for high income countries as opposed to 0.03% of GDP estimated by Fay and Yepes. For details of OECD author estimates, see OECD (2006), *Infrastructure to 2030: Telecoms, Land Transport, Water and Electricity*.
3. OECD (2006b), "SOCX: Social Expenditure and Recipiency Data", DELSA/ELSA/WP1(2006), Working Party on Social Policy, Directorate for Employment, Labour and Social Affairs, Employment, Labour and Social Affairs Committee, OECD, Paris.
4. OECD (2004), "The Social Conditions of Older People: Achievements and Challenges", *Revised Theme and Outlined Draft Issues for Discussion for the Ministerial Meeting*, DELSA/ELSA/PG(2004)6/REV1, Directorate for Employment, Labour and Social Affairs, Employment, Labour and Social Affairs Committee, OECD, Paris.
5. OECD (2005a), *Financial Market Trends*, No. 89 Supplement, November, OECD, Paris, pp. 21-22.
6. *Ibid.*
7. Data from the OECD Privatisation Database, and The Privatization Barometer.

8. Samuel-Lajeunesse, Denis (2005), in *The PB Newsletter*, Issue No. 3, July, The Privatization Barometer, Milan.
9. HM Treasury (2006), *PFI: Strengthening Long-term Partnerships*, March, HM Treasury, London.
10. OECD (2006e), "Pension Markets in Focus", October, Issue 3, OECD, Paris. For country-by-country details of restrictions by quantity and asset class, see *OECD Survey of Regulations of Pension Funds*, 2006.
11. OECD (2007), *Recommendation of the Council on Principles for Private Sector Participation in Infrastructure*, C(2007)23/FINAL, OECD, Paris.
12. These OECD instruments and guidelines include the *OECD Policy Framework for Investment* (2006), the *OECD Codes of Liberalisation of Capital Movements and Current Invisible Operations*, the *OECD Declaration on International Investment and Multinational Enterprises* and the *OECD Guidelines for Multinational Enterprises*.

Bibliography

Albrecht, Christian (2006), "Infrastructure Funds in Switzerland: How They Contribute to Reducing the Gap Between Short-Term Thinking in Politics and the Need for Long-Term Infrastructure Planning", paper prepared for the Infrastructure to 2030 Project, OECD International Futures Programme (IFP), Paris.

Andrieu, Michel (2007), "A Cross-Sectoral Synthesis on the Long-Term Outlook for Infrastructure Business Models", in *Infrastructure to 2030 (Volume 2): Mapping Policy for Electricity, Water and Transport*, OECD, Paris.

bfinance (2006), "Infrastructure Investments on the Rise at Dutch Pension Giant ABP", 13 November, *www.bfinance.co.uk*, London.

Bickerstaff, Karen and Gordon Walker (2005), "Shared Visions, Unholy Alliances: Power, Governance and Deliberative Processes in Local Transport Planning", *Urban Studies*, Vol. 42, No. 12, November, Routledge, London, pp. 2123-2144.

Björkdahl, Joakim and Erik Bohlin (2002), "Financial Analysis of the Swedish 3G Market", paper presented at First International Conference on Mobile Business (mBusiness-2002), July, Athens.

Bruzelius, Nils (2005), "The Impact of Legal/Regulatory Frameworks on Transaction Costs for Private Sector Involvement in (Transport) Infrastructure Funding", Working Document 1: Consultant's Report, CEMT/OECD/JTRC/TI1/WD(2005)1, Working Group on Transport Infrastructure Investment, Joint OECD/ECMT Transport Research Centre, Paris.

Coe, Amanda (2005), "Community Participation and Public Infrastructure in the United States", John F. Kennedy School of Government, Harvard University, Cambridge.

Crotty, P. (2004), *Selection and Definition of Performance Indicators for Water and Wastewater Utilities*, American Water Works Association and American Water Works Association Research Foundation, Denver.

Crozet, Yves (2007), "Strategic Issues for the Future Funding and Operation of Urban Public Transport Systems", in *Infrastructure to 2030 (Volume 2): Mapping Policy for Electricity, Water and Transport*, OECD, Paris.

Eddington, Sir Rod (2006), *The Eddington Transport Study, Main Report: Transport's Role in Sustaining the UK's Productivity and Competitiveness*, December, HM Treasury and UK Department of Transport, London.

European Commission (2003), "New ERA for Electricity in Europe – Distributed Generation: Key Issues, Challenges and Proposed Solutions", EUR 20 901, Directorate-General for Research, Brussels.

European Conference of Ministers of Transport (ECMT) (2002), "Implementing Sustainable Urban Travel Policies: Key Messages for Governments", OECD, Paris.

Fay, Marianne and Tito Yepes (2003), "Investing in Infrastructure: What is Needed from 2000 to 2010?", Policy Research Working Paper WPS 3102, Infrastructure Vice Presidency, The World Bank, Washington DC.

Flyvbjerg, Bent, Nils Bruzelius and Werner Rothengatter (2003), *Megaprojects and Risk: An Anatomy of Ambition*, Cambridge University Press.

Glaister, Stephen and Daniel J. Graham (2006), "Proper Pricing for Transport Infrastructure and the Case of Urban Road Congestion", *Urban Studies*, Vol. 43, No. 8, July, Routledge, London, pp. 1395-1418.

HM Treasury (2006), *PFI: Strengthening Long-term Partnerships*, March, HM Treasury, London.

Hanson, Royce, Hal Wolman, David Connolly and Katherine Pearson (2006), "Corporate Citizenship and Urban Problem Solving: The Changing Civic Role of Business Leaders in American Cities", The George Washington Institute of Public Policy, discussion paper prepared for The Brookings Institution Metropolitan Policy Program, Washington DC.

Heuer, Fred (2006), "Innovation of Infrastructure Management: The Anglo-Dutch Experience", Netherlands Ministry of Transport, Public Works and Water Management, Directorate for Knowledge and Innovation.

International Energy Agency (IEA) (2005), *Lessons Learned from Liberalised Electricity Markets*, OECD/IEA, Paris.

International Risk Governance Council (IRGC) (2006), "Managing and Reducing Social Vulnerabilities from Coupled Critical Infrastructures", Scientific and Technical Council of the IRGC, Geneva.

Kitchen, Harry (2006), "A State of Disrepair: How to Fix the Financing of Municipal Infrastructure in Canada", *C.D. Howe Institute Commentary*, No. 241, December.

Leape, Jonathan (2006), "The London Congestion Charge", *Journal of Economic Perspectives*, Vol. 20, No. 4, Fall, American Economic Association, Nashville, pp. 157-176.

Levina, Ellina (2006), "Domestic Policy Frameworks for Adaptation to Climate Change in the Water Sector. Part II: Non-Annex 1 Countries: Lessons Learned from Mexico, India, Argentina and Zimbabwe", COM/ENV/EPOC/IEA/SLT(2006)11, Environment Directorate and International Energy Agency, OECD, Paris.

Löwik, Lonneke and Peter Hobbs (2006), "European Infrastructure Market: Exploring Current Trends in a Changing Market", June, RREEF Research, Deutsche Bank Group, London, p. 10.

Mackie, Peter J. and Nigel J. Smith (2007), "Road Transport Infrastructure: Business Models, Trends and Prospects", in *Infrastructure to 2030 (Volume 2): Mapping Policy for Electricity, Water and Transport*, OECD, Paris.

Mahboobi, Ladan (2002), "Recent Privatisation Trends in OECD Countries", *Financial Market Trends*, No. 82, June, OECD, Paris.

Morgan, Trevor (2007), "Assessing the Long-Term Outlook for Business Models in Electricity Infrastructure and Services", in *Infrastructure to 2030 (Volume 2): Mapping Policy for Electricity, Water and Transport*, OECD, Paris.

NISTRA (2003), *Nachhaltigkeitsindikatoren für Strassenprojekte (Sustaining Indicators for Road Projects)*, Swiss Federal Road Office, Bern.

OECD (2002), *Financial Market Trends*, No. 82, June, OECD, Paris.

OECD (2004), "The Social Conditions of Older People: Achievements and Challenges", *Revised Theme and Outlined Draft Issues for Discussion for the Ministerial Meeting*, DELSA/ELSA/PG(2004)6/REV1, Directorate for Employment, Labour and Social Affairs, Employment, Labour and Social Affairs Committee, OECD, Paris.

OECD (2005a), *Financial Market Trends*, No. 89 Supplement, November, OECD, Paris, pp. 21-22.

OECD (2005b), "Regulatory Reform in Switzerland: Seizing the Opportunities for Growth", SG/SGR(2005)5, Special Group on Regulatory Policy, OECD, Paris.

OECD (2005c), "Structural Reform in the Rail Industry", DAF/COMP(2005)46, Directorate for Financial and Enterprise Affairs, Competition Committee, OECD, Paris.

OECD (2005d), "Evaluation of National and International Projections and Scenarios on Long-Term Infrastructure Requirements", paper prepared for the Infrastructure Project Steering Group, OECD International Futures Programme, Paris.

OECD (2006a), *Infrastructure to 2030: Telecoms, Land Transport, Water and Electricity*, OECD, Paris.

OECD (2006b), "SOCX: Social Expenditure and Recipiency Data", CELSA/ELSA/WP1(2006)7, Working Party on Social Policy, Directorate for Employment, Labour and Social Affairs, Employment, Labour and Social Affairs Committee, OECD, Paris.

OECD (2006c), *Economic Outlook*, No. 80, November, OECD, Paris.

OECD (2006d), "Projecting OECD Health and Long-Term Care Expenditures: What Are the Main Drivers?", Economics Department Working Papers, No. 477, ECO/WKP(2006)5, OECD, Paris.

OECD (2006e), *Pension Markets in Focus*, Issue 3, October, OECD, Paris.

OECD (2006f), *Financial Market Trends*, No. 90, April, OECD, Paris.

OECD (2006g), "Regulatory Reform in Sweden", SG/GRP(2006)2, Group on Regulatory Policy, OECD, Paris.

OECD (2007), "Recommendation of the Council on Principles for Private Sector Participation in Infrastructure", C(2007)23/FINAL, OECD, Paris.

OECD and ECMT (2005), *National Systems of Transport Infrastructure Planning*, Round Table 128, OECD, Paris.

OECD and ECMT (2007), *Transport Infrastructure Investment: Options for Efficiency*, OECD, Paris, forthcoming.

Palaniappan, Meena, Heather Cooley, Peter Gleick and Gary Wolff (2007), "Water Infrastructure and Water-Related Services: Trends and Challenges Affecting Future Development", in *Infrastructure to 2030 (Volume 2): Mapping Policy for Electricity, Water and Transport*, OECD, Paris.

Post and Telestyrelsen (2005), "3G Rollout Report", PTS-ER-2006:26, 23 June, PTS, Stockholm.

Samuel-Lajeunesse, Denis (2005), in *The PB Newsletter*, Issue No.3, July, The Privatization Barometer, Milan.

Sharma, A.K. (2006), "Country Report on India's Transport Infrastructure: Visions, Plans and Programme", paper prepared for the Infrastructure to 2030 Project, OECD IFP, Paris.

Siemens Financial Services (2003), *Project Finance Yearbook* 2002/2003, Siemens Financial Services GmbH, Munich.

Swiss Federal Council (2005), "Message about the Infrastructure Funds for Urban Agglomeration Traffic and the Network of National Roads", 2 December, Bern.

Sydney Morning Herald (2006), "Tunnel Goes Under", 27 December, Sydney, *www.smh.com.au*.

TD Bank Financial Group (2006), *Creating the Winning Conditions for Public-Private Partnerships (P3s) in Canada*, TD Economics Special Report, TD, Toronto.

Thompson, Louis S. (2007), "Key Trends and Implications for Policy Change in Long-Term Rail Freight Traffic and Infrastructure", in *Infrastructure to 2030 (Volume 2): Mapping Policy for Electricity, Water and Transport*, OECD, Paris.

Transport for London (2006), "London Underground Publishes Third Annual PPP Report", 24 July, London, *www.tfl.gov.uk*.

UK Office of Science and Technology, Foresight Directorate (2006), *Intelligent Infrastructure Futures (Project Overview)*, Department of Trade and Industry, London.

Unterrainer, Maria (2006), "Approaches to Infrastructure Financing in OECD Countries and Major Non-OECD Countries: An Overview of Risk Sharing, with Selected Case Studies", OECD IFP, Paris.

Van der Krabben, Erwin, Bas Zonnenberg and Rob van der Heijden (2007), "Understanding the Implementation of Infrastructure Projects: Speed of Decision-Making Processes, Participation and Complexity Levels of Dutch Infrastructure Projects", paper prepared for the Infrastructure to 2030 Project, OECD IFP, Paris.

Vander Ploeg, Casey (2006), "New Tools for New Times – A Sourcebook for the Innovative Financing; Funding, and Delivery of Municipal Infrastructure", Western Cities Project Report No. 35, Western Cities Project, Calgary.

Virtuosity Consulting (2005), *Successful Examples of Public-Private Partnerships and Private Sector Involvement in Transport Infrastructure Development*, written for the Joint OECD/ECMT Transport Research Centre, OECD, Paris.

Wiesmann, Gerrit (2007), "Deutsche Bahn 7bn Float Plan" and "Rail Chief Determined to Stick to Timetable", *Financial Times*, 26 February, London.

World Bank (2007), *Global Economic Prospects: Managing the Next Wave of Globalization*, World Bank, Washington DC.

ANNEX 1.A1

Selected Websites for Further Information on Case Studies

Box 1.2. The British experience with PFI

HM Treasury, The Private Finance Initiative, Key Documents, *www.hm-treasury.gov.uk/documents/public_private_partnerships/key_documents/ppp_keydocs_index.cfm*.

Box 1.3. Creative financing and funding of infrastructures – the Confederation Bridge, Canada

Transport Canada, Policy Group, Canada's Transportation System, Confederation Bridge,
www.tc.gc.ca/pol/en/Report/brochure/confederation_bridge.htm.

The Confederation Bridge, Canada,
www.confederationbridge.com/en/about_the_bridge/.

Box 1.4. The Alameda Corridor Project, US

The Alameda Corridor Transportation Authority (ACTA),
www.acta.org/projects_completed_alameda.htm.

Box 1.5. Integrating land value capture, land use and new infrastructure – the Copenhagen metro, Denmark

The Ørestad Development Corporation,
www.orestadsselskabet.dk/en/odc.

The European Commission's Urban Benchmarking Initiative, Reports, *www.transportbenchmarks.org/publications/reports.html*.

Box 1.6. Water utility performance indicators – an example

American Water Works Association Research Foundation, Selection and Definition of Performance Indicators for Water and Wastewater Utilities (2003), *www.awwarf.org/research/topicsandprojects/execSum/2633.aspx*.

American Water Works Association, Benchmarking Performance Indicators Survey and Report (2005 and forthcoming 2007), *www.awwa.org/science/benchmarking/*.

Box 1.8. Private operation of motorways, shadow tolls and real tolls in Portugal

Brisa Auto-Estradas de Portugal (Portuguese motorway operator), *www.brisa.pt/Brisa/vEN/Investidores/A+Brisa/Profile/*.

Tollroadsnews (online newsletter on tollroads, turnpikes, toll bridges, toll tunnels and pricing), article on Portuguese motorways dated 13 October 2004, *www.tollroadsnews.info/artman/publish/article_678.shtml*.

Box 1.9. The Eddington Transport Study – an economic approach to long-term strategic policy frameworks for transport in the UK

HM Treasury and UK Department of Transport, The Eddington Transport Study, December 2006, *www.hm-treasury.gov.uk/independent_reviews/eddington_transport_study/eddington_index.cfm*.

Box 1.10. Strategic planning of urban infrastructures for an expanding population in India

Government of India, Jawaharal Nehru National Urban Renewal Mission (JNNURM), Modified Guidelines for the Sub-Mission on Urban Infrastructure and Governance (September 2006), *http://jnnurm.nic.in/toolkit/modified_guidelines.pdf*.

Box 1.11. The management of water systems in France

Fonds national pour le développement des adductions d'eau (FNDAE) (French National Fund for the Development of Waterworks), website in French only, *www.fndae.fr*.

Box 1.12. Securing adequate and stable levels of long-term investment in surface transport infrastructure – the Swiss infrastructure funds

Swiss Federal Office for Spatial Development (ARE), documents on the Infrastructure Fund for Agglomeration Traffic, The National Motorway Network and Main Roads in Mountain Areas and Peripheral Regions, *www.are.admin.ch/themen/verkehr/00250/00460/index.html?lang=en.*

Box 1.13. Public involvement in infrastructure planning in France

French National Commission for Public Debate (CNDP), website in French only,
www.debatpublic.fr.

European Conference of Ministers of Transport, Round-table documents, National Systems of Transport Infrastructure Planning, Conclusions of Round Table 128 (2004),
www.cemt.org/online/conclus/rt128e.pdf.

Box 1.14. The Betuwe Line in the Netherlands – determining the public and commercial objectives

Railion Nederland, freight operator of The Betuwe Line,
www.railion.nl/gbpage.asp?id=1509.

The Netherlands Court of Audit (Algemene Rekenkamer), Policy Information on the Betuwe Line (2000),
www.rekenkamer.nl/9282400/v/.

Box 1.15. HSL-ZUID – fast-track processing of contract bids in high-speed rail in the Netherlands

HSL-Zuid website, including information on its PPPs,
www.hslzuid.nl/hsl/uk/Organization/index.jsp.

Siemens Netherlands, HSL-Zuid Project, Turnkey Project,
http://references.transportation.siemens.com/refdb/showReference.do?r=1908&div=3&div=2&div=8&l=en.

Railwaypeople online news, article on the HSL-Zuid Project, *www.railwaypeople.com/rail-projects/hsl-zuid-project-56.html.*

Box 1.16. Non-negotiated proposals in the procurement process in Spain

OECD/European Council of Ministers of Transport (ECMT), Working Group on Transport Infrastructure Investment: Funding Future Investment Needs, Documents,
www.cemt.org/JTRC/WorkingGroups/Infrastructure/infrdocs.htm.

Spanish Ministry of Public Works (Ministerio de Fomento), Contracting information,
www.fomento.es/MFOM/LANG_EN/INFORMACION_MFOM/CONTRATACIONES/DG_PLANIFICACION/.

Box 1.17. Network congestion management and pricing in the Nordic market

International Energy Agency, Free Publications, "Lessons from Liberalised Electricity Markets" (2005), Annex 2: The Nordic Electricity Market, *www.iea.org/Textbase/publications/free_new_Desc.asp?PUBS_ID=1589.*

European Commission, Directorate-General for Energy and Transport, Electricity Directive and Regulation on Cross-Border Trade,
http://ec.europa.eu/energy/electricity/legislation/index_en.htm.

Box 1.18. Efforts by the international group to improve the quality of rail transport in Corridor A (IQ-C)

European Commision, Directorate-General for Energy and Transport, Rail Transport and Interoperability, "IQ-C Action Plan 2006-2010 for Rail Freight Corridor Rotterdam-Genoa",
http://ec.europa.eu/transport/rail/market/doc/action-plan-rdam-genoa.pdf.

Box 1.19. International agreements on water between the US and Mexico – adapting to changing climate conditions

United States Section, International Boundary and Water Commission, *www.ibwc.state.gov/.*

Mexican Section, International Boundary and Water Commission, *www.sre.gob.mx/cila/.*

OECD, "Domestic Policy Frameworks for Adaptation to Climate Change in the Water Sector, Part II: Non-Annex Countries, Lessons Learned from Mexico, India, Argentina and Zimbabwe", COM/ENV/EPOC/IEA/SLT(2006)11, 2006, *www.oecd.org/env/cc/aixg.*

Box 1.20. The problems of 3G rollout in Sweden

Post and Telestyrelsen, Documents related to 3G Rollout, *www.pts.se/Dokument/dokument.asp?Sectionid=&Itemid=5522&Languageid=EN*.

Chalmers University of Technology, CITISEN Project the School of Technology Management and Economics, Prospects for Third Generation Mobile Systems, Research by Erik Bohlin and Joakim Björkdahl, *www.mot.chalmers.se/citisen/project01.asp*.

Box 1.21. The Foresight Project on Intelligent Infrastructure Systems in the UK

UK Office of Science and Technology, Foresight Directorate, Intelligent Infrastructure Futures documents, including Project Overview, *www.foresight.gov.uk/Previous_Projects/Intelligent_Infrastructure_Systems/Reports_and_Publications/Intelligent_Infrastructure_Futures/Index.html*.

ISBN 978-92-64-03131-9
Infrastructure to 2030 – Vol. 2
Mapping Policy for Electricity, Water and Transport

Chapter 2

A Cross-Sectoral Synthesis on the Long-Term Outlook for Infrastructure Business Models

by

Michel Andrieu*

This chapter takes a cross-cutting view of the five infrastructure sectors examined in this book – electricity, water, rail freight, urban public transport and road transport. The purpose is to arrive at some broad insights and conclusions on how infrastructure development should be addressed in future. The chapter assesses and draws out implications from the expert chapters on appropriate economic and business models for the successful implementation of infrastructure projects in the future and what role may be played by public and private actors.

* Consultant to the OECD International Futures Programme, Paris.

1. Introduction

This chapter takes a cross-cutting view of the five infrastructure sector chapters in this book. The purpose is to arrive at some broad insights and conclusions on how infrastructure development should be addressed in future. More specifically, the chapter assesses and draws out implications from the expert chapters on appropriate economic and business models for the successful implementation of infrastructure projects in the future and what role may be played by public and private actors in the future.

In addition to the main findings contained in the five expert chapters, account is also taken of the conclusions reached in the first two phases of the project (the content of which was published by the OECD in July 2006 as an interim report *Infrastructure to 2030: Telecom, Land Transport, Water and Electricity*). Moreover, special attention is given to the role of information and communication technologies (ICT) as an enabler in infrastructure development and management, and as a possible substitute for some infrastructure services (*e.g.* for transport).

Throughout this chapter, the term "business model" signifies "economic and business models". This is partly for the sake of convenience and partly because the use of the term "economic model" could be confusing, as the general understanding of economic model is quite different from the definition used here. In the context of this chapter, the term "business" is given a broad interpretation which extends beyond purely private activities. However, it focuses on the same quest as that in the business world, *i.e.* how to create value for money.

This chapter contains four main sections:

- Section 2 introduces the concept of business model and explains its potential usefulness in the formulation of public policy for infrastructure development.
- Section 3 assesses the strengths and weaknesses of the business models that currently prevail in the five sectors examined in this book, focusing on their capacity to meet a broad range of economic, social and environmental objectives. The assessment is based on consideration of the key technical and institutional factors that shape the design of these models.
- Section 4 examines how such an assessment may be modified in the coming decades under the influence of major drivers of change. These drivers may have impacts not only on the future viability of existing business models, but

also on the balance of objectives that policy makers are likely to pursue (*i.e.* some objectives are likely to become more or less important; and the balancing of a new configuration of multiple policy objectives in the future may raise new issues).

- Section 5 outlines some of the lessons that may be drawn from the analysis conducted in Sections 3 and 4 for the future design of business models and related supportive measures.

2. Business models and infrastructure development: basic concepts and key features

This section introduces the concept of business model and explains its potential usefulness for the formulation of public policy for infrastructure development.

2.1. *Business models in a business context*

The concept of business model has become popular in business literature in recent years in various contexts. For instance, with the emergence of e-commerce, much attention has been given to the formulation of business models that are more suitable for cyberspace than the traditional models, which were mostly designed to meet the needs of "real space". Indeed, the new reality of B-to-B (business to business) and B-to-C (business to customer) e-commerce has forced firms to go back to square one and fundamentally rethink their overall business strategy. In this context, the "business model" has been one of the main conceptual tools used, and completely new models have emerged (*e.g.* Google).

In a *business context*, business models primarily provide an overall description of the nature of the business at hand, that is, how the entrepreneur is trying to create value so as to generate profit. This includes consideration of the nature of the product, how it is produced and at what cost, why it is expected to generate value that customers are prepared to pay for, who the potential customers are, and what revenue streams may be expected. Business models also identify the various actors who have a bearing on the outcome of the activity and describe how such actors interact with one another.

The key objective for the entrepreneur is to create "value for money", *i.e.* to create a product or service that customers recognise as valuable and are prepared to pay for in a way that generates sustainable and profitable revenues.[1] Profits are maximised by using resources as efficiently as possible. Hence, the main purpose of the business model is to define a business that is both *effective* (creates value) and *efficient* (maximises profits).

2.2. Business models and infrastructure development: basic concepts

While it is originally a business tool, the business model can also be applied usefully to public policy making. This is notably the case when such policy relates to the provision of services (whether public or private) which have a strong economic dimension and require large investments over long periods of time, such as infrastructure services. Like business entities, governments should be interested in the effective and efficient creation of value in a sustainable manner, even though their definition of "value" and their motivation for creating such value may differ.

More specifically, in the public policy context of infrastructure development and management, the business model should contain at least four elements:

1. ***Economic logic.*** The business model should give details of the nature of the services provided, how those services are produced and for whom, who the key players are, and how they interact with one another. The model should clearly specify how *sustainable revenue streams* are generated to finance the maintenance and development of the infrastructure, so as to ensure its durability. Such revenue streams may not necessarily be profitable and may have to be complemented by sustainable public funding. Or the financing could be entirely public and the service provided free of direct charge.
2. ***Value created.*** The business model should describe the value provided to society at large, where value is not defined in monetary terms, but in terms of the policy objectives pursued by the government (*e.g.* economic, social and environmental objectives). For example, an infrastructure service that is more environmentally friendly could be preferable from a collective public policy perspective (*e.g.* public transport), even if it may be judged inferior by individual users who may prefer the flexibility and time-saving feature of private transport.
3. ***Public oversight.*** The business model should spell out whether the infrastructure is under public or private control, what type of regulation is applied, if any, and how.
4. ***Allocation of risks.*** When several actors are involved, including private ones, the business model should also describe how risks are allocated amongst the different actors. Typically, risks should vary inversely with oversight; the greater the freedom of action given to a particular actor, the greater the share of the risk assumed.

2.3. Business models and infrastructure development: key features

Two main elements need to be clearly spelled out in the formulation of business models for the development of infrastructure: *a)* the policy objectives that are being pursued (as they provide the general rational for infrastructure development and shape the overall architecture of the model); and *b)* the main building blocks of this overall architecture and the way they relate to one another.

Policy objectives

Whereas in private business models, the main objective for the private firm is to make a profit, public decision makers typically need to take into account a multidimensional mix of policy objectives that need to be carefully balanced in the light of the overall public policy agenda. This is the case for infrastructure development because infrastructure services cannot generally be considered as purely private goods. In this context, the fine-tuning of policy objectives is particularly important, given the central role played by infrastructure in our society.

A broad range of objectives needs to be considered in the development of infrastructure:

1. ***Economic objectives.*** The provision of services needs to be effective, efficient, reliable and resilient, and should also contribute to improving the competitiveness of the economy (*e.g.* electricity supply, rail and road transport).
2. ***Social objectives.*** The service provided may have a strong social dimension either because it is essential for life (*e.g.* clean water), and/or it has strong positive externalities (*e.g.* urban public transport).
3. ***Environmental objectives.*** The provision of services may have an adverse environmental impact which needs to be taken account (*e.g.* road transport, electricity).

The various objectives to be pursued may not be mutually supportive. For instance, the social objective of extending the provision of clean water needs to be balanced against the objective of limiting water withdrawals, so as to protect ecosystems and reduce the impact of water use on the environment. In addition, in the case of transport, the objective of providing increased mobility for economic and social reasons need to be balanced against the objective of limiting the environmental effects of increased traffic.

The mix of policy objectives may also induce governments to make arbitrages between different types of infrastructure or encourage particular forms of infrastructure over others (*e.g.* attempts to favour rail over road; to encourage the development of renewables, even if they cost more; to encourage the use of public transport even if individual travellers prefer private transport).

Even when the service provided by the infrastructure may be considered a purely private good, public scrutiny may be justified if large components (typically the network components) are subject to substantial economies of scale, hence subject to market failures as natural monopolies.

Main building blocks

It follows from the previous discussion that the formulation of business models for the provision of infrastructure services is a rather complex affair and that particular attention needs to be given to key building blocks of the models.

What is to be produced? In a private business environment, what is to be produced is what potential customers are prepared to pay for.[2] This is not the case in infrastructure where what is to be produced (the operational objective) is what best meets policy objectives. This means that changes in policy objectives may have a major bearing on the business model that is used. For instance, in urban public transport, the operational objective of the authorities in the past may have been to increase road capacity so as to improve mobility (policy objective). However, as concentration and traffic keep rising, increasing physical road capacity may no longer be a viable proposition, and a more holistic approach to infrastructure development may need to be adopted. In this context, the policy objective may be to increase accessibility (new policy objective) through the pursuit of an appropriate mix of public and private transportation (operational objective). In such a case, the business model needs to be extended to cover both public and private transport and the interaction between the two. It may even be extended to land use management because of its impact on the geographical distribution of economic activities, and hence on traffic flows.

How is output produced? Since we are dealing with networked infrastructure, one segment of the sector at least is subject to large economies of scale, justifying some degree of public oversight and regulation regarding access rights. Upstream and downstream activities may be unbundled and open to competition. However, this may not be an appropriate solution if there is a strong need to co-ordinate closely the operations of all segments of the sector along the value chain, *i.e.* if there are strong economies of vertical integration. Moreover, the presence of economies of scope may result in cross-subsidies between different services and may complicate the regulatory process in a context of regulated competition, since it is not easy in such a case for the regulator to assign costs to specific network services when attempting to establish equitable access charges.

By whom? Whether a particular infrastructure is public or private will depend on the degree of public oversight deemed necessary to meet public policy objectives and how this oversight is to be exercised. This, in turn, will depend on the economic nature of the service and the conditions of production.

A complicating factor is that the concept of "public oversight" is multidimensional. At the national level, several ministries may have a legitimate claim to oversee a particular infrastructure (*e.g.* health and environmental authorities over water infrastructure). Oversight may also be exercised at various levels of government (regional, local, and also transnational in some cases).

Between the two polar cases of purely public and purely private models, a broad range of mixed models can be considered, reflecting various degrees of involvement of private actors and different forms of oversight.

How is production and investment financed? A broad range of options is possible (from general public funding, earmarked public funding and public debt to fees imposed on direct and indirect beneficiaries and private debt). These options involve different allocations of the risks between the main actors. In some cases, advertising may also be a source of funds (*e.g.* most public broadcasters and subway systems, among others, use advertising as a complementary source of revenue).

Typology of business models

The traditional typology is based on the role assigned respectively to the public and private sector (public models, mixed public-private models and private models). However, this only gives a partial picture. Perhaps more importantly, one needs to take into account the nature and extent of the public oversight (*total*: public department under direct political control; *heavy*: public corporation or private company under rate of return regulation; *heavy to medium*: private company under price-X regulation; *medium*: regulated competition; *light*: application of standard competition rules). Typically, the policy objectives to be pursued should dictate what degree of public oversight is required, which in turn has a bearing on ownership. This also influences the allocation of risks: the heavier the public oversight, the greater the share of risks assumed by the public sector; inversely, more freedom of action for the various private players means also more risk assumption on their part. Together with expected returns, the balance between freedom of action and the degree of risk assumed will be a major determinant in the decision of private actors to participate or not in the development and management of infrastructure.

From a public policy perspective, the mere fact that a company is in a monopoly position does not automatically imply that it should be subjected to strong public oversight or transformed into a public monolith. The risks of "private failure", *i.e.* abuse of dominant position in the case of a private monopoly, need to be balanced against the risks of "public failures" (*i.e.* public mismanagement) in the case of a public monolith.

The concepts of "business model" adopted in the sectoral chapters

The five sectoral chapters have adopted different approaches to the definition of business model. Some definitions are explicitly spelled out; others are merely implicit, but may be inferred from the way the term is used. On balance, they are all generally consistent with the approach adopted above.

Although Morgan (2007) uses the term a lot, he does not give a formal definition of "business model" in the context of the *electricity* supply industry. One may nevertheless conjecture that he thinks of business model at the industry level rather than at the firm level. His main focus is on industry structure, operation and ownership, thus he adopts an industrial organisation approach to business models.

Regarding the *water* sector, Palaniappan *et al.* (2007) are more explicit, but their definition is narrower: "by a 'business model', we mean the actors that provide water services (water supply, wastewater, or storm water/flood control)". The authors readily admit that it is indeed a narrow definition that excludes the context within which the actors exist. However, this multidimensional context is described later in the paper (*e.g.* water-quality regulation, water-rights law, sources of capital). According to the authors, "the dimensions can be thought of defining the space or 'stage' on which the actors perform. Changes in technology, policy, and other drivers, can open up or make more attractive parts of the stage that were not previously accessible or desirable for the business models".

Thompson (2007) adopts a more traditional definition of "business model". For him, it determines how the assets will be deployed in meeting the market and social demands placed on the *railways*. He notes that railway business models are broadly defined in two dimensions: structure and ownership. Again in broad terms, there are three types of structural organisation: *integral*, where infrastructure and all operating services are operated under unified control (this is often called "the monolith"); *owner-tenant* models, where the owning dominant operator remains integrated with the infrastructure, and the minority tenant operators pay for their access to the infrastructure; and, *separated* models where (in principle) the infrastructure is separated from the operator or operators. Further variants of the separated model deal with whether or not the "separation" is merely an accounting separation or an actual institutional separation, and with the level of separation among the operators (there may be an integrated operating company, or the passenger and freight operators may be separated into distinct entities).

Like Morgan, Crozet (2007) does not provide a formal definition of "business model" in the case of *urban public transport* (UPT). However, one may infer from his analysis that he views business models as conceptual tools for describing the overall institutional architecture of the infrastructure (including who designs the infrastructure, who operates the infrastructure, who funds the infrastructure and who uses the infrastructure) and the relationships that exist between the different key actors.

Mackie and Smith (2007) point out that in *road transport* "precise definitions of 'business models' in this sector, which is still evolving, are not standard or universal". But in essence, their definition is similar to the one adopted by

Crozet to the extent that the main focus is on the institutional arrangement and the relationships that may exist between the key actors. Mackie and Smith propose five categories of business model ranging from the purely public sector model to the purely private sector model.

In summary, despite various wordings, all the authors in this book adopt a rather similar definition of business model that does not depart fundamentally from the approach taken above. The key questions are: who are the key actors; how do they relate to each other; and how are they organised to create value.

3. Strengths and weaknesses of existing business models

This section assesses the strengths and weaknesses of the business models that currently prevail in the five sectors in terms of their ability to meet a broad range of economic, social and environmental objectives, on the basis of a consideration of the key technical and institutional factors that shape the design of these models.

At first sight, this may seem an overwhelming task when one considers the very different circumstances that prevail across countries and across sectors.

However, the range of the business models that currently exist is in fact rather limited because such models are largely determined by a relatively small number of "shaping factors". Some of these factors reflect *technical* conditions of production (*e.g.* economies of scale) and hence apply across countries, while others relate to *institutional* arrangements which are likely to vary from country to country, but still follow relatively predictable patterns.

In a way, business models may be thought of as possible solutions to problems raised by technical conditions of production and institutional arrangements for achieving particular objectives. Strengths and weaknesses reflect how well (or how poorly) the solutions provided by the business models meet the objectives being pursued.

From an analytical perspective, it is possible to use such shaping factors as a guiding thread for identifying the main business models that currently exist, their key characteristics as well as their strengths and weaknesses, when such characteristics are measured against a set of *policy objectives*. This approach is illustrated in Figure 2.1 below.

The shaping factors that are considered here include the nature of the service provided by the infrastructure, economies of scale, economies of scope, vertical co-ordination/integration, technology and institutions. Moreover, the role of public and private actors and financing are singled out, as key dimensions of business models that deserve particular attention.

Figure 2.1. **Assessing the strengths and weaknesses of business models**

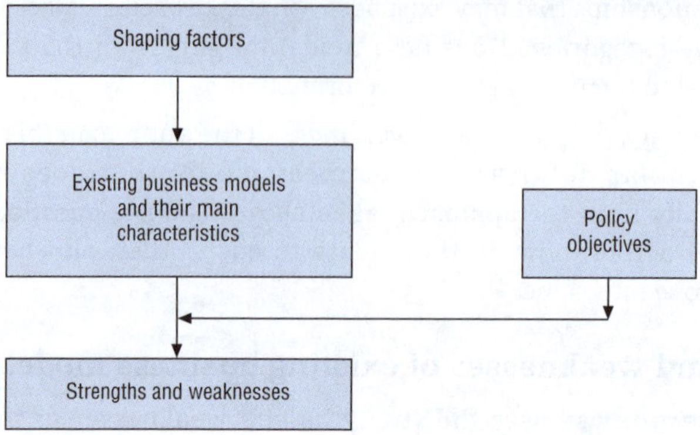

As discussed in Section 2, "strengths and weaknesses" are relative concepts that need to be assessed against a set of policy objectives. These include:

- *Economic objectives.* The provision of services needs to be effective, efficient, reliable and resilient, and should also contribute to improve the competitiveness of the economy (*e.g.* electricity, transport).
- *Social objectives.* The service provided often has a strong social dimension because it is essential for life and/or has strong positive externalities (*e.g.* clean water, urban public transport).
- *Environmental objectives.* The provision of services creates positive or negative externalities which need to be taken account (*e.g.* road transport, electricity).

As was already noted in Section 2, the different objectives to be pursued may not be consistent with each other. Moreover, the mix of policy objectives may also induce governments to make trade-offs between different types of infrastructures or encourage particular forms of infrastructure. Finally, one needs to keep in mind that policy objectives may vary from country to country, reflecting different cultural and institutional contexts in which the particular models are applied (*e.g.* ideologies and cultural values which have a bearing on the relative importance given to different policy objectives and on the policy formulation process, general attitude towards the role of government in society). Hence, a model that is perceived as "strong" in one country may be viewed as "weak" in another, if different policy evaluation criteria are applied in the two countries.

In what follows, the main factors shaping the design of existing business models and the consequences they may have for the strength and weaknesses of these models are first considered in Section 3.1. This provides the basis, in Section 3.2, for an overall assessment of such models in terms of three main policy concerns. Finally, Section 3.3 highlights in a systematic manner some of the key points that emerge from the discussion for each of the sector under consideration.

3.1. Main shaping factors

Nature of the service

From an economic perspective, a key consideration in the design of business models is whether the services to be provided by the infrastructure can be viewed as "private goods" and if not, in what way they differ from the concept of private goods.[3]

Electricity services may be considered to be private goods. In most cases, those who do not pay their electricity bills can be disconnected, while consumption by one consumer prevents consumption by others. However, the provision of electricity is often viewed as an "essential service" from two different public policy perspectives. First, as noted by Morgan, given the economic, social and political importance of "keeping the lights on", policy makers and regulators must develop effective mechanisms for ensuring that an adequate reserve capacity is maintained at all times, that power failures are minimised and that when they occur their consequences are as small as possible. Second, from a social perspective, a minimum level of service needs to be provided to all. This typically implies some degree of subsidy to some users, either by the state or by the utility itself.

As further noted by Morgan, this situation may create conflicts for the state between its responsibilities for maintaining a financially viable electricity industry and protecting taxpayers' interest, on the one hand, and its responsibilities for protecting consumers' interest in the short and long term, on the other hand.

The problem is illustrated by the situation that currently prevails in India, where large subsidies to electricity consumers – notably farmers and households – have caused the state electricity boards to incur huge financial losses. This has undermined the boards' ability to invest, meet growing demand for electricity and maintain reliable supply.

Another difficulty results from the fact that electricity supply suffers from "market failure", since the production and transmission of electricity create negative environmental externalities which are not effectively internalised in existing business models. This state of affairs is unsatisfactory from an environmental policy perspective, and it also has deleterious effects from an economic point of view. The lack of clear environmental policy direction in most countries creates uncertainties for sectoral operators regarding the costs associated with the measures governments are likely to take in the future. This means increased risks for potential investors with detrimental effects on the level of future investment.

Water, like electricity, might also be considered, *a priori*, a private good. However, even more so than for electricity, the provision of clean water and effective wastewater services is considered to be essential for life itself, as well as for public health and the environment. Hence, as noted by Palaniappan *et al.*, water cannot really be treated as a private good.[4] Protecting public health, as well as ensuring water quality standards and the equitable provision of supply, requires significant public oversight and governance. Thus, business models for the water sector need to factor in the central role that needs to be played by public authorities at the local, regional, national – as well as at the transnational level. The models also need to cover a broad policy front: economic and financial, as well as social, health and environmental.

Freight rail transport is more of a private good and so is more amenable to a strictly business approach, involving essentially economic considerations (*i.e.* how to cope with natural monopoly conditions). One approach adopted in the US in the past to deal with this problem was to foster intermodal competition by favouring the development of alternative means of transport (road and water transport) that offered better scope for intramodal competition. In this regard, Thompson notes that, historically, US policy heavily favoured trucks and barges over rail because of a deeply rooted political perception of railways as "public be damned" monopolists. The private good perception of freight rail was also detrimental from a revenue perspective since it induced the authorities to favour passenger traffic (because of its perceived social benefits) over freight transport. It is only since deregulation that freight rail has been able to operate more or less on a business basis in North America, although US (and Canadian) policy may still favours trucks over rail.

Faced with a similar dilemma, other countries chose to nationalise railways and to create public monoliths – often generating "public failures" at the same time. However, the private good nature of freight rail is increasingly recognised today, as well as the advantages of rail over road transport from a safety and environmental perspectives. Efforts are afoot in a number of countries outside North America to promote a more liberalised model of freight rail services, with the hope that it will lead to improved services with both economic (more efficient transport system) and environmental advantages (a higher share of freight carried by rail).

According to Crozet, the services offered by *urban public transport* networks have strong public good features because of the economic characteristics of their infrastructures (local monopolies that require public action at the design and planning stage, at least); the socio-economic benefits they provide (only reliable means of urban transport for the poor, allows everyone to participate in the economic life of the city);[5] as well as the environmental advantage they offer compared to private car journeys (less adverse effect per passenger-kilometre).[6]

In this context, business models must feature a central role for the government not only in the design and planning stages, but also the financing of the system, as fares collected from users will not cover costs if they are set at marginal cost (or even below marginal cost if the social and environmental advantages are taken into account) as they should logically be.[7] Today, for most UPT systems, operating costs are not even covered.

Road transport services do not meet the criteria established above for private goods. While they are rivalrous, they are not excludable in the business model that prevails in most countries. Road space is allocated to traffic on a first-come, first-served basis and is free at the point of demand. This model inevitably leads to congestion in densely populated areas (once capacity is reached) and to an inefficient allocation of scarce road space. The mixture of vehicle and fuel taxes that currently exist in most countries is not only inefficient but also unfair for rural users who pay a disproportionately high share of road transport costs.

Given the physical limitations of the extension of the network in already congested areas, the current model is clearly not sustainable. However, introducing a model that is both more efficient from an economic perspective, and at the same time considered "fair" by a large majority of people, is a formidable, if not impossible, task from a political perspective, as noted by Mackie and Smith.

Economies of scale

Technical conditions vary from sector to sector. However, all business model designers face a common problem: the models they build need to be suitable for the production and delivery of *networked* services over a single infrastructure, *i.e.* they need to take into account the fact that monopolistic conditions prevail in at least one segment (the network segment) of the value chain. However, the nature of this monopoly element varies from sector to sector. In the electricity sector, economies of scale prevail at the transmission and distribution stages and only at the regional level. In the water sector, economies of scale vary from stage to stage. For instance, water distribution systems are natural monopolies but may be very small indeed (according to Palaniappan *et al.* there are about 54 000 community drinking water systems and about 16 000 wastewater systems in the US) or very large in the major metropolitan areas. In the rail sector, Thompson notes that there is no particular benefit of system size beyond a few thousand kilometres, but that there are increasing returns to traffic density on a specific line. The same conditions apply in the UPT sector and in road transport.

The key question for business model designers is whether such monopoly conditions call for special public scrutiny and what form such public scrutiny should take. In most cases, the solution that has been adopted is to set up a public monolith for the networked segment (monolith that may or may not be extended to the other segments of the value chain).

This approach has a number of strong but also weak points. A business model that puts responsibility for a network in a ministry gives political decision makers direct control over its management and development. Hence, such a model should ensure that, in principle, the infrastructure is operated in the public interest and is responsive to the policy objectives set out by the government. The problem is that in a number of cases using this model decision making may be "too responsive" to the desires of politicians with short-term policy horizons (the next elections). In this context, important decisions for the future development of the infrastructure may be taken for short-term opportunistic reasons rather than on the basis of long-term sustainability considerations. As noted by Morgan, this is often the case with regard to electricity.

One solution to the problem has been to corporatise the activity so as to foster accountability and to remove it from direct political control by creating an arm's-length regulatory agency for its supervision. However, short-term political interference is still possible in this model, although perhaps more difficult.

Another problem with the public monopoly model – whether regulated or not – is that it can suffer from "public failures", as it offers little incentive to keep costs down. This problem prevails in all sectors and, as noted by Crozet in the case of UPT, is easier to identify than to solve. For instance, in the case of UPT and railways, it is typically reflected in excessive investment in infrastructure and rolling stock, overextension of the network to unprofitable lines and overstaffing, which for rail is hard to trim back under private ownership.[8] Moreover, the monolith typically tends to be relatively insensitive to users' needs to the extent that such users are captive with no alternative sources of supply.

Regulatory oversight can help to a degree. However, regulators may be "captured" over time by the regulated entity, whether it is a public or private corporation.[9] And, even when they remain independent, the regulators are not always well equipped to exercise their mandate. One of the many problems associated with regulating a utility is asymmetry of information skewed in favour of the regulated corporation.

This problem arises, for instance, when a concession has been granted to a company for operating a water system. Concessionaires have first-hand information about expenditures and degree of effort to reduce or control cost and achieve contract deliverables. These elements are largely unobserved by the regulators and are liable to be overblown. The concession agreement (CA hereafter) provides that the Regulatory Office (RO hereafter) approves tariff adjustment petitions by the concessionaires which cover prudent and legitimate costs and to disapprove otherwise. This requires the RO to have some idea of prudent costs and the reasonable toll taken by unforeseen events and *force majeure*. In a complex operation such as a water utility, precious information, while known to concessionaires, is hard to pin down by the RO (Fabella, 2006).

One solution to the problem is to break up the monolith on a geographical basis and introduce some form of *benchmark competition*. This is feasible, for instance, when the monolith operates at the national level, and economies of scales are actually reached at a lower level. This is the case for electricity. Electric utilities already operate *de facto* at the regional level in federal states (*e.g.* US, Canada) or have already been regionalised in some countries (UK). It is also feasible in other sectors, such as the water and UPT sectors, where monopoly conditions exist only at the local level.

As noted by Fabella (2006) in the case of water concessionaires, the idea behind benchmark competition is that a concessionaire may have features similar to those of other concessionaires, as well as features specific to its particular situation. Indeed, the literature (Laffont and Tirole, 1994) distinguishes between two types of features: "systemic features" which are subject to "systemic shock", and "idiosyncratic features" subject to "idiosyncratic shock". The existence of comparators applied to systemic features helps the RO in determining systemic shocks and the reasonable responses thereto (*e.g.* impact of currency fluctuations or of changes in the international price of resources on the costs faced by concessionaires). Assessing the significance of idiosyncratic shocks (*e.g.* impact of a local storm) is more difficult, unless comparators in the same locality and the same domestic and political environments are available (*e.g.* damage to several concessions in the same area hit by the same storm). They can provide valuable knowledge that contributes to reducing the information advantage of the concessionaire over the RO. The usefulness of benchmark competition depends on how systematically similar the concessionaires are and how easily they can collude to minimise being "shown up" by the other. While this does not eliminate the monopoly problem, it does tend to circumscribe it.

In North America, a third model prevails, the "owner-tenant model", where the owning dominant operator remains integrated with the infrastructure, and the minority, tenant operators pay for their access to the infrastructure (Thompson). This model allows railways to take advantage of increasing returns to traffic density on a specific line by sharing the same lines through owner-tenant relationships.

The successful operation of the model depends largely on the ability to set access charges that bear some relationship to marginal cost and that can be shown to relate in an appropriate way to the cost of different types of users. Unfortunately, marginal cost is a more useful concept in theory than in practice and is subject to abuse if the tenant operator is politically powerful (Thompson).

Economies of scope

If significant economies of scope exist in production, several services (which are distinct from a demand perspective) may be provided by the same infrastructure. In such cases, the business model needs to take into account all the actors involved and the relationships that may exist between them, as well as how costs are allocated between the different services. For instance, although the *provision of electricity* may be considered to be a single homogenous service, opportunities for economies of scope may arise in the future as technology evolves (*e.g.* production of electricity from waste treatment, the use of transmission and distribution lines to deliver telecom services). From a business model perspective, the challenge is how to best integrate these different services and ensure that institutional arrangements allow such joint production effectively and efficiently. For instance, if it becomes profitable for waste treatment operators to produce electricity, they should be allowed to do so and to sell their electricity to the distribution network on the same basis as other electricity generators. This means that barriers to entry in the electricity generation industry must have been largely eliminated and that an adequate regulatory oversight has been put in place for maintaining a level competitive playing field.

The same kind of issues arises in the other sectors. In the *water* sector, Palaniappan *et al.* note that economies of scope may be substantial in some cases (storm and sanitary sewers), but not in others (sanitary sewers and wastewater treatment). In the rail sector, the infrastructure can carry both freight and passenger traffic.

By contrast, there are no economies of scope in *urban public transport* systems, as such systems are not currently used for freight, although there are some historical precedents.[10] Freight subways could make a come-back in the future. For instance, Andrew Looney in *The Empty City* describes a "city of the future" where freight subways play a key role, as cars and trucks have been banned from the centre of the city (see Box 2.1). However, even in Looney's vision, the freight and the passenger subways are kept separate.

The lack of economies of scope in mass transit systems means that their economic viability is highly dependent on frequent usage by paying customers if other sources of revenues (*e.g.* public subsidies) are limited. This means that such systems will be highly vulnerable to overextension of the network to areas where population density is too low to generate an adequate level of paying traffic.[11]

However, significant economies of scope exist in road transport since the road network is a ubiquitous multipurpose infrastructure by excellence, which offers unique flexibility and door-to-door service. Moreover, the value of roads

Box 2.1. **Mass transportation and the "City of the Future" according to Andrew Looney**

In the *Empty City*, Andrew Looney describes the transformation of a city under the guidance of a "visionary" mayor, which involves an extensive use of mass transit systems both for commuters and for freight:

"The entire downtown area was, one piece at a time, evacuated, demolished and rebuilt. The small, worn-out old buildings and the tiny, narrow, traffic-clogged streets were all destroyed. In their place sprouted a true City of the Future. Homes, offices, shops, government agencies, mass transportation, and public parks were all combined and intertwined in the new City.

You could take an elevator from your apartment in a towering condominium down to the subway, ride the train across town to your job, work in a sunny office, and return home via the supermarket, all without ever once stepping outside. The towering office and apartment buildings were linked together by a vast underground system of shops and subways. And when you did go outside, you entered a land of beautifully landscaped parks and lush gardens. No roads penetrated the downtown area at all, and in much of the outlying regions, cars were only permitted by special pass. Everyone relied completely on the complicated, comprehensive mass transit system.

Since trucks were not permitted in the downtown sector, an additional network of subways had been built to provide shipping of goods into and out of the centre of the City. These 'freight subways' rumbled back and forth, very deep below the surface of the earth, bringing cargo in from depots on the outskirts of the City that could be reached by truck. Large freight elevators brought the shipments up to the surface from the freight subway stations deep underground.

The freight subways did not overlap with the normal subways at all, and few people other than employees ever saw them. Everyone knew they existed, of course, and those who lived and worked downtown relied on the freight subways for everything-but they never saw them, which was just as well. The freight subways were darker, mustier, and far more utilitarian than the normal subways. The stations didn't even have names, they were simply numbered. However, the people who drove the freight subways did have names for the stations, names like 'The Abyss', 'Hell's Crossover', and 'The Armpit'."

Source: Looney, Andrew (2002), *The Empty City*, *www.wunderland.com/WTS/Andy/EmptyCity/chapter36.html*.

extends beyond transportation, since the road network also provides space for accommodating lifelines, such as waterworks, sewage systems, gas and electricity.

Vertical co-ordination/integration

A key question in the design of business models is whether substantial needs for co-ordination exist between the various segments of the value chain and how best to achieve that co-ordination.

If co-ordination requirements are indeed strong and transaction costs between segments are high, then vertical integration may indeed be the best option. However, when one segment is subject to large economies of scale (as is the case for all the network services considered here), this means that the monopoly will be extended upstream and downstream.

If the need for vertical co-ordination is not too strong, one may envisage a *structural separation* between the networked monopoly component of the value chain from the other segments that can then be open to competition (if the benefits of doing so in terms of improved efficiency outweigh the burden resulting from higher transaction costs and higher risks for the operators in the competitive segments). Breaking down the monolith on a regional basis, as discussed above, can strengthen the economic viability of the unbundled model.

The need for co-ordination along the value chain has in the past justified the creation of all-inclusive monoliths in a number of sectors, including the electricity supply industry, the railways and urban public transport systems. In the water sector, the case for vertical integration has not been so compelling, although the merit of vertical co-ordination between the various segments of the value chain at the level of the watershed is increasingly recognised (such co-ordination may significantly contribute to improving the quality of service and cut costs). The benefits of vertical co-ordination are illustrated for instance by the New York City example given in Palaniappan *et al.*[12]

In the *freight rail* sector, the "separated model" involves a structural (or at least functional) separation between the infrastructure and freight trains, where the infrastructure remains a regulated monopoly, and freight trains can be privately owned and operated.

This approach has been adopted for instance in the UK where the infrastructure is now privately owned by Network Rail and regulated by the Office of Rail Regulation (ORR) established on 5 July 2004 under the Railways and Transport Safety Act 2003.[13] The role of ORR is to ensure that Network Rail, the owner and operator of the national railway infrastructure (the track and signalling), manages the network efficiently and in a way that meets the needs of its users; to encourage continuous improvement in health and safety performance; to secure compliance with relevant health and safety laws, including taking enforcement action as necessary; to develop policy and enhance relevant railway health and safety legislation. ORR is also responsible for licensing operators of railway assets, setting the terms for access by operators to the network and other railway facilities, and enforcing competition law in the rail sector. The Department of Transport looks after passenger and train-related matters.

By contrast, in the *road transport* sector, there is a clear separation of infrastructure services from freight transport, coaches and other transport services that use the infrastructure. Unlike rail services, these are rarely or never vertically integrated with the infrastructure and are essentially competitive (or at least contestable). Vertical co-ordination is assured by the formulation and enforcement of standards regarding the kind of vehicle allowed on the roads and the technical requirements they have to meet (size, safety features, etc.) as well as rules that govern the behaviour of users.

Regarding the road infrastructure itself, however, the various elements of the value chain (road planning, building, maintenance and operation) have traditionally been kept under the same public roof. This need not necessarily be the case. First, several public agencies may be involved. Moreover, opportunities may also arise for engaging the private sector through various forms of PPP (public-private partnership), ranging from concessions for running and maintaining the infrastructure (such as motorways in France), to BOT (Build-Operate-Transfer) models. The same argument applies to water systems and UPT systems.

Technology

Technology largely influences the way infrastructure services are provided and how business models are formulated. For instance, it largely determines the existence of economies of scale and scope, the need for co-ordination along the value chain and the way such co-ordination can best be achieved. Business models based on a particular technology may become obsolete if new technologies offer opportunities for doing things differently or provide new services. Moreover, the pace of technical change itself has a bearing on vertical integration. Typically, rapid technological change tends to undermine the advantages of vertical integration, as producers at each stage of the value chain will want to keep their options open so as to be free to choose the best technology available in a timely fashion, whether it is provided or not by the vertically integrated supplier. An interesting historical example in this regard is the vertical disintegration that has taken place in the telecom sector between telecom operators and telecom equipment suppliers, as the pace of change in ICT technologies accelerated in the 1970s with the introduction of digital technology.

In the case of *electricity supply*, the emergence of distributed generation and the development of renewables are having far-reaching consequences for the business models used in this sector. First, they contribute to reducing the needs for transmission and improving the security of the system. Moreover, they also offer opportunities for more robust competition, contributing to make more viable the "unbundled model" described by Morgan.

In the *water sector*, closed loop systems reduce the need for extensive sanitary sewage systems and offer great opportunities for recycling. In addition, advances in desalination technologies offer new decentralised water collection opportunities, since more than half the world's population lives within 60 km of the sea.[14]

Finally, as already noted, new technology may make the production of electricity from waste more cost effective, offering new opportunities for the design of business models combining electricity generation and waste treatment.

By contrast, technological progress in *freight rail* has been incremental with only minor impact on business models. However, it is in the countries where the liberalised model prevails that the adoption of new technology has been most effective in generating productivity gains. For instance, as noted by Thompson, significant gains in efficiency have been achieved in North America, *inter alia*, as a result of progress in rail metallurgy that allows increases in load, while better traction has reduced energy costs significantly over the last few decades. Gains have also been achieved by the introduction of better operation techniques (block trains, dedicated unit trains), more productive use of human resources and the more effective exploitation of ICT technology (enhanced signalling, scheduling and control).

The business models used in *urban public transport* systems have not been significantly affected by new technology, although the operation of such systems have benefited from some technical advances. For instance, the application of ICT contributes to enhanced signalling, scheduling and control. Automated systems are slowly starting to emerge and could offer opportunities to reduce labour costs (which represent today about 60% of operating costs, according to Crozet).[15]

One factor that explains such relatively slow progress is the fact that most UPT systems have been underfinanced in the past with little resources available to improve the system and little incentive to do so in the public monolith model. Moreover, as the equipment becomes obsolete, it becomes increasingly difficult to retrofit newer equipment. Also, strong unions typically prevail in the UPT sector. They often have the ability to oppose effectively the adoption of new technology that may lead to a drastic job reduction in the sector. This does not mean that the technology will not be implemented eventually, but that the rate of adoption is likely to be slow.

Progress in ICT also has an indirect bearing on urban public transport, to the extent that it offers possible alternatives to urban travel in the form of telework, teleshopping, distant education and telemedicine. However the impact on urban travel has remained marginal to date. This could change in the future as projects to develop high capacity networks are underway in a growing numbers of cities (Tokyo, Seoul, San Francisco, Philadelphia and Paris, for example).[16]

Technology has had only a minor effect on business models for *road transport* to date. However, things could change drastically in the future. First, research into multifuelled vehicles, fuel cells, biofuels, hydrogen-based fuels, as well as electric batteries, could bear fruit as shortages in more traditional fuels are encountered and bring about drastic reduction in the environmental impact of road transport.[17] Moreover, ICT could be used to regulate road traffic (including road pricing), lane usage and speed and to improve safety, reducing the need for new investment.

Over the next few decades, the development of intelligent infrastructure systems (IIS) could indeed have far reaching implications, not only for the economy but also for society at large and the environment. (See Chapter 1, Box 1.21 on the Foresight Project on Intelligent Infrastructure Systems in the UK.)

Clearly, IIS have great potential over the longer term to help address some of the challenges that will be raised by the further development of the transport network. However, their deployment faces a number of serious challenges, as noted in the UK Office of Science and Technology Foresight Directorate's *Intelligent Infrastructure Futures Project Overview* (2006).

First, new technology will need to be accepted as safe by the population at large, both in terms of security of any information surrendered to the system and physical safety. There will also be questions of who owns any data collected by the system and where liability rests if the system fails, as it will do from time to time.

Second, the success of the system will largely depend on the ability to model realistically complex processes in transport and other related activities. Although our ability to do so will increase, we will need to establish a means of quality assurance for those simulations. This will be a challenge, especially as more and more software programs work out for themselves how to meet their objectives, but the programmer will not necessarily have complete knowledge of how it works.

Third, widespread use of agent-based software approaches to support decision making could create social division between those who can and those who cannot afford the best software agents. Also, what will the effect be of the use of agents on the psychology of the user if people become dependent on and, in some cases, emotionally attached to an agent or avatar?

A further question concerns the ability to connect different computerised systems to provide seamless IIS. Integration could fail for a number of reasons. To begin with, the cost could be prohibitive. Systems running on different standards might not be able to talk to one another. Unexpected emergent behaviour could also prevent effective co-operation between systems. These obstacles could drive us more towards a situation where there are many systems, only some of which are integrated.

More fundamentally, policy making in this area faces two major uncertainties: will society embrace a world where we track, and perhaps control, the movement of all goods and people? The second is whether or not we develop an alternative source of energy for transport that has minimal impact on the climate. If we do have this energy source, we would want to use IIS to support as much movement of goods and people as possible. If we do not have such an energy source, we would want to use IIS to minimise the movement of goods and people, while still supporting economic growth.

Institutions

The constitutional arrangements that prevail in a given country play a major role in determining which actors will be involved in a particular business model and how they will interact. For instance, in unitary states, *electricity services* typically tend to be provided by national monoliths. By contrast, in federal states, the main responsibility for electricity provision generally falls under regional (provincial or state) jurisdiction. In Canada, the federal government has jurisdiction over electricity exports, as well as international and designated interprovincial power lines; the provinces and territories have jurisdiction over generation, transmission and distribution of electricity within their boundaries, including restructuring initiatives and electricity prices.[18]

This regional arrangement offers perhaps more opportunities to experiment with different business models than is possible in a unitary state where the public monolith has a vested interest in maintaining the *status quo*. For instance, in the Canadian context, both industry structure and policies vary considerably across provinces. While most provinces have adopted the monolith model, two major provinces, Alberta and Ontario, have established markets characterised by wholesale and retail unbundling, although their specific market designs differ. In the two provinces, an independent system operator (ISO) sets and administers policies for grid interconnection, transmission planning and spot market operation.[19]

Canada also provides an interesting example of what the impact of liberalisation in one country (the US) may have on another (Canada). In most cases, Canadian provinces are moving to the *unbundled* model, that is, separated business units (generation, transmission and distribution) to comply with orders from the US Federal Energy Regulatory Commission (FERC) related to competition, allowing them to export into the US market.[20]

In the *water* sector, institutional arrangements vary from country to country, although the main responsibility for the provision of water typically rests at the local level in all countries. However, a growing recognition of the multidimensional nature of the issues at stake is gradually forcing the adoption of a more holistic approach to the management of water resources everywhere.

For instance, the fact that consumption of water by one consumer upstream affects the quality of the water available to other consumers downstream means that water should logically be managed at the water basin level, irrespective of administrative boundaries. In some cases, a transnational approach needs to be adopted when the water basin straddles the territories of several countries. This water basin approach has been adopted in many countries already and has been advocated by the European Council (EC) in its Water Framework Directive.

A complex web of institutional relationships needs to be established across agencies at different levels of government. The national government has an important role to play not only in setting and enforcing standards, but also in funnelling the necessary resources to operational agencies at the local level for the effective implementation of such standards.[21] For instance, in France responsibilities for water management shared between the state and other levels of government. (See Chapter 1, Box 1.11 on the management of water systems in France.)

The formulation of water standards may also be formulated at the transnational level. For example, over the years, the EC has issued a number of water directives after extensive consultation throughout the EU. These directives are gradually reflected in national laws and implemented in member states. On balance, these efforts have had positive effects on the quality of water in Europe. For instance, the quality of bathing water has improved in the UK over the last ten years or so as a result of the application of the 1976 Bathing Water Directive (see Box 2.2).[22]

In the *freight rail* sector, national institutional arrangements do not seem to influence much the business models adopted in the various countries. For instance, the monolith model can be found in unitary states, such as France, as well as federal states, such as Germany. Liberalised models prevail in federal states (US, Canada), as well as unitary states (UK). However, as noted by Thompson, the institutional framework may have an impact on the way some major projects are carried out. In this regard, he points to the complex arrangements that were needed for the construction of major new terminals in California and the Chicago area, and the lack of involvement of the federal government in such projects, despite their importance at the national level for the US economy.

Box 2.2. **Application of the EC Bathing Water Directive in the UK**

Since 1995, water companies in England and Wales have invested over GBP 1 billion to upgrade sewerage infrastructure. This has resulted in a steady improvement of bathing water quality.

Compliance with mandatory standards in England has improved from 88.9% in 1995 to 98.8% in 2005, and the proportion of sites meeting all bacterial guideline standards has shown a marked increase from 41.1% to 73.7% between 1995 and 2005. Further improvements are planned at sewage treatment works and overflows at an additional 99 sites in England and Wales over the next five years (up until 2010), bringing additional benefits to bathing water.

However, despite significant improvements to the surrounding sewerage infrastructure, several bathing water sites continue to be affected by diffuse water pollution, *i.e.* fecal pollution from agricultural and/or urban runoff after heavy rain. Diffuse water pollution, particularly from agricultural sources, contributed to the "failure" of at least two of the five English bathing water sites which did not meet the mandatory microbiological standards of the directive in 2005.

Tackling sources of diffuse water pollution is the next big challenge if we are to see further significant improvements in bathing water quality. This will be delivered through initiatives such as the Catchment-Sensitive Farming Project, with the UK Department of Environment Food and Rural Affairs (Defra) working closely with farmers and other stakeholders to improve farming practices.

Source: www.defra.gov.uk/environment/water/quality/bathing/default.htm.

Institutional arrangements at the transnational level can also play a key role. For instance, EU institutions are major actors actively promoting the adoption of a *more liberalised rail* business model in Europe where railway systems and the rail markets largely still consist of a patchwork of badly interconnected national systems. Without the EU, progress would probably have been much slower than it is.

The Treaty of Rome and the Common Transport Policy have provided the basis for the formulation of pertinent legislative measures. Several regulations and directives have been adopted by the EC which contain detailed provisions on the opening of markets for rail transport of freight and passengers; on the interoperability of high-speed and conventional rail systems; on the conditions under which state aids can be granted and public service obligations and contracts can be concluded; on the access to the networks; and so on.[23]

UPT systems are typically developed and operated at the municipal level. However, since the fares generally cover only a fraction of operating expenses, public coffers need to be tapped one way or another for their financing. This may include revenues from a municipal tax as well as subsidies from the regional or national authorities. Moreover, whenever a metropolitan area extends over several municipalities, special institutional arrangements need to be made for managing the UPT system at the metropolitan level.

In some cases, considerable autonomy has been granted to local authorities. In the UK, the mayor of London is the key figure in urban public transport for the capital city since the devolution of power to the local level, enacted by the Greater London Authority (GLA) Act in 1999, which created the GLA as a corporation and defines the roles and responsibilities of the mayor and the authority's assembly. Having made transport a priority, the current mayor, Ken Livingstone (re-elected in June 2004 for a four-year term), has chosen to chair Transport of London (TfL), the main transport authority, which has been responsible for most transport in London since July 2000. This includes buses, major roads, river transport, cycling, taxis and private hire (the Public Carriage Office), and trams. Since July 2003, it has also been responsible for the "Tube" (the London Underground).

As chairman of the board of TfL, the mayor:

- Sets the budget, appoints the board and can direct the actions of TfL.
- Sets the fares for the Tube, buses, Docklands Light Railway, Croydon Tramlink and taxis.

From a legal perspective, TfL is a corporation treated as a local authority for accounting purposes. It is allowed to borrow without prior approval from the Department of Transport (DfT).

The autonomy given to the mayor of London and the resources put at his disposal reflect the high priority given by the UK government to the upgrading of the London transport system. Recognition is thus given to the key role played by capital cities in international competitiveness, and in this context, the crucial importance of urban transport for the economic development of the megalopolis (mobility of the workforce, efficiency of the communications network, quality of life for residents, etc.). This also underscores the many challenges of London in comparison with other large capital cities (New York, Paris and Tokyo) and the need for a major upgrading of its facilities. The success of London's Olympic bid in July 2005 has underlined the commitment of central government to support the upgrade of the capital city's transport network.

It is interesting to note, however, that the autonomy given to the mayor has been severely constrained by the setting up of a PPP for the upgrading of the Tube prior to its transfer to the local authority and despite strong opposition by the mayor and TfL. The PPP, aimed at providing a GBP 16 billion upgrade and maintenance programme for the Tube, was decided upon and organised by the government, leading to a political and judicial dispute with the mayor and TfL.

Different levels of government are typically given responsibility for the development and management of different types of *roads* (national, regional, local). In some cases, national governments may delegate their responsibility for the maintenance of national roads to regional authorities (as in France). This layered approach provides opportunities for experimenting with different types of business models. This may include, for instance, concessions at the national level for the operation of major motorways in some countries, or PPPs involving several levels of government for major new facilities. (See Chapter 1, Box 1.3 on the creative financing and funding of the Confederation Bridge, Canada) or concessions at the local level for the upgrading of roads at the municipal level.[24]

Public and private roles

It was noted earlier that in all five infrastructure sectors in this project the nature of the service as well as the monopoly conditions that prevail in its provision call for public scrutiny in at least some stages of the value chain. However, this leaves an important role to play for the private sector. Indeed, in all sectors one can find examples of private operation and private ownership.

As Mackie and Smith note in the case of *road transport*, the major challenge for business model designers is to find the best way to harness the expertise and resources that the private sector can bring to the development and maintenance of infrastructure. This challenge, which applies to other sectors as well, is no easy task.

Logically, the closer the service is to a purely private good, the greater the participation of the private sector should be. Thus, one would expect to find significant private ownership in the electricity and the freight rail sectors. Yet, this is clearly not the case in most countries. One reason is that the creation of a public monolith addresses, in principle at least, the market failure related to monopoly provision. Another one is that non-economic considerations have historically played a key role in business model choice in both sectors.

A key question is whether the alleged benefits of these non-economic considerations are worth their costs. For instance, *railways* were long viewed as strategic assets for the industrial and economic development of European nations and played a crucial role in the conflicts that split Europe for so many years. Railways were almost considered as being part of the state itself. This state involvement, however, had, and still has, its price for the taxpayers. State aids and other public contributions to the sector accounted for almost EUR 40 billion in 2001 in the EU.[25]

In addition, in the *electricity* sector, the choice of business model often hinges on the trade-offs to be made between economic and non-economic considerations. For instance, at the European level, there is on the one hand a long-standing project for lower prices led by the EC designed to liberalise the market and to enable producers and distributors to compete freely within and across national borders. On the other hand, there is a camp that argues with growing confidence against further freeing the market. In its view, long-term security and stable prices can best be preserved in managed national markets that are dominated by strong quasi-monopolistic companies that can withstand bullying input fuel suppliers (such as, gas from Russia) and sudden shifts in demand and supply.[26]

In the other three sectors (*water, UPT, road transport*), the role of public actors remains dominant at the design planning and ownership stage, while private operation is becoming more common. In some cases, the separation between ownership and operation may involve two public entities. There are some exceptions of course to this general rule. For instance in the water sector, the development of closed loop systems offer more scope for private ownership. In addition, Mackie and Smith give examples of purely privately owned and privately operated roads.

A potential advantage of separating ownership and operation is that it allows injecting some degree of competition in the process. Although competition *in* the market may not be possible, competition *for* the market might be feasible. However, successful co-operation between public and private actors is difficult to achieve in practice for a number of reasons. First, it must be feasible to delegate responsibility for the operation to a third party. This means that the public agency should be able to clearly define in advance the tasks to be performed by the concessionaire and how responsibilities and risks are shared between the different parties to the agreement. The contract should also define the conditions under which changes in circumstances may justify a revision of the contract, as well as the procedures (*e.g.* arbitration) to be applied in case of disagreement between the parties.

These last two elements are particularly important because of the long duration of most infrastructure contracts. Indeed, such contracts are particularly vulnerable to bounded rationality and lack of perfect foresight by the parties to the agreement. For instance, events unforeseen when the contract was signed, may nevertheless drastically affect its execution. The fact that one of the parties to the agreement is a public agency further complicates the situation for the concessionaire since such an agency may not be bound by contract law in the same way as a private company would be.

The experience of the London Underground with PPP (see Box 2.3) is an interesting case in point from all these perspectives.

Even when contracts can be drawn up effectively, the bidding process will be ineffective if bidders collude. This may occur for instance when there is only a small number of bidders. The problem may arise in all sectors, including the UPT sector as illustrated by Crozet.[27]

Box 2.3. **The London Underground PPP gamble**

The problems associated with attempts to harness private sector resources and expertise in a major infrastructure project are well illustrated by the 30-year PPP signed in March 2003 by the UK Department for Transport with two infrastructure companies (Infracos), Metronet and Tube Lines, for the maintenance and renewal of London Underground trains, stations, track and signalling. This followed a five-year procurement process costing some GBP 455 million. The PPP provides for spending an estimated GBP 15.7 billion over 30 years at present values, of which GBP 9.7 billion in the first seven and a half years.

The PPP split the Underground business in a new, complex way. London Underground retains responsibility for operations and safety, while Infracos maintains and renews the infrastructure over 30 years. London Underground pays Infracos largely on the basis of delivery of specified outputs, such as asset availability, rather than on the cost of the work. There is a built-in periodic review mechanism, untried in any other PPP arrangement, which enables the parties to respecify requirements within the PPP scope and reprice the deals at least every seven and a half years.

Independently of the political aspects, the disagreements that have emerged between the major public parties involved and the choice of Infracos, one may wonder if the expected benefits of this approach are worth the costs.

The government saw the PPP as the best way of ensuring stability of funding for the maintenance and renewal of the Tube, continued public sector management of operations, and the benefits of private sector management of a major infrastructure programme.

Critics point out that an alternative option – public sector management of maintenance and renewal financed by bonds raised by Transport of London (TfL) – would have allowed a simpler structure. They further point out that bond financing would have been cheaper than the PPP financing costs.

The crux of the matter seems to be the incentive scheme resulting from the allocation of risks. In the PPP approach, some of the risks are assumed by the private actors who are also responsible for the management of the infrastructure project. By contrast, in the public approach, the risks of non-performance fall directly on the public sector. Hence, the key question here is whether the gains to be achieved by the incentive structure and the greater scope for private initiative created by the PPP are worth the additional costs of the PPP (time and cost of negotiation, complexity of the structure, risk of conflicts, and so on).

So far the performance of Infracos has not lived up to expectation. However, this is only the beginning, and users do not seem unduly concerned. Up to almost four out of five Tube users appear to be reasonably satisfied with the operation of the infrastructure, despite the construction work. Only time will tell whether the results achieved are worth the PPP gamble.

Source: UK House of Commons Committee on Public Accounts (2005), *London Underground Public-Private Partnership*, Seventeenth Report of Session, 2004-05.

It is also common in the *water* sector where only very few companies operate at the global level. Three French companies (Suez, Veolia Water and Saur/Bouygues) account for 70% of the market world wide, and in most cases contracts have been awarded without genuine competition between bidders. Indeed, the largest companies in the sector (Suez and Veolia Water) sometimes submit joint bids. Abuses of dominant position have been found in France for instance.[28]

Competition is further restricted by the fact that construction and other contracts are frequently awarded to other subsidiaries of the company which holds the concession, without public tendering. This allows inflated charges to be imposed.

Even when there are enough bidders, the bidding process may be biased when some bidders "are more equal than others", that is, they have particular advantages over others because of access to information other bidders may not have or can take advantage of a monopoly position in one market to cross-subsidise their bid in another market. This situation which is not unusual in the UPT sector has induced the EC to issue the Public Service Obligation (PSO) directive which addresses the problem. The directive stipulates that no enterprise, notably if under state control, can reply to a call for tender if, in its area of origin, it benefits from a delegation of public service without any competitive process. The idea is to put an end to suspicions of "incompatible" aid while preserving recourse to an internal operator and margins of flexibility in the tendering process.

Financing

Financing is a major issue in the design of business models because all infrastructures require large investments over long periods of time. And increasing claims on the public purse not related to infrastructure development (such as health expenditures) mean that public funding (which was the major source of funds up to now) may be less readily available in the future. This is leading to a search for the formulation of models featuring private sector involvement, not only for the operation, but also for the financing of the infrastructure in all sectors. (See Chapter 1 for policy recomendations.)

As noted by Mackie and Smith, this search is somewhat illusory to the extent that whether financing is provided by public or private actors, "it comes from the same bank" anyway. Indeed, public agencies may get a better deal from the bank when borrowing money than private actors who may be perceived as more risky by financial institutions.

More important than the source of funding is whether the arrangement is financially sound, that is whether the lender has a good chance to recoup the money.[29]

In the *electricity* sector, financing depends largely on the revenues generated by providing the service. It follows that investment will be very much affected by the way electricity rates are set and what social obligations, if any, are imposed on operators. As already noted, the long-term soundness of the infrastructure may be undermined by price caps or requirements to subsidise particular categories of clients.

Changes in business models that affect risk allocation may also have a bearing on financial conditions and the outcome of projects involving public and private actors. Typically, liberalisation means in most cases that individual decision makers assume a greater level of risk, *i.e.* greater freedom of action implies more risk taking. For instance, a private actor will accept to manage a risky project and take responsibility for achieving specific objectives only if given sufficient leeway in the way the project is carried out. Successful business models will be those that provide an effective balance between the two: too much risk and not enough freedom of action can be a recipe for disaster for private actors. Conversely, low risk and high degree of freedom may allow the private actor to earn rents at the expense of the taxpayer.

An interesting case in point is the move to the unbundled model in the electricity supply sector, which is *shifting the business risk* from users and taxpayers to the different actors along the value chain (electricity generators, transmission and distribution networks operators, wholesalers and retailers). These actors, notably electricity generators, may be unwilling to make the investment necessary to meet increasing demand if they perceive the business risks resulting from higher price volatility and uncertainties about input supply to be too high.

In principle, this process should be self-correcting over time to the extent that reduced investments today should lead to higher electricity prices tomorrow which, in turn, should boost the perceived profitability of future investment, encouraging further investment. However, the process could generate serious price instability over time, if investors overreact to price signals and investment is subject to substantial bunching (an argument advanced by those who oppose the liberalisation of electricity markets in Europe). This can be corrected, in part at least, by appropriate mechanisms such as the formulation of long-term supply contracts and the development of more sophisticated futures markets for electricity.

In the *water* sector the bulk of the financing of capital expenditures come from the public sector, largely at the local level. In most countries, the sector has suffered for years from chronic underfinancing, as public authorities have not been able to provide the proper level of funding, while user charges often do not cover operating and maintenance costs. Private financing by large multinational enterprises (MNEs) have taken place in the past. However, the experience has not been very successful when water prices have been set too low to cover costs or when attempts to raise prices have met with strong political opposition. This has been the case in emerging markets, forcing most such companies to abandon their forays outside their traditional markets.

In *the rail freight* sector, the financing of investment depends largely on revenues generated by the operation of freight trains. However, such financing is often undermined by obligations to cross-subsidise passenger traffic and/or public policies that favour other modes of transport over rail. Thompson notes that where rail freight is provided privately or, at least fully commercially, and where governments do not unduly support highway or water competition, there is reason to believe that the wholly market-driven needs for freight infrastructure and operating investment will be met (one way or the other). The rail infrastructure challenge lies more in the willingness of governments to identify social benefits and costs transparently, and to fund them.

Thompson also notes that an important question arises with regard to the role that should be assumed by national governments for the financing of major infrastructure projects, such as the construction of intermodal terminals. In a globalising world, such terminals are likely to become increasingly important for international competitiveness, notably those involving maritime to rail transfers, as maritime to road transport terminals become increasingly saturated. This could justify public support at the national level for such facilities on economic as well as on environmental grounds. This is the approach adopted in Canada by the federal government in its decision to contribute to the financing of the major box container terminal of Prince Rupert, British Columbia, which is viewed as a strategic investment for the country as a whole. The Canadian policy contrasts with the hands-off approach of the US government noted by Thompson.

In Europe, progress in *intermodal* maritime/rail traffic is very much linked to the adoption of a more liberal business model for rail. This will give maritime companies additional freedom for integrating more effectively the maritime and terrestrial legs of their operation, so as to offer door-to-door service to their clients.[30]

In the *urban public transport* sector, outside sources of financing need to be found since revenues generated from passenger fares typically do not even cover operating costs. Even in London, where Tube tickets are among the most expensive in the world, fare revenues still represent a smaller share of revenues (41%) than grants (45%) for TfL.[31] In some countries, additional funding may come from those who benefit indirectly from the UPT system, including employers (such as, in France) and landlords.[32]

Another way to fund UPT systems that has been used in London is to impose a congestion charge on private cars entering the central area and to use the proceeds to improve the UPT. However, success has been mixed. While the scheme has been very effective in reducing private car traffic (down 30%)

and in encouraging the use of buses, it has generated less revenue than originally anticipated.[33]

In the *road transport* sector, financing depends on the business model: from the public purse in most cases; from private sources if the BOT approach is adopted. Regarding public financing, Mackie and Smith note that several approaches have been developed when more than one level of government is involved, including new two-tier models of public sector funding. In this respect, an interesting model quoted by Mackie and Smith is the Grant Anticipation Revenue Vehicle (GARVEE) programme and the Transportation Infrastructure Finance and Innovation Act (TIFIA) adopted in the US.[34]

Several approaches have also been used to take advantage of private sector resources and expertise. For instance, Mackie and Smith note that in the UK road infrastructure projects have been procured using the Design-Build-Finance-Operate (DBFO) model. This model is based on "shadow tolls", that is payments made to the private sector concession holder in regular instalments by the public sector, usually based on traffic usage, availability and service quality indices.

In France, the use of concessions for developing the highway system is well established since the first such concession for toll roads was signed in 1956. In 2004, the French highway system was more than 10 000 km long. About 75% was managed by concessions.

In Canada, the federal government also participates in the financing of roads, although road transport is largely a provincial responsibility. The Canadian experience with PPP has been limited to date, and the results have been mixed.

3.2. Overall assessment

The strengths and weaknesses of a particular business model can be measured in terms of its ability to provide solutions to problems raised in the pursuit of policy objectives. In assessing the merit of various business models, one can therefore examine how effectively the solutions they offer – in particular the way that public oversight is exercised – deals with the problems at hand.

Three evaluation criteria can be established on this basis:

- ***How effectively does the model deal with private and public failures?*** The need to correct for market failures often justifies government intervention. However, such public action may introduce some forms of "public failure". Hence, when assessing a business model, it is important to determine how it copes with both types of failures, and if the "solutions" are not worse than the problems to be solved.

- ***How well does the model take into account public obligations?*** Public action is often taken to meet social needs that would not otherwise be fulfilled by the market. Thus, business models can be assessed in terms of their ability to offer solutions to public obligations, without undermining the long-term viability of the infrastructure.
- ***How effectively does the model deal with environmental concerns?*** The provision of infrastructure services generates externalities that are ignored by traditional market mechanisms. Business models can be assessed on their ability to find appropriate solutions.

Dealing with private and public failures

It follows from the above discussion that two polar models typically tend to prevail in the five sectors under consideration:

- The *monolith model*. All segments of the value chain are vertically integrated. The monolith can be public (ministry, public corporation) or private under some form of public scrutiny (*e.g.* rate of return regulation).
- The *unbundled or separated model*. Only those segments (the network) of the value chain that are monopolistic are run as public or regulated private monopoly. Other segments are open to competition.

As discussed at length in the sectoral chapters, the monolith model is widely used in a number of sectors including electricity supply, water and water treatment, freight rail, UPT, and road transport. The separated or unbundled model is found in road transport and is gradually being introduced in rail transport and the electricity supply sector.

Each model has its strengths and weaknesses. The *monolith model* typically offers greater scope for vertical co-ordination and long-term planning, when appropriate financing mechanisms are put in place. Monoliths may also be in a stronger position to resist monopsonistic tactics of input suppliers (*e.g.* supplier of natural gas to electricity generators).

Conversely, the monolith model is more vulnerable to public or regulatory failures reflected in inefficient operation, lack of responsiveness to user needs, overextension of the infrastructure, capture of the regulator by the utility, high rents received by workers in the sector, lack of accountability, and vulnerability to political short-termism, leading to unsustainable levels of investment and poor maintenance of existing assets.

The weaknesses outlined above are particularly glaring in the water sector (notably short-termism and inefficiency), the rail and UPT sectors in OECD and non-OECD countries alike, as well as in the electricity sector in developing countries.

The *unbundled or separated model* is less vulnerable to public failures. It offers greater scope for efficiency and for responsiveness to users needs. It may also be less sensitive to political short-termism. However, the co-ordination of activities over the value chain may be more difficult to achieve in some sectors, resulting in increased uncertainty for key actors. This may lead to lower levels of investment than those that may be deemed desirable from an overall social perspective.

In practice, introducing the unbundled or separated model in sectors dominated by monoliths has proved difficult. For instance, in the electricity supply sector, effective reform has been more complex to achieve than originally anticipated. In the freight rail sector, the benefit of introducing some degree of competition whether following the US or UK/EU model is more clear-cut, but faces very strong opposition in Europe by legacy actors.

Dealing with social obligations

As already noted, social obligations are largely determined by the nature of the service provided by the infrastructure. Such obligations are relatively limited when the service is considered to be essentially a private good (freight rail, electricity). They are more extensive when the service is perceived to have a strong social dimension, either because the service is essential for life (water) or because it is viewed as important for fostering social cohesion (water, UPT, road transport).

In most existing models, social obligations are met by pricing the service below cost. For instance, in most countries, the price of water is very low and the main users (farmers) pay only a fraction of the cost, if at all. In addition, in the vast majority of public transport systems in the world, fares do not cover operating costs and do not rise in line with inflation (as an example, in the New York City subway, the "nickel fare syndrome" existed, where the fare remained set at a nickel, that is five cents, for more than forty years). In the rail sector, passenger rail fares typically do not cover costs, and passenger rail service is cross-subsidised by freight rail. Road transport provides free access at point of demand. Electricity is offered at highly subsidised prices in many developing countries (such as in India).

Putting the burden of social obligations on the infrastructure itself through below-cost pricing in such a way is inefficient and leads to the wastage of scarce resources (such as water). Moreover, it may have perverse distributional impacts (*e.g.* in a number of developing countries, the rich benefit from subsidised water rates, while the poor who are not connected to the network have to pay much higher prices to street water merchants). It is also clearly detrimental to the long-term sustainability of infrastructure and largely explains the chronic "infrastructure investment gap" that currently prevails in most countries.

The low priority attached to infrastructure development and maintenance at the political level arises in democratic societies from an "agency problem", that is from the fact that elected representatives only have a short-term political horizon (the next elections) and that future generations are not represented in the political process. Even when infrastructure-related issues attract political attention, such attention is more likely to focus on the development of new infrastructures rather than on the maintenance of existing ones.

This agency problem could be corrected in part at least by a greater emphasis on participatory democracy. Indeed, encouraging individual citizens directly concerned by a particular infrastructure – and who typically have a longer time horizon than the next election – to participate effectively in the decision-making process related to its development and management, could correct, at least in part, for the short-termism of elected representatives. Unfortunately, this is not the case in most instances. As a result, the need to ensure the long-term sustainability of the infrastructure is not fully taken into account in public decisions, leading to serious underinvestment.

Dealing with externalities

In most cases, the provision of infrastructure services does not reflect the externalities such provision generates. For instance, in the case of *electricity*, the pricing of services does not take into account the greenhouse gases (GHG) produced by the use of fossil fuels for electricity generation (coal-fired generators alone are responsible for 25% of the CO_2 released each year in the atmosphere). In addition, most users of *water*, notably farmers do not pay for the pollution they generate. In the *rail and UPT* sectors, the overextension of networks for political reasons under the monolith model results in wasteful energy use. In road transport, there is no incentive to pollute less because of the free access model.

Not only are the costs of externalities not reflected in the price of the infrastructure service, but less polluting infrastructure are not given preference over more polluting infrastructure. For instance, in the US, public policy typically tends to favour road transport over rail. In Europe, although the official policy is to promote rail transport, the patchwork organisation of railways prevents rail operators to compete on equal terms with trucks, in practice.

3.3. Sectoral perspective

The overall conclusion one may draw from the broad analysis in Section 3.2 above is rather pessimistic. Indeed, existing business models suffer from a number of weaknesses: 1) market and public failures prevail in many sectors, causing inefficiencies and lack of effectiveness; 2) the use of pricing for meeting social obligations contributes significantly to such inefficiency and results in unsustainable levels of investment; 3) the environmental consequences of providing infrastructure services are still largely ignored.

It is interesting to see how these general conclusions are reflected at the sectoral level. This is the purpose of the summary assessment presented below. It draws on the analysis above and attempts to put the findings in perspective, by highlighting some of the key points that emerge from the discussion for each of the sectors.

For each of the five sectors, the nature of the service provided by the infrastructure, as well as the main business models, are identified succinctly. This is followed by a quick overview of strengths and weaknesses from the three main policy perspectives considered here, that is, economic, social and environmental.

Electricity

Nature of the service and main business models. *Nature of the service.* Electricity is generally viewed a private good. However, it is considered to be an essential service from a security and social perspective. Moreover, electricity generation and distribution create negative externalities from an environmental point of view.

Main business models. Although a broad range of models exist, two polar models tend to dominate: the monolith and the unbundled models.

Strengths and weaknesses of existing models. From an *economic perspective*, the monolith model is strong for vertical co-ordination and long-term investment planning and implementation, provided the level of revenue generated is adequate and interference for short-term political gains is kept to a minimum. However, it tends to be inefficient and not very responsive to user needs. The unbundled model is more efficient, more responsive, but vertical co-ordination can be a problem. Moreover, systemic long-run planning is more difficult, as risk is born by individual private decision makers in a competitive context, rather than by captive users and taxpayers. This raises questions about future supply conditions with regard to reserve capacity. Conversely, the unbundled model offers greater opportunities for network interconnection across regions and across countries, which should reduce some of the risks of supply disruption and should allow a more efficient handling of peak demand across the different markets. It is nevertheless interesting to note that, in practice, the interconnection of networks may increase the risk of failure or at least the adverse consequences of failure as illustrated by the black out of 2003 in the north-eastern part of North America that affected close to 50 million people.[35] Although the outlook for deregulation was rather upbeat a few years ago, the impact of deregulation today is generally viewed as mixed, underscoring the difficulty of introducing effective market reforms in this sector. (See Annex 2.A1 for more details on this point.)

From a *social perspective*, the monolith model offers more scope for political interference. While interference is still possible with the unbundled model, its adoption encourages a more sound approach to meeting social objectives, by inducing governments to avoid actions that could undermine the sustainability of the infrastructure and the ability of the utility to undertake the necessary investment. However, concerns have been raised regarding the social implications of unbundling on the price of electricity charged to domestic users, to the extent that market conditions are likely to induce suppliers to adopt a Ramsay pricing approach to maximise revenues, *i.e.* discriminate in favour of large (industrial) users who have more options for meeting their demand for electricity than domestic users who typically have a more inelastic demand.[36]

From an *environmental perspective*, both models have failed so far to take into account the externalities generated by the industry, although the unbundled model may be more environmentally friendly to the extent that greater concern for efficiency results in reduced use of costly inputs and greater efforts to minimise transmission losses.

The design of an effective business model from an environmental point of view is a major challenge. The creation of a market for emission rights is a promising step in this direction as well as efforts to develop renewable energy sources. However, there is a danger that technology-specific incentives may be counterproductive. Moreover, uncertainty regarding the measures that will eventually be put in place by governments is creating uncertainty for the industry and may delay investment, notably in the unbundled model.

Water

Nature of the service and main business models. *Nature of the service.* Although water may seem to be a private good, it has strong public good characteristics (social, health, environmental). This justifies extensive public scrutiny, not only at the local level, but also at the regional, national and even the transnational level.

Another major consideration is the fact that urban use of water is only a relatively minor use of water.[37] Urban dwellers must therefore compete with other users for access to water supplies and also must bear the cost of the pollution generated by these users. This contributes to making the management of urban water systems particularly difficult. Indeed, urban water systems will not be able to satisfy surging urban demand unless rural supplies of water are also properly managed.[38]

Main business models. The public monolith model organised at the local level largely dominates in the world, although private concession models play an important role in some countries (for instance, in France).

Strengths and weaknesses of existing models. From an *economic perspective*, water systems under public monolith regimes have typically suffered from underinvestment over prolonged periods of time. This has lead to a serious deterioration of the infrastructure in most countries, resulting in significant inefficiencies while in emerging markets water systems remain largely underdeveloped.[39]

The seriousness of the problem faced by BRIC countries is well illustrated by the situation that currently prevails in Delhi where the city's water board, the Delhi Jal Board (DJB), is only able to meet a small fraction of actual demand for water (while 40% is lost to leakage) and receives revenues that cover only 60% of its operating costs.[40]

Growing pressures from financially hard-pressed governments and threats of privatisation have put pressures on public systems to improve performance via a "re-engineering" of existing systems. Corporatisation has also contributed to improved accountability.

Models involving strong private sector participation have met with mixed results outside the traditional markets of the private players. This has induced a number of players to be more selective and concentrate on contracts involving only limited risk. However, it is interesting to note that in France, where public oversight is strong and there is a clear policy that the management of water should be financially balanced ("l'eau doit payer pour l'eau", that is "water must pay for water"), private companies have been very effective in running water and water treatment systems. This suggests that these two conditions (strong public oversight and clear policy to set water prices at cost recovery levels) may be two important prerequisites for the effective participation of private actors in water management elsewhere.

From a social perspective. Concerns about meeting the needs of low-income users have kept user charges low, undermining the economic viability of many systems. However, models have often failed to pay sufficient attention to the key role public involvement and transparency play in the success and sustainability of water sector projects.

From an environmental perspective, existing models have not proved very successful. Water pollution and water stress is on the rise in a growing number of countries. Most of the problem, however, results from the wasteful use of water and water pollution in agriculture.

In the developing world, increasing industrialisation, population growth and lack of effective wastewater treatment are polluting future sources of water supply.

Developing country governments are typically more focused on providing water than with treating of wastewater. Continuing in this vein will certainly drive up costs for water provision as future sources of water supply become increasingly difficult to find, transport and treat to standards.

In OECD countries, the public awareness of problems is increasing, and a number of corrective actions have been implemented in recent years, including at the transnational level (for example, the water directives in Europe).

Hence, one may wonder whether current business models are up to the challenges they face. Are they able to channel the massive flows of additional finance needed to further extend infrastructure (to reach new segments of population, or to achieve more stringent health and environment standards) and to enhance maintenance of existing assets, in both OECD member and non-member countries? Alternative technologies may generate innovative approaches, harnessing such newcomers as the financial community (carriers of long-term savings), domestic operators and property developers.

Freight rail

Nature of the service and main business models. *Nature of the service.* Perhaps more than the other four infrastructure services covered in this book, freight rail may be viewed as a private good. This means that, in principle at least, economic considerations should dominate the policy agenda. However, the environmental advantage of rail over road transport should also be taken into account.

Main business models. Three main models seem to dominate the sector: the public monolith model which is still the dominant model world wide, the separated model (first introduced in the UK and which should be extended gradually to the rest of Europe in the coming years) and the owner-tenant model that prevails in North America.

Strengths and weaknesses of existing models. *From an economic perspective*, the monolith model offers some advantage in terms of co-ordination between infrastructure development and operation of rolling stock. However, it is vulnerable to political interference, and there is no strong incentive for efficiency while the service is not very responsive to user needs. The monolith model is also not conducive to long-term investment, when such investment requires substantial subsidies from the government (*e.g.* BR before privatisation in the UK, and the SNCF today in France).

The separated model should in principle allow for more efficient operation and greater responsiveness to user needs. In Europe, the EC has high hopes that this could eventually lead to a reversal of the gradual decline of freight rail, in competition with road and water transport. However, many obstacles remain to be overcome, including the strong resistance of legacy monoliths in a number of countries.

In the aftermath of the Stagger Act of 1980, the North American model has proved very successful, allowing freight railways to improve significantly the efficiency of their operation and increase their market share of the freight market, despite a bias by the US federal government in favour of road and water transport.

From a social perspective, both the monolith model and the North American models were vulnerable in the past to public policy aimed at cross-subsidising passenger service by freight. The problem has been largely resolved in North America by the creation of AMTRAK and VIA Rail which are funded directly by the government.[41] It remains very serious in other parts of the world. This includes Europe where investment plans clearly favour passenger traffic over freight traffic.

From an environmental perspective, freight rail is receiving growing attention from policy makers. This could have beneficial effects for rail across all models if it results in efforts to divert part of the growth in road transport to rail and to promote multimodal transport. In North America, such diversion is likely to be modest given the high share of freight already carried by rail. The potential is much larger in Europe where rail accounts for only 8% of the freight traffic. Doubling this share is doable according to the experts, but it would require more forceful efforts to move to a more liberalised (separated) business model, allowing private freight trains to move freely over a truly pan-European railway network and beyond.

Urban public transport (UPT) systems

Nature of the service and main business models. *Nature of the service.* Urban public transport systems are natural local monopolies and the services they offer have a strong "public good" dimension.

Main business models. Although a number of UPT systems were historically developed by private investors (notably the London and the New York City subway systems), today most are run as public monopolies. However, private sector participation occurs in some cases, either for the operation of the systems, or for the maintenance and upgrading of the infrastructure.

Strengths and weaknesses of existing models. *From an economic perspective,* as noted by Crozet, the public monolith model is vulnerable to political interference that can lead to significant inefficiencies. In most instances, UPT systems do not cover operating costs.[42]

Introducing competition for the market can help, but the tendering process is vulnerable to collusion among the bidders; and setting up a level playing field is not easy when incumbents of existing systems that have not had to go through a tendering process are allowed to bid on new contracts.

The use of PPP for maintenance and upgrading of the infrastructure is more controversial (see the London Underground example in Box 2.3).

From a social perspective, UPT systems fulfil an important social role by providing access to all within the city. However, setting fares too low and preventing such fares to rise in line with costs undermines the ability of the system to maintain and upgrade facilities with adverse consequences for all users.

From an environmental perspective, UPT systems offer an effective alternative to private cars in densely populated areas, and it is indeed the main reason often given in recent years for their implementation. However, overextension of the network to less densely populated areas – which may very well occur in the public monolith model – is questionable, both from an economic and environmental perspective. Moreover, the development of cleaner cars (such as, "plug in" electric cars), combined with effective road pricing and greater reliance on ICT (for telework, teleshopping, telemedicine, and distant education) may weaken the environmental advantage of UPT systems in the future.

From a planning perspective, it is becoming increasingly necessary to approach the planning process from a metropolitan-regional point of view, so as to ensure that all relevant institutional actors (national government, regions, municipalities, etc.) are involved. The same applies for certain other infrastructure sectors.

Road transport

Nature of the service and main business models. *Nature of the service.* Road services do not meet the criteria established for private goods: while they are rivalrous, they are not excludable in the business model that prevails in most countries. Road space is allocated to traffic on a first-come, first-served basis, and is free at the point of demand

Main business models. The large majority of roads in the world are owned and operated by the state and different levels of government. However, there is scope for private sector participation as concessionaires of motorways or, in some cases, as owners and operators of private roads.

Strengths and weaknesses of existing models. *From an economic perspective*, the model of free access at the point of demand inevitably leads to costly congestion in densely populated areas, once capacity is reached, resulting in an inefficient allocation of scarce road space. However, introducing a system that is both more efficient (*e.g.* road pricing) and viewed as fair by the majority of users is a politically formidable task. Nevertheless, as demonstrated by the London experiment with cordon charges, the imposition of such charges over a limited geographical region can be quite successful in reducing congestion and in encouraging greater use of public transport, even if the scheme is costly to implement and does not generate as much revenue as originally anticipated.

From a social perspective, the current regime may be considered unfair to rural dwellers who have to pay a disproportionately high share of the cost of the network, through the mixture of vehicle and fuel taxes that prevail in most countries.

On balance, the distributional impact of cordon charges may be positive. On the face of it, such charges seems to favour the rich, since they are better able to shoulder the extra burden of the charge, while they can take advantage of reduced congestion to move more quickly than previously in the city centre, saving economically valuable time. However, low-income commuters who were taking the bus before also benefit from a better service too, without having to pay for the charge. Those who might be most negatively affected are the middle-class users who are forced to abandon their private vehicle for public transport. However, their overall cost of commuting may be reduced, and they benefit too from reduced congestion in the central area.

From an environmental perspective, the current model of free access at the point of demand is inefficient since it encourages overuse of the facilities by vehicles that create negative environmental externalities.

4. Future prospects

This section examines how the assessment conducted in Section 3 above may be modified in the coming decades under the influence of major drivers of change, taking into account the impact that such drivers may have, not only on the future viability of existing business models, but also on the balance of objectives that policy makers are likely to pursue (*i.e.* some objectives are likely to become more/less important; the balancing of a new configuration of multiple policy objectives in the future may raise new issues).

The analysis above suggests that, on the basis of the current state of play alone, substantial changes should be made to existing business models. But given the long term nature of infrastructure development and management, considering the current situation is not enough for effective policy making. Ideally, one should also look into the future in order to take into account – to the extent possible – the future prospects of existing models, *i.e.* how such models may fare in the future in the light of changing circumstances, as well as likely changes in the public policy agenda.

This is a highly speculative undertaking since it is impossible to predict the future. However, the future is not completely open. Indeed, the set of possible futures is largely determined by a number of drivers of change. While it is not possible to determine in advance how such drivers will play out in the end, one can nevertheless speculate on the way each one may influence the future of our economy and society at large and on the consequences this may have for infrastructure development.[43]

Some of these trends may directly affect the strengths and weaknesses of the business models (*e.g.* a new technology may render an existing model obsolete); others may have indirect impacts, by changing the relative weight that may be assigned to various policy objectives (*e.g.* growing concerns about the environment may induce decision makers in the future to favour models that deal more effectively with externalities).

On the basis of work conducted in earlier phases of this project, several drivers of change have been identified as having a particularly important bearing for infrastructure development in the future.[44] The drivers which are considered below include the changing geopolitical environment; the growing importance of security considerations; the challenges raised by future economic growth, globalisation and expected changes in the structure of economic activities; key demographic trends (population growth, population ageing and urbanisation); new opportunities that may be offered by technological change; and the consequences of growing concerns for the environment. Attention is also given in this section to the increasing demands that are likely to be put on the public purse, the changing role of private actors and the general trend observed in OECD countries and beyond towards a more participatory form of democracy. These trends may also have important consequences for the formulation of public policy and the conditions under which infrastructure services will be provided.

4.1. *Geopolitics*

Growing interdependence in the coming decades will create an environment where geopolitical relations will be more complex and involve a larger set of actors beyond nation-states. This will have important implications for infrastructure development.

First, because of growing international interdependence, individual countries will become more vulnerable to the actions of other actors. This is the case for electricity generation and distribution, where concerns about security of supply of input fuel will become increasingly important.

Second, the management of common resources will require increasing co-ordination across countries and may lead to the formulation of transnational regulation and the establishment of transnational standards (*e.g.* water, road and rail transport).

Third, geopolitical considerations will significantly influence the development of some infrastructure. This applies, for instance, to the proposed extension of railways beyond Europe to the Middle East and Asia.

These developments will have important implications for *business models*. For instance, in the case of the *electricity* supply industry, as supply chains become increasingly globalised, the volatility of input fuel prices will be felt more quickly everywhere, increasing risk for investors. This could have a detrimental effect on investment and call for the adoption of risk mitigation measures, such as the storage of larger input fuel reserves and the development of more effective fuel switching capabilities.

The need for managing common resources more effectively across jurisdictions will call for a greater role for transnational governance. For instance, although the day-to-day management of *water* systems will remain largely local, transnational actors will play a growing role in shaping infrastructure development. This role will need to be reflected in business models both at the local and national levels. Standards established at the transnational level will increasingly influence the level and nature of infrastructure investment that will need to be carried at the local and regional levels (*e.g.* EC water directive). Moreover, as water becomes scarcer, co-ordination across countries sharing the same water basin will become increasingly critical, as access to water could become a growing source of conflict.

Finally, favourable geopolitical conditions will increase the potential for international exchanges, as well as the economic benefits that can be derived from such exchanges, resulting in an increased demand for the development of effective and efficient transnational *transportation* links (including multimodal terminals). These benefits will be better achieved with models that foster carriage competition than in monolith models.

The *implications for policy* will also be substantial. First, international relations will become increasingly important, and the distinction between "international" and "domestic" policy will become more blurred. In this context, national governments will increasingly have to negotiate international agreements with their neighbours and assist local authorities in the implementation of such agreements, including financially. The role of international organisations is also likely to grow, particularly in areas where specialised expertise is required.

The *electricity* supply industry is an interesting case in point in this regard. Governments in fuel-importing countries will have to pay particular attention to their relationship with input fuel supplying countries and will have to co-ordinate their position with other fuel-importing countries more effectively.[45] Efforts will also have to be made to strengthen links across electricity markets so as to be better able to cope with disruptions of supply. In addition, measures designed to foster the responsiveness of electricity demand to fluctuating electricity prices should help. This could be encouraged, *inter alia*, by the widespread adoption of smart metering so as to allow users to respond to price changes in real time.

When making policies affecting input fuel choices, governments will have to make difficult trade-offs between conflicting policy objectives. For instance, security of supply considerations may favour the use of coal as input fuel; whereas relying on gas supplies from abroad, although more risky, might be preferable from an environmental perspective. Such choices, however, will be increasingly constrained by international commitments (such as those under the Kyoto Protocol) unless new technological advances modify the balance of power between users and suppliers.[46]

Geopolitical factors will also be important in other sectors. For instance, beyond purely economic or social considerations, *transportation and communications networks* will continue to be given high priority by government as a tool for nation-building (or regional integration) and for forging links with other countries (*e.g.* TEN-T in Europe and plans to expand it to 26 neighbouring countries).

4.2. Security

As was noted in Andrieu (2005), in the future security will encompass a broad range of concerns beyond purely military ones. Such concerns will focus on a multiplicity of systemic risks (both natural and man-made) that could cause major devastation in terms both of loss of lives and loss of property. The increasingly sophisticated and ubiquitous infrastructures that we depend upon more and more could be particularly vulnerable in this regard.

For instance, in the case of the *electricity* supply industry – and in addition to the geopolitical threats outlined above – major disruptions at key choke points in the energy supply chain resulting from accidents, natural phenomena or terrorist attacks could have devastating effects throughout the world on input fuel supply. In this context, models featuring high dependence on the import of gas and a highly centralised network with limited interconnection to other networks are likely to be increasingly vulnerable. Moreover, such disruption could have far-reaching domino effects on other infrastructures that depend heavily on electricity, such as water treatment systems, road and rail transport and electronic financial networks.

Increased security threats will also have an adverse effect on investment in all models. In the case of public models, increased attention by government to security will put further constraints on the public purse, reducing the ability of government to devote resources to infrastructure development and maintenance. In addition, in the face of higher security risks, private sector actors will be more reluctant to invest in infrastructure. In both cases, this could have a vicious circle effect to the extent that underinvestment undermines the robustness of the network and makes it more vulnerable to future disruptions.

Security concerns may also open a debate on whether centralised or decentralised models should be adopted. For instance, in the case of *water*, security consideration may favour the adoption of more centralised governance and may make the use of private actors less attractive. Plus, in the case of *freight rail*, security risks may induce governments to favour public ownership and centralised systems that can more easily be monitored and controlled. A similar argument in favour of centralisation has been made regarding *electricity* supply in Europe, as already noted above.

Functionally, however, decentralised systems may be less vulnerable to some risks. For instance, in the case of *electricity*, distributed generation and interconnection across networks are thought to reduce vulnerability to disruption and to alleviate the need for capacity reserve. The risk of massive disruption is also reduced in decentralised water systems, while increased interoperability in the case of *rail* increases the robustness of the network.

In all cases, there is a clear message that security concerns will increase the need to monitor effectively the state of the network so as to be in a better position to take appropriate action in a timely manner. For instance, in the case of *water*, Palaniappan *et al.* note that security factors also make water quality monitoring more important: it should be well informed, well funded, publicly controlled and nationwide. This could put greater emphasis on the development of ICT-based monitoring technology and more investment in instrumentation for water systems.

In some cases, security concerns may affect the choice of infrastructure. For instance, terrorist attacks on *public transport* systems might induce commuters to favour the use of private cars. However, other security considerations could induce government to favour rail over road transport. *Rail transport* is not only safer, but it is also less vulnerable to fluctuation in the price and availability of oil than road transport.

Security concerns will also result in the development and stricter enforcement of security standards. For instance, in the case of *electricity*, more attention will be given to the development and enforcement of mandatory standards, including close monitoring of the condition of transmission lines.[47]

4.3. *Economic growth and structure*

Economic growth is generally viewed as the major driver of the demand for infrastructure services. However, changes in the composition of output also have a bearing (*e.g.* growing share of services in overall consumption) on infrastructure use, as well as the growing globalisation of economic activities.

In the case of most infrastructures, economic growth will fuel an increased demand for infrastructure services, creating pressures for increased production. Doing so can be achieved either by more efficient use of the existing infrastructure and/or an increase in its physical capacity.

Serious questions have been raised however, regarding the ability of existing business models to deliver the necessary investment. For instance, Morgan notes that there is no certainty that with existing business models all of the investment needed will, in fact, be forthcoming. If actual investment falls short of that required or is delayed, some part of demand might go unmet, leading to temporary or persistent power shortages. The main uncertainties surrounding the adequacy of electricity investment world wide relate in part to the impact of liberalisation and market reforms and the adoption of the unbundled model which will affect incentives to invest and access to capital (see Annex 2.A1). However, the monolith model could also be under strain, notably in countries where the revenue generating capacity of the model is insufficient, as already noted for instance in the case of India.

In the case of *water*, Palaniappan *et al.* note that underinvestment has been a serious problem for decades under largely public business models, as there is a failure of public governance to take the necessary action in a sustainable long-term manner. Underinvestment is also a serious problem for the *rail network* and *road transport* under the public monolith model.

In this context, the key issue for governments will be the adoption of business models that are *responsive to growing demand*, that is, models where prices better reflect the cost of providing the service and which take into account the need to adopt a long-term approach to infrastructure development in a sustainable manner. In many cases, this will call for regulatory reform so as to provide a more supportive environment to infrastructure development. An interesting case in point in this regard is Brazil where government must rely on the private sector, including foreign investors, for infrastructure development. This is forcing the adoption of more business-friendly policies by the authorities, as well as efforts to put in place more effective regulations.

Globalisation will also have an impact on business models and related public policy. As the volume and scope of international exchanges increase in the future, greater attention will need to be given at the national level to business models that effectively support the development of efficient transport and communication systems. This will create growing pressures for the adoption of more liberalised business models in these sectors (*e.g.* freight rail). Growing attention will also be given to urban development, as cities will likely be the major engines of growth in the future. Their effectiveness in this regard will depend in part on the availability of an efficient *urban transport* system that allows city dwellers to fully exploit agglomerations' economies.

Economic growth, however, will also have adverse consequences that will increasingly need to be taken into account. In some cases, expanding the capacity of the existing infrastructure will not be feasible. This will raise three key questions for policy makers: 1) how the existing capacity should be rationed, taking into account social and political objectives; 2) to what extent it is possible to induce infrastructure users to switch to other types of infrastructure services that are considered more desirable from an overall public policy perspective; and 3) how the use of the existing infrastructure can be improved.

In other cases, greater attention will be given to the externalities generated by the operation of the infrastructure. This will call for far-reaching changes on the supply and on the demand sides that will need to be reflected in the business models (*e.g.* for reducing environmental effects of electricity generation or road transport).

4.4. *Financing*

Given the growing constraints on the public purse, not least those stemming from ageing populations and the prospect of a possibly shrinking tax base, alternative sources of funding will have to be tapped to reach the necessary levels of investment.

In *monolith business models*, the key questions will be whether users are solvable or not and whether there is a political will to charge users a price that reflects costs. In traditional OECD *electricity* markets for instance, where the risk is largely borne by users, this should not be a problem. However, the situation is quite different when users are not solvable. This is the case for electricity distribution in countries such as India where the rates charged to users are deliberately kept low for political reasons. In addition, this applies to monolith models used in the *water* sector, in *UPT*, as well as *in rail transport* where passenger services may be cross-subsidised by a shrinking freight rail service (*e.g.* experiences of BR in the UK, and of SNCF in France where non-TGV infrastructure has suffered from underfunding as reported by Thompson). The situation is even worse in models where the service is provided free of charge (road transport), unless the fuel tax and tax on vehicles can be tapped for road network upgrading, as is the case in the US.

In *liberalised models*, the situation may be quite different to the extent that risks are borne by those who make the investment decision, rather than by captive final users. Investment will be forthcoming if the revenue stream received by the investor provides a rate of return in line with market rates, taking into account the specific risks facing investors in that sector.

The *electricity* sector seems to be where such conditions are most likely to be met in the future, provided that adequate instruments can be developed to mitigate risks and encourage investment.

In the *freight rail* sector, even in liberalised markets such as the US, private operators may not always have the resources necessary to expand capacity. Rail operators are typically very cautious when making investment decisions because of the long duration of rail assets and the long depreciation periods that apply from a fiscal point of view (such as, 30 years in Canada). Moreover, when investment involves the construction of major intermodal terminals of national interest, the question arises regarding the role that should be played by the state in such investment.

In the *water* sector, there are reasons to believe that the contribution of users could be strengthened; new technologies allow the development of on-site and closed-cycle systems that can be provided on a commercial basis. However, when considered from an overall policy perspective, all models should provide a minimum service to the poor. This should not be a problem in OECD countries, but this could undermine the financial viability of business models in the future in many developing countries, unless multilateral sources of funding can be tapped effectively.

In the *UPT* sector, public funding is essential. Regional and national authorities can be expected to continue to play an active role in this regard, because of the growing recognition of the regional and national significance of well-functioning cities in the overall economy and society. However, users may assume a larger share of the burden as such systems expand. Moreover, indirect beneficiaries of the systems (landowners, employers, private car commuters) could also be called upon to contribute more financially.

In *road transport*, public funding is likely to remain dominant, except in very specific cases. However, private finance initiative (PFI) models for rehabilitation schemes could be envisaged (the Portsmouth model in the UK as described by Mackie and Smith). Toll highways may also be progressively introduced in countries where they remain the exception today. This is likely to start first in situations where a "free" (but congested) alternative exist. However, strong public resistance may delay the implementation of this model, as illustrated by the Canadian experience in this regard (Highway 407, Fredericton-Moncton Highway).

4.5. *Demography*

When considering the impact of demographic development on infrastructure, several dimensions of such evolution need to be taken into account, beyond the mere increase in number. This includes for instance population ageing, urbanisation and international migration.

Growth in population by itself will put growing strain on existing infrastructures and create pressure for increases in capacity. The strain will be particularly severe in sectors where the available resources are limited (*e.g.* water services) or where there are physical limits to the extension of the network (*e.g.* roads). This will put existing business models under jeopardy, notably those that are not on a sound financial footing today. This problem is a major one for developing countries, since it is there that population growth of the poorest is expected to be the fastest.

Perhaps, it is in the case of the *water* sector that such problems are most severe. As noted by Palaniappan *et al.*, growing populations will contribute to rising demand for water in the future while, at the same time, the increased pollution generated by such populations will reduce readily available supplies of fresh water. Population is growing fast in areas that are already water-stressed. By 2025, two-thirds of the people in the world could live in water-stressed areas. In these regions, water systems already suffer from severe underinvestment and are clearly not on a sound financial footing. This implies that water-related issues will become increasingly prominent in the future, including the search for business models that can deal effectively with the problem. Particular attention will need to be given to wastewater treatment and recycling, an area that currently is not given much attention in developing countries. A key question will be the role that can be played by the private sector, including large multinationals specialising in this field, but also domestic operators and the financial community, *i.e.* how to develop "win-win" partnerships where the expertise of these companies are fully exploited for the benefit of all users, including the poor who do not currently have access to potable water.[48]

Growing populations will also have an adverse effect in other sectors. In the *electricity* sector, this will contribute to increased strains on energy resources. In the *road* sector, it will exacerbate road congestion. Larger populations will also have an impact on *freight rail*, not only on the demand side (because of the increased volume of goods that will need to be transported), but also on the supply side, as noted by Thompson, because of the increase in passenger train traffic it will generate. This could undermine the economic viability of existing rail freight business models to the extent that heavier passenger traffic may result in a higher burden on rail freight operators (more cross-subsidies from rail to passenger traffic), while priority given to passenger rail traffic means more disruption of freight rail traffic. This may lead to renewed efforts to more clearly separate passenger rail and freight rail traffic, *inter alia*, by developing freight corridors.

Population ageing will also have an impact on infrastructure development and business models. First and foremost, business models relying heavily on public funding will be under stress as population ageing will put increasing pressure on the public purse, reducing the ability of the central governments to finance infrastructure. This will encourage government to favour full cost pricing business models and to push financing to the local level whenever it is feasible to do so.

Population ageing will also be reflected in lower population growth in the OECD area and beyond, or even population decline in some cases. This means that particular attention should be given in these countries to business models that provide for effective maintenance of existing capacity. This is no easy task in light of the short-termism that prevails in democratic societies.

However, population ageing could have some *favourable* consequences for some infrastructures. Although this question is not addressed by either Crozet or Mackie and Smith, it would seem that, *ceteris paribus*, as population gets older, UPT could become more viable and the stress on the road network could be reduced, to the extent that older people are likely to prefer public transport over private cars in congested areas where the supply of public transport is adequate to meet their needs. Moreover, older people typically have the choice of travelling during off-peak periods. Finally, the elderly tend to move away from large cities, thereby contributing to reducing population density in large metropolitan areas.

Urbanisation is a major trend that will be particularly important in developing countries. It will strongly influence infrastructure development and the business models that will be used for this purpose. This will be the case notably for *water* infrastructure. Palaniappan *et al.* note that rapid urbanisation will call for significant investment in the development of centralised systems that may be the cheapest option to serve large population concentrations. Financing the development of such systems will be a major challenge given that a large share of the populations to be served will be poor. Business models involving financing in part by multilateral institutions such as the World Bank may be the most promising option for this purpose. Bringing in the private sector is unlikely to be successful except at the technical level.

It is clear that urbanisation will significantly increase the strain on *transport* systems, notably on the public transport systems in the large cities of the developing world, since most of the growth in population over the next few decades will be in urban areas in these countries. In this regard, one may wonder whether the countries involved will try to adopt the centralised segregated public transport model advocated by Crozet, given the heavy level of funding involved and the serious danger of public failures that such systems involve. Instead, they may attempt to build on the relatively successful informal private models found in many cities of Africa and Latin America that rely largely on the management of minibuses. Crozet notes that such a private transport offer is often least costly and of better quality than the public one and points out that this private model may offer an interesting example for developed countries, including notably the development of "car sharing" and "car pooling".

4.6. Technology

In all the infrastructure sectors, advances in technology are expected to have important consequences for existing business models and may allow the emergence of new ones. Overall, technology is not "business model-neutral". By multiplying options and opportunities, advances in technology tend typically to undermine "monolith-type models" and to favour a more distributed and diversified approach to infrastructure service provision.[49]

In the case of *electricity*, Morgan notes, for instance, that technology has significantly contributed to the adoption of the unbundled model in a number of countries. He notes further that the growth of small-scale renewables-based generation technologies, as well as other forms of distributed generation, such as small-scale fossil-based co-generation plants and fuel cells, could radically alter the structure of the electricity industry.

Policy makers in many countries are actively encouraging the development and deployment of *distributed generation* because of the economic, environmental and energy security benefits they can bring. On-site power production by fossil fuels generates waste heat that can be used by the customer, reducing overall primary energy needs. Distributed generation may also be better positioned to use inexpensive fuels that would otherwise go to waste, such as landfill gas. Distributed generation facilities located at an end-user's site or at a local distribution utility, and supplying power directly to the local distribution network, can also reduce the need to invest in long-distance high-tension transmission lines. Increased use of distributed generation technologies could avoid around USD 130 billion (in year-2000 dollars) of global investment in transmission networks between 2001 and 2030 – equal to 8% of total transmission investment (IEA, 2003). The reliability of electric power systems can be enhanced by distributed generation, as the system is less dependent on centralised facilities. The use of distributed generators at selected locations can also help distributors overcome local bottlenecks.

The widespread deployment of distributed generation would require profound changes in the way the electricity networks are organised, constructed and operated. Networks would operate in a much more decentralised manner. This could expand opportunities for small generators. More power would be generated and managed by the system operator at low voltages. In such a system, the high-voltage network would need to provide back up for the local decentralised systems.

In the case of the *water* sector, Palaniappan *et al.* notes that new technology will contribute to reducing the cost of water development and to increasing the quality of water as well as the security of water systems. It can also bring about the emergence of new business models, as such new technology makes smaller scale, decentralised systems cost-competitive.

On-site systems developed and managed *locally* will increasingly allow peri-urban, rural and greenfields to opt out of conventional large-scale centralised water and wastewater systems. Such a move should result in considerable savings, compared to extending the centralised system far afield, and will shift the burden of investment from the centralised system to property owners.

Desalination technology could provide a useful option in water-stressed regions. Advances in the technology have already brought the price of such units to levels not too far removed from more traditional source of waters (*e.g.* water pumped from rivers). Private entrepreneurs may apply this solution in a growing number of water-stressed areas in a decentralised manner, since more than half the world population lives within 60 kilometres of the sea.

The ability to generate energy from waste through *biotechnology* could considerably alter the business models of wastewater treatment. Up to now, the anaerobic digestion that creates biogas has been a niche technology. If energy can be generated profitably, such as through the development of microbial fuel cells, the cost of waste treatment could decline drastically and become more attractive for the private sector.

The development of "low impact technologies" could considerably reduce runoff water quality problems. But these decentralised solutions may be difficult to implement in a centralised water system context.

However, some technological development may favour centralised systems. *ICT and GPS-based technologies* will allow a closer remote real-time monitoring of water systems, improving the ability of managers to make decisions related to water sourcing and water pollution on a large scale (*e.g.* watershed level) and will provide for greater system robustness. ICT technologies will also allow systems to be effectively managed at larger scale.

New technology will also raise important *policy issues*. Governments will need to pay particular attention to the obstacles that may exist in business models regarding the application of new technologies. This includes rules and regulation and standards that are technology biased (*e.g.* a requirement that the new development be connected to a centralised system may discourage the adoption of on-site and closed water cycle solutions). Moreover, new technology that makes fresh water available where it was not previously will raise water rights issues. It will change the nature of who owns the water.

In the case of *rail freight* transport, technological progress is expected to have only a moderate impact on business models, although new technology is more likely to be adopted quickly in "separated models" where competitive pressures on operators will be the greatest than in monolith models. Progress is expected to be gradual, including increased freight wagon cargo capacity; increasing freight train loading; increasing maximum axle load; enhanced signalling, including the possible adoption of "moving block" signalling;

improved traction of locomotives and reduced energy consumption; improved operating techniques (including the use of block trains and dedicated unit trains). However, public monoliths may be in a stronger position to introduce breakthrough technologies (*e.g.* TGV) since all the risks are borne by users or taxpayers, while the public authority has the necessary clout to remove regulatory and institutional obstacles, if the political will is strong enough.

Governments keen to shift traffic from road to rail are likely to pay particular attention to the development of technologies that could contribute to giving rail an edge over road, hence to improve the efficiency, security and reliability of rail freight services.

However, as noted by Thompson, it seems quite possible that the single most important advance in technology aiding the growth of railway freight traffic will be in highway tolling, which should contribute to create a more level competitive playing field for rail freight carriers. However, the impact of highway tolling will very much depend on the business model used in the rail freight sector. In Europe, it will benefit EU freight rail traffic only if the management model for rail freight is changed to promote private ownership and operation of rail freight carriers at the European level, and if border barriers are considerably reduced.

Although Crozet does not address technology specifically, it is clear that it will have an important bearing on the business models used in *urban public transport*. First, technological advances could foster the efficiency and effectiveness of UPT systems by improving their carrying capacity through improved signalling, control and more widespread adoption of automation, reducing labour costs that currently represent 60% of operating costs, as noted by Crozet.

But technology could also improve the effectiveness of more decentralised models. ICT will contribute to improved road traffic management and should facilitate the introduction of demand management scheme (road pricing). It may also make decentralised solutions such as car pooling, car sharing or private minibus services more viable.

The development of ICT could help reduce the need for physical mobility within cities (telework, teleshopping, tele-education, telemedicine). In this regard, efforts in a number of cities to offer city-wide very high capacity Internet connections are interesting developments. But ICT may undermine the very *raison d'être* of cities by reducing the significance of agglomerations' economies, and by promoting the development of Internet-based communities outside large cities. However, the evidence on this score is not clear. Indeed, ICT seems to have favoured increased physical concentration up to now.

Finally, the enthusiasm for UPT, which has been largely motivated, as noted by Crozet, by environmental considerations, may be dampened by the development of emission-free vehicles, such as electric cars.

From a public policy perspective, technology raises a number of issues in an urban transport context. To what extent should the deployment of ICT technologies be encouraged (*e.g.* development of Wi-Fi in cities)? What changes should be made to regulations so as to encourage the development of new innovative business models (*e.g.* elimination of quotas on taxi licences that currently limit the offer in a number of cities and prevent the development of private minibus initiatives)? What policies should be adopted to encourage telework, e-commerce, tele-education, telemedicine?

Many of the remarks made regarding urban road transport are also pertinent for *road transport* in general, particularly those that apply to the application of ICT, and the role it could play for demand management and the introduction of business models based *on road pricing schemes*. The development of new fuel technologies could also contribute to reducing dependence on foreign oil as well as the adverse environmental effects of road transport. Research into multifuelled vehicles, fuel cells, biofuels and hydrogen-based fuels is promising and likely to be stepped up as shortages in more traditional fuels are encountered. This could help induce policy makers to consider further expansion of the network more favourably, especially if congestion becomes so widespread that the economic and social costs of reduced mobility become unbearable.

As noted by Mackie and Smith, the challenge in introducing road pricing schemes is not technical feasibility but cost effectiveness and political/social acceptability. They point out that it would be essential to think in terms of tariff reform, with road user charging for congestion and environmental reasons associated with reforms to fuel taxation and vehicle ownership taxes, so as to ensure that a strong coalition of road users would be willing to accept the package. In the UK (and probably in other countries as well), there is acute political sensitivity in the treasury to such a concept. The other point is that it appears that implementation would be hugely expensive.

The introduction of *tolls* in exchange for a reduction in fuel tax raises significant fiscal policy issues because of the weight of fuel taxes in public budget (these taxes are used for other areas and not only road transport). With a toll system, users will logically expect a closer link between the toll charged and the road service provided. Hence, the introduction of tolls could induce a sea change in the way the road network is managed, with greater emphasis on maintaining a sustainable level of quality of service over time.

4.7. *Environment*

The future evolution of the environment (in particular, climate change) and the growing concerns engendered will have a profound impact on infrastructure development and may bring about significant changes that could affect the viability of existing business models and induce governments to reassess their overall approach to infrastructure development and maintenance. In this regard, the *Stern Review on the Economics of Climate Change* (United Kingdom, 2006a), may be as J.F.O. McAllister of *Time* magazine puts it "a tipping point, one of those moments when a lot of trends converge to make old obstacles look punier".[50] For policy makers, the merit of the Stern report is that it considers climate change mitigation policies in a benefit/cost context, that is, to what extent the future benefits of mitigation are worth the costs they will impose on society today.

With regard to the consequences of climate change, the general conclusion reached in the report is that the scientific evidence points to increasing risks of serious, irreversible impacts from climate change associated with business-as-usual (BAU) paths for emissions. Climate change threatens the basic elements of life for people around the world: access to water, food production, health, and use of land and the environment.

The authors of the Stern report further point out that the damages from climate change will accelerate as the world gets warmer. Higher temperatures will increase the chance of triggering abrupt and large-scale changes. The impacts of climate change are not evenly distributed; the poorest countries and people will suffer earliest and most. And if and when the damages appear, it will be too late to reverse the process.

Of course, infrastructures will not escape unscathed. The findings of the Stern report most relevant in this regard focus on four consequences of climate change: greater weather variability, more extreme weather events (storms), permafrost melting and rising sea levels.

Greater weather variability. The impact of climate change will be particularly severe in the *water* sector. Greater weather variability will mean that rain precipitation will become more uneven and less predictable, increasing the occurrence of runoff, the amount of water that flows over the land surface. This will not only mean potential changes in water availability to people, but also will amplify the need to invest in infrastructure to help manage patterns of water supply. More frequent water shortages will raise the investment required in infrastructure, reduce agricultural output and exacerbate infrastructure damage from subsidence.

Water-related issues will be particularly challenging in developing countries which are highly dependent on water – the most climate-sensitive economic resource – for their development. Indeed, many developing countries do not have enough water storage to manage annual water demand based on the current average seasonal rainfall cycle. This will become an even greater bind with a future, less predictable cycle.

More extreme weather events. Critical infrastructure, which is often concentrated around coastlines, including oil refineries, nuclear power stations, port and industrial facilities will be increasingly vulnerable to violent storms.

Infrastructure damage will rise sharply in a warmer world because of the combined effects of increasing potency of storms from warmer ocean waters and the increasing vulnerability of infrastructure to rising wind speeds. Indeed, such damage will increase substantially from even small rises in sea temperatures because: 1) peak wind speeds of tropical storms are a strongly exponential function of temperature, increasing by about 15-20% for a 3 °C increase in tropical sea surface temperatures; and 2) damage costs typically scale as the cube of wind-speed or more (see Figure 2.2). Storms and associated flooding are already the most costly natural disaster today, making up almost 90% of the total losses from natural catastrophes in 2005 (USD 184 billion from windstorms alone, particularly hurricanes and typhoons).[51]

Figure 2.2. **Relationship between building damage cost and peak wind speed**

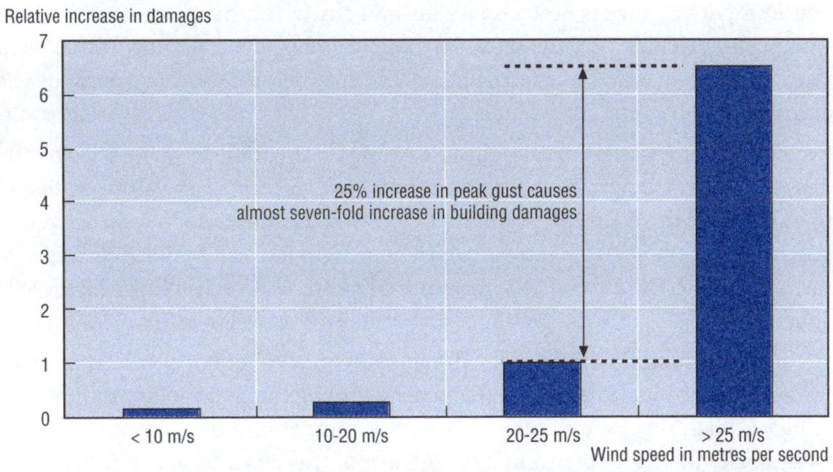

Source: United Kingdom (2006a), *Stern Review: The Economics of Climate Change*, HM Treasury, London.

Melting permafrost. Climate change will also have a detrimental effect on infrastructure in colder regions. High latitude regions are already experiencing the effects of warming on previously frozen soil. Thawing weakens soil conditions and causes subsidence of buildings and infrastructure. Climate change is likely to lead to significant damage to buildings and roads in settlements in Canada and parts of Russia currently built on permafrost.

Melting permafrost risks damaging high latitude oil and gas installations, pipelines and other infrastructure, including railways, such as the Russian Federation's Baikal-Amur railway, and will also require expensive remedial investment. Stormier seas could raise the attraction of land routes from Asia to Europe, including the planned new Eurasian railway across Kazakhstan.

Rising sea levels. This will increase the risk of damages to coastal infrastructure and accelerate capital depreciation. Costs of flood defences on the coast will rise, along with insurance premiums. A government study calculated that in the UK the average annual costs of flood damage to homes, businesses and infrastructure could increase from around 0.1% of GDP currently to 0.2-0.4% of GDP if global temperatures rise by 3 to 4 °C. Greater investment in flood protection is likely to keep damages in check. Similarly, preliminary estimates suggest that annual flood losses in Europe could rise from USD 10 billion today to USD 120-150 billion (EUR 100-120 billion) by the end of the century. If flood management is strengthened in line with the rising risk, the costs may only increase two-fold. According to one recent report, storm surge heights all along Australia's East Coast from Victoria to Cairns could rise by 25-30% with only a 2 °C increase in global temperatures.

From a policy perspective, the main message of the Stern report is that while climate change is real, dangerous and costly, it is much cheaper to solve – equivalent to just a 1% tax on everything we buy – if we act now rather than later. Indeed, it may be impossible to correct the situation as many of the damages will become irreversible.

Even though, in principle, climate change mitigation measures are highly desirable from a longer-term environmental perspective, they can be expected to undermine the economic viability of existing business models. Moreover, in practice, some measures may prove to be misguided and result in a waste of resources without clear environmental benefits (*e.g.* technology-dependent subsidies).

Environmental regulations will typically impose higher costs on existing infrastructure operators and developers by forcing them to modify their *modus operandi*. Such regulations may also reduce their ability to generate revenues by imposing heavier constraints on the use of the services they produce. The impact can be expected to be greater in liberalised models – where decisions tend to reflect market conditions – than in monolith models which are relatively immune to market changes and are better able to weather the imposition of new constraints which are ultimately born in any case by captive users or by taxpayers.

In the *electricity* sector, the application of environmental policies is clearly a necessary but also highly complex matter. Uncertainties about the measures that will actually be put in place in the coming years and their financial implications for investors are increasing the business risk faced by entrepreneurs in the unbundled model, which may delay needed investment. As noted by Morgan, some environmental policies may cause market distortions and inefficiencies, particularly where cross-border trade is possible. Subsidies for particular technologies, or non-transparent barriers that impede the development of others, may not lead to the optimal fuel mix or choice of technology in the long term given the unpredictability of technological development and imperfect information. The challenge, here, is to establish a legal and market framework that ensures that environmental objectives are met flexibly and at least cost, encouraging innovation without distorting business incentives and competitive conditions unduly. One such approach which is likely to receive growing policy attention is to cap and trade emission allowances.[52] The United States was one of the first countries to introduce such a system for sulphur dioxide emissions from power plants and large industrial facilities under the 1990 Clean Air Act Amendments. In January 2005, the European Union launched an Emission Trading Scheme for carbon dioxide, the largest multicountry, multisector greenhouse-gas emission-trading scheme in the world.

In monolith models, uncertainties regarding environmental policies can be very costly, too. In Europe, political uncertainty regarding the future of nuclear energy for the generation of electricity has had adverse effects in a number of countries. This includes the controversy raised by the Superphénix programme in France, and the political uncertainties that prevail regarding the future of the European Pressurised Water Reactor (EPR).

As already noted, in the *electricity* supply sector, governments may favour the unbundled model (assuming that an appropriate regulatory framework can be established), despite increased sensitivities to environmentally related uncertainties. This may encourage the development and deployment of distributed generation because of the economic, environmental and energy-security benefits they can bring.

In the *water* sector, with large potential increases in costs from climate change, water pollution, and more stringent regulations, environmental drivers will make it more difficult for utilities to recover all costs from user fees. This will mean that tax revenues or government support will most likely continue to be needed to finance major projects that address climate change impacts. Full cost pricing does not account for the external costs of climate change or water pollution that will affect the water system's sustainability.

Environmental concerns will contribute to shifting the level of governance to the regional and national levels, so as to ensure a better overall abstraction and discharge policy, as well as the more effective formulation and enforcement of water quality standards. At the same time, the management of water and water treatment systems will become more challenging technically, forcing greater reliance on outside expertise. As the claims on scarce water resources increase, greater efforts will also be required for ensuring that the needs of the poor are properly met in an environmentally sound manner.

In contrast to the two previous sectors, environmental concerns could have a positive impact on the *rail freight* sector. Indeed, concerns over the environment will give rail freight transport an edge over road transport as measures designed to reflect the environmental cost of transport services are put in place. In such a case, business models leaving a large place to competitive private actors are likely to be more successful in taking advantage of the situation, to the extent that private operators are closer to the market and their customers, hence better able to compete successfully with truck and water operators that have always be private than monoliths. In this context, the regulation of rail freight tariffs will be largely eliminated, replaced by enhanced intermodal competition or in some cases, with intramodal competition.

Shifting traffic from road to rail for a broad range of reasons including environmental ones (reduced pollution and reduced emission of GHG) has become a priority in a number of countries. For instance, in Europe, many countries, as well as the EC, have an explicit policy to shift freight and passenger traffic from highway to rail in order to reduce highway congestion and to achieve a number of desired social benefits (reduced pollution and CO_2 emissions, improved safety, changes in urban design, etc.). In fact, the EC has set an explicit goal of raising the rail market share in freight from 8% ton-km to 15% ton-km. The tools for doing so in the rail sector appear to be: 1) to encourage rail access charges to be set at incremental cost;[53] 2) to foster adequate investment and maintenance of the EU rail infrastructure; and 3) to separate the accounts of freight and passenger operators in order to ensure that freight operators are not asked to cross-subsidise passenger losses from freight profits (a policy that is clearly in operation in most of the eastern European railways, and the Russian Federation).

In other countries, the *opposite trend* may be observed and may continue to prevail in the coming years, reflecting their move to a market economy, as well as the changing composition of output. For instance, in China, current policies favouring rapid construction of highways may have the effect of shifting the modal balance toward highways. But given the trends in the Chinese economy towards higher valued products, especially for export, some shift away from overdependence on rail may well be rational from an economic point of view, although it may not be so from an environmental one. Indeed, the rail freight market share in China has been falling for many years from 72.3% in 1971 to 47% in 1981 to 39.2% in 1991 to 30.6% in 2001 (ton-km share).

Although Crozet does not address environmental issues *per se*, he does recognise that environmental concerns have been a major driver behind the renewed interest in *urban public transport systems* in recent years. This is likely to be even more so in the future.

Critics of UPT systems are not convinced. They point first to the high costs involved in the development of such systems and the long time it takes to build them. Moreover, the development and widespread adoption of emission-free cars could undermine the environmental arguments in favour of UPT. For mass transit critics, the UPT solution also contradicts the prevailing worldwide trend toward more personal transportation, in which people maintain control over their starting point, destination, route and time of travel. Hence, in this view, UPT systems will work in the future only if they integrate well with a flexible and mobile society, that is, when they run frequently, run to outlying stations with plentiful and inexpensive parking and connect easily to airports and each other.

Technology can help. In particular, the development of automatic transport systems such as driverless taxis could help alleviate traffic in congested areas.[54] However, technology is likely to provide only a partial solution to the gridlock problem to the extent that installing a big new transportation infrastructure in an established city will be extremely difficult.[55] In this context, non-technology approaches such as the application of the polluter pays principle is likely to be increasingly adopted and the development of car-free areas, as well as attention to the development of "environmental infrastructure" will become a more prominent on the public policy agenda. Greater attention may also be given to road-based approaches to urban transport such as the minibus solutions used for example in Latin America, as well as to improving the governance of taxis in urban areas.

Nevertheless, given the high costs that gridlocks impose on society from economic, social and environmental perspectives, some solution is "inevitable", as Peter Schwartz puts it, although it is not clear when and where it will occur first. Cities with well-designed transit and traffic infrastructure will thrive, if only because the best and the brightest will want to move there (Schwartz, 2003, pp. 86-88).

Regarding *road transport*, growing concern about the environment will induce governments to use price mechanisms to internalise the external cost of road transport and to use price as a tool for demand management. Moreover, greater efforts to shift traffic from roads to rail are likely.

4.8. *Private and professional actors*

The construction of models – whether they are business models or not – inevitably involves a simplification of reality. Modelling is clearly a useful analytical tool. However, there is always a danger of misspecification and oversimplification if important relationships are omitted from the analysis or if major players are not properly represented in their proper cultural and institutional context.[56]

The previous section indicated that it is not enough to refer only to "public actors". Depending on institutional arrangements and cultural values, several different types of public actor may play a key role in infrastructure development at the local, regional, national and transnational levels. The relationships that exist between these various actors may also vary from country to country. For instance, Thompson notes in the case of *railways* how national cultures influence the policy approaches adopted in North America and Europe.

Cultural and institutional factors are also important regarding the role played by non-public actors. Two categories of actors can be considered in this context: "expert" private and professional actors (discussed here) and "non-expert" civil society (discussed in the next section).

Private and professional actors include private firms involved in the development and maintenance of infrastructure and financial institutions, as well as professional and trade associations (*e.g.* for the engineering, urban planning and construction sectors) that contribute to the development of the necessary expertise, the formulation of standards and shape public policies.

Typically, such actors are large corporations that have developed specialised expertise and operate at the global level. For instance, as noted by Palaniappan *et al.*, the *water* sector is dominated by three or four large MNEs (Suez, Veolia Water, RWE and Bouygues/Saur) which have played a major role in their home market but have had mixed experience elsewhere.

A few large private actors also prevail in other sectors such as the *UPT* and *road transport* sectors. They typically form consortia with other firms when bidding for particular projects.[57] Because so few companies operate in these sectors and because they often submit joint bids, the bidding process may be ineffective or undermined by collusion among the bidders. Another danger is conflict of interest when experts participate in consortia in some instances, while in other cases governments retain them to assess bids.[58]

A few major private actors play a key role in the financing of infrastructure projects, although most investors have been wary of such ventures in the past because of the potentially large risks. In OECD countries, there is always a danger that *citizen protests* over high tolls or changes in political priorities may undermine the economic viability of expensive projects. In the developing world, the risks are even greater, as war, famine, political unrest and corruption all threaten investments. When financing large projects in a foreign society, the key question for investors is often how to tie the hands of the government so as to guarantee that it is not going to seize the property illegally, fail to abide by important terms of the contract or take actions that adversely affect the investment.

In the optimistic atmosphere that prevailed in the first half of the 1990s, large private investors became involved in infrastructure development throughout the world. But in the wake of large economic crises at the end of the 1990s, many projects became distressed or failed, and some governments, including those of Argentina and Indonesia, repossessed the infrastructure that foreign investors had helped to build.

After this painful episode, the situation is still uncertain today. On the one hand, investment risks may be lower than in the past to the extent that recent international laws have made it possible for investors to hold foreign governments responsible for the assets they seize and to arbitrate disputes in a neutral court.[59] On the other hand, the trend toward privatisation of infrastructure has been fiercely opposed in some quarters on the grounds that profit-hungry investors could cut corners, potentially endangering citizens with poorly designed or poorly maintained roads, bridges and airports.

Despite such concerns, it is clear that the "infrastructure gap" which currently exists throughout the world will not be met in the future without increased private sector participation. If political risks could be kept to a minimum, infrastructure investment could indeed be an attractive proposition for investors. For instance, according to Macquarie Bank, a major actor in the sector, the main reason for such infrastructure investment is that its defining characteristics offer long-term stable returns with the opportunity for capital growth:[60]

- ***Long life.*** This is created through the security of long-term concessions or agreements, government regulations or licenses.
- ***Sustainable competitive advantages and barriers to entry by competitors.*** These barriers can be exclusive concession periods or licences provided by legislation or regulation, natural barriers such as planning restrictions or availability of land, the high cost of new development, or long-term contracts for a significant portion of demand.
- ***Low variable cost base.*** Highly predictable operating costs create greater certainty in cash flows and returns to investors.
- ***Low demand variability.*** Demand for products or services provided by infrastructure assets is generally stable and often grows with underlying economic or demographic growth. This creates stable operating cash flows and reduced volatility in returns to investors.

Indeed, Macquarie Bank has demonstrated by its own actions that infrastructure can be profitable, earning an average return of 19% on its infrastructure investments over 11 years.[61]

Although infrastructure projects may be attractive for private investors, one clearly needs to be selective. Even without major crises looming on the horizon, some sales of public assets to private actors are likely to generate growing public discontent, hence fuel hostility towards privatisation, depending on the particular motivation for the sale and the intrinsic nature of the project. For instance, when a publicly owned asset, say a bridge, is sold to a private actor and the proceeds of the sale are used to fund public operating budgets rather than improving the road network, the users of the bridge are likely to be irritated since they have now to pay a toll for an access which was previously free. They are bound to become even more irritated over time if the toll increases without noticeable improvement in service. Moreover, selling the asset may undermine the ability of the public authorities to manage the regional transportation network in a co-ordinated manner, adding to the frustration of motorists. For instance, higher tolls on the asset will increase the congestion on neighbouring roads, with adverse consequences on citizens living near the privatised asset. Opposition to privatisation may therefore increase over time leading to growing pressures on the authorities to reclaim the asset.

Private investors need to be particularly careful to avoid this kind of situation that can only backfire on them in the medium to longer term and that involves "the outsourcing of political will", as John Foote (a senior fellow in the Kennedy School of government at Harvard) puts it in a recent testimony to Congress.[62] The private actor becomes in effect a scapegoat for politicians who are not able to muster the political will to confront voters with the reality regarding the cost of providing services to the public.

John Foote concludes his testimony by pointing out the three tests in his view that the sale of existing roads should meet:

- First, a significant portion of the proceeds of the sale should be reinvested in improving and enlarging the particular region's transportation infrastructure.
- Second, the private owner should be held accountable for the externalities – the non-cash costs – of operating the road.
- Third, if the road is part of a regional network, the toll regulation needs to accommodate regional solutions.

Applying these tests may reduce the amount of money that can be raised by state and local governments through these sales, but maximising the dollars should not be the sole objective. Improving the mobility of our citizens should be the overriding goal.

4.9. *Civil society*

"Civil society"[63] includes universities, non-governmental organisations, environmental movements, indigenous peoples' associations, organised local communities and trade unions. Their participation is essential for ensuring the success of infrastructure projects, as civil society actors help define what is the "public interest" or common well-being in infrastructure development.

Public administrations were reluctant in the past to engage a dialogue with civil society actors on the grounds that they were non-experts, hence not in a position to make a useful contribution in the decision-making process or that they would offer a view coloured by their narrow personal interest.

However, the faith in experts and in the ability of public administrations to deliver on the services that citizens want has been undermined over the years. In this context, a growing interest has been expressed in the institution of a "deliberative form of democracy" where "non-experts" can air their views and participate actively in the decision-making process.[64]

For advocates of deliberative democracy, deliberation is primarily a discursive approach to decision making in which citizens come together in a non-coercive environment to solve public problems. *Citizen engagement* is not about replacing representative government, but rather about making the current system more participatory by strengthening the deliberative input of the represented within a culture of democratic governance. Citizen engagement is a process of interaction between government and citizens. It is about creating the opportunity for effective dialogue and deliberation among and between citizens and elected representatives, so that the views and concerns of citizens are taken into account in the policy and decision-making processes.

Several arguments have been advanced for fostering citizen participation. First, such participation in policy formulation and decision making can reduce conflict. Experience suggests that by involving all the perspectives of community members who will be impacted by the policy outcome – and the competing interests – in governance processes, consensus develops around politically reasonable outcomes and lays the groundwork for successful implementation.

Second, citizen participation can lead to better, longer lasting, and wiser policy choices with better outcomes. This argument makes the case that the privately held knowledge of citizens – grounded largely in local experience – is "uncovered" through deliberation and can contribute valuable information to the policy process and outcome that would otherwise be overlooked. Citizens have a good sense of their needs; involving them may yield a different set of proposals.

Third, citizen participation builds citizen competence. It also gives citizens control of their lives, the opportunity to problem solve and, ultimately, better their lives through mechanisms that impact outcomes.

Fourth, citizen participation cultivates mutual understanding, builds bonds of trust among citizens, decision makers and governing institutions, and can effect changes in political attitudes and behaviour.

In summary, for citizen participation advocates, mechanisms of participation serve three important democratic values: they can make public decisions and actions more legitimate, more just, and more effective.

Citizen participation is thought to be particularly important in the case of infrastructure development. Indeed, infrastructure projects should be viewed as a collaborative effort, whereby citizens act as "partners" in the process of priority setting, planning and implementation (Perlman, 2000). Ideally, it should be seen as an ongoing process. "While one-shot deliberative efforts can be powerful catalysts for community change, citizen participation ultimately needs to be connected to processes that monitor and evaluate implementation. Without an enforcement mechanism, such efforts at community involvement will do little if economic development steers off course, or partners back out of their commitments. Thus, mechanisms for ongoing involvement in a self-correcting process of community development must be set up to ensure that the vision, motivation, and ends of citizen participation are not lost" (Lukensmeyer and Torres, 2003, p. 13). Ongoing engagement will help insure accountability.

However, it is important to ensure that greater citizen participation in the decision-making process does not result in more red tape at the planning stage and that the exploitation of the review process by special interest groups does not cause economic harm by unduly delaying the development of infrastructure projects which are important from an overall public interest perspective.[65]

5. Lessons learned for the future design of business models and public policy

This section outlines some of the lessons from the analysis in Sections 3 and 4 for the future design of business models and related supportive measures.

These "lessons learned" are presented here in terms of four main policy thrusts:

1. Improving economic performance.
2. Improving social performance.
3. Improving environmental performance.
4. Ensuring more sustainable financing of infrastructure development.

5.1. *Improving economic performance*

In all sectors, it has been clearly established that the public monolith model suffers from public failures, which adversely affect its economic performance. It follows that governments should explore the possibility of adopting business models that offer greater scope for introducing some degree of competition and private sector participation.

This can be achieved first by promoting competition *in* the market whenever potentially competitive components of the value chain can be unbundled. When this approach is not feasible, it might still be possible to promote competition *for* the market. In any case, whatever approach is adopted, models that contribute to align prices more closely with costs are highly desirable from an economic perspective as they bring about a more efficient use of scarce resources.

Promoting competition in the market

Enhanced competition should contribute to reducing both market and public failures. This calls whenever possible – and notably when the service is close to an economic good (electricity, freight rail) – to the adoption of models featuring a structural separation between the monopoly components of the value chain (typically the network component) from those components that can be open to competition. However, such structural reform is not always easy to achieve in practice and may take a long time to implement fully and effectively.

In the case of *electricity*, adoption of the unbundled model requires "deregulation", market reforms or "market restructure" that involves the implementation of a market design that transforms an electricity sector dominated by regulated integrated utilities into one that relies on competition to deliver generation and retail services. In this model, customers can choose to buy electricity directly from wholesale generation markets (which are the pool and the bilateral market), or through load-serving entities (LSE), such as distribution companies and retailers that procure from wholesale generation markets to meet their load obligations. Buyers and sellers may manage electricity spot price risk using hedge instruments (*e.g.* forward contracts) traded in a financial market. Moreover, a transmission company operates the grid and offers open and comparable access to all market participants (such as, in the UK). Alternatively, an independent system operator (ISO) leases transmission facilities from transmission owners to perform the same functions (*e.g.* California, New England, New York, PJM, Texas, Alberta, and Ontario).

Experience with this type of reform has been rather mixed to date. First, market reform has proved to be costly; the cost of setting up and operating an ISO is substantial. Second, deregulation has lead to the creation of complicated market design which invites gaming by traders and retailers. Third, because electricity cannot be stored, electricity spot prices are very volatile. This has resulted in considerable price uncertainty and offered ample opportunities for the exercise of market power in generation markets. Fourth, because of increased uncertainty, generation and transmission investment has been inefficient and the service has become less reliable as capacity reserves have declined. This has forced regulators to impose capacity obligations on LSEs. Fifth, efficiency gains have not always been achieved in generation because lower operation costs have been at least partially offset by higher capital cost in a more volatile environment. Moreover, higher transaction costs have contributed to dissipate the potential benefit of deregulation. Finally, even when deregulation has resulted in net benefits, such benefits have often been captured by electricity producers rather than by households and business customers.[66]

The obstacles to successful deregulations that have been encountered in a number of countries (see Annex 2.A1) clearly point to the need for a more careful approach to market reform. Particular attention needs to be given to the design of the model in the way risks are handled and to the responsiveness of supply and demand to price signals, notably when the price of input fuels are subject to severe fluctuations.

On the supply side, this requires first of all that all the barriers to electricity generation activities be removed as well as any restraint to transmission capacity. In this latter regard, appropriate incentive schemes should be put in place to stimulate construction to remove bottlenecks (*e.g.* node pricing).

To reduce risks, utilities should be allowed to enter into longer-term contracts at fixed price and to hedge through the futures market. Greater price stability could also be achieved by building a large reserve capacity. However, this is an expensive way to do so. Indeed, one of the reasons to move to a competitive market structure is to help reduce electricity prices by lowering the costs of the utilities' reserve capacity. In a competitive market, producers' investment in reserve capacity should be consistent with the amount of price stability (or, equivalently, supply security) that consumers are willing to pay for in the form of long-term supply contracts. The model must also allow the forging of alliances that can generate synergies (*e.g.* between the electricity and gas networks). This may involve some degree of re-integration of activities that were unbundled.

The ability of the unbundled model to withstand shocks can also be improved if greater flexibility is achieved on the demand side. First, consumers need to face the *real cost* of electricity. Exposing consumers to price changes will induce them to increase their use of power when prices fall and curtail it when prices rise. When prices do not change along with costs, and when the amount of power demanded cannot respond to prices in that way, a greater adjustment must be made on the supply side of the market.

Second, price signals should encourage consumers not only to buy more or less power now but also to invest in the ability to adjust their future power use. Some of the same demand responsiveness that results from having consumers pay market prices may also be achieved if utilities either compensate customers for reducing their consumption at peak demand time or allow customers to resell power to others (in which case, a third party is paying them to reduce their use).

In addition, electricity consumers should be encouraged to acquire devices that allow them to reduce use on short-term notice. For example, several approaches can make real-time pricing easier, such as technologies that monitor electricity use and prices, and contracting arrangements with electricity suppliers that permit the customer (or a designated agent) to interrupt the service when the price rises. In many cases, large industrial customers already have the capacity to monitor and adjust their demand in the face of rising prices and, in fact, do so. Successful restructuring may necessitate that residential and commercial customers acquire many of the same demand-management capabilities that industrial consumers have.

In the case of *rail freight*, the advantage of the deregulated model over the monolith model is clearly illustrated by the contrasting performance of railways in North America and Europe. While North American railways have been able to maintain or even increase their market share, despite stiff competition from trucks, the volume of freight carried by European railways under the monolith model has been steadily declining, both in relative and absolute terms. The decline experienced by European railways is largely linked to the business model that prevails on the old continent.

As noted by the European Commission, a careful analysis of the reasons for this decline, points at the organisation and structure of rail transport in the member states.[67] Historically, both passenger and freight transport have been organised along national lines. Rail transport was carried out by national railway undertakings, which were also responsible for the construction and maintenance of the rail infrastructure, railway safety and the rolling stock. Rail transport between member states was, and still is, organised as co-operation between national railway undertakings, which prevented railway undertakings from starting operations in other member states. International rail transport suffered from this structure as national rail networks were hardly interoperable. For example, locomotives had to be changed at the border as they were unable to run on the network of another member state due to different signalling systems, electrification systems or even gauge widths. Train staff very often could only operate in one member state, and had to be replaced at the border as well. Administrative and technical formalities to be complied with at the border added to long waiting times at the border which made rail transport less and less attractive, compared to other modes of transport, such as road or inland waterways. The organisation according to national lines prevented, and still prevents, railway undertakings from realising economies of scale and optimisation of market segments, such as rail freight.

Promoting competition for the market

When competition *in* the market is not possible, promoting competition *for* the market through the use of PPPs and the development of appropriate tender mechanisms could be a good way to foster the efficiency of infrastructure services. This approach can be applied for instance to the *water and water treatment* systems, as well as to *UPT* systems and the *road network*. However, as illustrated by the French experience, it requires strong public oversight, calling for the development of the necessary expertise and mindset in the public sector.

For advocates of this approach, the advantages for government and the economy at large are substantial. It allows the state to focus more effectively on its core role as regulator and task master. It brings about a reduction in the cost of construction and enables faster development of the infrastructure. It also offers opportunities for lower operating costs, reduced public funding needs, as well as lower risks for the state.

Let us examine these claims in greater detail:

More focus on core competence. The main function of the state is to conceive the development of infrastructure services and to ensure that they are effectively and efficiently provided to users. However, this does mean that government should develop the infrastructure and produce the service. In a democratic society, the state is the only entity with the legitimacy to make trade-offs between various policy objectives and to define the policy and regulatory environment for the provision of the service. The role of governments is to make decisions, to make trade-offs, to protect social justice and to keep the decision-making process transparent. In this context, greater private sector participation in the development and operation of infrastructure is not a retreat of the state but rather a redefinition of its role.

Reduction of construction costs. Contract clauses in PPPs that provide maximal cost for construction allow for a stricter control of budgets than the traditional construction approach. According to the UK auditor general, 73% of projects done in the conventional way have cost overruns compared to only 22% for PPPs.

Faster delivery of the infrastructure. PPPs allow for faster delivery because the returns to the private partners are linked to the availability of the infrastructure and penalty clauses in case of delays are often included in contracts. As a result, infrastructures are more often delivered on time than in conventional technique (76% compared to 22% in the public service). They are even sometimes completed ahead of schedule. Moreover, if the concession extends over a substantial number of years, the concessionaire is more likely to pay particular attention to the quality of the construction up front, so as to reduce maintenance costs over the life of the concession to a minimum.

Reduced operating costs. By using PPPs, the state is able to take advantage of expertise it does not have. For instance, in *water treatment*, savings of more than 30% in operating cost have been observed in some major US cities, such as Indianapolis, Seattle and Milwaukee. In Alberta, savings of more than 25% have been realised in the maintenance of *roads*.

If the advantages of PPPs are so great, then why are they not used more often? Four main reasons are usually given:

PPPs are most suitable for infrastructures where access can be controlled. As noted by Mackie and Smith, suitable *highways for toll* represent roughly 1% of the road network, although they probably carry a much larger share of the traffic. In other sectors, the scope for PPPs is greater. For example, in France, as already noted, 75% of *water* systems are run by concessions. Concessions are also widely used in *UPT*.

Contractual complexity. Second, one of the major obstacles to the use of PPPs is the need to negotiate the agreement. By definition, a PPP implies a long-term commitment by the private partner, as well as a large investment. An effective sharing of risks, gains and responsibilities must be done to the satisfaction of all parties to the agreement, a very complex task.

This task is not only complex but may be fraught with dangers if the public partner does not have the in-house expertise needed to properly assess all pertinent aspects of the project and to negotiate effectively with the potential concessionaires. This danger is higher in early experience with PPPs, *i.e.* when the attitude of the state has not yet fully evolved from a "doer" to a regulator and task master. In this regard, it has been noted that it is often difficult to find unbiased expertise both inside and outside the government and that in some cases the potential for conflicts of interest or corruption of public officials is real. Moreover, in practice, the number of potential bidders on large projects is limited, not only in the *water* sector but also in the *UPT* and *road* construction sectors.

In contract negotiations, particular attention also needs to be given to penalty clauses to ensure that they can be effectively enforced, if and when the need arise.

Political risk. Third, another major hurdle is linked to the political risk: the irreversible nature of the commitment and its length generate a high political risk. For instance, both in the case of Highway 407 and the Fredericton-Moncton Highway in Canada, new governments attempted to renegotiate the agreement signed by the previous government. In the case of Highway 407, it even went to court. This sends a negative signal to all companies interested in PPPs.

Political opposition to PPPs is often fuelled by various lobby groups (*e.g.* local construction firms) that benefit from the cosy relationship they have been able to establish with government officials over the years. Unions that have taken advantage of their strong bargaining position to earn economic rents are also likely to be hostile to PPPs that may undermine their position. In addition, there is a danger that the selection of the concessionaire could be influenced by job creation or job protection considerations. In such a case, the choice of concessionaire may not necessarily be in the best interest of users of the infrastructure or taxpayers.

Public perception. A fourth stumbling block is the perception of the population that the provision of public services should not be for profit. There is also a persistent view that public services should be free. Hence, efforts to inform the population, seek their views and ensure that the bidding process is fully transparent play a critical role in the success of PPPs.

Promoting cost pricing

Whatever the model adopted, in order to ensure a proper balance between the demand and the supply of infrastructure services, the price of services should be set as close as possible to cost recovery levels (taking into account externalities caused by the production and consumption of the service), and cross-subsidies that distort competition (*e.g.* in rail transport) should be eliminated.

Regarding *electricity*, Morgan notes the predicament of the Indian Electricity Board which is unable to generate sufficient revenues for maintaining the network because it is forced to provide electricity at tariffs that are too low and no alternative source of funding is available.

Chronic underinvestment prevails in the *water* sector because rates have been kept too low for too long as noted by Palaniappan *et al.* More generally, water management is grossly inefficient. First, some activities (*e.g.* agriculture) consume far too much water when compared to their contribution to GDP. Moreover, in urban areas a large share of available water is wasted because of leaky pipes or is stolen. Furthermore, at the watershed level, water is often polluted upstream with little regard for the need of users downstream.[68] Finally, the price of water varies considerably across users, suggesting gross misallocations of resources. For instance, in Australia, the driest continent in the world, Australian households pay on average about AUD 1.30 a kilolitre, compared to only a few cents per kilolitre paid by irrigators (farmers).

As the demand for water continues to increase in the future and as water resources become increasingly valuable, a major effort to improve the management of water is inevitable. Governments will have to implement effective business models for getting such water to high value users, despite the tensions between the historical and the new users this will create.

As illustrated by Crozet, the same problem exists regarding *UPT* systems. Typically, the fare charged to users does not cover operational costs. Moreover, as mentioned previously, fares tend to be subject to the "nickel syndrome", *i.e.* they are not allowed to rise over time in line with rising costs. Over time, the system becomes increasingly run down as maintenance is increasingly neglected, causing declines in ridership that, in turn, further reduce the ability of the operator to finance maintenance.

In the case of *rail freight*, cross-subsidy obligations have been a heavy burden on operators throughout the world and have significantly affected their economic viability. The problem has been largely solved in North America since deregulation and the creation of AMTRAK in the US and VIA Rail in Canada, although freight rail operators still complain about the low access charge they have been forced to grant the passenger rail operators.[69]

In Europe, the situation is much less favourable for freight operators. Cross-subsidies have contributed to the steady decline of rail freight in that region. Time will tell whether the efforts of the European Commission to remedy the situation will bear fruit in the coming years. One solution that is increasingly popular is to develop rail freight corridors, so as to separate passenger and freight traffic on some routes.

In *road transport*, free access at the point of demand leads to congestion. While this can be accommodated for a while by an expansion of the road network, there comes a time when such physical expansion is no longer feasible or is increasingly resisted because of the adverse side effects it creates. This is a situation that largely prevails today in north-western Europe, as noted by Mackie and Smith. Daily traffic over time remains paralysed for increasing hours, resulting in growing economic and environmental costs. This is clearly an unsustainable situation that can only be solved in the short term by introducing a form of demand management which rations scarce road space more efficiently. In the longer term, changes in land use patterns or the delocalisation of major activities to less populated regions may be the only viable option.

5.2. Improving social performance

Dealing more effectively with social obligations

In affluent countries there is no reason why infrastructure services should be subsidised for the vast majority of the population. Given the distortionary effect of taxes, it is more effective to pay directly for service rather than through increased taxation. Special targeted relief mechanisms can be devised for the poor, although broader income distribution schemes are likely to be the most effective way of dealing with the problem.

For instance, in the case of *water*, there is no good reason why the vast majority of (middle-class) users in OECD countries should not pay the true cost of water. Maintaining water prices artificially low can only by achieved by subsidies that middle-class users will have to pay anyway in the form of higher taxes. The alternative is to accept a deterioration of the service over time. Moreover, low water prices only encourage an economically wasteful and ecologically harmful use of water resources.[70]

Social obligation to the needy should be met directly either in the form of an income subsidy, or a more targeted subsidy, for instance through the use of "water stamps" for whatever minimum amount of water is deemed necessary to maintain a reasonably healthy life.[71] Alternatively, a price schedule involving rising price with usage could be implemented. This requires, however, effective metering of the water actually used.[72]

The same argument applies to electricity and passenger rail traffic. However, the situation may be somewhat different for *UPT* systems because of the social advantages that such systems offer. The cost balance should nevertheless largely be made up by those who benefit indirectly from the system (employers, landowners, landlords, private car commuters).

In some cases, efforts to foster efficiency involve a reallocation of resources from one category of users to another. While beneficial from an economic perspective, such reallocation may be detrimental from a social perspective if the "losers" are not adequately compensated. One possible solution to this problem may be to introduce a market for *tradable entitlements*. This solution, in particular the introduction of water markets, has been used, in Australia to promote a more efficient use of *water* resources without penalising the poor. (See Box 2.4 for more details on the use of water markets for the management of water resources in Australia.)

Water markets are more flexible than command-and-control instruments in moving water to higher-valued uses in a manner agreeable to all parties, thus promoting economic growth and diminishing social tension from competition for scarce water resources. The adoption of the user pays principle is more difficult in developing countries since the large majority of users is typically poor, hence cannot be expected to pay much for services. This means that new innovative solutions will need to be found with the support of multilateral funding institutions.

Encouraging participatory democracy

Greater attention should be given to fostering participatory democracy. Citizens affected by a particular infrastructure should be consulted and given a chance to participate in the decision-making process. Although this may at first be viewed as a cumbersome process that may delay implementation, it should contribute to ensuring that the infrastructure better meets the need of users in the longer run and may induce such users to be more inclined to pay directly for the full cost of the service they receive.

According to Palaniappan *et al.*, experience supports the views expressed by citizen participation advocates as outlined above. *Water* users are often willing to pay for improvements in service when such improvements are designed with their participation and when improvements are actually delivered. Broad participation by affected parties ensures that diverse values and varying viewpoints are articulated and incorporated into water-sector decision making. It also provides a sense of ownership and stewardship over the process and resulting decisions. Water is a resource that is essential for life and health and plays vital social, economic, and environmental roles. Water management is linked to issues of poverty alleviation, public health, social equity, and the sustainability of ecosystems. The best way to balance the multiple roles of water is to ensure that water-resource decisions involve multiple stakeholders and the public at large in needs assessment, planning, and implementation of any potential project. Governments must ensure that the public is aware of and educated on water sector decisions. They should also provide access to information, and include public input into all decisions and plans made about water resources.

Public involvement is important for both private and public actors. Increased transparency and public involvement may improve public trust in the private sector and increase the ability of the private sector to float private bonds. Increasing transparency and public communication will also allow public sector providers and governments to float bonds and successfully advocate for more public financing.

Palaniappan *et al.* also note that the importance of public involvement varies depending on the nature of the project. It is particularly important for large projects involving private actors. Small-scale private operations tend to be far enough from the public eye that it may continue unimpeded. For example, private operation of a particular wastewater treatment facility, private management of billing operations, and other specific functions tend to be under the purview of the water utility, and are rarely subject to public protest.

Public involvement is likely to greatly influence the future development of water systems. First, public pressure will probably keep large built system assets in public hands. Moreover, the public will be profoundly affected and undoubtedly involved in any changes to water rights regimes and accompanying legislation. Furthermore, international and local NGOs and public employees have always voiced the concern that the profit motive is ill-suited to the successful provision of water. Finally, the public and international and local NGOs will continue to be suspicious of private sector involvement in the water sector, primarily because of its impacts on the poor.

Despite its potential benefits, public involvement faces a number of political obstacles. For instance, it is noted in the case of the US that without federal mandates tied to federal programmes, it is unlikely that most municipal governments would voluntarily seek to share power with neighbourhood-based organisations.[73]

Although the issue is not addressed specifically in the other sectoral chapters, it is clear that citizen participation can play a key role in the other sectors under review. For instance in the *electricity* sector, many projects currently face widespread difficulty associated with facilities siting. This rising difficulty is due to a variety of causes, including public opposition and not-in-my-backyard (NIMBY) protests. Efforts to mitigate public opposition have focused on improving citizen participation, but many participatory programmes have still resulted in opposition and project delays. Taken as a whole, there is a growing need for: 1) better characterisations of siting difficulty and the relative role of public opposition; and 2) new strategies for facilitating timely, inclusive, and effective public participation (Vajjhala, 2005). Similar problems arise in the road transport network. For instance Mackie and Smith note the growing local opposition to the creation of new roads or highway in north-western Europe.

Dealing more effectively with labour relations issues

Infrastructures may also raise social issues from a labour relations' perspective. Because they are ubiquitous and vital in our daily life, they are highly vulnerable to crippling strikes.

In the case of *UPT* systems, transport workers' unions have acquired considerable clout, which they have been able to exercise successfully to obtain wage increases above those granted to workers of equivalent qualification, as noted by Crozet. This raises the question of whether urban public transport workers' right to strike should be reduced or abolished.

Some countries have indeed limited the right to strike by imposing minimum service obligations (*e.g.* Italy, Portugal). In a number of jurisdictions, what constitutes an "essential service" has been defined by law (for instance in Quebec labour law, a public service is deemed to be "essential" when withholding it would threaten the health or the security of the population) and a precise list of essential services has been drawn up, as well as rules for establishing a minimum service.

In other jurisdictions, subway strikes are forbidden by law. This is the case for instance in New York City with the Taylor Law, which was put into affect in 1967. One of the most controversial parts of the Taylor Law is Section 210, which prohibits New York state public employees from striking, compelling binding PERB (Public Employment Relations Board) arbitration in the event of an impasse in negotiations.[74] The fine for striking is twice the employee's salary for each day the strike lasts. Since its declaration, the law has been cited in averting several potential transit strikes, but did not prevent the 1980 and 2005 strikes. In both cases, the fine was applied.

5.3. *Improving environmental performance*

From a public policy perspective, environmental considerations play an important role for each of the infrastructure sectors under review. In some cases, it is because of their adverse effects. For instance, the generation and transmission of *electricity* generate negative externalities; the overexploitation of *water* resources represents a threat for ecosystems; *road transport* is a major source of pollution and the main source of GHG.

In other cases, public interest results from the fact that the use of the particular infrastructure is considered to be more desirable from an environmental perspective than alternative options. For instance, *UPT* commuting is less environmentally damaging than private car commuting (assuming the UPT network is not overextended to low population density areas); rail freight is more environmentally friendly than road transport.

In this context, the main challenge from an environmental public policy perspective is the adoption of measures that more strictly enforce the polluter pays principle and encourage greater use of more environmentally friendly infrastructures. Moreover, governments have an important role to play in fostering basic research on environmentally friendly technologies, not only at the national level, but perhaps more importantly at the international level.

Enforcing the polluter pays principle

Enforcing the polluter pays principle is highly desirable, but no easy task in practice. First, it needs to be applied gradually over a significant period of time because of the serious disruptions it may cause to important segments of the economy (*e.g.* heavy industry, agriculture). Second, its application often faces strong political opposition because of the adverse income distribution effects it may have. Third, to be effective and avoid damaging distortions of competition in an open international economic environment, the principle needs to be applied in a consistent manner over broad enough geographical areas, if not at the global level.

There are no easy solutions to this challenge, but a few approaches may be promising:

Emissions trading schemes. Capping emissions and creating a market for the trading of emission rights could be an interesting option for curbing GHG, notably those generated by industry and the electricity supply sector. As already noted, efforts in this direction have already been initiated in Europe.[75]

Although the scheme faces a number of problems, as might be expected, the market is growing fast. In the first half of 2006, carbon to the value of EUR 12 billion (USD 15 billion) was traded, five times more than in the same period in 2005. It has made some headway in reducing GHG. Last year it got rich-world consumers to invest USD 2.7 billion to cut developing-country greenhouse-gas emissions by around 374 million tons of CO_2 equivalent. That is only about half of Texas's annual emissions – but it's a start.[76]

Water markets. In addition to stricter enforcement of water quality and water treatment requirements, a water market approach might offer opportunities for more effective management of water resources and ecosystems, as illustrated by the Australian example in Box 2.4.

The greatest impact of water trading schemes is that they disconnect water rights from land property rights. This means that water access entitlements are commodities that can be traded.

The water trading schemes set a cap on current water use and allow trading of current allocation licenses to enable new users to obtain water supply and current licence holders who do not use their full allocation ("sleepers" and "dozers") to sell excess water entitlements for economic benefit.

In addition to providing a cap on water use, water trading schemes regulate different types of water use (ranging from agriculture to service provision) through the establishment of different water access licence types.

Water licences have been allocated a priority rating, so that in times of scarcity those with less "secure" licences will be the first to lose entitlements while "permanent security" licence holders such as drinking water providers and year-round irrigators (such as rice farmers) will be protected. In NSW for example, rights are organised on a priority basis and increases in scarcity result in reduction in licence rights of access entitlements beginning with the lowest priority licence holders.

A justification for water trading has been the capacity for water to be purchased for environmental flows. For example, the Australian federal government (under COAG) has allocated AUD 500 million to purchase water for the environment in the Murray-Darling Basin. An interest in environmental flows has resulted from increasing awareness of ecological degradation in Australia's river basins. Salinity has been particularly bad and has affected agriculture and altered flows in the Murray-Darling river system. Trading is represented as a means by which to improve water quality and quantity in rivers while providing current water with the appropriate market value in compensation. However, "the environment" still has to compete for its water needs with other users operating within the water market and is less represented at the political decision-making level. Furthermore, there is much debate concerning how much water is needed to maintain a healthy river system; the extent to which the environment can compete within the water market to obtain environmental flows in accordance with changing knowledge of ecosystem requirements remains to be seen.

Box 2.4. **The management of water resources in Australia**

As the driest continent in the world, Australia represents an interesting case in point regarding water management. The solutions adopted there could be a harbinger of things to come elsewhere.

The majority of water consumption in Australia is due to irrigation n (75%). Water use has increased by 65% since 1985. This is primarily due to irrigated agriculture, while only small increases or decreases have occurred in urban water consumption.

Prior to the introduction of the current regime of water trading, the country was faced with inefficient use of scarce water resources. Water was fully allocated and poorly used for irrigation purposes. Much irrigated land was unsuitable for irrigation; and many irrigators were low-value producers.

Water trading reform. In response to this situation, the government decided to introduce water trading as a way to gradually reallocate water from existing users and land.

This regime is largely determined by Australian constitutional arrangements. Under the Australian system of co-operative federalism, constitutional power for water management is vested in state and territorial governments. In most states, a licensing system regulates water access and distribution. These licences are often equated with water "ownership"; however, water in Australia remains a public good in legal terms. Licences do not equate with water ownership, but give the licence holder the right to use an amount of water at a particular time and place. Governments can withdraw or alter water rights without any statutory guarantee in most cases. Whether there exists a common law right to compensation for the removal of water rights has not yet been established.

Following a Council of Australian Governments (COAG) agreement in 2004 to establish a new national market to trade water rights, water trading has now become mandatory under the National Competition Policy. Although water markets are under state legislation, and although the rules vary considerably from state to state, two distinct markets exist: 1) Informal markets transfer the right to use a given volume of water for a given period of time; and 2) formal markets transfer the long term right of access to water.

Expectations. Regarding the *formal market*, the expectation was that it would move water resources to higher value and more efficient users and that water would be used in more suitable location and better soil. It was expected that such action would result in more economic activity per unit of water and a reduction in environmental damage.

Box 2.4. **The management of water resources in Australia** *(cont.)*

Regarding the *informal market*, it was expected that it would facilitate the adjustment of water use between seasons and within seasons in response to fluctuation in supply and in commodity prices. In addition, it was thought that it would allow retiring or unviable farmers to stay in the community and permit unviable farmer assets to be split and used in the most beneficial way.

Outcomes. In practice, informal markets have worked as expected. They are popular because they alleviate communities fear about change in long-term ownership. Water exchanges have emerged that are easy, quick, cheap, safe and predictable.

Formal markets have resulted in higher value use of water. But they remain limited (only 1% of entitlement per year; 60% of the water was previously unused). Farmers only sell if under strain or ill-informed. The reasons why it is not more widely used include: policy uncertainty, policy decisions regarding unused water; irrigator perception; community concern; a cumbersome and expensive procedure compared to the informal market. Moreover, many farmers cannot afford to buy water on the formal market.

The combined impact of water trading has been significant: 20% of the farmers have been involved in both the formal and informal markets and such markets have substantially assisted irrigators in managing the increased risk associated with water supply uncertainty.

Source: Bjornlund, Henning (2005), various papers on water trading in Australia, University of South Australia, School of Commerce, Division of Business. For more information, see *www.unisanet.unisa.edu.au/staff/homepage.asp?Name=Henning.Bjornlund*.

In the long run more sophisticated water markets may emerge. This may include for instance, the *water resource observations network* developed by the Australian Commonwealth Scientific and Industrial Research Organisation (CSIRO), Australia's national science agency. According to CSIRO, the network, which is about ten years from completion, will allow instant trading of water entitlements, adjustment for seasonal and natural flows, and the creation and trading of derivatives, such as water futures, options and hedges. It will be better able to allocate optimal environmental flows, remove uncertainty from the market process, optimise prices, find the most willing buyers and sellers, and signal scarcity.

Road transport. The cost of pollution could be better reflected in the price of gasoline, car ownership taxes and environmental fees imposed on trucks for instance. However, there is some degree of controversy regarding whether cars and trucks currently pay their "fair share". For instance, research by David Newbery, a professor of economics at Cambridge University, suggests that the cost to society imposed by the various pollutants, including carbon, produced from car engines works out to around 42p per litre of petrol burned and 47p for diesel in the UK. With fuel taxed at 47.1p per litre, this implies that road transport is, if anything, paying too much. By contrast, housing is getting off lightly, according to Newbery. Heating fuel, for example, receives substantial tax breaks. But at a time of soaring utility bills, ending these concessions would be as politically unpalatable as squeezing motorists.[77] This suggests that there is a clear need to establish a better factual and conceptual basis for the formulation of policy in this area.

Encouraging the development and greater use of environmentally friendly infrastructures

In the case of *rail freight*, this includes the removal of the obstacles to its development in Europe and perhaps a reduced bias against rail in North America, including tax law reform and greater public support to major intermodal rail to ship terminals. Efforts to foster the development of rail freight corridors in developing countries are also desirable. An interesting example in this regard is the Golden Quadrilateral freight corridor project in India which should link the largest Indian cities (Delhi, Mumbai, Madras and Calcutta) with financial support from the Japanese ODA agency.

Policies to encourage greater use of *UPT* include not only initiatives to improve the quality of service but also measures to provide a more effective demand management of traffic; and from a long-run perspective, changes in land use pattern to promote a more mixed land use pattern.

First of all, efforts to promote the adoption of sustainable transportation practices may involve for instance measures to encourage people to take fewer and shorter vehicle trips (*e.g.* ridesharing, telecommuting and parking management); balancing more carefully the traffic needs of new developments with the broader social and environmental objectives for the city as a whole; exploiting new technologies that improve urban travel conditions and help protect the environment.

But such measures need to be complemented by supportive land use planning initiatives. The development of an effective urban transport system requires that land use and transportation planning policies be closely linked to create an effective strategy for accommodating future trip growth in a way that reduces auto-dependency by making transit, cycling and walking more attractive alternatives. Such measures could include the *promotion of mixed use development* to increase opportunities for living close to work and to encourage walking and cycling for local trips. Moreover, in the targeted growth areas with good transit service, consideration should be given to: minimum development density requirements; lower parking standards; enhanced pedestrian facilities.

Security considerations play also a key role. For instance in the US, it is probably the most important single factor for revitalising city centres and inducing those who have fled the city for the suburbs in the past to come back. As already noted, demographic factors should favour such a move in coming decades. Finally, urban sprawl could be slowed perhaps by reducing the disparity in taxation between downtown and suburban residence.

Encouraging the development of environmentally friendly technologies

Governments also have a key role to play in encouraging the development of environmentally friendly technologies. In the case of *electricity* this includes efforts to foster renewable energies and perhaps having a second look at the nuclear option. An interesting programme in this regard is the GIF (Generation IV International Forum) which was set up in 2000 to foster international co-operation for the development of future nuclear reactors. The 13 participating countries (now including the Russian Federation and China) intend to spend USD 6 billion over 15 years to develop the fourth generation of reactors that should come on stream by 2030.[78]

As already noted, further research leading to the development and widespread adoption of clean coal technologies could also have far-reaching implications for the electricity supply industry, including from a geopolitical perspective. Moreover, it is expected to play a critical role in the mitigation effort until 2100.[79]

Public support to research efforts is clearly desirable in the early stage of development of these technologies. Current initiatives include a subsidised scheme unveiled in 2003 by the Bush administration to build a zero-emissions "integrated gasification combined cycle" (IGCC) plant called "FutureGen" by 2013. Such technology is promising because IGCC plants, aside from their carbon-capture potential, produce fewer traditional pollutants and also generate hydrogen, which can either be put to industrial uses or burnt. Research efforts are also under way in Europe on IGCC plants and other carbon capture technologies. Altogether it is estimated that the extra energy required to capture carbon would reduce a state-of-the-art supercritical plant's overall efficiency by about 10%.[80]

Electricity infrastructure services and their management would also change fundamentally with the emergence of small-scale decentralised generation and CHP (combined heat and power), and with hydrogen as an energy-carrying and storage medium for the transport and heat markets. There will also be new opportunities for demand management through new metering and information and control technologies.

In the case of *water*, new water treatment technologies are very promising, as already noted. Desalination may also become an attractive option for water-starved cities close to the sea. Indeed, desalination is becoming increasingly efficient. Despite controversy about its high energy use, new technologies have driven efficiencies up and costs down to nearly half the price for urban water. One major advantage of desalination is that it is not climate-dependent. The water is available continuously and just in time: it does not need to be stored and does not evaporate while waiting to be used.

Road transport is still likely to remain oil-based for several decades, and efficiency gains will be important for keeping emissions down. Incremental energy efficiency improvements are expected to continue in the transport sector. These will be stimulated both by fuel savings and, as they have been in the past, by government regulation. Increasing use of biofuels will also be important. In the long term, decarbonising transport will also depend on progress in decarbonising electricity generation and on developments in hydrogen production. The main technological options currently being considered for decarbonising transport (other than the contributions of biofuels and efficiency) are hydrogen and battery-electric vehicles. Both the hybrid car, and later, the fuel cell vehicle, will be capable of doubling the fuel efficiency of road vehicles. Much will depend on transport systems too, including road pricing, intelligent infrastructure, public transport and urban design (United Kingdom, 2006a).

As noted in the Stern review, it is critically important that the long-term investments over the next two decades *not* be made in high-carbon infrastructure. In this regard, the credibility of policies is key. This is particularly important in the *electricity* supply sector which is largely geared to the use of fossil fuels and where new low-carbon technologies do not easily fit.[81] Policy uncertainty not only undermines climate change policy, it can also undermine security of supply, by creating an incentive to delay investment decisions.[82]

5.4. *Ensuring more sustainable financing of infrastructure development*

As financial pressures on the government increase, notably to meet health and social obligations, fewer public resources will be available for infrastructure development. It follows that new ways of financing infrastructure will need to be developed.

Some of the measures already discussed in this section should help. Moving closer to *cost pricing* by expanding the scope of user charges should not only be beneficial from an economic point of view, but it should also provide utilities with a more stable and reliable source of funds than public grants that are often vulnerable to short-term political considerations. As already noted, the impact of short-termism can also be reduced by the corporatisation of utilities, which provides for greater accountability of their activities, the adoption of arm's-length regulatory schemes, so as to remove the decision-making process from the short-term political arena and by putting a greater emphasis on participatory democracy so as to give a greater voice to users, hence ensuring that the services provided are more responsive to their expectations, including their sustainability over time.

Another complementary approach is to seek greater private sector participation to the operation and development of infrastructure and to look for new financial partners with complementary interests. Finally, it is also important to ensure that resource for infrastructure development and management be effectively allocated between the various levels of government.

Encouraging greater private sector participation to the financing of infrastructure

It has already been discussed that greater private sector participation should contribute to fostering efficiency in the development and management of infrastructure. In addition to the benefits of greater focus on core competence, reduced construction and operating costs and faster delivery of the infrastructure than under traditional contractual arrangements, PPPs offer opportunities for reduced public funding and contribute to reducing the project-related financial risks incurred by the state.

The concept of PPP is based on the transfer of risk from the state to the private sector. This results in a greater control of costs by the state and higher incentives for private actors because their profits are linked to performance. This is reflected in reduced construction and operation costs and a faster implementation.

Success stories. The merits of PPPs are clearly demonstrated by a number of success stories, such as the Confederation Bridge in Canada (see Chapter 1, Box 1.3) or the Millau Viaduct in France, the tallest bridge in the world, that offers the fastest and cheapest link from Paris to the Mediterranean. In this latter case, for instance, all the risks (construction, financing, operation, maintenance, ownership over the period of the concession) except for the conception of the work were assumed by the private partner (Eiffage).[83]

The full cost of construction (EUR 320 millions) was born by Eiffage. The concession is over a 78-year period. After that, the overpass will be turned over to the state. The concessionaire guarantees that the overpass will remain fully operational for at least 120 years. The toll should not increase faster than inflation. It has been set at a rate that is well accepted by the population although no alternative "free road" is available.

The PPP is clearly a win-win solution. For the "concédant" (the state) the advantages are substantial:

- It allows the construction of a major infrastructure without public funding.
- Most of the risks are transferred to the private sector.

- The state will recuperate the infrastructure at the end of the contract.

There are also tangible benefits for the concessionaire: although Eiffage assumes most of the risk, the expectations of profits are substantial. The expected internal rate of return calculated by the École Nationale des Ponts et Chaussées ranges from 9.2% to 17.3%.

The cost of capital. From a financial perspective, one of the main arguments often raised against PPP is that the cost of capital for private actors is higher than for the state, hence that the infrastructure ends up costing more than it would have if the traditional public contract route had been used.

This is a somewhat simplistic analysis of the situation. First of all, the cost of capital is only one of the costs of the project. If indeed it is higher for the private actor than for the state, this may be more than compensated by the fact that the project is likely to be cheaper and has a better chance of being completed within budget and on time as noted above. Moreover, the extra cost of capital can be viewed as an "insurance policy" to the extent that most of the risks are transferred to the private partner. Furthermore, one needs to take into account the down sides of the alternative option: if instead of the PPP, the government chooses to issue more debt, this could reduce its freedom of action and may even lead to a reduction in the rating of government bonds, increasing the cost of capital for the whole debt. Finally, the lower cost of capital of governments is predicated on their ability to raise taxes to reimburse their debt. However, this is becoming increasingly difficult politically and unwise economically.

Hence, on balance, if appropriate governance mechanisms are put in place with a clear focus on users and taxpayers interests, the PPP route is an attractive option for the development and operation of infrastructures, not only because they can potentially provide best value for money but also because they can contribute effectively to the financing of infrastructure. For instance, in France, 75% of the highways built in the post-World War II period have been in the context of concessions (the first one dates to 1956). Thanks to concessions, the highway network was developed with minimum financial participation by the state. This has allowed the general population to take advantage of the network faster than if it had to be financed publicly. Moreover, the concession is temporary; the infrastructure returns to the state after the concession.

So far, the discussion has focussed largely on PPPs involving the private ownership of assets (including cases where the assets return eventually to the state, such as in the Millau Viaduct example). This is not the only way public sector actors can tap the expertise and resources of the private sector. Indeed, a Private Finance Initiative (PFI), another form of PPP, has been gaining growing attention in recent years (notably in the UK) and may become more prevalent in the future in the OECD area and beyond.

In PFI, the public sector contracts to purchase quality services on a long-term basis so as to take advantage of private sector management skills incentivised by having private finance at risk. This includes concessions and franchises, where a private sector partner takes on the responsibility for providing a public service, including maintaining, enhancing or constructing the necessary infrastructure (United Kingdom, 2003).

To be effective, PFI needs to be managed as a mature relationship between the public and private sectors that recognises their mutual responsibilities. PFI ensures that contractors are bound into long-term maintenance contracts and shoulder the responsibility for the quality of the work they do. With PFI, the public sector defines what is required to meet public needs and remains the client throughout the life of the contract. The public sector also ensures, by contract, delivery of the outputs it sets and has rights under those contracts to change the output required from time to time. Consequently, with PFI the public sector can harness the private sector to deliver investment in better quality public services while maintaining frontline services in the public sector.

The key to the success of PFI is to ensure that the sharing of risks between the public and private partners is done appropriately and effectively. The benefits PFI can offer, in terms of on time and on budget delivery and whole-of-life costing, all flow from ensuring that the many different types of risks inherent in a major investment programme – for example construction risk or the risk associated with the design of a building – are borne by the party who is best placed to manage them. In this way, the private sector is incentivised by having its capital at risk to perform well, and takes responsibility for the work it undertakes.[84]

While the private sector takes on the major project performance risks, such as cost overruns and delay, key risks in an investment project are retained by the public sector in both conventional procurement and in a PFI scheme. These include the need to make alterations in the delivery of services necessary to reflect changing needs of the public sector in the future. The government also needs to protect the ongoing delivery of public services. For those services provided through PFI, the contract entered into with the private sector builds in major protections for the public sector to safeguard the standards of delivery by PFI schemes in public services, and their flexibility in future.[85]

For further details regarding the British experience with PFI, see Chapter 1, Box 1.2. Experience in the UK has been largely positive to date, although PFIs are thought to be a suitable form of procurement for only 10-15% of total investment in public services.

Encouraging more funding of infrastructure by pension funds

As noted in the previous section, infrastructure investment offers long-term stable returns with the opportunity for capital growth. Such features could be particularly attractive to pension funds managers if political risks can be kept to a minimum. Indeed, pension funds are following a global trend by moving away from volatile stock markets into infrastructures that provide stable returns needed to pay future pension payments. The fact that traditional real estate has become too pricey in almost every market has prompted them to seek out alternate investments, including a broad scope of infrastructure projects like shipping ports, airports, communications, utilities, natural gas networks, health care, educational facilities and forestry. One of the attractive by-products of this strategy from the pension funds perspective is increased diversification, leading to lower portfolio risk since infrastructure has a low correlation to other asset classes. Some pension fund managers see infrastructure investment as somewhat between equities and bonds: some growth prospects and a very good running yield.[86]

An interesting case in point in this regard is the recent proposal (April 2006) by Treasurer Angelides that California's pension funds – the California Public Employees' Retirement System (CalPERS) and the California State Teachers' Retirement System (CalSTRS) – invest USD 15 billion in urban, smart growth infrastructure projects in California. This is in order to finance the projects that California needs, create jobs and earn a return for the pension funds and taxpayers. The Treasurer's Cal-Build initiative would provide a new source of capital for state and local infrastructure projects, supplementing the financing available from tax-exempt municipal bonds. And it would create a secure new investment for the pension funds to help them meet their need for solid, long-term financial returns.[87]

Proponents view investing pension funds in infrastructure as a way to kill two birds with one stone, *i.e.* meeting the needs of future pensioners while at the same time reducing the infrastructure investment gap. As Ryan Orr, executive director of the Collaboratory for Research on Global Projects (CRGP) at Stanford University puts it:

> *The (pension fund) money belongs to the school teachers and public employees. Why not invest it back into the roads and the infrastructure that they all use every day? Why not have the pension funds both earning their returns and improving the lifestyle for all?*

Canadian pension funds are also investing in infrastructure. For instance, two major funds, the Canada Pension Plan Investment Board and Ontario Municipal Employees Retirement System recently struck billion-dollar deals to acquire stakes in a British water company, AWG PLC, several Fairmont luxury hotels and MDS Diagnostic Services, Canada's largest laboratory operator.

Time will tell whether this interest of pension funds in infrastructure projects is a major new trend in OECD countries that may eventually extend to the developing world.

Indeed, the current enthusiasm for infrastructure investment is causing concern in some quarters that we may experience an asset bubble over the next few years.[88]

Moreover, even in the OECD area, infrastructure investment is not without risks. First, although regulatory regimes are clear and predictable, risks and rewards of investing in utilities can be skewed: high returns in one period cause the regulator to adjust his calculations for the next, so that the upside is capped whereas the downside is not. Second, it is clear that some infrastructure investments have proved disastrous for some investors, such as the tolled Cross City Tunnel in Sydney, which has just gone bankrupt, or Eurotunnel.

However, it is likely that in the longer run, the current surge of investor demand will be counteracted by a wave of supply from governments in light of the growing constrains on the public purse. The idea of privatising is probably most deeply embedded in Britain and Australia. The growing acceptance of the concept in the US is opening a huge new market. Success will critically depend on the putting in place appropriate institutions for managing risk as well as ensuring that risks are taken by those most able to assume it.

Pension funds in the OECD area have grown sharply over the last decade, from USD 5.9 trillion in 1994 to USD 15.6 trillion by 2004, representing a compound growth rate of 10.2% per annum.

According to the third edition of OECD's new bulletin, *Pension Markets in Focus*, the ratio of total OECD pension fund assets to GDP increased from 84.1% in 2004 to 87.6% in 2005. Some countries recorded fast growth, albeit from a low base. Total pension fund assets amounted to USD 17.9 trillion in 2005, up from USD 13 trillion in 2001. (See Chapter 1, Figures 1.5 and 1.6.)

Even if only 1-5% of these funds were devoted to infrastructure projects, as suggested for instance in Vives (1999), this would translate into a total infrastructure investment of USD 179-895 billion. The same logic could be applied in developing countries where pension funds have been expanding as a result of pension fund reform, building up a pool of financial resources in search of attractive investment opportunities that the local market can supply (*e.g.* Latin America).[89]

Promoting a more effective allocation of public resources across the various levels of government

Two main approaches have been discussed above to putting the financing of infrastructure on a more sound footing: greater reliance on user fees; and greater private sector participation in the development, operation and financing of infrastructure. It is also important to ensure that public resources are properly allocated between the various infrastructures (taking into account their specific features but also their complementarities) and between the various levels of government on the basis of their responsibilities and existing institutional arrangements.

For instance, *municipalities* often bear the greatest share of the cost of infrastructure development, in particular because of their responsibilities regarding *water and water treatment* systems. However, they do not always have the tax base necessary to carry out this responsibility. Hence, it is critical that appropriate mechanisms be put in place to ensure that adequate funding is made available to meet their needs, notably when they face added costs resulting from the imposition of stricter standards by national or transnational authorities. In addition, it is legitimate to expect higher levels of government to be involved in the financing of infrastructure that can be considered as strategic from a national perspective, such as *major intermodal terminals* or the development of *UPT* systems in large cities. Such issues arise in particular in federal states where co-operation between various levels of governments is essential whatever the jurisdictional distribution of responsibilities. For such co-operation to happen, a strong impulse is required from *higher* levels of government.

In the case of infrastructures financed essentially by *user fees*, it may be desirable to give municipalities a greater ability to issue bonds. The use of tax-free bonds appears an attractive way to give municipalities more freedom of action while at the same time providing for a transfer of resources from the state (forgone tax revenues). To encourage the greater use of user fees, federal grants can be made conditional on their adoption at the local level. For instance in Canada, one condition imposed on municipalities for receiving financial funding for a municipal water project under the Canadian Strategic Infrastructure Fund (CSIF) is that the issue of water metering and pricing be addressed in the project.[90]

6. Concluding remarks

Infrastructures are key determinants of the way our society is organised, and they affect all aspects of our daily lives. In the future, we will become more and more dependent on their effective, efficient and ubiquitous operation. In this context, the concept of "business model" offers a useful analytical tool for assessing the effectiveness and efficiency of existing arrangements from a policy perspective. It puts the emphasis on the need "to create value for money": how effective and efficient are our infrastructures and what can we do to make them more so in the face of changing conditions, both on the supply and on the demand side?

When considering the present situation, it is clear that we are confronted by a legacy of business models rooted in history, many of which are becoming increasingly inadequate in our rapidly changing world. Such inadequacy, which has lead to serious market and public failures, goes a long way in explaining the "infrastructure investment gap" that currently prevails throughout the world. Obsolete models no longer produce enough value for satisfying either the requirements of investors, the needs of users or for meeting the objectives set by policy makers.

A Darwinian selection process fuelled by globalisation is under way to eliminate the weakest models. Indeed, as a growing range of activities are globalised, underperformance becomes ever more visible, not only in the eyes of experts but also of individual citizens that have to bear the cost of obsolete infrastructures, both as users and taxpayers. However, this process is painfully slow, as it is often opposed by powerful legacy players. Moreover, the direction and the pace of reform are not always clear. And to be successful such reforms generally require the implementation of far-reaching innovative measures that need to be carried out with undaunted determination over extended periods of time – a formidable task for politicians with only a short policy horizon. Finally, because of cultural and institutional differences, the advances achieved in one country cannot be easily transposed to another, slowing down the adjustment process.

As business models slowly adjust to changing conditions in the coming years, they will be confronted by new challenges. First of all, they will need to take into account an increasing range of actors as *interdependence* between nations increases at the international level. They will also need to be more responsive to the needs of individual citizens at the local level, as the concept of participatory democracy is likely to be increasingly embraced, leading to a more proactive and ongoing participation of individual citizens regarding decisions that affect the key infrastructures that shape their daily life.

Greater attention should be given in the future design of business models to the need to ensure the *longer term financial viability* of the infrastructure in the face of *shrinking public budgets*. This will include efforts to reduce the scope for inappropriate interventions by opportunistic politicians, as well as efforts to make infrastructures more self financing by appropriate increases in the fees charged for the use of the infrastructure. Particularly important in this context will be ensuring that social obligations are effectively met but do not bear unduly on the financial viability of the infrastructure.

New technology will offer opportunities to provide service more effectively and efficiently and to reduce the burden on the public purse. In this regard, business models will need to be flexible enough so as to ensure that new technology, even when it is disruptive for legacy players, can be adopted rapidly for the benefit of all users and taxpayers alike.

This will call in particular for the more widespread adoption of ICT in order to develop intelligent infrastructure systems capable of responding in real time to changing conditions and providing incentives for effective modifications in the behaviour of users. In addition, this will contribute to greater flexibility and resilience when coping with security risk.

Business models will also need to allow key actors to be able to take into account new constraints, such as those related to the *environment*. This may call for the introduction of new market mechanisms to allocate resources more effectively and *internalise externalities* and the adoption of technology-neutral incentive schemes.

Notes

1. It is interesting to note that "customers" and "users" are not necessarily the same in all models. For instance, in the Google model, the sponsors (advertisers) are the customers, while usage of the service is free. But to be valuable for the customer, the service needs also to be valuable to the user. In a way, the Google model is very similar to the model used by private broadcasters or "free" newspapers. The main difference is that Google offers a superior ability to target the advertising message to users.
2. As noted above, "customers" and "users" are not necessarily the same. In the Google model or a private broadcaster type model, customers (advertisers) are prepared to pay for what users want, only if it is profitable for them to do so.
3. Private goods (or services) are defined here as goods that are *excludable* (*i.e.* it is reasonably possible to prevent a class of consumers – those who have not paid for it – from consuming the service) and *rivalrous* (*i.e.* consumption by one consumer prevents simultaneous consumption by other consumers).
4. One needs to be careful not to extend unduly the concept of "good essential for life" as a justification for strong public oversight. For instance, food is essential for life, but it does not follow that it cannot be provided under normal business conditions. Indeed, this is what markets are for. What is important for the state from a social perspective is to guarantee minimum access to all and to control the quality of the service provided. Provision can be left to the private sector, as long as environmental rules are fully respected.
5. It is worth noting though that, historically, subway systems were originally developed by the private sector in large cities, such as London and New York.
6. This argument holds only as long as the UPT networks are not overextended to low density areas and that such networks are properly maintained and upgraded.
7. It is interesting to note though that considerable price discrimination prevails in the setting of UPT systems' fares. However, such discrimination reflects social concerns rather than attempts to maximise revenues, as would be the case if a form of Ramsay pricing was adopted.
8. For instance, in the UK, rural rail services receive 60% of the subsidies but account only for 16% of the passenger kilometres travelled. (*Source: The Economist*, 2006a, "Cattle Class", 6 June, London.)
9. George Stigler, winner of the 1982 Nobel Prize in economics, has argued that interest groups will spend resources in an attempt to gain access to the rents created by regulations, *i.e.* that interest groups will spend resources in an attempt to increase the probability that they will be given a large rent. The probability of

receiving a rent can be increased by lobbying regulators in order to get sympathetic regulators elected or appointed, or, more directly, to influence regulators with monetary bribes.

10. An interesting historical example of a freight subway is the Chicago Freight Subway that was in operation from 1906 to 1956 and which was used largely to deliver coal to heat buildings in the city. (*Source: www.reference.com/browse/wiki/Chicago_Freight_Subway.*)

11. Economies of scope exist when taking into account other infrastructures. Subways offer a conduit for other infrastructures, such as communications, electricity or water.

12. In order to meet a new more stringent federal requirement for water filtration, New York City faced the prospect of having to build a new filtration facility at considerable cost (USD 6 billion). It chose instead to meet the new requirement by working with local residents in the upstate watershed to reduce contamination from local septic and sewer systems, to protect land from inappropriate uses that contributed to water contamination, and to locally manage storm water runoff. By implementing a wide range of watershed management tools, the City was able to meet its water quality obligations for about a third of the cost of a new centralised filtration infrastructure. This is a clear application of Coase theorem which suggests that in the absence of transaction costs, all government allocations of property rights are equally efficient, because interested parties will bargain privately to correct any externality. In this case, the upstream externalities have been internalised through bargaining between the City of New York and residents in the upstate watershed. This can work only when transaction costs are modest, as seems to be the case here. Alternatively, it might have been more efficient from a public policy perspective to impose more stringent requirements on upstate residents, *i.e.* more forcefully apply the polluter pays principle.

13. Network Rail took over the UK rail network (former British Rail) by the acquisition of Railtrack plc in October 2002 for GBP 500 million. Railtrack was managing the network since privatisation and was close to bankruptcy. Although Network Rail is a private company, it has a special and rather ambiguous status: it is a not-for-profit company. The shareholders do not receive dividends; profits being invested in the maintenance and upgrading of the network. Their position is similar to the managers of a public enterprise.

14. According to industry experts, the cost of producing drinking water from seawater is now 0.8 to 1.1 EUR/m^3 compared to 0.6 to 0.8 EUR/m^3 for water drawn from rivers and 0.4 EUR/m^3 for water pumped from aquifers. (*Source: Le Monde*, 24 July 2006, p. 7.) Desalination is becoming increasingly popular in some parts of Asia. For instance, the development of Binhai, a high priority area for the Chinese authorities, will depend on water diverted from the Yangtze river, but also from desalinated seawater. (*Source: The Economist*, 22 June 2006, London.)

15. Automated trains are by no means new. In San Francisco, Bay Area Rapid Transit (BART) trains have been completely automated since the 1970s. And New York City had a fully automated train between Grand Central and Times Square for two years in the early 1960s. More recently, driverless, computer-controlled train lines have emerged in Paris, London, Vancouver, Kuala Lumpur, Singapore and elsewhere.

16. In Paris, it is envisaged that 80% of Parisians will have access to very high transmission capacity (100 Mb), with 10 000 km of new optic fibre installed by 2010, as well as free Wi-Fi access in several municipal locations. (*Source: Le Monde*, 6 July 2006, Paris, p. 14.)

17. For instance, General Motors has recently unveiled a "plug-in" hybrid which can be recharged by plugging it into the mains. The principal drawback so far is the cost of the battery pack. However, as batteries improve in the future, all electric vehicles will become more feasible. (*Source: The Economist*, "Plugging In", 6 January 2007, London, p. 53.)
18. Comments from Infrastructure Canada in 2006 to the OECD IFP Project Team.
19. *Ibid.*
20. *Ibid.*
21. Institutional arrangements also have a bearing on the ability of the national government to issue standards. For instance, in Canada there is no standard set at the federal level for the quality of water.
22. A new EC Bathing Water Directive was adopted on 15 February 2006 to tighten but simplify the health standards for bathing water; to improve the management of bathing sites and the provision of public information about them; and to streamline water quality monitoring programmes.
23. European Commission, Rail Transport and Interoperability, *http://ec.europa.eu/transport/rail/overview/fascinating_en.htm*.
24. See for instance the Portsmouth example given by Mackie and Smith (2007). The project, which was signed in July 2004 by the Portsmouth City Council, will put the management and maintenance of all 414 kilometres of Portsmouth roads in the hands of a private company for 25 years. In addition to management and maintenance the contract also includes road cleansing, pot-holes, bringing street lights up to modern standards bridges, structures, street lighting, maintenance of traffic management equipment, highways-related tree and grounds maintenance, winter maintenance and street cleansing and managing the highways with regards to licences and inspections.
25. *Source*: EC, Rail Transport and Interoperability, *http://ec.europa.eu/transport/rail/overview/fascinating_en.htm*.
26. *Source: The Economist* (2006b), "The Politics of Power", 9 February, London.
27. See Crozet (2007) for a French example.
28. On 11 July 2002, the French competition council ("Conseil de la concurrence") ruled that Suez (Lyonnaise des Eaux, SLDE) and Vivendi (Générale des Eaux, CGE) had been abusing their market dominance in France, where they control 85% of private water. The two companies have created joint subsidiaries in a number of towns and regions, so that they are sharing the profits of a water concession instead of competing against each other. Twelve joint ventures in France were listed, including cities such as Marseille and Lille – two involving SAUR as well. The council also said that since June 1997 more than 40 tenders had been made uncompetitive by the groups' behaviour ("le Conseil a constaté à l'occasion de plusieurs appels d'offres publics que le jeu de la concurrence a été 'faussé' dans plus de quarante marchés à partir de juin 1997"). CGE failed to bid on 37 occasions, and SLDE on 33 occasions. (*Source: La Tribune*, 2002, "Vivendi et Suez accusés de fausser le jeu de la concurrence", 18 July.)
29. Recourse to the private sector to finance large infrastructure projects also raises ethical questions when inexperienced investors are lulled into investing in a project on the basis of incomplete or misleading information, as illustrated by the Panama Canal scandal in France in the 1890s and the more recent ordeal of small shareholders of Eurotunnel.

30. Gouvernal, Élisabeth (2003), "Les lignes maritimes et le transport terrestre : quels enseignements peut-on tirer du cas 'Rail Link'?", *Les Cahiers scientifiques du transport*, No. 44, pp. 95-113.

31. Fares are an important source of income for the TfL budget (41% of revenue in 2005), and represent a growing and much higher proportion than in many European transport systems (28% in Greater Paris). Annual Tube travelcards for zones 1 to 4 cost approximately 6% of the average wage of a London worker, which is much higher than the equivalent for Paris and Berlin (2% of the average wage). Single Tube tickets are among the most expensive in the world: GBP 1.52 (approx. EUR 2.2) for a single trip in zone 1 when paid via the new Oyster fare system; GBP 3 (approx EUR 4.4) when paid with cash (*i.e.* more than three times the price paid in Paris). The fare structure is, however, highly sophisticated, with pricing innovation (off-peak prices, family discounts, etc.), and is much more market-orientated than in other cities. (*Source:* FitchRating – Transport for London [TfL], International Public Finance, United Kingdom Credit Analysis, 10 March 2006.)

32. For instance, in Toronto property taxpayers pay 95% of transit costs according to Juri Pill, chairman of the Toronto Office Coalition. (*Source: National Post*, 17 October 2006, p. 1.)

33. On 17 February 2003, TfL launched the congestion charge, which aims to reduce the number of private cars entering the most congested central area. The congestion charge system is operated by a private contractor. Although it has been extremely successful as far as the restriction of car traffic (minus 30%) and the increase in bus patronage are concerned, the congestion charge is generating less revenue than initially expected. The congestion charge was raised from GBP 5 to GBP 8 as of 4 July 2005. In September 2005, the mayor approved the extension of the congestion charging zone to include the western portion of central London as of 19 February 2007. However, the revenues yielded by the extension are expected to be largely offset by the costs of administering this area. (*Source:* FitchRating – Transport for London [TfL], International Public Finance, United Kingdom Credit Analysis, 10 March 2006.)

34. Both programmes use leveraged federal assistance and access to capital markets. The GARVEE programme enables states and other public authorities to issue debt-financing instruments, such as bonds, to pay for current expenditures on transportation construction projects and repay the debt using future federal apportionments. However, reimbursement of construction costs occurs only when debt service is due. The main benefit is that upfront capital is generated to keep projects moving forward at tax-exempt rates, and the cost of the infrastructure is spread over its useful life rather than just over the construction period.

35. The Northeast Blackout of 2003 was a massive power outage that occurred throughout parts of the north-eastern United States and eastern Canada on Thursday, 14 August 2003. Although not affecting as many people as the later 2003 Italy blackout, it was the largest blackout in North American history. It affected an estimated 10 million people in the Canadian province of Ontario (about one-third of the population of Canada), and 40 million people in eight US states (about one-seventh of the population of the US). Outage-related financial losses were estimated at USD 6 billion. (*Source: http://en.wikipedia.org/wiki/2003_North_America_blackout.*)

36. In order to maximise revenues, suppliers of electricity are tempted in effect to apply the pricing strategy used by airlines: *i.e.* price discriminate on the basis of demand elasticity. In the case of airlines this pricing strategy results in outcomes that are generally considered to be "socially acceptable" to the extent that the discrimination is in favour of individual consumers and leisure travellers (and at

the expense of business travellers). In the electricity market, on the other hand, the burden of the discrimination would be born by households, if this pricing model was to be used.

37. It has been noted by a commentator that in a number of developing countries, such as Egypt, the management of rural water is even more challenging than urban water because capital costs per unit of water sold are much higher than in urban areas and the ability to pay of rural households is usually lower than that of city dwellers.

38. For instance in California, well-connected farmers grow rice in the desert, even as Los Angeles begs for water. Altogether, the Californian agriculture sector accounts for 80% of water use in the state although it contributes only 2% to California GDP.

39. In this regard, *The Economist* noted in 2000 that most governments have so mismanaged supplies that much of the world's fresh water is wasted. That is the main reason nearly one in five of the world's people lacks access to safe, reliable water. This is most visible in the sprawling cities of the developing world. With the encouragement of international donors, governments have invested in urban water infrastructure, and they provide water at rates well below the cost of provision. Unfortunately, this strategy born of good intentions has in practice created a morass of bureaucracy and corruption. Though governments spend a fortune on urban water utilities, the main benefits flow to the middle and upper classes. The poor rarely have access to sewerage or piped water. Out of desperation, they endure open sewers and have to buy water, often of dubious quality, from private vendors from the backs of lorries. Even in Haiti, the poorest place in the Americas, slum dwellers pay 100 times what the "morally repugnant elites" (as they take perverse pride in calling themselves) pay for water piped to the hillside mansions that rise above Port-au-Prince. (*Source: The Economist*, 23 March 2000, London.)

40. The DJB says it supplies some 2.9 billion litres (650 million gallons) of water a day, against demand of 4.2 billion litres. But that understates the gap. It estimates demand only from those with water connections, variously estimated at 60% and 80% of Delhi's 16 million people. As for supply, some 15% is stolen and 40% lost to leakage. Many people queue at tankers, standpipes and boreholes fitted with handpipes. (*Source: The Economist*, 11 August 2005, London.)

41. While the elimination of the cross-subsidy has been beneficial for the freight rail operators, the passenger rail operators have suffered; For instance in the US, AMTRAK has been caught in a double bind where, on the one hand, Congress requests that the company breaks even, while on the other hand politicians, including senators, individually urge AMTRAK to extend its service to clearly unprofitable services for political reasons. The net result is that despite repeated injunctions made by Congress for the company to break even, AMTRAK is still losing money. Altogether it has cost the taxpayer USD 31 billion in 25 years of operation and serves only a tiny portion of the population.

42. In the Paris area, in 2005, the largest share of operating costs of all public transport systems in the area (*i.e.* EUR 3.7 billion) were covered by public funding, including a special tax on firms employing more than 9 employees. Fare revenues amounted only to EUR 2.63 billion over the same period. (*Source: www.stif-idf.fr/IMG/pdf/presentation_stif-2.pdf.*)

43. In this regard, Peter Schwartz, a well-known futurist in the business community, notes that there are many "surprises" that we can anticipate, and we can make fairly good assumptions on how most of them will play out. Even the most devastating surprises – like terrorist attacks and economic collapses – are often predictable

because they have their roots in the driving forces at work today. In short, we know many of the surprises to come, although we can only speculate in advance on their consequences or how they will affect us. (*Source:* Schwartz, 2003, p. 3.)

44. See Andrieu (2005).

45. In this context, pipeline projects are very revealing regarding the long-term energy strategies adopted by key players.

46. It is worth noting though that improvement in the design of coal-fired power stations and the possibility of substituting biomass for some of the coal burned could reduce the emissions of carbon dioxide to the same level as those stations using natural gas. Given the abundance of and easy access to coal reserves, such a technological advance by itself (without even considering carbon dioxide capture technologies) could significantly modify the geopolitics of input fuel supply over the coming years. (*Source: The Economist*, 2006, "Can Coal be Clean?", 30 November, London.)

47. *E.g.* the North American Electric Reliability Council. (*Source: The Economist*, 29 July 2006, London, p. 46.)

48. A recent conference co-organised by the OECD, the World Bank and the Agence française de développement has scrutinised the emergence of domestic operators in non-member countries. This dynamic is seen as an opportunity to serve new communities (including the poor) and to develop expertise via innovative partnerships between large international and local players. (*Source:* OECD Global Forum on Sustainable Development "Public-Private Partnerships in Water Supply and Sanitation – Recent Trends and New Opportunities", 29-30 November 2006, Paris.)

49. This is not always the case, though. In the telecom sector, fibre optics – because of its huge capacity – clearly favours monopoly provision for trunk traffic.

50. McAllister, J.F.O. (2006), "Warming to a Global Theme", *Time*, 13 November.

51. Storms are currently the costliest weather catastrophes in the developed world, and they are likely to become more powerful in the future as the oceans warm and provide more energy to fuel storms. Many of the world's largest cities are at risk from severe windstorms. Miami alone has USD 900 billion worth of total capital stock at risk. Two recent studies have found that just a 5-10% rise in the intensity of major storms with a 3°C increase in global temperatures could approximately double the damage costs, resulting in total losses of 0.13% of GDP in the US each year on average or insured losses of USD 100-150 billion in an extreme year (2004 prices). If temperatures increase by 4 or 5 °C, the losses are likely to be substantially greater, because any further increase in storm intensity has an even larger impact on damage costs. This effect will be magnified for the costs of extreme storms, which are expected to increase disproportionately more than the costs of an average storm. (*Source:* United Kingdom, 2006a, The Stern Review.)

52. Although technologies for eliminating carbon dioxide emissions from coal-fired plants already exist, such technologies will not be adopted without strong regulatory incentives from governments, such as long time caps or taxes on such emissions. (*Source: The Economist*, 2006, "Can Coal be Clean?", 30 November, London.)

53. This is no easy task in practice, as noted by Thompson (2007).

54. For instance, a new European Union-funded project will see the introduction of driverless taxis at Heathrow, "cyber cars" in Rome and an automatic bus in Castellón, Spain. Under the auspices of the European Union's "Citymobil" project, companies and research institutes representing ten countries have come together to develop small automatic transportation systems. Currently, three model

projects are planned with funding of about EUR 40 million. (*Source: www.spiegel.de/international/0,1518,435805,00.html.*)

55. A good example of the difficulties involved is the "Big Dig" project in Boston. Big Dig is the unofficial name of the Central Artery/Tunnel Project (CA/T), a megaproject to reroute the Central Artery (Interstate 93), the chief controlled-access highway through the heart of Boston, Massachusetts, into a 3.5 mile (5.6 kilometre) tunnel under the city. The project also included the construction of the Ted Williams Tunnel (extending Interstate 90 to Logan International Airport), the Zakim Bunker Hill Bridge over the Charles River, and the Rose Kennedy Greenway in the space vacated by the previous I-93 elevated roadway. Initially, the Big Dig plan included a rail connection between Boston's two major train terminals (North Station and South Station, North-South Rail Link). The Big Dig is the most expensive highway project in the US. Although the project was estimated at USD 2.8 billion in 1985, over USD 14.6 billion had been spent in federal and state tax dollars as of 2006. The project has incurred criminal arrests, escalating costs, leaks, poor execution and use of substandard materials. The Massachusetts Attorney General is demanding contractors refund taxpayers USD 108 million for "shoddy work". The final ramp opened 13 January 2006. (*Source: http://en.wikipedia.org/wiki/Big_Dig.*)

56. As noted in Tukiainen *et al.* (2006), "cultures" may be viewed from a social science viewpoint as emerging and evolving in response to human need for answers to a set of problems common to all groups including issues related to basic assumptions concerning the relationship between mankind and nature; the nature of reality and truth; the nature of humanity; the nature of human activity; and the nature of relationships between persons. In order to survive and to exist as a social identity, every group, regardless of its size, has to find its solutions to these problems. These solutions then become distinctive for the group separating them from others. Closely intertwined and emanating from culture is the concept of "institutions". Institutions can be defined as relatively stable collections of practices and rules defining appropriate behaviour for specific groups of actors in specific situations. They consist of informal (sanctions, taboos, customs, traditions, and codes of conduct), and formal rules (constitutions, laws, property rights). The major role of institutions in a society is to establish a stable (but not necessarily efficient) structure to political, economic and social interaction.

57. For instance, for the Sea to Sky bypass in British Columbia (BC), three consortia – Black Tusk Highway Group, S2S Transportation Group, and Sound Highway Development Consortium – bid for the project. Each of these entities was composed of several companies. A total of 32 were involved in the bid, eight of them with headquarters in BC, 11 elsewhere in Canada and the rest abroad in France, the UK, US, Germany, Australia, and Hong Kong, China. Each consortium involved large corporations such as Vinci Concession, a division of the French Vinci Groupe, with revenues over USD 22 billion in 2003. Vinci is a world leader in concessions. In Canada, it owns nearly half of the consortium responsible for financing, constructing and operating the Confederation Bridge. Through a local subsidiary, it has a stake in the USD 640 million Fredericton-Moncton Highway. In France, Vinci Concessions' biggest asset is a two-thirds stake in Cofiroute, a concessionaire that operates a 985 kilometre network in France, as well as toll highways in the US, the UK, Germany, Greece and Chili.

58. For instance, in the British Columbia Sea to Sky bypass project, SNC-Lavalin Group, a large engineering and construction firm, was hired as an advisor to the government, while it was bidding at the same time on another BC project, RAV.

59. Arbitration of overseas investment disputes is one of the fastest growing areas of international dispute resolution. The exponential growth of international

investment in recent years has led to the signature of over two thousand Bilateral Investment Treaties (BITs) between foreign states, in addition to a wealth of multilateral treaties and other forms of concession agreements. Disputes that have arisen are often resolved through the forum of international arbitration, and typically involve claims by an investor company for compensation when an investment has been illegally expropriated or adversely affected by the state's activities. (*Source:* McLachlan, Campbell *et al.*, 2007, *International Investment Arbitration: Substantive Principles*, Oxford University Press, forthcoming.)

60. See *www.macquarie.com.au/au/corporations/sfpc/infrastructure_funds/overview.htm*.
61. See *www.innovations-report.com/html/reports/economy_finances/report-66444.html*.
62. See for instance John Foot's 24 May 2006 testimony to the US Transport and Communication Committee regarding the privatisation of the Chicago Skyway. (*Source: www.ksg.harvard.edu/ksgnews/OntheHill/2006/foote_052406.htm.*)
63. Several definitions of "civil society" can be found in the literature. The term generally refers to all of the organisations which are not public or for-profit institutions. For instance, in Anheier (2004), civil society is defined as "the sphere of institutions, organisations and individuals located between the family, the state and the market in which people associate voluntarily to address common interests". Examples of groups in civil society include universities, non-governmental organisations, environmental movements, indigenous peoples' associations, organised local communities and trade unions.
64. Deliberative democracy rests on the core notion of citizens themselves, and their representatives, deliberating about public problems and solutions under conditions that are conducive to: reasoned reflection and refined public judgement; a mutual willingness to understand the values, perspectives, and interests of others; and the possibility of reframing interests and perspectives in light of a joint search for common interests and mutually acceptable solutions (O'Hara, 1998).
65. In the UK, the long delay to the building of Terminal 5 at London's Heathrow Airport is often cited by business as unacceptable in a modern economy.
66. In the case of France, an argument has also been made that the monolith model may be preferable from both an efficiency and a security perspective when heavy reliance is made on nuclear generation. Given the relatively limited role of nuclear generation at the global level, being able to build a large number of identical plants result in substantial economies of scale and offers opportunities to acquire considerable experience over time. This experience can be used to improve plant design, including safety features.
67. European Commission (2004), Proposal for a Directive of the European Parliament and the Council, amending Directive 91/440/EEC on the development of the Community's railways to gradually open up the market for international passenger services by rail – Extended Impact Assessment, Commission Staff Working Paper, COM(2004)139 Final.
68. For instance in London, Ontario, a relatively prosperous mid-size Canadian city, large amounts of untreated wastewater are still regularly dumped today in the Thames river when it rains because in the older part of the city the storm and sanitary sewers share the same pipes. (*Source:* London Free Press, 23 September 2006.)
69. In Canada, the contract between VIA and CN regarding access charges is coming up for renewal in 2007. There is a concern that VIA may face much higher charges, which will further undermine its financial viability.

70. This position is echoed for instance in a recent report to Canadian Council of Ministers on the Environment by Marbek Resource Consultants where it is argued that developing accounting and pricing rules that fully reflect the full cost of water and water sewage treatment is the single most important thing that municipal and regional governments could do to promote efficient water use. (*Source: www.ccme.ca/assets/pdf/ei_marbek_final_rpt_e.pdf.*)

71. In Santiago, Chile, for example, the municipal government introduced a "water stamps" programme that covers part of the cost of water for low-income residents. The result is that more people have access to water, and water use is more efficient. (*Source: www.globalexchange.org/campaigns/wbimf/Shultz.html* and *www.globalexchange.org/campaigns/wbimf/Shultz.html.*)

72. An additional advantage of water metering is that it can contribute to reducing water usage. According to Environment Canada, universal water metering has proven to reduce overall residential and ICI (Industrial-Commercial-Institutional) water consumption by 15 to 30%. (*Source: www.ec.gc.ca/water/en/manage/res/e_res.htm.*)

73. See *www.nhi.org/online/issues/76/books.html.*

74. The New York State Public Employment Relations Board (PERB) was created as an independent neutral agency to administer the Taylor Law.

75. The second phase of the scheme required European countries to submit to the European Commission a national plan of CO_2 quota allocations by the end of June 2006, so as to establish at the European level the volume of CO_2 that large industrial firms and electricity utilities (11 400 plants in Europe) will be allowed to release in the atmosphere over the 2008-12 period. The response of member countries has been mixed: some have met the deadline (*e.g.* UK), other are dragging their feet (*e.g.* France) while five countries (including Italy and Spain) still have to submit a plan and may be sued by the Commission before the European Court of Justice. (*Source: Le Figaro*, 30 November 2006.)

76. *Source: The Economist*, "Selling Hot Air", 7 September 2006.

77. *Source: The Economist*, "Moving Target", 17 August 2006.

78. *Source: Le Figaro*, 2 December 2006.

79. The IPCC special report on CCS (IPCC 2005) suggested that it could provide between 15% and 55% of the cumulative mitigation effort until 2100. The IEA's Energy Technology Perspectives (IEA 2006) uses a scenario that keeps emissions to near current levels by 2050, with 14-16.2% of electricity generated from coal-fired power stations using CCS. This would deliver from 24.7-27.6% of emission reductions. Sachs and Lackner (2005) calculate that, if all projected fossil-fuel plants were CCS, it could save 17 Gt CO_2 annually at a cost of 0.1% to 0.3% of GDP, and reduce global emissions by 2050 from their 554 ppm BAU to 508 ppm CO_2. IEA modelling shows that, without CCS, marginal abatement costs would rise from USD 25 to USD 43 per ton in Europe, and from USD 25 to USD 40 per ton in China, while global emissions are 10-14% higher. This highlights the crucial role CCS is expected to play. (*Source:* United Kingdom, 2006a, The Stern Review.)

80. *Source: The Economist* (2006), "Can coal be clean?", 30 November.

81. National grids are usually tailored towards the operation of centralised power plants and thus favour their performance. Technologies that do not easily fit into these networks may struggle to enter the market, even if the technology itself is commercially viable. This applies to distributed generation as most grids are not suited to receive electricity from many small sources. Large-scale renewables may

also encounter problems if they are sited in areas far from existing grids. Carbon capture and storage also faces a network issue, though a different one; the transport of large quantities of CO_2, which will require major new pipeline infrastructures, with significant costs. (*Source:* United Kingdom, 2006a, The Stern Review.)

82. If a decision is expected at some point in the future about whether or not a new climate change policy will be introduced, a company which makes its investment decision now, risks a loss later if it makes the wrong call on policy. If it waits until the policy is agreed, it can make a more informed choice. Given this uncertainty, a much higher expected profit level would be required to trigger the investment now. In the energy sector, such delays in investment could create serious problems for a country's security of supply. Modelling work by Blyth and Yang (2006) indicates that an increase in the period of relative carbon price stability from 5 to 10 years (which could equate to increasing the length of an allocation period in a trading scheme) could reduce the size of the investment thresholds arising from uncertainty by a factor of two or more. (*Source:* United Kingdom, 2006a, The Stern Report.)

83. Eiffage is one of the largest construction groups in Europe with annual sales of EUR 8.5 billion and a staff of 50 000 employees in 2005.

84. Examples of contracts where risks have been passed on from the public sector at some cost to the private sector include the London Tube PPP (see Box 2.3) where one of the two private consortia is facing penalties, and the construction of Wales' Millennium Stadium in Cardiff.

85. Another interesting development has been the creation of a secondary market in PFI contracts, mainly for UK projects. While this unsettles some stakeholders who anticipate long-term commitments from the initial private partners, it can also be read as an expected outcome in a dynamic market where risks and responsibilities will come to reside with those most willing and able to nurture the contract. This market development underlines the need for the government to negotiate well-constructed contracts which ensure continuity of service, including provisions for equitable sharing of benefits as appropriate if the project is refinanced post completion.

86. *Source: The Economist*, 20 January 2007, p. 79.

87. *Source: www.treasurer.ca.gov/calbuild/ calbuild.pdf#search=%22infrastructure%20pension%20funds%22.*

88. For instance, Michael Wilkins of Standard and Poor's, a rating agency, gave warning last year: "The infrastructure sector is in danger of suffering from the dual curse of overvaluation and excessive leverage – the classic symptoms of an asset bubble." He estimated that USD 100 billion-150 billion of capital was raised last year to invest in infrastructure. As money pours into the industry, prices are going up and future returns are being revised down.

89. Vives (1999) suggests in this regard that an ideal financial instrument could be securities of a fund invested in many carefully selected projects, with some form of credit enhancement (*e.g.* multilateral participation, credit guarantees, political risk insurance) over several sectors (heavy on energy, light on water, with a mix of transportation subsectors), covering several countries, mostly in operation stage, with shares quoted in some exchange, preferably in a developed market.

90. The CSIF is a USD 4 billion fund directed at projects of major federal and regional significance in areas that are vital to sustaining economic growth and enhancing the quality of life of Canadians. Maximum federal funding is 50% except for broadband and Northern infrastructure projects where it is 75%. Special conditions are imposed

on the use of these funds. For instance: mass transit projects must explore option for transit demand management strategies as a condition of federal funding; water systems must address issues of metering and pricing; new municipal buildings must exceed energy efficiency requirements codes.

Bibliography

AEA Technology Rail (2006), *Review of National Rail Trends*, A Report for John Larkinson, Office of Rail Regulation, Reference: LD31152, Issue 4, United Kingdom.

Andrieu, Michel (2005), "The Long-Term Global Outlook for Investment in Infrastructures", paper prepared for the OECD IFP project on Infrastructure to 2030, Paris, 12 December 2005.

Aubert, Benoit A. *et al.* (2005), *Synthèse critique d'expériences de partenariats public-privé*, CIRANO (Centre interuniversitaire de recherche en analyse des organisations), Canada.

Banks, F.E. (2004), "Economic Theory and the Failure of Electricty Deregulation in Sweden", *Energy and Environment*, Vol. 15, No. 1, 1 January 2004, United Kingdom, pp. 25-35.

Bertram, Geoff *et al.* (2005), "Price-Cost Margins and Profit Rates in New Zealand Electricity Distribution Networks Since 1994: the Cost of Light-Handed Regulation", *Journal of Regulatory Economics*, Vol. 27, No. 3, May 2005, United States, pp. 281-308.

Blyth, W. and M. Yang (2006), "The Effect of Price Controls on Investment Incentives", presentation to the Sixth Annual Workshop on Greenhouse Gas Emission Trading, IEA/IETA/EPRI, September 2006, Paris, *www.iea.org/Textbase/work/2006/ghget/Blyth.pdf*.

Carrard, Naomi (2005), "Water Governance in Context, Case Study of Australia", presentation to the South East Asia Geography Conference Panel, Australian Mekong Resource Centre, University of Sydney.

City of Toronto (2005), *Building a Transit City*, Toronto.

CIDA (2001), *Infrastructure Service Performance Review: Executive Report*, Canadian International Development Agency, Gatineau, Quebec.

Coulson, N. Edward (2006), "Current Events: The Effects of Electricity Deregulation on State Economies", *Journal of Regional Science*, Vol. 46, No. 1, February 2006, United Kingdom, pp. 147-168.

Coyle Eugene P. (2000), *Price Discrimination, Electronic Redlining, and Price Fixing in Deregulated Electric Power*, report prepared for the American Public Power Association, Washington DC.

Cornwall, Claudia (2004), "World's P3 Kings Bid in B.C.", TheTyee.ca, *http://thetyee.ca/News/2004/09/20/P3KingsInBC*.

Coe, Amanda (2005), "Community Participation and Public Infrastructure in the United States", John F. Kennedy School of Government, Harvard University, Cambridge.

Crozet, Yves (2007), "Strategic Issues for the Future Funding and Operation of Urban Public Transport Systems", in *Infrastructure to 2030 (Volume 2): Mapping Policy for Electricity, Water and Transport*, OECD, Paris.

CSIRO (2006), "Irrigation in Perspective: Irrigation in the Murray and Murrumbidgee Basins: A Bird's Eye View", Co-operative Research Center for Irrigation Futures, Australia.

DREIF (2003), *Le déplacement des Franciliens en 2001-2002 : Enquête globale de transport*, Direction Régionale de l'Équipement, Île-de-France.

Daniels, Alan (2004), "Prince Rupert Box Terminal Will Be 'Midwest Express'", Nationwide News Service, Canada, *www.nationwidenews.ca*.

DELCAN *et al.* (2005), *Costs of Congestion in Canada's Transportation Sector*, final report to Transport Canada Sustainable Development Branch, Contract No. T8080-01-1593.

European Commission, *Rail Transport and Interoperability*, Brussels, *http://ec.europa.eu/transport/rail/overview/fascinating_en.htm*.

European Commission (2004), Proposal for a Directive of the European Parliament and the Council, amending Directive 91/440/EEC on the development of the Community's railways to gradually open up the market for international passenger services by rail, Extended Impact Assessment, Commission Staff Working Paper, COM(2004)139 final, Brussels.

Fabella, Raul (2006), *Shifting the Boundary of the State: the Privatization and Regulation of Water Service in Metropolitan Manila*, Working Paper Series Paper No. 123, University of the Philippines, School of Economics, Centre on Regulation and Competition.

FitchRating (2006), *Transport for London (TfL)*, International Public Finance, United Kingdom Credit Analysis, 10 March 2006.

Foote, John H. (2006), "Understanding Contemporary Public Private Highway Transactions – The Future of Infrastructure Finance", testimony to the Highways, Transit and Pipelines Subcommittee of the House Transportation and Infrastructure Committee, United States.

Foresight Directorate (2006), *Intelligent Infrastructure Futures Project Overview*, UK Office of Science and Technology, London.

Franco, Guido *et al.* (2006), *Climate Change and Electricity Demand in California*, report from California Climate Change Center, February 2006, CEC-500-2005-201-SF.

Frank, M.W. (2003), "An Empirical Analysis of Electricity Regulation on Technical Change in Texas", *Review of Industrial Organization*, Vol. 22, No. 4, June 2003, United States, pp. 313-331.

Gouvernal, Élisabeth (2003), "Les lignes maritimes et le transport terrestre : quels enseignements peut-on tirer du cas Rail Link ?", *Les Cahiers Scientifiques du Transport*, No. 44/2003, France, pp. 95-113.

Hall, David (2002), *The Water Multinationals 2002 – Financial and Other Problems*, report funded by Public Services International (PSI), United Kingdom.

IEA (1999), *Electricity Reform: Power Generation Costs and Investment*, OECD, Paris.

IEA (2006a), *Energy Technology Perspectives: Scenarios and Strategies to 2050*, OECD, Paris.

IEA (2006b), *Energy Technology Scenarios and Strategies for a More Secure and Sustainable Energy Future*, OECD, Paris.

Intergovernmental Panel on Climate Change (2005), "IPCC Special Report on Carbon Capture and Storage", Cambridge University Press, Cambridge, *www.ipcc.ch/activity/ccsspm.pdf*.

Johnston, David Kay (2006), "In Deregulation, Power Plants Turn into Blue Chips", *New York Times*, 23 October.

Klein, Michael (2003), "The Cost of Water", BBC News, *http://news.bbc.co.uk/2/hi/in_depth/2957398.stm*.

Looney, Andrew (2002), The Empty City, *www.wunderland.com/WTS/Andy/EmptyCity/chapter36.html*.

Lukensmeyer, Carolyn J. and Lars Hasselblad Torres (2003), "Deliberation for Community Planning and Economic Development", paper prepared for the Charrette Institute, United States.

Mackie, Peter J. and Nigel J. Smith (2007), "Road Transport Infrastructure: Business Models, Trends and Prospects", in *Infrastructure to 2030 (Volume 2): Mapping Policy for Electricity, Water and Transport*, OECD, Paris.

Marbek Resource Consultants Ltd. (2005), *Analysis of Economic Instruments for Water Conservation*, report submitted to the Canadian Council of Ministers of the Environment, Water Conservation and Economics Task Group.

Mayor of London and Transport of London (2006), *London Underground and the PPP: The Third Year 2005/06*, report for financial year ending 31 March 2006.

McLachlan, Campbell *et al.* (forthcoming 2007), *International Investment Arbitration: Substantive Principles*, Oxford University Press.

Morgan, Trevor (2007), "Assessing the Long-Term Outlook for Business Models in Electricity Infrastructure and Services", in *Infrastructure to 2030 (Volume 2): Mapping Policy for Electricity, Water and Transport*, OECD, Paris.

O'Hara, Kathy (1998). *Securing the Social Union*, Canadian Policy Research Network, Ottawa.

OECD (2002), "Regulatory Reform in Gas and Electricity and the Professions", *OECD Reviews of Regulatory Reform, Regulatory Reform in the United Kingdom*, OECD, Paris.

OECD (2006), *Infrastructure to 2030: Telecom, Land Transport, Water and Electricity*, OECD, Paris.

Palaniappan, Meena, Heather Cooley, Peter Gleick, and Gary Wolff (2007), "Water Infrastructure and Water-Related Services: Trends and Challenges Affecting Future Development", in *Infrastructure to 2030 (Volume 2): Mapping Policy for Electricity, Water and Transport*, OECD, Paris.

Perlman, Janice (2000), "Citizen Participation in City Planning and Development", The Mega-Cities Project (Publication MCP-004, 2000).

Sachs, J. and K. Lackner (2005), "A Robust Strategy for Sustainable Energy", *Brookings Papers on Economic Activity*, Issue 2, The Brookings Institution, Washington DC.

SACTRA (1999), *Transport and the Economy: Summary Report*, Standing Advisory Committee on Trunk Road Assessment (SACTRA) to the UK Secretary of State for Transport.

Schwartz, Peter (2003), *Inevitable Surprises: Thinking Ahead in a Time of Turbulence*, Gotham Books, New York.

Stabile, Tom (2006), "New York's Subway System Finally Starting Major Expansion", The McGraw-Hill Companies, *http://construction.com/NewsCenter/Headlines/RP/20060523ny.asp*.

STIF (2005), *Baromètre 2005* (survey of Ile-de-France residents on travel and modes of transport in Île-de-France), Syndicat des Transports d'Île-de-France (transport organising authority of Île-de-France).

STIF (2006), *Présentation du STIF*, Syndicat des Transports d'Île-de-France.

Tabors, Richard D. *et al.* (2006), "Price Discrimination in Organized/Centralized Electric Power Markets", proceedings of the 39th Hawaii International Conference on System Sciences.

The Economist (2006a), "Cattle Class", 6 June, London.

The Economist (2006b), "The Politics of Power", 9 February, London.

Thomas, Stephen (2004), "Evaluating the British Model of Electricity Deregulation", *Annals of Public and Co-operative Economics*, Vol. 75, No. 3, September, United Kingdom, pp. 367-398.

Thompson, Louis S. (2007), "Key Trends and Implications for Policy Change in Long-Term Rail Freight Traffic and Infrastructure", in *Infrastructure to 2030 (Volume 2): Mapping Policy for Electricity, Water and Transport*, OECD, Paris.

Transport Canada (2006), *Review of International Urban Transportation Policy Frameworks, Strategies and Governance Models*, Metropolitan Knowledge International, Markham, Ontario.

Tukiainen, Sampo *et al.* (2004), Effects of Cultural Differences on the Outcomes of Global Projects: Some Methodological Considerations, mimeo.

United Kingdom (UK) (2003), *PFI: Meeting the Investment Challenge*, HM Treasury, London.

UK House of Commmons Committee on Public Accounts (2005), *London Underground Public-Private Partnership,* Seventeenth Report of Session, 2004-05.

UK (2006a), *Stern Review: The Economics of Climate Change*, HM Treasury, London.

UK (2006b), *PFI: Strengthening Long-term Partnerships*, HM Treasury, London.

Vajjhala, Shalini P. (2005), *Mapping Alternatives: Facilitating Citizen Participation in Development Planning and Environmental Decision Making*, PhD thesis, Department of Engineering and Public Policy, Carnegie Institute of Technology, Carnegie Mellon University, Pittsburgh, Pennsylvania.

Van Doren, Peter *et al.* (2004), "Rethinking Electricity Restructuring", *Policy Analysis*, No. 530, Cato Institute, United States, *www.cato.org/pub_display.php?pub_id=2609*.

Vander Ploeg, Casey (2006), *New Tools for New Times: A Sourcebook for the Innovative Financing, Funding, and Delivery of Municipal Infrastructure*, Western Cities Project Report No. 35, Canada West Foundation.

Vanier, Dana J. (ed.) (2006), *Decision Support Systems in Infrastructure Management*, National Research Council of Canada, Ottawa, *www.itcon.org/2006/13/*.

Vanier, Dana J. *et al.* (2006), *Review of Commercial Municipal Infrastructure Asset Management Systems*, National Research Council, Canada.

Vives, Antonio (1999), "Pension Funds in Infrastructure Project Finance: Regulations and Instrument Design", Sustainable Development Department Technical Papers Series, Inter-American Development Bank, Washington DC.

Zielinski, Sue (2004), *Integration Technologies for Sustainable Urban Goods Movement*, report of "Moving the Economy" to Transport Canada, Toronto.

ANNEX 2.A1

The Impact of Deregulation on the Electricity Sector

At the end of the 1990s, the outlook for deregulation in the electricity sector was rather upbeat. For instance, a study conducted at the time by the International Energy Agency (IEA) to examine how electricity reform was expected to reduce generation costs confirmed the scope for cost improvements, although it was pointed out that it is the market which ultimately will determine their extent (IEA, 1999).

The study also considered how investment in the power sector would be affected by market liberalisation. It was acknowledged that some observers feared at the time that the additional uncertainties to which the transition gives rise would result in inadequate investment in new generation capacity or an inappropriate plant mix. The IEA analysis suggested that these issues would not deter investment, provided reform was well designed in the first place and effective regulation was put in place. However, the IEA warned that a residual responsibility rested on governments to monitor market developments and maintain an adequate regulatory framework. Governments must ensure that adequate incentives are in place to attract new investment well before capacity shortages appear. The IEA study concluded that, in the end, experience will demonstrate how well electricity reform measures up to expectations, but the authors were of the view that their analysis provided good grounds for confidence in the benefits of deregulation.

Observers are less upbeat today. The outlook for deregulation does not seem as rosy as it did then. Indeed, the impact of deregulation in the electricity sector is generally viewed as "mixed". On the one hand, there is some evidence that, on balance, deregulation has been beneficial in some countries at least. For instance, Coulson (2006) finds that panel regressions indicate that state electricity deregulation in the US is associated with higher housing prices, increased activity in the housing market, and lower wages, all of which are consistent with a model of compensating differentials wherein deregulation (which is shown to indeed lower electricity prices) increased the utility of state residents.

There is also some empirical evidence that the rate of technical change in the sector is higher in a deregulated environment than under a rate-of-return regulatory regime. This is found for example by Frank (2003) in the case of Texas, a state which offers a rather unique opportunity to assess historically the impact of regulation on innovation. In Texas, regulation was relatively limited until 1975, after which time state legislators imposed rate-of-return regulation. Utilising a translog cost framework on annual data covering the years 1965 to 1985, Frank was able to compare the rate of technological change both before and after the imposition of rate-of-return regulation. The findings indicate that before the implementation of rate-of-return regulation, costs decreased significantly because of technological progress. After the implementation, however, it was found that costs increased significantly due to technological regress brought on by regulation.

Other studies, however, draw a very different picture. In the case of New Zealand, there is evidence that "light-handed regulation" (limited to mandatory information disclosure) over the 1994-2003 period has resulted in large increases in the price-cost margin (Bertram *et al.*, 2005). The authors found that this regime has allowed profits to exceed the levels which would have been acceptable under the old rate-of-return regulatory framework, by about USD 200 million per year, on an ongoing basis.

Some authors are also rather critical of the impact of deregulation in the UK. In particular, it is noted that an expected result has not been fulfilled, that is, the replacement of monopolies in some areas by markets and price-setting using a simple incentive formula has not lead to "light" regulation. Incentive regulation has evolved into a complex and intrusive form of rate-of-return, while regulation of industry structure has allowed the industry to descend into a concentrated, vertically integrated structure, at odds with the aims of the reforms (Thomas, 2004).

Banks (2004) also raises questions regarding the deregulation of electricity in Sweden. The author notes that since the beginning of the deregulation 'experiment', the trend price of electricity has increased much faster than the consumer price index, especially during recent years. More importantly, because of: 1) the lack of investment in domestic generating (and perhaps transmission) facilities by Swedish power companies; 2) the questionable strategy employed by these firms to manage hydroelectric reserves; 3) increased and to some extent irrational energy taxes; and 4) the beginning of nuclear "disengagement", households and businesses are vulnerable to a prolonged "spike" in electricity prices.

In addition, concerns have been raised in the US that while some investors have profited handsomely by buying and sometimes quickly reselling "unbundled" power plants, electricity customers, who were supposed to be the biggest beneficiaries of the new system have not fared so well (Johnston, 2006). Indeed, the expectation that customers would benefit from healthy competition among a growing number of electricity producers has not been realised because not enough new competitors have emerged. Many of the new power plants failed because, unlike many of the old plants, they almost all used natural gas to produce electricity. Demand for natural gas soared, and the price for that fuel tripled, making electricity from these plants too costly to be competitive.

Moreover, many of the power plants that were sold by utilities are still owned by the utilities' parent companies; they were simply transferred from the regulated utilities to unregulated sister companies. Some regulators allowed utilities to favour the sister companies with long-term contracts, even if they did not offer the best price for electricity. As a result, truly independent electricity producers face significant barriers to entry. They complain that their modern generating plants often sit idle, while older, inefficient plants owned by politically powerful utilities and their unregulated sister companies whir around the clock under long-term contracts.

Barriers to entry also result from the way power plants have been transferred from regulated utilities to unregulated sister companies. In a number of cases, the potential savings from a competitive electricity industry were undercut by favouritism that regulators showed to utility companies. For instance in Ohio, regulators allowed an extremely favourable price when unregulated sister companies acquired power plants. The lower the price a sister company pays for a power plant, the more difficult it is for an independent power producer that must build an expensive new plant to compete.

These developments have induced many consumer advocate groups to lobby for a re-regulation of the industry. Even the Cato Institute, a strong advocate of *laissez faire*, has been very critical of restructuring in the US, arguing that attempts by bureaucrats and politicians to force unbundling on the industry is bound to fail. As the best alternative, Cato Institute experts recommend total abandonment of restructuring and a more thorough embrace of markets than contemplated in current restructuring initiatives, allowing utilities in effect to structure their operations as they see fit and to exercise fully their market power. However, recognizing that such reforms would be politically difficult to achieve, they argue that a second-best alternative would be for those states that have already embraced restructuring to return to an updated version of the old, vertically integrated, regulated *status quo*. In their view, it is likely that such an arrangement would not be that different from the arrangements that would have developed under *laissez faire* (Van Doren *et al.*, 2004).

This rather mixed picture of deregulation efforts to date that emerges from the literature suggests that the jury is still out on the gains that can realistically be achieved and the time it will take to achieve them. Whether deregulation and restructuring can deliver substantial benefits critically depends on three questions:

- How significant are the losses associated with vertical disintegration brought about by restructuring? In this context, the implementation of new technology could play a critical role. In particular, distributed generation and increased use of ITC should logically make arm's length operations more viable.
- To what extent can such losses be compensated by long-term contractual arrangements, appropriate market mechanisms and regulatory incentives?
- To what extent can barriers to entry for new comers in the industry be reduced to a minimum? These barriers have clearly played a critical role in preventing competition to emerge. As a consumer advocate puts it, utilities have been able to kill the market before it could be started.

While it would be unwise to abandon deregulation and restructuring, it is clear that greater efforts will be needed in the future to improve the regulatory framework, provide appropriate incentives and to reduce drastically the barriers to entry in the electricity generation segment of the electricity supply industry.

ISBN 978-92-64-03131-9
Infrastructure to 2030 – Vol. 2
Mapping Policy for Electricity, Water and Transport

Chapter 3

Assessing the Long-Term Outlook for Business Models in Electricity Infrastructure and Services

by

Trevor Morgan*

Rising electricity demands call for greater investment in electricity supply infrastructure. What are the long-term drivers of and prospects for business models in the construction and operation of electricity infrastructure and the provision of electricity services? This chapter describes electricity industry structure and patterns of ownership and the reasons for differences among countries and regions. It examines the challenges that governments face, including establishing and sustaining competitive markets in electricity supply, pricing network services efficiently, and ensuring security of supply.

* Menencon Consulting, France.

Summary

The adequacy and timeliness of investment in physical electricity infrastructure will remain closely linked to the long-term structural evolution of the industry, to sources of finance and to financing mechanisms. Several factors – including the pace of demand growth, government policies on market structure and ownership, technological change and growing cross-border trade – will strongly influence business models and prospects for investment. Policy and regulation, in turn, will have to continue to adapt in order to meet a number of challenges, including establishing and sustaining competitive markets in electricity supply, pricing network services efficiently and ensuring security of supply.

Liberalisation of the electricity industry – involving greater private sector involvement, the introduction of competition in generation and supply and new regulatory structures – will continue to have a profound impact on business models. Privatisation has largely run its course in most OECD countries, with the bulk of the industry now in private hands. But rapidly rising electricity demand in developing countries and emerging market economies, where the electricity industry is often owned by the state, will increase the pressure on governments to look to the private sector for at least part of the capital needed to expand infrastructure. Market and regulatory reforms will remain the primary driver of changing business models in OECD countries and may become increasingly important in many other parts of the world. Unbundling of vertically-integrated monopolies will impose new models in generation and supply.

How successful privatisation and market reforms, which are still being implemented in many countries, are judged to be will clearly have an enormous impact on future policy directions in all regions and, therefore, business models. In most cases, the implementation of reforms is far from complete and their effects on sector organisation and structure are not yet fully evident. Although experience so far suggests that competition in electricity generation and supply can in principle bring major benefits through gains in efficiency and lower prices, there are growing concerns about whether the new business and regulatory models that are emerging involve adequate incentives for investment in generating and network capacity as market players adapt to the new environment. Continuing difficulties in financing independent or merchant power plants in many parts of the world could hinder market entry, the development of competition and new investment. There will undoubtedly be profitable opportunities for new power generation investments in the future, but an improvement in the financing climate will call for changes in corporate governance, better risk management strategies and more transparency in accounting practices.

New developments in technology – particularly in power generation – and costs of supply will also have a major impact on the structure of the electricity industry. Upheavals in international energy markets and surging fossil fuel prices, if they persist, would have major consequences for future choices of technology and fuels. Faster growth of small-scale renewables-based generation technologies, as well as other forms of distributed generation, such as small-scale fossil-based co-generation plants and fuel cells, could radically alter the structure of the electricity industry.

The development of interconnections between national or regional networks and the subsequent expansion of cross-border trade will be both a major driver and a consequence of structural change throughout the electricity supply industry. Rising electricity demand will expand opportunities for profitable investments in interconnectors in liberalised markets. But how much new capacity is actually built and used will depend to a large extent on the regulatory framework.

Utilities are adopting varying business strategies in response to the changing market and regulatory landscape and the associated shifts in business risk. In general, the industry is consolidating and converging with other sectors, mainly through mergers and acquisitions. These trends are likely to continue. Risk management and economies of scale and scope will continue to underpin the business rationale for vertical and horizontal integration, reversing to some extent the initial restructuring where market reforms have been introduced. However, competition authorities may take a tougher stance on future horizontal deals in generation and supply amid growing concerns about the impact of concentration on the effectiveness of competition on wholesale and retail markets.

Electricity utilities are likely to become more integrated with gas and other network sectors, because of potential synergies, economies of scale and the potential to hedge fuel-price risk. The traditional boundaries between the utility sector and upstream oil and gas will become increasingly blurred, as upstream companies move downstream to protect market share and downstream companies seek to secure fuel supply and storage assets. In the longer term, utilities may seek more global reach. Opportunities and incentives to invest in emerging markets and developing countries will depend on national policies and their implications for perceived risk and potential returns. Further unbundling of networks would yield new opportunities for private investors to buy relatively low-risk regulated assets.

Many non-OECD countries will continue to struggle to attract private domestic and foreign investment in their electricity industries because of poorly developed domestic financial markets and the higher cost of capital caused by higher risk. Private investment is expected to play a growing role in the medium term, but this will hinge on the economic, political, regulatory and legal environment. The multilateral lending institutions are likely to remain a major source of much-needed capital in many countries for as long as the number of active international investors in developing countries remains small and national and regional finance modest.

Policy makers and regulators will increasingly need to focus on incentives for investment in generating and network capacity. In principle, competitive electricity markets can provide incentives for timely and efficient investments, as long as the market is well designed and the regulatory framework is appropriate. There are growing concerns about the adequacy of generation and transmission investment in liberalised markets – notably in Europe, the United States and parts of Asia. Reserve margins are falling in several countries as a result of a downturn in investment in recent years. Given the economic, social and political importance of "keeping the lights on", establishing efficient mechanisms for remunerating reserve capacity and network investments, streamlining procedures for approving new power plants and transmission lines and ensuring that utilities meet minimum standards for transmission-system reliability will remain of critical importance.

1. Introduction

This chapter assesses the long-term drivers of and prospects for business models in the construction and operation of electricity infrastructure and the provision of electricity services. Modern economies are becoming increasingly dependent on grid-based electricity services. Investment in expanding and upgrading electricity supply infrastructure – including power generation plants and transmission and distribution networks – will, therefore, continue to be of crucial importance to economic development and growth.

In its broadest sense, the term "business model" refers to the way an industry or an enterprise goes about doing business. This chapter focuses on the aspects of the electricity industry that set it apart from other industries – namely, the way the industry is structured and patterns of ownership. How the organisation of the electricity supply industry evolves will affect whether the industry is willing and able to invest in a timely manner, as well as sources of finance and financing mechanisms. Several factors, including the pace of demand growth, government policies on market structure and ownership, technological change and growing cross-border trade, will strongly influence business models and incentives to invest. But policy and regulation, in turn, will have to continue to adapt in order to meet a number of challenges, including establishing and sustaining competitive markets in electricity supply, pricing network services efficiently and ensuring security of supply.

The next section summarises existing models of industry structure, operation and ownership, and the reasons for differences among countries and regions. The chapter then goes on to review the principal drivers of change in the structure of the industry and markets for electricity services. This is followed by an assessment of how the industry could evolve in the medium to long term and what this will mean for financing and investment. The final section considers the policy and regulatory challenges posed by possible future developments in industry structure and ownership.

This chapter builds on the findings of Chapter 3 "Outlook for Global Investment in Electricity Infrastructure" (Morgan, 2006) in the OECD book *Infrastructure to 2030: Telecom, Land Transport, Water and Electricity*.

2. Current business models in electricity supply

2.1. *Vertical and horizontal integration*

There are many ways in which the electricity industry in its broadest sense – covering the construction, operation and maintenance of generating plants and networks that deliver electricity services to end-users – can be organised. The structure of the electricity supply industry is most obviously characterised by the degree of vertical and horizontal integration (Figure 3.1).

Figure 3.1. **Functional activities in electricity supply**

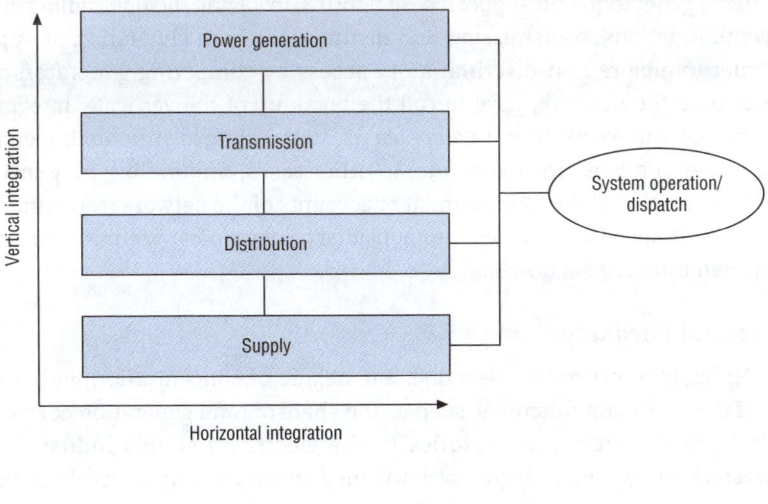

Vertical integration

Vertical integration describes the linkage between the main functional activities within the electricity supply chain – power generation, transmission, local distribution and supply.[1] An electricity industry or utility[2] is said to be fully vertically integrated if it is responsible for, owns or controls all four functions. At the other extreme, each function may be owned or controlled by different entities or companies. In practice, the actual structure of an electricity industry usually lies somewhere between these extremes. For example, a company may own and operate generation and transmission assets, but have no involvement in distribution.

Traditionally, the electricity supply industry in most countries has been characterised by a high degree of vertical integration because of the cost savings that could be realised from integrated planning of investment and capacity, especially in generation and transmission, and operational co-ordination. The highly capital-intensive nature of the industry, the large economies of scale in electricity supply, the importance of maintaining reliability and the natural monopoly[3] characteristics of the electricity industry were also seen as arguments in favour of vertical integration. Supply to final end-users was always the exclusive activity of distribution or transmission companies.

In the last two decades, however, several factors, including the emergence of new power-generation technologies with smaller efficient scales, the development of information and communications technology and growing support for market-based approaches to regulating network industries, have led governments to introduce market reforms aimed at encouraging competition in electricity generation and supply. These reforms, involving the unbundling of the network functions (transmission and distribution) from generation or supply in order to ensure non-discriminatory access by competing generators and suppliers to the network, have forced the break-up of the vertically integrated structure in some countries. In some cases, unbundling is structural, meaning that ownership is entirely separate. In other cases, unbundling may involve simply separation of the management or accounts of the network (sometimes by spinning off specific activities into subsidiary companies) within a vertically integrated firm (see Section 3).

Horizontal integration

Horizontal integration describes the degree of concentration within any one of the four main functions, such as the share of total generation controlled by individual generators. Historically, the electricity supply industry was characterised by a high degree of horizontal integration at all levels in most countries, at the national or, in large countries such as the United States, the regional level. Governments typically granted exclusive or monopoly rights to companies to take responsibility for planning, building and operating the generating plant or the network on the grounds that this was the most effective and efficient way to ensure that sufficient capacity was built and made available to meet national or regional demand.

The degree of horizontal integration in generation and supply has fallen in those countries that have successfully introduced market reforms. Indeed, horizontal *dis*integration is a necessary condition for competition to develop. In practice, policy makers or regulators may encourage investment by independent power producers or require incumbent generators with a large market share to divest assets to create multiple power wholesalers, especially where there is little opportunity or need to build new capacity. Reforms may also involve encouraging or obliging incumbent firms to reduce their share of retail supply, by breaking up and selling off their marketing functions piecemeal. In contrast, market reforms *per se* have not directly concerned the degree of horizontal integration in transmission and distribution, as these activities remain regulated as natural monopolies. In deregulated electricity markets, there is no centralised planning of generation capacity, though the authorities may continue to play a key role in identifying the need for new transmission and distribution capacity and encouraging private network operators to invest.

While horizontal integration is declining *within* many markets undergoing reform, many utilities are responding by acquiring or building assets or merging with other utilities in other markets overseas or by moving into other domestic or foreign network industries – such as natural gas, telecommunications and water. The past decade had seen the emergence of large multinational multiservice utilities, driven by economies of scale and scope (see Section 4). In some countries, notably Germany, municipal multiutilities were established long before the introduction of market reforms.

Co-operative arrangements

Regardless of the structure of an individual utility or of the electricity industry within a given country, co-operative arrangements often exist between networks both within countries (such as in the United States) or across national borders (for example, in Europe). These arrangements usually involve interconnected systems operating in synchronous mode. The system operator of each participating network is obliged to fulfil certain operating conditions, aimed at ensuring a minimum level of reliability across the entire interconnected system, and may be required to undertake certain actions in the event of an emergency. Co-operative arrangements can reduce both capital and operating costs, mainly by taking advantage of economies of scale, by establishing joint merit orders, by lowering the need for reserve capacity within a particular country or region and by reducing the overall system peak load.[4] They also make possible a larger market in power supply, increasing the potential for more effective competition between generators and marketers. Examples of co-operative arrangements include the North American power pools, some of which involve both US and Canadian utilities; the Union for the Transport of Electricity (UCTE) in western and central Europe; and Nordel, which groups the four Scandinavian countries (Denmark, Finland, Norway and Sweden).

The above discussion concerns the day-to-day operation and maintenance of the physical assets that comprise the electricity *supply* industry and related commercial activities. The electricity *services* industry, which provides maintenance and construction services to utilities, is normally structurally separate from the supply industry. In most cases, major maintenance and rehabilitation programmes are outsourced to specialist firms, because it is usually less costly than keeping such a capability in-house. Similarly, the design and construction of generating plants and network facilities are usually carried out by different entities. A contract to build a power plant usually involves start-up operations and training of the staff of the owner and eventual operator of the plant.

2.2. Ownership

Various models of ownership exist, ranging from wholly state-owned national utilities through municipality-owned local distribution companies and mixed private-public enterprises to private energy companies. In many countries, the electricity industry was developed initially by private companies, while the period of rapid expansion in the second half of the 20th century was carried out with a high degree of public ownership. This was especially the case in Europe and most developing countries, where the supply of electricity was, and often still is, regarded as a public service and of strategic importance in economic and social development. The United States and Japan, where electricity generation and transmission are still dominated by privately owned utilities, are the main exceptions. In contrast, the electricity services industry, which is becoming increasingly international, has always been dominated by private companies. A notable exception is France, where the state still holds a controlling stake in Areva, the world's largest nuclear services company.

Patterns of ownership have changed enormously in recent years, with a move back towards more private ownership in many parts of the world. In some cases, this has involved privatisation of state-owned utilities, through stock market flotations or private sales. In other cases, the electricity industry has been opened up to private investment solely in new power projects with public utilities retaining their central role in the industry.

Despite the increasing involvement of the private sector, the overwhelming majority of countries both in the OECD area and in the rest of the world still have at least some publicly owned electricity companies. Public ownership and a high degree of vertical and horizontal integration generally go hand in hand. State ownership and a highly integrated, centralised structure enable the authorities to retain direct control over the industry. Most countries that have introduced market reforms have also privatised at least some parts of the industry – except where the industry was largely privately owned already.

The structure of cross-ownership of electricity and other utilities, within and across national borders, can be complex in some countries, involving both public and private companies. Usually, subsidiary or sister companies operate at arm's length, for commercial reasons or because of regulatory requirements aimed at ensuring non-discriminatory access to networks and competition among generators and suppliers. Some utilities also hold stakes in electricity services companies.

2.3. Typologies

Today, there is a considerable diversity of industry structure and ownership across countries. This reflects primarily historical differences in the development of the electricity industry, the stage reached in the liberalisation process, the regulatory framework and the overall business and investment climate. Table 3.1 provides a snapshot of the typology of the electricity supply industry as it is

Table 3.1. **Industry structure and ownership in the world's 15 largest national electricity markets**

	Electricity consumption, 2003 (TWh)	Horizontal integration				Vertical integration (structural)	Ownership of infrastructure (predominant)
		Generation	Transmission	Distribution	Supply		
United States	3 475	Mixed	Low	Low	Mixed	Mixed	Private
China	1 483	High/moderate	High	Moderate	Moderate	High	Public
Japan	934	Moderate	Moderate	Moderate	High	High	Private
Russian Federation	632	High	High	High	High	High	Public
Germany	509	Moderate	Moderate	Low	High	Mixed	Mixed
Canada	504	Moderate	Moderate	Moderate	Mixed	High	Public
India	418	High	High	High	High	High	Public
France	408	High	High	High	High	High	Public
UK	337	Low	High	Low	Low	Moderate	Private
Brazil	329	Moderate	High	Low	Low	Moderate	Private
Korea	318	Moderate	High	High	Low	High	Public
Italy	291	Moderate	High	High	Moderate	High	Public
Spain	218	Moderate	High	Moderate	Moderate	Moderate	Private
Australia	190	Low	Moderate	Mixed	Low	Moderate	Private
Chinese Taipei	182	High	High	High	High	High	Public

Note: Mixed means that different utilities have different degrees of vertical and/or horizontal integration; *moderate* means that generation, transmission, distribution and supply are not fully integrated vertically or horizontally within each utility or country.

Source: IEA (2005a); Menecon Consulting analysis.

currently organised with respect to the degree of horizontal and vertical integration and the ownership of physical assets in the 15 largest countries world wide by domestic consumption. These countries account for just under three-quarters of total final electricity consumption world wide.

Among these countries, vertical integration is usually more pronounced than horizontal integration. In some countries, reforms have required or encouraged the break up of the horizontally integrated structure of power generation or supply, either through the divestment of assets or through new entrants, while allowing a degree of vertical integration to remain, at least for the time being. In several EU countries, for example, distribution and retail supply remain partially integrated, though this will change when full retail competition is introduced in July 2007. In other cases, it is down to the regionalisation of the industry within a given country. In China, for example, there exist several provincial utilities responsible for power generation, regional transmission, local distribution and marketing within clearly demarcated areas.

In general, transmission and distribution are more integrated horizontally than generation or supply because market reforms have generally not involved any requirement on the incumbent utilities to divest assets, as these activities are considered to be natural monopolies. In many countries, the authorities have organised transmission into a single monopoly company with responsibility for the entire country or state, in order to exploit economies of scale and facilitate network planning and operation. Distribution is usually less integrated than transmission, especially in big countries, as it is carried out in geographically distinct areas.

Market reforms are generally most advanced and the degree of vertical and horizontal integration lowest in OECD countries, though reforms have stalled or are progressing slowly in several of them. Today, the United Kingdom, where reforms were first introduced, has perhaps the most competitive market with a relatively low level of public ownership. In several EU countries, including France, Germany and Spain, contestability and the intensity of competition remain limited, and the industry remains largely in public hands. Korea today has one the most integrated electricity sectors in the OECD area, though the government is pressing ahead with plans to privatise state companies and promote competition.

Most non-OECD countries have taken steps in recent years to liberalise their electricity industries, but few of them have succeeded in establishing truly competitive markets even at the wholesale level. In China, the Russian Federation, India, Brazil and Chinese Taipei – the five largest non-OECD electricity consuming countries – the industry is highly integrated and predominately publicly owned.

3. Principal drivers of change

3.1. Rising electricity demand and investment needs

Business models in the electricity supply industry will be influenced by sector with rising electricity demand and investment needs in all major world regions. The International Energy Agency (IEA) projects that global electricity demand will grow at an average annual rate of 2.5% through to 2030 in a Reference Scenario, which assumes no new government policies are adopted. In this scenario, the world consumes twice as much electricity in 2030 as it does today. Developing countries and emerging market economies are expected to account for most of the increase in global demand. Their electricity consumption is projected to grow at about the same rate as their GDP, so that it more than triples by 2030. In the OECD area, the projected pace of demand growth is markedly slower, at 1.4% per year. Nonetheless, the 1.3 billion people in the OECD would still be consuming more electricity than the 6.5 billion people in the developing world a quarter century from now. Outside the OECD area, the Asian economies experience the highest growth in electricity demand. Increasing economic activity, partly linked to rising population, is the main factor behind higher demand in all regions. The Reference Scenario projections assume that the world economy grows on average by 3.2% through to 2030.

In an Alternative Scenario, which assumes that governments around the world adopt policies to curb energy demand for energy security and environmental reasons, electricity demand grows less rapidly. In 2030, electricity demand is 12% lower than in the Reference Scenario, an increase of 70% over 2003 compared with 94% in the Reference Scenario. The annual average rate of growth, at 2%, is 0.5 percentage points lower than in the Reference Scenario. Energy-efficiency measures for industrial processes, appliances and lighting are the main causes of these saving in all regions.

Factors other than government policies could lead to significantly faster or slower growth in electricity demand than projected in these scenarios.[5] For example, climate change could result in pronounced changes in demand for electricity for heating and cooling in the long term. This would have major implications for the amount and type of investment needed as well as policies for ensuring energy security (see Section 5.4). Similarly, faster economic growth – especially in developing regions – could boost electricity demand and infrastructure needs.

The rate of growth of demand will determine how much investment is needed in supply infrastructure. Projected demand growth in the Reference Scenario implies a need for total cumulative investment in electricity infrastructure world wide of USD 9.8 trillion in year-2000 dollars over 2003-30, equal to about USD 350 billion per year. Developing countries account for more than half of world electricity investment. China needs the largest increase, exceeding USD 2 trillion (Figure 3.2). New investment is also substantial in North America and Europe. More than half of global electricity investment is required in transmission and distribution networks. The share of transmission and distribution is generally highest in non-OECD countries, where there is the greatest need to extend and expand existing networks. In the Alternative Scenario, worldwide cumulative investment is about USD 1.5 trillion (in year-2000 dollars), or almost 16%, less than in the Reference Scenario. Although the average unit capital cost of power generation is 14% higher in the Alternative Policy Scenario than in the Reference Scenario (because of the greater use of more capital-intensive nuclear power, renewables and distributed generation), this effect is more than offset by slower demand growth, which reduces the need for new power plants and new network capacity.

Figure 3.2. **Cumulative electricity investment by region, 2003-30**

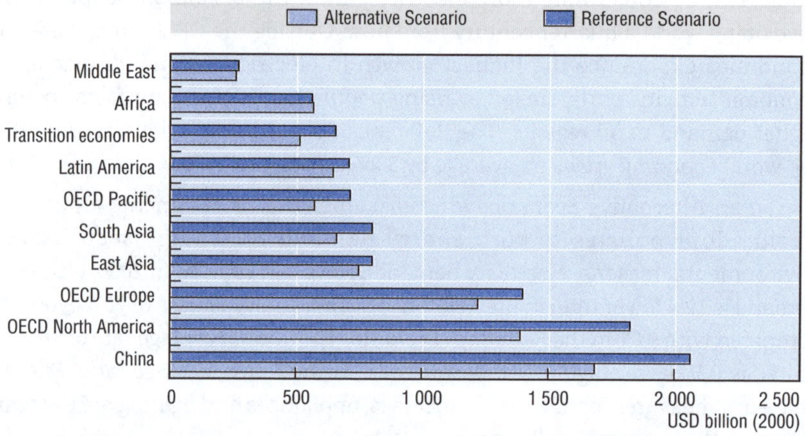

Source: IEA (2004).

There is no certainty that all of the investment needed will, in fact, be forthcoming – in either scenario. If actual investment falls short of that required or is delayed, some part of demand might go unmet, leading to temporary or persistent power shortages. The main uncertainties surrounding the adequacy of electricity investment world wide relate to the impact of liberalisation and market reforms, which will affect incentives to invest and access to capital. Any shortfalls in investment, especially where the industry is state owned, might lead to pressure to reorganise the sector, possibly involving opening it up to private capital. Environmental policies, notably affecting the siting of new power plants and transmission lines as well as airborne emissions, may also constrain investment. Investment opportunities and incentives will, in turn, affect the evolution of business models, regionally and globally.

3.2. *Corporatisation and privatisation*

The way in which state-owned electricity utilities are run and government policies on allowing private companies to invest in the sector will be of major importance to how business models evolve – especially in developing countries and emerging market economies. Corporatisation and privatisation have been widely adopted in the past two decades as ways of achieving more efficiency in electricity supply. Corporatisation involves the reorganisation of state-owned assets and the transfer of responsibility for operating them from a government ministry to a separate commercially oriented entity. This can be either a transitional step towards, or an alternative to, privatisation. Where privatisation is the objective, the assets are allocated to a joint stock company and the shares transferred to the treasury before they are sold. In either case, the aim is to introduce management and accounting structures and disciplines, and to improve operational efficiency. In practice, corporatisation and privatisation can have a dramatic impact on the way the industry operates.

Corporatisation

Corporatisation aims to separate the two roles of the state: as the owner and as the regulator. Where there is no such separation, there is a risk that the government will use its control of the industry to pursue social objectives for short-term political reasons, often in an *ad hoc* and non-transparent way. The most common example of this phenomenon is the direct imposition of price caps that results in operating losses that have to be financed out of the state budget. This creates conflicts between its responsibility to maintain a financially viable electricity industry and protect taxpayers' interest on the one hand, and its responsibility to protect consumers' interest in the short and long term on the other. In India, large subsidies to electricity consumers – notably farmers and households – have caused the state electricity boards to incur huge financial losses, which have undermined the boards' ability to invest, to meet growing demand for electricity and to maintain reliable supply.

Generally, publicly owned corporations have a statutory objective to be commercially successful businesses and to maximise the net worth of the assets. They normally have a management structure similar to that of a private company, with an independent board of directors elected by the representatives of the shareholders (municipal, state or central government). The board is responsible for service delivery and commercial performance. The corporation would typically agree with the shareholders on strategic goals by means of a planning agreement or agreed business plans. In this way, the corporation operates at arm's length from the public authorities.

In contrast to electricity boards controlled directly by a ministry, commercial functions are separated from any social obligations the government may impose, such as price discounts for poor households, which would then be funded separately. In practice, however, there remains considerable scope for governments to intervene in the day-to-day running of the electricity utility. For example, the government may decide to extract an exceptional unplanned dividend in response to short-term budgetary pressures, undermining the utility's ability to meet its investment and performance targets. Moreover, corporatisation does not by itself provide incentives for the utility to behave efficiently or competitively.

Privatisation

Privatisation policies are driven by two main forces. First, the perception exists that state ownership is a barrier to efforts to supply electricity efficiently and at the lowest possible cost to end-users – in large part because of political interference in the running of the business. Second, the highly capital-intensive nature of the industry places a heavy financing burden on the government, which may want to give priority to other sectors and types of spending in allocating scarce capital. Rising electricity demand in developing countries and emerging market economies will increase the pressure on governments to look to the private sector for at least part of the capital needed to expand infrastructure. In addition to relieving the financial obligation, privatisation may also yield a substantial one-off injection of cash into the state coffers. In most cases, privatisation has been accompanied by market reforms aimed at promoting competition in the construction of electricity infrastructure and provision of electricity supply services. This is likely to remain the case in the future.

There are various ways in which electricity companies can be privatised. The first issue to be addressed is whether to restructure the utility (or industry in the case of a fully integrated monopoly) before selling it, with a view to introducing market reforms aimed at creating the conditions for competition to develop (see below). Experience around the world has shown that restructuring is far easier prior to privatisation. The UK government decided to restructure the industry before privatising it in 1990 at the same time as introducing market reforms. In contrast, the French government did not undertake any major restructuring before selling off a tranche of shares in the state-owned utility, Électricité de France (EdF), in 2005.

In many cases, privatisation involves only the generation and distribution companies, with transmission-related activities (including dispatch and, in some cases, operation of the wholesale pool or spot market) kept under state ownership and control following corporatisation of the entire industry. For example, the recent restructuring of the Pakistan Water and Power Development Authority resulted in the creation of a structurally separate National

Transmission and Dispatch Company, a commercial enterprise that will remain in state ownership. In contrast, the three generation and eight distribution companies created at the same time are due to be privatised in the near future.

Other important issues include to whom the assets are to be sold and how, and the size of the stakes to be sold. Public flotations have been the most popular approach in most countries where sales have been large. This has often fitted with policies aimed at extending share ownership generally or, in the case of the former communist bloc countries, with the goal of redistributing wealth among the population. In many cases, a tranche of shares is reserved for institutional investors in order to ensure a degree of stability in ownership and effective oversight of management in the longer term. In the case of smaller companies, governments usually prefer to sell the assets directly to a single buyer – typically a well-established firm in the industry either domestically or internationally – to ensure that the privatised entity will be properly managed. Whatever the preferred approach to selling the assets, the government may decide to sell the state's entire stake, a majority of the shares or a minority – for practical or political reasons. Recent large electricity privatisations in France and Italy have involved minority stakes. In Italy, the decision to sell off an initial stake of about 30% in the national utility, ENEL, in 1999 was driven by practical considerations related to such a large flotation. Subsequent share offerings have reduced the state's stake to about 20%. In France, the government decided to limit the sale of shares in EdF to 10% in the face of strong opposition from the trade unions to the state losing its majority control of the company.

Privatisation and, to a lesser extent, corporatisation will remain controversial policies. Efforts to privatise electricity infrastructure – and other economic sectors – have often met with fierce political, social and institutional opposition. Most recently, there have been public protests in China, India, Indonesia, Korea, Thailand, Peru, Ecuador and Paraguay. Such opposition usually rests on arguments about economic nationalism and the strategic advantages of direct government control of the sector, fears of job losses associated with a more commercial approach to the business and concerns that prices may increase (Buresch, 2003). Underpricing of assets in past programmes and in other sectors or countries has contributed to public resistance to electricity privatisation.

Scepticism concerning the supposed benefits of privatisation is supported by research suggesting that public or private ownership makes little difference to efficiency of public utilities generally.[6] As a result of public opposition and doubts about the effectiveness of privatisation, governments have either abandoned plans or are proceeding more slowly and carefully with privatisation programmes, while placing more emphasis on explaining the long-term benefits of privatisation to the general public (Section 4). International financial institutions, including the World Bank, are now noticeably more cautious about supporting heavy reliance on private investment in the electricity sectors (World Bank, 2004). It seems likely that power companies in many developing countries will remain in public ownership for the foreseeable future.

3.3. Market and regulatory reform

Market and regulatory reforms will remain the primary driver of changing business models in OECD countries and in many other parts of the world. In most cases, the implementation of reforms is far from complete and their effects on sector organisation and structure are not yet fully evident. Although experience so far suggests that competition in electricity generation and supply can in principle bring major benefits through gains in efficiency and lower prices, there are growing concerns about whether the new business and regulatory models that are emerging involve adequate incentives for investment in generating and network capacity as market players adapt to the new environment.

The term "liberalisation" is normally used to describe a process involving the opening up of the electricity to both private investment and to competition between generators and possibly between suppliers too. Market reform, and the accompanying regulatory reform, normally refers only to the introduction of competition. In fact, the two elements are distinct: it is possible to privatise or allow private investment in the electricity sector without introducing competition and *vice versa*. Nonetheless, where market reforms have been introduced into a predominately state-owned industry, it has usually been preceded by privatisation. This was the case in Chile and the United Kingdom – the first countries to privatise their electricity industries, in the 1980s. A notable exception is New South Wales, where state-owned power generators were broken up and transformed into public corporations, and competition introduced at the wholesale (through participation in Australia's National Electricity Market) and retail levels.

Competition in various forms

Competition in the electricity sector can take different forms. At a minimum, it can involve a competitive tendering process for the long-term supply of wholesale electricity from independent power plants. The process may be organised by the authorities or by the incumbent utility that holds monopoly rights over transmission. This approach was adopted by the United States in 1978, with the adoption of the Public Utility Regulatory Policies Act (PURPA), which enabled utilities to choose between building their own capacity or contracting with independent producers under long-term contracts. Many other countries subsequently chose this route.

In most OECD countries – including the United States – and several non-OECD countries, reforms are being taken much further, with the extension of competition to real-time wholesale supply and, in some cases, also to retail supply under a system of open or third-party access to physical power networks. This has been achieved through the establishment of wholesale markets in electricity supply and related activities. Generators are free to sell power to wholesalers, retailers or directly to end-users. Generators, wholesale suppliers and retailers remunerate the transmission and distribution network operators for the actual use of their services, based on a pre-determined schedule of charges, in some cases adjusted *ex post* according to capacity constraints and actual grid losses. Independent regulators normally play a critical role in overseeing compliance with electricity laws, ensuring that the market operates efficiently and fairly, and in establishing cost-based network tariffs. With this approach, existing or new generators are free to decide when, where and how much capacity to build, subject to licensing procedures and conditions.

Process of market and regulatory reform

The process of market and regulatory reform involves several key components:

- The vertical separation of competitive segments (generation and supply) from the natural monopoly regulated segments (distribution, transmission and system operation), either through legal unbundling of the network entities or through unbundling of ownership. The latter is often considered to be a more effective way of ensuring that network operators do not discriminate in granting third parties access to the network. Unbundling effectively replaces the centralised decision-making system found in vertically integrated utilities with a decentralised system in which a number of players make commercial decisions within a markets framework.
- The reorganisation of transmission and network operations to create a geographically inclusive wholesale market and the establishment of a single system operator to manage the operation of the entire network, to schedule generation and dispatch power to meet actual load, and to maintain frequency, voltage and stability of the network. Where the network is not structurally (or legally) unbundled from generation and retailing, an independent system operator is typically established to handle dispatch so as to ensure non-discriminatory access.
- The setting up of a formal wholesale market in electricity and operating reserves to support the need for real-time balancing of supply and demand, to handle unplanned outages of transmission or generating facilities and to facilitate economically efficient trade among generators, wholesaler buyers and sellers, and retailers. The wholesale market determines a price for

power supplied for any given time period (and possibly delivery point, or node, on the transmission system) according to the marginal cost of supply to meet estimated load.

- Unbundling of retail tariffs for retail power supplies and network services to ensure non-discriminatory access by third parties to the network and a level playing field for competitors in supplying end-users. Retailers buy their power in wholesale markets, or own generating facilities to support their retail supply commitments, and deliver the power for a fee over the regulated distribution network. Where retail competition is restricted to large consumers, distribution companies remain responsible for supplying other customers by purchasing power in wholesale markets. In the case of full retail competition, no end-user has any direct contractual relationship with the network operators (Figure 3.3).
- The design and implementation of detailed regulatory rules and institutions to promote access to the transmission network by third parties, including mechanisms to allocate scarce transmission capacity and procedures for determining the use-of-network charges.

Figure 3.3. **Contractual relationships and physical electricity flows in a competitive market with full structural unbundling and retail competition**

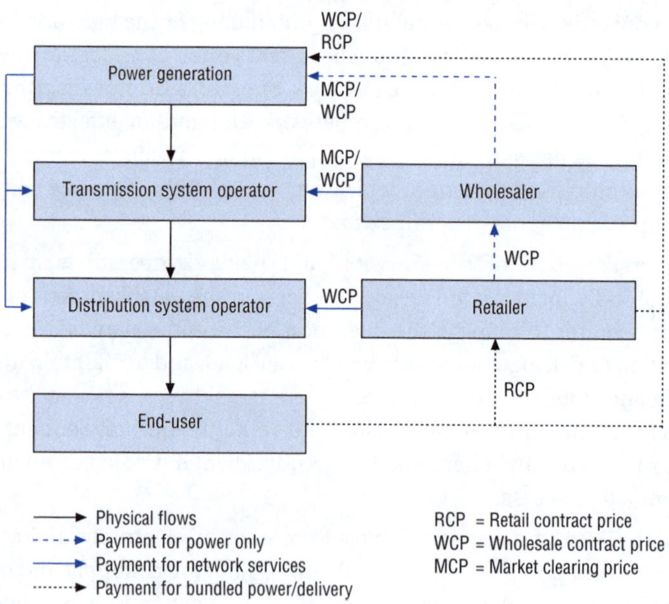

Source: Menecon Consulting analysis.

Country experiences

England and Wales pioneered the introduction of wholesale competition in 1990, with the extension of retail competition to all consumers being completed in 1999 (Box 3.1). Norway followed in 1991 and was joined by the other Scandinavian countries – Sweden, Finland and Denmark – in Nordpool during the second half of the 1990s. In Australia, regional competitive markets were launched in 1994 and the National Electricity Market started in 1998. In North America, several markets in the north-east of the United States were formed in the late 1990s, the largest of which operates across Pennsylvania, New Jersey and Maryland (PJM). The Californian market opened in 1998, but was suspended following the catastrophic power shortages of 2001. Texas and the Canadian province of Alberta opened their markets in 2001.

Member countries of the European Union are opening up their markets to competition at varying speeds. Under a 2003 directive, they are legally required to introduce full retail competition from 1 July 2007. However, competition is actually developing only very slowly, as evidenced by the limited degree of switching by eligible customers to alternative suppliers and the continuing dominance of the traditional incumbent utilities (Box 3.2). Japan launched electricity market reform towards the end of the 1990s. The 2003 Electricity Utility Network Law sets out the time frame for the full roll-out of retail competition by 2007. End-users accounting for more than two-thirds of total electricity consumption are already eligible to choose their supplier. Faster development of competition in both Europe and Japan will hinge on more proactive measures by regulators and policy makers to reduce the dominance of the big generators in regional and national markets (see Section 5).

Experience in Great Britain, Australia, Scandinavia, the north-eastern United States and elsewhere suggests that the process of market and regulatory reform involves three distinct phases. The initial phase, which may take several years, involves political negotiations, the adoption of formal legislation, the creation of new regulatory institutions, the preparation and implementation of regulations and the design and establishment of technical and management systems. This is followed by a phase of market development, involving the fine-tuning of wholesale trading arrangements, the gradual opening up of retail markets and the emergence of a number of competing generators and suppliers. The final phase involves a maturing of the market and the regulatory framework. It is debatable whether any market has passed beyond the second phase. In reality, the full process of market reform culminating in the establishment of a robust and relatively stable market might last at least one to two decades, and perhaps as long as the economic lifetime of existing assets.

Monitoring, oversight and decision making by governments and regulators will continue to drive the development of the electricity sector. How market

Box 3.1. **Development of competition and restructuring in the British electricity market**

The English and Wales monopoly utility, the Central Electricity Generating Board, was corporatised, restructured and then privatised under the 1989 Electricity Act, creating three generating companies, one transmission company and 12 regional distributors. The Act also established a competitive trading system, known as the pool. It also granted the right to consumers above 1 MW access to the grid. Eligibility was gradually extended, covering all end-users from June 1999. In 1993, the largest generator, National Power, agreed to divest capacity in order to increase competition in the pool and avoid an anti-trust inquiry. In 1998, the National Power and PowerGen, the other main non-nuclear generator, agreed to divest more capacity in return for approval to buy shares in the regional distributors. These divestitures had the effect of partially re-integrating the industry vertically, while reducing the degree of horizontal integration. The entry during the 1990s of a number of new independent power producers that built gas-fired power stations further reduced the shares of the three big generators in total generating capacity, from 91% in 1990 to 37% in 2004.

Following a detailed review by the regulator of the functioning of the pool, the government decided to redesign the trading arrangements to prevent dominant generators from "gaming" the pool and to lower prices. In 2001, the pool was replaced by a fundamentally different system, called the New Electricity Trading Arrangements (NETA). NETA replaced the obligation on generators to dispatch power through the pool with a voluntary, decentralised, bilateral trading system. The only formal market under NETA is for balancing, operated by ELEXON (a subsidiary of National Grid Company), in which prices are set through an auction. A capacity payment mechanism that had been set up with the pool, which had proved prone to manipulation by the dominant generators, was scrapped.

It was hoped that informal over-the-counter markets for different market segments, corresponding to the length of time before actual dispatch, would develop. In practice, however, spot trading has remained illiquid. One day-head exchange, called APX, is currently in operation, but trading volumes are very small. This has raised concerns about price transparency and, therefore, pricing efficiency, as well as transaction costs. Day-ahead balancing prices are nonetheless publicly available from ELEXON. Prices fell significantly immediately after NETA came into effect, though the extent to which NETA was responsible is still a matter of debate. Questions remain about the efficiency of the balancing market in signalling scarcity of capacity. In April 2005, NETA became BETTA (British Electricity Trading and Transmission Arrangements), with the integration of Scotland.

The British electricity supply industry has recently continued to re-integrate vertically, with large generating companies acquiring retail-supply businesses. The main driver of this trend appears to be the need for generators to hedge against fuel-input and wholesale electricity price movements. They can achieve this by securing the retail market for their physical output, through the acquisition of a retailer – despite the high transaction costs and the inflexibility associated with such a strategy. To some extent, this may reflect the lack of cost-effective alternatives in the form of liquid financial contract markets.

Box 3.2. **Obstacles to the development of competition in the EU electricity market**

Electricity market reform is progressing at varying speeds across the European Union. An EC directive adopted in 1996 together with a second directive and regulation on cross-border trade adopted in 2003 set minimum requirements for market reform. By 1 July 2004, EU countries were required to open their electricity markets to retail competition for all non-household consumers, to establish at least legal unbundling of the transmission system and set up an independent regulator. The deadline for countries to complete full retail market opening is 1 July 2007. Some countries have gone further and quicker, but the majority of member states have missed, or are likely to miss, EC deadlines. In general, competition has developed very slowly, markets are illiquid, and prices have not come down as much as originally hoped – notwithstanding the general rise in fossil fuel prices on international markets.

The European Commission has identified several obstacles to the development of a truly competitive single market in electricity (EC, 2005a and 2005b):

- A lack of integration between national markets, reflected in the absence of price convergence across the EU and the low level of cross-border trade. This is generally due to the existence of barriers to entry, inadequate use of existing infrastructure and insufficient interconnection between many member states, resulting in congestion.
- A high degree of concentration of the industry in many countries, impeding the development of effective competition. Switching by end-users – especially small consumers – remains limited and the market share of new suppliers from other member states remains small in most member states.
- Unbundling rules are not yet fully effective in practice, partly as a result of the late implementation of the directives by some member states. In around half of the member states, ownership of the transmission network is structurally unbundled (Table 3.2). However, most have taken advantage of derogations, by exempting smaller distributors from both legal and functional unbundling and postponing legal unbundling for larger distributors until July 2007.

In April 2006, the EC announced 48 legal challenges in one of the biggest court assaults ever initiated by Brussels. Most of the cases concern specific market practices, such as whether governments have implemented unbundling legislation adequately. Spain and Luxembourg already face action before the European Court of Justice over infringements in implementing unbundling rules. The EC has also launched an inquiry into electricity competition, focusing on the functioning of wholesale markets. The inquiry will consider the extent to which the lack of market integration and cross-border trade affects prices and barriers to market entry. Concerns about market concentration and dominant players are growing with the announcement of several large mergers and rising national protectionism surrounding corporate takeover attempts in France and Spain (see Section 4.1).

Table 3.2. **Status of electricity market reform in EU countries as of January 2005**

	Declared market opening (% of total)	Large eligible customers switch[1]	Small eligible customers switch[1]	Unbundling	
				Transmission	Distribution
Austria	100	22 (78)[2]	3	Legal	Legal
Belgium	c. 90	35	19[3]	Legal	Legal
Denmark	100	> 50	5	Ownership	Legal
Finland	100	> 50	Not known	Ownership	Accounting
France	70	22	Market not yet open	Legal	Management
Germany	100	35 (65)[2]	6 (25-50)[2]	Legal	Accounting
Greece	62	0	Market not yet open	Legal	None
Ireland	56	> 50	1	Legal	Management
Italy	79	c. 15	Market not yet open	Ownership	Legal
Luxembourg	57	10	Market not yet open	Legal	Management
Netherlands	100	30	35	Ownership	Legal
Portugal	100	9	1	Legal	Accounting
Spain	100	18	0 (18)[2]	Ownership	Legal
Sweden	100	> 50	Not known	Ownership	Legal
United Kingdom	100	> 50	> 50	Ownership	Legal
Estonia	10	0	Market not yet open	Legal	Legal
Latvia	76	0	Market not yet open	Legal	Accounting
Lithuania	Not known	17	Market not yet open	Ownership	Legal
Poland	52	10	Market not yet open	Legal	Accounting
Czech Republic	47	Not known	Market not yet open	Ownership	Accounting
Slovak Republic	66	10	4	Legal	Management
Hungary	67	24	Market not yet open	Ownership	Accounting
Slovenia	75	10	Market not yet open	Ownership	Accounting

1. Since market opening. The split between large and small customers is around 1 GWh/year.
2. Others that have renegotiated in parentheses.
3. Flanders only.

Source: EC (2005a and 2005b).

players anticipate policy and regulatory developments and respond to the risks they generate will have major implications for business models. A strong reaffirmation of political commitment to reform can create the necessary market response and avert actions that could undermine the long-term development of competition. But political interventions to address short-term issues – such as price caps to protect consumers from market volatility – can have a detrimental impact on investment, market stability and supply security (IEA, 2005a).

Measuring the success of reforms

How successful market reforms are judged to be will clearly have an enormous impact on future policy directions and, therefore, business models. It is misleading to take a snapshot of the industry at a particular stage of the reform process and use that as proof of success or failure. Nonetheless, evidence from a number of markets that have made good progress in implementing reforms suggests that they have had a significant positive impact on industry performance, when those reforms have been designed and implemented well. The performance improvements have stemmed from a combination of market, regulatory and organisational reforms, including privatisation or corporatisation of state-owned utilities and the introduction of competitive pressures (Joskow, 2003). These improvements have been manifested in a number of ways, including more efficient planning of generating and network capacity, construction of infrastructure and operation of those assets; reduced thermal and network losses; lower operating and maintenance costs through improvements in labour productivity; lower prices to end-users; and the extension of electricity service to households previously denied service. In some developing countries, investment has increased sharply, relieving shortages of capacity and boosting economic development.

Reforms have also run into serious problems and led to disappointing results in some cases, making ongoing adjustments necessary. During the first two phases of market reform, problems with abuse of market power have frequently emerged, which have had to be addressed through changes to the design of trading systems and legal or regulatory action to reduce horizontal integration and market concentration. Efforts to mitigate market power with restrictions on bidding behaviour and price caps, rather than with structural remedies, have often caused more harm than good by discouraging investment in new generating capacity. The ability to finance independent, or merchant, power plants has emerged as a major obstacle to market entry (see next section). Many markets have also encountered a supply crisis – often resulting in blackouts or brownouts – which effectively serves as a test of the robustness of the new market structure. In some countries, especially those with relatively immature electricity sectors, reforms have been delayed or suspended. How governments deal with these issues will directly affect utilities' business strategies and the organisation of the sector. Section 5 considers the main challenges facing policy makers and regulators.

3.4. *Technological and cost developments*

Developments in technology – particularly in power generation – and costs of supply will continue to have a major impact on the structure of the electricity industry. Traditionally, power generation was dominated by very large centralised fossil fuel, nuclear and hydroelectric plants. The emergence of combined-cycle gas-turbine (CCGT) technology, using natural gas as the fuel input, has dramatically altered the structure of the industry in many parts of the world. Upheavals in international energy markets and surging fossil fuel prices could have major consequences for future choices of technology and fuels.

Decisions about new generating capacity are largely driven by financial evaluations of different technologies and fuels, taking into account market, technical and policy risks. In competitive markets, the smaller economic size and shorter construction times of CCGT plants – together with their lower overall production costs – made them the favoured option for new capacity in many parts of the world, at least until the recent surge in gas prices (Figure 3.4). CCGTs account for almost all the new fossil fuel fired capacity brought on line in North America and Europe in the last ten years.

Figure 3.4. **Indicative mid-term generating costs of new power plants**

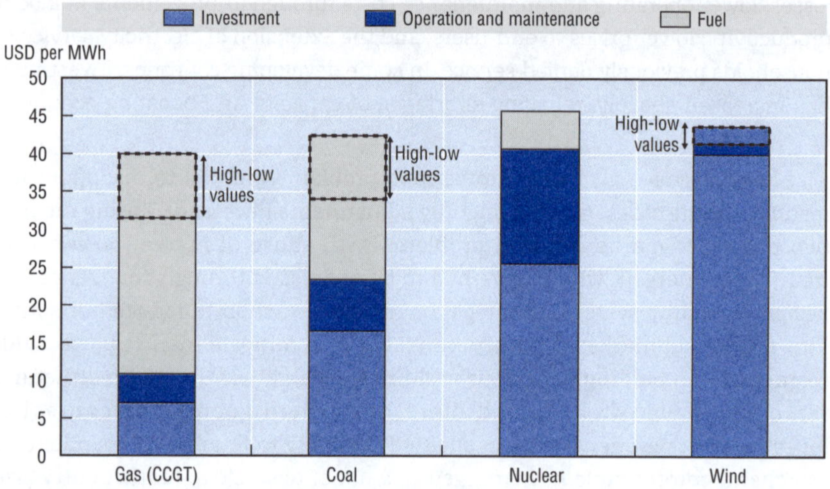

Note: Assumes a natural gas price in the range of USD 3.00-4.50/Mbtu, a coal price of between USD 35 and USD 60/ton, and a discount rate of 7%.
Source: IEA (2004).

Higher gas prices since 2003, in absolute terms and relative to coal, and concerns about the long-term availability of gas in several major markets have curbed the interest in building more gas-fired capacity and boosted the competitiveness of coal-fired plant, nuclear power and renewables technologies. If prices were to remain at current levels, all three options would most likely see their shares in generation increase significantly. In most parts of the world, hydropower and wind power are the most competitive of various renewable technologies under development. But advances in biomass, solar thermal and photovoltaic power and other advanced technologies could boost their market prospects in the longer term. The latest Reference Scenario projections from the International Energy Agency show a marginal increase in the share of renewable technologies in power generation from around 18% at present to 19% in 2030 (IEA, 2004). The US Department of Energy projects the share to remain broadly constant through to 2025 (DOE/EIA, 2006). Both organisations project the share of non-hydro renewables to increase significantly: from about 2% to 6% in 2030, according to the IEA.

Distributed generation

The growth of small-scale renewables-based generation technologies, as well as other forms of distributed generation, such as small-scale fossil-based co-generation plants and fuel cells, could radically alter the structure of the electricity industry. Distributed generation represents a small share of the electricity market today, but the wide range of potential applications and favourable government policies for combined heat and power and for renewable energy technologies could boost their market share over the coming decades.

Policy makers in many countries are actively encouraging the development and deployment of distributed generation, because of the economic, environmental and energy-security benefits they can bring. On-site power production by fossil fuels generates waste heat that can be used by the customer, reducing overall primary energy needs. Distributed generation may also be better positioned to use inexpensive fuels that would otherwise go to waste, such as landfill gas. Distributed generation facilities located at an end-user's site or at a local distribution utility, and supplying power directly to the local distribution network, can also reduce the need to invest in long-distance high-tension transmission lines. Increased use of distributed generation technologies could avoid around USD 130 billion (in year-2000 dollars) of global investment in transmission networks between 2001 and 2030 – equal to 8% of total transmission investment (IEA, 2003). The reliability of electric power systems can be enhanced by distributed generation, as the system is less dependent on centralised facilities. The use of distributed generators at selected locations can also help distributors overcome local bottlenecks. However, distributed generation has some drawbacks, which may limit the extent to which it will penetrate the power generation market. Unit capital costs per kilowatt can be higher than for large plants, especially if any associated heat is not captured and used. For some types of technology, there is a need for reserve capacity to deal with the non-availability of distributed power because of operating variability, where power output is tied to heat demand, and natural intermittency (such as with wind power).

The widespread deployment of distributed generation would require profound changes in the way the electricity networks are organised, constructed and operated. Networks would operate in a much more decentralised manner. This could expand opportunities for small generators. More power would be generated and managed by the system operator at low voltages. In such a system, the high-voltage network would need to provide back-up for the local decentralised systems.

The opening up of the retail market to competition, allowing access by generators and end-users to the local network, and appropriate regulation may prove critical to the development of distributed generation. If market reforms are limited to wholesale liberalisation, the incentives for distributed generators would depend on the terms and conditions offered by the monopoly distribution company. Government policies may oblige the distributor to offer favourable terms, but this approach is unlikely to be economically efficient as the price signals would not reflect market conditions. For example, excess capacity in the Dutch market can at least partly be attributed to policies that encouraged the creation of decentralised generation regardless of need (IEA, 2002).

In some markets that have not been fully liberalised, only high-voltage consumers have the ability to choose suppliers. Smaller customers and independent producers are required to notify the incumbent vertically integrated utility of their intent to install distributed generation facilities. The utility may respond by offering to discount the regulated electricity price in order to discourage the installation of those facilities. Distribution companies that continue to own generating capacity to supply their customers directly will also have an incentive to discriminate against distributed generators. Separation of distribution from generation and retail removes this incentive to discriminate. Conversely, a restriction on distributors owning and operating small generating plants may result in some inefficiencies. In certain cases, for example, the operation of distributed generation at a transformer station to relieve distribution system congestion may be the most efficient solution.

3.5. *Cross-border trade and network interconnections*

The development of interconnections between national or regional networks and the subsequent expansion of cross-border trade will be both a major driver and a consequence of structural change throughout the electricity supply industry in many parts of the world. Rising electricity demand will expand opportunities for profitable investments in interconnectors in liberalised markets. But how much new capacity is actually built and used will depend to a large extent on the regulatory framework.

International trade can bring important mutual economic benefits by exploiting comparative advantages. This yields a more efficient allocation of overall investment in transmission and generation and the creation of a larger, more liquid wholesale electricity market. Cross-border transmission can be an economically efficient alternative to building new generation capacity in a home market, where lower-cost spare capacity exists in a neighbouring market. For many countries, cross-border trade will be an important means of realising benefits from market reform, especially for small countries with geographically close neighbours; cross-border trade may prove to be the easiest and quickest way to enhance competition by enhancing the size of the market. The

Pennsylvania-New Jersey-Maryland (PJM) Interconnection provides an example of how network integration paved the way for the development of a wholesale market (Box 3.3).

Box 3.3. **Wholesale market development in the PJM Interconnection**

PJM is a power pool that co-ordinates trade between the states of Pennsylvania, New Jersey, Maryland and Delaware. It was actually formed in 1927 but only started to transform itself into an independent organisation in 1993, primarily through the formation of the PJM Interconnection Association to administer the power pool. PJM became a fully independent body in 1997, when a bid-based wholesale spot market for power was launched. PJM was the first independent system operator in the United States to be approved by the Federal Energy Regulatory Commission (FERC) under Order 888, which restructured the wholesale electricity business. In 2002, PJM was officially recognised as a regional transmission operator.

The initial day-ahead spot market was based on a single market-clearing price for the entire region. High costs for congestion management and poor operational flexibility in the utilisation of the system, largely due to security restrictions, led to the introduction of locational (or nodal) marginal pricing (LMP) based on reported costs, in which market-clearing prices were calculated for each node in the system. In 1999, a capacity market was introduced involving daily, monthly and multimonthly auctions, as well as a new pricing system based on competitive bidding. In 2000, the day-ahead market was extended with the introduction of a real-time market and a market for spinning reserves. In 1999, PJM introduced an auction of allocated financial transmission rights, enabling market participants to hedge price risk across nodes. These were replaced in 2003 with a more sophisticated system of auction revenue rights.

The geographical coverage and trading volume of the PJM market has grown considerably since its inception. In 2002, Allegheny Power joined PJM, added more regions of Pennsylvania, large parts of West Virginia, parts of Virginia and small parts of Ohio. In the same year, American Electric Power, Commonwealth Edison (Com Ed), Illinois Power and National Grid agreed with PJM to develop an independent transmission company that would operate within a western part of the PJM system. Dominion also joined PJM, integrating a large share of the electricity system in Virginia and a small share in North Carolina into PJM's system and market operation. These moves were completed in 2004-05. The integration of Com Ed alone expanded PJM's market by 20%. Midwest ISO (MISO) and PJM have worked together since 2004, with the aim of developing an integrated wholesale market across 24 states and the province of Manitoba in Canada. MISO launched a LMP-based market in 2005. Today, PJM serves approximately 51 million people, dispatching 163 806 MW of generating capacity over 56 070 miles of transmission lines.

Most of the states covered by the PJM market have decided to introduce retail access for all consumers. The first state was New Jersey, in 1999, followed by Pennsylvania, the District of Columbia, Delaware, Ohio, Maryland and Illinois between 2000 and 2004.

Source: PJM website *www.pjm.com.*

Opportunities for expanding cross-border trade in a given market will depend on the availability of transmission capacity. In liberalised markets, efficient prices on both sides of a congested transmission line signal the need to invest in new generation or transmission capacity. The pricing of access to interconnector capacity can reflect congestion, providing an incentive for the transmission system owner to expand capacity. In practice, however, the congestion rent earned by the owner of that capacity (or the rights to use it) might undermine incentives to build new capacity. This disincentive would be exacerbated if the interconnector owner is a dominant vertically integrated utility with a clear interest in limiting the development of competition in its home market. For this reason, the way the industry is structured and the way cross-border transmission access and charges are regulated are of critical importance to investment in interconnectors and cross-border trade.

In practice, approaches to handling these issues vary. The business model that has been adopted in the PJM and Australian markets involves the separation of transmission operation from ownership, as an alternative to full structural unbundling. This approach ensures that all congestion can be priced, that transmission needs are transparent and access is non-discriminatory. In these markets, there are two possible ways in which investments in transmission capacity can be remunerated within the current regulatory framework. The first involves a competitive or merchant approach, whereby the return on investment depends entirely on the difference in market prices between the two connected markets. In effect, the interconnector owner buys power at the end of the line where prices are lowest and sells into the market at the other end. The investor may be able to extract rent if a large enough price differential can be maintained for long enough, but runs the risk of losing money if this is not the case. The second approach involves pre-determined regulated tariffs to finance the extensions. In the PJM and Australia, most investment still relies mainly on financing through regulated tariffs. This approach is likely to remain predominant in these and other markets where opportunities for expanding interconnector capacity emerge in the medium term.

The European market

The model used in Europe keeps transmission ownership and system operation together in a monopoly arrangement. This approach allows for co-ordinated planning of transmission lines to fulfil both reliability and trading requirements, but may not lead to economically efficient investment in interconnector capacity. The incumbent monopolies have an incentive to maximise congestion rents and limit capacity expansion. Fear of distorted incentives is one of the main drivers behind the European Union's efforts to promote investments in new transmission lines relieving serious congestion points. Cross-border flows of electricity between western European countries in 2004 stood at around 10.7% of total consumption – an increase of only around two percentage points over 2000 (EC, 2005). The construction of priority electricity infrastructure is supported under the TEN-Energy programme, which the EC plans to reinforce.

The EC is also studying interconnector pricing approaches with a view to increasing incentives for enhancing investment. Barely half of the 34 country-to-country interconnections between the 24 member countries of the association of European Transmission System Operators (ETSO) are allocated according to market-based principles. ETSO and the association of European Power Exchanges have proposed a pricing approach that integrates trade of power with that of transmission capacity involving an implicit auction of transmission capacity – the approach known as market coupling used in the Nordic, Australian and various US markets (ETSO/EuroPex, 2004). Power exchanges in the Netherlands (APX) and France (Powernext) have agreed with the Belgian system operator (ELIA) to establish an exchange based on market coupling between all three exchanges. The proposal uses a methodology that partially takes into account loop flows. The proposal focuses on cross-border trade between jurisdictions but does not address the need for congestion management within countries and control areas. Statnett, the Norwegian system operator, and TenneT, the Dutch operator, are building an interconnector, the capacity of which will be allocated using market coupling.

The Nordic market

Transmission system operators in the Nordic market collaborate on interconnector capacity operation, planning and investment through Nordel. Substantial progress has been made in harmonising the operation of the national systems, adopting measures to improve reliability and developing pricing approaches to allocate scarce capacity efficiently. The capacities of the six Nordic cross-border interconnectors are allocated according to market-coupling principles. In 2004, the national system operators agreed to give priority to considering five major projects costing a total of EUR 1 billion to alleviate congestion on these lines. Four of these projects have so far been given the green light. The investment decisions are being taken on the basis of the net economic benefits to the entire Nordic market, rather than to local markets. The investments will be financed by grid users through tariffs.

Increased cross-border trade will also create opportunities for integrating the management of reserve capacity and markets for ancillary services, enhancing system reliability and security. In Australia, for example, the national Electricity Market Management Company (NEMMCO) was able to cut minimum reserve levels by more than half through sharing of reserves and by exploiting differences in load profiles among regions. Trade in ancillary services across jurisdictions has also reduced the aggregate need for reserves in the PJM. Summer peak demand increased by 30% as a result of expansion in the coverage of the market, but the demand for spinning reserves increased by only 20% – a clear illustration of the value of system co-ordination. National systems in Europe have long co-ordinated the use of reserves and other ancillary services, largely through agreements within UCTE and Nordel. But the only case of trading of reserves across borders was in 2003, when Eltra, the western Danish transmission system operator (TSO), bought operational reserves in Norway in agreement with the Norwegian TSO, Statnett. This led to a reduction in the need for reserves

3.6. Managing increased business risk

Changes in the risks of doing business in different regions and activities will play a major role in driving the evolution of industry structure and business practices in the electricity supply industry. Liberalisation radically alters the allocation of business risk, leading to the development of new ways of managing that risk. Prior to liberalisation, investment in the power sector carried relatively low risk. Utilities were guaranteed the ability to recover reasonable costs incurred in providing service to their customers. As a result, they had no need to hedge against unforeseen increases in the prices of their fuel inputs and the costs of other factors of production. For state-owned utilities, access to debt capital was easy. Even for independent power producers, the use of a long-term contract, which allowed market risk to be passed on to the single buyer, made it possible to finance investment at a low risk premium. Regardless of ownership, business risk – as well as any costs of excess capacity, inappropriate technology and inefficient operations – was largely borne by consumers.

Market reform and restructuring make risks more transparent and allocate risks more closely to the decision makers themselves. The nature of risk changes in different ways for generators, transmission and distribution companies, suppliers/retailers and end-users. The development of wholesale markets exposes generators to price risk, as their output is sold at unregulated prices, either into a real-time market or under bilateral contracts with suppliers. Price risk grows with increased volatility of both fuel input prices (especially natural gas) and electricity prices. For example, in the late 1990s, during a boom in construction, finance was relatively easy to find for independent or merchant power plants in US markets. Increased price risk, together with other events (notably California's electricity crisis, the bankruptcy of Enron and lower spark spreads in the early part of the current decade), has led to a sharp increase in the cost of capital for new plants in the United States and, consequently, a slump in investment.

In the United States and elsewhere, generators, merchant interconnectors, suppliers and large end-users are being forced to seek out ways of hedging price and other market risks. In principle, business risks can be effectively managed through contracts. Market participants can agree on quantities, timing, prices and other terms and conditions in a way that meets each participant's need for certainty. Such contracts can take the form of a bilateral deal between a generator and a supplier or end-user, or a futures contract traded on a formal exchange. The more liquid electricity markets become and the greater the degree of competition that develops, the greater the scope for introducing sophisticated risk management tools. Most competitive wholesale markets involve arrangements for day-ahead and real-time trading, but trading in long-term contracts remains limited in many markets (Table 3.3). In the United States, NYMEX began offering electricity derivatives in March 1996, and the Chicago Board of Trade and the Minneapolis Grain Exchange have also offered electricity derivatives. NYMEX had the most success, at one point listing six different futures contracts. Trading in electricity futures and options contracts peaked in the second half of 1998. However, by the end of 2000, most activity had ceased. NYMEX has since relaunched a monthly PJM contract, but trading remains relatively thin. In Great Britain, liquidity on the APX power exchange, launched in 2000, is even smaller.

Table 3.3. **Share of spot and futures trade in total electricity consumption in selected markets, 2004**

	England and Wales (%)	Australia (NEM) (%)	PJM (%)	Nordic market (Nord Pool) (%)	Germany (European Energy Exchange) (%)
Real time	5	100	35	3	n.a.
Day ahead	n.a.	n.a.	26	43	11
Further ahead (exchange)	n.a.	13[1]	24[3]	151[5]	29
Further ahead (over the counter)	n.a.	125[2]	58[4]	309[6]	34[7]

1. d-cyphas trade.
2. Australian Financial Market Association.
3. NYMEX.
4. ICE.
5. Nord Pool.
6. Nord Pool Clearing.
7. EEX Clearing.

Source: D-cypha trade; AFMA, FERC, Nord Pool and EEX websites.

Geopolitical risks will also influence where utilities will seek to invest, their long-term sources of fuel inputs to power generation, their choice of technology and their business strategies. Generators in many parts of the world will become increasingly dependent on imported oil and gas to meet their fuel needs. A growing share of those import needs will most likely be met by a small group of countries with large reserves, primarily Middle East members of OPEC and the Russian Federation (IEA, 2005d; DOE/EIA, 2006). In addition, more of the oil and gas traded internationally will pass through critical maritime chokepoints, such as the Straits of Hormuz in the Persian Gulf and the Straits of Malacca in South-east Asia, heightening the risk of a disruption through piracy, terrorist attacks, accidents or military conflict. Recent events in the Middle East, the Russian Federation, and Latin America, civil unrest in Nigeria and surging prices have drawn attention to the growing threat of supply disruptions.

Hedging risks

Organisational hedges are now emerging as an increasingly popular way of dealing with the investment and operational risk associated with price volatility and unpredictability and threats to the security of fuel supply for generators. Increasing risk resulting from the intensification of competition, made possible by vertical disintegration, leads to pressure on utilities to re-establish the original vertical structure through mergers and acquisitions, especially where it is difficult to replicate it through contractual arrangements. Other strategies include integration upstream, typically though the acquisition of natural gas or coal production assets, which provides a hedge against rising fuel input prices and the threat of a major supply disruption. Expansion into market overseas or into other network industries, such as gas distribution and supply, can reduce risk through diversification. Large consumers may also hedge their risks by developing their own power plants, with the potential to sell surplus to other consumers.

Transmission and distribution utilities are not faced with the same level of risk insofar as they remain regulated as natural monopolies. In this case, business risk will remain generally low, reflected in the relatively low rate of return on assets that network owners will be allowed to earn. Risk will remain lowest when all costs are allowed to be recovered regardless of whether they are judged to be reasonable or not. Risk is greater with incentive regulation, an approach pioneered in the United Kingdom. The regulated utility is allowed to earn an above target rate of return if it is able to provide service at a below target cost, allowing for inflation. But it is exposed to the risk of making a lower return if it is not able to keep costs down to at least the level deemed to be achievable by the regulatory authorities. In some countries, regulators have introduced measures aimed at increasing incentives to improve efficiency in investment and operation of networks. In Europe, the United States and Australia, several interconnectors between national or regional networks have been allowed to operate on an unregulated or merchant basis, on the grounds that they are effectively competing with spare generating capacity. This regulatory framework provides opportunities for network owners to earn higher returns, but at the cost of higher market risk.

4. Prospects for business models

4.1. Consolidation, concentration and globalisation

Utilities are adopting varying business strategies in response to the changing market and regulatory landscape and the associated shifts in business risk. Overall, there is a clear trend towards consolidation and convergence in the industry, achieved mainly through mergers and acquisitions (M&A), at the national level and, increasingly, regionally and internationally, too. M&A is the preferred mechanism for improving the prospects of stable cash flows as a source of finance for large, capital-intensive investments, as the cost of capital is typically lower than equity financing. Electricity utilities are likely to become more global in their activities and integrated with gas and other network sectors because of the potential synergies and economies of scale. In markets that are already liberalised, there may be a tendency for concentration to increase once again for similar reasons. However, competition authorities may take a tougher stance on future horizontal deals in generation and supply amid growing concerns about the impact of concentration on the effectiveness of competition on wholesale and retail markets.

The last few years have seen a boom in electricity M&A activity throughout the world. After falling back in 2002 and 2003, the total value of electricity sector deals world wide (including downstream gas) surged to a record high of USD 196 billion in 2005 – an increase of more than half over the previous year and more than twice the level of 2001 (Figure 3.5). This spending is almost equal to all the capital invested world wide in oil and gas exploration and production.

Domestic deals have dominated recent M&A activity, accounting for 71% of the value of all deals world wide in 2005, up from 54% in 2004 (PwC, 2006). In fact, the true scale of home market activity was probably even higher; a significant share of the other deals classified as cross-border were either moves by European companies to grow further in foreign markets where they were already present (such as E.ON's PowerGen subsidiary acquiring additional assets in the United Kingdom), to build scale in adjacent countries within a relatively contiguous home market (for example, Vattenfall's acquisition in Denmark) or were the public offerings of three big European privatisations. M&A activity in 2005 was strong on all continents, but Europe overtook North America for the total value of deals. European firms accounted for 58% of all targets and 44% of all bidders world wide. Three deals in Spain, Italy and France accounted for almost half of the value of the ten largest deals globally (Table 3.4).

The value of cross-border deals has grown less rapidly than domestic deals in recent years. Nonetheless, cross-border M&A spending – mostly within the main regions – in 2005 equalled the record of over USD 55 billion reached in 2001. Cross-border spending is becoming increasingly concentrated in markets geographically near to the home country.[7]

Figure 3.5. **Value of electricity and downstream gas and acquisitions mergers world wide**

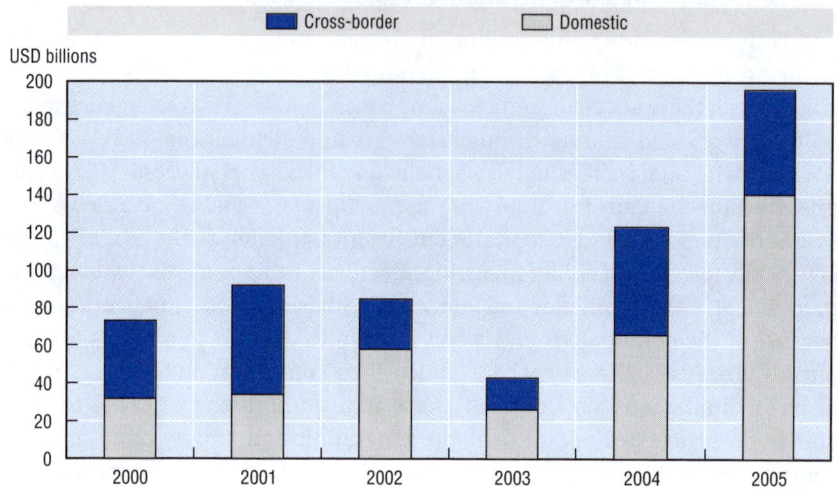

Source: PwC (2006).

Table 3.4. **Top ten electricity mergers and acquisitions world wide, 2005**

No.	Value of transaction (USD billions)	Target name	Target nation	Acquirer name	Acquirer nation
1	28.3	Endesa SA	Spain	Gas natural SDG	Spain
2	14.3	Cinergy Corp	US	Duke Energy Corp	US
3	13.9	Electrabel SA/NV (49.9%)	Belgium	Suez	France
4	11.2	Constellation Energy Group	US	FPL Group	US
5	10.3	Italenergia Bis	Italy	AEM/EdF	Italy
6	9.4	Pacificorp	US	Midamerican (Berkshire Hathaway)	US
7	8.3	Texas Genco LLC	US	NRG Energy	US
8	7.2	Électricité de France (10.4%)	France	Market purchase	International
9	5.6	Gaz de France (20.5%)	France	Market purchase	International
10	4.9	Enel (9.3%)	Italy	Market purchase	International

Note: Includes gas.
Source: PwC (2006).

Infrastructure fund investors are playing an increasingly important role in electricity sector M&A as they build global portfolios of assets, for the most part comprising network assets. These funds are starting to account for a significant share of total electricity industry assets, especially in Europe and North America. In 2004, GC Power Acquisition LLC, a US fund, bought Texas Genco Holdings for USD 2.9 billion – the largest acquisition of US power plants by a non-utility company since deregulation began.

With competition limiting the opportunities for businesses to grow organically, utilities are increasingly looking to M&A opportunities to deliver growth, both horizontally and vertically up the electricity supply chain. The bulk of the mergers and acquisitions world wide in recent years have been motivated by horizontal integration, even if they have generally involved vertically integrated utilities merging with or acquiring the same. More than half of all domestic and cross-border deals over the period 2002-04 involved firms operating predominantly in the same functional segment of the supply chain (PwC, 2004). New entrants, including fund investors, account for a growing share of M&A activity – close to a third in 2004. Convergence between electricity and gas utilities represented 15%. Vertical integration accounted for less than 10% of all deals world wide in 2005, down from about 20% in 2004. The impetus for vertical integration is coming largely from the supply end of the chain; many retail companies have adopted aggressive strategies to increase their assets in generation and fuel-supply sources. In Australia, for example, Origin Energy, a retailer, has moved into power generation to hedge against rising wholesale prices.

High wholesale electricity, natural gas and carbon prices have contributed to the surge in M&A activity, by pushing up generation asset values and reinforcing the need for utilities to hedge against price risk. The surge in international gas prices has reduced interest in building or acquiring CCGT plants and increased the attractiveness of other generating technologies, including nuclear power, clean coal and renewables. Growing worries about the security of oil and gas supply are also strengthening the drive to diversify and acquire assets, particularly in Europe. So far, the European competition authorities have not stood in the way of major deals, but there are signs that the competition authorities may take a tougher stance in the future because of concerns about the impact of concentration in national markets and in the European market generally on competition and pricing (Box 3.4).

Considerable room remains for further consolidation in the electricity sector at national, regional and global levels. Risk management and economies of scale and scope will continue to underpin the business rationale for vertical and horizontal integration, as well as convergence with gas and other activities. The traditional boundaries between the utility sector and upstream oil and gas will become increasingly blurred, as upstream companies move downstream to protect market share and downstream companies seeking to secure fuel supply and storage assets. The unbundling of network assets will continue to generate opportunities for infrastructure and pension funds and for other investors to buy network assets that yield steady returns with relatively low risk. Investor appetite remains strong for now, fuelling M&A activity. The attitude of competition authorities will play a key role in determining the extent of future megadeals in the power sector. In the longer term, utilities may seek more

Box 3.4. **Consolidation in the European electricity industry**

In continental Europe, "The Seven Brothers" – EdF, E.ON, RWE, Vattenfall, Endesa, Electrabel and Enel – have emerged as the dominant electricity utilities. Consolidation will increase further if the recently proposed merger of France's Gaz de France and Suez and E.ON's acquisition of Endesa go ahead. The E.ON bid is a record in terms of overall deal size and the amount of cash involved. The run-up to full retail market opening in 2007 may give momentum to consolidation. At the same time, the number of genuine newcomers to the European market has been declining recently. Only a very limited share of new electricity generation projects has been commissioned by non-incumbents in recent years.

Growing vertical integration between generation and supply activities has raised concerns about its impact on liquidity on wholesale markets. In addition, convergence of gas and electricity utilities may reduce incentives for competitors to build new gas-fired plants. The French government's role in promoting the GdF/Suez merger and the Spanish government's attempt to block the E.ON/Endes deal have raised concerns about national protectionism. The European Commission is monitoring these developments carefully and is investigating the concentration and consolidation of the industry in more detail as part of the inquiry into wholesale electricity pricing launched in June 2005. Following recent changes anti-monopoly rules and a revision to the Merger Regulation, the EC is adopting a more proactive approach to enforcing competition rules in the liberalised utility sectors (EC, 2004).

global reach. Renewed interest of the largest western utilities in investing in emerging markets and developing countries will depend on national policies and their implications for perceived risk and potential returns (see below).

In Europe, worries about security of gas supply from the Russian Federation and the need for a major increase in investment in gas infrastructure could drive further convergence between the gas and electricity sectors across Europe and the transition economies. Further consolidation and regionalisation are likely in other parts of the world too. In the United States, federal and state regulation will continue to play a key role in the pace and pattern of deals. The recent repeal of the 1935 Public Utilities Holding Companies Act (PUHCA), which limited the ownership of electricity utilities, will help to accelerate consolidation and the emergence of large regional players. The US market remains highly fragmented and regionalised, offering considerable scope for consolidation.

Similarly, regional consolidation in the more mature markets of Asia Pacific, spurred by the gradual implementation of market and regulatory reforms, will most likely continue. Geopolitical risks to the security of oil and gas supplies, notably from the Middle East, may accentuate this tendency. Some Asian companies – mainly private, but some nationally owned – have started expanding or are seeking to expand internationally, and others are considering doing so. In some cases they have taken over companies sold by western multinationals. Investment by Asian electricity utilities in Australia, for example, is now comparable to total private electricity investment by OECD-based utilities in Asia (Hall, Corral and Thomas, 2004).

4.2. Ownership and financing

Electricity sector ownership and financing issues differ greatly between the rich, industrialised countries on the one hand and emerging market and developing countries on the other. Privatisation has largely run its course in most OECD countries. Generally, a majority of generation assets are now in private hands. In some countries, state ownership is now limited to transmission and distribution. France and Korea are the main exceptions. Neither country plans to sell off a majority of its stake in generation in the foreseeable future.

There is little doubt that enough capital will potentially be available for required electricity investments in most OECD countries. But there are concerns about whether adequate incentives exist to ensure that all the investment will be made in a timely way and in the right areas. At present, electricity utilities finance new projects largely through a mixture of equity (internally generated cash or equity issued as public shares) and debt (through borrowing from banks or bonds). The current debt-equity structure of OECD utilities varies considerably. For example, Japan relies heavily on debt, while US utilities rely more on equity. On average, debt accounts for a little over half of electricity companies' shareholder capital structure (Figure 3.6). Some highly leveraged companies,

Figure 3.6. **Capital structure of electricity companies by region, 1992-2001**

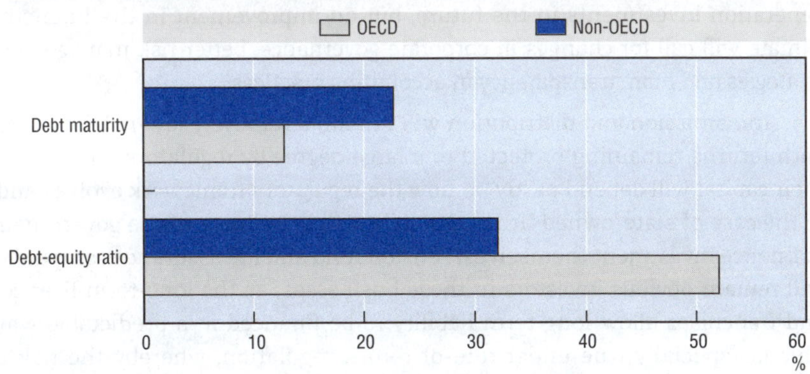

Note: The debt-equity ratio is debt as a share of the sum of shareholders' total debt and equity. Debt maturity is short-term debt as a share of total debt.

Source: IEA (2003).

such as in Japan and France, have reduced their debt in anticipation of the emergence of competition. In other cases, increased investment has been funded largely through borrowing, for example in the United States.

It remains to be seen how market reforms and the development of competitive electricity markets will affect the debt-equity structure of OECD-based utilities in the future, and in particular whether the share of equity will increase towards the higher levels typical in the oil industry. Electricity utilities will most likely remain relatively highly leveraged, *i.e.* they will keep their high debt-to-equity ratios. The growing involvement of infrastructure funds and other financial investors could push these ratios even higher. Returns on investment could fall as competition develops, which could drive up borrowing up especially for the most leveraged firms and for power-generation companies.

The environment for financing new independent, or merchant, power projects, has changed dramatically in the last few years. It has become extremely difficult to obtain debt financing for merchant plants, partly as a result of financial looses incurred by companies in Europe, the United States and other regions in the late 1990s and early part of the current decade. A combination of other events, including the collapse of Enron, the retreat of US firms from overseas markets (notably the United Kingdom) and the Californian power crisis, have added to the reluctance on the part of banks and other lenders to provide finance. The credit ratings of most power-generation companies have fallen in recent years; investment-grade ratings are now extremely difficult to achieve for new projects. Investors are looking for stable market rules and longer term contractual commitments before they will commit capital. The absence of liquid forward markets and corresponding supply contracts of more than a few years duration, such as in Great Britain, increases the risk of merchant plant investments. There will undoubtedly be profitable opportunities for new power-generation investments in the future, but an improvement in the financing climate will call for changes in corporate governance, better risk management strategies and more transparency in accounting practices.

Transmission and distribution will remain a relatively low-risk business, with returns remaining protected to a large degree by regulators. The cost of their capital will depend partly on how the regulatory framework evolves and, in the case of state-owned firms, the ability and readiness of the government to finance investment themselves. Pension fund and life assurance companies will remain obvious investors in these businesses, as the long-term licences and franchises allow long-term liability to be financed in a predictable way. This is especially true under rate-of-return regulation, whereby the risk is almost entirely transferred to customers, and equity risk is minimal. Under incentive regulation, equity risk is greater, rendering network investments less attractive to long-term institutional investors.

The prospects for further privatisation and opening of state monopolies to private capital in non-OECD countries are very uncertain. Most countries that have tried to privatise their electricity companies in the past few years have suffered serious delays, largely due to strong public resistance. In several cases, privatisation has been held up by a lack of credible buyers. At the same time, investment in independent power projects has plunged in response to deteriorating local business conditions and disillusionment with past investments (see Morgan, 2006). Yet the budgetary pressures on governments to seek greater private involvement in the electricity sector will not go away. Investment in electricity infrastructure in developing countries has traditionally been the responsibility of governments. Public utilities in several large developing countries are unprofitable – often because of underpricing of power for social reasons – and so are not able to finance new projects themselves. Governments will need to find an acceptable balance between private and public ownership that ensures adequate funding for development of electricity infrastructure and energy security (see Section 5.4).

As a result of political and practical difficulties with privatisation and often disappointing results, policy is undergoing a fundamental reassessment in many non-OECD countries. The World Bank and other multilateral lending institutions are also reviewing their policies in the light of the failure of privatisation and market reform policies to deliver the necessary investment, as well as sharply reduced private capital flows in many developing countries. They nonetheless remain committed to the same principles of power sector restructuring, including privatisation where possible. Accordingly, future policies are unlikely to remain based solely on the standard approach adopted in the industrialised world, involving the sale of assets to private investors, unbundling and independent regulation. Instead, the onus of policy may shift towards seeking ways of securing international financing through bonds and loans while retaining a central role for the public sector where straightforward privatisation is problematic.

The multilateral lending institutions are likely to remain a major source of much-needed capital in many non-OECD countries for as long as the number of active international investors in developing countries remains small and national and regional finance modest. The utilities' ability to borrow is much lower than in OECD countries, reflected in low debt/equity rations and reliance on short-term debt. There are signs that domestic and regional investors are becoming more prominent in the electricity sectors, especially in Asia (Estache and Goicoechea, 2004). Maintaining the momentum of the growth in financing from this source will hinge on policies that improve the investment climate. For now, private participation in the electricity sector remains relatively low across developing countries, especially in transmission and distribution. The Middle East and South Asia have been least successful or interested in attracting private capital.

In many cases, financing will remain difficult, especially in Africa, the transition economies and South Asia, because of poorly developed domestic financial markets and the higher cost of capital caused by higher risk. Private investment is expected to play a growing role in the medium term, but the success of efforts to attract private capital will depend critically on the economic, political, regulatory and legal environment in each country.

5. Policy and regulatory challenges

5.1. *Role of government*

Government has a critically important role to play in the provision of electricity services, regardless of the business model. It is responsible for ensuring that electricity is produced and supplied efficiently, that market failures – such as the failure of the market to place an appropriate value on public goods – are properly addressed and that the electricity sector develops in such a way that social, economic and environmental goals are met. Governments intervene through legislative and regulatory processes, and may directly involve themselves in the running of the industry through state ownership.

In a liberalised market, the government's role is fundamentally changed. Policy objectives, including industry structure and market design, must be expressed in legislation and implemented through regulation. In practice, the legal framework ranges from relatively light legislation, such as in New Zealand, to a more detailed legislative framework, such as in the United Kingdom. The roles of different players and the approach to liberalisation also differ considerably from country to country, reflecting *inter alia* differences in legal and political traditions, industry structure and the stage reached in the reform process. In particular, differences exist in the division of jurisdictional powers between government, the courts, the general competition authorities, the national regulatory authorities and, in federal countries, state regulators. Experience so far with liberalised markets suggests that relatively detailed rules are needed to prevent market abuse and regulatory uncertainty.

In most cases, an independent regulatory body is given responsibility for enforcing regulatory rules and requirements, including issuing and enforcing licences, setting tariffs for network services (and for supply to captive customers) and monitoring market behaviour. However, their sectoral scope, responsibilities, powers and degree of independence from government differ greatly from country to country. Transmission system operators and other market participant may also play an important role in establishing and adapting market rules. Effective regulation requires good information about the costs, service quality and comparative performance of the network companies, as well as qualified staff to regulate effectively the prices charged by distribution and transmission companies and the terms and conditions of access to these networks by wholesalers and retailers. Adequately resourced regulatory institutions are an essential condition of successful electricity market reform. Inadequate regulatory institutions have undermined the effectiveness of reforms in many countries, especially in the developing world.

There is no single best-practice approach to regulation. Regulatory structures and procedures need to be tailored to meet the particular circumstances of each jurisdiction. By its very nature, liberalisation results in markets that are in a continuous state of flux. Actual experience of operating competitive markets provides the impetus for modifications to trading arrangements and further reform of the regulatory framework, aimed at making the market work better – especially where problems of market manipulation and lack of transparency emerge. Changes in the physical electricity system brought about by network expansion and increased interconnection of previously independent networks or technological developments may also call for regulatory change.

Regulatory arrangements and structures must, therefore be *flexible* if they are to be able to adapt to the evolving competitive landscape. The need for a responsive regulatory system may clash with the benefits to investors of stable and predictable rules. Minimising regulatory uncertainty helps to encourage timely and adequate investment. Some regulatory uncertainty is unavoidable, as the regulatory framework needs to adapt to changing circumstances and deal with problems as they arise. Nonetheless, policy makers and regulators can take action to minimise uncertainty for investors, including improving access to market information, refraining from *ad hoc* interventions in the way markets operate (such as price-capping) and establishing transparent procedures for licensing. The procedures for regulating network pricing also need to be clear, transparent and predictable. Close interaction between system and market operators, generators and suppliers can help to reduce uncertainty and unpredictability.

Addressing environmental effects

The environmental effects of electricity generation are not automatically addressed by financial incentives in competitive markets. Pollution and global warming caused by rising concentrations of greenhouse gases in the atmosphere are prime examples of market failure; the market fails to put a financial value or penalty on the cost of emissions generated by power generators or other users of fossil fuels. Air quality and the weather are, in economists' parlance, public goods, from which everyone benefits. Damage done to the environment is known as an external cost or externality. Governments therefore have a responsibility to correct these failures, to discourage activities that emit noxious or greenhouse gases and to make sure that each polluter pays for the harm he causes to public goods. Placing a value of the pollution caused or emitted is effectively a way of internalising these environmental externalities. Policies motivated by environmental and climate change concerns are already having, and will continue to have, major effects on the functioning of competitive electricity markets.

Addressing environmental effects in the power sector is a highly complex issue. Some environmental policies may cause market distortions and inefficiencies, particularly where cross-border trade is possible. Subsidies for particular technologies, or non-transparent barriers that impede the development of others, may not lead to the optimal fuel mix or choice of technology in the long term given the unpredictability of technological development and imperfect information. The challenge here is to establish a legal and market framework that ensures that environmental objectives are met flexibly and at least cost. One such approach is to cap and trade emission allowances. The United States was one of the first countries to introduce such a system for sulphur dioxide emissions from power plants and large industrial facilities under the 1990 Clean Air Act Amendments. In January 2005, the European Union launched an Emission Trading Scheme for carbon dioxide – the largest multicountry, multisector greenhouse-gas emission trading scheme in the world.

5.2. *Promoting effective competition in generation and supply*

The intensity of competition in wholesale and retail electricity supply is a key measure of the success of market reform. A critical challenge for policy makers and regulators is, therefore, to establish a framework that allows for genuine contestability and, where necessary, measures to actively stimulate the development of effective competition. The benefits of competition come from the incentives for higher efficiency and more innovation through price signals that reflect the true cost and value of producing, transporting and consuming electricity. The number and types of participants in the market and how wholesale markets are designed and regulated are of vital importance. A high level of concentration and opportunities for dominant generators to earn monopoly profits remain serious problems in several markets, especially where the transition to competition is at an early stage.

For competition to flourish there must be a multitude of buyers and sellers in the market for wholesale and retail supply along the load curve.[8] If a single generator dominates one particular type of capacity, such as mid-load, it will be able to force up wholesale prices along that part of the load curve to the level of the next lowest cost generator, making abnormally high profits. In addition, the wholesale market must ensure that prices are driven by actual short-run marginal generation costs and that power plants are always dispatched in cost or merit order. Liquid bilateral forward wholesale markets for physical and financial contracts for electricity supply are also needed to ensure efficient pricing.

Governments and regulators can seek to enhance competition *ex ante* in various ways, including mandatory or negotiated restructuring and asset divestments – either before or after the market has been liberalised. In Great Britain, for example, the two largest generators created out of the old monopoly utility in 1989 later agreed with the regulator to divest assets to reduce their market shares and enhance competition in the wholesale pool as a condition for allowing them to acquire stakes in distribution companies. A second-best solution to mitigate the market power of dominant firms is to cap the prices they are able to charge through regulated forward contracts, but this is unlikely to result in an optimal outcome and can undermine incentives to build new capacity. This was a primary cause of the shortfall in capacity that contributed to the electricity crisis in California in 2001.

An *alternative approach* to the forced sale of physical assets is to require the dominant generators to sell the rights to their capacity to other generators or new entrant to the market under long-term contracts. In Europe, where France, Belgium, the Netherlands and Denmark have adopted this technique, these contracts are called virtual power plants (VPPs). Similar rights are also traded on financial markets in the form of options contracts. The buyer of VPP capacity, usually in an auction, gains the right to draw electricity from a plant or set of plants at a pre-determined price. The auction price corresponds to the option premium (the price the buyer of the options contract pays for the right to buy or sell power at a specified price in the future), while the pre-determined power price corresponds to the strike price in the options contract. The VPP auctions in Europe have all been used as part of an agreement in connection with a merger or acquisition. Experience suggests that this approach has helped to reduce the market power of the large generators and enhance competition.

The *ex ante* implementation of competition rules in connection with mergers and acquisitions provides another opportunity for the regulatory and competition authorities to strengthen the competitiveness of electricity supply. The authorities can make approval of a merger conditional on the utilities concerned divesting assets so as to reduce market concentration in the wholesale and/or retail market. This approach has been used on several occasions by the European Commission and national authorities. For example, the European Commission and the German Cartel Office imposed such conditions in approving mergers that led to the creation of the two German utilities, E.ON and RWE.

Ex post regulation of competition plays an important role in deterring and preventing anti-competitive behaviour and practices. In almost all countries, it is illegal to exercise or abuse market power. In practice, however, it is often hard to prove such behaviour, partly because of the complexity of the market and difficulties in measuring normal profit. The willingness of the competition and regulatory authorities to investigate and deal with allegations of market abuse may be compromised where the incumbent utility is regarded as national champions or is publicly owned. Market monitoring is an important element in detecting abuse of dominant position. Both PJM in the United States and Nord Pool in Scandinavia have independent market monitoring units with responsibility for monitoring and analysing market trade to detect breach of rules that support market manipulation. Nordic transmission system operators and regulators co-operate to model market power on a continuous basis.

In the long term, new entrants to the generation sector are vital to creating a *truly competitive wholesale market.* The incumbent dominant generators have an incentive to withhold capacity from the market and delay investment in new capacity as a way of forcing up prices. Easing the access for new entrants can be a particularly effective way of enhancing competition in countries where electricity demand is growing quickly. This requires regulators to introduce smooth, clear, rapid and transparent procedures for approving the construction of new power plants. Another way of achieving the same result is to extend markets across countries and regions, thereby importing competition. This can be particularly effective in small markets where the scope for a large number of players is restricted by the economies of scale in generation. The FERC has adopted this approach through the formation of Regional Transmission Organisations across the United States. Market integration to enhance competition has been critical to the development of the National Electricity Market in Australia. The European Commission also sees market integration through cross-border interconnections as the main path to a competitive single European electricity market.

The *design of wholesale trading arrangements and systems* is a vital factor in ensuring effective competition. There is no consensus on the most appropriate design of the wholesale market among market participants and experts. A central issue concerns whether the market should be built around a voluntary or mandatory pool for real-time and day-ahead supply or around bilateral contracts. Mandatory single-price pools encourage transparency and liquidity, but may be prone to gaming, where there is a small number of generators. Other issues concern the role of locational pricing of power and ancillary services in enhancing competition and achieving efficient pricing and the allocation of scarce transmission capacity (see below). Theoretical benefits have to be balanced against the costs and difficulties of implementing trading arrangements in practice. Because the physical characteristics of national or regional electricity systems differ, there is no single prescriptive model that can be applied to all markets. Nonetheless, experience with market design in Great Britain, North America, the Nordic market, Australia,

Chile and elsewhere suggest that certain features are likely to contribute to the smooth functioning of wholesale markets, where practical. These include:

- Voluntary spot markets for day-ahead and real-time balancing for electricity supply and reserve capacity combined with bilateral contracts.
- Locational pricing of power to reflect the marginal cost of congestion and transmission losses at each location
- The integration of spot wholesale markets for energy with trade in transmission capacity to ensure that scarce capacity is priced and allocated according to its value to different users.
- Allowing the possibility of demand responses to spot-price signals.

Up to now, the potential contribution of *demand responses* in setting prices has not been fully exploited in any liberalised market. By enabling end-users – typically large industrial consumers – to adjust their load according to short-term changes in spot prices, the need for peak capacity and the threat of price spikes at times of peak load can be reduced. In this way, the potential for market abuse by dominant generators can be restricted. Demand response also enhances system security, as load is usually highest at nodes on the network where congestion is most frequent and network security most vulnerable. The United States and Great Britain have gone furthest in trying to incorporate demand-response programmes into wholesale and retail markets, but considerable potential remains to expand their coverage and effectiveness.

Transparency is critical to well-functioning competitive electricity markets. All the necessary information to enable market participants and the regulatory and competition authorities to analyse and understand market conditions must be made easily available. Market participants will only collect and publish fundamental market data and statistics if they are required to do so. Therefore, the authorities must devise a clear set of rules and requirements governing the disclosure of information. Access to basic market prices is most important. In the PJM, British, Nordic and Australian markets, day-ahead and/or real-time balancing prices are made public through the market operators' websites. In the Australian and Nordic markets, all spot market-sensitive information, such as unplanned outages, plant re-connections and changes in schedules for planned outages, must be disclosed immediately.

Competition in retail markets in many cases remains largely limited to large industrial and commercial customers – even where contestability has been extended to all customer categories (as in the British, Nordic, PJM and Australian markets). Extending competition to small residential consumers is an ongoing challenge. The principal barrier is the relatively high cost of implementing retail switching programmes, mainly because of the need to monitor closely actual consumption. This requires the installation of meters that can be read remotely on a daily basis or a system that uses calculated load profiles based on monthly, quarterly or annual meter readings. Replacing meters is very expensive. In both cases, the operating costs are high. Technological advances and cost reductions may pave the way for more widespread residential switching in the long term.

5.3. Regulating networks

Regulation of transmission and distribution networks is of central importance to the operation and the overall efficiency of the entire electricity supply industry. Network-related costs typically account for between 30% and 40% of the average cost of delivering electricity to end-users and as much as half of the cost of supplying residential customers. Even in liberalised markets, networks are generally regulated as natural monopolies. Charges for network services to third parties or, in the case of an unbundled monopoly industry, the costs of running the network that are passed through to final customers are controlled by the regulatory authorities to prevent the network owner from overcharging and earning monopoly rents. The challenge for regulators is to establish procedures and rules for allocating capacity rights and setting tariffs that reflect true costs so as to encourage efficient operation of the network and investment in new capacity as and when required. Non-transparent management of congested interconnections is a major barrier to trade and competition. In liberalised markets, how networks are regulated shapes the development of wholesale and retail competition as well as interregional and cross-border trade. It also affects how generating capacity is used and investment in new capacity.

Traditionally, network regulation was based on some form of *cost-plus approach*, which involved network owners passing through to customers all costs considered reasonable and approved by the regulator as well as a profit margin. This form of regulation, which is still widely used in many liberalised markets, guarantees a return on investment and, therefore, the long-term financial stability of the network owner. But it provides little incentive for efficient operation or investment. In some liberalised markets, incentive regulation, typically built around price or revenue caps, has been introduced to encourage network owners to improve the efficiency of their operations. Great Britain was the first to introduce such an approach, which allowed average network tariffs to increase with consumer price inflation but required continuous efficiency improvements of a pre-determined percentage amount each year over the price-review period (known as CPI-X). In the event that the regulated firm is able to cut costs by more than X% per year, it would be able to make a larger return on capital than that allowed in setting the initial tariff.

Although this form of incentive regulation has proved successful in lower operating costs, it has not provided sufficient incentives for efficient maintenance and investment. There is now increased focus on quality. Great Britain, Norway and Sweden have recently reformed their regulations to incorporate service quality and reliability, involving a reduction in the revenues to the utility if performance falls short of fixed benchmarks. The Spanish regulator recently introduced a system in which network companies must compensate electricity consumers for poor service quality.

The incorporation of *locational pricing* is an increasingly important focus and highly controversial aspect of network regulation. In principle, efficient network pricing requires that tariffs reflect the actual costs associated with inputs and off-takes of power at specific locations or nodes in the grid. In practice, however, shifting patterns of generation and load result in constant changes in costs, making it hard to match them with tariffs. Furthermore, resistance in electricity networks creates losses, which add to transportation costs.[9] This has important implications for the pricing of the power itself and economically efficient dispatch. At the margin, dispatch of the generator with the lowest marginal cost might, at another location on the network, trigger higher losses that more than outweigh its competitive advantage over the next generator in the merit order. In this case, it would be more efficient for the entire system to dispatch the higher-cost generator, a practice known as out-of-merit-order dispatch. Dispatch of the generator with the lowest marginal cost may also lead to congestion somewhere else in the network, blocking access for other relatively cheap generators. Efficient pricing requires that these considerations are taken into account.

Nodal pricing principles seek to price use of the network at different nodes taking into account transmission capacity and grid losses. Typically, each transformer station in the transmission grid is designated a node. All flows and constraints between nodes, including loop flows, are priced (using computer models) and those prices are made public, signalling congestion and the need for investment in additional capacity. In the trading arrangements used in the PJM market, transmission congestion is priced and managed simultaneously with the settlement of bids and offers for power. Transmission capacity is thus priced implicitly in the spot prices. However, there are drawbacks with this approach: trading is fragmented into separate nodal markets, reducing liquidity, increasing the risk that one or more players may exert market power and raising transaction costs. In some cases, technical factors can prevent nodal pricing from always being applied.[10] An alternative approach, which has been adopted for pricing interconnector capacity in Europe, is to make the auction of transmission capacity explicit. In 1999, the German and Danish transmission system operators set up an auction of capacity for the Danish-German interconnector. Other countries have since established similar auctions along several other European borders, including the Netherlands-Germany and England-France borders. The European Commission has ruled that implicit and explicit auctions comply with EC directives and the 2003 regulation on cross-border power trade.

Zonal pricing, an alternative to nodal pricing, sets uniform prices for use of capacity for groups of nodes that correspond to the main congestion points in the grid. The aim is to simplify pricing, maintain liquidity and facilitate transparency. This approach is used in the Nordic market (see Chapter 1, Box 1.17), as well as in Australia. In both cases, networks are more radial and less intermeshed, with few loop flows. Each Australian state in the National Electricity Market together with the hydropower capacity in the Snowy Mountains region constitutes a zone. The system operator calculates network losses for each zone on the basis of loss factors, assessed annually, for specific nodes. Losses are taken into account in determining the dispatch schedule.

In Great Britain, BETTA introduced uniform balancing charges across the entire British system with the integration of Scotland in 2005. As a result, there are no locational pricing signals. A shortfall in physical transmission capacity between Scotland and the rest of the network has resulted in a sharp increase in constraint management charges, which the system operator recovers from all network users regardless of their location.

Regulation of *regional and cross-border interconnectors* may be treated differently to meshed networks. One approach is to simply let it compete with generation on equal terms without any price controls. Such merchant interconnectors would be financed purely by congestion rents. Several merchant interconnectors, built prior to liberalisation, currently operate in Europe, North America and Australia. In theory, greater reliance on competitive merchant lines would support more effective use of price signals to strengthen incentives for efficient transmission network performance and to promote cross-border trade. But this approach may undermine economies of scale and raise costs if several lines were built by competing utilities. Merchant lines might also be built without regard to reliability requirements (Joskow and Tirole, 2005). As a result, it is unlikely that policy makers will be able to rely primarily on a merchant model to drive interconnector investment. The objective is to develop regulatory mechanisms that provide opportunities for merchant investors to develop projects when they are the most efficient options. Experience in Europe suggests that strong incentives or active intervention in the form of publicly backed investments are needed to bring forth investment in interconnectors, because of the inherent self-interest of incumbent utilities in limiting cross-border exchanges in order to protect their dominant positions in their home markets.

The amount *of transmission capacity* that is made available for trade is a critical factor when incorporating the locational aspects into efficient electricity pricing. System operators typically restrict the transmission capacity available for trade below the actual physical thermal capacity of the line for reasons of security. Capacity held in reserve may be used in the event of an emergency. The methods used for analysing system security needs have changed little since liberalisation. In many cases, these methods are extremely conservative, are not based on probabilities of critical events occurring and rarely exploit the information on costs and prices revealed by the market (IEA, 2005c). There is considerable scope for better aligning such practices with the competitive market framework to maximise available transmission capacity. This, in turn, would allow for more trade and lower prices.

5.4. *Ensuring energy security*

Ensuring the security of electricity supply hinges on *timely investment* in generating and network capacity (and related infrastructure to supply fuel to power stations) and adequate systems for maintaining reliable uninterrupted operation of transmission and distribution networks. Threats to the reliability of supply could increase substantially in many parts of the world as a result of unexpectedly rapid increases in demand, which may squeeze reserve capacity and increase congestion in transmission systems. Underinvestment in transmission and distribution networks may compromise system reliability. Climate change might also lead to more frequent natural disasters, such as hurricanes, storms and flooding. Transmission and distribution systems would be most at risk from such events. Major changes in climate patterns would, therefore, make electricity supply less reliable unless electricity infrastructure is made physically more robust or additional back-up facilities are put in place to handle emergencies. Geopolitical factors may also affect the supply of natural gas, oil and other fuel inputs to power generation, with knock-on effects for electricity supply security. Increased risk of a disruption in fuel supplies increases the need for reserve capacity, fuel-switching capability or flexible demand responses.

At any given moment, the adequacy of generation and network capacity to meet all demand at all times depends on whether enough investment is forthcoming at the right location and in a timely manner. A lack of capacity forces system operators to impose blackouts and brownouts. System security depends, to some degree, on available network capacity and, therefore, the amount of investment. But it also depends on operating tools and co-operative arrangements that allow the system operators' to effectively monitor and flexibly control flows in real-time and to respond to emergencies. Many power outages, such as the major blackouts in North America and Europe in 2003, are caused by the sudden failure of the transmission system.

The costs of power outages or poor-quality electricity service can be extremely high. The economic cost of the disruption in electricity supply in the north-east United States and eastern Canada in August 2003 has been estimated at between USD 4 billion and USD 10 billion for the United States and close to CAD 1 billion in Canada (IEA, 2005c). For all of 2003, the total cost of all power disruptions throughout the United States is estimated at USD 52 billion for the information and communication industries and USD 100 billion, or 1% of GDP, for the economy as a whole (EPRI, 2003a).

In principle, competitive electricity markets can provide incentives for timely and efficient investments, as long as the market is well-designed and the regulatory framework is appropriate. There are growing concerns about the adequacy of generation and transmission investment in liberalised markets – notably in Europe, the United States and parts of Asia. Reserve-capacity margins – the difference between peak demand and available generating capacity – are falling in several countries as a result of a downturn in investment in recent years. In most cases, market reforms were introduced at a time of overcapacity, so the initial focus was on reducing operating costs. The focus is now shifting to the adequacy of incentives to invest in new capacity – particularly peaking – and streamlining regulatory procedures for authorising new investment in generating plant and high-tension transmission lines.

There are increasing doubts about whether markets for power only can provide sufficient incentives and whether prices need to be uplifted by formal capacity payments. Theory suggests that energy-only markets with spot prices that are allowed to fully reflect scarcity rents at peak will generate sufficient income to generators to allow the full recovery of their initial investment in capacity (Roques *et al.*, 2005). But, in practice, the perceived increase in investment risk, which has raised hurdles rates, may be skewing investment away from capital-intensive base-load and peaking plant. In poor developing countries, financing much-needed investment in infrastructure to meet rising demand and maintain reliability will be a major challenge in view of the limited availability of public funds, limited access to capital markets and the difficulties in attracting private capital.

Given the economic, social and political importance of "keeping the lights on", policy makers and regulators are considering *alternative mechanisms for remunerating reserve capacity*. These include capacity payments, determined by a formula for calculating the value of lost load (VOLL), and capacity obligations. The electricity pool established in 1990 in England and Wales incorporated a fixed VOLL-based capacity payment (increased each year in line with inflation). How much of the VOLL that was actually paid to generators for each half-hour settlement period was determined by the probability of a shortage occurring, computed according to available capacity and the assessed load for each period. Problems with gaming led to the payment scheme being phased out with the introduction of the New Electricity Trading Arrangements in 2001. Capacity payments are still used in Spain but the amount is fixed each year for all hours regardless of the actual supply and demand. Capacity obligations require retail companies to contract for an amount of generation capacity that meets a fixed percentage of contracted load plus a reserve. PJM, New England and New York have adopted this approach, together with a cap-and-trade system in which capacity can be traded using a competitive market mechanism.

In a draft proposal for an EC directive concerning security of electricity supply, the European Commission has proposed that member states can use either a one-price-only market or capacity obligations to maintain balance between electricity supply and demand. But if this leads to different arrangements in neighbouring states, investment would be distorted because of free-riding across borders and pricing differences. This is a major issue in the north-eastern United States, where different approaches to remunerating capacity have emerged.

Private investment in networks depends largely on the incentives provided by the regulatory framework. Many countries have adopted regulatory approaches to network-tariff setting that incorporate strong incentives to cut operating costs. This has led to concerns about whether reliability is being compromised – particularly following a series of large-scale blackouts in 2003 and 2004 in a number of OECD countries, notably in North America, Italy, southern Sweden, and eastern Denmark. Often, the costs of establishing effective communication and monitoring systems, training staff and managing vegetation[11] are far outweighed by the economic benefits of fewer outages (IEA, 2005c). In several countries, network regulation is being adjusted to provide direct incentives for maintaining reliability, including through investment. The regulated rate of return remains a critical factor in ensuring the adequacy of investment.

Obtaining permission to build electricity supply infrastructure is a vital factor in securing supply. Non-transparent and bureaucratic *approval procedures* – whether to use a particular technology, to build a power plant at a particular site or to build a transmission line along a particular route – remain a major barrier to investment in most markets (IEA, 2005b). The so-called "not-in-my-backyard" (NIMBY) syndrome was a major cause of the power shortages that emerged in California in 2001 and that persist today. In some European countries, the long lead times in obtaining approval to build new transmission lines in the face of public opposition is the most serious obstacle to expanding supply capacity.

Increased cross-border trade can bring major benefits, as described in Section 3.4, but they must be carefully managed by system operators in such as way as to prevent them undermining system security. One lesson learned from the recent blackouts in North America and Europe was the importance of co-ordination and co-operation between system operators, including the full implementation of bilateral agreements. Such agreements were subsequently made legally binding in the United States. Another lesson concerned the importance of monitoring compliance with reliability standards. For example, a failure to trim trees adjacent to power cables played an important role in the failure of the transmission system in Italy and north-east America in 2003. Although liberalisation does not *per se* affect these issues, it is clear that it has fundamentally changed the way transmission systems are used and managed and that regulation of the industry has to adapt to these changes. There is a growing consensus among policy makers on the need for better monitoring of the impact of market developments and changes in industry structure on energy security. Governments may need to intervene in electricity markets to respond to a looming capacity crunch and to ensure that system operators take appropriate steps, including co-operation with neighbouring operators, to ensure system reliability (IEA, 2005b). For example, in July 2006, the US National Electricity Reliability Council – a self-regulatory industry body – took on new powers under the 2005 Energy Policy Act to develop and enforce mandatory reliability standards, including the imposition of fines on utilities that fail to meet those standards.

Notes

1. Generation, transmission and distribution are physical activities, while supply – wholesale trading among generators and marketers and retailing to end-users – is a transactional function. Other functional activities include system operation/dispatch, which covers all levels of the physical supply chain, and risk management.
2. The term utility is used throughout this chapter to refer to any company or entity involved in one or more of the four main functional activities that comprise the electricity supply industry.
3. The supply of any commodity or service is defined as a natural monopoly if the economies of scale are such that the overall cost of supply is lower if there is a single supplier. Grid-based energy transportation and delivery, including electricity, natural gas and district heat, which require more or less permanent connections with customer premises, are widely recognised as natural monopolies.
4. Differences in load patterns across an interconnected system result in a lower overall peak load compared with the sum of the peak loads of the individual sub-systems.
5. The drivers of and prospects for electricity demand and investment are described in detail in Morgan (2006).
6. On balance, research has shown that private electricity utilities tend to be more efficient than public ones and that efficiency improvements are usually faster, though this may depend on efficient markets being established. See, for example, Pollitt (1995 and 1997) and IMF (2004).
7. The 1990s saw a number of European and US companies expand aggressively into foreign markets on different continents. Électricité de France (EdF), Spain's Endesa and Iberdrola (Spain) and Portugal's EdP acquired assets mainly in Latin America. The other large European companies, such as E.ON, RWE, Vattenfall and ENEL, have not invested to any significant extent outside Europe. EdF is now looking to sell its assets outside Europe. A number of US companies acquired assets in the United Kingdom during the 1990s, but have since largely divested them.
8. The ranking of load or demand in each hour or other period of the year, with peak load at the top and base load at the bottom.
9. Electricity follows along the path of least resistance ignoring any path that may have been envisaged in a contract. On any given line, resistance and losses increase with load. As these relationships are neither linear nor constant, determining the cost of transportation is extremely complex – especially with

highly meshed networks where different flow paths, or loop flows, are possible. Where loop flows exist, it is not possible to define the available transmission capacity at a point in time without the existence of complete information about the use of the overall network.

10. In the PJM, for example, it is sometimes necessary to dispatch capacity out-of-merit order dispatch for reliability reasons, usually to deal with heavy congestion in certain parts of the network. This results in additional costs, which are spread evenly across all users.

11. Trees touching transmission cables are a leading cause of system failures.

Bibliography

Buresch, M. (2003), "The Declining Role of Foreign Private Investment", paper presented at World Bank Energy Forum, Washington DC, 24-27 February.

Department of Energy (DOE)/Energy Information Administration (EIA) (2006), *International Energy Outlook*, US DOE, Washington DC.

European Commission (EC) (2003), "Regulation No. 1228/2003 of the European Parliament and of the Council of 26 June 2003 on Conditions for Access to the Network for Cross-Border Exchanges in Electricity", *Official Journal of the European Union*, L 176/1, CEC, Brussels.

EC (2004), *A Pro-active Competition Policy for a Competitive Europe, Communication from the Commission*, COM(2004)293 final, Brussels.

EC (2005a), *Fourth Benchmarking Report: Annual Report on the Implementation of the Gas and Electricity Internal Market*, CEC, Brussels, *http://europa.eu.int/comm/energy/electricity/benchmarking/index_en.htm*.

EC (2005b), *Report on Progress in Creating the Internal Gas and Electricity Market*, CEC, Brussels, *http://europa.eu.int/comm/energy/electricity/report_2005/doc/2005_report_en.pdf*.

Electric Power Research Institute (EPRI) (2003), *Electricity Technology Roadmap 2003: Summary and Synthesis – Power Delivery and Markets*, EPRI, Palo Alto, California.

European Transmission System Operators (ETSO)/Association of European Power exchanges (EuroPex) (2004), *Flow-based Market Coupling: A Joint ETSO-EuroPEX Proposal for Cross-Border Congestion – Interim Report*, September 2004, Brussels, *www.etso-net.org/upload/documents/ETSO-EuroPEX_Interimreport_Sept-2004-.pdf*.

Hall, D., V. Corral and S. Thomas (2004), "Electricity privatisation and restructuring in Asia-Pacific", paper submitted to the Public Services International meeting in Changmai, Thailand, December 2004, *www.psiru.org/reports/2004-12-E-Asia.doc*.

International Energy Agency (IEA) (2002), *Distributed Generation in Liberalised Electricity Markets*, OECD, Paris.

IEA (2003), *World Energy Investment Outlook*, OECD, Paris.

IEA (2004), *World Energy Outlook*, OECD, Paris.

IEA (2005a), *Electricity Information*, OECD, Paris.

IEA (2005b), *Lessons from Liberalised Electricity Markets*, OECD, Paris.

IEA (2005c), *Learning from the Blackouts: Transmission System Security in Competitive Electricity Markets*, OECD, Paris.

IEA (2005d), *World Energy Outlook: Middle East and North Africa Insights*, OECD, Paris.

International Monetary Fund (2004), Public Investment and Fiscal Policy, 12 March, IMF, Washington DC, IMF, *www.imf.org/external/np/fad/2004/pifp/eng/PIFP.pdf*.

Joskow, P. (2003), "Electricity Sector Restructuring and Competition: Lessons Learned", *Cuadernos de Economía*, 40, No. 121 (December 2003).

Joskow, P. and J. Tirole (2005), "Merchant Transmission Investment", *Journal of Industrial Economics*, 0022-1821, Vol. LIII, June 2005, *http://econ-www.mit.edu/faculty/download_pdf.php?id=910*.

Estache A. and A. Goicoechea (2004), *How Widespread were Private Investment and Regulatory Reform in Infrastructure Utilities during the 1990s?*, The World Bank, Washington DC.

Morgan, T. (2006), "Outlook for Global Investment in Electricity Infrastructure", in *Infrastructure to 2030: Telecom, Land Transport, Water and Electricity*, OECD, Paris.

Pollitt, M.G. (1995), *Ownership and Performance in Electric Utilities*, Oxford University Press/Oxford Institute for Energy Studies, Oxford.

Pollitt, M.G. (1997), "The Impact of Liberalisation on the Performance of the Electricity Supply Industry: an International Survey", *Journal of Energy Literature*, Vol. 3, No. 2, pp. 3-31.

PriceWaterhouseCoopers (PwC) (2004), *Power Deals: Mergers and Acquisitions Activity Within the Global Electricity and Gas Market*, 2004 Annual Review, PwC, London, *www.pwc.com/extweb/pwcpublications.nsf/docid/63a2c46a51cea74285256fa8005b592c*.

PriceWaterhouseCoopers (PwC) (2006), *Power Deals: Mergers and Acquisitions Activity Within the Global Electricity and Gas Market*, 2005 Annual Review, PwC, London, *www.pwc.com/extweb/pwcpublications.nsf/docid/8568b30a425291458525712400757e46*.

Roques, F., D. Newberry and W. Nuttall (2005), "Investment Incentives and Electricity Market Design: The British Experience", *Review of Network Economics*, Vol. 4, Issue 2, June 2005.

World Bank (2004), *Reforming Infrastructure Privatization, Regulation, and Competition*, World Bank/Oxford University Press, New York.

ISBN 978-92-64-03131-9
Infrastructure to 2030 – Vol. 2
Mapping Policy for Electricity, Water and Transport

Chapter 4

Water Infrastructure and Water-related Services: Trends and Challenges Affecting Future Development

by
Meena Palaniappan, Heather Cooley, Peter H. Gleick *and* Gary Wolff*

The water sector faces serious challenges in both developing and OECD countries. For all water systems there is a growing focus on the best ways to finance and implement improvements in operation and maintenance of systems. How are business models in the sector being affected by the challenges of financing, demand management, scale of water systems, public involvement and equity, competition and climate change? This chapter analyses the evolving dynamics of the water and wastewater sector and discusses policy implications and a range of options for sustainable solutions.

* Pacific Institute for Studies in Development, Environment and Security, Oakland, California, US. This chapter was jointly commissioned and financed by the OECD International Futures Programme and the OECD Environment Directorate.

Summary

The water sector faces serious challenges. The failure to meet basic human needs for water; difficulties in meeting the financial requirements for maintaining, extending, and upgrading both new and ageing water systems; new regulatory requirements for water quality; increasing water scarcity; competition for limited capital, and global climate change will continue to affect the development of the water sector. In addition, the water objectives of the Millennium Development Goals add impetus to efforts in developing countries and the Big 5 economies[1] to halve the proportion of people without access to safe drinking water and sanitation. As existing water infrastructure hits the century-old mark, the developed OECD countries are facing immediate needs to replace and upgrade infrastructure, respond to new water quality regulations, and ensure the security of water supplies in response to climate change, pollution and growing populations. For all water systems, there is a growing focus on the best ways to finance and implement improvements in operation and maintenance of systems.

Business models

Different business models involving various relationships between private and public roles have emerged and become predominant in France, UK, Canada, the US, Germany, and in other OECD countries. These models range from the purely public, to a mix of public and private, to purely private. These models vary in terms of level of decentralisation, who owns system assets, who finances investments and who defines the price and level of service. Different water sector forms, however, do share some common characteristics: water provision is a natural monopoly; it is often capital-intensive in its need for infrastructure for water collection, purification, distribution and waste treatment; and it typically offers a low "return on investment" common to other regulated utility industries. While most water-sector investments have been local and public, private sector participation has also played an important role in some parts of the world.

Key issues

Some key issues affecting the robustness of business models become apparent in the analysis of the future trends in the water sector. These are briefly detailed below:

Financing. Financing is critical for ongoing operation and maintenance as well as responding to needs for new infrastructure. Ashley and Cashman (2006) estimate that by 2015, an average annual investment of USD 772 billion will be needed in OECD and BRIC countries. Water services are more capital intensive than other utilities, requiring twice the capital compared to electricity utilities with the same annual operating expenses. With growing financial needs, along with a decline in public investments in water, and the lack of private investment being directed to this sector (only 5% of private investments tracked by the World Bank went to the water sector), new strategies need to be found to make needed investments. Full cost pricing is a key tool being considered to address funding gaps. Full cost pricing through user charges that account for all the costs of providing water and wastewater services are being considered in communities throughout the world to address water sector needs. Yet, very few systems world wide are currently fully funded by existing or future customers, depending instead on taxes and international aid.

Demand management. Demand management – by reducing the amount of water and wastewater services that are needed through efficiency, conservation, and structural changes – can substantially reduce the capital requirements of existing water systems. A demand management approach to water increases the productivity of water use, rather than seeking endless new sources of supply. Demand management changes the industrial dynamics, increases the time scale of planning efforts (long term *vs.* short term), focuses on the end-goal instead of the path to reach it, involves fewer technical risks and uses less money.

Scale of water systems. In order to address challenges in the water sector, various approaches are being tried that either expand or reduce the scale of water systems. In the US and Canada, approaches to regionalise water systems capture economies of scale by banding together several municipalities. Regionalised water systems can lead to reduced costs, the sharing of expertise, improved performance, enhanced water supply security in uncertain climate conditions, and water systems managed at a more appropriate watershed scale. An emerging area is that of on-site, point-of-use, and closed loop systems where the water and wastewater system is integrated into a residential dwelling or industrial or commercial establishment. This introduces new actors and methods of financing into the water sector including property and landowners, flat complex developers in water-stressed areas, and engineering firms who provide design-build-operate (DBO) functions.

Public involvement and equity. Public involvement will facilitate much larger investments in the water sector. Ultimately, water utilities will be subject to the court of public opinion to determine whether they have convinced ratepayers, taxpayers, and stockholders of the need for new infrastructure investments and the utility's ability to manage those infrastructure improvements effectively. Lack of public involvement can, and has, led to the failure of projects and investments. Because water is fundamental for life and health, ensuring equity is a key goal and a driver in the water sector. Pressures for full cost pricing will make it increasingly difficult to ensure that water is affordable for the poor, and will require the involvement of a health agency to ensure that the needs of the poor are being met.

Competition. Seeing the success of the introduction of competition in the telecommunications sector in terms of reduced cost and improved service, competition is being tried in the water sector. Because of the high costs of infrastructure and the key public health nature of the service, introducing competition in water has been more difficult. It is being done in a few key ways: third party access, or allowing a third party to use the capital intensive water distribution network, is being tried in England; water transfers are being used to reallocate water among users; and benchmark competition in the form of performance scorecards has been used in Australia and the UK.

Climate change. Climate change and water pollution are considered by Ashley and Cashman (2006) to have the greatest impact on increasing the cost of water services. In different regions of the world, climate change will affect where, when, how much and how water falls; increase the vulnerability of water supplies; increase the severity of droughts and flooding events; threaten coastal aquifers, among other impacts. Investments will be needed to protect water security, and the diversity of sources of water, as well as to introduce low cost methods of increasing supply, including demand management.

Changes to existing business models

Existing business models are changing in significant ways to respond to challenges in the water sector and to take advantage of key opportunities. We expect these trends to continue into the future. Public models are responding to competition from private actors by instituting efficiency through re-engineering their operations and services. Private sector models are also changing the nature and role of their investments. After a decline in private investments in 2002, we see private investments picking up again with changing actors and new strategies.

Having been stung by public backlash against previous privatisation agreements, the private sector is embracing the need for transparency and stakeholder involvement in successful privatisation agreements. Local private actors are also taking a much more significant role in the water sector, particularly in China and the Russian Federation. Private companies are also moving from concessions, which involve high capital risk, to operation and management contracts in some regions. There has also been a growing trend towards wastewater contracts *versus* water contracts, possibly because wastewater contracts are less politically charged. Companies are also focusing on key regions and withdrawing from others. We anticipate that in the future, local private actors will become more predominant, and that concessions will continue to be attractive in some stable economies, but in others Operation and Maintenance (O&M) contracts will be preferred.

Through all of this, we expect water sector actors to continue to depend on public finance, while seeking to expand innovative mechanisms of financing that take advantage of local capital, as well as get rewarded for positive externalities. Robust business models will integrate new scales of service, including regionalisation when appropriate and on-site systems as they emerge. The nature of the landscape is also changing and will require business models to interact and partner with numerous actors, including local governments, other water providers and regulators, in a more fluid and effective manner. The ability to communicate with and involve the public in decisions about the water system will be critical for success, as will managing system assets effectively, effective staffing, and adaptive management approaches that identify the problem before arriving at solutions.

Policy implications

Governance in the water sector is critical to protect the social and public goods aspects of water and wastewater services. The need to reduce epidemics of waterborne disease gave birth to the public health movement in the 1880s, and positive externalities from investment in water and wastewater are significant, ranging from USD 4 to 12 per USD 1 invested. Protecting public health, ensuring water quality standards, and the equitable provision of supply requires significant public oversight and governance.

With the changing dynamics of the water and wastewater sector, sustainability in the water sector will require supporting and regulating a range of options within an enabling policy framework. The goal in the policy arena will need to be the creation of a pro-competitive framework, while supporting a range of business models and scales to address water and wastewater needs. This will involve creating opportunities and removing obstacles to new entrants into the water sector, creating opportunities for multiple financing mechanisms, strengthening the regulatory system, focusing on transparency and public education, providing incentives for competition, and funding more research and development in the sector.

1. Introduction

The water sector continues to face serious challenges. The failure to meet basic human needs for water; difficulties in meeting the financial requirements for maintaining, extending, and upgrading both new and ageing water systems; new regulatory requirements for water quality; increasing water scarcity; competition for limited capital, and global climate change will continue to affect the development of the water sector. New ways of delivering water and disposing of waste, emerging players in the water sector, and innovative ideas about sustainable water planning, demand management and community transparency are creating new opportunities in water management. As a result, existing business models are innovating or giving way to emerging business models that may reshape the sector.

World wide, estimates of revenues in the water sector range from USD 350-650 billion (Maxwell, 2005). The scope of the water sector is complex, owing to its diversity, interactions and synergies with other industrial, commercial and financial sectors, and its international nature. Most traditional estimates of the scope of the water sector have focused on urban water services because of better availability of data and challenges in defining boundaries to water services. While these estimates are valuable, globally about 70% of water used by people goes to the agricultural sector for the production of food and fibre (although this varies widely from country to country). Thus, estimates of the current and future role of water in the agricultural sector are also critical, though the primary focus here will be on urban needs.

Water services are provided through a variety of approaches, though most involve centralised systems with large supply, distribution and treatment facilities – what has been described as the "hard path" (Wolff and Gleick, 2002; and Gleick, 2003). Increasingly, however, there is a realisation that the hard path alone may not provide for a range of unmet and new needs, and that combining centralised infrastructure with new approaches for water supply, demand management and community engagement may be more successful, and are often less costly.

Decreasing water availability, declining water quality and increasing water withdrawals are placing greater demands on limited water resources. This increasing water stress is already constraining socio-economic growth in some countries. Global climate change is likely to have significant impacts on water availability, quality and demand (IPCC, 2001). No good estimates are available of the additional costs (or reduced costs) that climate change may impose on water resources in different regions, nor the effects it may have on the effectiveness of any particular business model. Nevertheless, the importance of the problem must be acknowledged, and more comprehensive efforts must be made to better understand climate change impacts and adaptation costs and benefits.

The *social benefits* that water and wastewater services provide are well known, including reduced mortality and morbidity from waterborne diseases. Most of these benefits accrue outside the financial accounts of the infrastructure investor, creating a significant gap between "project" and "social" rates of return. Since the development of water and wastewater infrastructure grew out of the public health revolution in the late 1800s, there is a strong link between public health and the development of water and wastewater utilities. Public capital has often been used provide backing for infrastructure bonds, or to provide low-cost or no-cost capital to undertake infrastructure projects that protect public health. The increasing drive to full cost pricing from customers is shifting some of the underlying capital and operating costs from governments to water users; a drive that to some extent fails to consider the positive externalities generated by the services. It is also well recognised that increasing public involvement in water decisions can lead to greater willingness to pay for water and wastewater services, which will be required to sustain and increase investment levels to meet needs.

The importance of water as a social good and a *human right* has been well recognised in numerous international fora. The United Nations Committee on Economic, Social and Cultural Rights declared access to water a fundamental human right, entitling everyone to affordable, safe and accessible water supplies for domestic uses. While water is recognised as a human right and a social good that should be affordable to all people, this does not mean that water should or can be free for all people. Extracting, collecting, treating, testing and distributing water all require certain levels of infrastructure and resources. In order to deliver potable water to the tap, maintain system infrastructure and expand to underserved areas, a sustainable source of funds needs to be maintained.

Finance plays a key role in the water sector. The gap in required financing in the water sector and projected financing is enormous and growing, and chronic underinvestment in the water sector is an ongoing problem. Although there have been efforts to increase the role of private capital as a way of reducing the burden on public funding, such privatisation approaches have run into public opposition. The participation of private actors in recent years has not been particularly successful as a means for increasing capital investment in the sector. Indeed, some participation has been highly polarised and controversial. If substantial additions to private participation are to be encouraged and successful, new models will have to be developed that satisfy basic public interests and generate political and social acceptance. Private capital may also be generated through the use of municipal, public or private bonds, where future system users pay for current system investment needs.

One of the contributions of economics to public policy is its focus on incentives and their effects on behaviour. Greater levels of infrastructure investment, and different types of investments, will be encouraged or

Box 4.1. **Definition of privatisation**

We also note that "privatisation" has been defined in many ways, and no single definition is used consistently. For the purposes of this assessment, privatisation in the water sector involves transferring some or all of the "assets" or "operations" of public water systems into private hands. There are numerous ways to privatise water, such as the transfer of the responsibility to operate a water delivery or treatment system, a more complete transfer of system ownership and operation responsibilities, or even the sale of publicly owned water rights to private companies. Alternatively, various combinations are possible, such as soliciting private investment in the development of new facilities, with transfer of those facilities to public ownership after investors have been repaid. Over the last decade, offers to privatise water services were coming from newly amalgamated, large multinational corporations. There seems to be a cooling in this trend as we describe later in this chapter, with regional actors playing a greater role. Opposition to privatisation continues at local, regional and international levels.

When the service being privatised has "public good" characteristics, like water, government regulation or oversight has traditionally been applied. Economists and others argue that goods and services previously provided by public officials or agencies may become less vulnerable to political manipulation when privatised, but private entities may also become less responsive to public interests. Examples include protection of water quality, commitment to efficiency improvements that reduce the volume of water used, maintenance of basic service levels, transparent prices and billing practices, and investments in water reclamation or additional sources of water supply.

discouraged by different patterns of incentives. In this chapter, we discuss *incentive patterns* mostly through the lens of "business models", by which we mean the entities providing the water, wastewater and stormwater management services.

2. Current business models

2.1. *Functions common across business models*

Every water system includes a variety of functions, such as maintenance of underground pipe systems or collection of revenues. Box 4.2 presents a useful and relatively complete categorisation of functions from Gleick *et al.* (2002). The list in Box 4.2 is not the only such list one could create. For example, one could combine the operation and maintenance (O&M) functions into one, as is usually the case. Or one could divide a water system based on

Box 4.2. **Water system functions**

1. Capital improvement planning and budgeting (including water conservation and wastewater reclamation issues).
2. Finance of capital improvements.
3. Design of capital improvements.
4. Construction of capital improvements.
5. Operation of facilities.
6. Maintenance of facilities.
7. Pricing decisions.
8. Management of billing and revenue collection.
9. Management of payments to employees or contractors.
10. Financial and risk management.
11. Establishment, monitoring, and enforcement of water quality and other service standards.

Source: Gleick *et al.*, 2002.

geographic area, as in Manila, Philippines, where potable water services were divided into areas served by different contractors when its water system was privatised in the 1990s.

2.2. Current business models

Current business models are successful based on their ability to attract capital, maintain and expand water services, protect water assets, communicate with the public, and provide safe water and wastewater services to users.

The traditional focus on public *versus* private ownership or operation of built assets does not allow one to fully distinguish the entire context within which business models in the water sector operate. For example, water rights are valuable assets that affect service provider behaviour perhaps as much as "built" assets. The context in which business models operate should be defined to include other important characteristics, such as:

- Where does investment capital come from?
- Who repays the capital?
- How is the service organised (*i.e.* central systems, decentralised systems, etc.)?
- How are service quality, potable and ambient water quality, and economic factors, such as tariffs or rates of return to invested capital, regulated?

Table 4.1. **Current and emerging business models in OECD countries**

	French (*affermage*)	Concession	English/Welsh	Canadian	German	US	Closed loops
Status	Stable	Some decline in OECD and non-OECD countries	Limited dissemination	Stable	Stable	Stable with some emerging private	Emerging
Level of decentralisation	Municipality	Municipality	Regional	Regional or municipal	Municipality	Municipal/regional	Condominium
Who owns the assets	Municipality	Municipality	Utility	Municipality	Municipality	Municipality or regional district	Property developer
Who pays for investments	Municipality/basin organisation	Utility	Utility	Municipality	Municipality	Municipality or regional district	Property developer
Who defines the service	Municipality	Municipality	Regulator	Municipality	Municipality	Public utility or service commissions	Property developer
Who sets the price	Municipality	Municipality	Regulator	Municipality or Regional District Board	Utility	Public utility or service commissions	Property developer
Robustness *vis-à-vis* key drivers	Attracts no private capital. Depends on municipal capacity to raise funds.	Depends on emergence of domestic operators and their capacity to raise private funds.	Fails to attract private capital. Apparent shift towards mutual funds.	Attracts no private capital. Regional models capture economies of scale, particularly useful in less dense areas surrounding urbanised areas.	Until recent reform due to EU regulation, service provided by multi-utilities (water, energy, urban transit), with cross subsidisation.	Attracts no private capital. Depends on municipal capacity to raise funds.	Best qualifies in new, extensive, peri-urban habitats.

A range of business models exists currently in OECD and non-OECD countries. These business models vary as to who owns the assets, who makes investments, the scale of the system, who sets the price, and how robust the business model is at attracting investment. A few existing models and their context are laid out in Table 4.1.

It should be noted that some countries (France, Germany) have allowed the development of *régies*, where the utility belongs to the municipality and has no legal identity (it exists only as a service of the municipality). This model is now criticised, typically in the EU, as being opaque. There is a general tendency to sever the service provider from the municipality and to corporatise it (French *régie*, or German *Eigenbetrieb*), with, at least, a separate budget.

United States and Canada

There are a number of purely public examples in the United States and in Canada. By purely public, we mean systems where built assets are entirely owned and operated by public entities. An old and venerable business model is that of a water, wastewater or flood-control department within a general-purpose unit of government (*e.g.* a city, county, province, state or federal government).

Funding for public systems might come from a tax base or fee-for-service revenue (*e.g.* water sales). Revenue sources that are earmarked for water sector services and sequestered from general revenue, are referred to as "enterprise funds". Both departments whose budgets are supported by commingled general funds and those supported by sequestered funds are purely public models within general-purpose government, but the incentives these models face may be quite different.

Special districts separate not only revenue but also governance from the general-purpose government entity. Such districts usually have a separately elected governing board whose sole duty is (usually) to provide water, wastewater or flood-control services. Residents within the service area may vote, whether they own property or not. Businesses within the service area do not have direct say in who sits on the governing board. This business model is common in the western US.

Another model is that of a corporatised public utility. This model is like a special district, but is managed like a corporation with one shareholder. The shareholder can be a city, as in Louisville Water, a water-supply utility owned by the City of Louisville, Kentucky in the US; or a state, as are the water-supply utilities throughout Australia. Corporatised utilities typically have appointed rather than elected boards, where appointments are made by the owning entity. These boards are often composed of experts in various areas (*e.g.* engineering or finance), and need not represent the stakeholder groups in the community.

In both the United States and Canada, geographically interdependent municipalities have taken advantages of economies of scale to consolidate their operations into regionalised water service providers. This is discussed further in the following section of the report.

French and German models

Some systems maintain full public ownership of all assets but involve various degrees of operation and maintenance management by private companies. Operating contracts and design-build-operate (DBO) method for procuring new assets are becoming more common. Under most of these contracts, the public entity collects payments from customers or raises revenue from other sources, and pays the contractor for their services.

Concession and franchise agreements are often similar to design-build-operate-transfer (DBOT) in that the private investor typically owns assets until the end of the agreement, but at least in concept there is no requirement for a design-build component. For example, a concessionaire or franchisee might be granted the right to operate an existing system, collect revenues, pay for operation and maintenance, and make minor improvements. In some cases, ownership of the system resides with the public, but the concession grants an exclusive licence to operate and maintain the system. Major improvements might be negotiated under a separate agreement with the concessionaire or franchisee, or might be designed and constructed by others, then included in the concession or franchise. Concessions often include the exclusive right to construct new assets, while franchises tend to be more limited in that regard. The franchisee or concession holder usually collects revenues from customers.

Another variation of the public ownership/private management business model is the French system of *affermage*. In this model, publicly owned assets are leased to the private operator. The operator pays a fee for use of the assets, which is then recovered from customers as part of the water or wastewater service charge. Capital improvements are usually budgeted and funded by government. A unique incentive sometimes exists for the leasing company in *affermage*. If they can defer the need for a capital improvement, they are allowed to keep the interest on the deferred investment sum in excess of the increase in investment cost due to inflation. This creates an incentive for high-quality maintenance and creative measures (*e.g.* water main leak reduction) to reduce demand for new facilities.

Dutch model

The Dutch water companies often have mixed public-private ownership, with public operation of assets. This creates an incentive for efficiency because the private owners would like to earn higher dividends on their investments, but regulation moderates the profit motive by requiring that more than 50% of the ownership interest is public.

English/Welsh models

In 1973, England passed the Water Act, which placed the responsibility for managing the entire water cycle from collection, distribution, conservation, sewage collection, and pollution abatement in the hands of Regional Water Authorities (RWA). In 1974, the water industry was restructured into ten Regional Water Authorities (RWA). A few water agencies retained their autonomy and were designated Water Supply-only Companies (WSCs). Some district councils chose to retain sewerage collection, public health and land-use planning functions, and they collected sewage fees and paid the RWAs for treatment services.

Despite the improvements in the 1970s and early 1980s, a number of major challenges remained. During this period, the British economy slowed, decreasing resources available for system improvement and management. At the same time, new standards developed within the EC put pressure on water agencies to upgrade facilities. Huge capital investments were required, but underinvestment by public agencies worsened overall conditions. By the mid-1980s, an estimated GBP 26 billion was needed to bring the old water system to EC standards of water quality and environmental protection.

These trends were supplemented by the ideological goals of the Thatcher government to push for privatisation of many public services, including transportation, energy, telecommunications and water utilities. As a result, the Water Acts 1988 and 1989[2] were passed, privatising the water systems and services in England and Wales. The acts gave the privatised water companies 25-year concessions for sanitation and water supply, and protected concessionaires against any possibility of competition.

There was no formal public consultation at the time the industry was privatised despite (or because of) polls that suggested that 75% of the public did not support privatisation (Saunders and Harris, 1990). Since 1997, the new Labour government has made an effort to widen public participation in concession agreements.

As a result of the initial structure and form of privatisation, a variety of problems materialised early that led to changes, modifications and revisions in the government agencies responsible for oversight, customer protection and regulation. We offer here a summary of the most relevant issues that arose, and the responses by public agencies. Among the problems:

1. Tariffs rose sharply following privatisation, necessitated by huge investments in water-system improvements, with little public input. The different regulatory authorities with different mandates sent conflicting signals to the water companies.
2. Public opinion was divided on how much should be spent on environmental protection.

3. The rise in tariffs led to an increase in water debt and disconnections, drawing widespread public criticism.
4. There was public anger over the fact that water companies were continuing to earn substantial profits even in drought years, when consumption restrictions had been imposed on the public.

In response to strong public opposition, strong government regulatory oversight and a reorganisation of government regulatory authorities eventually helped improve service, stabilise and monitor rate increases and ensure water quality protection. The model is now stable, and regulators are working to improve competition and introduce new actors into the water sector.

Small and/or domestic private

It is also worth differentiating between locally owned private companies and multinational private companies, which we explore later in the chapter. In many developing countries another model of private provision exists: small private companies act as vendors of water and water-treatment equipment. Water vendors sell water from tanker trucks in peri-urban areas of the world, particularly in parts of Brazil, India, China and Indonesia. The quality of water sold in this way is typically unregulated, although licensing these actors as part of municipal supply is growing in some countries. In addition, private vendors of water-treatment equipment often operate the equipment under contract. A typical client for these service providers is an industrial or large commercial facility that needs on-site wastewater or water treatment. This business model seems to be growing rapidly as on-site and smaller scale technologies become more reliable and economical, and are increasingly used in residential and commercial applications.

2.3. History, importance and future of business models in the OECD and Big 5 countries

Private sector participation in the provision of water and sanitation services is not a new concept. Private entrepreneurs, investor-owned utilities, and other private entities have provided water and sanitation services in different parts of the world for many years. In England, for example, private water services began in the 16th century and lasted for over 300 years before local governments took a more active role (NRC, 2002). In France, private water services began in the mid-19th century under the reign of Napoleon III (Gentry, 2000). Water services in the US were largely provided by the private sector during the 18th, 19th and early 20th centuries. Commencing in the latter part of the 19th century, however, local governments throughout Europe and the United States substantially increased their investments in public water supply, and took over many formerly private systems, to ensure service coverage for all segments of society, reduce the incidence of waterborne diseases, including cholera, and provide water for fire fighting (Gleick *et al.*, 2002; NRC, 2002). Public sector investment continued to grow throughout the 20th century as governments recognised the broader economic and social benefits that a safe, reliable water supply provides.

In the 1990s, public and private entities looked to privatisation in a range of sectors to meet a variety of needs. During this period, private sector participation in the water and wastewater sector increased in many countries throughout the world. Private sector participation in water and sanitation, however, varies considerably among countries. Table 4.2 shows the per cent of

Table 4.2. **Per cent of the population served by the private sector in 2005**

	Water	Sewerage
United Kingdom	90	93
France	76	57
Czech Republic	68	65
Spain	45	52
Greece	44	37
Italy	41	29
Hungary	26	25
Australia	22	6
Brazil	20	14
Portugal	19	16
Germany	17	14
Mexico	16	9
United States	15	5
Austria	7	0
China	5	3
Canada	4	2
Russian Federation	4	1
Belgium	3	40
Indonesia	3	0
Slovak Republic	3	3
New Zealand	2	6
Poland	2	2
Turkey	2	1
Ireland	1	36
Norway	1	5
Sweden	1	1
Denmark	0	1
Finland	0	1
India	0	0
Japan	0	0
Korea	0	7
Luxembourg	0	0
Netherlands	0	11
Switzerland	0	0
Iceland	n.a.	n.a.

n.a.: Signifies no data available.
Source: Pinsent Masons, 2006.

the population in each country served by the private sector in 2005. While this includes those served by purely private and mixed public-private schemes, this table does not include the use by public utilities of private vendors for functions such as outsourced billing or administration. This table also does not characterise the extent of informal, or small-scale private sector involvement, including water tankers and bottled-water providers. These unregulated private actors are very common in countries like India.

The private sector is dominant in the United Kingdom, France, and the Czech Republic and plays a significant role in Greece, Hungary, Italy, and Spain.[3] In most OECD and Big 5 countries, however, the private sector plays a relatively minor role in the provision of water and sewerage services.[4] Variation in private participation among countries is due to a number of factors, including the existence of supportive policies, a stable political and financial climate, local history and conditions, and public perception.

The data available for all the 35 countries of interest (OECD plus Big 5 countries) does not provide the level of detail on type of contract needed to assess which types of private sector arrangements are most common in which regions, and which models are growing over time. More detail is provided below on the emerging and developing economies.

Trends in private sector involvement in emerging and developing economies

The World Bank maintains data on the number, amount and type of investment (concession, greenfield,[5] divestiture, and management and lease contract) involving private participation in the water and sewerage sector in middle- and low-income countries. Eleven of the 35 countries included in this study fall within that category (Table 4.3). The following discussion will focus on these countries.

Table 4.3. **Countries in World Bank PPI database included in this study**

	Category
Czech Republic	Upper Middle Income
Hungary	Upper Middle Income
Mexico	Upper Middle Income
Poland	Upper Middle Income
Slovak Republic	Upper Middle Income
Turkey	Lower Middle Income
Brazil	Upper Middle Income
Russian Federation	Lower Middle Income
India	Low Income
China	Lower Middle Income
Indonesia	Lower Middle Income

Source: World Bank PPI database.

Between 1990 and 2004, a total of 177 projects representing USD 11.2 billion (in year 2000 dollars) were initiated in the countries listed in Table 4.3. Figure 4.1 shows the number of projects involving private entities by the year that they reached financial closure. The number of projects rose sharply in the early to mid-1990s, peaked in 2000, and dropped precipitously between 2000 and 2003. The number of projects, however, appears to be rebounding, as they more than doubled between 2003 and 2004. Over 70% of the projects initiated between 1990 and 2004 were in Brazil, India and Mexico.

Figure 4.1. **Number of water and sewerage public-private partnership investment projects, 1990-2004**

In the eleven OECD + BRIC countries listed in Table 4.3

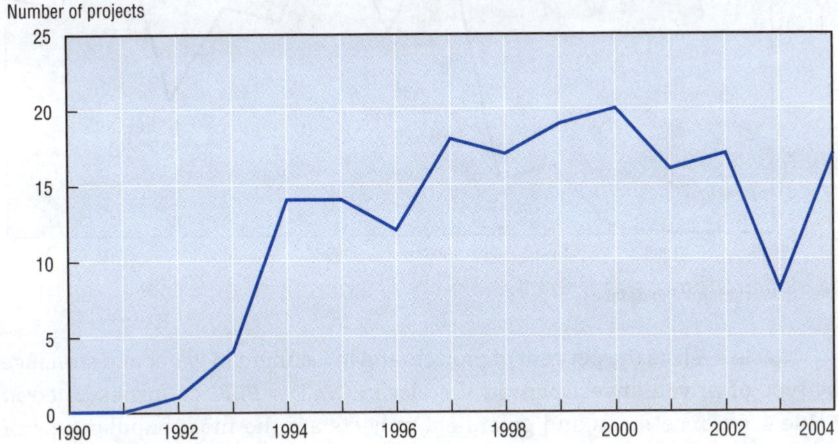

Source: World Bank PPI database.

Large privatisation projects are riskier investments. By 2004, seven out of 177 of the projects (representing 11% of the total investment) initiated in those countries listed in Table 4.3 (11 out of 35 OECD + BRIC countries) between 1990 and 2004 were either cancelled or in distress.[6] By comparison, 7% of projects (representing 37% of the total investment) initiated during the same period in all middle- and low-income countries were either cancelled or in distress. Thus the failure rate of projects initiated in those countries listed in Table 4.3 is less than the average of all middle- and low-income countries, suggesting that the countries addressed in this chapter may be more capable of supporting privatisation efforts.

Total public-private partnership investments in the water and sewerage sector in the eleven OECD + BRIC countries listed in Table 4.3 were USD 11.2 billion (in year 2000 dollars) between 1990 and 2004. Investments in the water sector, however, exhibit high annual variability, particularly since 1996

(Figure 4.2). Current investments in the eleven OECD + BRIC countries listed in Table 4.3 are nearly 30% below their 1998 peak level of USD 1.6 billion (in year 2000 dollars).

Figure 4.2. **Total project investment in water and sewerage public-private partnership investment projects, 1990-2004**

In the eleven OECD + BRIC countries listed in Table 4.3

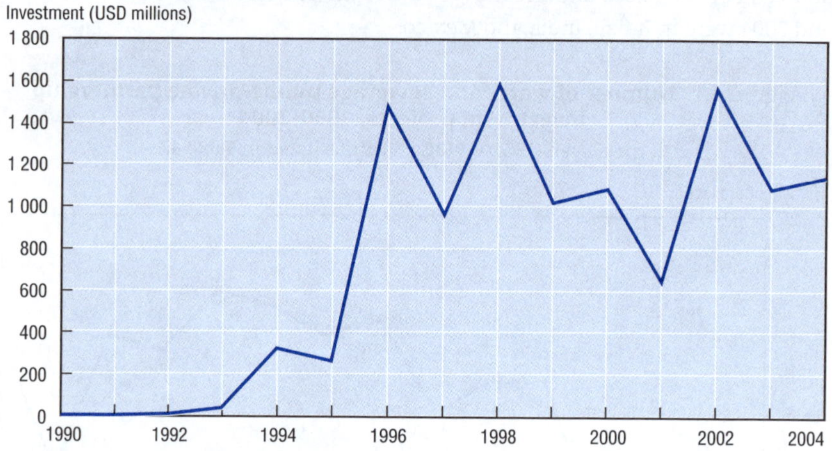

Source: World Bank PPI database.

Table 4.4 lists the per cent of projects and investment in water and sewerage by type of private investment in the eleven OECD + BRIC countries listed in Table 4.3. Concessions and greenfield projects are the most popular type of arrangement, accounting for 39% and 37%, respectively, of the projects between 1990 and 2004. Similarly, investment in these types of projects was also high. Divestiture was the least common type of arrangement, but accounted for 20% of cumulative investment, indicating that these projects are among the most expensive. Concession and greenfield contracts are likely more common because ownership of the asset potentially provides greater protection for the investor against abuse by the governmental contracting entity.

Table 4.4. **Per cent of projects and cumulative investment of water and sewerage projects, by private investment type, 1990-2004**

In the eleven OECD + BRIC countries listed in Table 4.3

Type of private investment	Projects (%)	Investment (%)
Concession	39	40
Divestiture	7	20
Greenfield project	37	37
Management and lease contract	17	3

Source: World Bank PPI database.

Trends in private sector involvement in OECD countries

Country-specific information on water privatisation in developed countries is not collected in a consistent manner.[7] The Privatization Barometer maintains data on privatisation efforts in Europe, but does not provide specific information on contract type, *i.e.* concession, BOT, divestiture, etc. Thus, it is difficult to quantitatively assess private sector involvement in OECD countries other than those included in Table 4.3. Anecdotal evidence, however, suggests that the prominence of various contract types depends upon a number of factors, including the existence of supportive policies, a stable political and financial climate, local history and conditions, and public perception. England and Wales, for example, have divested most of their assets to private companies, although clearly divestiture is the least common type of contract in developed countries. In the United States, however, DBO and pure O&M contracts are more common than, for example, DBOT contracts because public financing of privately owned assets (private activity bonds) is limited under the tax code, while earnings to those who lend to government for construction of public assets is tax exempt. In France, concessions and leases are more common. In the Czech Republic, concessions are dominant. And in Ireland, BOT contracts are more common.

3. Key drivers and opportunities in the water sector

After carrying out a detailed analysis of the water sector's characteristics and the impacts of the drivers presented by Ashley and Cashman (2006), we believe that there are a few key principal drivers of change and opportunities that have the potential to transform the water sector. In this section, we look more closely at the principal drivers, which include financing, demand management, the scale of water systems, climate change, and public involvement and equity.

3.1. Financing

The key challenges of the water and wastewater sector include the need to expand access to water and wastewater services, invest in replacing and maintaining ageing infrastructure, and address security and environmental concerns. Addressing these challenges will require both large capital investments for new infrastructure, ongoing investments in maintenance, repair, upgrading and operation of existing facilities, and integration of new ways of organising, funding and producing revenues and reducing costs within utilities.

In most of the countries that are the focus of this chapter, the networks developed for water supply, distribution and treatment are generally considered well developed and the most valuable assets, comprising some 60-80% of the total value of all urban water and wastewater systems. According to Ashley and Cashman (2006), the current value of existing sewerage assets in the UK alone is some USD 200 billion, and it is several times larger than that in the United States. Comparable levels of investment and development, however, have not been made in some of the OECD and Big 5 countries. In transition economies, the need for maintaining and upgrading existing infrastructure is combined with sometimes significant needs to expand coverage and at the same time address the challenges of poor governance, institutional neglect and inefficiency, and deterioration of the water asset base.

There is a range of estimates of required annual expenditures in the water and wastewater sector. Ashley and Cashman (2006) estimate the needed annual expenditures based on income categories. In the high-income countries, they estimate that 0.35 to 1.2% of GDP will be required to finance needed infrastructure, maintenance and services. In middle-income countries, they estimate 0.54 to 2.60% of GDP is needed and in the low-income countries, an estimated 0.70 to 6.30% would be needed. Because financing infrastructure needs in low-income countries requires a larger percentage of GDP than in other countries, these requirements will reinforce and worsen income disparities, suggesting that attempts should be made to rectify this problem.

Table 4.5 provides an estimate of the projected annual expenditures on water and wastewater services and includes the influence of the drivers on projected needs (Ashley and Cashman, 2006). The total projected needs in the OECD and Big 5 countries approach USD 800 billion by 2015, which is consistent with a recent study by Andrieu (2005). Scenarios of future expenditures for water vary widely and should be viewed sceptically. No standardised method for estimating needs is used. Moreover, most scenarios tend to focus on "investment" needs and exclude recurring expenditures for operations, maintenance, repairs, replacement and overhead. While these expenses are sometimes covered by revenue, shortfalls often lead to inadequate expenditures for operations and maintenance, and a resulting increase in future investments. While considerable uncertainty is involved in these estimates, it is clear that water-related infrastructure investment needs could be huge and that governments will need to pay particular attention to water in the future.

Access to capital

There are major drivers affecting the ability of OECD and non-OECD countries to make needed investments and finance the expansion and maintenance of water and wastewater infrastructure and services. Limited tax revenue that is available to support financing these investments will be increasingly constrained by growing demands on public resources, including the need to support ageing populations. Currency risks in the Big 5 economies are causing a shift to more local financing in these countries. Increasing demands on water and wastewater services also increase the financial pressures on the sector. Ashley and Cashman (2006) project that socio-economic changes including

Table 4.5. **Projected expenditures on water and wastewater services**

Average annual investment (in USD billions)

	By 2015	By 2025
Australia	6.86	9.95
Austria	2.59	3.91
Belgium	2.75	4.38
Canada	10.27	15.74
Czech Republic	3.12	2.83
Denmark	1.82	2.74
Finland	1.35	2.15
France	16.86	25.84
Germany	23.38	35.84
Greece	2.17	3.34
Hungary	2.02	2.79
Iceland	0.09	0.14
Ireland	1.35	2.15
Italy	16.83	25.23
Japan	46.98	63.41
Korea	12.76	18
Luxembourg	0.24	0.39
Mexico	167.78	153.65
Netherlands	5.43	7.88
New Zealand	1.14	1.63
Norway	1.58	2.55
Poland	7.93	7.18
Portugal	1.96	2.97
Slovak Republic	1.35	1.22
Spain	10.97	15.96
Sweden	2.26	3.6
Switzerland	1.97	3.19
Turkey	9.33	9.66
United Kingdom	19.14	27.96
United States	101.65	167.63
Russian Federation	11.49	26.41
India	74.8	108.31
China	182.1	247.18
Brazil	19.8	32.02
Total	**772.12**	**1 037.83**

Source: Ashley and Cashman (2006), "The Impacts of Change on the Long-Term Future Demand for Water Sector Infrastructure", in *Infrastructure to 2030: Telecom, Land Transport, Water and Electricity*, OECD, Paris.

population growth, age profile changes and rising expectations for water services; environmental challenges such as climate change and water pollution; and internal politics, including governance challenges and urbanisation, will increase water infrastructure and services costs. Technologies that increase efficiency are estimated to reduce unit costs of water services.

Ultimately, in financing water services, the questions of who pays for what, what the scale of financing is, whether financing is protected, and the venues for accessing capital are critical. Water systems typically acquire funds to maintain and expand service through the general budget, local budgets, consumers, taxpayers and the system operator (reinvestment of profits). New models are also accessing capital through involvement of mutual funds that seek long-term fixed rates of return on capital, engineering service firms that build an on-site water system and obtain an ongoing service contract to service their capital investment, and landowners or homeowners who purchase an on-site system as part of the purchase of an existing property or the construction of a new one.

Accessing the capital is critical, and it depends on establishing trust among investors and users that the water system is operating efficiently and effectively. Capital can be accessed through general budgets, local budgets and private lenders. Accessing private capital and public capital will require a high credit and bond ratings and guaranteed returns on the investment.

Capital must be serviced. This needs to be done through adequate cost recovery mechanisms that maintain service and infrastructure quality while accruing funds to service debt. Debt should be serviced by users of the water system. This is the most appropriate way of ensuring the longevity and sustainability of the water system. Debt is also sometimes serviced by taxpayers paying into a general or local budget that subsidises the debt servicing.

The role and nature of traditional actors in the water financing sector are changing significantly. General budgets which funded much of the construction of water infrastructure are shifting away from ongoing funding because of competition for government funds and decreasing funds. Infrastructure Canada documents very compellingly a situation faced in many OECD countries:

> *Trends in the past 30 years indicate that the proportion of the national pie devoted to public infrastructure has been declining. Not only has public investment been on the decline, but also investment requirements to maintain, upgrade, and expand infrastructure have been on the rise. Thus a gap has developed between what is needed to bring public infrastructure to satisfactory levels and current expenditures on this infrastructure. A 1984 study by the Federation of Canadian Municipalities estimated that this gap was 25% of annual investment in urban infrastructure.* (Infrastructure Canada, 2004, p. 10.)

The private sector is being looked to fill in this funding gap in the water sector. The private sector has not met the demands of huge investments in the water sector, nor does it appear that the private sector can do this alone. What has been demonstrated is that a very small portion of private investments in developing countries have been made in the water sector (Figure 4.3).

Figure 4.3. **Five per cent of private investments in World Bank PPI database directed to the water sector**

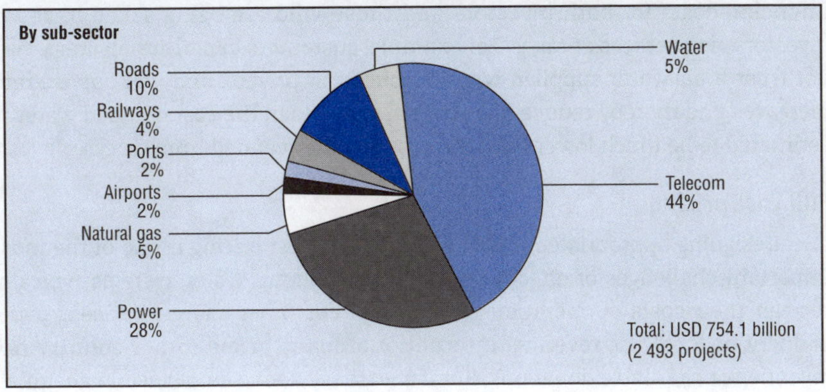

Source: Moss, J. *et al.* (2003), p. 12.

A critical dimension of the context within which water business models operate is that of access to capital. It is clear that the sector's capital needs are not being fully met, although there is still much debate about the specific types of investments needed (*e.g.* dams *versus* efficient appliances). Advocates of increased private involvement in the water sector often claim that private capital is essential if these needs are to be met. Certainly that is true in some sense since most government investments in the water sector are paid for with bonds sold to private investors. But it is not true unless private water companies are more attractive to investors than government bonds. Sometimes, they are less attractive (*e.g.* when government bonds are tax exempt as in the US). Investing in a private water company is more attractive than buying a government bond only when the rate of return on the private investment is relatively high or is guaranteed to some extent (*i.e.* it is low risk). If government can credibly make such guarantees, it can also borrow and invest directly.

In some parts of the developed world, bond financing is a primary vehicle for investments in the water sector. When investor-owned utilities exist, equity investments in the stock of those companies are also an important source of capital. Because equity investors demand higher rates of return than bond investors, however, debt is often a significant source of finance even for investor-owned utilities. Direct investment of tax revenues is also sometimes a source of finance, especially in rapidly growing economies like China and India today. However, that same tax revenue can be used to amortise large loans; a more effective way of raising capital than pay-as-you-go financing with tax revenue. Consequently, the vast majority of capital invested in the water sector is borrowed or raised (as equity investments) in private capital markets, regardless of the business model that delivers services.

Stated differently, the key issue in accessing sufficient capital is usually not the source of that capital. Instead, there are other issues that affect the risk and financing costs for both investors and those who are being asked to repay investors via user fees or taxes. For example, customers in peri-urban areas may not trust their water supplier, whether public or private, and will oppose rate increases and thereby reduce investment, even when the cost of piped water is estimated to be much lower than the cost of water vended from trucks.

Full cost pricing

Designing appropriate rates that ensure full cost pricing is one of the most important challenges of effective water management. Water systems typically recover their costs of operation via a mix of customer charges (prices), own-country or local tax revenue, international loans or aid (other-country tax revenue), or charitable donations. But if a water system cannot sustain adequate levels of finance via these sources – and many cannot – it will not be able to extend services to poorer, marginal areas that lack water and sanitation, nor will it be able to properly maintain existing systems. Multilateral banks and others have increasingly put pressure on utilities in developing countries to increase funding by increasing user charges. This is often labelled as a trend toward "full cost recovery" but is more accurately labelled as a trend toward "full cost pricing". The strategy of moving toward full cost pricing requires that utilities increase rates for water and wastewater services to meet maintenance and expansion goals. Doing so is not possible without effective communication with, and trust between, customers and utility management.

The inability or unwillingness of governments to finance needed infrastructure and maintenance, and increasing demands on public finances, is driving the move towards a greater portion of system costs paid through user fees. There will continue to be overt pressure to recover infrastructure and operation and maintenance costs through full cost pricing as the water sector grows. The issue of full cost pricing is often combined with calls for more private sector involvement in the sector, and as costs become increasingly covered by user fees, this will be more attractive for private sector business models.

Currently, very few systems throughout the world are fully funded by current or future customers of the service. Indeed, some believe that the pressure for full cost pricing by international lending institutions and others in developed parts of the world, toward less developed parts of the world, is inconsistent with the history and current practices in much of the developed world. It is very common for water sector business models to involve a mix of customer charges and general tax revenue.

Whenever possible, local levels of government have worked together to obtain financial support from higher levels of government, thereby reducing the need for local agencies to increase customer charges. Complicating the issue of full cost pricing are inherent failures of market capitalism that affect all actors. For most industries and public welfare utilities, we need to consider the extent to which all benefits and costs are internalised. The costs of poor ambient water quality from ineffective wastewater treatment are borne by downstream users, while many of the benefits of adequate supplies of clean drinking water accrue externally in reduced health costs in the community. Many external costs may be internalised through government regulations and enforcement, including regulations governing the quality and disposal method of treated wastewater and sludge. External benefits, however, may also be internalised via subsidies. This is in fact the most common rationale for tax revenue supported spending in the water sector, rather than full cost pricing.

It is of course, in theory, possible for full cost pricing to account for additional anticipated costs from climate change or water pollution. Full cost pricing could also internalise the external public health benefits of water and wastewater service provision by requiring annual payments from the public health department as part of the overall revenue stream. If well designed, rates should incorporate the costs of externalities and the costs of removing water from in-stream uses. Anticipated climate change or water pollution infrastructure needs could be incorporated into prices borne by water system users. For pollution outfalls into the water system, *point-source charges* could be levied which could feed into water system revenues.

Investments in water interventions often pay enormous dividends, but in unconventional ways. Table 4.6 shows the estimated "cost/benefit" ratio for water actions in developing regions and Eurasia. As these data indicate, the investment of a dollar may return as much as USD 4 to 12 in health, social and financial benefits, but often those benefits accrue to parties other than those making the investment. Overall, the UN concluded (UN, 2003) that an investment of USD 11.3 billion dollars per year to meet the Millennium Development Goals for water could produce an overall benefit as large as USD 84 billion a year. This disparity in who bears the costs and who receives the

Table 4.6. **Benefit/cost ratios for water interventions in developing regions and Eurasia**

Type or result of intervention	Benefit/cost ratio
Halving the proportion of people without access to improved water sources by 2015	9
Halving the proportion of people without access to improved water sources and improved sanitation by 2015	8
Universal access to improved water and improved sanitation services by 2015	10
Universal access to improved water and improved sanitation, and water disinfected at the point of use by 2015	12
Universal access to a regulated piped water supply and sewage connection in house by 2015	4

Source: Modified from WHO/UNICEF (2005).

benefits is rarely openly discussed or considered in water policy decisions. Measuring these varying costs and benefits, and identifying ways of capturing the benefits and reinvesting them in the water system, are key components and challenges to those looking to expand old or develop new business models.

Good governance is critical to addressing financing needs. Well-governed countries and utilities are typically able to borrow enough to meet their investment needs. Similarly, better governance reduces the risk premium required to induce investment. Selected national or regional policy interventions may be necessary to improve credibility and reduce risk premiums in the most neglected and backward parts of countries where investments in water systems are risky at present.

Well-developed civil courts capable of resolving contract disputes in reasonable time frames and at reasonable cost would also be helpful. This is especially important for the development of business models that include numerous smaller projects and actors. The transaction costs associated with development of these models are large. Administration costs, as noted above, are larger per dollar of investment in small projects, and even a few contract disputes among hundreds of contracts can prevent return on investment from being adequate to promote yet more investment.

Communities are often concerned that when a private company takes over a local water system, the drive for full cost pricing and profits will lead the company to increase water rates that are paid by users. The drive for *greater public involvement* will be integral to the success of any efforts towards full cost pricing. In cases where rate changes need to be made, improved services should be clearly described and rate changes should be tied to comprehensive consumer education and information programs describing the changes and their reason. While the driver of public involvement won't affect how many business models try to more fully recover costs from users, it will determine how successful these attempts will be.

With large potential increases in costs from climate change, water pollution and more stringent regulations, environmental drivers will make it more difficult for utilities to recover all costs from user fees. This will mean that tax revenues or government support will most likely continue to be needed to finance major projects that address climate change impacts. Full cost pricing does not account for the external costs of climate change or water pollution that will affect the water system's sustainability.

3.2. Demand management

The amount of capital and financing needed to satisfy water supply and sanitation needs depends in large part on the size of those needs and on choices made to satisfy them. In some cases, substantial reductions in capital

Box 4.3. US drinking water revolving fund

As noted earlier, water systems must make significant investments to install, upgrade, or replace infrastructure to continue to ensure the provision of safe drinking water. These investments include installation of new facilities to improve the quality of drinking water as well as maintenance necessary to sustain ageing infrastructure. In the United States, a mechanism was created to help states meet federal requirements under the Safe Drinking Water Act. This bill established the Drinking Water State Revolving Fund (DWSRF) to make funds available as grants to finance infrastructure improvements. The programme also emphasises providing funds to small and disadvantaged communities and to programmes that encourage pollution prevention as a tool for ensuring safe drinking water.

The DWSRF programme awards capitalisation grants to states, which in turn are authorised to provide low-cost loans and other types of assistance to public water systems to finance the costs of infrastructure projects. States may also use a portion of their grants to fund a range of set-aside activities including source water protection, capacity development and operator certification (US EPA, 2000). The federal appropriation for this programme in 2005 was USD 843 million split among all US territories though less money than this is usually dispersed. Figure 4.4 shows actual federal grants from 1997 to 2005.

Figure 4.4. **US drinking water state revolving fund grants**

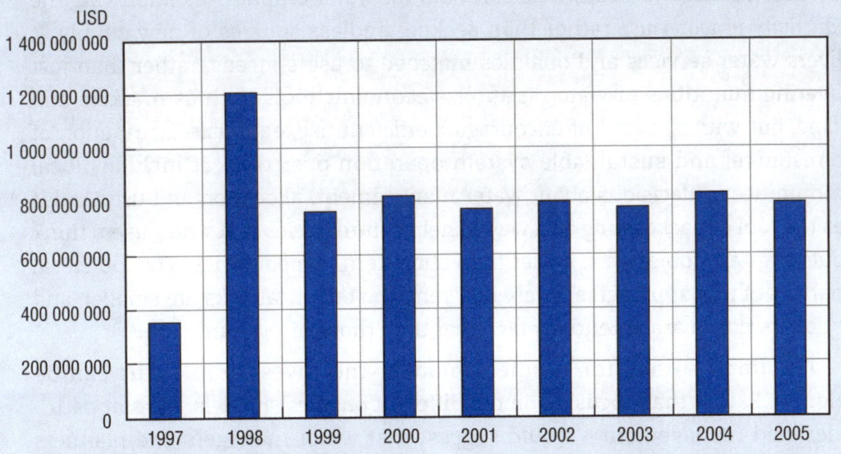

Source: www.epa.gov/safewater/dwsrf/nims/dwus06.pdf.

requirements can be achieved by expenditures to reduce demand through technological improvements, structural changes to water use, or other approaches. Below we offer a few examples on experiences in the United States and Canada.

The world is in the midst of a major transition in water management and use. Over the past century, the construction of massive infrastructure in the form of dams, aqueducts, pipelines and complex centralised treatment plants, funded with a limited set of financial tools and approaches dominated the water agenda. This "hard path" approach, focused on expanding water supply, brought tremendous benefits to billions of people, reduced the incidence of water-related diseases, expanded the generation of hydropower and irrigated agriculture, and moderated the risks of devastating floods and droughts. But the hard path also had substantial, often unanticipated social, economic and environmental costs. Tens of millions of people have been displaced from their homes by water projects over the past century, including more than one million displaced by the reservoir behind the Three Gorges Dam in China alone. Twenty-seven per cent of all North American freshwater fauna populations are now considered threatened with extinction, a trend mirrored elsewhere around the world. Adequate flows no longer reach the deltas of many rivers in average years, leading to nutrient depletion, loss of habitat for native fisheries, plummeting populations of birds, shoreline erosion and adverse effects on local communities.

A new way of thinking is emerging: called the "soft path" or *demand management* by some analysts. The soft path continues to rely on carefully planned and managed centralised infrastructure but complements it with small-scale decentralised facilities. The soft path for water emphasises improving the *productivity of water use* rather than seeking endless sources of new supply. It delivers water services and qualities matched to users' needs, rather than just delivering quantities of water. It applies economic tools such as markets and pricing, but with the goal of encouraging efficient use, equitable distribution of the resource, and sustainable system operation over time. It includes local communities in decisions about water management, allocation and use. And it uses the tool of backcasting as a way to help communities and water users think about long-term objectives, rather than short-term expediencies. The industrial dynamics of this approach are very different, the technical risks are smaller, and the dollars risked are potentially far fewer than those of the hard path.

The implications for business models and investment paths can be profound. Rather than focusing on the different business models, the soft path – or demand management – would suggest that water managers and planners focus on the long-term objectives, such as meeting basic needs, or integrated sanitation and ecosystem restoration, and then explore different financial paths for satisfying those objectives. Thus, society's goal should not be promoting specific business models, but might instead focus on improving the social well-being associated with the use of water and the provision of water services.

The concept of increasing the productivity of a unit of water is central to the idea of demand management. In many cases, water is not needed itself, but performs certain functions, whether it is to carry away human waste, cool industrial processes or grow crops. Each of these functions that water provides is actually not dependent on the actual amount of water used, but on how effectively the water that is used satisfies the end goal. If a smaller amount of water can perform the same function, this increases the productivity of a unit of water. For example, water efficient shower heads use less water but serve the same purpose of allowing people to clean themselves. Drip irrigation systems used in agriculture use significantly less water and reduce evaporation losses by directing water to where it is most needed, underground, while fulfilling the function of growing crops.

The traditional approach to meeting increasing water needs has been to augment availability by building massive water-supply projects. Increasingly, these projects are becoming more expensive as communities need to go farther and farther a field to find and access new supplies still uncontaminated by pollution and sewage from growing urban centres. The cost of water per cubic meter increases each time a new water source is tapped, increasing the costs to the utility and the end-user (Wegelin-Shuringa, 1998).

A demand management approach that focuses on *efficiency and conservation*, including reducing unaccounted for water in the water sector is often the best "new" source of water to satisfy the social and environmental needs of growing populations. It was often thought that improving economic prosperity required increases in water use. But technology improvements have severed this link. While producing a ton of steel in the 1920s required as much as 200 tons of water, today it requires less than 4 tons of water. This is a fifty-fold increase in the *productivity* of a given unit of water. One of the cornerstones of a demand management approach to providing water services is increasing water productivity, the amount of output – whether it is satisfying a human need or producing a ton of wheat – for a given unit of water that is used.

In Singapore, an aggressive strategy to improve efficiency and conservation was implemented to significantly reduce the water losses in the system. Rates of unaccounted for water in badly run or decaying systems can reach as high as 60% of water produced, which is a huge financial drain on any utility and ratepayers. Reducing the rates of unaccounted for water in the system achieves social and environmental objectives while improving efficiency and reducing costs. The Singapore PUB developed a comprehensive and proactive strategy to detect and control leakage. As the city seeks new methods of meeting its water needs, Singapore's demand management approach focusing on efficiency and conservation in the water sector has proven to be a more effective "new" source of water and permitted the city to avoid or delay the huge capital expenditure associated with new supplies in a region with few natural alternatives. Singapore saved nearly SGD 26 billion in avoided capital expansions by reducing unaccounted for water levels from over 10% to 6% over the course of six years.

Water efficiency improvements in many parts of the western United States have greatly reduced per capita water use and eliminated the need for a wide range of new supply investments. New reservoirs costing billions of dollars have been *cancelled* by investing in conservation improvements. For example, the Two Forks Dam outside Denver – a billion dollar project designed to boost Denver's water supply – was cancelled in 1990 due to opposition from local and federal governments over its ecological impacts, together with the belief that conservation and efficiency were appropriate and adequate alternatives. Denver then succeeded in reducing demand, successfully demonstrating how to replace large capital projects with improved management.

A recent study in Kings County, Washington State, found that a small community could cost effectively reduce the size of a planned wastewater treatment plant by aggressively implementing indoor water conservation measures (Wolff, 2004). Water in this community was quite inexpensive, so unlike the example above, water-use efficiency was not justified by avoided costs for water supply. Instead, water-use efficiency was justified by avoided costs for new sewer lines and wastewater treatment facilities. These new facilities were driven by an environmental concern – groundwater pollution from septic systems. But the capital required to respond to this driver was not as large as initially believed, once indoor water-use efficiency was included in the plan. Similarly, Australia recently cancelled plans for a desalination plant to serve Sydney after alternative approaches, including groundwater, improved conservation and efficiency, and new recycled water efforts, were found to be cheaper and less controversial to develop.

Investments in conservation and efficiency could limit the growth in new demand so effectively that few new centralised supply investments would be required. While investment would be required for conservation and efficiency programs and technologies, these are likely to be far less costly than large infrastructure projects (Gleick *et al.*, 2002; Gleick *et al.*, 2005). A study by the Pacific Institute compares a high-efficiency scenario developed for California to the year 2030, along with the "Current Trends" scenario from the official state water plan (Figure 4.5). The difference between the two represents nearly 10 billion cubic kilometres per year in supply investment that can be avoided (Gleick *et al.*, 2005).

Another classic example of avoiding a multibillion dollar infrastructure investment is the experience of New York City in developing innovative policies for satisfying a new federal requirement for water filtration. In order to meet the new standard, the City of New York would have had to spend an estimated USD 6 billion for a state-of-the-art filtration system. Instead, they petitioned the US government for permission to work with local residents in the upstate watershed to reduce contamination from local septic and sewer systems, to protect land from inappropriate uses that contributed to water contamination,

Figure 4.5. **California statewide trend in total water demand between 1960 and 2000**

With projections to 2030 in the current trends and high efficiency scenarios

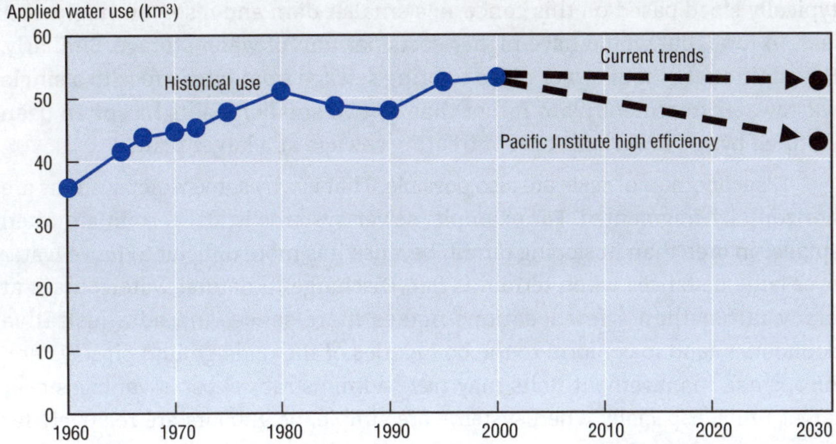

Source: Gleick et al. (2005).

and to locally manage stormwater runoff. By implementing a wide range of watershed management tools, the city was able to meet its water quality obligations for about a third of the cost of the centralised infrastructure.

Infrastructure Canada notes the key role that demand management can play in reducing the need for new infrastructure through reducing water consumption and peak demand for water and wastewater, reducing unaccounted for water in the system, and increasing water recycling. They also note the key role that adequate water pricing can play in reducing demand, improving efficiency and increasing conservation. A critical piece of demand management is effective public outreach that communicates the value of water and the importance of conservation. Often, in water rich countries like Canada, and parts of the United States, the perception is that water is abundant and can be used without fear of scarcity. This has led to some of the most wasteful water consumption rates in the world.

3.3. Scale of water systems

Water systems have typically been governed at municipal, regional and subnational levels. Water systems are often local or regional in scope, conducting abstraction, treatment and delivery within relatively small areas, compared to the distance that other utilities (such as telecom or energy) may travel. While water regulations are typically made at the national level, governance over water supplies and systems is usually done at the municipal level. Water and wastewater services have historically been a function of the municipal government, with some financial assistance from national governments.

An economy of scale exists when enlarging a facility or programme will lower the cost per unit of the product or service being delivered.[8] Economies of scale often exist in water systems. Dams and reservoirs, for example, are typically sized based on this concern; a smaller dam and reservoir might cost less, in total, but would have higher costs per unit of water storage. Similarly, the additional cost of sewer pipes to bring sewage from large areas to a single wastewater treatment plant rather than to two smaller plants has often been justified by the lower unit cost of treating sewage at a larger plant.

Diseconomies of scale are also possible. That is why some water systems are horizontally fragmented. For example, sewer systems in flat terrain are often smaller in area than in sloping terrain because it is more difficult to move water over large distances when terrain is flat. Discharge to natural watercourses at many rather than a few locations makes more sense, and administrative boundaries tend to conform to the boundaries of the underground pipe system. Also, small management units may have administrative cost advantages over larger units, especially when systems are simple, neighbours are relatively far away, or they have different management priorities and objectives.

Regionalisation of water systems

Numerous regions are beginning to take advantage of economies of scale through the regionalisation of water systems. While water services are typically managed at the municipal level, watersheds are typically larger than municipal boundaries. Different municipalities also have different capacities to manage water systems (McFarlane, 2003). Regionalised water systems can take advantage of managing water systems across many municipalities to reduce costs, share expertise, improve performance, enhance the security of water supply in uncertain climate conditions, and address and manage water systems at a more appropriate watershed scale.

The river basin or watershed approach has been used in many regions including in parts of the US and Canada, and is now supported by the European Union. The regions using and promoting this approach have found that management at the river basin level is ideal for water resource planning, demand management, infrastructure development, financing and other functions. The river basin approach considers all of the water falling into one river basin or watershed and manages the needs of all residents in the watershed. This will require supramunicipal levels of co-ordination and government, and will help manage all water inputs, extraction, loss, and in-stream uses in the entire river basin system.

Environmental drivers that increase the costs of the system, including climate change, water pollution and environmental regulations (supranational and national), will potentially make it more attractive to manage systems at larger scales. Environmental concerns are creating greater awareness of and planning for the interconnectedness of water systems at the watershed scale. Previously, water-system boundaries were defined politically, and little attention was paid to watershed boundaries. Consequently, this driver will help to focus attention on the possible economic benefits of management at the watershed scale; benefits that, if real, will help to overcome parochialism common in local government.

Ensuring water security is also a key benefit of regionalised water systems. As water becomes polluted, or climate change impacts water security in certain regions, management of water and wastewater systems may need to be undertaken at a larger scale allowing water systems to develop partnerships with other systems as added security. The scale of systems may need to expand as the regional scope of water resource abstraction increases, as more regions seek to obtain water from greater distances. By banding together several municipal water systems, or urban with rural systems, each water system can benefit from having several water supply sources at their disposal in the event of failure of any particular source. With climate change impacting the nature of water supply in many regions, increasing the number and type of water sources will enhance water security.

Decentralisation of governance in some countries (*e.g.* Brazil, the Russian Federation, India, China, Indonesia and parts of eastern Europe) may help to reduce costs by shedding the diseconomies of scale embedded in large bureaucracies. Such bureaucracies have large transaction costs; that is, their actions require the involvement of so many parties at so many levels that relatively small opportunities for improvement cannot be captured without significant spending for meetings, memoranda, and so forth.

The development of *international standards* may create economies of scale as well. Vendors of equipment, in particular, can reduce their costs if sizes (*e.g.* metric *versus* imperial), public health codes or tests, and enforcement approaches are standardised.

Financial concerns have and will continue to drive discussions about water-system consolidation, especially smaller ones, into regional entities or via private companies that can provide economies in purchasing or administration even when the systems are physically separate (Beecher, 1996). There is evidence that both of these approaches can reduce costs significantly. For example, Wolff and Hallstein (2005) also report that consolidation of wastewater operations in three small communities in Minnesota resulted in a 30-50% reduction in bulk chemical purchasing, back-office functions like utilities billing, and so forth. On the other hand, Wolff and Hallstein (2005) also report that a regional consolidation in Kentucky failed to achieve expected cost reductions. Financial pressure will drive the search for economies of scale, but they are not always possible.

In "Regional Water Works: Sharing Urban Water Services", Susan McFarlane (2003) of the Canada West Foundation documents the usefulness of regional water management and key principles for moving it forward. Case studies on two successful regional approaches in Vancouver and Edmonton are documented.

That paper posits that regional water services can improve water availability, quality and affordability in rural areas; enhance management, planning, and protection of watersheds; and increase cost effectiveness of urban water services by expanding the coverage area. There are financial benefits that can be gained if regionalisation of water services leads to increased revenue, reduced costs and improved efficiency. Municipalities that are adjacent to one another are connected because water usage or disposal of wastewater by one municipality affects the water security of another municipality. By consolidating services, municipalities can share water wealth and protect existing water supplies. Smaller municipalities often find it difficult to meet more stringent government standards. Banding together to form a larger entity or joining with a larger municipality may help smaller towns gain the resources and expertise needed to implement new standards.

Also documented are a series of challenges and pitfalls in the regionalisation of water services. These include problems if a municipality is not able to pay the costs of extending the water service to its town. Smaller municipalities are often suspicious of their larger city neighbours and may be concerned that water system sharing may lead to further erosion of autonomy in other arenas. If there is a fear that water is scarce, this may lead to more contentious rather than collaborative relationships between neighbouring municipalities.

MacFarlane's paper offers a series of key recommendations in moving toward a regional approach to water systems:

- Large cities should be open to exploring the development of shared water services.
- Ensuring the safety of drinking water should be viewed as a shared responsibility.
- Water service sharing agreements should fully account for their environmental effects.
- Water service sharing agreements should account for the full cost of water services including the long-term replacement of infrastructure and maintenance of watersheds.
- Water conservation mechanisms should be built into water service sharing agreements.
- Formal structures for managing regional systems should be created.
- Provincial governments should become more involved in facilitating regional water systems.

- Water management and land-use planning should occur at both an integrated level and at the larger regional level.

On-site, point-of-use, and closed loop systems

At the same time, advances in technology are reducing the diseconomy of scale associated with small systems. Membrane bioreactors may make high-quality treatment available at low cost at much smaller scale than was previously available. And microfiltration, reverse osmosis, electrodialysis and advanced technologies make it possible to treat small, intermittent water flows that are not easily treated with biological processes like activated sludge or membrane bioreactors. On-site wastewater recovery (so called "closed loop systems") is much more economical now, and may become even more attractive in the future, so long as energy costs are manageable.

New technologies that reduce costs and improve efficiency in the water and wastewater sector are important drivers that will have significant impact on provision of infrastructure. World wide, the provision of water and disposal of human waste has followed a particular technological trajectory, involving massive centralised projects that abstract, treat, deliver water, depend on water to transport and dispose of human waste, and require significant energy inputs. The dominant technologies were developed in relatively rich societies where capital was available to undertake large centralised projects.

The transfer of these systems in the developing world through multilateral aid and government support has faced numerous challenges, including lack of capital, population growth, and inability to fund or conduct ongoing maintenance. At the same time, developed country governments need significant investments to maintain and repair ageing infrastructure, as well as meet increasingly stringent standards. In addressing these challenges, a host of technologies have emerged or become more predominant over time.

On-site and closed loop systems are a small but growing share of the water and wastewater sector. On-site systems are varied in form and function. They can be low-energy and low-cost systems for water collection, storage, disinfection and waste treatment. On-site systems can also be expensive and energy intensive, such as conventional mini-water plants (using, for example, reverse osmosis or ultraviolet technologies) and wastewater treatment plants (*e.g.* membrane bioreactors).

Drinking water. On-site water provision can be as simple as rainwater harvesting (mandatory in many parts of India and growing in Australia), where untreated rainwater is used for washing and gardening, and treated rainwater (through UV or filtration) is used for drinking. Many urban residents in developing countries depend on groundwater to supplement limited supplies of piped water.

In some places, individual homes and apartment complexes often maintain their own well or borewell, pumping it to an overhead tank for use throughout the day for washing and other non-consumptive uses. This water is also used for drinking when other drinking water is not provided to or purchased by the household.

A small number of "point-of-use" systems for drinking water have recently been developed to test the idea of solving problems with access to safe water for individual users, rather than municipalities, regions or villages. This approach relies on private market forces to distribute water purification options to end-users directly, eliminating community, municipal or centralised private water development requirements. For example, the Centers for Disease Control and other private and public groups developed the Safe Water System of chlorine disinfection solution, which has been launched in numerous African countries and India. The PuR system developed by Procter and Gamble Company provides a sachet to safely disinfect drinking water at the point of use. There are advantages and disadvantages to the use of these options to meet the needs of individual water users, which will not be discussed here. But the commercial availability of such options suggests that some consider this an appropriate business model for meeting water needs.

In some regions, for example in Mexico and India, drinking water is critical to provide on-site to attract potential residents to water scarce areas without adequate piped supply. Developers and builders in these areas in India are integrating mini-reverse osmosis (RO) facilities on-site. Developers in peri-urban areas either contract this service out to third parties, who then maintain the RO or wastewater treatment plant, or sell this service as part of the housing package, to be managed by the homeowners association through dues.

Wastewater and waste. The use of on-site systems to treat waste in peri-urban areas in developing countries is growing. Two low-cost on-site and closed loop methods for sanitation are popular and supported by overseas development aid.

One is *ecosanitation*, a method promoted by the Swedish government, which is based on closing the nutrient loop in sanitation and moving away from conventional waterborne sanitation. The traditional sanitation path was developed in countries rich with water resources, and is not often a good fit in countries facing water scarcity. In addition, a core tenet of ecosanitation is that human excreta contains valuable nutrients that can be used to provide food security when treated and handled properly.

Ecosanitation involves separation of urine and fecal matter, applying sterile urine directly onto plants, and composting the fecal matter (mostly drying) until it is safe for land application. Ecosanitation approaches have been implemented in India, China, Sweden and parts of eastern Europe.

Ecosanitation facilities are growing rapidly in China and India and both countries host ecosanitation offices. These are often used along with a set of toilet blocks, in areas with high groundwater levels, and in areas where there is no sewerage (peri-urban and rural).

The Dewats system, or decentralised wastewater treatment, is promoted by Germany's overseas development agency, BORDA. Dewats is sometimes referred to as "wet" ecosanitation. Dewats provides a series of modules to achieve tertiary treated water through sedimentation, baffled reactors, anaerobic filters and polishing ponds. The relatively low-cost, low-energy systems use the natural grade to move water. The Dewats system is growing in its application in peri-urban areas, and small- and medium-sized enterprises, particularly in areas that traditionally use water in latrines. Dewats is popular in India and South-east Asia.

Numerous private companies have emerged to provide small-scale conventional treatment for water and wastewater. Emerging economies are increasingly requiring on-site treatment for wastewater instead of connection to overburdened centralised systems. New legislation in India requires all large generators of wastewater to treat all their waste on-site. This has led to an explosion of service providers developing water and wastewater treatment plants for offices, apartment complexes, and other users.

Speaking with developers and consultants in India, we found that many builders of flat complexes are integrating wastewater treatment and water treatment into their buildings because that is the only way to attract residents, particularly in water-scarce urban areas. While developing a mini-conventional wastewater treatment may seem expensive, we found that costs are often one-fifth the cost of water purchased from tanker trucks or other sources. Treated wastewater can be used for gardening, toilet-flushing and groundwater recharge.

The trend is for more peri-urban and rural areas in developing and emerging countries, and in greenfield areas in developed countries, to opt out of conventional large-scale water and sewage treatment systems. Small-scale systems can require less energy, less maintenance (if they are modelled after Ecosan or Dewats), and be far less costly than extending pipes and the centralised system far afield. Small-scale systems often require more space, and may not be appropriate for dense, built-out urban areas.

The growth of on-site systems particularly in emerging economies and in the greenfield areas of developed countries changes the landscape of business models in the water sector. New business models are emerging including flat developers who are now in the business of water and wastewater provision – they are required to do so to develop a saleable property. New consulting firms and full service firms are emerging locally and internationally to provide on-site water and wastewater services not only for industrial use, but also for residential and commercial uses. These firms tend to operate on a DBOT or a DBO basis. This is reducing the pressure on centralised water-system expansion needs, but is complicating traditional regulatory mechanisms because drinking water or water for other purposes (*e.g.* toilet flushing or landscape irrigation) is provided by a variety of different sources, and waste is treated and disposed of in numerous places.

Stormwater management. Technologies for addressing runoff water-quality problems (called "non-point source" pollution in the US and "diffuse" pollution in Europe) are experiencing rapid innovation and development. This is because runoff problems cannot be completely solved by street sweeping and other best management practices, and are very expensive to solve by end-of pipe treatment. Storm runoff is highly variable in quantity and quality and, unlike sanitary sewerage, is often not piped together to one or a few points. There are numerous places where polluted urban or farm runoff enters streams, rivers or other water bodies.

Consequently, decentralised solutions for preventing diffuse pollution or treating it near the source are being pursued and are increasingly recognised as feasible and desirable. These solutions often involve so-called "low impact development" techniques (*e.g.* see *www.lowimpactdevelopment.org*) that maximise rainfall retention near its source, increase percolation to groundwater aquifers, or filter runoff through vegetation prior to entering concrete channels or other large, conveyance structures. They also involve the use of constructed natural systems such as small "bioswales", "biocells", or wetlands and marshes specifically designed and operated to protect ambient water bodies from diffuse pollution in runoff (Box 4.4).

These techniques are directly applicable to business models that operate combined sanitary and storm sewer systems. Reducing the quantity of rainwater that must be managed by the system can significantly reduce costs for peak hydraulic loading. Cleaner rainwater can significantly reduce costs for treatment or regulatory compliance. These techniques are also indirectly applicable to all business models in the sense that growing public pressure to solve diffuse pollution problems creates opportunities for new actors in the water sector (*e.g.* housing or commercial developers).

3.4. *Public involvement and equity*

Public involvement, if welcomed and managed appropriately, will facilitate much larger investments in the water sector. The large multinational water companies seem to have recognised this in recent years, and increasingly try to communicate with citizen groups as well as governments when they are developing new business. Since customers must repay investments in many cases, it is essential that they trust both the service provider's ability to deliver

Box 4.4. **Constructed wetland for treating urban runoff**

A 55-acre freshwater marsh in Alameda County, California, was designed to remove pollution from urban runoff before it reaches the San Francisco Bay. Water from a 46 square-mile area drains into the marsh. A Gross Pollutant Trap (GPT) collects large pieces of trash behind a series of weirs before they reach the main body of the marsh. Water then flows into one of two ponds. The first is a five-acre, six-foot-deep lagoon with a central island. Incoming water mixes with marsh water containing bacteria and other micro-organisms that remove pollutants. The large surface area of this system provides wind exposure, which contributes to increased mixing and more effective chemical and biological processes. The second pond is a four-acre section of shallow water averaging three feet in depth and covered in aquatic plants.

The plants take up nutrients through their roots. Bacteria in the pond sediments break down biological matter and mediate the removal of nitrogen to the atmosphere. Sediments are trapped in the plant roots along with attached nutrients and other pollutants such as agrochemicals. Water from both ponds then flows through a channel before being released to a natural marsh that borders the bay. The large surface area of this channel allows sun, soil, bacteria and plants to provide a final removal of pollutants before discharge. Fish and plant tissue, sediments in the marsh, and water exiting the marsh have been tested for a wide range of chemical constituents. These tests showed that suspended solids, nutrients and urban toxic materials were removed by the marsh. The marsh itself remains a healthy and viable ecosystem, despite the fact that urban runoff has been flowing through the system since the early 1980s.

Source: Alameda Countywide Clean Program (1998).

services *and* the provider's ability and willingness to transparently and credibly account for the spending necessary to provide those services. This issue applies as much to public as to private providers.

Improving public involvement and *transparency in water decisions* are key drivers in the water sector, as experience has identified the key role public involvement and transparency play in the success and sustainability of water sector projects. In decades of working on the global water and wastewater problem, development professionals have learned that social, economic, and political factors are just as important as technological factors and must be considered at the beginning of any potential project. Officials at multilateral lending agencies have also found that lack of transparency in decisions has played a key role in the failure of many urban infrastructure projects.[9]

Business models can be more or less transparent in their decision-making processes or their access to data and resources. When decisions in the water sector are not adequately disclosed or publicly vetted, controversy can develop around the resulting projects. When the public does not have access to documents, information or decisions being made about the water resources upon which they depend, they may perceive that these decisions are not in their best interests, that government or the private sector is hiding potential problems or flaws in a project, or that these decisions are the result of corruption or bribery. In fact, both theoretical and empirical evidence points to the fact that transparency and external accountability in the workings of government can reduce bribery and corruption (Kaufmann, 2002).

In the case of private sector involvement in water and wastewater services that were formerly provided by the public sector, the importance of maintaining public access and transparency is even more critical; and a closed process can lead to outcomes that are not in the best interests of the public. A lack of transparency in the selection and design of a privatisation scheme can lead to subversion of the competitive bidding process, corruption or collusion, subjective awarding of contracts, or favourable treatment of the selected private sector partner (Kaufmann, 2002).

A lack of transparency can transform broad support to outright opposition from other political parties or the public at large and can precipitate project failure. For example, the Buenos Aires water concession of Aguas Argentinas, a subsidiary of the French companies Vivendi and Suez, is often held up as an example of successful privatisation, with significant improvements including greater coverage, better service, more efficient operations, and lower prices for consumers. At the low point of the economic crisis of the late 1980s, 59% of Buenos Aires' residents favoured privatisation, and just 16% opposed it. Four years after the concession was put in place, those numbers had essentially reversed. According to a case study on the Buenos Aires Water Concession by the World Bank: "... public confidence in the process has eroded. The Buenos Aires concession shows how important transparent, rule-based decision making is to maintaining public trust in regulated infrastructure" (Alcazar *et al.*, 2000).

Transparency and public involvement in decisions about rate increases are also important drivers in the water sector. As the events in Cochabamba, Bolivia, highlighted, rapid and large increases in water rates can cause strong social and political reactions. Public protests and political demonstrations over price increases have also taken place in Tucuman, Argentina; Puerto Rico; Johannesburg, South Africa, and elsewhere. In Argentina and Bolivia, rate concerns along with other factors led to privatisation efforts being cancelled. Across South-eastern Asia, disputes over water tariffs are raging. In Malaysia, rate increases just prior to privatisation led to protests.

Rate increases, whether under public or private provision, may need to happen to cover system operating and maintenance costs. These rate increases need to be clearly tied to communication and public involvement efforts. There is abundant evidence that people – even those with low incomes – are willing to pay for water and sanitation when the services are reliable and the cost of delivering services is reasonably transparent and understandable to customers. This suggests that dissemination of detailed information about the improvement in services, and the capital investments needed to create those improvements, is essential to public acceptance of increases in overall water prices.

Equity and water

Because water is fundamental for life, ensuring equity is a key goal and a driver in the water sector. Addressing the key link between water and poverty is being recognised as a key responsibility for water sector actors (see Box 4.5). Lack of access to water is a factor in ongoing poverty for numerous reasons. The economic costs of poor health and disease due to lack of water are borne by the individual as well as the state. The United Nations includes access to water services as a key component in their Human Poverty Index (UNDP, 2004). The Millennium Development Goals (MDGs) adopted by the United Nations in September of 2000, among other explicit targets by the year 2015, called for the world community to halve the proportion of people who are unable to reach or afford safe drinking water, and to halve the proportion of people without adequate sanitation. The MDGs are key drivers in developing services in underserved areas globally.

While most OECD countries have nearly universal coverage, the *affordability* of water is a critical component for the health of populations. Even in wealthy OECD countries, rapid increases in rates have affected public health among the poorer sections of society. When water was privatised in England in 1989, price increases led to customer dissatisfaction with costs, consumer defaults, and non-payment. In 1994, for example, two million customers defaulted on water payments. These defaults, in turn, led to thousands of disconnections for non-payment of bills. A 1996 study by the Save the Children Fund showed that 70% of low-income customers were taking health-endangering measures to reduce consumption, such as flushing less frequently, sharing baths and washing clothes less often. It concluded that vulnerable groups could not make any further reduction in household water consumption without eliminating essential uses of water. Another study by the British Medical Association correlated the rise in dysentery rates with water disconnections. These studies served to consolidate the negative public image of water companies and led to changes in disconnection rules.

Box 4.5. **The human right to water**

The human right to water remains a vital issue that has begun to play a role in national and institutional choices about meeting basic human needs. A growing number of organisations are arguing that the human right to water means that fundamental changes are needed in the way water is priced, financed and managed.

There is a clear legal human right to water. Far less clear, however, are the rights and responsibilities that such a right implies, and how it is to be implemented in the context of different business models for water supply and sanitation. Gleick (1999) explores the historical precedents, legal background, and rationale for the human right to water in existing international laws, covenants, conventions and state practice. In 2002, the UN issued General Comment No. 15, a far more definitive assessment of human rights law in this context.

While there are serious unresolved concerns about definition, and especially, implementation of such a right, the simple existence of a right to water, from a legal, historical, ethical and moral point of view is increasingly established, and many governments are now trying to resolve uncertainties about implementation.

As noted elsewhere in this chapter, water is both a public good and an economic good, and the serious debate about water privatisation and the role of the private sector has spilled over into every water discussion in the past decade, including the debate over the human right to water. General Comment No. 15 quite explicitly notes that some forms of private participation in water service delivery may be appropriate but it also offers some limits and bounds to the role of private entities in providing this public good and service.

General Comment No. 15 tackles the question of water pricing by noting that water must be affordable and does not have to be provided for free, even for the most basic quantities for human survival. It also leaves open the possibility of governments providing free water, if they choose such an approach and it also addresses the need for increased cost-recovery through user charges and a sustainable economic structure to permit operation and maintenance of water service systems over time. Along with these principles for financing, General Comment No. 15 also pays special attention to concerns about equity and socially disadvantaged groups and the need to ensure that their water needs are met affordably. It also notes specific obligations for transparency and information exchange as a key element of any water management and financing approach.

Source: Gleick (1999) and Riedel, Eibe and Peter Rothen (eds.) (2006), *The Human Right to Water*, Berliner Wissenschaftsverlag.

The question of how to provide water to the poor is of critical importance and affects the pricing structure of utilities, their plan to achieve full cost pricing, and their ability to provide the key public health benefits that water and wastewater services entail. Affordability is an important dimension of the policy discussion that is different than willingness-to-pay. While cost recovery via rate increases may be essential for the sustainable operation of a water utility, it can force the poor to pay more than they can afford for water. An economic willingness to pay does not imply that the payment is affordable or socially desirable. Gutierrez *et al.* (2003) pointed out that the urban poor in Accra pay as much as five times more than other users per litre to fetch water from distant sources. Paying five times more demonstrates that willingness to pay is high, but it also demonstrates that water is essential and the purchaser has no choice.

Pressures for full cost pricing will make it increasingly difficult to ensure that an affordable basic amount of water is provided to the poor, and that the poor do not pay excessive costs for water. This may require that an external public actor, such as a health agency, provide subsidies to the poor to ensure that the health benefits of water and wastewater provision are protecting the poorer sections of society. There are numerous successful strategies to ensure that water is provided for the poor, including rising block tariffs, where prices increase over a certain minimum block of water; free basic amount of water; and subsidies provided to poor consumers. These strategies are either written into contracts with private utilities or guaranteed outside contractual obligations by the state.

A good example of a strategy to ensure water services for the poor without altering the price of water is the approach taken in Santiago, Chile. In the early 1990s, Chilean officials introduced a "water stamps" scheme that covers part of the cost of water purchases for the poorest residents. Until the late 1980s, Chile had used a cross-subsidy programme to address the needs of the poor, but the water utility was not recovering the costs of providing water service, and could not extend service to peri-urban populations. In 1988, Chile reformed its water sector, designing tariffs that recovered the costs of providing service to each zone. When Santiago privatised its water system, tariffs went up by 90% in four years. In order to meet a WHO goal that households not spend more than 5% of income on water, a "water stamps" scheme was introduced. By the end of 1998, 450 000 customers representing 95% of the target population were using water stamps. About 77% of the subsidy went to the poorest section of the population, while about 23% "leaked" to moderate and higher income customers (EMOS, 1995; Gomez-Lobo, 2003).

Governments are ultimately responsible for ensuring that the poor are provided with water and wastewater services. While this responsibility is likely to remain at the national level, new international efforts to develop accepted guidelines, including the ISO standards setting process on water and wastewater services, may provide new tools for helping to ensure that the poor are provided with a basic amount of affordable water.

3.5. Competition

As policy makers in the water sector seek to capture the benefits of competition to improve efficiency and service in the sector, new approaches and opportunities are emerging. The benefits in terms of reduced cost and improved service that have followed the introduction of more competition and deregulation in the telecommunications sector have been looked to as models. It is far more difficult to introduce competition in the water sector because of the high costs of infrastructure (it is a natural monopoly), and the essential public health nature of the service, since introduction of poor water quality water into an existing system is a health concern. Options that are being considered to introduce a measure of competition into the water sector include third party access, water transfers and benchmark competition.

Third party access

"Third party access" or "common carriage" in the water sector is the use of the water or wastewater system network by a third party to supply water and wastewater services. Water and wastewater transportation networks are highly capital intensive, with capital costs representing 60% of the cost to provide water and wastewater services to a property. These networks are uneconomic to duplicate (Tasman, 1997). Common carriage has governed the telecommunications industry since the 1900s.

Similar to what happened in the telecommunications industry, allowing access to capital-intensive network assets by third parties could increase competition either at the supply end or the demand end of the network. In England and Wales, common carriage has been viewed as an opportunity to encourage competition in upstream markets, including abstraction and treatment. In Australia, common carriage is thought to improve competition in the downstream markets and retail supply.

The implementation of common carriage is furthest along in England and Wales. The Competition Act of 1998 opened up the scope for common carriage. The act, brought into effect in March 2000, requires incumbent companies to develop a code identifying the terms on which they would provide access to their system infrastructure. The act requires the incumbent company to respond directly to new entrants or competitors requesting access to its infrastructure. If the incumbent company does not provide adequate justification for rejecting an application for common carriage or only offers access on unreasonable terms, they are subject to investigation and potentially financial penalties. This was meant to facilitate new entrants and more competition between established players in the English water market (Ofwat, 1999).

The UK Water Act of 2003 further extended opportunities for competition. From August 2005, new market entrants could enter into common carriage or bulk water purchase agreements with water companies to supply non-households consuming more than 50 megalitres of water a year. New and established water providers are able to use other providers' pipe networks or treatment works, and customers using over 50 megalitres annually can purchase water from their existing provider or from a water supply licensee. The Water Act of 2003 also extends competition in the laying of water mains, sewers, and service pipes (Ofwat, 2004). Australia is considering the use of common carriage to increase competition in their system.

Common carriage could have major implications for improving competition in the abstraction, treatment, and delivery of water and wastewater services. Currently it is still in a trial period in the UK, with consideration of moving common carriage competition to household users as well in the next three years.

In other parts of the world, common carriage seems to be happening on a limited case-by-case basis. For example, Poseidon Resources, Inc. is attempting to build desalination plants for Carlsbad and Huntington Beach in California. They will be contracting with municipal governments to provide water to be used directly in the municipal water supply system. Desalination is a clear case of a new abstractor/treatment facility requiring entry into the water system through common carriage. Because the source water for desalination plants is not regulated there is an unlimited amount of water that can be produced and distributed through new desalination plants, so long as revenues cover costs. This could require some sort of California-wide common carriage rule, or some standards for undertaking it on a local level.

Common carriage or third party access, although probably 10-20 years out in many countries, has the potential to have a significant impact on the water sector. Common carriage can introduce new public and private sector competition in abstraction and treatment of water as well as in the retailing. This may mean new business models that include desalination facilities entering water directly into the water network, private players that introduce efficiency gains as a new source of water, private players that cater to green markets on the retail side by paying for efficiency, and green system improvements (*i.e.* similar to Working Assets Telecommunications in the US).

Another way to conceptualise third party access, although not traditional, is to consider "extending" the water system through licensing arrangements with small and informal water vendors. This allows two regulated systems to exist side by side, providing service in different ways in different neighbourhoods. This is happening in urban and peri-urban areas in developing countries.

Water transfers

A water transfer is defined as "a change in the point of diversion, type of use, or place of use of water" (Gomez and Steding, 1998). Water transfers have both environmental and socio-economic implications, including changes in water quality and employment. While they are not a new phenomenon, water transfers are becoming increasingly common due to scarcity concerns and the need to reallocate water among users. For example, the Imperial Irrigation District and two Southern California water utilities recently entered into a water transfer agreement by which water (but not water rights) from agricultural users is transferred to urban users in Southern California due to land fallowing and on-farm water efficiency measures. In addition, the Chinese government is building a north-south water transfer scheme by which water from the Yangtze River will be transferred to the North China Plain, where land is better suited for agriculture than in the South.

Water transfers will have implications for the water sector business models, including the emergence and expansion of new players. While water transfers can occur on an informal basis, more formal systems that involve water brokers are gaining popularity. Water brokers, either private or public, facilitate transfers among buyers and sellers. In Australia, for example, anyone can act as a water broker, and "water brokers are not subject to any legal obligations other than the general body of law applying to commercial transactions" (Queensland government, 2006). While public institutions can serve as water brokers, private water brokers are more common. Water brokering is a specialised line of work, and it is unlikely that a single public entity will generate sufficient trades to staff and fund a water transfer programme.

It is important to recognise, however, that water transfers are only possible between actors that are capable of changing the point of physical delivery from the seller to the buyer. Either a piped conveyance system, or a tanker or water bag system across oceans, must both exist and have costs of operation that are small relative to the value of the transaction. These conditions are often not met for water. Water is very bulky per unit of value and therefore more difficult and expensive to move than electricity, oil, natural gas or telecommunications signals.

Benchmark competition

Advocates of increased private involvement in the water sector often claim that competition will reduce costs and improve performance in general. However, non-market as well as market competition is contributing to the trend (Wolff and Palaniappan, 2004). Performance measurement and accountability tools are emerging around the world, in both public and private business models within the water sector.

For example, performance scorecards published periodically (*e.g.* annually) can be used along with or instead of performance bonuses. This practice has been used successfully in Australia, the United Kingdom, and other parts of the world. Australian water utilities are municipal corporations governed by a technical board appointed by the state within which they operate. They are responsible for paying dividends to the state treasury and for providing the services and service quality desired by their customers. Standardised performance measurements are required by the state government, which are used by customers and senior managers to evaluate the performance of each utility. Reportedly, doing well in these appraisals has become a significant driver for utility boards and senior managers (based on discussions by author Wolff with utility and Australian Water Association staff in Brisbane, Sydney, and Melbourne in July and August 2005). Benchmarking in the water sector is discussed in further detail as an important enabling policy.

3.6. Climate change

Environmental issues, including climate change and pollution, may have the greatest impact on infrastructure needs and the costs of water and waste services. Ashley and Cashman (2006) indicate that these factors may increase costs by as much as 33%. Climate change will undoubtedly have considerable impacts on water resources, although the extent of the impact and the precise locations where major impacts will be felt is unknown. Climate change will increase the vulnerability of water resources to disruptions. With increasing climate variability, severe drought and flooding events are likely to increase. Sea level rise will threaten coastal aquifers that are already facing over extraction and salinisation. Projected increases in evaporation may reduce the efficiency and the attractiveness of future surface-water storage projects. Per capita water use may increase as climate warms. Agriculture may also need to shift locations as climate zones shift, increase cropping intensity and change cropping patterns to lower water usage products. Investments will be needed to protect the security of existing water supplies, and diversify sources of supply to protect against climate uncertainty. Demand side management, increasing the efficiency of water use and varying water quality will provide low-cost methods of reducing water demand and thus provide new "sources" of water.

The OECD paper on "Domestic Policy Frameworks for Adaptation to Climate Change in the Water Sector" (Levina and Adams, 2006) provides an analysis of the ability of four OECD countries – UK, Finland, USA, and Canada – to adapt to climate change impacts on water resources. The potential climate impacts on water resources include variations in snowmelt and water supply; increase in floods, flash floods and drought; insufficient water; and saltwater intrusion (Table 4.7).

Table 4.7. **Climate change impacts related to water in four countries**

	Country/state province basin	Climate impact					
		Snowmelt water supply	Flash floods	Floods	Drought	Insufficient water	Saltwater intrusion
USA	California	X	X	X	X	X	X
	Colorado	X	X		X	X	
	New York			X	X		X
Canada	British Columbia	X		X	X		
	Ontario	X		X	X		
USA/Canada	Great Lakes Basin				X		
United Kingdom	England and Wales			X	X	X	X
	Scotland			X			
	Northern Ireland			X			
Finland	All		X	X			

Source: Levina and Adams (2006).

Levina and Adams document climate change general circulation models which predict decreases in snowpack and frequent thawing and an increase in floods as well as summer droughts in Finland. In the UK, drought is predicted to have a major impact on water security, with decreasing runoff in the south-east and growing populations leading to greater water scarcity. Winter flooding is also anticipated to be an expensive problem. In the United States, the states of California, Colorado, and New York were profiled. California and Colorado both depend on winter snowmelt to provide water supply during the dry summer months. With earlier snowmelts, reduced snowpack and growing populations, these states will face significant water challenges as temperatures increase. The low lying state of New York will face concerns related to the effects of sea level rise and increased storm frequency on protecting the integrity of water infrastructure. While Canada is a very water rich country, climate change will also impact different regions of Canada with climate variability, decreased runoff in the summer, increased runoff in the winter and lower water levels in major fresh water bodies.

The impact of climate change on water resources will undoubtedly be significant. As climate change affects where and when water falls, those who previously had licences to extract water may be affected by water scarcity. This may cause water rights regimes to be reapportioned or recreated to address changes in water availability. The environmental driver of climate change will make it more challenging to operate and maintain built assets, and may require increasing levels of investment to keep up with changes in water security. Environmental regulations may require the development of new infrastructure or partnerships to create compliance with stricter standards.

Controlling the extent and speed of climate change may reduce the cost of adapting water-supply and flood-control systems to altered precipitation patterns. Any such avoided costs in the water sector are an offset to the cost of controlling climate change through investments in energy efficiency or low-carbon energy production technologies. Environmental drivers that increase the costs of the system, including climate change, will potentially move the level of governance to higher levels. As water becomes polluted, or climate change impacts water security in certain regions, governance of water and wastewater systems may need to be undertaken at a larger scale allowing water systems to develop partnerships with other systems as added security. The scale of governance may need to change as the regional scope of water resource abstraction increases, as more regions seek to obtain water from greater distances.

With large potential increases in costs from climate change, water pollution, and more stringent regulations, environmental drivers will make it more difficult for utilities to recover all costs from user fees. This will mean that tax revenues or government support might continue to be needed to finance major projects that address climate change impacts, although accurate full cost pricing should account for the external costs of climate change that will affect the water system's sustainability.

4. Influence of drivers on business models

The six key drivers and opportunities explored in this chapter will interact and shape the water sector in the decades to come. How will business models respond to these drivers, and which business models will be most robust in overcoming the challenges while taking advantage of the opportunities presented here?

Financing is an ongoing challenge in the water sector. Most countries are facing increased infrastructure maintenance and repair needs. Climate change, security concerns, and new and more stringent water-quality standards will have a significant impact on water resources and the provision of services, potentially greatly increasing projected financial needs in the water sector. The public sector, however, is reducing government expenditures, creating an increasing gap between capital availability and capital needs. The private sector also fails to invest the level of capital that is needed to fill this gap, a problem that is exacerbated by a recent shift from concessions to operation and maintenance contracts in some places, effectively reducing the amount of capital that the private sector is supplying.

How can business models achieve the financing necessary to meet current and future infrastructure needs? There are four opportunities outlined in the above section that can help business models meet infrastructure needs.

The first is *changes of scale*. Business models are emerging that are taking advantage of differences in scale to increase cost effectiveness of water services, increase revenues, and also introduce new models to achieve capital needs. Regionalisation of water services has improved efficiency, cost-effectiveness and watershed management in key areas in Canada and the United States. Expanding the scope of service can improve a water systems ability to finance needed investments. Decentralised, on-site systems are changing who is responsible for and paying for water infrastructure. Engineering firms are building water systems using private capital, and maintaining ongoing service contracts to finance this capital. And home and landowners are investing their own capital (or servicing the debt on needed capital) in order to build on-site systems for single family or multifamily complexes.

The second opportunity to meet infrastructure needs is through *demand management*. Demand management changes the nature of needs for infrastructure. Increasing water productivity and efficiency, and improving conservation, can reduce the need for new and expensive water supply or wastewater treatment projects. As new water supply projects become more expensive due to sourcing water from greater distances, the cheapest new source of water has often been water gained through conservation, efficiency and improved management. Demand management can reduce the amount of financing and new infrastructure needed in water systems. Funding would instead be used for ongoing efficiency and conservation measures.

Competition is a key opportunity to reduce ongoing financing needs and improve the capacity of utilities to access financing. Competition that increases efficiency and improves water system management will reduce costs, thus requiring less ongoing revenue to support water system operation. Competition that improves the efficiency and effectiveness of water utilities can also have a huge impact on improving the utility's credit worthiness, thus allowing it to access private capital and public bonds. By being able to demonstrate that all measures for efficiency and cost effectiveness are being employed, a utility can make a strong case for its ability to manage capital.

The final and ultimately most important opportunity to achieve financing needs is *public involvement*. In the end, the public, whether as ratepayers, taxpayers, or stockholders, will finance whatever debt is incurred to build new infrastructure. Ultimately, water utilities will be subject to the court of public opinion to determine whether they have convinced ratepayers, taxpayers and stockholders of the need for new infrastructure investments and the utility's ability to manage those infrastructure improvements effectively. Public communication about the water system, the state of water system assets and the need for repairing and upgrading of water infrastructure is critical for the success of any efforts by any utility, public or private, to meet its investment needs. Public involvement will facilitate much larger investments in the water sector. Since customers must repay investments in many cases, it is essential that they trust both the service provider's ability to deliver services *and* the provider's ability and willingness to transparently and credibly account for the spending necessary to provide those services.

Ultimately, business models need to meet the existing financing challenges and the new challenges posed by climate change. Existing business models must seek opportunities for demand management, improved efficiency through competition, and increased public involvement in order to sustain in the challenging decades ahead. Business models may also take advantage of scale changes, whether larger or smaller scales, to introduce new sources of capital and financing.

We can already see examples of public models seeking more efficiency, and a greater attention to public involvement by the private sector. The international private sector has given way to the local private sector, which is more connected to local populations. The private sector is also shifting in ways to manage financial risk, some of which are related to the drivers identified, and others of which are not. The changes in business models that are being observed and that we expect to continue are described below.

4.1. *Changes to existing business models*

Described below are key trends in each business model that we expect to continue over the next five to ten years. We anticipate that in the future, local private actors will become more predominant, and that concessions will continue to be attractive in some stable economies; but in others, O&M contracts will be preferred.

Public models

Greater efficiency. In the late 1990s and early 21st century, a growing trend toward privatisation in the United States led some public utilities to re-evaluate their efficiency and services in order to stave off privatisation pressures. These efforts were sometimes termed "re-engineering" and involved evaluating the complete water management system in an effort to identify potential efficiency improvements in operations that would permit a reduction in labour, energy and other costs. Business process "re-engineering" has been defined as the fundamental rethinking and redesign of existing processes to improve performance in areas of cost, quality, service and efficiency.

The East Bay Municipal Utility District (EBMUD) – a public water agency that serves over a million customers in northern California – recently implemented a "re-engineering" programme to help improve maintenance practices. EBMUD brought in auditors to review business practices around purchasing and handling materials, managing and scheduling maintenance, and setting priorities for system repair and preventive maintenance. They then implemented a series of actions that they estimated would lead to savings of nearly USD 7 million per year, with an initial outlay of only USD 1.2 million (US NAS, 2002).

A similar program was implemented by the Phoenix Water Services Department (PWSD) in Arizona. The city was especially concerned about the possibility of privatisation and worked to identify possible advantages of the private sector over public operations and then studied how to improve their performance in those areas. PWSD's efforts focused on labour relations and performance, dispute resolution and customer service. Improvements were also evaluated in the area of maintenance strategy and job training. After reviewing possible improvements, PWSD implemented a series of changes that saved more than USD 10 million in the first three years and permitted them to meet their goals while reducing the need for new staff. According to PWSD director Michael Gritzuk, "Privatization doesn't even begin to address the scope of what a re-engineering project can address" (AWWA, 1999).

Private and mixed private-public models

Scope. Privatisation failures, driven in part by financial and political factors, have shifted the types of contracts sought by private investors. In both developed and developing countries, companies are focusing on limited projects with a narrower scope, *i.e.* an individual component of a water system, rather than large, multiscope projects (VanDe Hei, 2006).

In addition, concession contracts are becoming less popular, while operation and management contracts seem to be increasingly attractive. In the United States, for example, VanDe Hei (2006) notes that concession contracts have been replaced by operation and management contracts in small communities. Izaguire and Hunt (2005) note a similar trend in developing countries, where the number and size of new concession and lease contracts has declined since 2000, while the number of management contracts has increased. Both VanDe Hei (2006) and Izaguirre and Hunt (2005) attribute this trend to privatisation failures and the resulting risk averse behaviour displayed by companies. Concessions involve a high degree of capital risk, and companies are pursuing ways to minimise this risk: "Renegotiations and cancellation of water contracts have raised questions about the viability of private participation in water, particularly in concessions with significant investment commitments" (Izaguirre and Hunt, 2005).

Table 4.8 highlights a fundamental shift in investment patterns among private companies world wide. Private contract awards in wastewater exceeded that in water in the late 1980s. In the 1990s, however, private contracts in water were over two times greater than contracts in wastewater. Contract awards in the water sector have fallen, and between 2000 and 2004 were 20% less than during the previous five-year period. But, since the early 1990s, wastewater

Table 4.8. **Worldwide contract awards in the water and wastewater sectors**

	1985-89	1990-94	1995-99	2000-04
Water	48.6	33.14	136.05	109.69
Wastewater	56.53	13.57	57.94	72.05

Source: Pinsent Masons (2005).

contracts have been steadily growing. This transition from investment in water to wastewater is particularly true in China, where investments in wastewater have exceeded those of drinking water in two of the last three years (Pinsent Masons, 2005).

Environmental and technological factors are driving growth in wastewater investments. Growth in wastewater investments is due to growing concern about water pollution and its associated environmental and human health consequences, as well as more stringent wastewater discharge standards. In addition, there is a greater need for sanitation services, as a smaller percentage of the world's population has access to adequate sanitation than has access to a clean water supply. Additionally, technological improvements that allow more economical wastewater re-use are driving investments in this sector.

Political factors are likely driving greater *private* involvement in wastewater investments. Water investments have drawn a substantial amount of opposition due to concerns about corporate control of water resources. This opposition has slowed and in some cases halted privatisation projects. Wastewater, however, is less visible and fundamental compared to water supply. As a result, it has drawn less public opposition and allowed private companies to steadily expand their role.

Greater transparency and stakeholder involvement. Public opposition to water privatisation contracts and a series of water privatisation problems, notably in Cochabamba, Atlanta, and Buenos Aires, are driving the private sector to seek greater transparency. Corporate transparency, however, has largely focused on reporting, rather than involving stakeholders in the decision-making process. Thames Water, for example, recently released an extensive corporate responsibility report, which provided information on 25 key performance measures, including water pollution incidents, percentage of operational wastes recycled, and length of rivers suffering from low flow due to abstraction. The report also describes the importance of building stakeholders relationships: "We recognise that importance of stakeholder engagement and are working hard to raise awareness, skills, and capacity at all levels within the company to help improve our stakeholder relationships" (Thames Water Utilities Ltd., 2005). However, they acknowledge that they do not presently have a formal system of engaging stakeholders.

Business trends. The role of multinational and local companies has changed significantly since the mid-1980s. Table 4.9 shows the distribution of contract awards by recipient globally. Between 1985 and 1989, local companies in developed countries were granted over 90% of contract awards. Buoyed by successes in their home countries, some of these local companies, most notably Suez, VE and RWE, sought contracts in the international market, marking their transition to multinational corporations. Between 1995 and 1999, multinational corporations were awarded nearly 70% of contract awards. Since 2000, however, there has been a shift away from multinational corporations toward local companies in developed and developing nations. In 2005 alone, 13 new companies, mostly local and regional players, entered the water market (Pinsent Masons, 2005).

Table 4.9. **Worldwide contract awards by recipient in the water and wastewater sector**

Water and wastewater	1985-89	1990-94	1995-99	2000-04
Local – developed	94.89	1.66	8.64	29.26
Local – developing	0.6	5.18	43.4	45
Expatriate Chinese	0	0	8.99	7.98
Multinational	9.64	40.17	132.42	99.7
Total	**105.13**	**46.71**	**193.99**	**181.74**

Source: Pinsent Masons (2005).

Political and financial factors as well as changes in governance are largely driving the trend toward more local and regional players. Strong public opposition to water privatisation schemes by multinational companies, especially in Latin America, resulted in a number of project failures. Foreign exchange risk, *i.e.* companies pay for the infrastructure in hard currency but are repaid in soft currency, has also created problems for multinational corporations. In addition, local capacity building may also be improving. In the Pinsent Masons Report (2005), Owens cautions that this trend may have negative implications: "This is not necessarily a good thing as while local or expatriate funding obviates exchange rate risk, it plays a limited role in mobilising new sources of funding needed to attain the Millennium Development Goals as expatriate funding has only been identified being used in China to date."

Table 4.9 also indicates that an increasing number of contracts have been awarded to expatriate Chinese companies. Proliferation of Chinese players working regionally is due, in part, to access to funds from local and regional sources, including Hong Kong, China, which help stabilise currency and thus reduce financial risk. In addition, a recently enacted Chinese law prohibits foreign companies from earning a fixed rate of return on investments (Pinsent Masons, 2005). Chinese companies, however, can earn a fixed rate, and municipalities can change regulations to suit their needs. These conditions favour local players and some multinational corporations have either exited the Chinese market entirely, *e.g.* RWE, or have opted to work with Chinese companies and municipalities under joint ventures. The needs in the water and wastewater sector in China remain high, and local and regional players have only partly filled the void left by multinational corporations who have exited the market.

In recent years, the international water market has contracted in some regions, but is growing in others. Suez, for example, has relinquished control of a number of projects, mostly in developing countries, and is focusing on expansion in Europe, North America and China; in Europe, their three priority markets are the Czech Republic, Hungary, and the Slovak Republic (Pinsent Masons, 2005). Veolia is focusing on China, which is projected to become its largest international market. And RWE AG has decided to shift its focus from the global water market to the European power market (Pinsent Masons, 2005).

4.2. Robustness of business models

In the face of a dynamically changing water sector, we also want to evaluate what underlying characteristics successful business models will share in the future. A few of these characteristics include the ability to incorporate multiple scales into water management, the ability to develop strategic partnerships in an ever widening circle of water sector actors, the ability to leverage innovative sources of financing while still maintaining a level of public funding, the ability to incorporate adaptive management and performance based incentives to improve performance, and the ability to communicate with and involve the public in decisions about the water system. Successful water system business models will also manage system assets effectively, staff their businesses effectively, and ensure proper assessment of the problem *before* proposing a solution.

Many of these determinants of success are detailed in the report *Beyond Privatization: Restructuring Water Systems to Improve Performance* by Gary Wolff and Eric Hallstein (2005). The analysis uncovered several problems in organisations, these included: insufficient funds, inefficient staffing, poor asset management, limited transparency and public participation, and ineffective performance measurement and reward. For these ailings, the authors propose a variety of solutions that they define as the *six determinants of success*. These six characteristics of high performance organisations would be present in either public or private models and are: effective staffing, consistently sufficient funding, detailed asset management systems, performance measurements and rewards aligned to organisational objectives, decision processes that are transparent and open to the public, and using an effective planning process that identifies and assesses problems before arriving at solutions. These and other determinants of success are detailed further in the discussion below.

As we saw in the discussion on scales of water systems, water utilities are seeking *economies of scale* through regionalisation and river basin approaches while at the same time new water actors are emerging that are taking advantage of technology improvements to implement small-scale on-site systems. Successful business models will have to leverage both opportunities by integrating economies of scale through regionalisation, while allowing small-scale systems to provide services in areas that are not cost effective for centralised system expansion. It may also be the case that regionalised or river basin approaches may work in some cases, particularly where water systems are well developed, while on-site systems will predominate in areas that lack water systems or are unattractive for centralised water systems.

With the increasing number of actors being introduced into the water sector, successful water utilities will need to *manage a network of relationships* with vendors, competitors, and regulators in order to provide water services. This is already happening in the most privatised water system in England. The introduction of third party access will presumably introduce new actors into the system that are providing water services which the "host" water utility will need to work with in order to provide access to the water network. English water utilities will need to not only manage these relationships, but also relationships with several regulatory agencies, Ofwat, the economic and service regulator, the environmental regulator, and the drinking water inspectorate.

Because of the importance of water as a social and public health good, *public financing* in the water sector will still make up a portion of the needed funding in most OECD and developing countries. Effective water utilities will combine dwindling public financing with new financing mechanisms, while mitigating the social and equity impacts of full cost pricing for water. Moving toward full cost pricing will be desirable as a goal. Successful water utilities will incorporate new financing mechanisms that access private capital by accessing private savings invested in local financial institutions and capital markets. These utilities will also seek to get paid for the positive externalities generated by water services, including being paid for the public health benefits and the property development benefits of providing water services. These could be paid through funds from the public health agency or developers that benefit from water access at their development.

Water sector actors that can continuously improve performance, reduce costs and improve efficiency will be the most successful over the long term. Outward measures of performance are sure to be incorporated in many regions to compare water utility performance. More and more public utilities are facing competition from newly emerging private actors. Successful business models will be prepared for competition in the market and for the market by integrating performance based incentives and adaptive management into their operations.

Those business models and water utilities that can *communicate with the public* that they serve are the most likely to be successful. Water utilities that can involve users of the water system in decisions about service, water rates, water quality, infrastructure investments and other key business decisions will be very successful in generating needed investments, achieving full-cost pricing, and building trust in the water system and its operators. In many OECD countries people take the massive underground system of pipes and hidden water and waste treatment facilities for granted. People simply expect clean water to flow from the tap. Proactive water utilities that can demonstrate the importance of the water system and the infrastructure and maintenance needs of the water system, and triangulate this with the needs of water system users, will be the most successful in generating needed investments, while protecting health and providing the desired level of water service.

Water system *assets need to be managed effectively* in order for business models to survive. As described earlier, the water sector is highly capital intensive, much more so than other sectors. This means that a significant amount of money is tied up in underground and overground infrastructure. These assets and this investment need to be protected and maintained on an ongoing basis. A successful business model would undertake a one-time system-wide asset condition assessment; this would be followed by ongoing inspection of assets. Long-term costs for lack of asset management would need to be factored into decisions on annual maintenance expenditures.

Efficient and effective staffing is also needed for business models to be successful. Staff need to be trained and have access to professional development that exposes them to new ideas and technologies in the field. In some cases, regionalisation may allow different agencies to share staff positions that could not have been funded by one municipality, and yet are critical for planning and management. Ensuring that technical and management skills that are not available on staff are contracted through outside firms is also important.

Planning processes undertaken at successful water utilities will start at *defining the problem* instead of jumping to pre-determined solutions. For ideological or political reasons, sometimes a particular solution is prescribed for a water utility, without even appropriately diagnosing the problem. Effective and sustainable water sector business models will undertake strategic planning efforts that define the problem, identify causes, evaluate options, before selecting and implementing solutions. In an adaptive management approach, these solutions will also be continuously evaluated for their effectiveness at addressing the root causes and solving the identified problems.

5. Policy implications

How can national and state governments facilitate the success of water, wastewater, and stormwater managers in the next few decades? As existing and new water sector providers respond to infrastructure needs and growing populations, the implications for government policy are significant. Governments can play an important role in creating the conditions necessary for water and waste system providers to make needed investments, achieve social and health goals, and protect against threats to water security, while at the same time providing strong regulatory oversight.

5.1. *Balancing multiple objectives*

Governments are balancing multiple objectives in the water sector, including those linked to environment, public health, affordability, reliability and allocative efficiency. Gleick *et al.* (2002) in "The New Economy of Water" identifiy a core set of principles that are critical to ensuring that the restructuring of water and wastewater services, particularly the move to private sector partnerships, adequately balances the multiple objectives listed above. These principles include: meeting basic human needs for water, subsidising water rates when necessary for reasons of poverty, ensuring that governments retain control over the water resource itself, and ensuring that negotiations over privatisation contracts should be open, transparent and include all affected stakeholders. These principles are summarised below in Box 4.6.

The Principles for the New Economy of Water create an overarching framework, within which further government actions can be identified that do not violate the principles, but that will enable a diversity of actors to succeed in fulfilling water and wastewater needs.

5.2. *Creating an enabling policy framework*

With the changing dynamics of the water and wastewater sector, sustainability in the water sector will require supporting and regulating a range of options within an enabling policy framework. We have identified an initial list of policy responses to provide for a robust response to the multiple drivers in the water sector. These policy responses will take advantage of technological opportunities to reduce costs, while assisting utilities in managing water and wastewater services in the face of environmental, security and financing challenges. The goal in the policy arena will need to be to create a pro-competitive framework while supporting a range of business models and scales to address water and wastewater needs. This will involve creating opportunities and removing obstacles to new entrants into the water sector, creating opportunities for multiple financing mechanisms, strengthening the regulatory system, focusing on transparency and public education, providing incentives for competition, and funding more research and development in the sector.

Box 4.6. Core principles in restructuing water and wastewater services from "The New Economy of Water"

1. Continue to manage water as a social good

1.1. Meet basic human needs for water.

Contract agreements to provide water services in any region must ensure that unmet basic human water needs are met first, before more water is provided to existing customers.

1.2. Meet basic ecosystem needs for water.

Basic water-supply protections for natural ecosystems must be put in place in every region of the world.

1.3. The basic water requirement for users should be provided at subsidised rates when necessary for reasons of poverty.

2. Use sound economics in water management

2.1. Water and water services should be provided at fair and reasonable rates.

Provision of water and water services should not be free. Rates should be designed to encourage efficient and effective use of water.

2.2. Whenever possible, link proposed rate increases with agreed-upon improvements in service.

Experience has shown that water users are often willing to pay for improvements in service when such improvements are designed with their participation and when improvements are actually delivered.

2.3. Subsidies, if necessary, should be economically and socially sound.

For example, subsidies to low-income users that do not reduce the price of water are more appropriate than those that do because lower water prices encourage inefficient water use.

2.4. Private companies should be required to demonstrate that new water-supply projects are less expensive than projects to improve water conservation and water-use efficiency before they are permitted to invest and raise water rates to repay the investment.

Privatisation agreements should not permit new supply projects unless such projects can be proven to be less costly than improving the efficiency of existing water distribution and use. Rate structures should permit companies to earn a return on efficiency and conservation investments, or to be financially rewarded in some other manner.

Box 4.6. **Core principles in restructuing water and wastewater services from "The New Economy of Water"** *(cont.)*

3. Maintain strong government regulation and oversight

3.1. Governments should retain or establish public ownership or control of ambient waters.

Permanent and unequivocal public ownership of ambient water sources gives the public the strongest single point of leverage in ensuring that an acceptable balance between social and economic concerns is achieved.

3.2. Public agencies and water-service providers should monitor water quality. Governments should define and enforce water-quality laws. Fortunately, this is the case in most of the countries addressed in this study, with the exception of bottled and vended water.

3.3. Contracts that lay out the responsibilities of each partner are a prerequisite for the success of any privatisation.

Contracts must protect the public interest; and good contracts will include explicit performance criteria and standards, with oversight by government regulatory agencies and non-governmental organisations.

3.4. Clear dispute resolution procedures should be developed.

It is necessary to develop practical procedures that build upon local institutions and practices, are free of corruption, and difficult to circumvent.

3.5. Independent technical assistance and contract review should be standard.

Weaker governments are most vulnerable to the risk of being forced into accepting weak contracts. Many of the problems associated with privatisation have resulted from inadequate contract review or ambiguous contract language. In principle, many of these problems can be avoided by requiring advance independent technical and contract review.

3.6. Negotiations over privatisation contracts should be open, transparent and include all affected stakeholders.

Numerous political and financial problems for water customers and private companies have resulted from arrangements that were perceived as corrupt or not in the best interests of the public. Stakeholder participation is widely recognised as the best way of avoiding these problems.

Source: Gleick *et al.* (2002).

Creating opportunities for innovative business models and strategies to succeed

Governments and water utilities face a range of uncertainties and vulnerabilities in the water sector, including climate change, water availability and financing challenges. In the face of uncertainty, it is important to cultivate diverse actors that can introduce an array of approaches that allow adaptation and innovation to respond to changing needs. Supporting a range of approaches is the best antidote to address uncertainties, challenges and risks.

The regulatory system in OECD countries is typically hardwired to regulate piped water supply and waterborne sewage treatment in centralised systems using a series of accepted technologies. This technological determinism toward conventional methods of water and waste treatment limits opportunities for new entrants into the sector and for innovative methods of achieving societal and water quality goals.

New actors attempting to provide on-site treatment of waste and provision of water may be limited because regulations require new and existing properties to connect to underground systems of water supply and waste disposal. There may also be no method to disconnect from the existing system or be served by a non-conventional entity. Ecosanitation proponents note that regulations often presuppose water-based transport for human excreta, ultimately excluding ecosanitation from the range of available options.

Standards for water and waste treatment need to be performance-based rather than technology-based. Technology-neutral standards afford providers in the water sector with greater flexibility and capability to innovate to meet needs. Standards should state quantitative and qualitative system objectives to achieve public health goals, rather than specify the type of technology that should be employed (Winbald and Simson-Hebert, 2004). In addition to providing a greater scope for on-site water and waste service providers, performance-based standards will also provide incentives for providers to seek out more efficient and cheaper ways of achieving set performance standards.

For example, New York City led a highly successful effort to manage watershed lands in order to protect ecosystems and water quality rather than build large new water-treatment infrastructure. In response to growing concerns over drinking water quality, the United States Environmental Protection Agency issued regulations in 1989 that required filtration of all surface water unless municipalities could employ other methods that would produce comparable water quality.[10] In lieu of constructing a filtration plant that would have cost city residents USD 6 to 8 billion, New York elected to design and implement an innovative environmental protection strategy to protect water quality in the entire watershed. This approach saved the city

USD 4 to 6 billion and brought many of the watershed's stakeholders into a collaborative process that both respected watershed landowners' economic well-being and protected the city's water quality. This approach has also spread widely since it was "discovered". For example, most water suppliers in the US have subsequently been required to develop plans for protection of their source watersheds based on the city's experience.

There are a range of policy approaches that can promote the entry of non-traditional service providers to operate on-site systems or for new entrants to come into the market. In India, for example, a series of rules implemented in the last few years require most new large generators of water to provide on-site wastewater systems. Ofwat, the economic regulator in England and Wales, has created a framework to facilitate effective competition in the water and sewerage industry through a series of legislative acts. Inset appointments allow the existing supplier of water to be replaced by another service provider in a specific site. All service providers need to be licensed as a water or sewerage supplier by Ofwat.

Third party access legislation, which quickly followed with the Competition Act of 1998 in England, promotes competition in the water sector, more so than in any other part of the world. There are many critics of the full privatisation/ competition route taken in England, and whether it has been successful at improving efficiency. While similar legislation may not be appropriate elsewhere, it provides an example of how incumbent operators can be regulated to allow for new entrants into the water sector.

Creating and supporting a range of financing mechanisms

Governments are ultimately responsible for the provision of water and waste services. The best mechanism to ensure that this happens is to continue to promote and support a range of financing approaches. While in the past, governments were more involved in financing in the water sector, providing national backing for municipal bonds and national grants or loans for water-system services, the current drive for private investment at the expense of public responsibility needs to be reconsidered.

Governments and water utilities will not succeed, in our opinion, at increasing the availability of capital in the water sector until lending organisations and governments focus on making funds available to the full variety of business models, not just those involving private actors. For example, Mexico's CNA (Comision Nacional de Agua) has restricted its loans to water utilities that are engaged in projects with a private partner. Although this has stimulated private involvement in the water sector, it has also created a public backlash that may eventually (or soon) undermine the very companies this policy has lured into the Mexican marketplace.

It is possible that reinsurance along the lines proposed in the Camdessus report released at the 3rd World Water Forum in Kyoto may eventually help reduce currency risk for investors in the water sector, and thereby promote more investment. But little has happened in that regard since the Forum, in part because the reinsurance scheme was designed to promote private participation in the water sector rather than investment across international boundaries in general.

Because of the national character of many of the water sector challenges, national governments will need to take a more active role in ensuring the success of municipal and regional water providers. Many of the new financing challenges facing municipal and regional water utilities, such as climate change and security concerns, are national and supranational in character. Some climate change impacts, for example, may only be mitigated through transnational treaties, in which only national governments have the capacity to engage. Additionally, protecting national security has also traditionally been a responsibility of national governments. As a result, national governments must develop cost-sharing policies with water utilities to address national challenges such as climate change and security.

Standard setting organisations, including national and transnational governments that implement new regulations in the water sector, must identify and support associated financing options for water utilities. Similar to what was done in the United States with the Clean Water Revolving Loan Fund, governments should consider specifically associating each new regulatory requirement with a sufficient number and type of financing mechanisms to ensure that the full range of business models has access to capital needed to satisfy the requirements.

In the United States, tax exempt status for earnings from municipal bonds has helped finance water infrastructure. Re-evaluating the role, particularly in OECD countries, that national governments can play in supporting a system where future users pay for needed water infrastructure, will be an important enabling policy. US overseas aid work in financing in the water sector, has also introduced water sector improvement bonds in India and other areas, partially backed by USAID. The partial backing has provided enough security that small Indian municipalities can go to local and international financial markets to procure loans.

It is also critical that financing be made available for non-traditional approaches to needs satisfaction in the water sector. New York City was able to finance their watershed protection programme without any changes in current US policy. Similarly, on-site systems can also be financed in conventional ways often enough that the market for these systems is growing. But the full impact of these new approaches may not be fundable with existing financial mechanisms because new ways of doing things involve risks that must be managed. Policy intervention to reduce risk or spread it via insurance mechanisms could be very helpful.

Improving the ability of water quality regulators to monitor a range of systems and sources

With the changing dynamics of the water sector, water sector regulators need to be prepared to monitor water quality from a variety of different sources. This includes regulating ground water extraction, regulating on-site systems, and ensuring adequate financing for monitoring and enforcement.

In the face of growing water scarcity and overextraction of groundwater supplies, governments will need to establish monitoring and control over groundwater sources. The typical water rights attribution in groundwater in most countries is that groundwater is the property of the landowner. This has often led to problems of overextraction and salinisation of coastal groundwater. Governments will need to systematically identify and monitor existing wells and borewells, and establish ongoing systems to regulate abstraction and groundwater quality.

The growth of on-site systems and providers will introduce new regulatory challenges. Governments will need to create opportunities for these actors to pre-dominate by removing regulatory obstacles, and creating new regulations allowing non-traditional arrangements for water and waste provision. In addition, governments will need to determine how to regulate these systems for drinking water quality and waste disposal to ensure that public health and the environment are protected. This may require the development of guidelines for on-site drinking water quality, quality guidelines for use of treated wastewater for landscaping, gardening, or toilet flushing, and quality specifications for the disposal of waste or wastewater effluent.

Governments will also need to develop a system to monitor these multiple sources of drinking water and waste treatment. This includes identifying who will be responsible for this monitoring and enforcement, whether it is municipal governments, health departments, environmental agencies, or existing water utilities. Regulators also need to identify where funding will come from to support these new and more complex regulatory functions, through on-site user fees or taxes. These multiple challenges need to be addressed in order to provide an environment where new business models can grow while being protective of public and environmental health.

Providing incentives for competition

Private sector involvement in the water sector was promoted with the idea that private actors could introduce more competition into the market. Public economists have long known that water and wastewater systems are natural monopolies that cannot compete in the usual way. This is being opened up in key ways with third party access requirements in England, and this is being considered in Australia. This has been discussed earlier. We will focus on the important enabling policy of benchmarking to introduce competition into the water sector.

Competition for the market is not limited to private companies, but can be achieved through benchmarking efforts. Specifying an appropriate set of performance standards and indicators may require considerable effort and refinement. Indicators must be both observable and measurable. The challenge is to select a set of standards and indicators that is sufficiently detailed to be meaningful for management and oversight decisions and which is, at the same time, available and attainable at a reasonable cost. A few dozen robust measures of performance are usually superior to larger numbers of indicators or standards.

Documents that provide both in-depth discussion and comprehensive lists of performance measures in the abstract include Alegre *et al.* (2000) and Matos *et al.* (2003). In this book, see Chapter 1, Box 1.6, for a list of water utility performance indicators from the American Water Works Association (AWWA) and Water Environment Federation (WEF). Lafferty and Lauer (2005) provide data on numerous US water utilities in comparison with the indicators in Crotty (2004). A World Bank initiative along these same lines, known as the Water and Sanitation International Benchmarking Network, is available at *www.ib-net.org*. Benchmarking is a growing field and the data available will likely increase significantly in the next few years, forcing business models to respond.

Continuing to focus on public education, public involvement and transparency

Ensuring that users know about water-system needs is undoubtedly the best way to ensure public support for funding and potentially increased user fees. Ideally, consumers and residents should be involved in the water service and rate decisions that affect them. Consumers are in the best position to be able to weigh service improvements against rate increases to determine the best strategy that meets their needs and fits their budget. This demand-driven planning approach ensures sustainable outcomes.

There is broad consensus in the water sector that that *openness and transparency* are critical elements to success in privatisation. But, governments need to go further than requirements for transparency during privatisation. Broad-based and ongoing education and communication with the public is a critical function of the water utility. This is important because of the public health and societal goods dimensions of water. This is also critical in ensuring public support for new facilities, rate increases, or restructuring efforts. Water users should not be consulted when rate increases are needed, but throughout the process of arriving at solutions for water-system challenges. If the public feels ownership of the water system, they will be in a better position to proactively choose solutions rather than react to solutions that are chosen by others.

Broad participation by affected parties ensures that diverse values and varying viewpoints are articulated and incorporated into water-sector decision making. It also provides a sense of ownership and stewardship over the process and resulting decisions. Water is a resource that is essential for life and health and plays vital social, economic and environmental roles. Water management is linked to issues of poverty alleviation, public health, social equity and the sustainability of ecosystems. The best way to balance the multiple roles of water is to ensure that water-resource decisions involve multiple stakeholders and the public at large in needs assessment, planning and implementation of any potential project. Governments must ensure that the public is aware of and educated on water-sector decisions, provide access to information, and include public input in all decisions and plans made about water resources.

Better decisions and better outcomes result from the *free flow of information* in the water sector. Ensuring open access to documents, information, and contracts instils public trust and inspires public confidence. As mentioned earlier, *transparency* in contractual negotiations also ensures that decisions are sustained from one political regime to another, and prevents corruption and collusion in contract awards. *Public access* to information ensures that government and potential private-sector partners are accountable for agreed-upon outcomes.

Water sector decisions should ensure public access and oversight, monitor the public interest, and ensure public participation and transparency. In the case of governments considering privatisation, this should include the following:

1. Ongoing public forums to educate the public and to obtain community input on water system issues.
2. Periodic third party assessments.
3. Public advisory committee with broad community representation to advise governments proposing privatisation or restructuring.
4. Formal public review of contracts and licences and responses to public comments in advance of signing agreements.
5. Public education prior to any transfer of public responsibilities to private companies.
6. Technical support to communities to assess restructuring impacts on equity, environment and welfare.

Many private companies are realising the importance of public involvement and transparency to help ensure stable business environments, and the long-term sustainability of their operations. Increased transparency and public involvement may improve public trust in the private sector and increase the ability of the private sector to float private bonds. Increasing transparency and public communication will also allow public sector providers and governments to float bonds and successfully advocate for more public financing.

Funding more R&D in the sector

Funding increased research and development in the water sector will be critical to capturing opportunities for efficiency and cost reduction that can help make water utilities more financially sustainable. As described earlier, the energy generation potential of wastewater processed through microbial fuel cells, and other technological opportunities, will need further development in order to be ready for wide-scale commercialisation. Subsidies to research are not always justified and can be abused. But in general there is a strong case for fundamental research that both has the potential to dramatically change how business is done and is so broad that individual investors could not possibly capture the full benefits of it, and therefore underinvest in it. Microbial fuel cells for energy production from wastewater are a good example, as are development of standardised methods for testing the performance of new technologies in water treatment, wastewater recycling, and so forth.

6. Conclusion

Ultimately, the water sector must include a *full range of financing approaches* in order to meet its investment needs and successfully maintain and expand service. Achieving that full range will require the development of *enabling policies*. This chapter has concluded with a limited policy discussion, because that is the next logical step in tackling the challenges of underinvestment while leveraging the opportunities emerging in the sector in the form of new ideas and approaches.

Based on the analysis in this chapter, we believe that policies which enable every reasonable type of financing mechanism, rather than a few chosen by "experts", have the greatest likelihood of success. Each OECD and Big 5 country will need to design policies grounded in their own institutional history and that are likely to work as next steps in the evolution of institutions in each country.

We need to move beyond the single-solution approach. By providing an environment where new financial mechanisms, technologies and solutions can emerge and become successful, within the boundaries of the principles described above, governments have a greater chance of success in meeting current and growing needs in the water sector.

Notes

1. Big 5 economies are Brazil, the Russian Federation, India, China and Indonesia. This chapter will focus on OECD countries and the Big 5 countries.
2. Public Utility Transfers and Water Charges Act 1988 (Chapter 15) and Water Act 1989.
3. "Dominant" is defined as having more than 50% of the population served by the private sector, and "significant" is defined as having 25-50% of the population served by the private sector.
4. "Minor" is defined as having less than 25% of the population served by the private sector.
5. The World Bank defines a greenfield project as one in which "a private entity or public-private joint venture builds and operates a new facility for the period specified in the project contract. The facility may return to the public sector at the end of the concession period." DBOT, BOT, and BOO fall within this category.
6. Distressed projects are defined as those that the government or the operator has either requested contract termination or are in international arbitration.
7. The privatisation database maintained by OECD was discontinued in 2001.
8. The services delivered by water systems are numerous and can be defined in a variety of ways. For example, flood-control services are often defined based on protection against flooding from a specified duration (*e.g.* one hour) and frequency (*e.g.* once every ten years, on average) of precipitation event. Flood protection in practice uses several or more duration-frequency objectives. Another example is water supply, which can be of potable or less-than-potable quality. Or one could enumerate the services provided by the water (*e.g.* human consumption, waste removal, irrigation) rather than the service of delivering water of a specified quality. Focusing on the ultimate services for which water is desired is essential when considering options for managing water demand (see Wolff and Gleick, 2002). Simpler "aggregate" categories (*e.g.* delivery of potable water) are sufficient, however, for the purposes of this chapter. This function represents the cost of delivering services without specifying the inputs (*e.g.* labour, capital, water, energy, knowledge) required to deliver them. There may be and often are numerous combinations of inputs that would deliver a specified level of services at a specified cost. For example, programmes to promote water use efficiency often substitute knowledge for physical water while maintaining the same level of end-use services to customers.
9. Much of this comes from the discussion on the World Bank Rapid Response website (*www.rru.worldbank.org*) moderated by Clive Harris on "Canceled Infrastructure Projects: Causes and Consequences".
10. The 1989 Surface Water Treatment Rule (SWTR).

Bibliography

Alameda Countywide Cleanwater Program (1998), *DUST Marsh Long-Term Evaluation*, *www.cleanwaterprogram.org/indexFlash.htm*.

Alcazar, L., M. Abdala and M. Shirley (2000), *The Buenos Aires Water Concession*, The World Bank Policy Research Working Paper 2311, April, Washington DC.

Alegre, H., W. Hirner, J.M. Baptista and R. Parena (2000), *Performance Indicators for Water Supply Services*, International Water Association, London.

Andrieu, Michel (2005), "The Long-Term Global Outlook for Investment in Infrastructures", paper prepared for the OECD IFP project on Infrastructure to 2030, Paris, 12 December 2005.

Ashley, R. and A. Cashman (2006), "The Impacts of Change on the Long-term Future Demand for Water Sector Infrastructure", in *Infrastructure to 2030: Telecom, Land Transport, Water and Electricity*, OECD, Paris.

AWWA (1999), *Water Quality and Treatment – Handbook of Community Water Supplies*, 5th Edition, McGraw Hill Co., New York.

Baumert, J. and L. Bloodgood (2004), *Private Sector Participation in the Water and Wastewater Services Industry*, Office of Industries, US International Trade Commission, Washington DC.

Beecher, J.A. (1996), *The Regionalization of Water Utilities: Perspectives, Issues, and Annotated Bibliography*, the National Regulatory Research Institute, Columbus, Ohio.

Blokland, M., O. Braadbaart and K. Schwartz (eds.) (1999), *Private Business, Public Owners: Government Shareholding in Water Enterprises*, Ministry of Housing, Spatial Planning and the Environment, The Hague, Netherlands.

Brown, L. and B. Halweil (1998), "China's Water Shortage", Worldwatch Press Release, Worldwatch Institute, Washington DC.

Byrnes, P., S. Grosskopf and K. Hayes (1986), "Efficiency and Ownership: Further Evidence", *The Review of Economics and Statistics*, Vol. 68, No. 2, pp. 337-341.

Camdessus, M. and panel (2003), *Financing Water for All*, the report of the World Panel on Financing Water Infrastructure, the World Water Council Report, the Third World Water Forum, Kyoto, Japan.

Center for Disease Control (CDC) (2006), *Safe Water System (SWS) Publications – PUR*, *www.cdc.gov/safewater/publications_pages/pubs_pur.htm*.

Crain, W. Mark and A. Zardkoohi (1978), "A Test of the Property-Rights Theory of the Firm: Water Utilities in the United States", *Journal of Law and Economics*, Vol. 21, pp. 395-408.

Crotty, P. (2004), *Selection and Definition of Performance Indicators for Water and Wastewater Utilities*, American Water Works Association and American Water Works Association Research Foundation, Denver, Colorado.

Empresa Metropolitana de Obras Santarias (EMOS) SA (1995), *Memoria* 95, Santiago, Chile.

Estache, A. and M.A. Rossi (2002), "How Different Is the Efficiency of Public and Private Water Companies in Asia?", *The World Bank Economic Review*, Vol. 16, No. 1, pp. 139-148.

Feigenbaum, S. and R.Teeples (1986), "Public *Versus* Private Water Delivery: A Hedonic Cost Approach", *The Review of Statistics and Economics*, Vol. 68, No. 2, pp. 337-341.

Fox, W. and R. Hofler (1986), "Using Homothetic Composed Error Frontiers to Measure Water Utility Efficiency", *Southern Economic Journal*, Vol. 53, No. 2, pp. 461-77.

Gentry, B. (2000), *Global Trends in Urban Water Supply and Waste Water Financing and Management: Changing Roles for the Public and Private Sectors*, OECD, Paris.

Gleick, P.H. (1999), "The Human Right to Water", *Water Policy*, Vol. 1, No. 5, pp. 487-503.

Gleick, P.H. (2003), "Global Freshwater Resources: Soft-Path Solutions for the 21st Century", *Science*, Vol. 302, pp. 1524-1528.

Gleick, P.H., H. Cooley, and D. Groves (2005), *California Water 2030: An Efficient Future*, Pacific Institute for Studies in Development, Environment, and Security, Oakland, California.

Gleick, P.H., D. Haasz, C. Henges-Jeck, V. Srinivasan, G. Wolff, K. Kao Cushing and A. Mann (2003), *Waste Not, Want Not: The Potential for Urban Water Conservation in California*, Pacific Institute for Studies in Development, Environment, and Security, Oakland, California.

Gleick, P.H., G. Wolff, E.L. Chalecki and R. Reyes (2002), *The New Economy of Water: The Risks and Benefits of Globalization and Privatization of Fresh Water*, Pacific Institute for Studies in Development, Environment, and Security, Oakland, California.

Gomez, S. and A. Steding (1998), *California Water Transfers: An Evaluation of the Economic Framework and a Spatial Analysis of the Potential Impacts*, Pacific Institute for Studies in Development, Environment, and Security, Oakland, California.

Gomez-Lobo, A. (2003), "Making Water Affordable: Output-based Consumption Subsidies in Chile", in P.J. Brook and S.M. Smith (eds.), *Contracting for Public Services: Output-Based Aid and its Applications*, The World Bank, Washington DC, *http://rru.worldbank.org/Documents/07ch2.pdf*.

Guttierez, E., B. Calaguas, J. Green and V. Roaf. (2003), *New Rules, New Roles: Does PSP Benefit the Poor? The Synthesis Report*, WaterAid and Tearfund, London.

Hodgson, S. (2004), *Land and Water – the Rights Interface*, FAO Legislative Study 84, Development Law Service, Food and Agriculture Organization in the United States Legal Office, Rome.

Infrastructure Canada, Research and Analysis Division (2004), *Water Infrastructure: Research for Policy and Program Development*.

Intergovernmental Panel on Climate Change (IPCC) (2001), *IPCC Third Assessment Report – Climate Change 2001*, Cambridge University Press, Cambridge.

Izaguirre, A.K. and C. Hunt (2005). *Private Water Projects: Investment Flows Up by 36 Per Cent in 2004*, Public Policy for the Private Sector, Note No. 297, The World Bank Group, Washington DC.

Jensen, O. and F. Blanc-Brude (2006), *The Handshake: Why Do Governments and Firms Sign Private Sector Participation Deals? Evidence from the Water and Wastewater Sector in Developing Countries*, World Bank Policy Research Working Paper 3937, June, Washington DC.

Kaufmann, D. (2002). *Transparency, Incentives and Prevention (TIP) for Corruption Control and Good Governance. Empirical Findings, Practical Lessons, and Strategies for Action based on International Experience*, The World Bank, Washington DC, *www.worldbank.org/wbi/governance/pdf/quinghua_presentation.pdf*.

Lafferty, K.A. and W.C. Lauer (2005), *Benchmarking Performance Indicators for Water and Wastewater Utilities: Survey Data and Analyses Report*, American Water Works Association.

Levina, E. and H. Adams (2006), *Domestic Policy Frameworks for Adaptation to Climate Change in the Water Sector. Part I: Annex I Countries*, OECD, Paris.

Matos, R., A. Cardoso, R. Ashley, P. Duarte, A. Molinari and A. Schulz (2003), *Performance Indicators for Wastewater Services*, International Water Association, London.

Maxwell, S. (2005), "How Big is the 'Water Business'?", *Journal of the American Water Works Association*, Vol. 97, No. 1, January.

McFarlane, S. (2003), *Regional Water Works: Sharing Urban Water Services*, Western Cities Project Report No. 28, Canada West Foundation, November.

Moss, J., G. Wolff, G. Gladden and E. Guttieriez (2003), "Valuing Water for Better Governance", CEO Panel for Water, Pacific Institute, Oakland, California, *www.pacinst.org/reports/valuing_water/valuing_water_paper.pdf*.

National Research Council (NRC) (2002), *Privatization of Water Services in the United States: An Assessment of Issues and Experiences*, National Academy Press, Washington DC.

Ofwat (1999), *MD 154: Development of Common Carriage. To Managing Directors of Water and Sewerage Companies and Water Only Companies*, *www.ofwat.gov.uk/aptrix/ofwat/publish.nsf/Contest/md154developmentofcommoncarriage*.

Ofwat (2004), *SLR 1/03 Water Act 2003: Self Lay and Requisitioning*, *www.ofwat.gov.uk/aptrix/ofwat/publish.nsf/Content/slr0103*.

Pinsent Masons (2005), *Pinsent Masons Water Yearbook 2005-2006*, Pinsent Masons, London.

Queensland Government (2006), *Water Trading: An Overview of Queensland Water Markets*, *www.nrm.qld.gov.au/water/trading/pdf/wat_trad_overview.pdf*.

Raskin, P., Gleick, P., Kirshen, P., Pontius, G. and K. Strzepek (1997), *Water Futures: Assessment of Long-Range Patterns and Problems. in the: Comprehensive Assessment of the Freshwater Resources of the World*, Stockholm Environmental Institute, Stockholm.

Saunders, P. and C. Harris (1990), "Privatization and the Consumer", *Sociology*, Vol. 24, pp. 57-75.

Tasman Asia Pacific (1997), *Third Party Access in the Water Industry: An Assessment of the Extent to Which Water Facilities Meet the Criteria for Declaration of Access*, prepared for the National Competition Council.

Thames Water Utilities Ltd. (2005), *Corporate Responsibility Report 2004*, Thames Water Utilities Ltd.

United Nations (UN) (2003), *Water for People, Water for Life*, World Water Development Report (WWDRI), UNESCO, Paris, and Berghahn Books, United Kingdom.

United Nations Development Programme (UNDP) (2004), *Human Development Report*. Data available at *http://hdr.undp.org/statistics/data*.

US Congressional Budget Office (US CBO) (2002), *Future Investment in Drinking Water and Wastewater Infrastructure*, November, Washington DC.

United States Environmental Protection Agency (US EPA) (1999), *National Characteristics of Drinking Water Serving Populations Under 10 000*, Washington DC.

US EPA (2000), *Drinking Water State Revolving Funds Interim Final Rule*, United States Office of Water EPA 816-F-00-026, Washington DC.

US EPA (2002), *The Clean Water and Drinking Water Infrastructure Gap Analysis*, September, Washington DC.

United States General Accounting Office (US GAO) (2002), *Water Infrastructure: Information on Financing, Capital Planning, and Privatization*, August, Washington DC.

United States National Academy of Sciences (US NAS) (2002), *Privatization of Water Services in the United States: An Assessment of Issues and Experience*, Water Science and Technology Board, National Academy Press, Washington DC, *http://fermat.nap.edu/catalog/10135.html*.

VanDe Hei, D (2006), "PPPs: Beware the Promises", *Underground Infrastructure Management*, January/February.

Wilkinson, R. (2003), *Integrated Water Resources Management: Landscape Planning in a Watershed Context*, Calfed Urban Water Use Efficiency Pilot Project, Inland Empire Utilities Agency, Rocky Mountain Institute, Snowmass, Colorado.

Winblad, U. and M. Simpson-Hebert (eds.) (2004), *Ecological Sanitation: Revised and Enlarged Edition*, Stockholm Environmental Institute, Stockholm, Sweden.

Wolff, G. (2004), Economies of Scale and Scope in River Basin Management. Pacific Institute for Studies in Development, Environment and Security, Oakland, California.

Wolff, G., R. Cohen, and B. Nelson (2004). *Energy Down the Drain: The Hidden Costs of California's Water Supply*, Natural Resources Defense Council, New York.

Wolff, G. and P.H. Gleick (2002). "The Soft Path for Water", in Gleick *et al.*, *The World's Water: 2002-2003*, Island Press, Washington DC.

Wolff, G. and E. Hallstein (2005), *Beyond Privatization: Restructuring Water Systems to Improve Performance*, Pacific Institute for Studies in Development, Environment, and Security, Oakland, California.

Wolff, G. and M. Palaniappan (2004), "Public or Private Water Management? Cutting the Gordian Knot", *Journal of Water Resources Planning and Management*, January/February.

World Bank (2006), Private Participation in Infrastructure (PPI) Database, Washington DC, *www.ppi.worldbank.org*.

World Health Organization (WHO)/UNICEF (2005), *Water for Life: Making It Happen*, Joint Monitoring Programme for Water Supply and Sanitation, WHO Press, Geneva.

ISBN 978-92-64-03131-9
Infrastructure to 2030 – Vol. 2
Mapping Policy for Electricity, Water and Transport

Chapter 5

Key Trends and Implications for Policy Change in Long-Term Rail Freight Traffic and Infrastructure

by

Louis S. Thompson*

Rail infrastructure serves freight and passenger operators. This chapter focuses on rail freight operations and infrastructure needs and examines the underlying economic and demographic forces which are creating growth pressures. What is the future demand for rail freight and how will demand be met by the public and private sectors? As this chapter discusses, management models and government policies vary greatly.

* Thompson, Galenson and Associates, Maryland, US. This chapter was jointly commissioned and financed by the OECD International Futures Programme and the Joint OECD/ECMT Transport Research Centre.

Summary

Studies have shown that the demand for rail services, and the need for the related infrastructure, will grow in the next three decades. Even though the extent of growth is subject to an unusually wide range of uncertainties, the underlying growth pressures and potential for growth are clear.

Rail infrastructure serves two types of operators – freight and passenger – with significant subcategories depending on national or regional conditions. Passenger services can be subdivided by commuters, regional trains, conventional longer-haul intercity trains, and (in some countries) High-Speed Rail (HSR) operating on exclusive rights of way. Freight services can similarly be subdivided by commodity (*e.g.* bulk commodities such as coal by comparison with finished goods), type of service (wagonload, multiple wagon shipment, unit – or block – trains), etc.

The infrastructure needs of freight *versus* passengers cannot be fully distinguished, except where there is an exclusive right of way. There is a complex three-way interaction among the characteristics of the infrastructure, the passenger services and the freight services. This chapter will focus on rail freight operations and infrastructure needs, but the problem of passenger/freight interaction and infrastructure use indistinguishability must always be kept in mind.

Underlying economic and demographic forces will manifestly create a *need* and an *opportunity* for added rail freight infrastructure capacity. This need will be reinforced by, *inter alia*, highway congestion, safety, security, environmental concerns, and deliberate public policies to shift traffic from road to rail.

Though the *need* for added rail freight infrastructure capacity will grow, the responses to this need are less clear. *Responses* by the rail sector and governments will be influenced by government policies, by the business models that the rail sector adopts, and by a number of exogenous factors such as technology.

What will actually happen will be heavily driven by the consensus that emerges (if and where it does) as to the relative roles of the public and private sectors. Where rail freight is provided privately, or at least fully commercially, and where governments do not unduly support highway or water competition, there is reason to believe that the wholly market-driven needs for freight infrastructure and operating investment can be met (one way or the other) from resources generated in the freight sector.

The rail infrastructure challenge lies equally in the willingness of governments to identify social benefits and costs of freight services transparently, and to fund them. Some governments (in the European Union in particular) have identified rail infrastructure public benefits, but have not reached a balanced and fully compensatory support policy among the transport modes. Others (the US and Canada) have still to reach consensus on the public *versus* private benefits of rail freight, and how to pay for them.

In the broadest terms, most rail *freight* services, and their related infrastructure, should be market-driven and, where the market is allowed to function effectively, could be financed and operated without major public involvement. Achieving additional *non-market* freight benefits (reduced highway congestion or air pollution) and minimising non-market costs (passenger-freight interference) will only be achieved with effective public intervention.

In summary, the investment in rail freight infrastructure could be put into two categories: primarily private and primarily public. The *private* investment is likely to be heavily focused in North America and in countries such as Australia and Brazil that have large, export-focused companies in mining and agriculture (where investments may have little benefit for the national system). North American investment is likely to be oriented to increasing capacity, especially on critical port/landside interfaces, on major nodes such as Chicago and, as always, on capacity for major bulk commodity flows such as coal and grains or for the growing internal container flows. There may well eventually be a public sector counterpart for the private investment, but the timing and scope are unclear. The bulk of the primarily *public* investment will clearly be in China and India with a focus on increasing system capacity, either by building new, high-capacity, freight-only lines or by building new passenger lines that will free-up capacity for freight movements. There will also be an EU programme to encourage freight rail flows (and capacity), but the impact of EU programmes on freight, as opposed to passenger, capacity is not clearly defined. There will clearly be a private counterpart for these public investments, especially in operating companies and their assets. The degree of private investment in infrastructure is harder to predict because public policies on freight privatisation are unclear, and because the priorities to be assigned in resolving capacity conflicts between freight and passenger access in open access systems are likely to favour passenger.

1. Introduction

This chapter has two broad themes: the future demand for rail freight infrastructure, and the factors that will influence how that demand is met.

Rail infrastructure is normally multipurpose, serving passengers as well as freight. There are subcategories of each type of service that also will influence the need for operating services on the infrastructure. As a result, it is not possible to clearly disentangle freight as opposed to passenger needs and related investment in infrastructure, except where the infrastructure is dedicated to a single purpose. Single purpose rail freight infrastructure is mostly restricted to the railways of North and South America (though Amtrak does operate over about 25% of the freight infrastructure in the US, and VIA operates over about 25% of the freight infrastructure in Canada), and some specialised railways in South Africa and Australia. Table 5.1 displays the degree to which railways are weighted toward freight or passenger. It is possible to disentangle the *operating* performance and investments, though many countries have delayed in doing so.

Table 5.1 shows the location and scale of most of the world's rail infrastructure. Several important points should be noted. First, infrastructure, rail freight traffic and rail passenger traffic are highly concentrated in a limited number of countries. For example, of the 99 countries in the basic dataset used for this chapter, the top 10 account for over 61% of all line-kilometre (km). The top 10 rail passenger carriers account for about 84% of all passenger traffic (passenger-km), and the top 10 freight carriers account for over 92% of all freight traffic (ton-km). This means that a reasonable forecast of the freight demand for infrastructure investment might be accurately based on only a limited number of countries. Note that the set of countries in the top 10 groups are different in each case, but there are only 16 countries that fall in the top 10 in any of the three rankings. These top 16 countries account for about 71% of the world's rail infrastructure. Second, while world rail freight traffic did increase slowly (by 14%) between 1980 and 2003, and passenger traffic increased somewhat more rapidly (40% over the same period), total infrastructure line-km actually *fell* by about 13% (mostly in the OECD countries).

There are a number of explanations for the shrinkage. The US Class I railroads accounted for about 62% of the shrinkage, which rises to 70% when the Canadian National (CN) and Canadian Pacific (CP) in Canada are added. In the US and Canada, many light density lines have become uneconomic in the face of highway competition, and the play of market forces on the private railroads has created intense focus on reducing costs. Another 13% of the shrinkage occurred in Germany, France and Poland, where light density rural tracks have been replaced by more efficient auto and bus services.

This should highlight the fact that rail infrastructure *capacity* (at least as measured by line-km) is not directly related to output. In fact, because there are increasing returns to line density (passenger-km or ton-km per line-km), economic forces have actually delivered a negative relationship between traffic and line-km since 1980 (though this is unlikely to continue). Table 5.1 shows that there is a wide variation among railways in line density. For the most part (India and Japan are exceptions), the highest densities are found on freight-dominant railways because freight trains can be longer and heavier than passenger trains.

Table 5.1. **Data table on worldwide rail infrastructure**

Passenger and freight line density

	Line-km					Pass-km (000 000)				Ton-km (000 000)			
	1980	1990	2003	% growth, 1980 to 2003	Shrinkage (km) 1980 to 2003	1980	1990	2003	% growth, 1980 to 2003	1980	1990	2003	% growth, 1980 to 2003
OECD North America													
Mexico	20 351	20 351	17 576	(13.6)	(2 775.0)	5 295	5 336	n.a.	(100.0)	41 330	36 417	65 260	58
Canada: CP + CN	63 127	52 327	50 551	(19.9)	(12 578.0)	–	–	–	–	185 219	224 751	405 499	119
Canada: VIA	–	–	–	–	–	3 110	1 266	1 350	(56.6)	–	–	–	–
USA: All Class I Railways	287 647	214 475	196 929	(31.5)	(90 718.0)	–	–	–	–	1 393 235	1 530 743	2 267 051	63
USA: Amtrak	1 100	1 100	1 100	0.0	0.0	7 637	9 769	8 862	16.0	–	–	–	–
USA: Suburban carriers	–	–	–	–	–	9 000	11 404	15 993	77.7	–	–	–	–
OECD Asia													
Korea	3 135	3 091	3 140	0.2	5.0	21 640	29 863	28 562	32.0	10 549	13 663	11 057	5
Japan	22 236	20 254	20 067	(9.8)	(2 169.0)	193 143	237 551	241 160	24.9	37 000	26 803	22 600	(39)
New Zealand	4 478	4 029	3 913	(12.6)	(565.0)	370	370	n.a.	(100.0)	3 226	2 744	3 500	8
Australia	40 000	40 000	40 400	1.0	400.0	n.a.	n.a.	11 320	n.a.	63 700	87 920	161 000	153
OECD EU													
Austria	5 857	5 624	5 655	(3.4)	(202.0)	7 380	8 575	8 150	10.4	11 200	12 158	17 852	59
Belgium	3 978	3 479	3 521	(11.5)	(457.0)	6 963	6 539	8 265	18.7	8 037	8 370	8 306	3
Czech Repbulic	9 501	9 501	9 501	–	–	11 728	12 568	6 483	(44.7)	42 705	38 371	17 069	(60)
Denmark	2 015	2 344	2 273	12.8	258.0	3 803	4 855	5 397	41.9	1 619	1 730	1 888	17
Finland	6 075	5 867	5 851	(3.7)	(224.0)	3 216	3 331	3 338	3.8	8 334	8 357	10 047	21
France	34 362	34 070	29 269	(14.8)	(5 093.0)	54 660	63 761	71 937	31.6	68 815	50 667	46 835	(32)
Germany	42 745	40 980	36 044	(15.7)	(6 701.0)	63 637	61 024	69 596	9.4	118 988	101 166	73 951	(38)
Greece	2 461	2 484	2 414	(1.9)	(47.0)	1 464	1 977	1 574	7.5	814	647	456	(44)

Table 5.1. **Data table on worldwide rail infrastructure** *(cont.)*

Passenger and freight line density

	Line-km					Pass-km (000 000)				Ton-km (000 000)			
	1980	1990	2003	% growth, 1980 to 2003	Shrinkage (km) 1980 to 2003	1980	1990	2003	% growth, 1980 to 2003	1980	1990	2003	% growth, 1980 to 2003
Hungary	7 614	7 617	7 730	1.5	116.5	13 550	11 298	7 300	(46.1)	24 041	16 593	7 568	(69)
Ireland	1 987	1 944	1 919	(3.4)	(68.0)	1 032	1 226	1 601	55.1	624	589	398	(36)
Italy	16 138	16 086	15 965	(1.1)	(173.0)	39 587	45 512	45 221	14.2	18 384	19 419	22 457	22
Luxembourg	270	271	274	1.5	4.0	246	208	225	(8.5)	664	615	600	(10)
Netherlands	2 880	2 798	2 811	(2.4)	(69.0)	8 910	11 060	13 848	55.4	3 468	3 070	4 026	16
Poland	27 185	26 228	19 900	(26.8)	(7 285.0)	46 300	50 373	19 643	(57.6)	132 576	83 500	47 394	(64)
Portugal	3 609	3 064	2 818	(21.9)	(791.0)	6 077	5 664	3 339	(45.1)	1 001	1 459	2 442	144
Slovak Republic	3 657	3 657	3 657	–	–	6 315	6 767	2 316	(63.3)	23 505	21 119	10 117	(57)
Spain	13 450	12 560	12 310	(8.5)	(1 140.0)	13 527	15 476	20 608	52.3	10 528	10 742	14 156	34
Sweden	11 377	10 081	9 882	(13.1)	(1 495.0)	6 787	6 076	5 733	(15.5)	15 914	18 441	12 829	(19)
United Kingdom	17 645	16 588	16 660	(5.6)	(985.0)	31 704	33 191	40 400	27.4	17 640	15 986	18 900	7
Non-EU European OECD													
Switzerland	2 943	2 978	2 990	1.6	47.0	9 167	11 049	12 290	34.1	7 220	8 127	9 341	29
Norway	4 242	4 044	4 179	(1.5)	(63.0)	2 394	2 104	2 204	(7.9)	3 014	2 568	2 092	(31)
Turkey	8 193	8 429	8 697	6.2	504.0	6 011	6 410	5 878	(2.2)	5 029	7 894	8 612	71
Total OECD	**670 258**	**576 321**	**537 996**	**(19.7)**	**(132 262.0)**	**584 653**	**664 603**	**662 593**	**13.3**	**2 258 377**	**2 354 629**	**3 273 303**	**45**

Table 5.1. **Data table on worldwide rail infrastructure** *(cont.)*

Passenger and freight line density

	Line-km					Pass-km (000 000)				Ton-km (000 000)			
	1980	1990	2003	% growth, 1980 to 2003	Shrinkage (km) 1980 to 2003	1980	1990	2003	% growth, 1980 to 2003	1980	1990	2003	% growth, 1980 to 2003
Europe non-OECD													
Slovenia	1 058	1 196	1 229	16.2	171.0	1 436	1 429	777	(45.9)	3 851	4 196	3 274	(15)
Estonia	993	1 026	959	(3.4)	(34.0)	1 553	1 510	182	(88.3)	6 515	6 977	9 283	42
Latvia	2 384	2 397	2 270	(4.8)	(114.0)	4 774	5 466	762	(84.0)	17 586	18 538	17 604	0
Lithuania	2 008	2 007	1 774	(11.7)	(234.0)	3 258	3 640	432	(86.7)	18 237	19 258	11 457	(37)
Bulgaria	4 341	4 299	4 318	(0.5)	(23.0)	7 055	7 793	2 517	(64.3)	17 491	14 132	5 274	(70)
Romania	11 110	11 348	11 077	(0.3)	(33.0)	23 220	30 582	8 528	(63.3)	78 390	57 253	16 584	(79)
Ukraine	22 600	23 316	22 079	(2.3)	(521.0)	60 160	76 038	52 558	(12.6)	469 643	473 953	225 287	(52)
Belarus	5 512	5 569	5 502	(0.2)	(10.0)	10 922	16 852	13 308	21.8	66 264	75 373	38 402	(42)
Big Five developing countries													
Brazil: all concessions	28 645	26 945	25 895	(9.6)	(2 750.0)	11 867	3 188	2 500	(78.9)	40 640	41 042	67 300	66
Russian Federation	82 600	85 969	85 500	3.5	2 900.0	227 300	274 000	157 100	(30.9)	2 316 000	2 523 000	1 664 300	(28)
China	49 940	53 378	60 446	21.0	10 506.0	138 037	263 530	456 000	230.3	570 732	1 060 100	1 609 000	182
Indonesia	6 458	5 000	5 300	(17.9)	(1 158.0)	5 900	9 290	17 000	188.1	1 000	3 190	5 000	400
India	61 240	62 367	63 122	3.1	(1 882.0)	208 558	295 644	515 044	147.0	158 474	235 785	353 194	123
All other countries	193 384	191 663	167 966	(13.1)	(25 418.0)	146 735	174 219	137 785	(6.1)	656 002	658 847	370 949	(43)
World total	**1 142 531**	**1 052 801**	**995 433**	**(12.9)**	**(147 098.0)**	**1 435 428**	**1 827 784**	**2 027 086**	**41.2**	**6 679 202**	**7 546 272**	**7 670 210**	**14.8**

Source: World Bank Railways Database.

Figure 5.1 shows a somewhat different measure of traffic intensity and freight role, that is, train-km/line-km and the percentage of freight train-km. The point in juxtaposing Table 5.1 and Figure 5.1 is to caution the reader that infrastructure "capacity" and the interactions between passenger and freight traffic and infrastructure operations are complex. This will be discussed in more detail later.

Figure 5.1. **Network complexity *versus* intensity of use (train-km/km of line basis)**

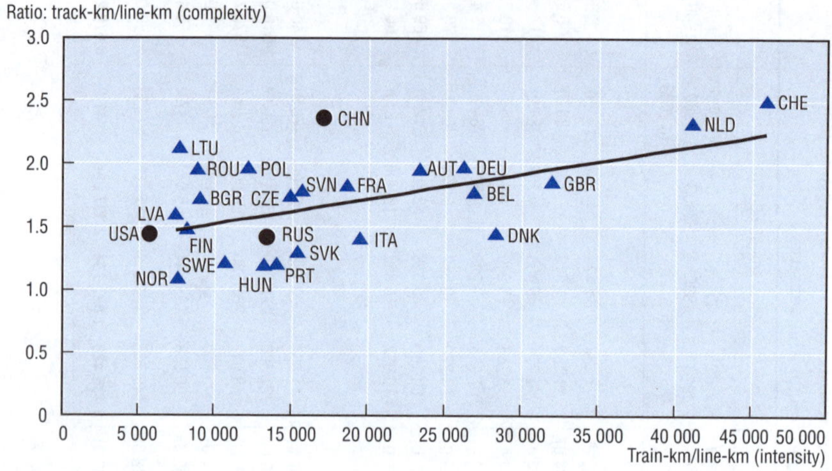

Note: Russian Federation, US and China added manually and do not affect the regression line.
Source: ECMT (2005), *Railway Reform and Charges for the Use of Infrastructure*, OECD, Paris, p. 42.

Stambrook (2006) provides new construction estimates for rail infrastructure between 2000 and 2030 of around USD 1.606 trillion, with the net asset value increasing by USD 711 billion.[1] No attempt was made to attribute amounts to passenger *versus* freight.[2]

Table 5.2 taken from a 2003 IEA study of future energy consumption in transport, provides insight into the relative roles of freight and passenger traffic in the need for added infrastructure. The IEA study is based on projections of a number of factors that influence energy demand, such as population, GDP and efficiency changes. In the rail area, it is also based on an analysis of past trends in rail traffic in relation to demographic changes. It reinforces the fact that most of the freight-driven need for added infrastructure is likely to be in North America and the Big 5. Other areas will be influenced as much by passenger traffic growth as by freight, and the interaction between freight and passenger services will be critical to the outcome.

Table 5.2. **Projected worldwide needs in freight and passenger trail traffic**

	2000	2005	2010	2015	2020	2025	2030	2035	Absolute growth 2005-35	Per cent growth 2005-35
Russian Federation GDP (2000 = 100)	100.0	117.1	134.1	159.1	188.2	216.5	245.6	282.2		
Frt ton-km index	100.0	110.8	122.9	136.2	151.0	167.3	185.5	205.6		
Ton-km projection	*1 197 495*	*1 327 362*	*1 471 314*	*1 630 877*	*1 807 744*	*2 003 792*	*2 221 102*	*2 461 979*	*1 134 617*	*85.5*
Passenger index	100.0	109.6	120.1	131.6	144.3	158.1	173.3	189.9		
Pass-km projection	*167 100*	*183 135*	*200 708*	*219 967*	*241 075*	*264 208*	*289 561*	*317 347*	*134 212*	*73.3*
CIS other than Russian Federation GDP (2000 = 100)	100.0	117.1	134.1	159.1	188.2	216.5	245.6	282.2		
Frt ton-km index	100	109.6	120.1	131.6	144.3	158.1	173.3	189.9		
Ton-km projection	*378 962*	*415 327*	*455 181*	*498 859*	*546 728*	*599 192*	*656 689*	*719 704*	*304 377*	*73.3*
Passenger index	100.0	107.7	116.0	124.9	134.6	144.9	156.1	168.1		
Pass-km projection	*83 953*	*90 419*	*97 382*	*104 882*	*112 960*	*121 659*	*131 029*	*141 120*	*50 702*	*56.1*
Eastern Europe/Turkey GDP (2000 = 100)	100	119.2	140.7	165.7	194.3	226.1	260.5	315.2		
Frt ton-km index	100.0	111.6	124.6	139.0	155.2	173.2	193.3	215.8		
Ton-km projection	*130 277*	*145 405*	*162 290*	*181 136*	*202 170*	*225 647*	*251 850*	*281 095*	*135 690*	*93.3*
Passenger index	100.0	107.2	114.9	123.1	132.0	141.4	151.6	162.5		
Pass-km projection	*65 908*	*70 639*	*75 709*	*81 143*	*86 967*	*93 209*	*99 898*	*107 069*	*36 430*	*51.6*
China GDP (2000 = 100)	100.0	133.7	174.5	223.1	276.2	336.2	406.3	485.7		
Frt ton-km index	100.0	115.9	134.4	155.8	180.6	209.4	242.7	281.4		
Ton-km projection	*1 333 606*	*1 546 015*	*1 792 255*	*2 077 715*	*2 408 641*	*2 792 275*	*3 237 012*	*3 752 584*	*2 206 569*	*142.7*
Passenger index	100.0	115.4	133.1	153.5	177.1	204.4	235.8	272.0		
Pass-km projection	*441 468*	*509 303*	*587 561*	*677 844*	*782 000*	*902 160*	*1 040 784*	*1 200 708*	*691 405*	*135.8*

Table 5.2. **Projected worldwide needs in freight and passenger trail traffic** *(cont.)*

	2000	2005	2010	2015	2020	2025	2030	2035	Absolute growth 2005-35	Per cent growth 2005-35
Other Asia GDP (2000 = 100)	100.0	121.4	149.2	181.5	217.6	258.5	305.2	360.7		
Frt ton-km index	100.0	109.1	119.1	130.0	141.9	154.9	169.1	184.6		
Ton-km projection	*31 032*	*33 871*	*36 970*	*40 353*	*44 045*	*48 075*	*52 473*	*57 274*	*23 403*	*69.1*
Passenger index	100.0	111.6	124.6	139.0	155.2	173.2	193.3	215.8		
Pass-km projection	*87 111*	*97 227*	*108 517*	*121 118*	*135 183*	*150 881*	*168 401*	*187 957*	*90 730*	*93.3*
India GDP (2000 = 100)	100.0	127.4	163.3	207.4	257.7	316.2	385.6	464.3		
Frt ton-km index	100.0	115.9	134.4	155.8	180.6	209.4	242.7	281.4		
Ton-km projection	*305 201*	*353 812*	*410 165*	*475 493*	*551 227*	*639 023*	*740 803*	*858 794*	*504 982*	*142.7*
Passenger index	100.0	113.7	129.3	147.0	167.1	190.0	216.0	245.6		
Pass-km projection	*430 666*	*489 641*	*556 691*	*632 923*	*719 594*	*818 134*	*930 168*	*1 057 543*	*567 903*	*116.0*
Middle East and North Africa GDP (2000 = 100)	100.0	113.7	129.0	146.8	169.1	193.7	217.7	241.6		
Frt ton-km index	100	109.6	120.1	131.6	144.3	158.1	173.3	189.9		
Ton-km projection	*29 892*	*32 760*	*35 904*	*39 349*	*43 125*	*47 263*	*51 799*	*56 769*	*24 009*	*73.3*
Passenger index	100.0	111.6	124.6	139.0	155.2	173.2	193.3	215.8		
Pass-km projection	*79 930*	*89 212*	*99 571*	*111 134*	*124 039*	*138 443*	*154 519*	*172 463*	*83 251*	*93.3*
Europe/OECD GDP (2000 = 100)	100.0	111.5	126.1	140.7	154.4	167.5	180.2	189.2		
Frt ton-km index	100.0	104.1	108.4	112.9	117.6	122.5	127.5	132.8		
Ton-km projection	*247 612*	*257 858*	*268 528*	*279 640*	*291 211*	*303 262*	*315 810*	*328 879*	*71 020*	*27.5*
Passenger index	100.0	106.1	112.5	119.3	126.5	134.2	142.3	150.9		
Pass-km projection	*300 916*	*319 134*	*338 454*	*358 944*	*380 675*	*403 721*	*428 163*	*454 084*	*134 950*	*42.3*

Table 5.2. **Projected worldwide needs in freight and passenger trail traffic** *(cont.)*

	2000	2005	2010	2015	2020	2025	2030	2035	Absolute growth 2005-35	Per cent growth 2005-35
US and Canada GDP (2000 = 100)	100.0	112.6	128.5	142.7	156.9	171.7	187.5	203.9		
Frt ton-km index	100.0	108.4	117.6	127.5	138.3	150.0	162.7	176.4		
Ton-km projection	*2 427 145*	*2 632 171*	*2 854 515*	*3 095 641*	*3 357 135*	*3 640 718*	*3 948 256*	*4 281 772*	*1 649 601*	*62.7*
Passenger index	100.0	104.1	108.4	112.9	117.6	122.5	127.5	132.8		
Pass-km projection	*47 947*	*49 931*	*51 998*	*54 149*	*56 390*	*58 723*	*61 153*	*63 684*	*13 752*	*27.5*
Pacific/OECD GDP (2000 = 100)	100.0	108.8	123.3	137.7	152.1	167.0	182.7	198.3		
Frt ton-km index	100.0	104.8	109.9	115.1	120.7	126.5	132.6	139.0		
Ton-km projection	*156 391*	*163 917*	*171 805*	*180 072*	*188 738*	*197 820*	*207 340*	*217 318*	*53 401*	*32.6*
Passenger index	100.0	107.2	114.9	123.1	132.0	141.4	151.6	162.5		
Pass-km projection	*241 113*	*258 419*	*276 966*	*296 845*	*318 151*	*340 985*	*365 459*	*391 689*	*133 271*	*51.6*
Latin America GDP (2000 = 100)	100	114	134	156	182	210	242	276		
Frt ton-km index	100.0	107.2	114.9	123.1	132.0	141.4	151.6	162.5		
Ton-km projection	*117 903*	*126 365*	*135 435*	*145 155*	*155 574*	*166 740*	*178 707*	*191 534*	*65 169*	*51.6*
Passenger index	100.0	104.1	108.4	112.9	117.6	122.5	127.5	132.8		
Pass-km projection	*13 659*	*14 224*	*14 812*	*15 425*	*16 064*	*16 728*	*17 421*	*18 141*	*3 918*	*27.5*
Africa GDP (2000 = 100)	100	120	145	174	208	247	291	339		
Frt ton-km index	100.0	109.6	120.1	131.6	144.3	158.1	173.3	189.9		
Ton-km projection	*114 609*	*125 607*	*137 660*	*150 869*	*165 346*	*181 213*	*198 602*	*217 659*	*92 052*	*73.3*
Passenger index	100.0	104.1	108.4	112.9	117.6	122.5	127.5	132.8		
Pass-km projection	*17 574*	*18 302*	*19 059*	*19 848*	*20 669*	*21 524*	*22 415*	*23 342*	*5 041*	*27.5*
Total ton-km projection	**6 470 125**	**7 160 469**	**7 932 020**	**8 795 159**	**9 761 684**	**10 845 019**	**12 060 442**	**13 425 359**	**6 264 890**	**87.5**
Total pass-km projection	**1 977 346**	**2 189 583**	**2 427 428**	**2 694 223**	**2 993 766**	**3 330 377**	**3 708 972**	**4 135 147**	**1 945 564**	**88.9**

Note: Frt = freight, pass = passenger.
Source: IEA (2003), ETP Transport Model, Spreadsheet version 1.28.

The probable need for enhanced rail infrastructure in the next 30 years, both in total and specifically for freight, is well established (see TRB, 2002 and TEN-T, 2005, both of which make this point). "Needs" generate different responses, however, depending on the way in which the "market" can balance all of the investment needs it faces. To be very clear, the actual "need" will be for the ability to haul more rail freight *ton-km*. The way in which the need is met (or not met) will be determined by a number of interacting factors, including:

1. The management model in place, which will influence the perception of economic and financial forces that make up the set of incentives the infrastructure provider and freight operators face.
2. Technology (signalling, tractive power, wagon size, axle loads, speeds of freight and passenger trains, energy costs, and a large number of other possible considerations).
3. The high capital cost of rail freight infrastructure by comparison with roads and (in some cases) water navigation combined with the single-purpose nature of rail freight-only infrastructure.
4. Government policies as to the role of the public and private sectors, regulation, modal promotion, rail infrastructure access charges and financial targets for the infrastructure provider, competition objectives (intramodal and intermodal), availability of information, and others.

The outcome of the interaction between "need" on the one hand and "response" on the other will probably differ significantly among countries. Management models will differ as a result of history, culture and political preference. All countries will have access to the same basic technology, but the way in which it is adopted will differ depending on passenger and freight balance, management model and government policy. Government policies will consider the same issues, but will clearly differ as a result of differing national objectives and perceptions.

As a broad generalisation, North American rail infrastructure investment is likely to be driven by the private sector for commercial reasons, and will be concentrated on profitable freight capacity. Government policies in North America are only now beginning to address the issue of public interest in private rail infrastructure (especially as it relates to freight rather than passenger needs), and government involvement in specifically freight infrastructure is only now emerging.

EU rail infrastructure will clearly be largely driven by passenger concerns (economically and politically) and specifically freight infrastructure is likely to receive second priority. Success at promoting rail freight growth and the infrastructure needed to support it will depend on creating commercially driven rail freight companies that can operate Europe-wide with reasonable access to infrastructure: this, in turn, will depend on the *implementation* (as opposed to the formulation) of EU transport policies.

Up to the present, at least, international rail freight operations in Europe have been limited by the higher access priority by passenger rather than freight, by interoperability issues in signalling and electric traction, by access charge regimes that discriminated in favour of the existing, large national freight operator, and by attempts by some countries to use high freight access charges to cross-subsidise passenger train use of the infrastructure. A recent ECMT study analysed the issues for freight use of the infrastructure in the ECMT countries and concluded that access charges applied to freight need to be simplified and that the high freight access charges in the CEE members will need to be reduced to the comparable practices in the original EU15 countries (ECMT, 2005).

Rail infrastructure in Japan has long been almost totally dominated by passenger traffic: this is likely to continue in the future, even though Japan has a significant highway traffic capacity problem for freight as well as passenger. Rail infrastructure in the Russian Federation and China will be heavily influenced by freight capacity needs, though the Chinese government intends to build dedicated passenger lines – partly to improve freight capacity by removing the passenger interference on vital freight lines. Though the Russian Federation has made progress in developing a business model that would permit rail freight to be provided competitively by new, private companies, the implementation of this model is only partially complete, and full implementation is uncertain. The Chinese model relies on a state-owned monolith that might, in the longer run, conflict with the increasing emphasis in China on the "socialist market" economic structure.

The Indian government is currently considering a proposal to construct new freight-only lines in the Mumbai, Delhi, Calcutta and Chennai "Golden Quadrilateral". The business model for financing and operating the new lines is under discussion, though Indian Railways already has a container operating company under separate ownership and management.

Andrieu (2005) argued that the "third conclusion one can draw is that – perhaps with the exception of the telecommunications sector – none of the other sectors have put in place an institutional framework that is up to the challenges of the future, including a regulatory framework which allows for the full and effective participation of private actors". This conclusion could be broadened to argue that there are as yet no countries in which the current public policy and institutional framework will fully suffice to meet the challenges of providing adequate rail infrastructure, specifically rail freight infrastructure, in the next thirty years.

In the US, the federal government is now initiating the process of identifying the specifically public benefits from rail freight (and passenger) infrastructure and services and highlighting those benefits that can only be achieved through public finance. This should also create a focus on locating the public resources required. Canada, with its recently privatised CN, is facing the same issues. In the EU, access to the infrastructure network (at least for freight operators) must be more clearly established and simplified. Some interoperability issues (less serious for freight than for passenger trains) need to be resolved. The structure of the freight operators, both for ownership and for competitive balance, must be defined (though it will likely differ among countries). Financial resources for the freight component of rail infrastructure (freight freeways, and the Betuwe Line, as well as for continued maintenance) need to be located (about EUR 130 billion remain unfunded in the TEN-T programme).

The Russian Federation faces the need for the freight rail infrastructure to recover from a decade of relative neglect during the years of economic transition. This will pose a difficult choice between a need for government support when financial resources are restricted and the need to generate more earnings, particularly on coal, when there will be pressures to hold tariffs down. In addition, operating cross-subsidies from freight to passenger services could seriously undermine the ability of the railway to finance infrastructure for whatever purpose.

China has announced a massive (perhaps grandiose), more than USD 200 billion plan of rail infrastructure investment, between now and 2020. However strong the merits of this plan, the railway (Ministry of Railways of China, MOR) cannot finance this growth from its current earnings or from credible sources of public debt. The institutional framework of MOR will need to adapt to generate new sources of finance and enable the entry of new train operators.

India clearly needs added rail freight capacity. The challenge is that the capacity of the current system is ineffectively managed as a result of social policies that encourage uneconomic passenger services (that rob the system of needed capacity for economic services such as freight and intercity passenger trains) and a policy of cross-subsidy from freight to passenger which absorbs earnings that could more productively finance new freight and intercity capacity.

In all of these cases, traditional approaches (however justified they might have been in the past) are now becoming barriers to meeting the future need for rail freight infrastructure and operating services.

2. Existing models of railways organisation

A "railway" consists in the most general terms of infrastructure (steel rails and sleepers, switches and signals, bridges, buildings and structures, electric traction catenary and associated electrical equipment), and operating assets (locomotives, freight wagons and passenger coaches – some independently powered). The "railway" faces an almost unlimited panoply of economic and social forces which determine demand for passenger and freight services (and thus the need for infrastructure) and set the values for non-market (social) functions that the railway must provide. It is the "business model" that determines how the assets will be deployed in meeting the market and social demands placed on the railway. At the same time, of course, society places restrictions on the business models that the railway can adopt.

Railway business models are broadly defined in two dimensions: structure and ownership. Again in broad terms, there are three structure types: integral, where infrastructure and all operating services are operated under unified control (this is often called "the monolith"); owner-tenant levels, where the owning, dominant operator remains integrated with the infrastructure, and the minority, tenant operators pay for their access to the infrastructure; and "vertically separated" models where (in principle) the infrastructure is separated from the operator or operators. Further variants of the structural model deal with whether or not the "separation" is merely an accounting separation or an actual institutional separation, and with the level of separation among the operators (is there a single, integrated operating company, or are the various passenger and freight operators separated into distinct entities?).

Countries have also varied greatly in the approach to ownership. The US freight railways have generally been owned and operated by private companies. With the privatisation of the largest Canadian railway (CN) in 1996 (CP was already private), and with the concessioning of the Latin American freight and passenger railways in the 1990s, most freight railways in North and South America are now operated privately, while there is a mix of public and private operation of passenger services. Outside the Americas, the traditional model of railway ownership and operation has been public, though the privatisation of British Railways in the mid-1990s and the trend toward franchising of passenger services in some EU countries (Germany, Netherlands, Denmark and Sweden) is enlarging the role of the private sector, at least in operations if not in infrastructure. The break-up of Japanese National Railways (JNR) led to the privatisation of the three largest pieces – East, West and Central Japan railways – creating among the largest passenger operators in the world. Table 5.3 shows the options and gives examples of a number of national examples in both the structural and ownership axes.

These ownership options have emerged over time in response to changing perceptions as to what railways ought to do and how they should do it. The structural options have developed in line with increasing complexity in the markets and purposes served.

Economic efficiency. Most expert analyses of rail economic have agreed that there are no particular benefits of system *size* beyond a relatively small level of a few thousand kilometres. There are, however, increasing returns to traffic density on traffic on a specific line. This has encouraged railways to share the same lines, either through owner-tenant relationships or through vertical separation with

Table 5.3. **The basic business model alternatives: structure and ownership interactions**

Structure	Ownership		
	Public	Partnership	Private
Integral (monolithic)	China, India	Network Rail, India Railway Container Corp., Latin American freight and passenger concessions	Smaller US freight railroads, East Japan, Central Japan and West Japan
Dominant operator Integral, tenant operators separated	Amtrak and VIA, Japan Rail Freight, Russia, Island JRs	US freight and commuter railways in the North-eastern Corridor, CN and CP	US freight railway trackage rights, JB Hunt
Separation	"Standard" EU model	Some UK franchises	Most UK franchises, Railtrack (but not Network Rail), EWS

several operators on the same line, and has been applied both to operators in the same market (for example, two freight operators) and to operators in different markets (for example, passenger operations on freight lines).

Market focus. When railways began, customer options and competition in both the freight and passenger markets were limited, and a monolithic model was possible. As competition has grown in severity and sophistication, it has become harder for a unitary management on the rail side to compete with cars, buses and air in the passenger markets and with trucks and barges (sometimes aided by government support) in the freight markets. The enhanced market focus associated with differentiated (or institutionally separated) management has become more and more important.

Competition. There are a number of countries in which the possibility of rail *versus* rail competition (intra- as opposed to intermodal competition) is seen as a significant weapon in limiting the potential market power of railways, especially in the freight market. In the US, this has taken the form of controls over mergers to protect competition on parallel (integrated) lines and of enforced access rights to retain competition that might otherwise be eliminated through mergers. In addition, private rail freight companies have voluntarily negotiated trackage access agreements ("trackage rights" give one railroad the right to run a specified set of services on the lines of another in return for a trackage use fee), where one railway company wants access to a market exclusively served by another.

Clarity of public involvement and funding. There are many situations in which governments would like to support specific aspects of the rail system or, at least, to support different parts of the system in different ways. This is difficult to do when the only information available is based on more or less arbitrary (and murky) accounting separations and allocations. Institutional separations with transfer prices where necessary give a much more defensible identification of costs and benefits. In the EU, for example, Community law permits public support of infrastructure (so long as access is non-discriminatory) and of social services (primarily suburban or regional passenger traffic), and restricts support to services that are "commercial" (such as freight or intercity passenger).

Table 5.4 shows how these objectives interact to influence the choice of the actual business model. There are generally six distinct types of markets being served by railways: infrastructure, freight, HSR, conventional intercity passengers, rural/regional passenger services and suburban services. Each of these has a characteristic commercial or social objective. Because of its high investment costs and the need to serve multiple users in a non-discriminatory way, multiple-use infrastructure is essentially a public utility. Freight, HSR and conventional intercity services compete directly with other private modes such as airlines, buses and cars, and are therefore mostly commercially driven. Rural/regional and suburban services are mostly socially determined because they serve lower income needs, or are provided to reach social goals such as reduced noise and air pollution or reduction of urban congestion (though these weights can change with location and will change over time, especially as alternative modes become more congested and less competitive). Each of the six has a distinct competitive implication, where some (especially freight, possibly conventional intercity or HSR) may justify competition *in* the market (*i.e.* rail *versus* rail competition) whereas most of the others are subject to competition *for* the market (that is, competitively awarded, exclusive franchises).

Table 5.4. **Markets and models: interactions**

Type of market	Purpose: commercial or social	Type of competition (if any)	Public and private roles
Infrastructure	Utility or commercial	None/FOR	Mostly public, though private ownership and/or contract operation is possible
Freight services	Commercial	IN	Currently often public, moving towards private ownership and operation
Passenger services			
HSR	Commercial	FOR	Currently public, could be privatised or franchised
Conventional Intercity	Commercial (social?)	IN	Currently public, could be franchised
Rural/regional	Social	FOR	Currently public, could be franchised
Suburban	Social	FOR	Currently public, could be franchised

The categories in Tables 5.3 and 5.4 are sometimes less distinct than they appear. A good example is the J.B. Hunt Company in the US. J.B. Hunt is actually one of the largest US truckload freight carriers. In the early 1990s, Hunt became convinced that problems of driver availability (at that time Hunt had more than 200% driver turnover each year) and of highway congestion would mandate a better combination of the short haul, pick-up and delivery capabilities of trucking and the long haul, high volume capabilities of rail. Hunt developed and negotiated with railways an arrangement in which Hunt provides all marketing, pick up and delivery and customer relations, while the railways handle only full trainload shipments of Hunt containers between Hunt terminals. This is in effect a wholesaler/retailer relationship in which each part plays to its strengths. The Hunt system is now nationwide and has grown from about 6 000 containers (then 48 foot standard) in 1990 to 600 000 containers (present 53 foot standard) in 2005 (Figure 5.2).

Figure 5.2. **JB Hunt intermodel traffic**

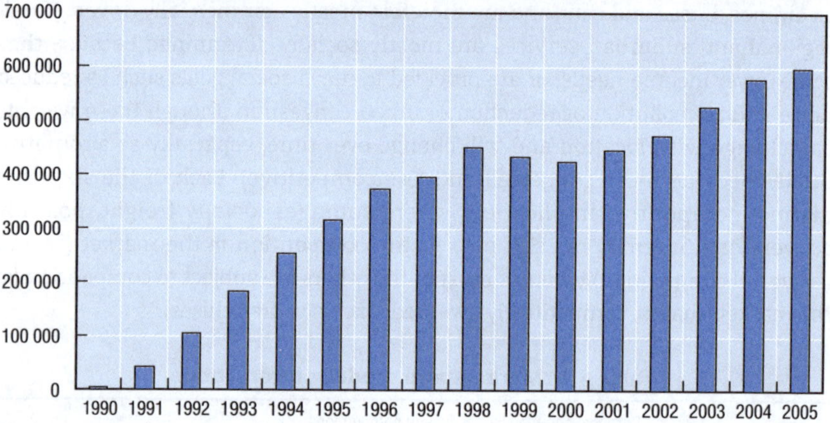

Note: Growth is slightly understated because container size has grown from 48 feet in 1990 to 53 feet in 2006.

Source: J.B Hunt.

Hunt's intermodal traffic has benefited from economic growth and increasing international trade, as well as from highway congestion and driver shortages in the US. The Hunt intermodal approach has been limited by rail capacity problems, particularly in terminal areas, and from less than optimum on-time performance that was partly caused by rail capacity problems and partly caused by the fact that US freight railroads normally do not operate freight trains on fixed schedules. The Hunt intermodal system is a good example of the interaction between market forces and enterprise structure – new business models do indeed arise and develop if they are permitted to do so.

The distinction between intercity passenger services and regional or long haul suburban services can also be blurred. In these cases, separation of commercial from social roles can be difficult.

The power of a change in business model is illustrated by the shift in Latin America. At the beginning of the 1990s, all Latin American railways were monolithic state agencies ("enterprises" has too favourable a connotation). By the end of the decade, essentially every freight railway was operated by private concessions (as well as the suburban passenger services and metros in Buenos Aires and Rio de Janeiro). Table 5.5 shows the dramatic results: traffic that had been shrinking or stagnant began growing rapidly, and labour and infrastructure productivity exploded. After successful concessioning with the resulting increases in efficiency and customer focus, freight rail services in Latin America are now poised for continuing growth, so long as the political environment continues to be supportive and the export economies in these countries continue to thrive as the have in the recent past.

Table 5.5. **Concessioned freight railways in Latin America**

		Km of line	Ton-km	Ton-km/employee	Ton-km/km
Mexico (old FNM)	1996	26 000	41 959	850	1 614
	2004	16 000	61 051	3 550	3 816
Brazil (old RFFSA)	1995	22 095	39 195	1 000	1 774
	2004	21 659	59 700	4 700	2 756
Brazil (old FEPASA)	1998	4 183	4 995	450	1 194
	2004	4 236	9 400	4 420	2 219
Argentina	1992	18 000	2 523	240	140
	2004	11 000	9 878	2 530	898

Source: World Bank Concessioned Railways Database.

3. Key economic and social trends affecting rail freight traffic and infrastructure

3.1. *Drivers of growth*

The basic drivers of growth in the potential demand for rail freight are well described by Stambrook (2006). Freight traffic, in particular, is a derived demand, that is, freight movement (whether by air, truck, rail or water) is not consumed for its own sake, but is, instead, generated by the need to move the goods and services being produced by the economy. Passenger travel is also, for the most part, a derived demand in that only a small part of personal travel is generated purely for the travel experience. Even for leisure purposes, most travel is to get there, not to look out the window. The most powerful driver of freight demand is, of course, underlying economic development.

Predicting economic growth is always difficult, and the results of predictions are always riddled with questionable assumptions and a large range of uncertainty. The basic data source for this OECD Futures Project seems to be the World Bank's "Global Economic Prospects 2005" (World Bank, 2005). Table 5.6 shows the GDP/capita forecasts in the World Bank 2005 report. Table 5.6 only extends through 2015, not long enough for the scope of this study. Table 5.7

Table 5.6. **Forecast growth of world GDP per capita**
Compound annual percentage

	1980s	1990s	2000 to 2006	2006 to 2015
World total	**1.3**	**1.2**	**1.5**	**2.1**
High-income countries	2.5	1.8	1.6	2.4
OECD	2.5	1.8	1.6	2.4
US	2.3	2	1.8	2.5
Japan	3.4	1.1	1.1	1.9
EU	2.1	1.8	1.4	2.3
Non-OECD countries	3.5	4	2	3.5
Developing countries	0.7	1.5	3.7	3.5
East Asia and the Pacific	5.8	6.3	6.4	5.3
Europe and Central Asia	0.9	–1.8	5	3.5
Latin America and the Caribbean	–0.9	1.6	1.2	2.3
Middle East and North Africa	–1.1	1	2.5	2.6
South Asia	3.3	3.2	4.5	4.2
Sub-Saharan Africa	–1.1	–0.5	1.8	1.6

Source: World Bank (2006), Global Economic Prospects 2006, p. 8.

shows population, GDP and GDP/capita estimates taken from an international energy study (based on the *IMF World Economic Outlook* 2002). Neither the categorisations nor the estimates from the two sources match up precisely; in fact, it would be a surprise if they did. The significant point is that both show significant GDP and GDP/capita growth, although they differ somewhat by countries and regions. This means that the underlying economic forces will encourage growth in freight traffic: no matter which source is used, this will be true.

Within the broader umbrella of economic growth, there are a large number of considerations that could act to restrain or accelerate the growth of freight traffic overall, and of the share of rail in the freight sector in particular.

Globalisation. "Globalisation" conjures up visions of worldwide trade, with emphasis on waterborne and long-haul air movements. While these are important, globalisation is also having a significant and positive impact on rail freight traffic. This can be seen in two ways: reduction of trade barriers generated by regional free trade agreements, and in the traffic to and from the ports involved in global trade.

Both the North American Free Trade Agreement (NAFTA) and the increasing size of the EU have created opportunities for increased rail traffic. NAFTA is a free trade agreement among the US, Canada and Mexico, signed in 1990, which began having an impact in 1992. Trade has grown rapidly by all modes, but rail freight traffic from 1992 to 2004 slightly more than tripled in value between the US and Mexico, and significantly more than doubled between the US and Canada

Table 5.7. **Growth rates in population, GDP and GDP/capita**

Compound annual

	2000	2005	2015	2025	2035	2000 to 2005	2005 to 2015	2015 to 2025	2025 to 2035
	Population (millions)								
OECD North America	405	426	466	504	537	1.02	0.90	0.79	0.64
OECD Europe	514	520	525	526	509	0.23	0.10	0.02	–0.33
OECD Pacific	197	201	205	204	200	0.40	0.20	–0.05	–0.20
Former Soviet Union	254	252	251	248	247	–0.16	–0.04	–0.12	–0.04
Eastern Europe	100	96	91	85	82	–0.81	–0.53	–0.68	–0.36
China	1 272	1 318	1 406	1 467	1 479	0.71	0.65	0.43	0.08
Other Asia	891	967	1 119	1 265	1 401	1.65	1.47	1.23	1.03
India	1 014	1 089	1 230	1 352	1 450	1.44	1.22	0.95	0.70
Middle East	168	192	245	300	353	2.71	2.47	2.05	1.64
Latin America	415	446	506	560	603	1.45	1.27	1.02	0.74
Africa	794	892	1 110	1 358	1 617	2.35	2.21	2.04	1.76
Total	**6 023**	**6 399**	**7 154**	**7 869**	**8 477**	**1.22**	**1.12**	**0.96**	**0.75**

Table 5.7. **Growth rates in population, GDP and GDP/capita** *(cont.)*

Compound annual

	2000	2005	2015	2025	2035	2000 to 2005	2005 to 2015	2015 to 2025	2025 to 2035
	GDP (USD billions)								
OECD North America	10 556	11 884	15 059	18 126	21 528	2.40	2.40	1.87	1.73
OECD Europe	9 637	10 744	13 555	16 145	18 237	2.20	2.35	1.76	1.23
OECD Pacific	4 366	4 749	6 011	7 293	8 657	1.70	2.38	1.95	1.73
Former Soviet Union	1 414	1 655	2 250	3 061	3 989	3.20	3.12	3.13	2.68
Eastern Europe	453	540	751	1 025	1 429	3.58	3.35	3.16	3.38
China	4 861	6 499	10 845	16 345	23 611	5.98	5.25	4.19	3.75
Other Asia	2 955	3 587	5 363	7 639	10 657	3.95	4.10	3.60	3.39
India	2 279	2 903	4 727	7 205	10 579	4.96	5.00	4.30	3.92
Middle East	952	1 083	1 398	1 845	2 301	2.61	2.59	2.81	2.23
Latin America	2 605	2 965	4 072	5 466	7 181	2.62	3.22	2.99	2.77
Africa	1 530	1 830	2 670	3 773	5 191	3.65	3.85	3.52	3.24
Total	**41 609**	**48 439**	**66 700**	**87 923**	**113 362**	**3.09**	**3.25**	**2.80**	**2.57**

Table 5.7. **Growth rates in population, GDP and GDP/capita** (cont.)

	2000	2005	2015	2025	2035	Compound annual			
						2000 to 2005	2005 to 2015	2015 to 2025	2025 to 2035
	GDP per capita (USD thousands)								
OECD North America	26.0	27.9	32.3	35.9	40.1	1.42	1.48	1.06	1.11
OECD Europe	18.8	20.7	25.8	30.7	35.8	1.94	2.23	1.75	1.55
OECD Pacific	22.1	23.7	29.4	35.7	43.3	1.41	2.18	1.96	1.95
Former Soviet Union	5.6	6.6	9.0	12.3	16.2	3.34	3.15	3.17	2.79
Eastern Europe	4.6	5.6	8.3	12.1	17.4	4.01	4.01	3.84	3.70
China	3.8	4.9	7.7	11.1	16.0	5.22	4.62	3.72	3.72
Other Asia	3.3	3.7	4.8	6.0	7.6	2.31	2.64	2.26	2.39
India	2.2	2.7	3.8	5.3	7.3	4.18	3.48	3.38	3.25
Middle East	5.7	5.6	5.7	6.2	6.5	–0.35	0.18	0.84	0.47
Latin America	6.3	6.6	8.0	9.8	11.9	0.93	1.94	2.05	1.96
Africa	1.9	2.1	2.4	2.8	3.2	2.02	1.34	1.55	1.34
World average	**6.9**	**7.6**	**9.3**	**11.2**	**13.4**	**1.95**	**2.04**	**1.88**	**1.81**

Source: IMF (2002), *World Economic Outlook.*

(especially in car parts as well as in basic goods). The basic reason for the rail participation is that the length of haul advantage of rail has been increased. This has been enhanced by cross-border ownership of railways both between the US and Canada (CN and CP both own significant railroad companies in the US and Norfolk Southern owns track in Canada) and between the US and Mexico (one major Mexican railway connecting the US to Mexico – TFM – is owned by a US railway, KCS, and the other major Mexican connector – FerroMex – has a significant US partner, UP). In addition, the government of Canada has created a Pacific Gateway, which is a multimodal network of transportation infrastructure focused on trade with Asia, mostly via the Port of Vancouver. This programme has included nearly CAD 590 million in investment in both public and privately owed infrastructure assets in the seaports, airports, railroads and road systems aimed at improving Canada's connectivity with Asian trade.

The EU may be an equally significant example of the opportunity that increasing lengths of haul can offer the rail sector. One of the underlying reasons that the Commission issued Directive 91/440 was the expectation that open access to rail infrastructure would eventually create rail freight companies operating more seamlessly and competitively across borders. Prior to Directive 91/440, the balkanisation of the EU railways meant that, in effect, the longest seamless rail freight trips were restricted by the boundary of each country, whereas the trucking competition has always been able to operate seamlessly across borders. If rail freight companies could easily operate across national borders, then the seamless haul for rail freight could in principle extend from the north of Sweden to the French/Spanish border (or beyond, if the effects of the gauge change can be overcome) and from Liverpool to Bratislava (or on to the eastern border of Turkey someday).

Evidence from the US and Canada (the largest truly single markets for which good data exist) and from China and the Russian Federation (also large single markets) gives an idea of the likely point at which rail gains more and more advantage over truck (see Table 5.8). The average rail length of haul in the US, Canada and the Russian Federation is about 1 400 km, and around 800 for China (and nearly 1 000 for Mexico) – all of which are in the range where rail has a cost advantage. By comparison, the EU countries typically have a freight length of haul from 130 to 400 km, which is clearly in the range at which rail does not have a natural advantage. To an extent, the actual length of haul by rail in the EU is probably underestimated, since each country reports the ton-km on its territory, but may well be double (or more) counting the tonnage handled. In any event, the creation of EU-wide freight rail operating companies will clearly offer the opportunity to increase the length of haul by rail. Expansion of the EU from 15 to 25 countries will also increase rail's length of haul and thus its competitive position.

Table 5.8. **Average lead for railway freight over truck**

In kilometres

	1980	2004	Per cent change
Brazil – FEPASA	367	468	27.5
Brazil – RFFSA	470	436[1]	–7.2
Mexico	682	935	37.1
Czechoslovakia	254	–	–
Czech Republic	–	185	–27.2
Slovak Republic	–	194	–23.4
Hungary	186	183	–2.0
Poland	284	293	3.2
Russian Federation	1 131	1 434[1]	26.8
China	526	743	41.3
Korea	224	235[1]	4.7
India	720	671[1]	–6.8
Austria	219	208	–4.7
Belgium	112	131	16.9
Denmark	250	260	4.2
Finland	283	237	–16.4
France	314	384	22.5
Italy	326	279	–14.6
Japan	303	597[1]	96.8
Netherlands	157	168	7.2
Portugal	270	235	–13.1
Spain	303	442	46.2
Sweden	297	300[1]	1.0
Switzerland	161	161	–0.1
United Kingdom	114	219	92.3
West Germany	201	–	–
Germany	–	288	43.4
Canada: Canadian National	1 093	1 440	31.7
Canada: Canadian Pacific	1 037	1 495	44.2
US: All Class I railways	1 029	1 452	41.1
Australia (bulk)	–	245	–
Australia (non-bulk)	–	1 636	–

Note: Average lead is defined as ton-km per tons originated.

1. Indicates data are from 2003.

Source: World Bank Railways Database.

Congestion in ports and in the port/landside interface is another facet of globalisation that could affect rail freight traffic, and truck or inland water traffic as well. Port side congestion is already occurring in a number of the world's ports (see UNCTAD, 2005). There are a number of ports in which rail access has become a significant determinant of the amount of traffic that rail ultimately receives (or ports in which highway access is sufficiently congested that improved rail access would have a significant impact on rail traffic). A good example of this is the Port of Rotterdam, where the Betuwe Line has been constructed to ease the flow of port traffic onto the EU rail freight network. (See Betuwe Line case study in Box 5.1. Betuwe Line data are also in the TEN-T case study in Box 5.3.)

Another example is the Alameda Project, a PPP project to improve rail access to the Port of Los Angeles and Long Beach, California (see Chapter 1, Box 1.4 on the Alameda Corridor Project).

The US ports of Los Angeles, Long Beach and New York/New Jersey are particular pressure points in world trade flows. These three are the primary West Coast and East Coast points of entry of containerised traffic, an area in which world growth was 23% between 2001 and 2004, and which is expected at least to double between 2005 and 2020 (assuming there is capacity to handle it – see US DOT, 2005). A less obvious, but equally significant container capacity issue for the US is the rail hub in Chicago, the nodal point for over one-third of all rail flows in the country (see Box 5.2 on the CREATE Program), and a potential pinch point for container traffic in the US. Beyond these cases, the US DOT (2005) has concluded that the US container movement network is rapidly approaching its capacity limits, and shows port capacity shortfalls of around 30% on the West Coast and about 25% on major East Coast ports. A major factor in the capacity issue is the landside connections to the ports, of which rail is a large actor, especially for container traffic that is travelling a significant distance inland.

It is clear that the US ports will not be alone in facing capacity issues due to growth in container traffic. Table 5.9 shows what has been happening in the top 20 world container ports in the early 1990s. This table has a number of critical aspects. First, on average, container movements grew by over 30% in only two years (2002 through 2004). Though this rate of growth would clearly be unsustainable for long, it does presage rapid growth – and strained landside capacity – nearly everywhere. Second, China accounts for three of the four largest container ports, accounting for 30% of the movements in the top 20 ports (and, in fact, Chinese ports in total account for 44% of the traffic in the top 20 ports). Next, the two major EU container ports, Rotterdam and Hamburg, experienced growth rates of nearly 30%, though growth has recently slowed. Los Angeles (19.8%), Long Beach (27.9%) and New York/New Jersey (17.3%) are also growing rapidly. Since rail access is critical to most of these ports (and all have highway congestion as well), it is clear that there will be a strong demand on the railway infrastructure to handle more traffic.

Table 5.10 shows that the port capacity issue, and the related land links, is likely to be go beyond solely the issues of container movement. "Dry cargo" in this table includes not only containers, but also all other bulk cargos such as iron ore, coal, and grains, among others (unfortunately it is not possible to separate the container tonnage from the rest of the dry cargo category).

Box 5.1. **The Betuwe Line, Netherlands**

International trade has always been especially important to the Netherlands: 20% of the Dutch GDP is attributed to activities in the Port of Rotterdam and the Schiphol Airport (US DOT FHWA, 2005). As a result, port access issues have taken a high priority in transport planning in the country, and landside port capacity issues are critical in a country that has among the highest population densities in the world.

Rotterdam, in addition to being one of the world's larger general cargo ports, is the largest *container* port outside Asia (Table 5.9). The Rotterdam container traffic, at over 8 million TEU (twenty-foot equivalent units), would amount to around 11 000 trucks/day – a serious challenge to the Dutch highway system, and a potentially significant creator of noise and pollution. It is important that as much of the container traffic as possible be shifted to rail and water (Rhine river) for inland movement.

The efficiency of the port is not just important to the Netherlands, because Rotterdam, along with Hamburg, is a major interface point in world trade. For example, 57% of all European distribution centers for US companies are located in the Netherlands, making Rotterdam a key link in transatlantic trade.

In 1990, the Dutch government announced its intention to proceed with a project to construct a new rail link from the Rotterdam area to a connection with the German railway network in order to speed up the connection of Rotterdam with inland, rail-based trade, to relieve the congestion on the existing railway (NS) lines that were already carrying large volumes of passenger trains (as Tables 5.1 and 5.15 show, the Dutch rail system has higher traffic density and a higher percentage of passenger traffic than any other EU15 railway), and to relieve congestion on the Dutch highways. This decision was apparently based on a "strategic" belief, but was not based on detailed analysis (see Netherlands Court of Audit, 2000). Subsequent planning studies led to a commitment to upgrade an existing 40-km rail line in the port area (from Maasvlakte to Kijfhoek, near Rotterdam), and to connect it with a new, 120-km line to Zevenaar where it connects with the German network. The overall project is called the Betuwe Line. The upgraded section has been used as an internal railway to integrate the Port of Rotterdam and to improve the existing linkages. The second section, which is now expected to be completed in early 2007, will complete the high capacity (up to 10 trains per hour each way), all-freight link with the German network.

The project has had a troubled history in a number of ways. The completion date has stretched from 2004 to 2007, and the cost in constant terms has doubled, from EUR 2.3 billion to around EUR 4.6 billion (about 60% of the escalation is due to scope additions, and 40% is due to cost escalation). The early traffic estimates (and the financial and economic viability of the project) have been called into question because the downward trend in overall rail freight traffic in the Netherlands has continued and official estimates of Betuwe Line traffic have been stretched out in time. At the same time, rail freight traffic to Germany has increased since 1994, so the future demand picture specifically for the Betuwe Line is not fully defined.

Box 5.1. **The Betuwe Line, Netherlands** *(cont.)*

The government's plans for the institutional management of the Betuwe Line have also evolved, partly in line with the evolution of the structure of the national railway. Originally planned to be part of the national rail infrastructure, the government gave serious consideration in the mid to late 1990s to setting the project up as a PPP. This has now been abandoned on grounds of "risk", which (the Netherlands Court of Audit suggests) apparently means that the cost of the project is too high to be recovered within the limits of the potential demand expected and the infrastructure access charges that the government is willing to allow to be charged.

The government has instead asked the national infrastructure agency (ProRail) to manage the facility for the first few years after completion until the actual traffic flows and operating costs can be determined. Current estimates are that the line will need public support of about EUR 20 million annually, over and above the funds generated from access charges (set at marginal cost), through 2011, after which no further government support to operations is expected. ProRail has announced the proposed 2007 access charges for the line, which include a discount from the national charge structure in order to promote traffic on the line.

It is interesting also that the predominant freight operator on the line is Railion, a subsidiary of the Deutsche Bahn holding company, though there are seven other licensed operators, including Rail4Chem. Railion is the only significant rail freight carrier serving both of the two largest EU container ports – Hamburg and Rotterdam – putting much of the traffic on the Betuwe Line under the control of a company that might feel conflicting pressures between promoters of traffic through the two ports.

The analysis of the project by the Court of Audit highlights the similarity of the Betuwe Line with a number of other major public rail infrastructure projects. On the positive side, the Dutch government has been quite aggressive in determining the public objectives in improved access to the Port of Rotterdam, and has been willing to make a clear distinction between commercial and public objectives, accompanied by public support for the public goals. On the negative side, the essential scope of the project appears to have been committed before any conclusive analysis was available, and not much re-examination has been done since. Because the real performance and structure of the line were not pinned down until recently, the institutional structure – especially the role of the private sector – could not be committed. In addition, the goal of keeping the access charges low in order to promote traffic conflicted with the stated goal of promoting private sector investment. Finally, because of the enormous size of the project (it is the second largest public works project in Holland's history after the Delta Works), the management team was not initially up to the challenge. Several years, and several reorganisations, were necessary before the project was brought under control.

It is not at all uncommon for projects like this to be over budget and over schedule. Flyvbjerg, Bruzelius and Rothengatter (2003) argue that these kinds of short falls are endemic in public megaprojects. Only the future years will tell whether the demand estimates, on which the benefits are based, were also too high (all too typical).

Box 5.2. **The CREATE Program**

The Chicago area is the nerve centre in the US railroad network, acting as the main connecting point for six of the seven Class I railroads (which includes the two largest Canadian rail companies). The Chicago rail infrastructure includes 78 switching yards, 4 500 km of tracks, and covers a total of 6 400 hectares. Approximately 1 200 trains (of which 500 are freight trains) handling 37 500 rail freight wagons are processed daily. The Chicago hub also handles 20 000 intermodal rail/truck operations daily. In total, the Chicago rail hub handles roughly one-third of all rail freight traffic in the US. Significantly, the states most affected by rail traffic movements through Chicago (aside from Illinois) are California, New Jersey, Texas and Ohio. This linkage with seemingly remote states is driven by the fact that Chicago actually handles much of the containerised rail traffic that originates or terminates in the ports of California (Los Angeles and Long Beach) and New Jersey (the Port of New York and New Jersey) as well as the petroleum cargoes originating in Texas (Houston, Beaumont and Corpus Christi). Ohio is a major consumer of containerised cargo from Asia via Pacific ports as well.

The Chicago Region Environmental and Transportation Efficiency (CREATE) Program has been under joint development since the concept was initiated in 1990. On the private sector side, the project involves the Association of American Railroads (AAR) along with six railroad members (BNSF, UP, CP, CN, NS, and CSX), plus three smaller railway switching companies (Belt Railway of Chicago, B&O Chicago terminal and Indiana Harbor Belt) that form the contact point among the line haul railways. Public authorities include the commuter rail section of the Chicago Metropolitan Area Transportation Authority (Metra), along with the Chicago Department of Transportation, the Illinois Department of Transportation and the Federal Highway Administration (part of the US Department of Transport). Amtrak is also a party to the planning.

The project originated through the recognition that highway and rail congestion in the Chicago hub area was reaching serious proportions. By the mid-1990s, congestion levels had grown to a point where congestion was costing the area about USD 400 per capita (the LA/Long Beach area was much higher). With all projections indicating that rail traffic would continue to increase, the objectives of the project were to (in the order listed in the project documents): reduce accidents at level crossings; eliminate rail and highway conflicts that caused highway congestion by constructing 25 rail/highway over grade bridges; eliminate conflicts in rail traffic and reduce rail/rail congestion (freight and passenger) by constructing better connecting points and building 6 rail/rail flyovers; reduce fuel consumption and emissions on rail and highway; reduce highway traffic congestion; re-route rail freight traffic more efficiently; modernise and increase rail capacity to meet future needs; and improve rail connections through the hub area to improve the flows of rail traffic, including international traffic.

Box 5.2. **The CREATE Program** *(cont.)*

The project developers recognised that there is a split between private and public benefits. Project estimates show that the private rail benefits should be worth USD 232 million out of the total project cost of USD 1.534 billion. The railroads have agreed to finance their share, with public funding from Chicago and Illinois making up the balance. Federal funding under the federal highway programme would ultimately finance a significant share of the Illinois share: for example, level crossing elimination would be largely financed with federal funds.

As with the ACTA, CREATE is an *ad hoc* response to a problem that appeared most serious at the local and railroad level. As the project has developed, however, the potential national significance has become clearer. Because of Chicago's role as the critical hub for rail interchanges among the major railways, the pressures for a larger and more direct federal role have grown. Unlike ACTA, however, the railroads are funding their share upfront, rather than trying to develop a payment per wagonload over time (six railroads cannot agree on the charge per wagonload).

Thus far, though the railroad and local shares are relatively secure, the need for federal funding through the state has not been satisfied (FHWA funding for level crossing elimination would be stretched and other states would have to be denied if the Illinois amounts were paid), nor have the proponents been able to generate a more direct federal grant role. At present, only about USD 300 million in funding is firmly committed to the project, roughly equally divided among the railroads, local government and state/federal sources. Despite the difficulties, the criticality of the project is likely eventually to support gradually increased funding along with a more balanced role that would permit the project to proceed in a planned, rather than piecemeal, way.

Though the growth rates of containers were clearly faster than the rest of the dry cargoes, because the bulk cargo demand is driven by underlying economic growth, dry cargo growth in and out of the EU, Australia/New Zealand, and the Asian developing economies is strong. The worldwide rate of tonnage growth of 4.8% between 1990 and 2004, which shows every sign of continuing into the future, would lead to a further doubling of tonnage by 2020. More significantly, it is likely that a higher percentage of the bulk cargo needs rail for port access than do containers, indicating that rail systems and port access facilities will be challenged in many ports that are not critical container facilities. Since many bulk cargo ports are related to specific commodity flows (iron ore in Brazil, coal and iron ore in Australia) this will have implications for private investors as well as public sector finance.

Table 5.9. **Top 20 world container terminals**

Throughput in TEU millions

	2004	2002	Per cent growth 2002-04
1. Hong Kong, China	21.93	19.14	14.6
2. Singapore	20.60	16.94	21.6
3. Shanghai[1]	14.57	8.81	65.4
4. Shenzen[1]	13.65	7.61	79.4
5. Busan (Korea)[1]	11.43	9.45	21.0
6. Kaoshiung	9.71	8.49	14.4
7. Rotterdam[1]	8.30	6.52	27.3
8. Los Angeles[1]	7.32	6.11	19.8
9. Hamburg[1]	7.03	5.37	30.9
10. Dubai	6.43	4.19	53.5
11. Antwerp[1]	6.06	4.78	26.8
12. Long Beach[1]	5.78	4.52	27.9
13. Port Klang	5.24	4.50	16.4
14. Qingdao[1]	5.14	3.41	50.7
15. New York/New Jersey[1]	4.40	3.75	17.3
16. Tanjung Pelepas	4.02	2.67	50.6
17. Ningbo[1]	4.00	n.a.	n.a.
18. Tianjiin[1]	3.81	n.a.	n.a.
19. Laem Chabang	3.62	2.66	36.1
20. Tokyo	3.58	2.71	32.1
Total for top 20	**166.62**	**121.63**	**37.0**

Note: If the flows in Ningbo and Tianjiin are estimated at 3 million TEU in 2002, the growth rate for the Top 20 would be about 31%.
n.a.: not available.
1. Indicates significant dependence on rail access.
Source: UNCTAD (2005), p. 76.

Security issues are becoming more important, especially in the port/landside interface, but also at land borders where rail traffic is significant. The NAFTA borders are facing greatly increased inspections as a result, and the same may be true of the EU borders with CIS and Balkan countries. To the extent that the issue is related to the control of the contents of containers as they are loaded, this is a common problem for all modes, and will not favour or disadvantage any particular mode. To a probably marginal extent, the ability of railways to stack and load containers in a way that retards illegal entry, and to keep containers moving on a defined and controllable path, may act to promote use of railways, especially for potentially hazardous cargo.

Congestion on highways as an opportunity for rail. Highway congestion is an increasingly serious problem in the US and in the EU. Highway congestion in the US was originally an urban phenomenon and is increasingly serious in the major urban *areas* (many of which have ports). Highway congestion is now spreading into the rural parts of the Interstate Highway System (the major network of

Table 5.10. **Exports and imports by world region**

Millions of tons

	1990	2004	Per cent of compound growth
North America			
Petroleum	355.6	725.6	5.2
Dry cargo	742.7	842.3	0.9
Europe			
Petroleum	905.9	642.4	–2.4
Dry cargo	1 245.4	2 536.4	5.2
Japan			
Petroleum	284.4	254.3	–0.8
Dry cargo	668.7	745.4	0.8
Australia and New Zealand			
Petroleum	26.5	53.3	5.1
Dry cargo	284.4	627.5	5.8
South America: Eastern Seaboard			
Petroleum	129.0	247.8	4.8
Dry cargo	349.7	462.7	2.0
Developing countries in Asia			
Petroleum	920.4	1 645.2	4.2
Dry cargo	753.4	2 243.3	8.1
World total			
Petroleum	3 515.7	4 634.0	2.0
Dry cargo	4 618.0	8 911.1	4.8

Note: All dry cargo figures include containers.
Source: UNCTAD (2005), pp. 119-122.

limited access highways commenced in 1956 and essentially completed by the end of the 1980s). Table 5.11 gives a stark picture of the problem, showing that highway traffic density (vehicle miles travelled/lane mile) has increased by 65% since 1980 on the urban parts of the Interstate Highway System, and by 102% on the rural parts of the Interstate System. Of the 19 major port-related urban areas, 14 are officially considered "congested", and most of those are "highly congested".

Highway congestion may, if anything, be worse in many EU countries.[3] For example, the strategy paper of the Association of Train Operating Companies (ATOC) in the UK includes "congestion on the roads" as one of the main factors that will affect growth of rail traffic (freight and passenger) in the future (ATOC, 2005). Unfortunately, ATOC also concludes that congestion at peak times on the *railway* will act to retard rail growth as well. The entire transport system faces capacity issues, and the UK may have to enhance *both* rail and highway infrastructure capacity.

Table 5.11. **US roadway vehicle-miles travelled (VMT) per lane/mile**

By class of highway

	1980	1985	1990	1995	2000	2001	2002	2003	2004
Urban VMT per lane-mile, total (thousands)	613	677	764	810	869	852	861	856	860
Interstate	3 327	3 773	4 483	4 784	5 323	5 370	5 440	5 436	5 479
Other arterials	1 451	1 556	1 751	1 829	1 974	1 997	2 025	2 012	2 019
Collector	572	552	634	686	718	728	743	741	745
Local	146	168	184	181	196	181	188	183	184
Rural VMT per lane-mile, total (thousands)	103	113	136	148	172	176	179	175	174
Interstate	1 031	1 170	1 473	1 693	1 993	2 035	2 080	2 070	2 088
Other arterials	518	555	640	695	778	787	797	780	771
Collector	132	141	164	167	189	192	195	190	189
Local	19	20	23	25	30	32	33	33	32
Index 1980 = 100									
Urban VMT per lane-mile, total (thousands)	100	110	125	132	142	139	140	140	140
Interstate	100	113	135	144	160	161	164	163	165
Other arterials	100	107	121	126	136	138	140	139	139
Collector	100	96	111	120	125	127	130	130	130
Local	100	115	126	124	134	124	128	125	126
Rural VMT per lane-mile, total (thousands)	100	110	132	143	167	171	174	170	169
Interstate	100	113	143	164	193	197	202	201	202
Other arterials	100	107	123	134	150	152	154	150	149
Collector	100	106	124	126	143	145	147	143	143
Local	100	105	120	131	159	167	175	171	170

Source: 1980-94: US Department of Transportation, Federal Highway Administration, *Highway Statistics Summary to 1995*, FHWA-PL-97-009 (Washington DC, July 1997), Table VM-202.

1995-2004: US Department of Transportation, Federal Highway Administration, *Highway Statistics* (Washington DC, Annual issues), Table VM-2; Internet site *www.fhwa.dot.gov/policy/ohpi* as of 18 January 2006.

Lane-miles:

1980-95: US Department of Transportation, Federal Highway Administration, Office of Highway Information Management, unpublished data, 1997, Table HM-260.

1996-2004: US Department of Transportation, Federal Highway Administration, *Highway Statistics* (Washington DC, Annual issues), Table HM-60. Internet site *www.fhwa.dot.gov/policy/ohpi* as of 18 January 2006.

Urbanisation is also impeding metropolitan rail freight flows in a number of major urban areas. A good example is the Chicago area, where rail freight flows through the city are slowed by level crossings with high amounts of highway traffic, awkward connections among the various railroads (Chicago is a major interchange point between the two major western railroads – UP and BNSF – and the two major eastern railroads, NS and CSX), and a lack of sufficient space to develop adequate marshalling yards in the urban areas. The response, the so-called CREATE Program (see case study in Box 5.1) is a proposed federal, state, local and private railroad project which will improve rail to rail connections, eliminate level crossings, and decongest the interactions among the local suburban rail agency (RTA), Amtrak passenger trains and the freight trains of the five or more freight rail companies in the Chicago area.

Rising energy costs. Rail freight consumes less energy per ton-km than trucking (a balance that varies from area to area, depending on both railway and trucking efficiency and technology). In general, then, rail's competitive position in freight markets will be enhanced *vis-à-vis* trucking, and rail traffic should increase if the costs of petroleum fuels remain high. The significance of the impact of rising fuel prices is not entirely clear, though, given the fact that trucking has a competitive advantage in markets where service quality is a factor. The effect will be to raise the value of cargo for which rail becomes competitive, but the actual effect on rail revenues and traffic is difficult to judge.

Government efforts to shift traffic from road to rail. Many countries within the EU, as well as the EC, have an explicit policy to shift freight and passenger traffic from highway to rail in order to reduce highway congestion and to achieve a number of desired social benefits such as reduced pollution and CO_2 emissions (freight railways consume less than one-third the energy per ton-km than do trucks),[4] improved safety (US fatalities per ton-km for rail freight are one-tenth the rate for heavy trucks),[5] and changes in urban design (both the Alameda Corridor and the CREATE projects are aimed at consolidating urban facilities and releasing land for better use), etc. In fact, the EC has set an explicit goal of raising the rail market share in freight from 8% of ton-km to 15% of ton-km. The tools for doing so in the rail sector appear to be to:

1. Encourage that rail access charges be set at incremental cost.
2. Foster adequate investment and maintenance of the EU rail infrastructure.
3. Separate the accounts of freight and passenger operators in order to ensure that freight operators are not asked to cross-subsidise passenger losses from freight profits (a policy that is clearly in operation in most of the eastern European railways, and the Russian Federation).

There are few other countries or country groups that have an explicit strategy to promote a shift to rail from highway. In fact, though US freight regulatory policy is now nominally "balanced", the actual financial role of the US government heavily supports large trucks and barges (prior to the rail and trucking deregulation, US regulatory policy also heavily favoured trucks and barges, because of a deeply rooted political perception of railways as "public be damned" monopolists). Fortunately, both the US and Canada have eliminated cross-subsidy from freight to passenger through creation of nationally funded rail passenger companies (Amtrak and VIA) that receive government support to cover operating losses and that pay access charges for use of private freight tracks. Current policies favouring rapid construction of highways in China may also have the effect of shifting the modal balance toward highways: but, given the trends in the Chinese economy toward higher valued products, especially for export, some shift away from overdependence on rail may well be rational. Indeed, the rail freight market share in China has been falling for many years: from 72.3% in 1971 to 47% in 1981 to 39.2% in 1991 to 30.6% in 2001 (ton-km share).

Figure 5.3 illustrates the same problem in many of the eastern European countries and the Russian Federation. Prior to the transition from socialism, many of these countries probably had *too much* rail freight traffic, partly because of over-industrialisation that produced too much bulk traffic, and partly because socialist planners, lacking a full appreciation for logistics costs (as opposed to transport costs alone), tended to overemphasise dependence on rail in the transport sector. As a result, the formerly socialist countries had a rail freight share that was inefficiently *high*. As these countries make the shift to market economies (some are further along than others, but none have completed the shift), rail freight market shares will inevitably need to fall – and *should* fall. The major limitation on this trend will be the availability of alternative modes, primarily trucking.

Despite the EC's desire to shift some freight traffic from highways back toward rail, the actual trend has been in the opposite direction, from about 21% in 1970 to 8.4% in 1998 (EC, 2001). As Figure 5.3 suggests, rail freight market shares will be under strong pressure to fall in the central and eastern countries that are EU members (and prospective members). This raises the question as to whether the EC can actually do anything that will achieve its objective.

Figure 5.3. **Rail share of rail + truck traffic (%) *versus* average rail length of haul**

1998

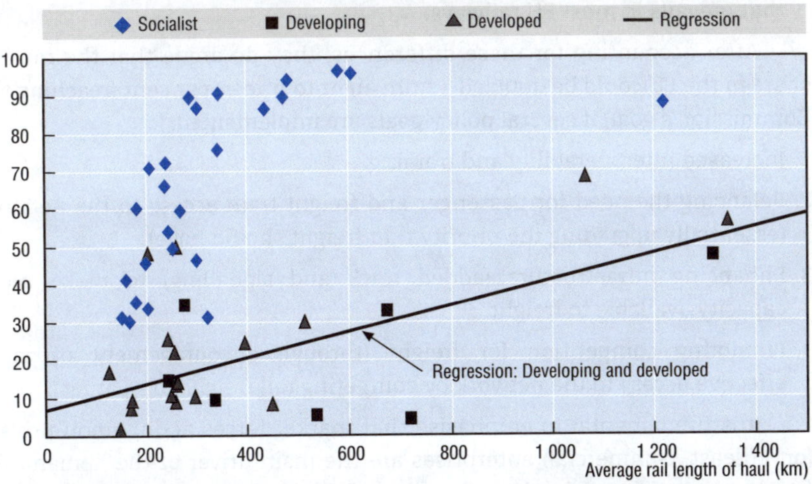

Source: ECMT (2001), "What Role for the Railways in Eastern Europe?", Round Table 120, OECD, Paris, p. 59.

The US example appears positive. As a result of years of unbalanced and intrusive tariff and entry/exit regulation, the market share (ton-km) of the US freight railroads had fallen from 56.2% in 1950 (just before the start of the Interstate Highway System construction) to a low of 37.5% in 1980, just before deregulation. In 1981, the transport regulatory system for trucks and railways was fundamentally changed, removing most tariff and entry/exit regulation from railways and trucks. As a result, railways were essentially free to set tariffs in accord with demand. They are free to sign confidential contract tariffs with shippers in which shippers can invest in unloading facilities and specialised freight rolling stock in return for tariff consideration. Since 1980, the US rail freight market share has increased to over 42%, and is at least stable if not climbing slowly. It deserves emphasis, however, that the change was only *regulatory*: there was no change in the fundamentally unbalanced federal and state financial support for heavy trucks.

A recent study analysed the question of increasing rail freight market share in the EU (see Vassallo and Fagan, 2005). Vassallo and Fagan argue that it would be unrealistic to expect that the eight per cent existing market share of the EU rail freight railways could ever be lifted to the North American levels, for several reasons:

1. The role of water transport is inherently higher in the EU than in North America.
2. Distances are greater in North America than in Europe (though this disparity can be reduced by further reducing the boundary effects of the existing infrastructure and operating companies).
3. The commodity mix in North America (high percentage of coal and grains) is more conducive to rail than the merchandise-dominated commodity mix that prevails in most EU railways.

After accounting for these differences, they do argue that the market share in the EU could be doubled – from eight to fifteen per cent (reaching the Commission's goal) if several policy goals are implemented:

1. Increased interoperability and training.
2. Balancing the need for passenger and freight train access to the network (essentially upgrading the priority that freight should have).
3. Enhancing infrastructure (added track and signalling) to make more capacity available to freight.
4. Promoting competition for freight (through encouragement of more effective access to the network by competing rail freight companies).

It is fundamental to emphasise that market forces acting upon private (or, at least, commercial) enterprises are the main driver of the demand for freight transport, and for the rail mode within the freight transport sector. As a result, the main battle for rail market share will be fought where it should be fought, in the transport market place. Governments can and will influence this market, but for the most part this influence should be aimed at providing a reasonably level playing field, without distorted support or hindrance to any mode. Second, governments can also influence market share by clearer identification of social needs that the market cannot or will not provide – congestion, safety and environmental impacts.

3.2. *Where and how will rail freight infrastructure grow?*

Rail infrastructure will "grow", but the definition of the term needs careful discussion. As discussed above, freight "capacity" does not directly relate to kilometre of rail lines. As Figure 5.1 showed, a kilometre of rail line can produce vastly different amounts of freight traffic. In fact, as will be discussed below, there is a nearly unlimited list of influences on the output of rail lines, each of which has a cost and an impact, and many of which interact or even conflict. For this reason, it is probably better to ask where the *investment* in rail infrastructure for the purposes of increasing the ability handle rail freight traffic will be. In this approach, "investment" will include not only kilometres of new line, but also all sorts of measures to increase freight throughput, including adding new track to existing lines (double- or triple-tracking, new signals, electrification, freight depots and yards, interoperability measures, and a host of productivity measures to be discussed below.)

Table 5.12 summarises the data from Table 5.2 to show, for the countries and groups developed, what the growth in rail ton-km and passenger-km will be between 2005 and 2035. The table also shows the percentage of freight and passenger traffic growth that can be attributed to each country or regional groupings, and it shows the percentage of the growth in each country that is freight traffic as opposed to passenger traffic (assuming that Traffic Units – the sum of passenger-km and ton-km is a useful measure of total traffic).

Table 5.13 restates the value of investment in railways presented in Stambrook (2006). Unfortunately, the country groupings are not the same in the IEA report (2003), and the data do not exist to make them entirely consistent. That said, at least some of the groupings (and individual countries) are the same, and some significant comparisons can be drawn. The calculations and amounts in both tables must be taken with a distinct "grain of salt", and quantitative inferences are probably impossible to draw. Nevertheless, it is intriguing to note, for example, that 76% of China's traffic unit (TU) growth will be in freight, and that China will be the fastest growing railway in the world in absolute terms (freight *and* passenger).The top four groupings (China, US/Canada, the Russian Federation and India) account for 88% of the freight traffic growth and 72% of the passenger traffic growth in the world. Adding Japan and the EU OECD countries to the passenger category brings the passenger percentage to 86%, and the freight

Table 5.12. **Growth in rail traffic from 2005 to 2035**

	Absolute growth 2005-35		Per cent growth 2005-35		Per cent absolute freight traffic growth	Per cent absolute passenger traffic growth	Per cent absolute growth as freight
	Ton-km	Pass-km	Ton-km	Pass-km			
China	2 206 569	691 405	142.7	135.8	35.2	35.5	76.1
US and Canada	1 649 601	13 752	62.7	27.5	26.3	0.7	99.2
Russian Federation	1 134 617	134 212	85.5	73.3	18.1	6.9	89.4
India	504 982	567 903	142.7	116.0	8.1	29.2	47.1
Non-Russia CIS	304 377	50 702	73.3	56.1	4.9	2.6	85.7
Eastern Europe, Turkey	135 690	36 430	93.3	51.6	2.2	1.9	78.8
Africa	92 052	5 041	73.3	27.5	1.5	0.3	94.8
European OECD countries	71 020	134 950	27.5	42.3	1.1	6.9	34.5
Latin America	65 169	3 918	51.6	27.5	1.0	0.2	94.3
Pacific OECD countries	53 401	133 271	32.6	51.6	0.9	6.8	28.6
Middle East, North Africa	24 009	83 251	73.3	93.3	0.4	4.3	22.4
Other non-OECD Asia	23 403	90 730	69.1	93.3	0.4	4.7	20.5
Total world	**6 264 890**	**1 945 564**	**87.5**	**88.9**	**100.0**	**100.0**	**76.3**

Source: IEA (2003), ETP Transport Model, Spreadsheet version 1.28.

grouping to 90%. Overall, Table 5.12 suggests that about 76% of the growth in railway TUs will be in freight. Though it would almost certainly be inaccurate simply to multiply the traffic growth percentages in Table 5.12 by the investment percentages in Table 5.13, it seems reasonable to argue that at least half, and maybe more, of the investment predicted in rail construction over the 2000 to 2030 period will be for addition of *freight* infrastructure capacity.

Of course, we know more than just these general percentages. Some countries have announced significant initiatives for investment that furnish more specific values.

China, for example, has announced a USD 220 billion programme between 2005 and 2020. This will include increasing the size of the network from 70 000 km to 100 000 km, increasing electrification and double tracking to at least 50% of the network, and construction of around 7 000 km of new, dedicated passenger lines. Of these, at least one (Beijing to Shanghai) will be designed for 300-plus km/hour speeds, and one is said to be a candidate for magnetic levitation. There is little doubt that the current traffic density of the Chinese network would support such a network. The challenge will be so see how to finance the additions, since the earnings of the railway alone will not support the required investment.

The Indian government has announced a proposal to construct all new, high axle load, dedicated freight lines to link Mumbai with New Delhi and Calcutta. The total cost of the project is currently estimated at EUR 3.6 billion.

Table 5.13. **Rail construction forecast**

USD billions

	2000 asset value	Construction value 2000-30	2030 asset value
High income industrialised	468.5	1 069	900.8
G7	329.7	679	583.2
United States	93.4	203	180.8
Japan	78.5	103	97.8
Germany	43.8	120	95.9
United Kingdom	24.8	54	44.9
France	28.0	78	61.6
Italy	46.3	83	72.0
Canada	14.9	37	30.2
Other – OECD	111.4	310	248.8
Europe and central Asia	84.0	246	194.1
East Asia and Pacific	22.0	46	39.4
North America (Mexico)	5.4	18	15.3
OECD industrialised	441.1	988	832.0
Non-OECD	27.4	82	68.8
East Asia and Pacific	1.6	15	12.5
Europe and central Asia	5.8	10	8.7
Latin America and the Caribbean	10.8	33	26.8
Middle East and North Africa	0.7	8	6.9
South Asia	–	–	–
Sub-Saharan Africa	8.6	16	13.6
Big Five	100.3	405	322.3
China	28.8	231	171.9
India	19.0	62	52.9
Brazil	7.4	30	24.3
Russian Federation	43.6	70	64.1
Indonesia	1.6	11	9.0
Developing	62.6	132	119.7
East Asia and Pacific	3.5	22	18.3
Europe and central Asia	30.5	43	39.8
Latin America and Caribbean	5.3	15	12.6
Middle East and North Africa	9.0	26	23.4
South Asia	4.1	14	13.0
Sub-Saharan Africa	10.3	13	12.6
World	**631.4**	**1 606**	**1 342.8**

Source: Stambrook (2006).

These lines are justified based the congestion on the existing lines, mainly caused by interactions between freight and passenger trains. The question here will be to see whether a more rational policy might be simply to raise the prices on the existing regional passenger services (which cause the congestion on the passenger/freight lines), and thus free up freight capacity.

The EC has announced a EUR 200 billion plan for upgrading the main passenger and freight lines in the EU (see case study on the TEN-T network in Box 5.3). The freight share of this amount is not clear, but is at most only a part of the EUR 105 billion allocated for conventional speed projects. The relative priority of passenger services *versus* freight services on the upgraded system is also not at all clear.

The US freight network is approaching an unacceptable level of congestion, primarily because freight traffic growth has, for the past 30 years, been matched by a determined effort to reduce unnecessary investment in rail trackage. Figures 5.4, 5.5 and 5.6 show the result of increasing rail traffic combined with shrinking network size: freight traffic density has more than tripled since the Staggers Act deregulation in 1981, and has more than quadrupled since the creation of Amtrak in 1971.

Figure 5.7 shows the impact: the freight railroads were able to manage the increases in density until about 1990. Since then, there has been a 20% deterioration in train speeds. Increased output since 1990 has been achieved in the face of increasing congestion and at the cost of decreased productivity of rolling stock and increased labour costs.

Coal flows out of the Power River Basin in Wyoming are of great significance; but, the high density flows from the Los Angeles/Long Beach area through Chicago and onward to the East Coast reflect the importance that rail container flows play in the output of the network. In terms of container traffic, West Coast to East Coast connections via Chicago are of great importance, as previously noted. These container flows are not balanced, however, so there is a net flow of empty containers from east to west that balances the predominantly loaded flows from west to east.

The issue in the Russian Federation is not specifically capacity, since the railway carried more traffic in 1988 than it is likely to carry anytime in the reasonable future and there are no present indications of line congestion. Instead, the issue is rehabilitation of a network that has operated for years without investment. The new Russian railway company (OAO RZhD) has reasonably healthy earnings, and has plans to rectify the infrastructure deficits either from earnings or from targeted government assistance. Significantly, the approach to obtaining new freight wagons is heavily dependent on ownership of new wagons by shippers or operators[6] rather than by OAO RZhD. As of now, over 30% of the Russian freight wagon fleet is privately owned, and the railway expects this percentage to rise to over 50% within the next few years.

None of the plans discussed above can be entirely financed from internal funds generation (though the US, Canada and the Russian Federation may come close on the infrastructure side). In all cases, outside financing (government, or other private investors in the case of freight wagons) will be

Box 5.3. **TEN-T rail programme**

The European Commission has long recognised that transport is critical to economic development and to the geographic integration of the members of the EU. The issues and problems of transport co-ordination have increased with additions of new countries to the EU, with a quantum jump when the EU increased its membership from 15 to 25 in 2005. In addition, the Commission is also concerned with promoting better connections between the EU and the countries adjoining it, and beyond.

The trans-European transport network (TEN-T) was developed in order to identify and alleviate problems limiting the free flow of passengers and freight within the Union. TEN-T covers highways (89 500 km), railways (in total 94 000 km of which about 20 000 km are to be higher-speed passenger lines operating at 200 km/hour and above), inland waterways (11 250 km) and 366 airports. The target for completing the TEN-T network improvements is 2020, although the approach contains a large number of specific corridors and investment components, some of which are already underway or completed.

The challenge is to meet demand for rail freight transport that is expected to grow by two-thirds by 2020 within the old EU15, and to double within the new member states. There will be a corresponding increase in passenger flows as well. The TEN-T programme in total is expected to reduce road congestion by 14% and to improve rail flows, a benefit that is estimated at EUR 8 billion annually. The Commission found that without TEN-T, the rate of growth in the EU would be slowed, and CO_2 emissions would increase. The total investment remaining to complete the TEN-T projects is estimated at EUR 252 billion (the total cost of all projects, including the non-priority axes, would total more than EUR 600 billion). The sources of finance for these projects could include direct funding from member states, EIB loans, ISPA, ERDF and Cohesion funding, as well as the TEN-T budget. As a supplement, the TEN-T programme looks to PPP projects, but recognises that these can never be more than about 20% of the total funding, and that making PPPs feasible will require new legislation to create a better investment climate for the private sector.

The specifically rail part of the TEN-T programme will include projects covering 19 271 km of line, and could cost about EUR 200 billion by current estimates (see Table 5.14 below). The entire panoply of rail projects will take until 2020 to complete although, as noted, some of the projects are already finished or are underway. As the table below shows, EUR 83.9 billion are to be used for solely passenger projects, EUR 10.7 billion are to be allocated for solely freight projects, and the remainder (EUR 105.6 billion) will be spend on projects that are at least nominally to benefit both freight and passenger services. Of the joint projects, it is difficult to allocate money as between freight and passenger; but, it seems safe to assume that a predominant share of the EUR 105.6 billion would benefit rail freight only peripherally, by way of moving some passenger traffic off combined lines and thus hypothetically creating more capacity for freight.

Box 5.3. **TEN-T rail programme** *(cont.)*

Table 5.14. **The TEN-T rail programme**

Priority axis	Description	Completion	Km line	Total cost EUR million	Spent to Dec. 2004 EUR million	Passenger or freight use
1.	Berlin-Vienna/Milan-Bologna-Naples-Messina-Palmermo	2007-15	1 798	45 611	13 232	Both
2.	Paris-Brussels-Cologne-Amsterdam-London	1993-2007	510	17 457	14 777	Passenger
3.	High Speed Rail Axis – France/Spain/Portugal	1998-2015	2 956	39 730	7 352	Passenger[1]
4.	High Speed Rail Axis East Luxembourg-Paris-Mannheim	2002-07	510	4 373	1 534	Passenger[1]
5.	Betuwe Line	2004-06	160	4 685	4 130	Freight[2]
9.	Cork-Dublin-Belfast-Stranraer	2001-05	502	357	357	Both
11.	Øresund fixed link	2000	53	4 158	4 158	Both
12.	Nordic Triangle rail/road axis	1995-2015	1 998	10 905	3 222	Both
14.	UK West Coast Main Line	1994-2008	850	10 866	9 680	Both[3]
16.	Freight rail axis Sines-Algeciras-Madrid-Paris	2006-20	526	6 060	0	Freight
17.	Railway axis Paris-Stuttgart-Vienna-Bratislava	1990-2015	882	10 077	2 396	Both
19.	High-Speed Interoperability Iberian Peninsula	2001-20	4 687	22 313	2 485	Passenger[1]
20.	Fehmarn belt railway axis (Hannover-København)	2006-15	448	7 051	4	Both
22.	Rail axis Athens-Sofia-Budapest-Vienna-Prague-Nuremburg-Dresden	2005-16	2 100	11 125	0	Both
23.	Rail axis Gdansk-Warsaw-Bratislava-Vienna	2005-15	1 291	5 488	852	Both
Total			**19 271**	**200 256**	**63 179**	

1. Also may release conventional line capacity for freight.
2. Specifically intended to serve the port of Rotterdam for distribution into the EU. Capacity: 74 million tons.
3. Mostly passenger objectives.

A later effort has been made to develop an analogous programme for improving the rail connections between the EU25 (Cyprus and Malta have no railways) and the 26 adjoining countries of the CIS, Middle East and North Africa. Traffic volumes between the EU and these countries are expected to double by 2020, with rail playing a major role because of the huge distances and inferior highway network in many of the CIS countries (and the Russian Federation in particular). This programme would have the added benefit of improving the longer-range connections with Asia. The total cost of this programme has been estimated at EUR 45 billion spread over five corridors, though this must be considered at most a rough estimate of such a massive programme extending over 20 years or longer, and hypothecated on improved relations and co-operation among a large number of countries. There is no separation of the programme as between rail and other modes.

Box 5.3. **TEN-T rail programme** *(cont.)*

Significantly, the extension programme puts a major emphasis on technical and institutional issues. Technical issues (interoperability and communications) are likely to be easier (though more costly) to resolve than the institutional issues (border formalities, common legal regimes for freight, etc.).

Overall, and in contrast with the US cases, national and EU government inputs dominate the TEN-T programme, with little direct participation by local governments or the private sector. A specific problem that has long accompanied the rail freight planning is that the networks to be improved are being planned by state-owned entities that are far more interested in infrastructure investment and passenger service than they are in freight services. This poses the clear risk that the "freight" investment may well go to the wrong place and for the wrong reasons, especially if the private sector eventually takes a larger role in the EU in operating freight services.

Also by contrast with the US cases, the TEN-T programme is heavily oriented to long range, comprehensive planning with a very limited role for *ad hoc* approaches. High-level planning has the advantage of ensuring coherence at the system level, but it often suffers for lack of direct contact with the actual users of the facilities.

It is unlikely that the full, ambitious TEN-T programme can be financed as planned, because the member governments may well not agree to support the EC's plans fully. For this reason, the EC is now focusing its effort on high priority and bottleneck segments of the proposal. It seems likely that actual financing will run 50-70% of plans. The effect of cutbacks on the specific modal plans is hard to predict though we might speculate that the brunt of rail sector reductions would fall more heavily on freight than on passenger investments.

Figure 5.4. **Ton-km in the US by mode**

In millions of ton-km

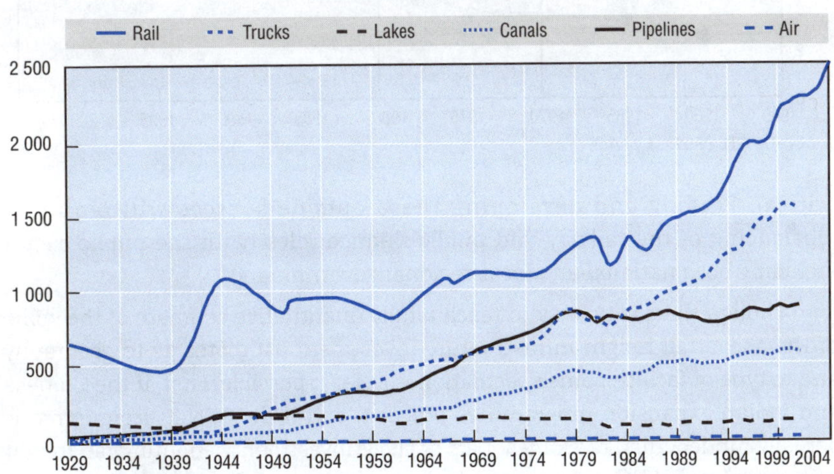

Source: AAR (2005), *Handbook of Railway Facts 2005*.

Figure 5.5. **Km of rail line in the US**

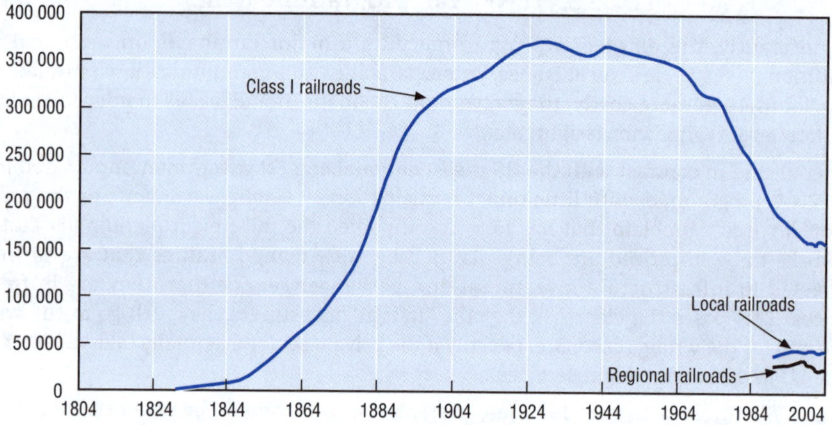

Source: Author based on AAR (2005) and US STB (various years).

Figure 5.6. **Ton-km/km on US Class I Railroads**

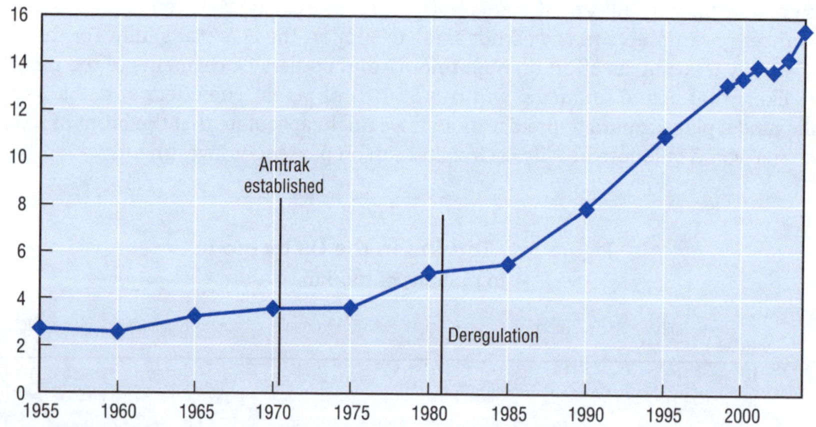

Source: US STB (various years).

critical. Finding and developing these outside sources will require a rebalancing of the railway and public finance roles (with the public sector including both national and local/regional governments).

Though there is no way to reach a fully quantitative estimate of the splits of the above rail freight infrastructure investment estimates as to geography and to type of facility, some speculation is at least possible. First, if the Chinese and Indian expansion programmes proceed, and if the TEN-T programme is actually funded, then the largest part of *public* investment benefiting rail freight infrastructure is likely to be made in China, India and the EU member states. There will clearly be private freight rail infrastructure investment in North

Figure 5.7. **Average US freight train speed**

Km/hour

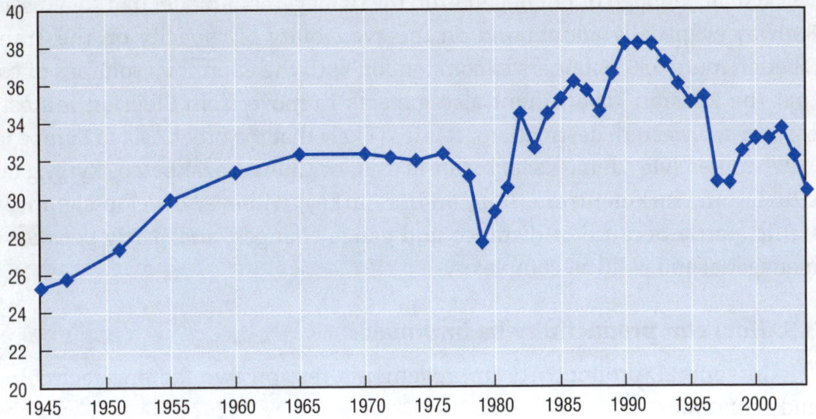

Source: US STB (various years).

America, but (without dramatic changes) there is not likely to be more than a 20-30% increase in the USD 7 billion average capital investment programme of the Class I railroads over the past 10 years. There are no significant prospects for major rail freight infrastructure programmes in Latin America, Africa, the Middle East and Asia (aside from China and India), though Brazil may be an exception if iron ore and soy export markets remain strong. Second, again with the possible exception of China and India, most of the foreseeable investment in rail freight infrastructure capacity will not be in new lines, *per se*. Instead, most investment will be in adding capacity to existing lines through double tracking, signalling, and electrification. Information management techniques for signalling and train controls as well as machine-aided dispatching will also be important.

Though not actually part of infrastructure, significant increases in line capacity will also be realised through enhancing the capability of locomotives and freight wagons (higher horsepower, improved tractive effort, higher net-to-tare ratios, etc.) and more effective management of capacity (unit trains, greater length of haul, reduced changes of locomotives, etc.). Finally, it is clear that port/inland transport network interfaces (port access from/to the land side) are going to be an increasing challenge, especially on the West and East Coast of the US (and in Chicago), the ports of Rotterdam and Hamburg, and the major ports of Asia (particularly China). Whether the port access issues are treated as a port problem or a rail (and highway) problem is harder to predict; but, it is clear that a significant amount of investment will be needed to reduce the impedance at the interface.

It is also possible that the Trans-Siberian route across Russia will develop into a significant actor in container transport from Asia to Europe. Whether this will actually happen or not depends on the management model that the Russian Railway eventually adopts and on the availability of capacity on the Trans-Siberian route for containers in competition with the enormous volumes of coal that the Russian government also expects to move from Siberian mines to eastern and western destinations. It is less likely that the other Asia to Europe rail "Silk" routes (via China-Kazakhstan-Russia, or China-Kazakhstan, Kyrgyzstan, Uzbekistan, Turkmenistan, Iran, and/or Turkey) will ever develop significant traffic, partly because of distance and gauge changes, and partly because of managerial and political complexity.

3.3. How can productivity be improved?

In general, productivity improvements rest on two factors: technology and economics.

Technological factors to improve freight rail productivity. There are many ways in which the "productivity" of freight rail infrastructure and operations can be enhanced, and there are a number of examples of freight railways in the world that illustrate these opportunities.

Increasing freight wagon (the North American term for freight wagon is freight car) cargo capacity is an important alternative because line capacity goes up directly with wagon size. For example, the maximum freight wagon loading in the US increased from 63.5 tons in the 1970s, to 90.7 tons in the 1990s. On selected lines, the maximum wagon loading can now rise as high as 113.4 tons. Since 1970, the *average* wagon load has risen from 54.9 tons to as high as 67.7 tons (in 1985) but has declined slightly since due to an increase in merchandise (as opposed to bulk) traffic. Table 5.15 shows the range of average wagon loadings in a number of railways for which the data are available.

Increasing freight train loading is another important option, at least up to the point that the length of the train might exceed the length of the passing sidings to be used (and assuming that the tractive effort assigned to the train, and the braking distance, are within the design plans of the signal system). Table 5.15 also shows the range of variation in train loading for a number of selected countries. To be precise, train loading is related to both the train length and the maximum load per wagon.

When wagon weights go up, then the maximum axle load goes up as well. It is the axle load that ultimately determines the strength needed in the infrastructure (rail, track structure and bridges), and increased axle loads cause increased track maintenance, with greatly increasing effect on mixed freight and passenger lines. At the same time, improvements in rail metallurgy have significantly reduced rail wear even when axle loads have risen. Maximum axle

Table 5.15. **Average wagon loading and train loading for selected railways, 2004**

In tons

	Railway	Wagons loaded	Tons loaded	Average wagon load	Average train load
AUT	ÖBB	2 356 630	90 569	38	357
BEL	SNCB/NMBS	1 529 358	69 040	45	408
CZE	CD	2 018 994	86 816	43	418
DEU	DB AG	6 839 397	269 884	39	343
FIN	VR	1 055 630	42 700	40	578
FRA	SNCF	2 991 561	117 415	39	348
HUN	MAV	1 346 342	45 270	34	419
ITA	FS	2 214 005	83 087	38	360
LTU	LG	802 411	45 555	57	1 334
LVA	LDZ	865 438	51 058	59	1 600
POL	PKP	3 495 452	163 488	47	615
PRT	CP	263 723	11 151	42	296
SVN	SZ	273 157	17 856	65	359
SVK	ZSSK	1 145 838	49 756	43	575
CHE	SBB CFF FFS	2 035 122	57 940	28	322
BGR	BDZ	429 310	20 387	47	401
ROU	CFR	2 758 919	62 771	23	485
TUR	TCDD	475 541	17 708	37	n.a.
IRL	RAI	516 586	29 453	57	n.a.
MAR	ONCFM	580 525	32 901	57	n.a.
CAN	Total Canada	5 359 972	251 746	47	n.a.
USA	AAR Class I	30 094 796	1 673 023	56	2 716
CHN	CR	n.a.	2 178 160	n.a.	2 565
IND	IR	n.a.	557 390	n.a.	1 288
JPN	JR	9 122 000	37 056	4	n.a.
RUS	RZhD	n.a.	1 229 000	n.a.	2 041

Source: International Union of Railways (UIC), *International Railway Statistics.*

loads can rise as high as 35.7 tons in the US, compared with 25 tons in the Russian Federation and 22.5 tons in most of the EU. On HSR lines, the maximum axle load is often restricted to 17 tons.

Enhanced signalling increases productivity by increasing traffic density (more train-km/line-km). Conventional methods of enhanced signalling are closer signal spacing, multiple-aspects (allowable speeds), centralised traffic control, and others. More recent innovations include versions of positive train control (PTC or ERTMS) and even "moving block" signalling in which train speed and spacing are determined by the schedule and by the characteristics of each train.[7] These types of signalling are dependent on methods of position determination (GPS, Galileo or other), clear and totally reliable digital communications, and computer-based control systems. The economic benefits of these newer systems also include other significant productivity gains and cost reductions such as better energy management, improved equipment condition reporting (reducing maintenance cost and improving reliability and availability), reduced energy consumption through better train speed management, and reduced crew costs (potentially through enabling a reduction in crew levels). All of these systems will improve the safety of operations significantly beyond the already safe levels of today.

Modern locomotive designs, including traction slip/slide controls (especially the switch from DC to AC traction), are reducing energy consumption significantly and improving output per locomotive. As an example, ton-km per litre of fuel has improved by 75% between 1980 and 2004 in the US. Class I railroads (AAR, 2005) and ton-km per installed locomotive horsepower increased by 53% over the same period (US STB, various years).

There are a number of operating techniques that yield improved freight productivity. The use of unit or block trains, for example, significantly improves the productivity of wagons, locomotives and labour. As a result, many EU railways have simply abandoned single wagonload traffic in favour of block trains (or, at least, multiple wagonload shipments). Dedicated unit trains offer another level of improvement because the rolling stock can be specialised for the service, and is often owned by the shipper rather than the railway. Dedicated, shipper-owned wagon fleets have long been the norm in tank wagons, but are now becoming common in many bulk commodities (such as coal for utility power plants) and specialised commodities (automobiles, finished steel, etc.) in North America, the EU and the Russian Federation.

A good example of a consolidated shopping list to enhance capacity is found in ATOC, 2005. Although this list is heavily passenger influenced, it does involve freight, and has most of the same elements to be found in any capacity enhancement programme. It includes:

- De-bottlenecking.
- Lengthening trains.
- Squeezing more train paths by better scheduling and control.
- Increasing equipment reliability.
- Increasing track capacity.
- Avoiding removing track or scrapping of rolling stock.
- Reducing the number of unproductive trains.
- Analyzing and employing world wide best practices.

Data on trends in improved productivity. Calculating and comparing railway freight productivity is notoriously difficult. Most important, the balance between passenger service and freight service affects all comparisons. The traditional approach – using the linear sum of passenger-km and ton-km to represent output – is at best an approximation (Transport Reviews, 2003, pp. 7-13). Analyses have suggested, for example, that passenger-km are far more labour intensive than ton-km. With this caveat in mind, Table 5.16 shows selected measures of railway productivity and its growth between 1980 and 2003. This table leaves no doubt that railways have worked hard to improve productivity, both of labour, infrastructure and freight wagons. Locomotive and coach productivity is not calculated because the use by some railways of independently powered coaches (called diesel or electric multiple unit equipment) makes passenger locomotive productivity calculations questionable.

The case of the US freight railways is particularly instructive because passenger service plays an insignificant role in the network and because the railway accounts make a complete separation between passenger and freight. It is therefore possible to look directly at freight railway productivity without confusing the impact of passenger service. In addition, the US case holds special interest because the railways were deregulated in 1981 and thus furnish a particularly interesting "before and after" illustration of the impact to a change in incentives and the management model. Moreover, the data are good enough to permit calculation of output trends per ton of wagon capacity (and not just per wagon, which is distorted because wagons were getting larger) and per installed horsepower in the locomotive fleet (locomotives were getting larger also).

Figure 5.8 shows the results of deregulation in the US – dramatic improvements in the productivity of all aspects of the industry. Figure 5.9 shows the results of the improvement from the point of the user of the system – equally dramatic reductions in the cost of rail freight and of the prices charged to the shipper. Table 5.5 showed a similar improvement after the concessioning of the Latin American railways.

Management models will also have a significant effect on productivity, both on determining how technology is employed to improve productivity and on how the required investment in infrastructure capacity will be financed. The US Class I railroads and the Canadian railroads have shown what the private sector can do in meeting commercial demand if the government policy framework is not impossibly biased. But the limits to this model are becoming clearer as the congestion throughout the US transport network (caused, in part, by flaws in the federal financing approach) grows. The role of the public sector in financing private rail freight capacity improvements seems certain to grow, and the Alameda and CREATE projects are one possible model for a more general approach.

The railway in China shows what a purely publicly owned railway can do with adequate financing within a socialist, planning context: this model, too, is showing signs of strain in the face of a need for rapid growth in the socially-driven parts of the system combined with a tariff policy that holds tariffs too

Table 5.16. **Railway productivity trends, 1980 to 2003**

	Traffic units (TU)/employee)			TU/km of line			Ton-km/wagon		
	1980	1990	2003	1980	1990	2003	1980	1990	2003
Argentina	227	211	2 530	643	537	420	213	233	430
Bolivia	158	129	1 060	327	251	300	283	265	310
Brazil	500	550	5 400	1 900	1 600	2 680	600	700	1 380
Mexico	591	501	2 500	3 278	2 052	2 800	948	781	2 070
South Africa	430	989	3 906	4 219	5 333	5 325	522	649	926
Bulgaria	335	342	226	5 654	5 100	1 804	n.a.	333	306
Czech Repbulic	n.a.	300	306	n.a.	n.a.	2 479	n.a.	n.a.	375
Slovak Republic	n.a.	300	337	n.a.	n.a.	3 400	n.a.	n.a.	422
Hungary	276	219	348	4 937	3 662	1 923	352	267	353
Poland	516	398	490	6 580	5 104	3 369	n.a.	650	427
Romania	537	355	339	9 146	7 740	2 267	620	397	256
Turkey	190	290	602	1 348	1 697	1 666	217	386	511
FYROM	210	186	127	1 537	1 614	665	n.a.	316	153
Serbia	247	246	121	3 741	3 633	800	554	445	n.a.
Croatia	283	253	299	4 613	4 102	1 435	n.a.	n.a.	536
Slovenia	366	358	536	4 997	4 703	3 296	n.a.	483	686
Russian Federation	1 700	1 751	1 400	30 791	32 535	21 303	2 624	2 983	2 800
Ukraine	1 075	1 236	740	23 443	23 589	8 000	n.a.	2 120	950
Kazakhstan	n.a.	2 152	1 500	n.a.	29 498	11 500	n.a.	3 818	1 664
Belarus	911	1 046	675	14 003	16 560	9 398	n.a.	2 529	1 748
Estonia	n.a.	947	2 446	8 125	8 272	9 870	n.a.	500	532
Georgia	n.a.	817	341	n.a.	11 021	3 762	n.a.	979	478
Latvia	1 006	1 011	1 318	9 379	10 014	8 091	n.a.	1 300	2 214
Lithuania	n.a.	1 219	1 020	10 705	11 409	6 702	n.a.	900	946
China	319	391	937	14 192	24 797	34 163	2 143	2 905	3 202
Indonesia	134	309	n.a.	1 068	n.a.	n.a.	n.a.	272	n.a.
Korea	840	1 151	1 449	10 268	14 082	12 618	623	876	765
India	233	323	590	5 993	8 521	13 755	395	681	1 730
Pakistan	187	196	250	2 757	2 926	3 300	218	164	n.a.
Austria	256	326	610	3 172	3 687	4 598	n.a.	354	792
Belgium	245	330	454	3 771	4 285	4 706	187	276	413
Denmark	257	324	664	2 691	2 809	3 205	235	373	n.a.
Finland	472	578	1 221	1 901	1 992	2 288	388	550	887
France	505	566	716	3 593	3 359	4 058	287	342	451
Greece	178	197	271	925	1 056	841	75	59	131
Ireland	92	154	400	834	934	1 042	141	322	247
Israel	538	911	1 532	n.a.	2 099	3 907	n.a.	1 141	927
Italy	263	324	720	3 592	4 036	4 239	n.a.	195	400
Japan	605	1 364	2 568	10 350	13 052	13 144	350	888	1 523
Netherlands	441	540	838	4 298	5 050	6 359	305	458	2 228
Portugal	289	322	644	1 961	2 325	2 051	171	319	614
Spain	360	527	1 127	1 788	2 087	2 416	258	285	557
Sweden	693	862	1 418	1 995	2 432	1 878	347	671	1 509
Switzerland	427	509	842	5 568	6 439	7 234	n.a.	n.a.	484
Germany	210	210	842	2 783	2 468	3 983	n.a.	350	463
New Zealand	154	326	n.a.	720	681	n.a.	115	213	n.a.
Canada: Canadian National	2 000	3 715	10 814	n.a.	3 955	8 426	n.a.	1 963	n.a.
Canada: Canadian Pacific	2 494	4 370	10 384	3 030	n.a.	7 509	1 288	2 291	n.a.
USA: All Class I Railways	3 040	7 073	14 659	5 241	7 925	14 250	814	1 263	1 757

Note: n.a. signifies not applicable or not available.
Source: World Bank Railway Database.

Figure 5.8. **Productivity in US railroads**

Index: 1980 = 100

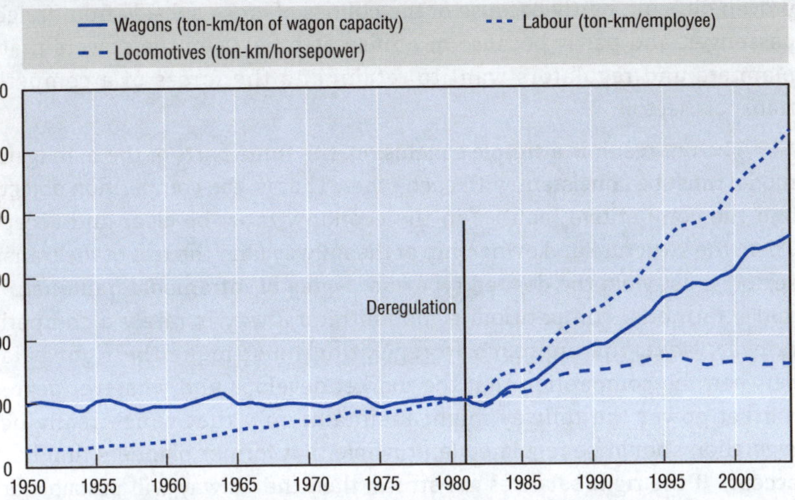

Source: US STB (various years).

Figure 5.9. **US Class I revenue per ton-mile**

Statistics of Class I railroads

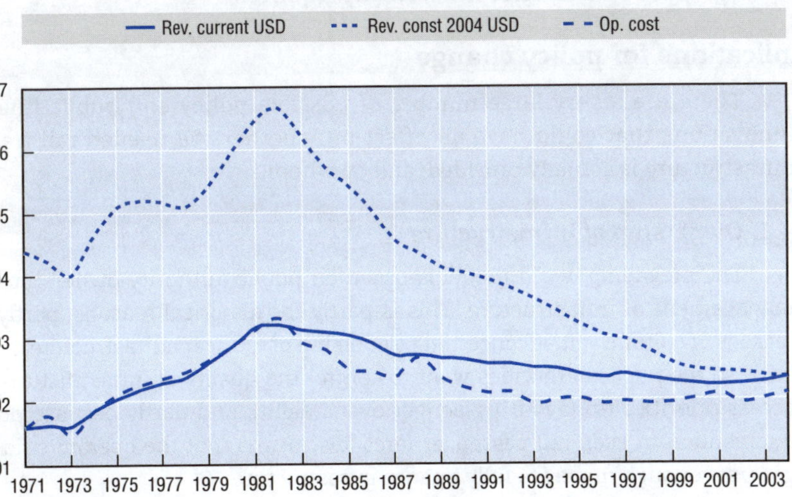

Source: US STB (various years).

low and effectively removes pricing flexibility from the railway. China will obviously need both an infusion of private investment in a number of areas along with a thorough re-thinking of government oversight policy. The Russian Federation illustrates the damage that can be done when the railway is still "planned", but the economy shifts to a market-driven approach: the result was a decade of underinvestment. The current attempts to reform the management model are reasonably comprehensive, but implementation has proven difficult, partly because of the politics of cross-subsidy from freight to passenger, and partly because of a mismatch between the powers that the planners and regulators want to retain, and the forces of a competitive transport sector.

The net result is a simple conclusion: the three parts of the management model must be consistent with each other. That is, the competition objectives and the competitive realities in the economy must be clear and accepted. Then, the structure and ownership of the railway (and the rest of the transport sector) must yield the desired type and degree of intramodal (rail *versus* rail) and intermodal competition: a monolithic railway is rarely a competitive railway. Next, the approach to regulation must make the right balance between the competition that the market develops and whatever degree of market power the railway might maintain; only that which really needs regulation should be regulated (a principle that former planners find hard to accept). If the right balances are struck, then the railway will probably do an effective job of finding the right technology and generating the financial resources needed to provide the right capacity. Finally, government promotional and financial policy must focus on defining, and paying for, whatever social rail services the economy requires.

4. Implications for policy change

There are a very large number of possible policy and public finance innovations that could have an effect on whether the needed rail freight infrastructure is actually provided, and by whom.

4.1. *Ownership of infrastructure*

The prevailing world model is based on public authority ownership and management of infrastructure. This is partly for historical reasons, partly for reasons of cultural values concerning ownership of "critical" infrastructure, partly because the public authorities want to control the quality of infrastructure and access priorities (to favour passenger over freight), and partly because public intervention to keep rail passenger fares low means that the operators do not generate enough money to fully finance infrastructure.

Private ownership and management of rail infrastructure is, of course, possible. The North American example is clear (in fact, the largest Canadian railroad – CN – was privatised in 1996 after years as a Crown Corporation). Among the largest passenger railways – the three large Japanese companies – are entirely private (though there is public investment in the infrastructure in cases where the private companies think the investment is unprofitable). In addition, about 30% of the line-km in Japan has always been owned by private companies operating commuter services. The infrastructure of British Railways (BR) was privatised to become Railtrack. For a number of reasons, this privatisation failed, and a new company (Network Rail) was formed that occupies a middle position between public and private (there are reports that Network Rail is considering issuing new equity, which would further blur the distinction between public and private). The Latin American countries all retained ownership of their rail freight infrastructure, though they concessioned operations.

Though governments have often insisted on owning rail infrastructure, they are somewhat less than insistent on meeting their obligations to fund the needed maintenance and investment. To an extent, this is due to a perennial problem with government budgeting (people want services but do not want to be taxed to pay for them – the reason why cross-subsidies from freight to passenger services are popular) and partly one of political priorities – what Andrieu (2007) calls "short-termism". This is a problem that has become public and serious in France, for example, where the SNCF (non-TGV) infrastructure has suffered from underfunding. A general conclusion is that the private sector has and will adequately fund the amount of rail freight infrastructure it needs for commercial purposes, if the regulatory and competitive environment are appropriate. Only the public can, and should, fund rail infrastructure that serves social or public needs.

Prognosis: With the exception of North America, the three large Japanese railways, and a few integrated bulk freight railways, there is little enthusiasm for private ownership of railway infrastructure. It is possible that some governments may view sale of their railway infrastructure as a source of cash for a strapped treasury (this was part of the motivation for the Railtrack privatisation and the sale of the Estonian Railway – both of which have subsequently faced significant challenges). For the most part, however, there will not be significant infrastructure privatisations or additions to private line-km because of a general perception that rail infrastructure is a nationally strategic asset. On the other hand, there may well be significant prospects for contracted maintenance or even award of concessions to *manage* public infrastructure, including freight infrastructure.

4.2. Ownership of the freight operating company

As with infrastructure, the traditional model in most of the world is for the freight operator (and passenger operators) to be owned and managed by government "enterprises". The only long-standing exceptions were in the US and the CP in Canada, and several mining railroads around the world (CVRD in Brazil, or Pilbara in Australia) that had railroads as part of the overall mining and transport function. This model is changing. The CN was privatised in 1996 – perhaps the largest railroad freight privatisation ever (with the possible exception of the privatisation of Conrail in the US in 1987). Essentially all of the operators of rail freight in Latin America (Argentina, Chile, Bolivia, Peru, Brazil, Guatemala and Mexico) were shifted to private concessions in the 1990s and no significant public rail freight operators remain. The BR freight operator (EWS) was entirely privatised in 1996 (it is *not* a franchise). The open access regimes in the EU and the Russian Federation have engendered the rise of new, private, usually own-account rail freight operators (such as Rail4Chem and Ikea) that operate paying access charges. New open access rail freight operators have arisen to compete with EWS in the UK, and UK operators are now negotiating to run trains through the Channel Tunnel and into the continental networks. Though not actually a privatisation, Railion (the freight arm of Deutsche Bahn) has bought the formerly national freight operators in the Netherlands and Denmark, and has offered to buy other freight operators in Sweden and Poland. The German government is now considering "privatising" DB, though in what format is still unclear. A privately owned freight rail operator (Connex) has recently commenced running trains on the public national infrastructure (RFF) in France. The paradox of government ownership of rail freight companies is that the trucking and water operators have always been private. Private companies are inevitably closer to the market and the customer. In addition, trucking companies do not suffer from the border effects that railways face in the EU, and trucking companies inherently offer better service than rail (albeit at higher prices) because their shipment sizes are smaller.

Prognosis: The trend toward private ownership and management of operators may well be the best hope for rail freight growth. It is entirely possible that the EU freight rail operators will be mostly privatised in the next decade, and it is even more likely that new, private, open access operators and carriers will be a significant competitive force in the EU and Russia.

4.3. *Competition policy*

Government competition policies towards railways hinge first on the degree of intermodal competition that exists in the transport market. In countries where ample intermodal competition prevails – generally the case in the EU, North America and Latin America, and increasingly the case in China – governments can be less concerned about the competitive structure of the railway sector. Where ample competition does not exist – as is the case in the Russian Federation, where over 80% of the surface transport goes by rail because the highway system is so limited – a structure fostering intrarail competition can be a significant tool. The US has, for example, seen a constant trend toward railway mergers, to the point that rail *versus* rail competition on parallel lines has been significantly reduced. In 1970, there were 71 Class I railroads; today there are nine, of which only four are significantly competitive. Of these, two (UP and BNSF) compete in the west, and two (CSX and NS) compete in the east.

The Russian Federation government is considering (but seems unlikely to adopt) plans to create parallel line competitive companies in the Third Phase of its railway restructuring. Even though intermodal competition is pervasive in most of the EU, the EC has fostered open access to infrastructure in order to create at least some cross-border competition among railway freight companies. In this regard, a situation in which one company (for example Railion) buys up a large number of formerly national rail freight operators might pose significant structural competition issues.

Prognosis: For the most part (except for some bulk traffic in the Russian Federation and China), regulation of rail freight tariffs will be effectively eliminated and replaced by enhanced intermodal competition or, in some cases, with intramodal competition as well.

4.4. Regulation

Regulation must be consistent with competition. In situations where competition is pervasive (high-valued cargoes that trucks can carry effectively, or low-valued cargos where barges operate, or between two market areas that are served by two railroad companies), there may be little need for regulation of railway tariffs and services. This was, for example, the rationale behind the trucking and rail deregulation in the US in the early 1980s. Even where the general level of competition is adequate, though there may still exist areas where the railways can exercise market power. For this reason, the Surface Transportation Board (STB) in the US retains power to regulate rail tariffs where three tests are met: railways have market dominance *and* railway earnings are inadequate *and* the proposed railway tariffs appear to be too high (there are numerical standards for all three tests). For the most part (including Latin America and Africa and most of Asia) there is little reason to expect that rail freight tariff regulation will be needed. There are, however, three significant exceptions: China, the Russian Federation and India.

China has already witnessed a rapid growth of trucking, and the rail share of intercity ton-km has already fallen below that of North America (and continues to fall, primarily because the rail system is congested with bulk traffic and because the railway is not commercially oriented and tariffs are overregulated). At the same time, the railway freight traffic in China does include a number of vital commodities, especially coal, on which the economy is heavily dependent and for which there is little effective competition. China will clearly need to retain control over railway pricing of coal, and possibly some other bulk commodities. Because of its geography and weather, Russia will always have a higher rail market share than in other countries, especially for long haul traffic from European Russia to Asian Russia. To some extent, this traffic can be subjected to open access competition: where this is infeasible, regulatory power over tariffs must be retained (albeit rationalised). India exhibits a distinct set of regulatory issues, partly because of an inadequate road network (though intracoastal shipping does furnish a competitor in some cases), and partly because of a distorted rate structure in which rail freight rates are held artificially high in order to cross-subsidise politically mandated passenger services. So long as this cross-subsidisation continues, both freight and passenger tariffs will have to be regulated, as will truck tariffs, if the system is not to collapse under its contradictions (as effectively happened in the US immediately prior to deregulation).

Prognosis: Cross-subsidies in railways from freight to passenger services are remarkably difficult to eliminate because policy makers find it easier to tax freight shippers than the public at large. The EC has thus far been unable to enforce its requirement for separate accounting of social from commercial services, and has been mostly unable to enforce the stricture against cross-subsidies. Given the current lack of information to support regulatory intervention (ECMT, 2006), and given that the new EU members are supporters of cross-subsidies, there is little reason to believe that the EC will be successful in improving its regulatory enforcement in the next decade. The Russian Federation government has proposed (but has so far not implemented) a reduction in cross-subsidies. India has weakened its rail network by cross-subsidies, but has been unable to change policy because of political interference. Fortunately, China has thus far avoided losses on passenger services, and the passenger services in Japan are profitable, or are supported directly from public funds. Both the US and Canada have successfully eliminated cross-subsidies by institutional separation of Amtrak and VIA and by direct public funding.

4.5. *Regulatory/investment interactions*

As suggested in the case of India, there is a direct linkage between tariff regulation and investment generation, especially for freight operations and infrastructure. If the regulator's actions are restricted to alleged abuse of market power and to political attempts to cross-subsidise passenger from freight, and if the regulator does not adequately consider the earnings need of the railway, then internally generated investment will be inadequate. Unfortunately, this is the rule in many of the world's railways, and will be a major source of weakening of the link between the rail freight infrastructure that is needed, and that which is actually provided.

Prognosis: Regulatory constraints on development of rail investment have been, or will be, removed in North and South America and the EU. Such constraints will remain serious in the Russian Federation (due to the policy of making coal exports appear more economic by forcing down long haul coal tariffs), India and China, all of which are pursuing explicitly social goals at the expense of adequate freight earnings for their railways.

4.6. Cross-subsidies and PSOs

Imposed cross-subsidies from freight to passenger services have a significant and adverse impact on the ability of the freight side of the railway to generate earnings and finance investment in infrastructure. This is not only a problem in India. In fact, most of the central and eastern European countries (including those that are new EU members) have traditionally used cross-subsidies to hold down passenger tariffs while also minimising government budget contributions. This is true not only of operating support, but also of infrastructure, where many of these countries charge high infrastructure access charges to freight in order to reduce the access charges to passenger operators (ECMT, 2005). The same problem can be seen in different guises (Japan Rail Freight Company, and Amtrak and VIA in North America) where the tenant operator is supposed to pay only "marginal cost" for track access. EC directives oppose cross-subsidies, and require that social services only be provided under a fully compensatory Public Service Obligation (PSO) contract. The question is whether, and how soon, the Commission will succeed in enforcing its directives in this respect.

Prognosis: Transparent PSO systems are usually more popular with economists and public managers than they are with politicians. The problems in the CEE countries with creating more transparent PSO regimes are a good example. It is clear that more and more PSO systems for supporting social services by railways will be developed. Unfortunately, the development will be slow, and full compensation (if it can ever be properly defined and measured) will be slow in coming.

4.7. Infrastructure access charges

The EU is the only multicountry regime in which infrastructure access charges are legally required and in which the rules for setting the access charges are formally developed. In most other countries (US, Canada, the Russian Federation, Japan, Argentina, Mexico), access charges apply to minority, tenant operators, and are set at an approximation of marginal or variable cost. Marginal cost is, unfortunately, a more useful concept in theory than in practice (see discussion on information below), and is subject to abuse if the tenant operator is politically powerful. In most of these countries, the owning railway argues that the tenant is not even paying marginal cost, especially when the lines over which the tenant operates are congested. The EU rules for access charges are by now well established: access to the infrastructure must be non-discriminatory; no user should pay below marginal cost; all users should optimally pay marginal cost with government making up the difference between economic marginal cost and the financial costs of the infrastructure provider; governments are permitted to require the infrastructure provider to pursue recovery of some (or all) of financial costs through imposed mark-ups, but the mark-ups must be levied in an economically efficient manner and must not be discriminatory; and, the infrastructure provider must, through the sum of user access charges and government support, collect enough to be financially stable from year to year (ECMT, 2005). These rules would be beneficial to infrastructure in general, and to freight operations in particular, if they were fully enforced. Unfortunately, they are not enforced, partly because of a lack of information, partly because of lingering political interference that favours priority access for passenger services, and because the new CEE members have been reluctant to deal with the cross-subsidy/PSO issue. The result has been a patchwork of inconsistent access charge regimes that almost certainly act to hinder the flow of rail freight traffic across national boundaries and, in the CEE countries, clearly are encouraging rail freight traffic to shift to trucks.

Prognosis: There is emerging support within the EU for adopting simple access charges for rail freight (that is, basing freight access charges on simple measures of use, such as net ton-km or gross ton-km or train-km). There is less support for complete harmonisation of the charge levels, both because of different cost circumstances and financial objectives among countries, and because harmonisation of freight access charges would expose internal cross-subsidies from freight to passenger services. In addition, some countries (*e.g.* Germany) argue that some aspects of rail freight access charging decisions are commercially sensitive and should be confidential.

4.8. *Inadequate information*

A fundamental challenge of access charge regimes (which are necessary for successful operation of either the owner/tenant models or the vertical separation regimes) is the ability to set access charges that bear some relationship to marginal cost and that can be shown to relate in an appropriate way to the cost of different types of users. In addition, all users and government need to know that the condition of the infrastructure is appropriate and stable from year to year. As discussed in a recent ECMT report (2006), the access to, and validity of, information about EU railways is inadequate to the task. Though the EC requires it, few EU railways actually separate their costs and revenues as between infrastructure, passenger operations and freight operations. It is thus difficult, if not impossible, to say that passenger losses are being adequately compensated or that the costs of infrastructure are being fully covered as required. Few railways maintain, and none report publicly, the data required to calculate the marginal cost of infrastructure as applied to each user. Equally important, there is no agreed or common method for calculating marginal cost anyway. Though the EC requires an annual Network Statement – and most countries comply (or will nominally comply shortly) – the Network Statements are too general to ensure that the condition of the infrastructure is actually appropriate or stable from year to year.

Prognosis: Developing better information will be a critical aspect of improved railway management and regulation in the EU. The EC is likely to push for improved information. Indeed, EC directives already require that most required information be developed. The issue is one of enforcement (always slow) and of development of improved and harmonised accounting systems (also slow). It could be decades before the required information is actually developed and reported in a fully useful way.

4.9. *Interoperability*

Interoperability at national boundaries is a significant issue in the EU. The need to change electric power voltage and frequency, signal systems and crew has made it difficult for any operator to provide service in more than one country. This is somewhat less serious for freight than for passenger services, since diesel locomotives could haul freight across boundaries with ease, but the signalling systems are still disparate and crews are rarely qualified to operate across boundaries. Given the slow progress in the access charge issues above, it may in the end be easier to resolve technical interoperability problems than the political ones.

Prognosis: Although the technical solutions to interoperability issues are reasonably easy to define, getting railways (and their governments) to agree on common solutions has not been simple. Moreover, the money involved is so large that a process of evolution as old systems are replaced seems to be the best approach. Despite a generally positive outlook, it will be decades before full interoperability is achieved, if ever.

4.10. *Priority access for passenger services versus freight*

Countries generally support passenger services (preferably through an explicit PSO system), while they do not usually provide significant support to freight: for example, NERA estimated that only 2.8% of EU rail funding went to support freight (NERA, 2004). Passenger services (especially commuter services in the major cities) tend to enjoy high political visibility. As a result, infrastructure providers are often under clear (usually non-verbal) orders to give access slot priority to passenger operators and let freight take what is left over. This obviously has an effect on the ability of the freight operator to compete and to finance any needed freight capacity.

Prognosis: The problem of non-discriminatory access to the EU rail infrastructure for freight services cannot be fully resolved because of the very high levels of passenger services on the networks. The concept of dedicated freight lines (or the Freight Freeways) has promise, but the costs of implementation may be so high as to make most dedicated freight lines uneconomic.

4.11. *Broader government policies influencing intermodal market shares*

There are at least three areas in which non-rail government policies will affect rail freight traffic and infrastructure.

First, as in the US, many governments have policies that include financial assistance to the various modes of transport. The US government (and state governments), for example, provides massive assistance to the construction of the national highway system. The revenue sources to finance the highways (principally a tax on fuel, but also on lubricating oils and tires and tubes, and on truck licenses) are roughly sufficient. However, within user categories, the car and bus users pay for their financial share of construction and maintenance whereas the heavy trucks pay 50-80% of what they should pay (FHWA, 2000) to recover financial costs. Second, neither trucks nor cars cover their marginal social costs (adding safety, congestion, environmental impacts).[8] Heavy truck subsidies are a significant determinant of the market share currently enjoyed by trucks. Third, the federal government in the US pays essentially the entire cost of constructing and maintaining the inland waterway system. The net result is that railways lose high revenue traffic to trucks and low revenue traffic to barges (where barge competition is possible).

Prognosis: It is unlikely that this problem will be resolved, at least in the US or Canada, due to the political power of the trucking and barge lobbies, though there is some indication of a growing awareness of transport congestion issues in the US. Railways will have to find a way to live with the problem. One potentially promising idea, though, is congestion tolling on the highways. At present, there is little political enthusiasm or understanding of tolling: if that changes, then railway freight traffic should definitely benefit.

Much the same situation prevails in Latin America where trucks do not pay their way in highway construction and maintenance costs. This has had the result of weakening the performance of the rail freight concessions. **Prognosis:** No significant change.

Even where trucks pay their way in a rough financial sense (as may be the case in the EU where fuel taxes are very high), they do not necessarily pay their way when externalities, especially congestion, are included. The problem is that there has been strong political resistance to highway use tolling, partly because of tolling administration costs and traveller delays, and partly because many people object to "paying twice" for their access to highways (they don't think that paying both fuel taxes and use tolls would be fair). This resistance has been compounded when users are asked to pay congestion-related tolls, such as time-of day and directional tolls (inbound in the morning, outbound in the afternoon). Many European countries, as highway congestion has mounted, are beginning to implement various types of congestion tolls in major urban conurbations. Advances in tolling technology that, at least in principle, will eventually permit congestion tolling whenever and wherever it occurs have aided this movement. It seems quite possible that the most important single advance in technology aiding the growth of railway freight traffic could be in highway tolling. It is an open question whether trucking demand will suffer more from low tolls and congested throughput or higher tolls and free flowing traffic.

Prognosis: Highway tolling is likely to increase. It will benefit EU rail freight traffic only if the management model for rail freight is changed to promote private ownership and operation of rail freight carriers. It would definitely benefit North American railways, but by how much is uncertain, since much of the competitive equation is driven by quality rather than cost considerations.

The form of financing can sometimes be as important as the level. For example, fuel taxes are purely variable with use. If the traffic does not move, the operator does not pay. By comparison, the fixed costs of private railways must be paid whether or not the business cycle is positive. Access charges for freight railways can have a very different effect if they are purely variable with use as compared with having a significant fixed component. For example, the Alameda Corridor Project was financed mostly with public funds, with the railways paying the money back through a charge per container hauled. The project might not have been feasible if the railway had been required to borrow all of the money up front.

Prognosis: As the Alameda Corridor Project shows (see Chapter 1, Box 1.4), the use of public money to convert a fixed charge into a variable charge has real promise. The actual use of the approach in the US depends on development of broader policies to support it, rather than the past reliance on *ad hoc* groupings of federal and local authorities with the private railroads. In cases where the user charges can reliably pay the expected share of public investment, this approach will probably grow. The Alameda Corridor Project also highlights a dilemma: if the user charges cannot be passed on the shippers, the enthusiasm of the railways is likely to be limited.

Government policies toward the method of promoting private involvement are also important. When facilities such as rail infrastructure are being privatised, governments have the choice of trying to value assets at book value or allowing them to be sold for going concern value (usually much less). In addition, assets can be sold for upfront cash (hard to finance) or for a stream of payments over time. Concessions or franchises can be either positive (payments to government for use of the infrastructure) or negative (payments from government to cover operating losses and maintenance of assets). Franchises can either be gross cost (in which the franchisee takes no demand or revenue risk, but only bids minimum cost to provide services) and "commercial" (in which the franchisee takes the demand revenue risk as well). Gross cost franchises (actually contracts) tend to be more appropriate for socially supported services whereas commercial franchises are more appropriate for services where market forces are fully at work. In all of these cases, government policy and expertise will determine whether the approach works.

Prognosis: The understanding of this set of issues has advanced, as a recent ECMT conference on franchising of railway services demonstrated. If the current EU trends toward franchising remain positive, then private involvement in both infrastructure and operations of freight (and passenger) rail will develop.

5. Conclusion

This chapter argues that a significant portion of future rail freight infrastructure investment will need to be approached as a *joint effort* between the public and private sectors because there are both public and private benefits of rail freight services. This suggests the use of PPP vehicles, for which there is an accumulated store of experience, some successful and some not (see the Australia case study in Box 5.4 for a discussion of the Darwin extension). A particular lesson that has emerged – the effect of the "megaproject" – needs to be emphasised. It is almost inevitable that the new PPPs for transport infrastructure, including rail freight, will be megaprojects, with impacts that reach virtually all areas in the society, and with resulting political challenges (poverty reduction, regional development, environmental and cultural preservation, etc.) that reach far beyond easy planning and management, especially for the private partner. As Flyvbjerg *et al.* (2003) discuss, the complexity of such projects, along with the irresistible tendency on the public side to overpromise benefits and underestimate costs, almost always leads to results that are delayed, over budget and under performing.

Prognosis: Most PPPs will be troubled ones, with optimistic schedules and inadequate budgets. In addition, political challenges from special interest groups will further aggravate budget and schedule problems.

Box 5.4. **Australian rail restructuring**

The details of railway ownership and operation in Australia, and the process by which they have evolved in the past 30 years, are far too complex to be covered in depth in this chapter.[1] It is useful, though, to summarise in a broad way what has happened as it illustrates and elaborates a number of the structural issues presented in Tables 5.3 and 5.4.

Australia has around 40 000 km of rail line, making it one of the world's larger freight networks (see Table 5.1). In total, in 2003/04 the Australian railways carried almost 600 million tons of freight (see below), of which about 580 million tons were bulk commodities (mostly coal, ores, and grains). Only two per cent of the total tonnage crossed a state line; 98% of the tonnage was short haul (238 km average), bulk moves for processing or export, and 42% was carried on private railways having no significant connections to the rest of the network.

Prior to the mid-1970s, railways in Australia had either been developed as private, dedicated railways, or they had been owned and developed to serve the needs of a single state. With no significant interconnections, the various rail systems used different gauges (see map below), with slightly over 4 000 km of broad gauge lines (1 600 mm), around 19 000 km or narrow gauge lines (1 067 mm) and the remaining 17 400 km of standard gauge lines (1 435 mm). Except for the private, dedicated railways, all common carriage railways were publicly owned and operated by state governments as vertically integrated systems.

Beginning in 1975, the process of development of a freight *system* began. Although the steps in the evolution are very complex, the end result is shown in the tables and map below. The common carriage network is now, for the most part, vertically separated, offering competitive access using published and regulated access charges (the private railways were, and remain, integrated without competition, and the Tasmanian Railway has no competitive operators at present). On the Queensland Railway Group (QRG) narrow gauge infrastructure, which is publicly owned by the state government of Queensland, the infrastructure provider is part of the group but is "ring fenced" from the remainder of the group and offers access to others. The Australian Rail Track Corporation (ARTC), owned by the Commonwealth government, owns, leases or has contracted access to a national network of standard gauge lines spanning the continent from Perth to Brisbane (via Adelaide, Melbourne and Sydney) and from the North (Darwin) to a connection with the transcontinental line at Tarcoola). The ARTC standard gauge line connects with a series of state-owned standard gauge lines, offering competitive access through a significant part of the country. The narrow gauge lines in Western Australia were privatised but have now been acquired by the QRG (and offer open access as in Queensland). The broad gauge system of the Victoria Railway is now managed by ARTC, and offers open access.

Box 5.4. **Australian rail restructuring** *(cont.)*

The freight operators have been separated from infrastructure. Most have been privatised, with the exception of the QRG freight operator (that recently bought the Western Australia freight operation). There are now four major privately owned freight operators: Pacific National, Asia Pacific Transport Consortium, Genessee and Wyoming of Australia, and NRG (Flinders Power). There are also a number of smaller, private, tenant operators, including SCT Logistics, P&O, Grain Corp, Southern and Silverton Rail, Patrick Portlink, Lachlan Valley and Southern Shorthaul R.R. Table 5.19 below has a description of the territories and operating conditions of the freight operators.

Vertical separation for freight also led to the creation of a national, long haul passenger operator, the Great Southern Railway (GRS). GRS is a private corporation providing overnight, tourist-based passenger services from Sydney to Perth and from Melbourne and Adelaide to Darwin. GRS operates on a "hook and haul" basis in which GRS provides the coaches and all passenger services and the operating freight carrier provides locomotives and drivers. Most of the suburban and local passenger services are operated on a vertically integrated basis by local authorities (Perth, Adelaide, Sydney and Brisbane) whereas the commuter services in Melbourne are provided by a private franchisee (Connex).[2]

Australia also furnishes an interesting example of a PPP project – the 1 420 km Alice Springs to Darwin Railway. This link had been a century-long dream of the Northern Territory, furnishing a direct rail connection with the rest of the country and, it was hoped, providing a "land-bridge" for containers between southern Australia and Asian markets via the Port of Darwin.

Construction of the link commenced in 2001, and was completed in January 2004. In addition, the 820 km link from Alice Springs to the East-West line at Tarcoola was acquired under lease. The AUD 1.86 billion cost of the link was financed through an AUD 191.4 million grant from the Commonwealth government, AUD 367.8 million from the State governments of South Australia and Northern Territory, and AUD 1.3 billion financed by the private sector. The project was overseen by a public company jointly owned by South Australia and Northern Territory (AustralAsia Railway Corporation), which awarded a BOOT concession to the Asia Pacific Transport Consortium. Freight operation on the line is provided by Freightlink (a partner of AustralAsia) and by the Australian Rail Group (now owned by QRG) under open access provisions for the infrastructure.

After only two years, it is not yet clear whether the project is financially "successful". Thus far, the land-bridge traffic has not developed as expected, but the potential for bulk freight may turn out to be greater than forecast, and the line appears to have gained about 85% of the entire surface freight transport traffic from the South to Darwin. Freightlink reportedly lost money in its first two years, and is now trying to sell part of its equity for AUD 350 million to obtain new financing (*source:* "The Australian Financial Review", 3 May 2006). The performance of the concession owner is not public, so its success cannot easily be assessed.

Box 5.4. **Australian rail restructuring** *(cont.)*

The Australian experience offers a number of potential conclusions bearing on the availability of infrastructure for rail freight:

- The completely market driven, private freight railways, carrying 42% of Australia's rail freight traffic, were able to finance their infrastructure needs without significant public intervention. Since these companies are serving a booming world commodities market and have low production costs, there is no reason to think that they will be unable to provide the capacity they need in future.
- The privatization of the freight operators has largely been successful (Williams, 2005, p. ix), offering better services at lower rates, and generating sufficient internal financing for operating needs.
- The primary interstate infrastructure provider, ARTC, seems to be an effective conduit for reaching a balance between public and private funding for rail infrastructure. For the fiscal year ended 30 June 2005, ARTC generated AUD 239 million in access revenues, AUD 88 million in services to regional and local governments, and another AUD 62 million in other non-operating revenues. To this was combined AUD 100 million in special Commonwealth government grants for improving the system. The total (AUD 489 million) comfortably exceeded the total costs for the year of AUD 342 million. In total, ARTC has received AUD 550 million in grants, and expects to receive AUD 550 million in grants for financing of specific infrastructure projects through the Auslink programme that deals with the national transport infrastructure (see ARTC Annual Report, 2005, pages 2 and 44). An additional AUD 820 million has been provided via Auslink to ARTC to upgrade the high density Melbourne-Sydney-Brisbane corridor in order to upgrade capacity and reduce trip times for freight as well as passenger trains. Overall, through ownership of ARTC and through funding in the rail activities of the Auslink programme, the government has clearly defined the public interest needs for rail infrastructure capacity, and has moved to ensure that these needs are financed.
- The separation of passenger operations has been effective in ensuring that the freight operators do not have to cross-subsidise passenger services. In particular, GRS has upgraded the quality of the service and is profitable on an operating cost basis. It is not yet clear whether GRS will be able to finance new equipment if that is needed.
- Under an acceptable balance of public and private finance, as the Alice Springs to Darwin project shows, PPPs can readily add capacity to the national rail freight infrastructure.

1. See Williams (2005) for a more detailed discussion of the overall organisation of the Australian rail sector, and Kain (2006) for a detailed discussion of the experience with passenger franchising in Australia.
2. Franchising of passenger services in Melbourne has been a troubled process that may still be evolving. See Kain (2006) for a detailed discussion. See also Williams, Greig and Wallis (2005).

Table 5.17. **Australian rail freight traffic, 2003/04**

Top bulk commodities	For hire carriage		Private carriage	Total
	Intrastate	Interstate		
	Million tons			
Coal	239.1	0	0	239.1
Ores	12.7	0	207.0	219.7
Grain	17.6	0.1	0	17.7
Other bulk commodities	55.2	3.0	44.0	102.2
Total bulk	**324.5**	**3.1**	**251.0**	**578.6**
Non-bulk traffic	**6.6**	**9.4**	**0**	**16.1**
Total traffic	**331.2**	**12.6**	**251.0**	**594.7**
	Billion ton-km			
Coal	45.5	0	0	45.5
Ores	3.5	0	69.1	72.5
Grain	5.5	0.1	0	5.6
Other bulk commodities	12.2	4.8	1.2	18.2
Total bulk	**66.7**	**4.9**	**70.2**	**141.8**
Non-bulk traffic	**4.0**	**22.3**	**0**	**26.3**
Total traffic	**70.7**	**27.2**	**70.2**	**168.1**
	Average length of haul (km)			
Coal	190.5	0	0	190.5
Ores	273.4	0	333.6	330.1
Grain	312.1	571.4	0	314.2
Other bulk commodities	221.5	1 605.4	26.6	178.1
Total bulk	**205.6**	**1 559.1**	**279.8**	**245.1**
Non-bulk traffic	**600.9**	**2 366.2**	**0**	**1 636.4**
Total traffic	**213.5**	**2 164.9**	**279.8**	**282.7**

Source: Australasian Railway Association (2006), Tables 3 and 4.

Table 5.18. **Australian railway structure, mid-2006**

	Infrastructure	Suburban and regional passenger operations	Intercity passenger operations	Intrastate freight	Interstate freight
South Australia	ARTC owns interstate freight line. State owns local passenger lines.	Trans Adelaide state operated.	Privately operated by Great Southern ("hook and pull").	PN.	PN, AP, G&W, NRG, SS, S&S, PP, P&O, Onesteel.
Tasmania	Privatised: Pacific National Tasmania.	–	–	Privatised: PN Tasmania.	Privatised: PN Tasmania.
Western Australia	WestNet (private), but ARTC has access to Perth.	Transperth publicly operated suburban; Transwa public regional.	Privately operated by Great Southern ("hook and pull").	PN, QR National, S&S, Pilbara, BHP Iron Ore.	QR National, S&S.
Queensland	QR Network Access (QRG).	Brisbane operated by QRG.	QRG.	QRG, Comalco.	QRG, PN.
Victoria	State, with interstate lines leased to ARTC.	Suburban franchised to Connex; V/Line passenger for regional.	Privately operated by Great Southern ("hook and pull").	PN, QR National, SS, S&S, PP, P&O	Pacific National.
New South Wales	State, with interstate line leased to ARTC.	Public "Railcorp".	Privately operated by Great Southern ("hook and pull").	PN, QR National, GC, SS, S&S, PP, LV.	QR National, PN.
Northern Territory (Alice Springs to Darwin)	50-year BOT concession, incl. lease of Alice Springs to Tarcoola line.	–	Privately operated by Great Southern ("hook and pull").	FreightLink (AP).	FreightLink (AP).
ACT	ARTC.	–	–	–	PN

Note: PN = Pacific National. AP = Asia Pacific. G&W Aus = Genessee and Wyoming of Australia. NRG = NRG Energy. QRG = Queensland Rail Group. GC = Grain Corp. SS = Southern Shorthaul. S&S = Southern and Silverton. PP = Pacific Portlink. LV = Lachlan Valley.

Source: ARA (2006).

Table 5.19. **Freight railway operators in Australia**

State	Private integrated				Pub integ	Public tenant	Private tenant						
	PN	AP	G&W Aus	NRG	QRG	QR Nat	PN	GC	SS	S&S	PP	P&O	LV
SA		X	X	X		X	X		X	X	X	X	
Tas	X												
WA						X	X			X			
QL					X		X						
Vic	X					X	X		X	X	X	X	
NSW						X	X	X	X	X	X		X
NT		X											
ACT							X						

State	Wholly privately and vertically integrated			
	Pilbara	BHP Iron Ore	Comalco	Onesteel
SA				X
Tas				
WA	X	X		
QL			X	
Vic				
NSW				
NT				
ACT				
State				

Source: ARA (2006).

Figure 5.10. **Australasian Railway Association map**

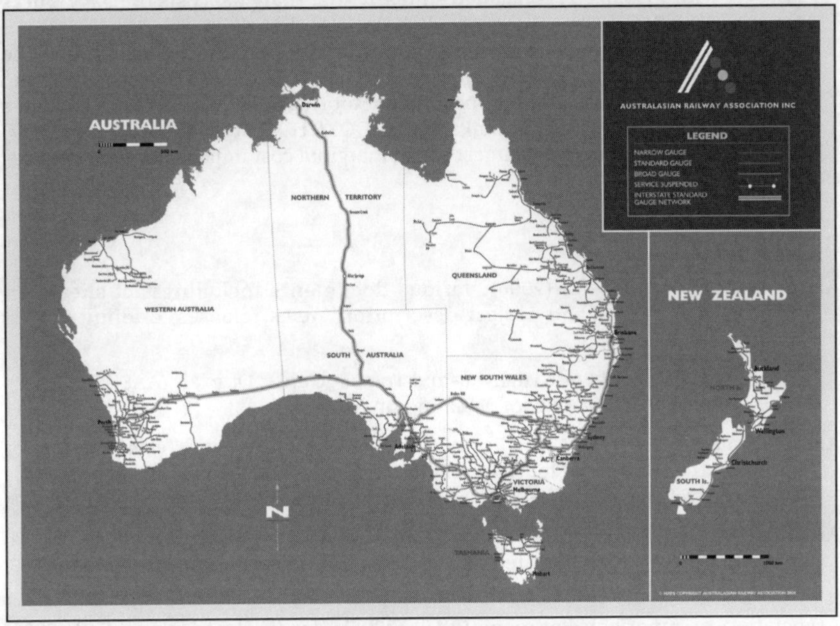

Note: Used by permission of the Australian Railway Association.

Notes

1. The definition of "new construction" is not precise. The amount given includes not only new construction, but also rehabilitation and, in some cases, major maintenance.
2. Correspondence with David Stambrook of Virtuosity Consulting, Canada, dated 11 April 2006.
3. The definition of "congestion" in the US may be different than in the EU, so common conclusions are always approximate.
4. See ORNL 2006, pp. 2-17. Conservatively assumes average load/truck of 20 tons.
5. See US Department of Transportation, Bureau of Transportation Statistics, "National Transportation Statistics", Tables 2-4 and Tables 1-46b.
6. In Russian practice, an "operator" is a company that owns freight wagons and asks the main carrier to haul trains with a discount reflecting wagons ownership costs.
7. "Moving block" signals, in which computers automatically calculate the position of each train and regulate the speeds of all trains, have so far been restricted to the controlled conditions of mass transit. They have not been proven yet on regular rail lines. If moving block signals can be proven safe and effective, they could have a significantly positive impact on line capacity.
8. Calculations of social marginal costs are difficult. Work done at Leeds University (see Sansom, *et al.* 2001, p. 49) suggested that Heavy Goods Vehicles impose social costs (the largest component of which is congestion) that fall far short of charges

paid. In fact, the same was true of all highway users. Comparable studies in the US (see, *e.g.* TRB 1996, p. 98) concluded similarly that marginal costs of heavy trucks far exceeded the charges imposed on them, and that the major components of social marginal costs were congestion and accidents. The report studied the specific case of containers moving by truck from Los Angeles to Chicago and found that congestion accounted for almost half of total social marginal costs. Though a direct comparison is harder to make, the US DOT/FHWA study (US DOT 2000, p. 17) found that congestion is the largest social marginal cost imposed by heavy trucks.

Bibliography

Alameda Corridor website (2006), various documents including fact sheets on history, governance and project description; news releases; briefing charts, *www.acta.org*.

American Association of State Highway and Transportation Officials (AASHTO) (2002), *Transportation: Invest in America*, Washington DC.

Andrieu, Michel (2007), "A Cross-Sectoral Synthesis on the Long-Term Outlook for Infrastructure Business Models", in *Infrastructure to 2030 (Volume 2): Mapping Policy for Electricity, Water and Transport*, OECD, Paris.

Andrieu, Michel (2005), "The Long-Term Global Outlook for Investment in Infrastructures", paper prepared for the OECD IFP project on Infrastructure to 2030, Paris, 12 December 2005.

Association of American Railroads (AAR) (2005), *Handbook of Railroad Facts 2005*, Washington DC.

Assocation of Train Operating Companies (ATOC) (2005), *Looking Forward: Contribution to Railway Strategy*, London.

Australasian Railway Association, Inc. (ARA) (2006), *Australian Rail 2004: The 2004 Productivity Report*, Kingston, ACT, Australia.

Australian Rail Track Corporation Ltd. (ARTC) (2005), *Annual Report 2004-2005*, *www.artc.com.au/company/annual.htm*.

Bureau of Transport and Regional Economics (2006), "Freight Measurement and Modelling in Australia", Report 112, government of Australia, Canberra.

Chicago Region Environmental and Transportation Efficiency Program (CREATE) (2005), *Final Feasibility Plan*, August, *www.createprogram.org*.

Dewey Shipping Consultants Ltd. (2005), *Annual Review of Global Container Terminal Operators – 2005*.

European Council of Ministers of Transport (ECMT) (2005), *Railway Reform and Charges for the Use of Infrastructure*, OECD, Paris.

ECMT (2006), "Public Accounting and Asset Quality Data: Reporting Requirements for Effective Regulation of Rail Infrastructure", CEMT/CS/CF(2006)2, OECD, Paris.

European Commission (EC) (2001), "White Paper, European Transport Policy for 2010: Time to Decide", Luxemburg.

EC (2005), "Networks for Peace and Development: Extension of the Major Trans-European Transport Axes to the Neighboring Countries and Regions", November, Luxembourg.

EC (2005), "Trans-European Transport Network: TEN-T Priority Axes and Projects 2005", Luxembourg.

Flyvbjerg, Bent, Nils Bruzelius and Werner Rothengatter (2003), *Megaprojects and Risk*, Cambridge University Press, Cambridge.

IEA (2003), ETP Transport Model, Spreadsheet version 1.28.

International Union of Railways (UIC), *International Railway Statistics*.

Kain, Peter (2006), "The Pitfalls in Competitive Tendering: Addressing the Risks Revealed by Experience in Australia and Britain", paper for 12 January ECMT workshop on competitive tendering of rail services.

McClellan, James (2006), "Railroad Capacity Issues", paper for TRB Conference in Railroad R&D Needs for the Future, Washington DC.

McCullough, Gerard (2005), "US Railroad Efficiency: A Brief Economic Overview", Department of Applied Economics, University of Minnesota, Minneapolis.

National Economic Research Associates (NERA) (2004), *Study of the Financing of and Public Budget Contribution to Railways*, London.

Netherlands Court of Audit (Algemene Rekenkamer) (2000), *Policy Information on the Betuwe Line*, *www.rekenkamer.nl/9282200/v/indexdom.htm*.

Penfold, Andrew (undated), "The Future of Seaborne Trade – Supply, Demand and Innovation", PIANC 2020 (Permanent International Association of Navigation Congresses) meeting briefing charts.

Prorail (2006), Network Statement 2006, Netherlands, *www.prorail.nl*.

Prorail (2007), Network Statement 2007, Netherlands, *www.prorail.nl*.

Quinlan, Howard G. (revised 2005), "Route-Kilometer Statistics Tracing the Evolution of Australian Public Railways to 20 June 1997", Australian Railway Historical Society (ACT Division), Canberra.

Sansom, Tom, Chris Nash, Peter Mackie, Jeremy Shires and Paul Watkins (2001), "Surface Transport Costs and Charges", Institute for Transport Studies, University of Leeds, United Kingdom.

Schrank, David and Tim Lomax (2005), "The 2005 Urban Mobility Report", Texas Transportation Institute, College Station.

Stambrook, David (2006), "Key Factors Driving the Future Demand for Surface Transport Infrastructure and Services", in *Infrastructure to 2030: Telecom, Land Transport, Water and Electricity*, OECD, Paris.

Thompson, Louis S. (2003), "Changing Railway Structure and Ownership: Is Anything Working", *Transport Reviews*, Vol. 23, No. 3.

Transportation Research Board (TRB) (1996), "Paying Our Way: Estimating Marginal Social Costs of Freight Transportation", Special Report 246, Washington DC.

TRB (2002), "Freight Capacity for the 21st Century", Special Report No. 271, Washington DC.

United Nations Conference on Trade and Development (UNCTAD) (2005), "Review of Maritime Transport, 2005", United Nations, New York and Geneva.

US Congressional Budget Office (CBO) (2006), "Freight Rail Transportation: Long-Term Issues", January, Washington DC.

US Department of Energy, Oak Ridge National Laboratory (ORNL) (2006), *Transportation Energy Data Book*, 25th Edition.

US Department of Transportation (DOT), Bureau of Transportation Statistics (2003), National Transportation Statistics.

US DOT, Federal Highway Administration (FHWA) (2000), *Addendum to the 1997 Federal Highway Cost Allocation Study*, May, Washington DC.

US DOT FHWA (2005), *International Freight Studies: Summary Report on Europe*, performed late 2000, updated June 2005, *http://ops.fhwa.dot.gov/freight/freight_analysis/euro_scan/index.htm*.

US DOT, Federal Maritime Commission (2005), *Report to Congress on the Performance of Ports and the Intermodal System*, June, Washington DC.

US Surface Transportation Board (STB) (1978 to present), *Statistics of Class I Railroads*, various issues, Washington DC.

Vassallo, Jose Manuel and Mark Fagan (2005), "Nature or Nurture: Why Do Railroads Carry Greater Freight Share in the United States Than in Europe", WP05-15, Harvard University, Kennedy School of Government, Cambridge.

Waterfront Coalition (2005), "National Marine Container Transportation: A Call to Action", May, Washington DC.

Williams, Robert, David Greig and Ian Wallis (2005), "Results of Railway Privatization in Australia and New Zealand", World Bank Transport Paper TP-7, September.

World Bank (2005), *Global Economic Prospects 2005*, Washington DC.

World Bank (2006), *Global Economic Prospects 2006*, Washington DC.

World Bank (undated), Railways Database, data covering 1980 to 2003/4, *www.worldbank.org/transport/rail/rdb.htm*.

ISBN 978-92-64-03131-9
Infrastructure to 2030 – Vol. 2
Mapping Policy for Electricity, Water and Transport

Chapter 6

Strategic Issues for the Future Funding and Operation of Urban Public Transport Systems

by
Yves Crozet*

This chapter provides a review of the operation and funding of urban public transport (UPT) systems and describes the challenges that the sector will have to meet in the future. How can diverse models of public transport systems contribute to urban dynamics? How will UPT be integrated into increasingly multimodal systems? This chapter details how UPT financing, pricing and organisation must be viewed from the more general perspective of urban policy.

* Professor, University of Lyon 2, and Director, Transport Economics Laboratory, Joint Research Unit (CNRS) No. 5593, France.

1. Introduction

Towns and cities account for a growing share of the global population, often over 80% in developed countries. They also produce the largest share of value added, in both industry and services. Urban quality and efficiency are accordingly key variables, as much for economic growth as for compliance with the requirements of sustainable development.

Yet the quality and efficiency of our towns and cities are directly related to transport, and more specifically passenger transport. In this field, urban public transport (UPT) poses specific problems and its role is currently undergoing change. Often viewed as a service for largely captive, low-income users, they once seemed confined exclusively to the public sector. But as the public sector everywhere is facing growing financial constraints, does this mean that urban public transport is under threat? Will the universal popularity of private cars one day sound the death knell of transport systems whose investment needs and operating subsidies are a drain on the public purse?

The answer to this question has changed over the past few decades. Following a period of relative decline, more large cities have decided to boost investment in UPT in light of projected needs to 2025/30, both in the industrialised world and in emerging countries such as Brazil, China and India. The new popularity of public transport, in particular projects involving segregated infrastructure, will not drive down public spending, quite the contrary. However, it does confirm the principle familiar to economists for a century now and known as "Wagner's Law", whereby the development of an industrial economy will be accompanied by increasing demand for public intervention. This is particularly relevant in urban areas where the smooth running of economic activities, as well as flourishing social and cultural activities, call for government policies that provide the community with the public goods it requires.

The law that A. Wagner formulated at the turn of the 20th century has been confirmed by the underlying rise in public spending as a share of GDP. But the very fact that it has proved to be true poses a problem in terms of logic. Public expenditure already exceeds 30% of GDP in the US and Japan, and 40% or even 50% (Sweden, France) in much of western Europe. So there is a need to rethink the forms that public policy can take in many sectors, including UPT. There should be no hesitation in conducting in-depth reviews of the situation in each of the sectors where government plays a strong role. These include education, health and research but also network industries such as water, energy, telecommunications and transport. Such industries, particularly transport, often make intensive use of government funds, owing to their infrastructure requirements. Consequently, given the budgetary constraints on government departments, every avenue should be explored with a view to optimising UPT services, while at the same time ensuring that public spending does not get out of hand.

This chapter endeavours to provide input for an in-depth review of the operation and funding of UPT systems and is divided into four sections:

1. The first section looks at the UPT systems in terms of their current mode of operation, rationale and limits. What is the reason for the significant differences found across countries and continents? Are these differences entrenched?
2. The second section is a reminder that the widely differing approaches to UPT operations and management reflect the highly diverse range of urban management approaches. Can we identify any typical "urban models" and how can public transport systems contribute, within each model, to urban dynamics?
3. The third section looks at current and future changes in the organisation and funding of UPT. Over and above the new demands for efficient and transparent financing, how can UPT help to promote sustainable mobility, and with what resources?
4. The fourth and final section looks at the challenges that the UPT sector will have to meet in 2030. How will UPT be integrated into increasingly multimodal systems? What funding mechanisms will be put in place? How will the UPC sector open the door to technical and institutional innovation? How will mobility policies be evaluated, and by whom?

2. Urban public transport: varied country responses

Tourists who are fortunate enough to visit many cities in the industrialised world will have the initial impression that they are all fairly similar. Everywhere there will be buses and sometimes trams, underground or subway systems and railway trains. Fares and pricing will be different, and network maps and timetables will be more or less easy to find. Even if cities try to personalise their public transport networks, users will find that nothing looks more like a metro line than another metro line.

However, if we stop looking through a tourist's eyes and view the situation from the standpoint of the researcher instead,[1] we discover that these apparent similarities conceal some very marked differences in the way UPT systems are organised. Some cities have genuine decision-making powers, while others come under a regional authority or central government. In some cases, commercial revenue covers most of the operating costs, and even investment. In others, government subsidies can cover as much as 80% of the costs. The UPT sector may be entirely government-run, or the private sector may predominate, with or without a detailed mandate. Insight is therefore required into this organisational diversity. To gain that insight, we shall first pose some key questions, before endeavouring to understand why the answers to those questions vary so widely across cities and across countries.

2.1. Key questions with regard to urban public transport

Although it may be a somewhat simplistic way of presenting the issues, there are four basic questions facing organisations providing UPT services:

- Who designs UPT?
- Who operates UPT?
- Who funds UPT?
- Who uses UPT?

Who designs UPT?

UPT provision seldom stems from private initiative. Bus, tram, underground and suburban train networks were set up by public bodies and not intended to be profit-making concerns. We are not dealing with a textbook example of market economics here.

UPT provision in some cities, particularly in the developing world, is entirely private. Individuals or firms, for instance, offer passenger minibus services, for which they charge fares set simply by supply and demand, on routes which are known solely to users and which can sometimes vary. However interesting those private initiatives may be,[2] they are not a benchmark for UPT systems in industrialised countries. And there is little chance that they will become one, for a simple reason linked to the nature of passenger transport services in urban areas. Even if UPT systems are used by individual passengers according to their needs, such services fall into the broader category of public goods. More specifically, the UPT sector has experienced several market failures, described in public economics over the past 50 years.

As a network industry, UPT – and in particular segregated public transport (SPT) – is characterised by increasing returns. It therefore features natural monopolies, or more specifically local monopolies requiring government policy upstream from service provision to determine routes, types of service, frequency and other details.

Such public policy is particularly necessary because of the social considerations involved. UPT is often the only reliable means of medium-distance transport for those on low incomes.

But economic considerations also enter the equation. Many in the low-income groups, who are more or less captive users of urban transport, are making a very worthwhile contribution to the economic vigour of their town or city. Consequently, just as road networks are developed and maintained under government supervision, UPT – whether segregated or not – is a government responsibility. It is a question of externalities.

The same applies to the environment. Well-organised UPT systems do less harm per passenger, or per passenger-kilometre, than private cars. This is one of the main reasons for recent expansion, namely potential, on segregated infrastructure, to ease road congestion problems.

The many different economic, social, environmental and other needs met by UPT make it essentially a political good. As one of the flagship components of the urban environment and of the city as a public good, UPT cannot leave elected representatives indifferent. For that reason it is increasingly included in policy plans that go beyond the confines of transport. When the policy planners decide to create or extend underground or tram lines, or map out bus routes, they are building our cities just as much as when they are building new roads, and just as much as any real-estate developer.

The answer to the question "who designs UPT?" is therefore fairly straightforward. UPT is very largely contingent, in the industrialised world, on government policy makers. But we should bear in mind the wide range of administrative departments involved in fleshing out the policy outline provided by politicians. It may therefore be worthwhile taking a closer look at the extent to which government policy making is decentralised. Do city councils really have the resources for their own UPT policy or are they hampered by national or regional constraints? How much weight, for instance, do city councillors carry *vis-à-vis* regional councillors? And when the city, as an administrative entity, is but one component of an entire urban community, are there political and administrative entities that are capable of acting on the right scale? To what extent, if at all, will regional rail services be co-ordinated with urban transport *per se*, for instance? This raises another question, of course, that of how systems are operated, but it also suggests that we bear in mind a lesson learned in public economics: while excessive government intervention may carry risks, too little or poorly targeted government intervention is a symmetrical risk that should not be underestimated.

With regard to large urban areas, the question is not just who designs UPT, but whether the entity in charge of service provision is working to the right scale or ensuring sufficient co-ordination with the neighbouring authorities, which amounts to the same thing.

Who operates UPT?

For a long time, UPT operations were closely tied in with design. Just as in railway networks there was originally no separation between design and operations, or between infrastructure provision and the operational side, in UPT systems, single operators were virtually the rule from the outset. However, the situation gradually evolved and a distinction was gradually made between owners and operators. This has led to diversification in the number of players involved, as shown in Figure 6.1 below, based on the EU's research programme named MARETOPE (Managing and Assessing Regulatory Evolution in local public Transport Operations in Europe).

Figure 6.1. **UPT systems: owner and operators**

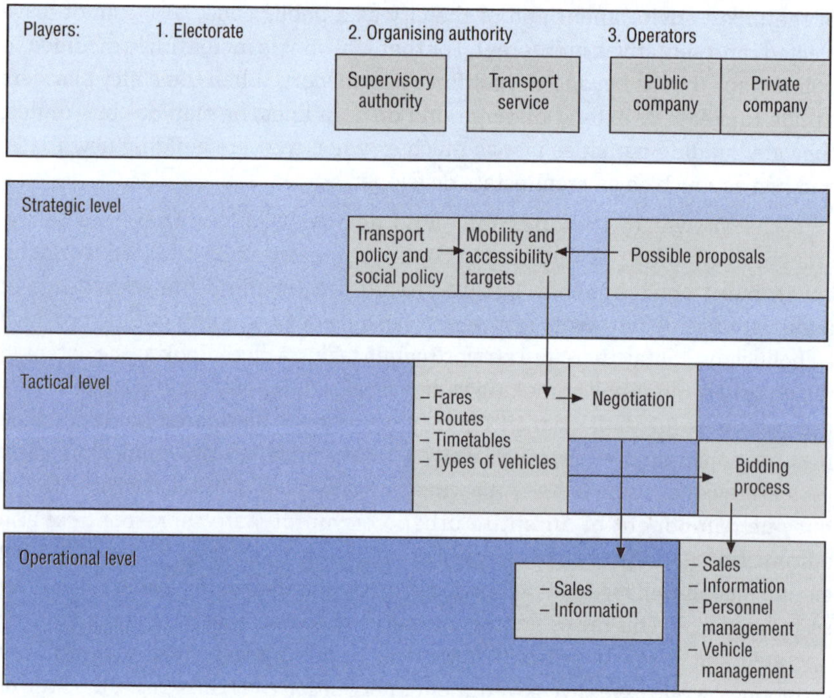

Source: Based on MARETOPE analysis.

The columns in the figure show the distinction between ownership by the organising authorities and management by operators (private, public or a partnership between the two).

The rows, at each level, show the strategic, tactical and operational issues. The purpose of this distinction is to reveal some of the very practical issues, such as routes and fares. In other words, service provision *per se* can be broken down into a host of separate components and the relevant responsibilities can be allocated in very different ways.

The distinction between the strategic, tactical and operational levels is interesting. A strategic situation is one in which there is some uncertainty as to the political and technical context. A purely tactical situation is one in which all of the parameters of the context are known. The difference between the two provides an insight into an initial form of responsibility sharing. The public sector, with its political and administrative components, retains responsibility for strategic decision-making. The operators merely make suggestions. While they are beginning to wield some negotiating powers on tactical issues, their real room for manoeuvre is confined to operations.

While the prime feature of this diagram is its logic, it is not set in stone. It allows the transfer of players to different levels of responsibility, and markedly alters the big picture by calling into question, for instance, direct service provision by the public sector (government department or agency) and replacing it with a concession or "public service delegation" (as in France). The UPT sector has long seen various forms of public-private partnership (PPP) aimed in particular at reducing operating costs in response to funding problems.

Who funds UPT?

By and large, UPT is expensive and the fares charged to users generally cover only a small share of the overall cost. Only a few cities in Asia with very heavy traffic receive enough operating revenue to cover not only their operating costs but also their investment costs. European cities, apart from some exceptions, are nowhere near breaking even. In most cases, commercial revenue covers no more than 50%, or even 30% of their current expenditure. The same applies to North America where public transport is heavily subsidised in that it targets what is very largely a captive market.

This means that other sources of financing have to be found. They are fairly varied and fall into the following categories:

- General taxes, by local or national authorities. In this case, the resources derived from government budgets are simply turned into subsidies.
- Special taxes, on those who benefit indirectly from UPT services.
  - One option is to tax businesses, whose employees are potential UPT beneficiaries. This is the case in urban France with the "*Versement Transport*", a payroll tax on firms with a workforce of 10 or more. This represents a substantial amount of funding, in some cases exceeding commercial revenue, and can have unwanted adverse effects on the labour market – not to mention the threshold effect which encourages very small firms to employ no more than nine people.

- In some cases, too, UPT may receive special funding, such as fines from illegal parking. Some cities (*e.g.* London, Singapore and Oslo) have introduced congestion charges for cars, some of which will go to improve public transport. In spite of initial hostility to the idea of charging urban road users, city councils are showing increasing interest in such schemes. The city of Stockholm has just launched a six-month experiment along these lines.
- Another form of special tax targets property owners. Whether it is regular (annual tax) or one-off (when new infrastructure is introduced), the idea is for the local authority to recuperate all or part of the capital gain linked to the presence of efficient UPT. Consequently such schemes mainly concern SPT, but are rather hard to organise.

- Along the same lines as capital gains, it is possible to envisage sophisticated forms of PPP, whereby the company operating SPT as a concession is also allocated a specific amount of land around the new line. It is then up to that company to utilise the capital gains on that land as a means of balancing its operating budget. This kind of scheme has been used in Asia and a few cities in the US. However, it cannot be readily brought into more widespread use.

So there are numerous different ways of funding UPT, and the fact that government subsidies and/or cross-subsidies are common shows that this is a sector marked by externalities. The idea is that the indirect beneficiaries of UPT should pay. But who are the direct beneficiaries of this kind of redistributive system?

Who uses UPT?

UPT users do not fall into a single category. To grasp just how diverse they are, we have to distinguish between cities (in terms of size, for instance), modes of transport, areas covered and even times of day.

To simplify matters, some UPT systems consist in a few bus routes, on which services are slow, infrequent and, in most cases, cheap. The passengers will generally be captive users who, for a variety of financial and other reasons, have no access to cars. They are on low incomes and are either elderly or young people who do not have access to a car. In such cases, there is almost a social stigma attached to using public transport ("I know what kind of person has to take a bus!").

At the other end of the customer scale are the users of rapid, segregated public transport systems in the larger city centres. In the heart of London, for instance, 85% of those who travel use public transport. They are probably not low-income passengers. The same applies to cities in Asia, and to most of the major world capitals. When UPT services provide comfortable services and acceptable overall journey times, the users become more high-profile. Of the 20 million US residents who take suburban trains every day, some are private-car owners who appreciate the reliability of UPT. In the same category are the users of SPT services between city centres and major airports (London Heathrow Express, Arlanda-Stockholm, Brussels, Amsterdam-Schiphol). The overall trip speed of these links, much faster than taxis in the rush hour, is such a persuasive business argument that fares can more accurately reflect real costs.

Between these two extremes, with on the one hand subsidised less affluent, captive users and, on the other, affluent users who pay the costs they generate, a whole range of contrasting UPT situations are to be found. Some of the main differences depend on the part of the city concerned. In European city centres, UPT are increasingly used by non-captive passengers who prefer public transport to car use or even car ownership. In Paris, for instance, half of all households do not have a car at their disposal in the city – usually out of choice. This raises the question of whether fares should not be more in line with their ability to pay. Another similar question relates to the status and efficiency of transport operators. These are just two of many questions which prove that the organisational form of UPT is not set in stone.

2.2. *Contrasts and change in national and local choices*

The main characteristic of the UPT sector is its diversity. It is hard to compare a small town with a handful of bus routes and a teeming metropolis with several million inhabitants and dozens of kilometres of SPT. But the differences stem not just from the geographical and social background alone, but from national and local traditions. Some countries choose to maintain government-run UPT whereas others resort more to competition and private initiative. Below is a broad matrix illustrating some of the standard models that have served to organise UPT systems. It will enable us to see how organisation patterns can change.

An organisational matrix

Returning to the four key questions (who designs/operates/finances/uses UPT?) and some typical responses, we have identified four "models" or cases that will illustrate how wide a variety of situations there is. In reality, there is a continuum in UPT organisation patterns, stemming from the fact that such systems are a mix of economic, social and political factors.

The public sector model describes a situation found in many European and North American cities, where UPT is viewed more or less as a social service, and the rationale is largely redistributive. Consequently it is designed, managed and funded mainly by government.

Table 6.1. **UPT organisation: four "models"**

"Models"	Who designs UPT?	Who operates UPT?	Who finances UPT?	Who uses UPT?
Public sector (increasingly rare)	Government	Government or agency	Mainly taxpayers	Mainly captive users
Private initiative (urban minibus services in Brazil and Turkey)	Many small operators	Many small operators	Users	Middle and lower-middle classes
Public service delegation (continental Europe)	Organising authority and to some extent operators	Private or semi-private operators	Users, special taxes and general taxes	Various social groups
Allocation (*e.g.* United Kingdom, Sweden)	Organising authority	Several operators	Users and specific/general taxes	Various social groups

In clear contrast with the previous model, and in many cases set up in response to public failures, the private initiative "model" is the kind of private scheme found in some major cities in Latin America and Africa, but also Istanbul. These are based on private initiative and consist in minibus services.

Back in Europe again, there are two "models" that are fairly typical of the changes currently taking place. The first seeks to transfer the government's responsibility for operating UPT to others via public service delegation (*délégation de service public*) or concessions. An operator is chosen to manage the entire UPT network. This means competing "for the market" rather than "in the market" as in the previous example. Competition is found only at the bidding stage. Operators compete to submit the best bids.

Another way of introducing more competition while allowing government to retain much of its control over design is to increase the number of operators. In the "allocation" system, the UPT network is divided up and auctioned off to various operators in a tendering process. London, for instance, has allocated around 700 bus routes via some 500 auctions. In such cases, operators become no more than owner/operators. They have extremely little room for manoeuvre other than to cut costs, which is precisely the aim of this "model". It is also common practice in northern Europe (Sweden).

The interesting point highlighted by this matrix is that systems are not stable. As there are many sometimes contradictory selection criteria, policy makers may want to change the system to prevent it from becoming too "permanent" and favouring a specific player. The key issue should therefore be the impetus for change. Can it come from UPT policy makers alone or from private initiatives? Should these not be encouraged as a means of breaking the inertia inherent in certain models?

Uneven progress in the role of competition and private players

The wave of deregulation in the early 1980s also affected UPT. Private operators emerged to play a growing role in many countries and become part of vast multinational firms like Veolia, Kéolis and Transdev. But it should be borne in mind that public transport provision is still very closely tied to policy, and even politics. Elected representatives do not readily relinquish this kind of political leverage. This is one of the factors that restricts competition in such cases. Figure 6.1 shows what changes are possible in the roles allocated to each player.

A comparison of Figures 6.2 and 6.3 illustrates that there is scope for some very different options. There could be change, for instance, in the way the various responsibilities (routes, fares, transport policy) relate to one another.

In some forms of deregulation (Figure 6.2), government intervention is reduced to monitoring compliance with the rules on competition. Much of the tactical side and even some of the strategic aspects then fall to the carriers.

Conversely (Figure 6.3), other forms of deregulation may reduce the carrier's role to that of owner-operator.

Figure 6.2. **Transferring responsibility to the private sector**

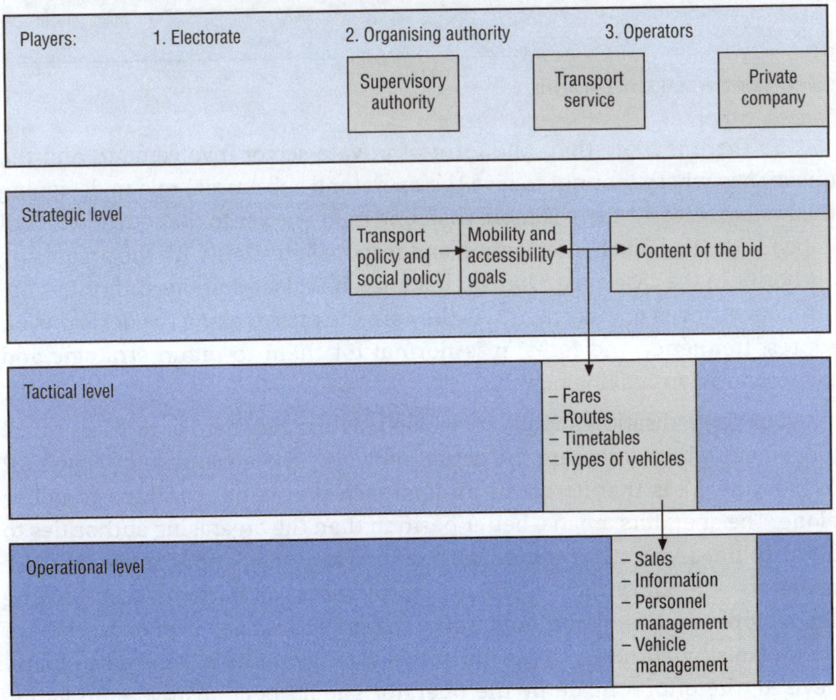

Source: Based on MARETOPE analysis.

Figure 6.3. **Private initiative reduced to the operational function**

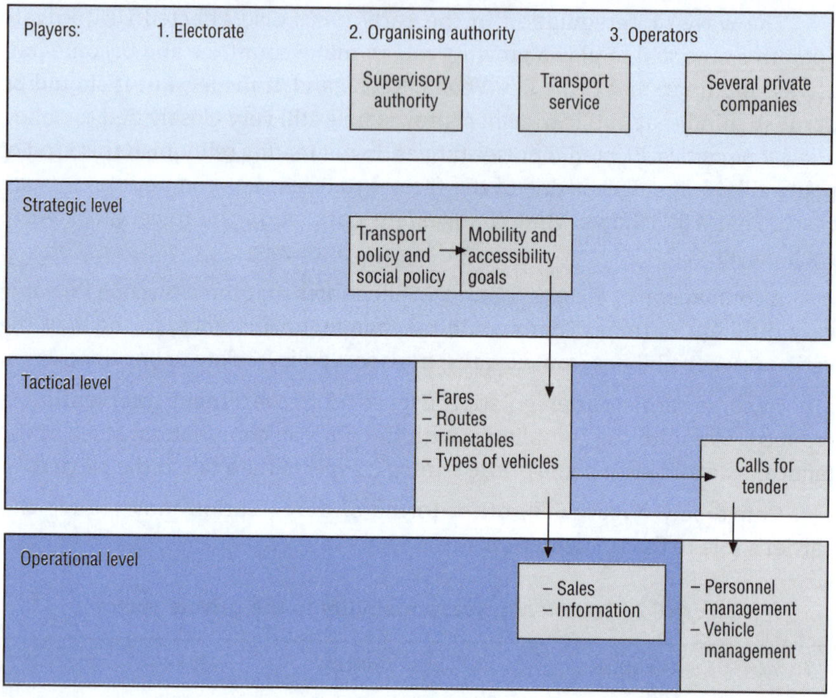

Source: Based on MARETOPE analysis.

So there is more than one form of private sector involvement, and the question is whether or not to give the operator a substantial role in designing the system. Clearly, there is more than one right answer to that question. It all depends on how much information and responsibility lies with the organising authority. In the case of London, for instance, it is clear that the authorities are familiar with bus management. As they are the ones making the decisions on routes, frequency and fares, it is normal for them to retain strategic and tactical decision-making powers.

But generalisation should be avoided, as the risk here is to lack critical judgement when designing the actual network. The advantage of Figure 6.2 over Figure 6.3 is that it reveals an approach that is not confined to policy alone. The operators are in a better position than the organising authorities to identify lines, routes or zones with a very low cost/utility ratio. It is the operators who know their customers and their travel patterns best. Leaving them scope to adjust provision is not necessarily a loss of power on the part of the organising authority. If the incentive arrangements have been properly devised, the efforts made by the operator should be a positive-sum game, *i.e.* improved cost-efficiency and a better situation for users and the public

Box 6.1. **Strategic questions for 2025-30**

- In the cities of the industrialised world, how much control do local authorities have over the design of UPT systems? Are they really holding the reins? If not, what should be done to ensure that they are?
- UPT systems are seldom funded by users alone. Other sources of finance therefore have to be found, one being the indirect beneficiaries. There is already some "good practice" in the form of contributions from employers or property owners. These will have to be developed. When users are genuinely in a position to pay, one option to be envisaged would be to increase their share.
- UPT remains a "policy goal" of prime importance at the local level. That does not mean that it should remain an entirely government-run concern. Recourse to private initiative and competition is possible, for instance by letting operators develop community-friendly innovation.

purse. In other words, innovation should be possible, just as it is in other sectors of the economy.

3. How does public transport contribute to urban dynamics?

Major cities are facing an ongoing challenge, namely accessibility. This is crucial, as three features now characterise metropolitan areas: urban sprawl, social segregation and road congestion. All three are accentuating distances, be they spatial, temporal or social. To prevent such developments from undermining the functional unity of urban areas, transport policies must clarify their goals, and this is where urban public transport can play a growing role. In years to come it is UPT that will be providing accessibility, the key to successful cities.

3.1. *The role of transport in successful cities*

Cities have occasionally been described as "organised proximity". This kind of rationale highlights the fact that urban activities are organised by combining location decisions and transport systems. The very existence of our towns and cities is based on the beneficial agglomeration effects that stem from density. We shall now look at some of the features that characterise urban density and the reasons why public transport is relevant in dense environments and, by the same token, less relevant in the kind of lower-density urban and peri-urban environments that are found in North America, for instance.

Key indicators in major cities

The information contained in the UITP (Union internationale des transports publics) database on "Millennium Cities" can be used to identify some of the salient features of cities around the world in terms of both similarities and differences. We have selected three main indicators, namely public transport use, overall trip speed and distance covered.

The modal share of UPT in daily urban mobility is the first sign that cities are not organised in the same way in the various geographical areas used in the UITP database. For instance, in the five typical Asian cities (Tokyo, Singapore, Hong Kong, China, Osaka and Sapporo), UPT accounts for over 50% of all passenger-kilometres in terms of motorised mobility. The ratio falls to 7.5% in five major cities in Oceania (Brisbane, Melbourne, Perth, Sydney and Wellington). Admittedly, the latter are smaller in size, which limits the relevance of public transport. But this should not mask the differences in public preferences, as in the comparison between Europe and North America.

In the UITP database, UPT accounts for only 5% of all motorised passenger-kilometres compared with 20% in the 32 European cities in the study. There is strong dispersal around the mean, and the salient features are not only national but local, as in the case of Geneva and Zurich, where UPT accounts for 10% and 25%, respectively, of motorised mobility. Across the Atlantic, UPT accounts for 12% to 13% of motorised mobility in Montreal and Toronto, compared with less than 1% in Phoenix and Houston. The latter are entirely given over to cars, which usually travel at faster average speeds than UPT. This is shown in Figure 6.4 below. With the y-axes giving average UPT speeds and the x-axes the average speed of private vehicles as indicated in the UITP database, it is easy to see that UPT speed exceeds average road speeds in only a few cities. This is the case in only two Asian cities and two European cities, those located above the first bisector.

However, we should point out that there is, here too, a substantial difference between European cities and those in North America, where the average speed of private cars may be fairly high, giving rise to a tendency to urban sprawl. This can be seen in Figure 6.5, which demonstrates the paradoxical effect of car speed. When average speeds are high, urban users tend to cover greater distances. As assumed over thirty years ago by Zahavi (1980), when the travel time budget (TTB) is constant, those who are mobile reinvest in travel the time that they save through speed. Hence the increase in distance covered, which is something of a paradox for the low-density cities of North America. It is as if the fact that North American car-drivers travel faster encourages them to cover longer distances, but also to spend more time travelling, as we shall see below.

Figure 6.4. **Overall trip speeds for UPT and private cars in 57 cities throughout the world**

In kilometres per hour

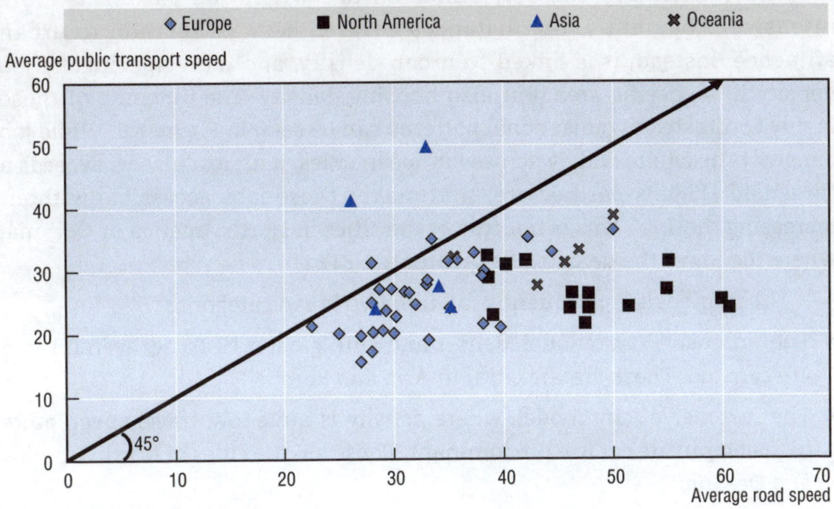

Source: UITP database on "Millenium Cities".

Figure 6.5. **Average daily distance covered per person and urban GDP per person in western Europe, North America, Oceania and major Asian cities**

In kilometres per day and USD thousands

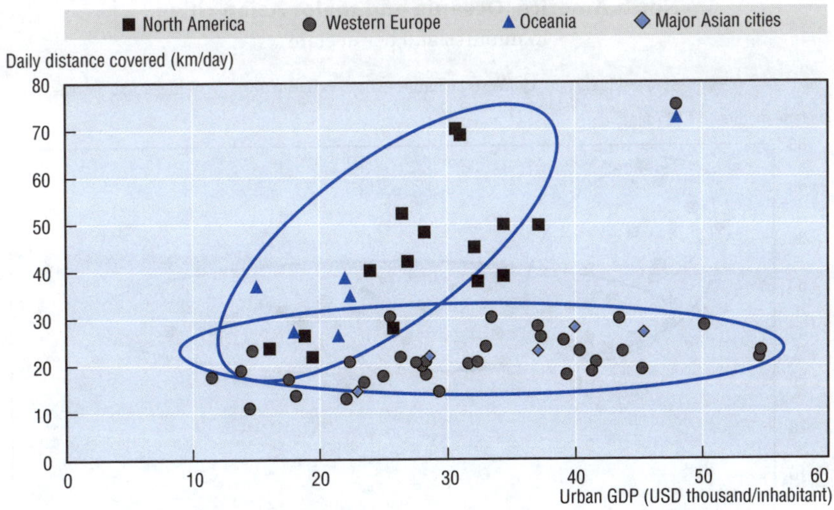

Source: UITP database on "Millenium Cities".

Two "urban models"?

The trend in US cities towards growth in distances and GDP is turning them into extensive entities, unlike Europe where the pattern is more intensive. Apparently, the distances covered bear no relation to urban affluence. Instead, it is linked to urban density, and more specifically job density in a specific area, but also housing density. The outcome of these highly contrasted organisational patterns can be seen in Figure 6.6. While job density varies quite widely across European cities, it almost always exceeds a threshold (15 jobs per hectare) that makes these jobs accessible without increasing the TTB. This is not true of the cities in North America or Oceania, where the lower the density, the greater the TTB.

Urban models consequently fall into two broad categories:

- The "intensive" city model, denser and with greater UPT use, even if there are cars too. These are the cities in Asia and Europe.
- The "extensive" city model, where density is quite low, travel speed quite high and private car use predominant. These are the cities of North America and Oceania.

In these cities, then, space and time are expanding, and this is an issue that needs to be addressed. With time becoming an increasingly scarce and probably the scarcest resource, we should be addressing the relevance of these two urban models and the role that UPT can play.

Figure 6.6. **Motorised TTB per person and job density in western Europe, North America, Oceania and major Asian cities**

In minutes and per hectare

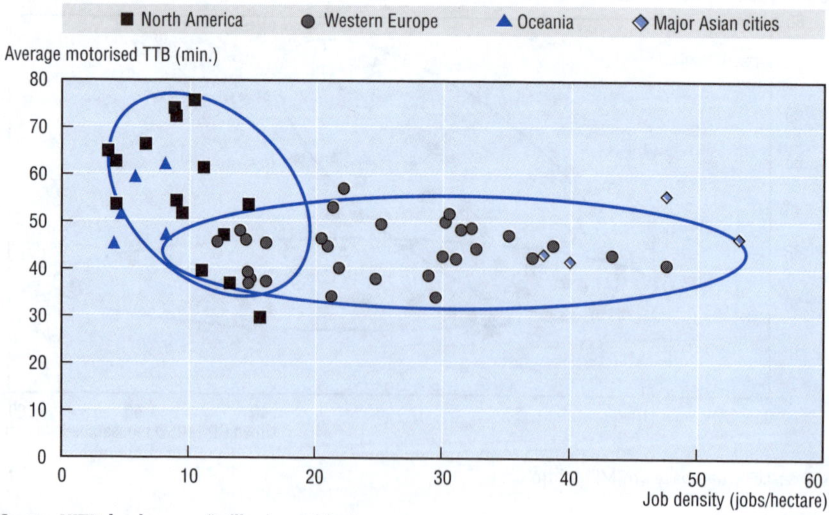

Source: UITP database on "Millenium Cities".

3.2. Public transport and accessibility

Whether cities are built according to the extensive or intensive model, they are increasingly having to cope with a lack of space, congestion (which suggests a lack of time) and the demands of sustainable development. For that reason, many are planning to develop UPT, in some cases as segregated PT. Going beyond the dictates of fashion and conventional wisdom on sustainable mobility, there is a need to show why UPT really does have a key role to play. We shall therefore reason on basis of the following assumption, namely that, if cities are to remain cities, if they are to continue producing agglomeration effects that benefit a majority of the population, then they should foster proximity among their residents. For a long time this issue was addressed in terms of space, but is now being approached in terms of time, via the notion of accessibility.

From proximity to accessibility: a new approach

If pedestrian cities have made accessibility rhyme with spatial proximity, motorised cities have done away with the location constraint. As far back as the 19th century in larger cities, the development of motorised transport enabled suburbs to develop at a distance from the city centre, thereby pushing back and spreading eroding the constraints imposed by a lack of space, expressed in economic terms as land rent. More recently, the widespread popularity of private cars and steady improvements in the road and motorway networks have allowed urban sprawl, or more precisely peri-urban development, *i.e.* urban fragmentation – to such an extent that most metropolitan areas no longer bear any relation to the official city limits or morphological city boundaries. It is increasingly common for people to live several kilometres, or tens of kilometres, away from their workplace, from the hypermarket where they do their shopping, or from the school that their children attend every day.

Addressing mobility merely as a transport issue, policies from the 1960s to the 1980s overlooked a hidden side effect of the drive to encourage faster travel, namely spatial and social distance. The advantage of extending the range of travel, largely thanks to cars, lies in the scope to segment (or segregate) urban functions. Today we know that there are limits to the rationales developed in the Athens Charter.[3] Dissociating housing and employment, housing and leisure or housing and stores not only puts a certain distance between urban functions, it may also put distance between social groups. Beyond the opportunities and constraints of daily mobility, cities are emerging in which the accessibility issue is becoming acute. How can we ensure that the residents of a metropolitan area, irrespective of social rank, continue to have access to all urban amenities? In other words, how do we prevent distances from growing, in terms of not only space but time (particularly because of road congestion)? This prompts another question: what is accessibility?

Box 6.2. **Accessibility: from transport costs to "density of opportunities"**

In 1959, W.G. Hansen developed a measurement of accessibility. He did this by first considering that travel patterns were proportional to the number of goods in the destination area and proportional to a decreasing function of generalised cost. He revealed the notion of choice indices by taking a transport link "ij" and varying urbanisation in "j" (*e.g.* increased job supply) and transport conditions between the two zones (increased cost of transport). He then applied the law of travel patterns to this link "ij" as follows: "For user satisfaction to remain constant (irrespective of change), any linear progression in the cost of travel should be associated with a progression multiplying the choices offered at the destination."

J.G. Koenig (1974) then formalised this second approach in an "economic theory of urban accessibility", taking up the microeconomic theory of consumption based on utility maximisation under constraints. The main purpose of the economic theory of urban accessibility is to evaluate access to jobs. To do this, Koenig assumes that consumers associate net utility (the difference between the advantages derived from a job, such as salary or job interest, and the costs relating to that job, such as the generalised cost of travel between home and work) to any job offered in the area. Koenig also assumes that the gross utility of a job is a random variable, of which the law of probabilities is a negative exponential function. The value of this theory lies in two key results. First, it establishes a link between the gravity model of traffic patterns and the microeconomic theory of consumption. Second, it allows a disaggregate analysis of utility according to various categories of consumer. However, while empirical studies have validated this theory based on microeconomic assumptions and the use of a negative exponential function for gross job utility, caution is advisable when moving from accessibility as a "service quality indicator" to its use in economic calculations aimed at assessing the economic value of a particular project.

In developing this economic theory of urban accessibility, Koenig considers a transport network as a vector of opportunities. Through the performance of a transport network, accessibility becomes a measurement of the supply of opportunities available to a household (or set of households), (Wachs and Koenig, 1979). Camagni, in 1996, takes up and develops the idea of accessibility as a source of new opportunities. For businesses, accessibility is viewed as scope to gather as much strategic information as possible before their competitors, while for individuals it is the scope to benefit from services confined to specific locations. In this approach, there is the positive nature of the accessibility concept, which is not confined to the costs inherent to any travel but also covers the advantages to be derived by the individual from using a transport network.

By establishing a link between opportunities and accessibility, these authors acknowledge the direct impact of accessibility on a person's activities. The more a destination area is accessible from the original area, the more people in that original area will increase their scope for potential activities and hence their satisfaction. This approach is in fact used in economic appraisals of urban transport projects,* which stipulate that the purpose of accessibility indicators is to measure the satisfaction that individuals derive from the transport system.

* For example, "Transports urbains et calcul économique", Working Paper No. 97-1, French Ministry of the Economy and Finance, Forecasting Directorate, Paris.

Following the work of Koenig (1974), economists and geographers were able to develop accessibility indicators, for a given point in space, by combining density and speed.

Density refers to the relative number of opportunities (including jobs and the number of inhabitants/shops/schools) in a particular area, accessible in what is considered to be an acceptable journey time, for instance one hour per day for a return journey.

Speed is a key component of the generalised travel cost, which associates monetary cost and the value of travel time. The greater the value of time, the greater the importance of speed in the generalised cost, particularly since improving speed automatically increases the accessible area and hence the number of opportunities available.

This rationale provides more insight into why government policy has been and still is drawn to the potential improvements in speed offered by new transport infrastructure. A motorway, or the widening of a trunk road, is a real step forward in terms of accessibility. The accessible area, and hence the scope for choice in terms of housing and potential jobs, grows substantially with the provision of rapid modes of transport. But this tendency to increase car speeds to enable users to "save time" runs up against two problems:

- First, it increases both spatial and social distances, while paradoxically increasing daily travel times. This steady creep tends to cause urban fragmentation, as in some North American cities where the growing number of "gated communities" is a negation of what cities should be.
- Second, it is an underlying factor that accentuates congestion, particularly for access to denser areas, density being the key feature of attractive cities.

It therefore comes as no surprise that, in dense urban areas, government policies have undergone a major shift. Without disregarding the lessons learned on accessibility, it is as if elected city representatives in Europe but also in Asia had ceased to bank on speed at any price and were instead opting for density and to reliability.

By developing relatively slow modes of transport such as tramways, new mobility policies have suggested that city-dwellers reconsider how they view accessibility. Rather than focusing on speed, and the distance it provides, residents are invited to make choices that reflect the advantages of density and to some extent proximity. There is accordingly a move towards denser urbanisation in the areas served by the new tram lines.

When warranted by the size of the city, in terms of both the distance to be covered and the number of daily commuters, the chosen option will be forms of SPT that move people faster than tramways. This will involve underground and regional express trains, a field requiring substantial investment in all of the world's major cities.

As if to show that reliability and speed were now the prerogative of public transport, many large cities have opted to curb or reduce average car speeds in urban areas by choosing not to reduce congestion. The initial grounds were road safety and the environment, but the main reason has been to break the spiral whereby increasing road capacity gradually induces traffic growth (see the Mogridge conjecture[4]).

Care should be taken not to be misled by the few cities that have introduced urban traffic charging (*e.g.* Singapore, London, Stockholm, Oslo, Bergen and Trondheim). In the charging zone, the aim is of course to keep traffic moving fluidly and thus at a guaranteed speed for those travelling by car. But this option is only available to a small section of the population. For the majority, it is public transport that will be ensuring access to urban opportunities. Controlling car flows by charging, as in London, or by road restrictions, as in Paris, are only two partially different forms of response to the same question, namely accessibility.

In the case of London, it should be borne in mind that the number of jobs in the "charging zone" far outstrips the number of residents (who pay only 10% of the daily EUR 12 charge). The purpose of charging is therefore to guarantee car access for a minority of working people with a high time value, the idea being that this will produce surplus revenue which goes to improving access by public transport.

In Paris, the ratio of residents to jobs is higher than one. This has dictated another rationale, whereby non-residents are dissuaded from driving into the city and invited to travel through Paris via public transport which, as explained above, is not financed solely by the city. Consequently, Paris has no objective reason to introduce charging.

The question of whether or not to introduce urban road charging is not the crux of the issue. The decisive question for the future of our cities is the quality of public transport and the accessibility it will provide.

Public transport and accessibility

The future of UPT lies in its ability to improve access to the denser urban areas with their wealth of jobs, shops, housing, entertainment and other urban amenities. Urban policies, particularly those promoting mobility, will therefore have to find a better fit between PT accessibility and the average speed of car trips.

Government policies should stop trying so hard to maintain car access over ever-vaster areas. On the contrary, they should try to foster – in conjunction with existing policies that promote public transport in the core cities of conurbations – improvements in public transport access for links between the centre and the outskirts. This would keep both jobs and residents in the core city, without creating a spatial, temporal and social divide with the outskirts, which by their very nature exist only in relation to the centre. Thus cities, or metropolitan areas, will extend beyond what are increasingly theoretical administrative boundaries and retain their functional unity. That unity should also be addressed in terms of the travel time budget, a neglected but vital factor in sustainable mobility.

Time has long been a factor in transport economics. Price-time models were developed in the 1960s and are now quite robust. But the basic assumption behind those models is that improving speed is a way of saving time. The travel time budget (TTB) is therefore viewed as a variable which consumers seek to minimise. Without denying the fact that consumers seek to maximise utility, we should nevertheless remember that the travel time saved through increased speed is usually reinvested in longer distance or in further travel for a new activity. This is what economists call the "Zahavi conjecture".

Without asserting that Zahavi's assumption is universal and irrefutable, we can nevertheless use this simple idea as a basis for understanding key mobility trends, which can be summarised in two terms: relatively constant TTB, and the search for increasing returns to public transport.

If individuals reinvest the time they have saved in a new journey (the constant TTB hypothesis), any improvement in car speed will translate into longer overall travel distances and increased demand for roads.

But as cars are not full, those roads are increasingly costly and cannot deal with the growing traffic flows. The decreasing returns to road infrastructure then become apparent in the form of congestion. City centres, in the rush hour, are functionally isolated. The time required to reach the centre by car is becoming longer and increasingly uncertain. Only SPT can offer the average speeds and reliability that will protect residents from growing uncertainty about travel times.

Consequently, rather than discussing the need for a modal shift to PT largely on environmental grounds, it would seem more relevant to explain that a modal shift would guarantee urban accessibility for the majority. The new phenomenon here is that roads, which dominated urban history in the 20th century, are no longer viewed as the travel mode of the future. For long-distance travel, they have been replaced on the high-speed list by air travel and high-speed trains; and for urban travel, congestion makes roads less attractive than SPT, provided it has been modernised and the network expanded.

So, by tying the idea of accessibility (travel time plus opportunity) in with the Zahavi conjecture, we can see why road use is now reaching certain limits in urban areas and why UPT should tackle the accessibility challenge. It is public transport that should increasingly be responding to the many challenges raised by the new scarcity constraints: scarce public funding, scarce environmental resources, lack of space, and – last but not least – loss of valuable time. Yet, as Figure 6.7 below suggests, is it not the cities with good public transport systems that are best at helping residents to control their travel time expenditure?

Figure 6.7. **Motorised TTB per person and market shares of public transport in western Europe, North America, Oceania and major Asian cities**

In minutes

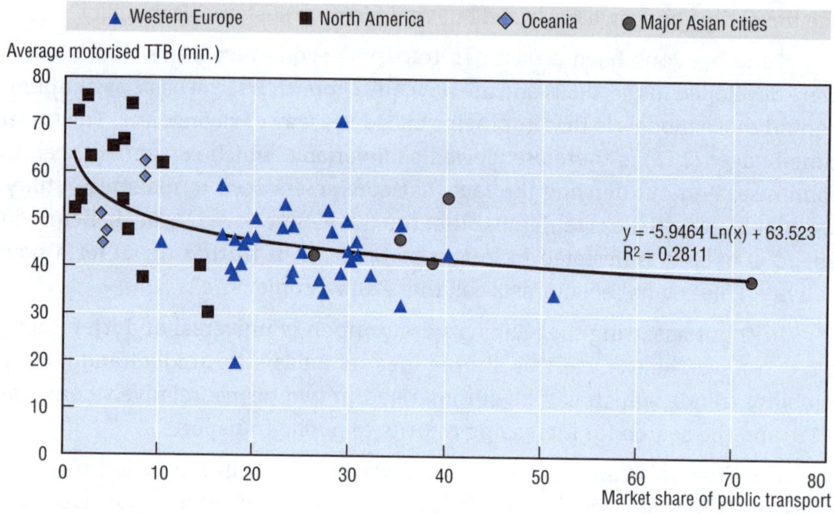

Note: TTB = travel time budget.

Source: UITP database on "Millenium Cities".

Figure 6.7 gives some unexpected results. It is usually accepted that for the same journey from A to B, door-to-door car use will on average be faster than public transport. Although this is often confirmed by our mobility patterns, there are still two points to bear in mind:

- The first is systemic and has already been mentioned above in respect of the distinction between extensive and intensive urban models. The latter offers less incentive for mobility, precisely because urban density is greater. There is more travel on foot (not included above) but it is spontaneously regulated, more than car mobility.
- The second is forward-looking and refers to the fact that, for certain types of travel, particularly from the centre to the outskirts, the door-to-door speed of SPT exceeds that of car travel in the rush hour. So on airport routes, for instance, airport officials and city councillors alike are doing their utmost to develop rapid SPT links. The presence of such links in London, Stockholm or Amsterdam has become a key factor in making those cities and their airports attractive.

This last example symbolises the expectations placed in public transport systems, for today's demands on them in terms of efficient airport links are tomorrow's demands over the next few decades in terms of the many strategic

Box 6.3. Strategic issues for 2025-30

- The appeal of a city has always been linked to agglomeration effects. Bringing together people and activities creates a host of opportunities. But this "organised proximity" is now being threatened as much by urban sprawl as its corollary, road congestion around city centres. The new dynamics of UPT seeks to meet the challenges posed by congestion and rising TTB.
- Grasping the potential role of UPT in large conurbations means reasoning in terms of accessibility. In order to tackle road congestion, even if flows are controlled by charging, it is up to UPT to provide the fullest possible access to the city and its denser areas. This can even be done by proposing faster and more reliable overall trip times than private cars.

links within metropolitan areas. It is public transport that will be making our cities accessible and attractive in the 21st century. They will accordingly face a host of challenges, most of them relating to organisation and finance.

4. Organisation and financing of public transport: new requirements

Given the changes in how cities work, and more specifically the factors that foster urban sprawl and road congestion, the role of UPT is going to become increasingly critical for certain forms of mobility. As a result, the capital investment needs are enormous. But this is no reason why investment and operating costs should start to get out of hand. Cost control is therefore vital. But the question of pricing and user contribution must also be posed, as Figure 6.8 suggests. Along the vertical axis we find the R/E ratio, *i.e.* operating revenue divided by operating expenditure; and along the horizontal axis is the market share of UPT in the major metropolitan areas. The relationship between the two variables is obvious. The coverage rate, or R/E ratio, tends to increase as UPT accounts for a larger proportion of motorised mobility.

But deviations from the overall trend are just as important to study. Amongst the group of European cities in particular, we see many cases that depart significantly from the regression line. In other words, whereas UPT market shares are in these instances relatively high, the R/E ratios remain low, which can be explained by either excessively high operating costs or an excessively low level of fares, or by a combination of both. We must therefore address these two questions in turn. We shall begin by looking at ways to enhance the efficiency of UPT by exploring possible adjustments to business models, after which we shall turn to sources of financing, pricing and other factors. In both cases we shall be looking for changes that could make UPT financing more sustainable.

Figure 6.8. **UPT market share and R/E ratio**

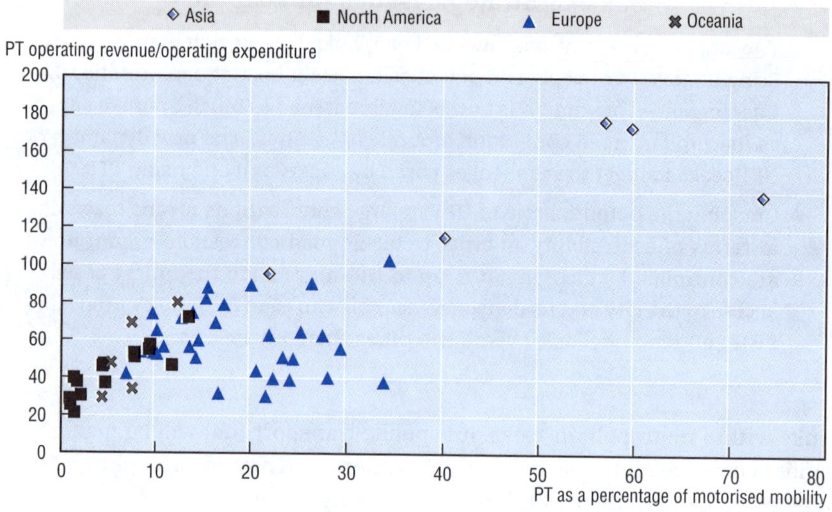

Source: UITP database on "Millenium Cities".

4.1. *Looking for ways to improve UPT performance*

In discussing the performance of UPT, it must first be made clear that there are many sources of UPT efficiency or inefficiency. We shall of course be looking at the companies that operate UPT and how they could be prompted to cut their costs without impairing the quality of service. But the firms we are dealing with here are not ones that are driven spontaneously by a self-regulating market to seek productivity gains: by breaking down the cost structure of UPT, we shall see that the business models in question are still very heavily dependent on government policy making, which is not geared spontaneously to a quest for efficiency.

The cost and supplemental cost of urban public transport

It is a given that public transport is costly in terms of public funds. As shown by Figure 6.8, few cities succeed in generating sales revenue that covers, let alone exceeds, operating costs. And spending on infrastructure is in virtually all cases financed by government subsidies. These subsidies are sometimes deemed exorbitant,[5] but such a claim needs to be put in perspective by comparing the subsidies with parallel spending on roadway infrastructure, which provides motorists with substantial benefits while, exceptions apart, imposing no across-the-board infrastructure toll charges. Our intention here is not to point a finger at any given government subsidy, but to show why it would be fairly easy for spending earmarked for UPT to get out of hand, generating supplemental costs that would be as easy to spot as they are difficult to combat.

Let us begin with capital investment costs, which can be broken down into two main categories: infrastructure and rolling stock.

- Infrastructure costs are low if there is no reserved-track public transport. More specifically, these costs are included in aggregate roadway expenditure. Nevertheless, outlays for items such as bus shelters and bus stations have to be added in. But facilities such as these, which in some cases pay for themselves via advertising (as do bus shelters), do not entail substantial expenditure if there is no reserved-track public transport. Consequently, it is only large metropolitan areas (that do have this type of transport), which must engage in substantial capital investment for UPT. In this case, however, the question arises as to the risks of overinvesting.
- The cost of rolling stock can also trigger supplemental costs. Whether these assets (buses, trams, metros, trains, etc.) are wholly owned by the local authorities or are provided by a private entity, lessee or operator does not alter the fundamental question: how to avert the risk of overinvesting? When the decision to acquire lies entirely with government, there are strong pressures to channel spending towards the most costly models (using clean energy and providing low floors in buses and tramways, for access by people with reduced mobility in particular). Since they are supposed to set the example in the realm of sustainable mobility, governments are prompted to act as guinea pigs by disseminating new technologies or, very simply, protecting market outlets for local or national vehicle manufacturers.

But the most widespread of these traditional tendencies of bureaucracies to spawn supplemental costs and excessive quality lies only indirectly in rolling stock. The main cause is actually in the tendency to increase the number of lines and frequencies in areas, or at times, when UPT occupancy rates remain very low. Thus in many metropolitan areas there are public transport lines that it would be preferable, given their amount of use, to replace by transport on demand – and this brings us to operating costs.

UPT operating costs have two main components: labour and energy.

- With respect to energy, it would be possible for operating costs to trend downwards, although the savings might be used up, in full or in part, by a rise in capital investment costs if they stemmed from the purchase of new stock. Given the current increase in fuel prices, the cost of energy is on the rise, in absolute value and in relative terms, but it is still easier to control than the other major component of operating expenditure – wage costs.
- Total wage costs, including social security and pension contributions, account in many cases for over 60% of aggregate operating costs. They

therefore have a major impact on total cost, compounded by the fact that they are difficult to reduce, in terms of either staff numbers or unit costs.

- The number of employees depends first on the volume of jobs on offer, but it is also directly tied in with productivity, *i.e.* primarily the length of the work week, the number of holidays and the volume of compensatory leave. Since the rate of union membership is generally high, and since strikes (when authorised) have a major impact in the media, the occupations concerned frequently obtain substantial relative advantages.
- The same holds true for compensation. For the same reasons as above, employees in the UPT sector are in a position of strength to obtain higher average wages than for equivalent occupations, as compared with either the economy as a whole or other components of the transport sector. This is shown, in the case of France, by Figure 6.9.

Figure 6.9. **Average net monthly salaries of full-time employees in 2000**

In euros

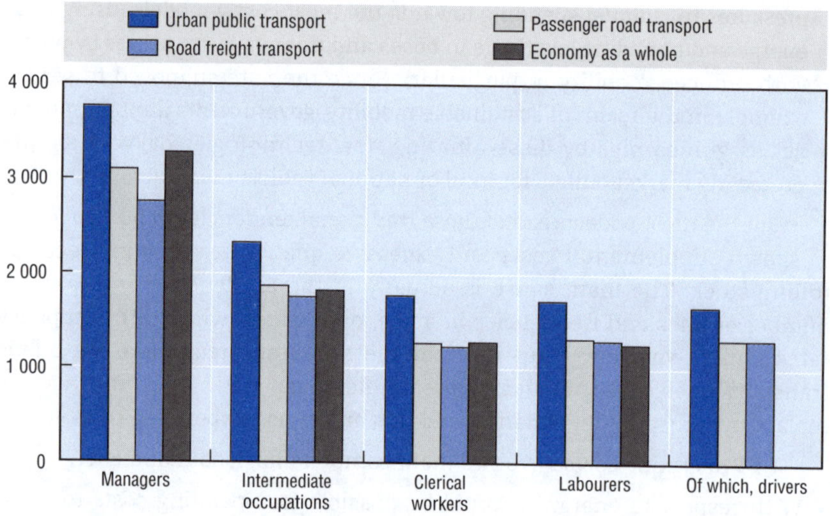

Source: INSEE, derived from annual company reporting ("DADS" surveys). INSEE (2003), Table C.03-3 and DAEI/SES-INSEE (2003), p. 88, Table III 2.6.

We are thus in a delicate situation because whatever transpires in the realm of labour relations is a reflection of what prevails over all decisions affecting public transport. Just as elected officials are prepared to disregard expenditure in order to acquire the most modern equipment or make costly urban investments in new infrastructure, they have a tendency to forget about economic constraints when setting headcounts and unit salaries. Here, it is not the market that dictates its law, but rather political and labour organisations, which tend frequently to agree on a consensus of underproductivity.

To guard against this tendency, a country like the United States, which has a flexible labour market, undertook back in the 1980s to limit the burden of payroll costs. Hiring women and part-time workers such as students effectively stemmed the rise in unit wage costs. At the same time, a variety of measures were taken to combat absenteeism and bolster employee commitment to the quality of services rendered. The United Kingdom followed this model in part, focusing more on working hours and organisational aspects than on unit salaries. But the UK was an exception amongst European countries, which held on to their more highly regulated job markets.

There are, however, a number of notable differences. Countries such as France and Italy have made no attempt to alter the UPT sector environment: labour unions remain powerful, their demands are great (lowering the retirement age to 55, or even 50; higher wages; shorter hours), and strike days abound. The same does not hold true in a country like Germany. While not engaging in US-style downsizing, German – but also Swedish – transport companies found themselves compelled by the opening-up of competition in the form of allotment to improve productivity without necessarily raising pay. The current discussions over a certain increase in working hours in Germany illustrate this new state of affairs resulting from incremental adjustments. Whether it takes the form of an Anglo-Saxon-style "big bang" or a gradual acclimatisation, will the opening-up to competition be capable of altering business models while sparing public finances certain costly increases in expenditure?

Opening up to competition: towards greater efficiency?

Competition is the keynote in the wave of deregulation that has swept through the industrialised world for the past quarter-century. A hidden motivation of the major comeback of this principle laid down by the founders of economics is a desire to rectify instances of bureaucratic and oligopolistic drift. As a result, competition has regained its place as the economic hallmark of network industries (water, energy, telecommunications, transport and so on). But in economic theory itself, competition takes a variety of different forms, and it does not eliminate government intervention, which in turn takes a variety of different forms, between which the choice is not readily apparent.

As is their custom, economists have proposed not one but multiple solutions to develop competition and improve the performance of firms operating in network industries.

The first idea is simply privatisation. Private management of a market activity generally outperforms public management, which is less sensitive to risks of losses and less apt to drive employees to show what they can do. But this "solution" proves impossible in a context of network activities in which increasing returns to scale prevail. What should be done, for instance, in the case of a natural monopoly, or a quasi-natural monopoly, as is often the case with UPT?

Here is where the theory of contestable (or disputable) markets, which emerged some twenty years ago, comes in. In the early 1980s, Baumol, Panzar and Willig substituted the idea of contestability for the idea of actual competition between a large number of competitors: the mere threat that a potential competitor might enter the market is enough to make the incumbent firm behave as if it were already in a competitive situation. Here the notion of barriers to entry becomes paramount, since any obstacle to a potential competitor's threat will cast doubt on the very principle of contestability. For this reason, the European Union has placed great emphasis on third-party access to networks, as we shall see later.

But contestability is not the only way to harness threats of competition so as to prompt players to improve their performance. Sometimes competition "by" the market has to be replaced by competition "for" the market (Demsetz, 1967). The community conducts a call for bids whereby operation of certain activities is contracted out to operators who are required to meet certain specifications at the lowest cost. It is this third type of competition that is practised most widely in the UPT sector.

It should be noted that in such a situation of Demsetz-style competition "for" the market, it is also possible to practise a complementary form of competition called "yardstick competition" (Shleifer, 1985). This consists in comparing the performance of various operators in comparable situations in order to uncover best practices.

With this in mind, we can seek out the various business models, taking care to distinguish between operators and the organising authorities. Given the eminently political nature of the supply of UPT, we cannot restrict our focus to operators alone. The hallmark of competition "for" the market is in fact the ongoing action of government, which cannot afford simply to privatise and then wash its hands of subsequent developments. On the contrary, public players, both upstream and down, retain an important role in laying down the rules for sector in question. We are not therefore in the classic agency theory situation that prevails when a principal delegates completion of a given task to an agent. While there is indeed delegation of a task, and that delegation can be evaluated, as we shall see, government action itself must in turn be evaluated because it plays a key role in determining the business model of UPT. As in Figure 6.10, we are going to explore ways in which competition can improve overall performance by working on one of the organisational components of UPT – efficiency.

Figure 6.10. **Coherence, relevance, efficiency and effectiveness of UPT**

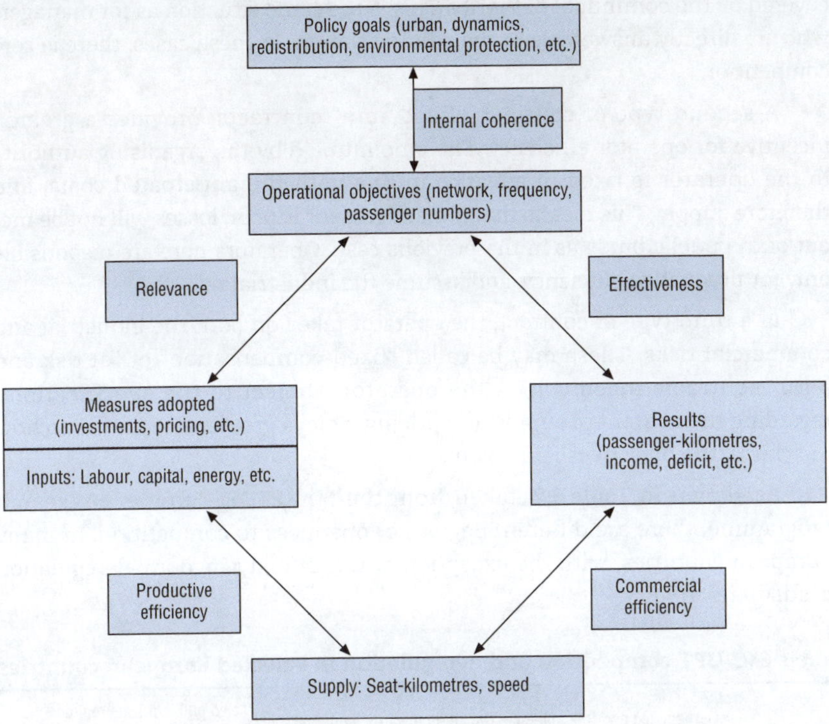

There are three key concepts for assessing the performance of organising authorities: relevance, coherence and effectiveness.

- Relevance concerns the relationship between policy goals and operational objectives. Do these match policy goals with regard to the environment or redistribution, for example.
- The concept of coherence involves comparing the resources adopted, in the broad sense of the term, with operational objectives. Have sufficient resources been provided to achieve goals?
- Effectiveness involves comparing the results of the operational objective.

These concepts of relevance, coherence and effectiveness are not the same as the overall efficiency of operators which can be broken down into two main parts, productive efficiency, which compares inputs and supply, and commercial efficiency which compares supply and passenger use.

Competition is usually introduced into UPT systems in the lower section of the diagram, in a very gradual way. Using an operator other than the administrations themselves can give increasing responsibility to the operator depending on the type of contract between him and the organising authority.

Other "management" contracts, operators are sure that their costs will be covered by the communal authority. This is the same situation as for managers who are directly answerable to the administration. In these cases, there is zero competition.

A second type of contract, "fixed-sum" contracts, provides a greater incentive for operator efficiency. The amount paid by the organising authority to the operator is fixed in advance in line with the anticipated costs, and therefore supply. This means that if management is poor, losses will not be met out of the public purse as in the previous case. Operators here are responsible only for productive efficiency, and assume the industrial risk.

In a third type of contract, the operator takes on both the industrial and commercial risks. These may be called "fixed-compensation" or "at risk and peril" contracts inasmuch as the operator, subject to the specifications regarding the content of supply and pricing, enjoys greater freedom as to how to achieve the objectives laid down.

As shown in Table 6.2, taken from the MARETOPE European research programme, there are different degrees of openness to competition. In many European countries, with the exception of the United Kingdom, deregulation is still in its infancy.

Table 6.2. **UPT competition and deregulation in selected European countries**

	Deregulated and free market	Transition towards tendering	Mixed public/private regime without tenders
Countries	UK.	Scandinavian countries, Netherlands, France.	Germany, Italy, Portugal, Belgium, Luxembourg, Austria.
Similarities	Private initiative. Deregulated market. Tenders for loss-making lines	Public tendering introduced (S). Not yet applied everywhere (FRA, NLD).	Not (yet) privatisation of (some) public companies. Not (yet) transition towards tendering.
Differences		Some countries already "in the new" (S). Some others in the middle of transition. France, still a lot of direct concessions.	Some experiments with subtendering of operations (BEL). Some countries already have legislation to introduce compulsory tendering (AUT, ITA).

Source: MARETOPE, D2 Report.

The development of tendering is one way of getting operators to be more efficient. This was shown by a study conducted in France of 135 towns with a bus network (not public transport on dedicated infrastructure). The technical efficiency of operators (level of supply compared to inputs) is slightly greater when the organising authorities have called for tenders in which the operator assumes the industrial risk or both the industrial and commercial risks. But the differences are not very large from one type of management to the other. Thus, the UPT sector shows similarities to the water sector for example. In both cases, it cannot be said that public production (under state control[6]) is always less efficient than private production since it all depends on the type of contracts and the incentives involved. Thus, still with regard to France, Marc Ivaldi showed that price contracts had a more favourable impact on UPT than cost plus ones.

Box 6.4. **Cost plus or price cap? What remuneration should the operator receive?**

With regard to remuneration of the operator, what types of incentive are the most effective? There are two possible methods here: *cost plus* or *price cap*. While, as we shall see below, the latter usually seems preferable, large areas of doubt remain as to its implementation. The cost plus method, which applies in the case of "fixed price" contracts, involves fixing prices in line with costs, at the same time guaranteeing for the operator a given and "reasonable" yield.

Although this approach seems at first sight sensible, there are many limits to it:

- The public authority must be in possession of a complex information system relating to operational costs, capital cost, assets required, etc.
- Not having any direct control over this information, unlike the operator, the authority is at an informational disadvantage. The operator might be tempted to inflate his costs and/or expenditures, passed on to passengers, without the authority being able to verify this or use dissuasive measures.
- If, in order to keep costs down, the regulator increases constraints too much, there will be a risk of underinvestment or under maintenance on the part of the operator.

The main drawback with the cost plus method is therefore that it offers no incentive to cut costs, thereby encouraging increased productive efficiency. To overcome these shortcomings, the price cap method* is the most commonly used form of incentive regulation. In the case of UPT, it sets in advance a ceiling on the amount of subsidy (fixed-compensation contract) in the knowledge that the fare levels are also fixed. In this way, prices are no longer subject to costs, any reduction in which is to the advantage of the operator. The operator therefore runs a risk with the price cap method (costs higher than prices), but also has the chance to make significant profits in the event of productivity gains. This has an impact on the public authority, the quality of whose work will be judged on its ability to maintain profits at a reasonable level.

* "Fixed cost" is often used instead of "price cap".

The form and content given to contracts following a call for tender are therefore very important. It can happen that the authorities are not demanding enough. What is more, as was confirmed in the French case, they are not faced with many competitors.[7] There is therefore a risk of cartels in the tendering process. As in the water sector, once again the tendering procedure is not a panacea. Far from discharging the public authority from its responsibilities, it results, as shown in Figure 6.4, in the operator being responsible only for efficiency. The requirements relating to coherence, relevance and effectiveness remain the responsibility of the public authorities. We should bear this in mind when looking at the way in which the European Union is pursuing a policy of opening UPT markets to competition.

The European draft regulation on public service obligations (PSO)

For some years, the European Commission has worked on introducing a certain degree of competition in the UPT sector. Considered as foreign to the concept of profit-making, UPT systems had been excluded from competition rules by European Regulations of 1969 and 1991 (1191/69 and 1893/91). But deregulation in the United Kingdom showed that other organisational formulae were possible while, at the same time, several studies showed that competition could be used to achieve efficiency gains. In addition, in 2003, in the Altmark judgment, the Court of Justice of the European Communities held that subsidies paid to an operator in charge of loss-making UPT lines should be assessed in comparison with an average, well managed and adequately equipped enterprise. This decision created a degree of legal uncertainty inasmuch as it became possible to contest the amount of certain subsidies before the courts. Such proceedings are naturally very tempting against operators who are given large subsidies and who are sometimes suspected of reaping profits on a protected market which means they can put in the lowest bid in response to certain calls for tender.

On 20 July 2005, the Commission therefore proposed a draft regulation concerning the public transport of passengers by road and rail. The purpose of this regulation is to harmonise and clarify the conditions for competition in the supply of public transport services in order to ensure greater transparency about the obligations of public service and the remuneration of services. The European Union has opted in favour of "regulated competition" which recognises the specificity of public subsidies in support of the supply of economic services of public interest. There is therefore a need to clarify the rights and obligations of each party in the knowledge that the social and territorial objectives specific to each competent authority are recognised. Encouragement is thus given to public service contracts which clearly identify SSOs and their costs.

In compliance with the principle of subsidiarity, the draft regulation gave territorial authorities the flexibility needed to meet the specificity or complexity of local public transport needs in line with their social cohesion and territorial objectives. Local authorities are thus given the right to choose the way in which their public transport services should be managed, in accordance with the legislation of most member states. Although authorities therefore are free to choose a management method, they must comply with the rule of geographical containment for internal operators (Article 5.2). This means that no enterprise, notably if under state control, can reply to a call for tenders if, in its area of origin, it benefits from a delegation of public service without any competitive process. The idea is to put an end to suspicions of "incompatible" aid while preserving recourse to an internal operator and margins of flexibility in the tendering process. Public service contracts can give rise to negotiations (Article 5.3) or be replaced by direct assignment in the event of an interruption of services (Article 5.5).

Thus, the draft regulation protects the room for manoeuvre of organising authorities which underlines their key role, and thus their responsibilities, which operate on two levels:

- *The level of operation.* If territorial authorities decide not to make a call for tender, they must keep a watchful eye on the questions of efficiency.
- *The level of the conception of the TCU offer.* Whether there is a call for tender or not, authorities are responsible for the coherence, relevance and effectiveness of TCUs.

It is therefore essential to undertake benchmarking studies not only about the efficiency of operation but also the relevance of the choices made earlier. Among these choices are the questions relating to financing and pricing.

As was shown in Figure 6.8 there are wide differences across western cities with regard to financing and pricing. While there is an obvious distinction between North American cities, where the R/E ratio is low, and cities in Asia, where this ratio is high, sometimes even above 100, the situation in European cities is less clear. It is easy to say that in Asia, the large market share of UPT is the key to its sizeable commercial revenue and that, conversely, the marginal role of UPT in North America explains its poor commercial record. But why, in Europe, is there such a difference between Barcelona and London on the one hand (R/E ratio of 102% and 89%, respectively) and Paris (38%), Amsterdam (31%) and Brussels (29.5%), on the other?

The main conclusion to be drawn from this diversity is that cities are not condemned to suffer a situation in which commercial revenue is very low. But this requires taking some clear decisions on UPT pricing and financing and on fare levels for urban journeys in general.

Pricing and other forms of financing

It could be thought that the large subsidies given to many UPT systems means that it is impossible to increase the share of commercial revenue. But the examples of London and Barcelona show that this is not the case. If these cities have achieved a relatively high R/E ratio, it is because they have not hesitated to introduce higher fare levels. Comparing Figures 6.11 and 6.12, it can be seen that the average price of a PT journey, expressed as a proportion of GDP per capita of the city in question, is significantly higher in cities like London and Glasgow.

Figure 6.11. **R/E ratio in large European cities**

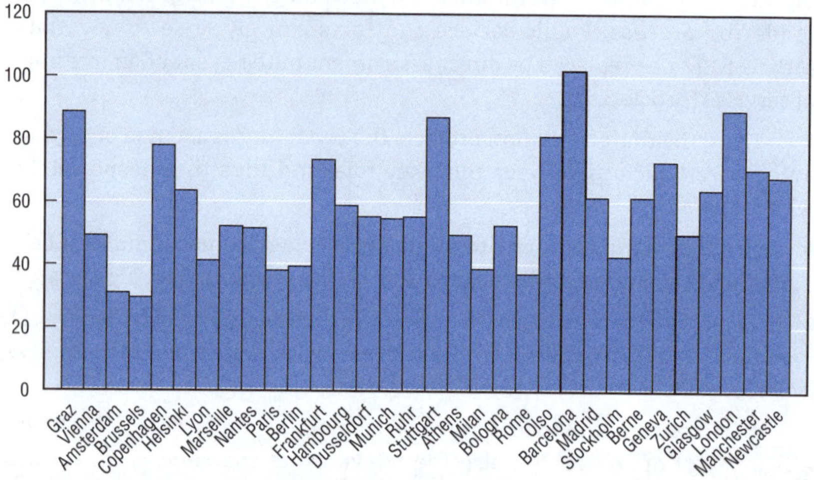

Source: UITP database on "Millenium Cities".

It could be tempting to point to national specificities. The cities in the United Kingdom (the four columns on the right) are visibly more demanding of their users than is the case in France, particularly in Lyon or Nantes. But national traditions cannot explain everything. UPT in Berne, for example, is twice as "expensive" for users as in Geneva. In Germany also, Berlin and Hamburg are twice as expensive as Dusseldorf and Munich. Organising authorities therefore need to think about the level of their operating revenue but not on the basis of the extreme case of the sell price for individual tickets. This latter is only one component of the fare structure. The problem is often to be found in the extremely low price of travel passes or special fares. Is it justified to offer such low prices to the whole population, including people on middle and high incomes? The organising authorities responsible for setting fares must reflect on these issues, especially when their customer base evolves and is increasingly composed of persons with money.

Figure 6.12. **Average fare for a UPT trip**

As a % of 1/10 000 of per capita GDP

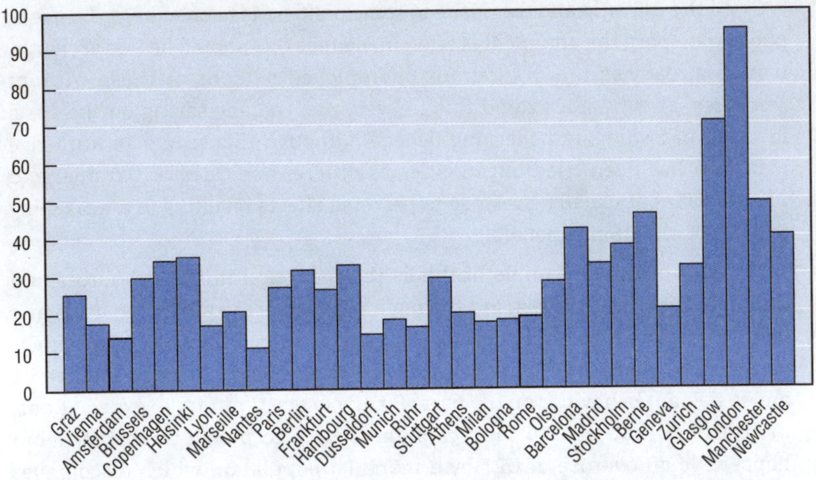

Source: UITP database on "Millenium Cities".

The R/E objective is not to reach 100% (or even more if it is wanted to cover investments) nor should it be to approach zero (see box). The idea is simply that public authorities should think about what level they want while avoiding, as far as possible, any move towards "fiscal translation". There is a constant search for sources of financing other than direct users as a positive external effect of UPT. But while it may be legitimate to obtain financing from indirect beneficiaries (real estate owners, employers), the distorting effect of certain taxes must also be taken into account. Payments by employers are particularly relevant here. Questions have to be asked when, for example, the French transport payment (*Versement Transport*) levied on employers with more than ten employees led to a disincentive to job creation. To answer these questions, account has to be taken of all modes of urban mobility and thought given to the validity of the all too often implicit principle that mobility should be subsidised.

Towards an integrated approach to fare setting?

Rising oil prices have been a constant since the early 2000s. This translates, for motorists, into more costly mobility which represents a break with 1985-2000 trends. Following the oil counter-shock of the mid-1980s, the price of petrol, in constant terms, was tending to fall as was the price of cars once the quality effect was discounted. Adding to this trend towards cheaper automobile mobility was the steady increase in average speeds resulting in network improvements. In terms of generalised cost, meaning monetary cost plus the cost of the time spent travelling, automobile mobility does became increasingly competitive. The car therefore increased its market share in both urban and interurban transport.

Box 6.5. **Free UPT for all: a bad good idea!**

Given the R/E ratio and the desire of some politicians to encourage the use of public transport, the argument is often made that UPT should be free of charge. It is so already in many cities for unemployed persons or those without resources. So why not extend this to everyone, thereby saving on the costs involved in issuing and checking tickets? Although this seems an attractive idea, and has been tried out in cities as different as Odessa (Ukraine) and Atlanta (USA), it usually gives rise to perverse effects resulting in a worsening of the UPT situation in general.

The first obvious example of this is the reduction in UPT resources and therefore capacity to invest. But the main problem is the impact on users and staff. As could be feared, in light of the work done by Hirshmann (Exit, Voice and Loyalty), making UPT free of charge leads to staff becoming demotivated and to deviant behaviour on the part of many users. Contrary to expectations, motorists do not give up their cars and switch to public transport. What happens is an overuse of UPT by a marginal population which discourages other potential users.

As described earlier, this situation is gradually changing, both for long journeys (because of rapid forms of transport such as aeroplanes and high-speed trains) and for daily travel, which is what interests us here. In the case of car journeys in cities, both facets of the generalised cost are on the increase: the cost in terms of time, due to growing congestion on the roads at rush hour, and the monetary cost, given the rise in petrol prices and in ancillary costs such as parking and, in some cases, urban tolls.

In sum, UPT financing and pricing can no longer be addressed as issues relating to UPT alone. Policy choices in this field cannot be dissociated from the general objectives adopted by a metropolitan area in terms of accessibility, attractiveness and sociability. The multiplicity and ranking, often implicit, of objectives explains why sources of financing, as well as their combination, are varied. Contributions by UPT users and by motorists must not be neglected. Nor should there be any hesitation in taxing the indirect beneficiaries of the transport system, employers and real estate owners, while avoiding as far as possible distorting or penalising measures.

5. Public transport and sustainable urban mobility

As we reach the end of this prospective overview, issues relating to UPT financing, pricing and organisation must be viewed from the more general perspective of urban policy. As our discussion has progressed, it has become increasingly clear that UPT primarily fall under the category of public goods, in

Box 6.6. **What type of urban toll?**

When looking at the whole of an urban system and not simply at a particular main road, it becomes very difficult to combine the objectives of increased fluidity, infrastructure financing and financial (and modal) transfer. The pressure from the demand for travelling by car remains very strong and any local improvement in fluidity leads to an overall increase in traffic. Other than providing systematically for overcapacity on the network,[1] or imposing levies which are socially and politically insupportable,[2] there is no point in adopting a vague and general objective of fluidity. The lesson to be learned from recent urban policy is, on the contrary, the need for a differentiated approach to the network. While on some highways, for example a ring road, it is desirable to maintain a certain speed, this is not the case for city centres or roads leading thereto. In the first case, it may even be necessary to envisage new infrastructures. In the second, on the other hand, authorities today are rather seeking to reduce speeds for reasons of safety but also, and above all, as part of the requalification of urban areas. Even if the thinking may seem paradoxical, since the objective is to limit traffic, the approach is rather to reduce road space. Experience shows that this leads to a reduction in traffic which does not excessively cut speeds but which gives that to city centres their commercial, residential and cultural functions.

With this type of approach, there is little space for imposing congestion charges since traffic is well organised at a local level. This does not mean that there should be no thought given to pricing, however, rather that another basis should be used for charging. Although we have in effect given up the idea of fluidity in city centres, there is no question of creating generalised congestion. It must be possible to make journeys without wasting excessive time. In order to do so, it will be necessary to develop public transport. This requires money, and it is legitimate for car drivers to make a contribution beyond what they already pay in the form of fuel taxes. However, charging for the use of new sections of road makes little sense since this will not reduce heavy traffic precisely where this should be done, *i.e.* on the three sections of the network, in city centres.

The idea of an infrastructure toll must therefore be abandoned since it does not meet the need for a comprehensive approach to pricing, covering the agglomeration as a whole. The same is true for a network toll under which certain major city highways would be profit-making, supposedly guaranteeing for their users a high quality of service in terms of speed. Apart from its technical complexity, such an approach faces problems of acceptance relating to "first-class roads", and has no impact on traffic flow on sections which remain free of charge. If policy is objective-based, this is exactly where, at least in Europe, the priority of urban authorities lies, to give back to city centres, or maintain, their attractiveness which means, according to the Rhine city model, reducing automobile access without however banning it since such traffic is necessary to the daily life of the inhabitants, businesses and their customers.

Box 6.6. **What type of urban toll?** *(cont.)*

In such a scenario, it is clear that any traffic which can avoid the city centre must do so. Peripheral roads must not therefore be penalised. This excludes any idea of distance-based pricing and, on the contrary, argues in favour of a zone-based toll. Anyone entering a defined zone (city centre) in a motorised vehicle must pay a fixed charge. This is precisely the idea already adopted by Norwegian cities, London and Stockholm. Deciding to introduce a zone-based toll is one thing, deciding on the toll amount is another. In London, the desire to generate significant income while at the same time reducing congestion considerably in the city centre, led to the adoption of a very high charge. In Norwegian cities, the unitary charge is lower although it is gradually growing. The question of the amount charged is directly linked to the size of the zone concerned. Issues of acceptability together with the desire to generate income gives rise to two main variants, a rather expensive toll in a limited urban zone; or a somewhat lower toll but covering the agglomeration as a whole.

1. A frequent misconception may be mentioned here. Many car drivers, and unfortunately local authority officials, state that their objective would be to be able to drive every day under the same conditions as during school holidays when traffic is reduced by 10-15%. They forget that on such days, there is quite simply an oversupply of road networks since activity in the city is operating at a slower rate as it were. This idea is simply an avatar of the dream of "country living in the city".
2. In this respect, the toll system introduced in Singapore is rather an example of what not to do.

the same way that towns and cities have themselves become public goods. The many challenges relating to the issue of sustainable urban development would therefore suggest that we reconsider our initial four questions, but this time from the perspective of the year 2030. Who will be using public transport in a generation's time? Who will pay for public transport? Who will operate the services and who will design and plan both individual UPT systems and urban mobility in general? These questions are the same as those which served as the starting point for the first part of this discussion; what we shall now do is simply review them here in reverse order, moving this time from users to planning authorities.

5.1. *Who will be using public transport in 2030?*

The main change we need to take into account in our understanding of the changes we can expect to see over the next few years is the concept of multimodality. Growth in the use of public transport in many European cities is driven as much by complementarity as competition with other modes. This can clearly be seen in the case of travel by foot. All types of trip by public transport entail some travel by foot at both the origin and the destination. This complementarity also exists for other environmentally friendly modes such as bicycle, and can clearly be seen in countries such as the Netherlands and Belgium where the railway stations all have enormous bicycle parks. This use

Box 6.7. **Future strategic issues 2025-30**

UPT can no longer be considered as a minor issue in the large cities of industrialised countries. It is increasingly becoming a distinctive element in a city as is shown, in international classifications of cities, by the good rankings obtained by agglomerations such as Geneva, Zurich and Vancouver. Cities do not take the same form in Switzerland and in British Columbia but in both cases, significant efforts have been made to promote urban transport.

From this general "urban performance" viewpoint, deregulation must not be seen as a way for local authorities to rid themselves of a sensitive issue. On the contrary, by making a clear distinction between the tasks of conception and execution, the idea is to highlight the project owner role of local authorities which must assume their responsibilities.

One such responsibility is to ensure that costs are kept in hand. This means that care must be taken not to overinvest and to ensure that operating costs do not get out of hand. A certain transparency is required for this and international benchmarking must systematically be carried out in order to flush out abnormal situations.

Cutting operating costs is not in conflict with the trend towards higher mobility costs for all users of motorised transport. Contributions from UPT users must match their ability to pay, and the same is true for car drivers. Transport infrastructures must less and less be considered as an abundant and free natural resource. On the contrary, given their cost, there is no reason why the direct and indirect beneficiaries should not be directly involved in financing them.

of bicycles plus public transport is also growing in other cities such as Berlin and Lyon where bicycles are made available to season-ticket holders. Even though such systems, which the city of Paris is also developing further, remain relatively marginal, they show that accessibility to the town centre can be improved not by means of a single solution, but through a combination of different modes of transport.

The same logic applies to peripheral urban areas where bicycles, as well as cars, can be used to travel to the main public transport corridors. From the user's standpoint, there is no conflict between private car use and public transport. The person who needs to travel does not make an *a priori* decision whether or not to use a given mode of transport. The choice amounts simply to an optimisation under constraint whereby the user combines the most efficient mode of transport for each given segment of the trip. The main change is therefore that car use has become less relevant for certain links. However, this reality does raise a number of new issues. For example, the Brussels conurbation is currently drawing up plans for a new railway network for the capital, comparable to the RER in Paris, which if implemented would offer commuters sharply improved travel times and reliability compared with the current supply of services. However, studies have shown (see the EU Scatter project) that unless other supporting measures are adopted, such an improvement could lead to a reduction in the population of Brussels. The reason for this is the improvement in travel times, since the time savings offered by public transport could be simply added on to other modes such as the car which in peripheral urban areas offers greater accessibility to areas where house prices are lower. Thinking in terms of transport infrastructure alone is not sufficient to ensure control over mobility. It is important, as in the "Vinex" project in the Netherlands, to consider the interface between transport and the localisation of activities (Sniellen and Hilbers, 2005).

It would therefore be best to avoid any over simplistic division into two opposing camps: "good citizens" who use public transport and "bad citizens" who use a private car. In reality, the situation is somewhat more complicated and in all probability is to some extent impossible to completely control. As the Swiss example shows, a highly activistic policy towards the development of public transport does not preclude a continuation of urban sprawl. And yet in countries that are particularly attached to the quality of UPT, private car use is gaining market share for the simple reason that more and more people live at a distance from their town centre and are clearly willing to increase their travel times in order to be able to live in a less densely populated area. Even though with population ageing we can observe the elderly moving back into the central areas of cities, it would be wrong to conclude that the peripheral areas will fall out of fashion. A more pertinent analysis would look at life cycles and the diversity of choice. Households with young children do not have the same needs or resources as households consisting of pensioners. Furthermore, choices and resources vary from one social group to another and also from one individual to another.

To meet this diversity of demand, public transport must therefore prepare itself to meet a demand based on multimodality that allows the inhabitants of major conurbations to optimise their mobility behaviour. To do this, however, the public transport sector will have to rethink its funding and open the door to technical and institutional innovation.

5.2. *Who will finance public transport?*

The introduction of urban tolls in cities like London, Oslo and Stockholm in the middle of a period of rising petrol prices must be seen as signalling a new approach which is gradually being adopted in large cities: the increasing generalised cost of mobility. For many reasons, mostly environmental and financial, local authorities no longer feel that mobility should necessarily be subsidised. This is an important change which does not concern cars alone. The example of London is important here, a city which not only has a very expensive toll for motorists (EUR 12 a day) but also a relatively expensive UPT system. As is often the case, UK policy can seem a little surprising whereas in fact it is simply somewhat ahead in terms of practice and opinions.

We must realise that urban mobility is gradually entering into a new age. This is not a sudden revolution but rather a gentle curve, a slow transition between two approaches, between two eras. But the extent of this transition is not easy to grasp since, measured by the components of the generalised cost of transport, it includes elements that seem to be moving in opposite directions:

- Certain policies aim to reduce the monetary cost of mobility, notably by making use of competition and public-private partnerships (PPPs).
- But at the same time, there is a trend to increase user contributions. An increase in prices for end-users thus goes hand-in-hand with the reduction of certain costs.
- In terms of the time cost of mobility, some decisions seek to reduce user perceptions of the time spent travelling (introduction of TCSP, improvements in frequency and comfort).
- Others accept *volens nolens* an increase in time cost (the organisation, more or less, of traffic congestion as in Paris[8]).

These decisions, however, only appear to be contradictory. In fact, the message to citizens is relatively clear (see Box 6.8). First of all, it is impossible to continue to provide large subsidies for urban mobility, whether by car or UPT. Users are therefore going to have to pay more. But what is to be done with this extra money (revenue from fines, parking fees, tolls, etc.)? The experience of cities which have introduced tolls provides a clear answer to this question. While toll revenue may in some cases be earmarked to pay for new infrastructure (a bridge or a tunnel), it is increasingly clear that another purpose is to generate financing for other public expenditures, notably for UPT. We have replaced the toll/infrastructure approach by a toll/zone one, which means that urban mobility is considered as a whole by public authorities. It is no longer a question of finding financing specific to each mode of transport but of developing a global pricing system for urban mobility.

All this shows evidence of a strong desire to price all types of journeys: regulate demand and find financial resources for the whole system. The price message, for both car drivers and UPT users, is more than simply wishing to make users pay for the costs they incur. Not only maintenance costs would then be covered, but also external costs while authorising an equalisation adjustment between modes, in particular to the benefit of UPT, which is more

Box 6.8. The generalised cost of transport and the messages being sent to users

One way of illustrating the new messages being sent to users of private cars and UPT in urban areas is to look at the generalised cost of mobility, which may be defined as follows:

$$C_g = p + hT_g$$

where:

p is the monetary price of travel between points A and B

Tg is the generalised time between A and B

h is monetary parameter representing the average value of the time as perceived by travelers.

It is interesting to note that the generalised cost takes account of the monetary price, the whole time needed for the journey and also a parameter relating to the way in which this journey time is perceived. Factors to be taken into account here are saturated lines, service frequency in the case of public transport, number of changes required, etc. There is, therefore, a qualitative dimension to journey time. In order to measure it, depending on the mode being studied, the Tg parameter could be made more detailed so as better to reflect not only the time spent on the journey itself but also on access, before and after, as well as the performance and qualities inherent to the mode in question.

Taking rail transport as an example, the following could be taken into account:

- Travel time in the form of the average time needed to complete the journey between starting point and destination in zones A and B.
- An indicator of the average interval between trains calculated on the basis of the hours covered by the daily timetable.
- The number of times the traveller has to change trains (saturation of lines).
- The frequency of trains on the line.
- A constant representing terminal travel times.

All of this gives an aggregate total time, a physical value which will have to be made compatible with the journey price by selecting an average value of time for travellers.

- The economic analysis used to measure this theoretical value is based on the concept of the scarcity of time. Individuals choose from among different possible activities by comparing the benefits derived and the share of total time available they consume. Thus, the time spent on travelling is that much less to spend on other activities.
- From a practical standpoint, this measuring process involves using the concept of the Value of Time (VOT), or monetary value of time, which can be assessed by studying individual behaviour patterns (a behavioural value): the readiness to pay more in order to save time.

Box 6.8. **The generalised cost of transport and the messages being sent to users** *(cont.)*

In the case of urban mobility, given the huge cost of building new infrastructure (roads or TCSP), it is no longer possible to offer users savings in time in the strict sense of the term, except in special cases like access to airports. It is more important to focus on the parameter h by improving the quality of transport by cutting down on required changes and improving UPT frequency of service. But if these improvements are to be made, the monetary cost will have to be raised. In sum, we are moving towards an increase in the monetary component and, at best, a slight improvement in the time cost, mainly on the grounds of quality. The result is simple: a trend towards a higher generalised cost of mobility!

suitable than motor vehicles for travel in densely populated areas. But beyond its accounting dimension, prices constitute a multifaceted incentive whose essential purpose is to ensure the best possible system for the urban area.

But this general goal of ensuring that cities work better must rid itself of certain naïve assumptions. Better pricing for travel, for example in the form of an urban toll, cannot be a panacea guaranteeing that traffic will flow better, that infrastructures will be financed and that there will be an important shift from private cars to public transport. This is for the simple reason that it is generally difficult, and therefore imprudent, to try to make a single tool serve three such diverse objectives. Each urban area must therefore prioritise its various objectives and then investigate what type of pricing would be more suited to the goals sought.

From the standpoint of tariff integration, a search will also need to be made for other sources of funding that might be secured by taxing the capital gains realised by the owners of land and real estate in the vicinity of transport infrastructure designed to improve accessibility. Here again, the funding issue cannot be conceived simply in terms of the allocation of costs to users, but as a comprehensive financing system for urban amenities. In the same way that a supplier of electricity or water puts in place complex pricing systems (dual or tripartite pricing systems, progressive tariffs varying over time and distance, etc.), sometimes involving cross-subsidisation between consumers, the funding of urban mobility can also use a sophisticated mix of resources from a wide variety of sources: user charges, urban tolls, employer taxes, real estate taxes, etc. The need for such diversity will be all the greater in that we shall undoubtedly find ourselves facing a *de facto* challenge to the public transport monopoly.

5.3. *Who will operate public transport services?*

Our reply to the first two questions (who will use and who will finance public transport?) consisted of two keywords: multimodality and integration. In reply to the third question as to who the operators will be, we could add a third keyword "innovation", and to be more precise technical and institutional innovation.

Technical innovation will come first, following the diffusion of new information and communications technologies (NICT) into the public transport sector. The first applications of NTIC in UPT can already be seen in new forms of payment (magnetic subscriber cards) as well as real-time information systems. But what is also starting to take shape at the moment, notably in less densely populated areas, is the use of special software to optimise on-demand transport services. The problems besetting public transport in such areas have been widely documented: the wide diversity of origins and destinations of potential customers makes it difficult to provide a proper match between supply and demand. The outcome is either an insufficient supply of public transport or very low rates of patronage and exorbitantly high costs. However, it is possible to organise services differently. By asking users to state several hours beforehand what their points of departure and destinations are, operators can plan tailor-made routes and match the size of their vehicles to the number of potential passengers. On-demand public transport therefore looks set to grow in the future.

However, before such technical innovations can see the light of day, the door needs to be opened to organisational innovations. Accordingly, the first step is to challenge the fact that in far too many cases a single operator is responsible for all transport services in a conurbation. Even if this can sometimes be justified on economic grounds (increasing returns), it also acts as a brake on innovation. As a result, in many cases these bodies have problems matching supply to demand. Vehicles that are too large, running on routes that are too rigid are used in areas where they are not particularly suitable. Political and trade union pressures conspire to maintain a situation that is scarcely productive. The only way in which this state of affairs can be challenged is through the entry of new operators. We must therefore work towards securing a major institutional innovation, namely the integration of a diversified supply, provided by different operators, while maintaining a context of tariff transparency. Multimodality, integration and innovation must therefore be brought together into a coherent whole, and for that we need an overseeing authority which itself will have to adapt to the new set of rules that assessment ill bring.

5.4. *Who will design the supply of public transport services (and how)?*

As we have already noted earlier, the supply of public transport is classed as a public good; in fact, to be more precise, public transport is a political good or a good controlled by politicians. These two different ways of describing UPT by varying the emphasis are a timely reminder that we are confronted with a very particular type of situation. Public decision makers have made UPT an object that is primarily under their control and use it to lend substance to their policies. Public decision making is therefore not driven by economic considerations but by political interests or even the personal interests of politicians.

However, because these decisions entail increasingly large financial commitments that can have decisive impacts on the way cities function, they must be subjected to both *a priori* and *post factum* evaluation.

- *A priori* evaluation. The decision by the public authorities must be taken on the right scale and must ensure that the resources deployed are both coherent and relevant. The match between the level at which decisions are taken and the area concerned by the UPT supply is a crucial issue. In too many cases decisions are taken at suboptimal level, *i.e.* at too high a level when the local authority is subject to decisions taken at the level of central government; and by default when small authorities are unable to co-ordinate their actions despite constituting the same catchment area for daily mobility. The first evaluation to be conducted therefore raises this issue of the optimum level for decision-making.
- An *a priori* evaluation also needs to be made of the relevance of the resources deployed, failing which *post factum* evaluation is essential. Even though elected representatives are usually highly reluctant to undertake such action, the content of supply needs to be closely examined. Is the UPT supply properly matched to demand? Is the occupancy rate high enough? More generally, are the costs of UPT development borne by the local population justified in terms of the services provided? Figure 6.13 suggests that international benchmarking studies should be more widely conducted. In this example, we are clearly confronted with two types of extreme situation: firstly, Italian cities where very high occupancy rates indicate an inadequate level of supply; and secondly, cities in the UK where occupancy rates are very low and therefore indicate oversupply, particularly in view of the relatively high unit prices.

The most sensitive aspect of this issue is undoubtedly the coherence, relevance and transparency of public decisions. To use a well-known metaphor, the issue of UPT operator performance is merely the tip of the iceberg. The main problem lies hidden within the operating procedures for public administrations and the political bodies which govern them. However, what history and economic analysis, notably the school of public choice, have taught us is that there is no guarantee that either of them will be efficient. To ensure that decisions regarding UPTs are properly matched to the needs of the population

Figure 6.13. **Seat occupancy ratio**

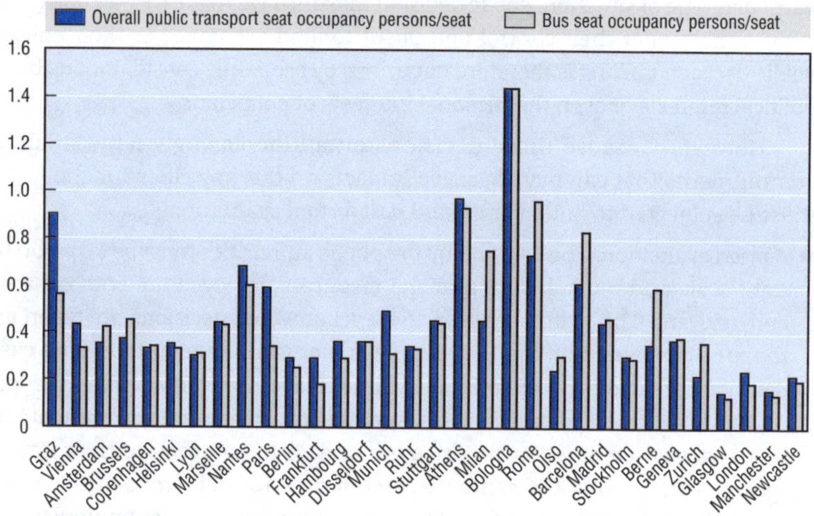

Source: UITP database on "Millenium Cities".

and the goals that local authorities have set themselves, decision-makers should not be left to their own devices. There are two ways to ensure this:

- The first would be to make systematic use of an assistant for the infrastructure owner. Private actors specialised in such arrangements can guide public decision makers. The aim is not only to delegate the management of buses or public transport, but also to consider the consistency and relevance of the choices made.
- The second is to make regular and documented comparisons of choices. If it is now possible to determine the comparative performance of a hospital or school, it is only fair that citizens should be able to consult comparative studies of UPT systems. The provision of information still remains the safest fallback, particular if, as we have suggested, the aim is not only to manage the bus network by also to put in place an integrated and innovative policy towards multimodal mobility.

Box 6.9. **Strategic issues for the period 2025-30**

UPT currently enjoys public support in many cities, particularly in Asia and western Europe. It attracts an increasing number of users, primarily due to the rising costs of car fuels.

This trend requires us to plan ahead by closely linking the future development of UPT to its relative costs with regard to private transport. To be more precise, UPT must be developed on a new and different basis for which keywords are multimodality, integration and innovation. Innovation must be pursued in such diverse areas as tariff systems, information, the matching of supply to demand and reduced production costs. To achieve this requires help from the private sector which can bring innovations, particularly when operating monopolies are challenged.

The mission of the organising authorities must also be recast. Even if they retain the ownership of the infrastructure used for the supply of UPT, they can seek help with the organisation and running of services. Public administrations are also subject to requirements with regard to efficiency, which are part of an overall approach towards the evaluation of urban policies. With this aim in mind, benchmarking studies are required. To ensure that mobility policies do not simply follow the least line of resistance, they need to be informed by developments taking place elsewhere.

Notes

1. Stance adopted, for instance, for the MARETOPE research programme or the benchmarking study conducted by the transport authority in Barcelona (EMT), or by the International Union of Public Transport (UITP) when building its "Millennium Cities" database. This chapter draws on all three sources.
2. In many cities in Africa and Latin America, private provision is less costly to the community and performance is better than public provision. Some of these experiments can probably serve as examples in the industrialised world, for instance the development of various forms of car-sharing or car-pooling.
3. As pointed out by Wiel (2002), Le Corbusier thought that faster speed was the key to a new urban order.
4. Mogridge, an Englishman, explained in the 1970s why any road investment in urban areas tends to reduce average car speeds as infrastructure supply boosts demand beyond what the new capacity can cope with, while at the same time leading to a deterioration in the quality of public transport provision.
5. In France, public expenditure on UPT totals EUR 10 billion – an amount decried by the representative of the International Road Transport Union, Christian Gérondeau, in a book entitled *Les danseuses de la République* ("The Dancing Girls of the Republic"), L'Harmattan, Paris.

6. We may note, however, the striking case of underproductivity of the transport system in Marseille (RTM). A recent study by the Cour des Comptes (the official body which oversees public accounts in France) showed a particularly worrying increase in costs without any improvement in the service.
7. There are three large private groups which operate UPT systems today in France (Kéolis, Transdev and Veolia). Some years ago there were thirteen. In 2005, the Competition Council imposed a heavy fine on these three groups for having entered into cartels.
8. An apparently anodyne decision by Paris Town Hall after the 2001 elections was to reduce by a factor of five the cost to residents of parking in the street while gradually eliminating free parking places. The result is that residents are strongly discouraged from using their cars during the week. Their cars "colonise" parking spots and limit to a large extent the turnover of parking places and hence the chances of finding one, which is one way, amongst others, of reducing the average speed of journeys by private car.

Bibliography

Ausubel, J.H., C. Marchetti and P.S. Meyer (1998), "Toward Green Mobility: The Evolution of Transport", European Review, Vol. 6, No. 2, pp. 137-156.

Baumol, W.J. and W.E. Oates (1988), *The Theory of Environmental Policy*, Cambridge University Press, Cambridge.

Becker, G. (1965), "Time and Household Production: A Theory of the Allocation of Time", *Economic Journal*, 75, September, pp. 493-517.

Beesley, M.E. (1965), "The Value of Time Spent in Travelling: Some New Evidence", *Economica*, 45, May, pp. 174-185.

Ben Akiva, M. and S.R. Lerman (1979), "Desegregated Travel and Mobility-Choice Measures of Accessibility", in Hensher, D.A. and Stopher P.R. (eds.), *Behavioural travel modelling*, Croom Helm, London, pp. 654-679.

Blayac, T. and A. Causse (2002), "Value of Travel Time", *Transportation Research*, Part B, pp. 367-389.

Bonnafous, A. and S. Masson (1999), "Évaluation des politiques de transports et équité spatiale", Working Paper.

Bonnafous, A. and H. Puel (1983), Physionomies de la ville, Les Éditions ouvrières.

Camagni, R. (1996), *Principes et modèles de l'économie urbaine*, Bibliothèque de sciences régionale, ASRDLF, Economica, Paris.

CERTU (2006), *Le transport à la demande, état de l'art, éléments d'analyse et repères pour l'action*, Collections du Certu, Lyon.

Crecy, R. (1979), "Quelques réflexions sur l'accessibilité", *Les cahiers scientifiques de la revue transports*, 4th quarter.

Crozet, Y. and I. Joly (2004), "Budgets temps de transport : les sociétés tertiaires confrontées à la gestion paradoxale du 'bien le plus rare'", *Les Cahiers Scientifiques du Transport*, No. 45, pp. 27-48.

Crozet, Y. and I. Joly (2006), "Budgets temps de transport et vitessse : de nouveaux enjeux pour les politiques de mobilité urbaine", in Bonnet, M. and P. Aubertel (eds.), *La ville aux limites de la mobilité*, PUF, Paris, pp. 287-296.

Crozet, Y. (2005), "Le temps et les transports de voyageurs", 127th ECMT Round Table, OECD, Paris, pp. 27-69.

Crozet, Y. (2005), "Réduire ou accroître les coûts du transport : les politiques européennes entre deux âges", in *Pouvoirs Locaux*, Vol. 2, No. 66, pp. 107-112.

De Palma, A. and C. Fontan (2001), "Choix modal et valeurs du temps en Ile de France", *Recherche, Transports, Sécurité*, No. 71, April-June, pp. 24-47.

Department of Transport (2004), *Measuring Accessibility for the Appraisal of Wider Economic Impacts*, TAG Unit 3.5.11.

ENEA, UITP and FAMS (2004), *Information Society, Demand Responsive Transport Services: Towards the Flexible Mobility Agency*.

Gruebler, A. (1990), *The Rise and Fall of Infrastructure: Dynamics of Evolution and Technological Change in Transport*, Physica, Heidelberg.

Hansen, G. (1959), "How Accessibility Shapes Land-Use", *Journal of the American Institute of Planners*, 25, pp. 73-76.

Hau, T.D. (1998), "Congestion Pricing and Road Investment", in Button, K. and E. Verhoef (eds.), *Road Pricing, Traffic Congestion and the Environment*, Aldershot, Elgar.

Hensher, D.A. (2001), "The Valuation of Commuter Travel Time Savings for Car", *Transportation*, pp. 101-118.

Koenig, J.G. (1974), "Théorie économique de l'accessibilité urbaine", *Revue Économique*, Vol. 25, No. 2.

Koenig, J.G. (1980), "Indicators of Urban Accessibility: Theory and Application", *Transportation*, No. 9, pp. 145-172.

MARETOPE (Managing and Assessing Regulatory Evolution in local public Transport Operations in Europe), various research studies.

Ministère de l'Équipement (2004), *Instruction-cadre relative aux méthodes d'évaluation économique des grands projets d'infrastructures de transport*, ministère de l'Équipement, des Transports, du Logement, du Tourisme et de la Mer, Paris.

Morris J.M., P.L. Dumble and M.R. Wigan (1978), "Accessibility Indicators for Transport Planning", *Transportation Research*, pp. 91-109.

Orfeuil, J.P. (2000), *L'Évolution de la mobilité quotidienne*, Les collections de l'INRETS, No. 37.

Schleifer, Andrei (1985), "A Theory of YC", *Rand Journal of Economics*, 16, pp. 319-327.

Snellen, D. and H. Hilbers (2005), *Evaluation of the Mobility Impacts of the Dutch "Vinex" Policy*, Netherland Institute for Spatial Research, Den Haag.

Stalinov, K. (2003), "Accessibility and Land Use: The Case of Suburban Seattle, 1960-1990", *Regional Studies*, Vol. 37, pp. 783-794.

Union internationale des transports publics (UITP), *Millenium Cities Database*.

Wachs, M. and J.G. Koenig (1979), "Behavioural Modelling, Accessibility, Mobility and Travel Needs", in Hensher, D. and P. Stopher (eds.), *Behavioural Travel Modelling*, Croom Helm, London, pp. 698-712.

Wiel, M. (2002), *Ville et automobile*, Edition Descartes and Cie, Paris.

Zahavi, Y. and A. Talvitie (1980), "Regularities in Travel Time and Money", *Transportation Research Record*, 750, pp. 13-19.

ISBN 978-92-64-03131-9
Infrastructure to 2030 – Vol. 2
Mapping Policy for Electricity, Water and Transport

Chapter 7

Road Transport Infrastructure: Business Models, Trends and Prospects

by

Peter J. Mackie *and* Nigel J. Smith*

World wide, roads are the backbone of the transport network. This chapter describes five main "business models" in the road transport sector, divided along the public-private financing spectrum. It looks at the sustainability of models in light of trends in demand growth, investment and pricing and rationing. Examples of successful and problematic road transport projects are provided. Implications for policy makers are outlined.

* Professors, Institute for Transport Studies, University of Leeds, United Kingdom.

1. Introduction

Road infrastructure is a key national asset and is an essential element in the free movement of people and goods, which in turn lies at the heart of the concept of a common market. Similar to other utility sectors, roads are characterised by increasing returns to scale at the planning stage and congestibility once delivered. Most of the network is a strong spatial natural monopoly. Competitive networks are largely unimaginable, except where traffic densities are sufficient to support both limited access expressways and general purpose roads in the same corridors.

In most parts of the globe, roads are the backbone of the transport network. There are exceptions – big, well-developed cities such as New York, London and Paris, where large volumes of passenger movements are undertaken by metro and rail. Rail also captures strong market shares in the intercity passenger market for movements of two to around four hours' duration, and in long distance movements of freight especially to/from ports in trainload quantities. But roads are the maids of all work, *the* common user transport infrastructure (see Tables 7.1, 7.2 and 7.3).

Here are a few debating propositions about roads:

- In the poorest countries, inadequate road infrastructure has frequently been a feature associated with rural poverty, difficulties of famine and flood relief, and problems of security against local militias.
- Very important countries, such as China and India, have come to the conclusion that a modern economy requires a national expressway network. China has gone a long way towards providing that in twenty years; India is now following.

Table 7.1. **Road network and traffic growth**

	All roads per 1 000 km^2			Road traffic in billion vehicle-km		
	1991	2001	% change	1991	2001	% change
Great Britain	1 566	1 707	+9.0	411	474	+15.3
Denmark	1 647	1 664	+1.0	37	47	+27
France	1 633	1 809	+10.7	449	500	+15.8
Spain	320	324	+1.2	110	202	+83.6
Sweden	302	473	+56.6	64	71	+10.9
Switzerland	1 719	1 724	+0.2	54	57	+5.5
USA	668	681	+1.9	2 266	2 532	+11.7

Source: Transport Statistics Great Britain (2004), Department for Transport.

Table 7.2. **Freight traffic by mode**
2001 freight market shares

	Road %	Rail %	Inland waterway %	Pipeline %	Total billion ton-km
Great Britain	83	11	–	6	181
Denmark	73	9	–	18	24
France	78	14	2	6	352
Germany	71	15	13	3	499
Spain	87	8	–	5	162
Sweden	61	39	–	–	50
Switzerland	70	29	–	1	34
USA (1991)	27	38	13	22	3 952

Source: Transport Statistics Great Britain (2004), Department for Transport.

Table 7.3. **National passenger traffic by land mode**
2001 market shares

	Cars and taxis %	Buses and coaches %	Rail[1] %	Total billion passenger-km
Great Britain	88	6	6	709
Denmark	80	12	8	73
France	86	5	8	843
Germany	83	8	9	848
Spain	81	14	5	379
Sweden	82	10	8	113
USA	96	4	–	6 747

1. Excluding metros.
Source: Transport Statistics Great Britain (2004), Department for Transport.

- Congestion in cities is a pandemic. Speeds in London – at least pre-congestion charge – are no higher than they were a century ago.
- In many western countries, the motorway age lasted from around 1955 to around 1980. Since the completion of the M25 around London in 1986, little new capacity has been added to the British network while vehicle-kilometres have roughly doubled. Unstable equilibrium is achieved through rationing by congestion. Many commentators believe that the policy mix is one of underpricing and underinvestment.
- Scarce public finance has been a significant constraint on the roads programme in many countries, and there remains much interest in the roads sector as one where the private sector can play a useful role.

The roads sector faces a number of conflicts, if not conundra. Travel as a freedom, demand growth, congestion and pollution, tax revenues several times allocated costs and constrained public finance investment are all features of the landscape. There are concerns about the true social returns on investment in roads and about their affordability using conventional public finance.

The purpose of this chapter is to consider the balance between public and private and the scope for alternative business models in the context of economic, social and technical trends. The potential scope of this chapter is daunting, and therefore we have limited it in two ways. First of all, we consider only road infrastructure, and not the ancillary services which are provided such as service stations. These may be bundled with the infrastructure, or more likely franchised out, or for old roads be in the hands of many private owners. Some form of market solution – however imperfect and ill-informed – will operate. Similarly, we do not address in this chapter the freight transport, coaches and other transport services which use the infrastructure. Unlike rail services, these are rarely or never vertically integrated with the infrastructure and are essentially competitive (or at least contestable).

Secondly, although we were invited to consider a very wide range of countries, it is impossible to do justice to the literature on several of these. Amongst very many recent World Bank papers are Estache, Romero and Strong (2000); Queiroz (2005); Irigoyen (2006); Bellier *et al.* (2003); World Bank (2005), which in turn open the door to many other references.

The statistics showing the extent of the road network, the motorway network and the concessioned network for many OECD countries and the US and Japan, based on the figures from Fayard (2003), are given in Table 7.4. A few countries such as France, Italy, Austria and Portugal rely heavily on concessions, usually toll concessions to operate their motorways. Most others have little or

Table 7.4. **Road infrastructure statistics**

	BEL	DEN	DEU	FRA	FIN	ITA	ESP	LUX	SWE
Total road network (km)	149 739	71 952	644 429	998 001	103 850	668 721	164 139	5 001	139 847
Total length motorway (km)	1 729	1 010	12 174	10 379	653	6 487	9 739	126	1 591
Total length of motorways concession (km)	14	34	4	7 840	69	5 593	2 610	0	16
Total billion vehicle-km	93.1	47.2	–	–	49.8	–	–	–	63

	GBR	NLD	AUT	GRC	PRT	EU15	USA	JPN
Total road network (km)	414 226	125 893	106 058	114 605	79 428	3 785 889	6 407 637	1 200 000
Total length motorway (km)	3 609	2 289	1 633	742	1 836	53 997	264 703	64 500
Total length of motorways concession (km)	580	4	1 600	742	1 771	20 877	15 793	10 500
Total billion vehicle-km	513	32	–	–	–	–	–	–

Source: Fayard, A. (2003), "Analysis of Highway Concessions in Europe, Conference on Highways: Cost and Regulation in Europe", University of Bergamo, Italy.

no experience of motorway concessions. Of course in all countries, the total motorway network is only a small percentage of the total highway network. The discussion in this chapter takes place within this context.

2. Road provider business models

The precise definitions of business models in this sector, which is still evolving, are not standard or universal. There is a plethora of variations on each of the main business models, and the location of the boundaries at which an approach changes from being a variant into a discrete and separate business model is a subject of much debate. We propose five categories of business model covering the complete range from the purely public sector model to the purely private sector model.

The five generic business models selected for the delivery of new highways, refurbishment and upgrading, and management services, whilst distinct, are similar in nature to the five categories adopted by Stambrook (2006) of Virtuosity Consulting concentrating on PPPs for the Operation and Maintenance (O&M) of highway networks. The models are divided along the public/private financing spectrum, as shown in the Figure 7.1, and consist of the following:

- *Public*. Traditional purely public sector funding drawn from taxation, together with a range of alternative public funding, often involving access to private finance and a necessary collaboration between national government and local government road providers.

Figure 7.1. **The public/private financing spectrum**

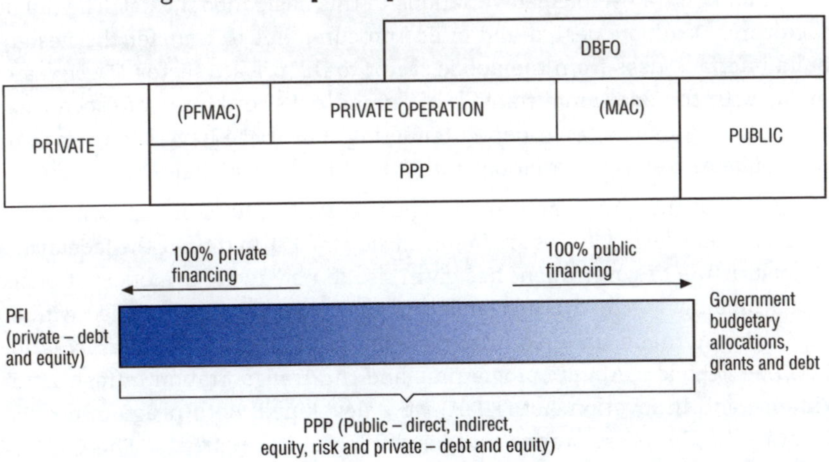

Source: Based on Ganon (2004).

- *Design-Build-Finance-Operate (DBFO)*. Privately financed projects remunerated by shadow tolls which cannot be regarded as true concessions.
- *Public-Private Partnership (PPP)*. Toll road infrastructure, including the widespread practice of franchising with mixed public-private funding and/or ownership of new build with private or public-private operation and maintenance. (Stambrook, 2006, calls this "mixed public-private".)
- *Private operation*. Range of variants with private finance instruments being used to address operation and repair, improvement and/or reconstruction. (Stambrook, 2006, names this "private concession O&M".)
- *Private*. Purely Build-Operate-Transfer (BOT) concession. (Stambrook, 2006, refers to this as BOT.)

2.1. Public business model

The traditional public sector funded business model is well known and understood. It was widely adopted in the UK and many other countries and is still in use for many road infrastructure projects. The need for a project is determined by the state, through appraisal and public inquiry, using either in-house staff or private sector consultants. Design is undertaken either by in-house public sector design staff or by private sector consultants. Competitive tendering is used to select private sector construction contractors, and the public sector usually takes on responsibility for operation and maintenance. In this model, use is made of private sector expertise but not private sector finance. Traditionally the revenue is raised from taxation.

A number of established variations to this basic model exist. The public sector might adopt "design and build" procurement to transfer the design-build interface risks from the public sector to the private sector. "Design and build" with the additional transfer of ground risks to the private sector has been utilised, as has "own period tendering" but these have been relatively unpopular and exist as variations rather than discrete models.

Some of the best examples of public sector business models with more complex financial structures are found outside the EU. In the US, the federal and state structure of government has given rise to new two tier models of public sector funding. Faced with problems of limited state finances coupled with an increasing demand for road infrastructure projects the Grant Anticipation Revenue Vehicle (GARVEE) programme and the Transportation Infrastructure Finance and Innovation Act (TIFIA) were developed. Both programmes use leveraged federal assistance and access to capital markets. The GARVEE programme enables states and other public authorities to issue debt-financing instruments, such as bonds, to pay for current expenditures on transportation construction projects and repay the debt using future federal apportionments. However, reimbursement of construction costs occurs only when debt service is due. The main benefit is that upfront capital is generated to keep projects moving forward at tax-exempt rates and the cost of the infrastructure is spread over its useful life rather than just over the construction period. The TIFIA programme provides assistance to projects with their own repayment streams, such as toll roads. Under TIFIA, the US Department of Transportation (US DOT) provides direct credit assistance of up to 33% of eligible project costs to sponsors of major transportation projects. Credit assistance can take the form of a loan, loan guarantee or line of credit. The benefits of TIFIA assistance include improved access to capital markets, flexible repayment terms, and more favourable interest rates than in private capital markets.

2.2. *DBFO business model*

In a market where experience of private financing of public infrastructure is scarce and when few projects have been undertaken to indicate likely levels of risk, the UK selected the Design-Build-Finance-Operate (DBFO) business model of procurement based on shadow tolls. This model is not a true concession, and in the UK payment was usually made to the private sector concession holder in regular instalments by the public sector based on traffic usage. A shadow toll means that vehicles are not physically stopped, and no direct charge is made on the highway user. Hence, the utilisation of the new highway is likely to be high. This in turn means that the revenue generation risk for the concession holder is low, encouraging competitive tendering.

DBFO concessions can be developed to reflect the availability of the highway and service quality indices in the shadow toll. Estimated traffic flows can be "banded" such that specified "bands" of traffic would attract different payment amounts with the top band generating no additional return for the concessionaire, so that the procuring agency's financial exposure would be capped. The DBFO concession agreement could provide flexibility for alternative revenue sources typically from land-development usage to complement the shadow toll. This public-private range is indicated in the Figure 7.1.

In the UK, traffic was further divided into vehicles below 5.2 metres in length and above 5.2 metres in length, as a proxy for light and heavy axles to reflect differential maintenance costs. This model was largely abandoned in 1998 following the Bates Review, although there are one or two very large projects, such as the M25 widening schemes for which shadow tolling may be adopted.

2.3. *Public-private partnership (PPP) business models*

The essential features of this model are public sector planning and feasibility leading to a decision to proceed, a concession or franchise arrangement to deliver the project using a mixture of public and private capital, financed by toll revenues and operating concessions over a concession period with reversion to government. The basic model has been modified to suit custom and practice in different countries, but the basic principles remain the same. It is useful to briefly outline the practice of this type of model in different markets.

The case of Hungary, as an example of an emerging market economy, demonstrates the lack of public money to finance new road infrastructure expenditure. Concession contracts were sought with international private sector consortia to finance, build, own, operate and transfer new physical toll motorways but the risks, including a non-convertible currency, were such that considerable public sector support was required from the Hungarian state and the European Bank for Reconstruction and Development participated in making the projects bankable.

The National Roads Authority of Norway ran a pilot PPP model with a private sector special purpose vehicle (SPV) responsible for construction operation and financing of construction and operation of the project. The SPV will receive an annual unitary payment over the period of the concession, but the actual level of payment is varied according to performance against a number of pre-defined criteria related to political goals of accessibility, performance and safety on the road network. Funding is from the state budget in addition to revenues from tolls. Tolls will be collected by an independent intermunicipal not for profit state company over the concession period. Repayment starts from the day the road is open for traffic.

The Great Belt project linking Denmark and Sweden uses a different variant of the PPP business model. The SPV has been established and is regulated according to a special agreement between the governments of the two countries, each retaining a 50% share in the consortium. Guarantees by the Kingdom of Denmark and the Kingdom of Sweden give a very high credit rating on the bonds issued by the SPV in the domestic as well as the international capital markets. Loans are repaid from tolls paid by road users in addition to income from the railway users paid by the Danish National Railways Agency and the Swedish National Rail Administration at a set annual fee. Other income derives from the sale of capacity of optical fibres used for the transmission of data and telephony. It is a fundamental condition of the model that the costs of building and financing the project will be borne by the users.

In the US, the Intermodal Surface Transportation Efficiency Act (ISTEA) of 1991 and its predecessors, Transportation Equity Act for the 21st Century (TEA-21) and Safety Accountability Fairness Efficiency Transportation Equity Act (SAFETEA) in 2005, created a major change to transportation planning and policy in the US. Greater decentralisation of decision making meant that individual states could now have more influence over the allocation of finance to transport projects in their area under three main programmes. The Interstate System Construction Toll Pilot Program enables 3 projects nationwide to collect tolls on an interstate highway, bridge or tunnel for the purpose of constructing interstate highways. The Interstate System Reconstruction and Rehabilitation Toll Pilot Program allows up three interstate highways to collect tolls on existing interstate highways to enable reconstruction or rehabilitation of other interstate highway corridors. The Value Pricing Pilot Program has funding of USD 59 million to support the costs of implementing up to 15 variable pricing pilot programmes nationwide on tolled roads to manage congestion and benefit air quality, energy use, and efficiency.

Japan has one of the largest toll road networks in the world (9 200 km). Nearly two-thirds of the 12 700 km of trunk roads and expressways are tolled. Roads were initially funded through the public sector dependent on a Road Improvement Special Account which was raised from tolls, central and local taxes on fuel and freight transport. Later, highway projects were promoted by large construction companies with subsidized debt. Companies injected equity, usually about 10% of the funding requirement and senior debt was provided by Japanese commercial banks, regional banks, or trust companies, with some participation by the Development Bank of Japan. Debt has been underwritten by government. There is no sign yet of "pure" financial investors or of bond issues. Six public expressway corporations are in charge of expressway construction and maintenance; East Nippon, Central Nippon, West Nippon, Metropolitan, Hanshin and Honshu-Shikoku Bridge.

Almost all high-grade highways in China, including new expressways, are toll facilities. Despite this, China still remains a very risky country for foreign investors, particularly due to previous investors' inability to repay loans mainly due to problems related to currency convertibility and repatriation of profit. This makes it difficult to raise long-term debt in the international capital market, particularly due to the absence of legal and regulatory frameworks. China is therefore trying to raise new equity capital in Hong Kong, China, and the domestic market by issuing new equity shares in provincial expressway companies by relying on the expressways with more mature traffic for income generation. Highway assets are sold to these public sector companies which can then leverage or securitise revenues and issue shares through international private finance. This technique is now widely used in China, and in several cases, new financing has been supported by the use of existing, revenue-producing toll facilities partially financed by the World Bank (Nickesen and Stanfield, 2001).

Several European countries have developed a public-private sector "franchise" model. Historically, roads were paid for largely by the state with only the operation passed on to the private sector by a concession. The object of the franchise contract was usually motorway maintenance and the provision of motorways services, although in some cases the franchise contract also included the construction of new roads. Tariffs were meant to generate revenues sufficient to cover costs and could be adjusted annually by the principal. In some countries franchisees were privatised and changes made to the regulatory framework whereby a public sector contribution to funding could be decided on a case-by-case basis, depending on the local conditions and on the expected social benefits, when the investment could not possibly be paid for by traffic revenues only.

2.4. Private operation business models

In the UK, the public sector owner of mainly urban and/or local highway networks have been contracting out the O&M services for many years. However, in 2001 the first Managing Agent Contractor (MAC) contract came into operation in September 2001. The contract allows the partner MAC organisation to design and undertake all projects up to a value of GBP 500 000 for a maximum period of seven years. The contract covers routine maintenance works aimed at keeping the network safe and in good appearance in addition to reactive works such as response to hazards, accidents or removal of ice. It is an incentive based contract that relies on key performance indicators set by the client. The contract is allocated on the basis of partnering skills rather than solely on financial criteria.

A private finance version of the MAC form of maintenance contract, a PFMAC, has been developed. The PFMAC partnership, often consisting of staff from the public authority, design consultants and a main contractor, are expected to finance the works in addition to the management of all operational and maintenance work. In this instance, consideration will be given as to whether the scope of this form of contract should include network communications and control equipment and also any elements of network operation. In addition it could be extended to provide a means of delivering major improvements either through public or private funding or a combination of both. The PFMAC partnership acts as almost a semi-autonomous agency. This concept is being considered in a wide form by Highways Agency in conjunction with Rijkswatersaat, Atkins and Grontmij in a study of Programme Infrastructure Management. PIM is an R&D programme to improve operations and maintenance of the national highways network by the exchange of knowledge and best practice. A key element is to improve interfaces and relations between national agencies and private companies, with pilot projects running in the Netherlands and UK.

PFMAC variations can be applied to cities and urban areas. In addition to management and maintenance for a given concession period, the contract also includes road cleansing, treatment of pot-holes, bringing street lights up to standard, bridgeworks, structural retaining walls, street lighting, maintenance of traffic management equipment, highways-related tree and grounds maintenance, winter maintenance and street cleansing and managing the highways with regards to licences and inspections. Typically, the ethos reflects a "Highway Asset Maintenance" approach, the essence of which is that the road network – substantially failing and suffering from lack of investment – should first be rehabilitated and then sustained at the improved level by planned life cycle maintenance. This offers better value for money than the traditional public sector annual works programme that responds only to immediate and acute need. Finance is often provided by the city local authority and central government but with a core investment funded by the SPV through a senior debt facility. Other services will be carried out concurrently to generate revenue streams that are paid by the city as infrastructure starts to meets specified standards. Revenue can also be raised by charging users and through land-usage options. The unitary charge being based principally upon availability and performance, but also includes an element related to usage by heavy goods vehicles. The main aim of the model is defined as the restoration of the condition of the network to a point where sustainable maintenance is achieved utilising the principles of whole-life costing.

Examples of purely private operation also exist. In China, the Transfer-Operate-Transfer (TOT) model is popular and is based on the transfer of an existing highway facility from the public sector to the private operator who is authorised to raise tolls. The revenue stream is then used to fund maintenance and/or upgrades and/or sections of new build or ultimate replacement depending upon the government's requirements, the cash flow and the source of additional funding, if any. At the completion of a pre-agreed period the facility is then transferred back to the public sector.

2.5. *Private business model (BOT)*

At the other end of the spectrum exists the wholly private sector funded model, often referred to as the Build-Operate-Transfer (BOT) model or in the UK the Private Finance Initiative (PFI). For a relatively small number of low-risk, high-profit toll road projects a model based on pinpoint equity and private sector debt finance can be utilised. Land development concessions may be bundled with the toll road to achieve a viable commercial proposition.

This type of project is usually the first transport project to utilise private finance in any country adopting a project financing strategy. The projects have a clear appeal to the private sector to outweigh the disbenefits of operating in novel cultural and contractual circumstances which does have adverse financial consequences. Often the concession is made more attractive by a lack of regulation over re-financing or tariffs which will be imposed as the market matures. As might be expected the number of projects that are both socially and politically desirable and are financially robust is normally very small, and hence the long-term market for purely privately financed projects is limited.

3. The policy context and implications for development

In previous work, the OECD (2006) has identified the following key economic, technological and governance-related trends and challenges. These are:

- Increasing constraints in coming decades on public finances due to conflicting priorities (*e.g.* ageing populations' claims on resources for health and pensions, security concerns) and higher costs associated with infrastructure (*e.g.* environmental impacts).
- Perceived mismatches in infrastructure planning cycles, budget cycles and electoral cycles.
- Availability of a wider range of innovative financing mechanisms, and greater acceptance of the use of these mechanisms.
- Policy directives that call for increasing consideration of externalities in pricing schemes related to transport, as well as the use of pricing as an instrument of demand management.
- Policy directives by which greater direct user contributions are sought as a means of funding transport infrastructure.
- The advent of new technologies (Galileo, advanced computing, etc.) that strengthen the focus on the potential for more effective user charging systems and eventually network-based pricing.
- The public's (un)willingness to pay for access to and use of road infrastructure and related services.
- Urbanisation and its impact on land use and prices.
- Congestion in given gateways and corridors as a result of growth in (international) trade.
- Broad-based trends towards greater democratisation (especially at local level) and decentralisation, accompanied by growing pressures for greater public transparency of reporting, accountability of performance, public consultation, resolution of conflicts, etc.

We would propose to add two bullet points to this list:

- Globalisation trends and the role of infrastructure in promoting competition within the EU and in enhancing EU performance *vis-à-vis* other trading blocs.
- Demographic and other social trends – ageing populations, saturation of the "propensity to drive" as the current generation replaces the "baby boomers" where women drivers were underrepresented.

For ease of discussion, we group these under headings before discussing the implications for policy.

3.1. Demand growth

In a business as usual scenario, we would expect to see continuing demand growth for road transport associated with GDP growth as the key feature of the landscape. Demand growth is driven primarily by car ownership growth with kilometres per car remaining roughly constant in this scenario. In the more prosperous countries, income elasticities will continue to fall, but will remain positive. Only extreme fuel price scenarios will be sufficient to offset the effects of income growth fully and such scenarios will stimulate technical change and fuel substitution. In middle-income countries, including the more prosperous accession states, fast growth in car ownership and use is to be expected, with income elasticities well above unity.

Demand growth will differ by location as well as income level. The last decade has seen little growth in UK urban areas as the system has reached capacity with growth only feasible at off-peak times. Ultimately however, this affects urban form and journey length, so growth may be partially displaced in space. In countries such as the UK and the Netherlands, the default policy scenario is increasing restraint due to capacity being reached over progressively wider areas and longer time periods. However, the price being paid in terms of congestion, unreliability, and environmental problems is becoming appreciable.

Social trends such as ageing, allied to technological developments such as internet which facilitate home-working, are likely to change the spatial and temporal pattern of demand for road use and may act to moderate some of the worst peak problems.

3.2. Investment

A simplistic view would be that demand growth should be matched by supply growth, the predict-and-provide principle. In parts of the European system especially on the interurban network, new capacity is part of the solution especially where the historic legacy is inadequate and fast growth is anticipated.

However, in the north-west of Europe, history suggests that the investment "solution" is rather unlikely to happen. The UK has seen almost no investment in new urban road capacity relative to stock since the early 1970s. The few schemes which have been completed, such as M8 Glasgow and M11-Hackney Wick in London, have been massively controversial. More grandiose concepts equivalent to some of the investment in the Paris region have not been seen as a credible option. In the last fifteen years, there have been, with a few exceptions including the M6 toll road, no greenfield road building and limited expansion of capacity on the core motorway network through widening schemes.

There are a number of reasons for this:

- Road capacity is very expensive and governments have been unwilling to provide it out of public budgets given other spending priorities and public budget rules to be met.
- Road capacity on new lines of route is unpopular with the public and therefore politically sensitive in North-western Europe – the not-in-my-backyard (NIMBY) syndrome.
- Increased environmental awareness (1) – biodiversity, loss of heritage and natural assets associated with new infrastructure provision.
- Increased environmental awareness (2) – local effects such as emissions and noise, global effects such as carbon emissions associated with transport operations.
- The "roads generate traffic" debate has, for congested axes, weakened the economic case for new capacity; so too has the belief that roads are underpriced relative to long-run marginal cost leading to an element of excess traffic. This is associated with the argument that we should get the prices right as a prerequisite to decisions on new capacity.
- Some lack of faith that the values in CBA especially the travel time values, can be converted into real economic benefits.

There are some signs that this agenda may be changing. There is concern in the more congested regions about the consequences for unreliability of a continued failure to invest. The system may be self-regulating but at a very low and unpredictable level of service quality. There is also renewed interest in the links between transport infrastructure investment and economic performance. Here the official view in some countries is that there is too much of a disconnect between concepts such as travel time values and the effects on the real economy which these concepts represent, and that political progress will only be made if this gap can be convincingly closed (DfT 2005, IASON, 2004).

3.3. *Pricing and rationing*

If demand growth continues and capacity fails to meet demand, then the question of how best to manage capacity will become increasingly loudly asked. We have the situation in Britain and the Netherlands and the Ruhr where extremely valuable scarce road space is allocated to traffic on a first-come first-served basis, free at the point of demand. Already, representatives of high-value users such as the CBI and the Freight Transport Association in the UK support road user charging "provided the revenues are recycled into road investment". It is difficult to say how bad network conditions have to be for the general public and politicians to accept the case for road user charging; it may be that some tipping point such as gridlock conditions occurring with monotonous regularity will be needed.

In terms of political and public acceptance (as opposed to economics), the feasibility of road user charging can be ranked as follows:

- *New capacity.* M6 toll, HOT lanes on motorways. Feasibility – high. The public and private users have to demonstrate their "willingness to pay" for something at acceptable toll levels otherwise, as in the case of the Skye Bridge in Scotland the project is not viable. This is where hybrid PPPs have a role to play.
- *City centre schemes.* Examples in London and Stockholm. Feasibility is moderately high for city centres of sufficient environmental quality and congestion problems especially with low residential population. The public may accept more of these schemes. The current Transport Innovation Fund in UK is funding studies for eight town and city schemes.
- *City area-wide schemes.* The Oslo, Bergen toll rings, and Singapore. Feasibility is moderate, but the failure of the Edinburgh scheme to gain acceptance in a referendum was a big disappointment and there is a need to overcome problems relating to boundary effects, treatment of residents and fear of activity migration out of the charged zone.
- *Motorway tolls.* Feasibility variable. These are common throughout Europe but there are few examples of introducing tolls on historically free roads. Politicians in UK and the Netherlands doubt the saleability of this concept; also there are many economic issues concerning diversion in the more dense congested areas because some traffic is removed from the purpose-built sections of the network to less suitable routes. Tolls work best where they are least needed for congestion reasons, *i.e.* on long distance interurban routes as a premium charge for better quality service. Casual observation in Spain, France, Italy suggests they are there to raise revenue, not to deal efficiently with congestion, although there have been some experiments with time of day pricing.
- *Network charging.* Feasibility – the "64 billion dollar question". Various methods are approaching technical feasibility (tag and beacon before GPS). Major issues, however, are political as demonstrated in the Netherlands. Could such a fundamental change in the social contract be negotiated with the public and under what conditions? Our view is that it would be essential to think in terms of tariff reform, with road user charging for congestion and environment associated with reforms to fuel taxation and vehicle ownership taxes so as to ensure that a strong coalition of road users was willing to accept the package. In the UK, there is acute political sensitivity in the treasury about such a concept because this could involve a reduction in central government control and discretion over tax instruments. The other point is that it appears that implementation would be hugely expensive. The challenge is not technical feasibility but cost effectiveness and political/social acceptability.

- *Rationing.* High occupancy vehicle lanes, high occupancy toll lanes and ramp metering have all been suggested but the fundamental practicability, efficiency and economics of such schemes remain unclear. More extreme physical analogues to pricing such as tradeable (or even non-tradeable) permits seem much less likely even than road user charging to be socially acceptable except as short term responses to world fuel crisis conditions.

3.4. *Governance issues*

There is a view which says that the mixture of:

- scarcity of public capital;
- inconsistency of electoral cycles with long-term infrastructure planning; and
- unpopularity of public decisions on tolls and charges;

points in the direction of some form of PPP or franchise model. This would probably be a mixed public-private finance model, using a mix of taxpayer funding possibly remunerated via shadow tolls and user funding via actual tolls. Politically, the creation of an independent agency gives a greater guarantee of stability and progress than the politicised environment of government roads departments. This could be an attractive model in eastern Europe where arguably the priority is to get the infrastructure designed and built. It also is attractive for those countries where versions of the franchise model already operate, including Spain, France and Italy.

However, we have reservations about very widespread applicability of this model to total networks as opposed to high-quality tolled motorways. Franchise at the network level raises difficult problems of private monopoly power over rights of access to land and property, discriminatory tariffs and other stories familiar from economic history. The regulatory regime would need to be so tight and prescriptive that there would be little advantage over conventional public ownership. The franchise model seems to us to work best where users are freely choosing and paying for a restricted access road offering a higher quality of service than the base network provides.

3.5. *The European "project"*

For most of western Europe, the road network can be considered to be complete. Here, new capacity is essentially incremental in terms of its impact in the economy. However, there are exceptions – the missing links such as the Messina, Oresund and Fehmarn Belt crossings where regional economic structure effects are to be expected. For eastern Europe, the position is rather different. At the political level, as was seen in Canada and the US in the 19th century, transport infrastructure is one of the few visible means of demonstrating achievement of a political ideal. Furthermore, the eastern TEN roads are much more of a step change relative to the existing networks and are more likely to bring with them effects on production locations, migration and European competitiveness. Relative to roads in France or UK which are very largely matters for national or regional government, there is a European dimension to these decisions (Community Value Added). This creates a multiparty aspect to the problem – the EU and several countries working together – where an independent agency with an element of toll finance, may be the best prospect for delivery of politically desired projects.

4. Sustainability of business models

The further we try to see into the future, the more difficult it is to have confidence in the outcomes. Yet it is essential to make these judgements if we wish to make progress. To illustrate this point, it is useful to recall the traffic and road infrastructure 60 years ago and then consider the practicalities of producing realistic, robust forecasts of traffic in 60 years time which will guarantee the sustainability of the project. Nevertheless that does not mean that a 60-year road infrastructure concession cannot be robust and sustainable when pooled in a portfolio with other infrastructure investment projects or that the business case cannot be rigorously evaluated. Many attempts (for example, the UK Department for Transport's Foresight Intelligent Infrastructure Project) have been made to forecast transport futures based upon technological developments, the pressures for sustainable development on a finite planet and the balance between freedom, revenue and performance or capacity. This section offers an assessment of the likely future sustainability of the main business models for road infrastructure in the context of the key development drivers identified earlier in the report. A summary is provided in Table 7.5 at the end of this section.

In terms of demand growth, most scenarios consider that a strong growth in road traffic within the EU at least until 2030 is inevitable. However, the growth is unlikely to be uniform. In several northern European countries birth rates are falling and in Germany in 2005 the actual population fell, however traffic growth is very high in some of the southern and eastern European countries where emerging markets almost by definition are likely to have demands for new road infrastructure and for increased growth on existing infrastructure. This traffic is not only national but creates traffic increases in northern European countries as well. The population in Europe is also ageing and in turn creating greater off-peak traffic movements.

Within countries the densities of population also affect the patterns of highway utilisation. Urban areas are experiencing increasing growth and there is widespread use of congestion charging schemes to facilitate the effective flow of road traffic. Although the UK is experiencing serious road traffic congestion in many urban areas the level of car ownership is still lower than many developed countries. This has resulted in cities adopting or proposing to adopt road user charging based upon a variety of technological solutions. The well-reported schemes in Durham and London (Dix, ECMT/TfL Congestion Conference, London, 2004), demonstrate both the effectiveness of these systems and the significant revenue raising capacity. The current system in central London utilises number plate recognition technology, database management computing and a range of communication types including so called "smart" cards to monitor daily traffic flows and to pursue and charge all non-payers.

The main urban areas in the UK are connected by heavily used motorways or major highways. Congestion problems, particularly at peak times are already causing difficulties. A range of tolling systems (M6) and active traffic management (M25 and M42) are already being used but in future management schemes will rely upon communications technology. Dedicated short-range communications (DSRC) and Global Navigation Systems will increasingly be used probably in conjunction with transponders in vehicles and intelligent route markers. This technology offers the potential to monitor all vehicles on all major routes at all times of the day and to apply variable tariffs accordingly. Hence, it should be possible to offer highway users a choice of routes and times to match budgets and schedules. Clearly the operation of the technology with its capacity for regulating and variably charging users will have a huge influence on the financial viability of the highway. It is unlikely that the public sector would be willing to allow the private sector to operate in an uncontrolled manner and any private sector business model would require strict limits on any change mechanisms. Although probably neutral for most business models, the increasing use of technology may favour business models under which the public sector retained the responsibility for regulation and tariffs.

In managing highway capacity, we are seeking cost effective and socially acceptable incentives to modify user behaviour in a manner likely to satisfy the objective we are trying to realise. To date, the incentives adopted have been either financial, usually in the form of road pricing strategies, or regulatory, usually some form of rationing access through technology or legislation. In order for an incentive to operate, it has to be perceived as a realistic opportunity. Negative incentives, such as the dissatisfaction with gridlock, are not normally regarded as effective unless the condition becomes persistent; rather, positive incentives, such as dedicated lanes for particular types of road user, are preferred. In areas of high traffic volumes, technology can be utilised to regulated lane usage and speed every few hundred metres along a motorway. If obeyed, these measures can significantly increase capacity but are frequently ignored by users. Research is ongoing into the use of technology to override manual operation of each vehicle and impose computer based "road-trains" of many vehicles travelling at the regulated speed in very close proximity. This would improve safety and increase capacity but would not differentially affect any of the business models, Bunker and Holdane, TRL (2003).

The growth trends are dependent upon assumptions about fuel, in particular, fuel types, fuel costs and taxation, and fuel availability. The current use of carbon-based fossil fuels is rapidly depleting a resource which is renewable over geological time frames but which is not sustainable in the short- to medium-term future. Research into multifuelled vehicles, fuel cells, biofuels and hydrogen-based fuels is promising and likely to be stepped up as shortages in more traditional fuels are encountered. Fuel of some sort is likely to be available and it is likely to be taxed and it is the future regulation of fuel tax that is likely to have the greater impact.

Regarding new investment, we think it is unlikely in most OECD countries in the short- and medium-term future that significant additional sources of public sector finance will suddenly become available. Equally, we believe that the purely private financing is only ever going to be viable for a small percentage of low-risk, high-revenue road projects which satisfy the requirements of social cost/benefit and a viable financial analysis. In most countries, if they exist at all, these types of road projects will be completed first and be unlikely to occur again. Therefore, neither of the models at the extreme ends of the spectrum is particularly robust, although the public sector is likely to retain a wider remit of responsibilities for the future construction, maintenance and operation of road infrastructure projects. However, it seems equally likely that the constraints on public sector finances will mean that an even smaller percentage of public sector investment will be made in the highway network through any of the business models.

Box 7.1. **Fuel taxes in adjoining countries**

There are current examples of a significant difference in tax levels between adjoining countries. For example, Luxembourg imposes a relatively lower fuel tax that renders its petrol 20% cheaper than in neighbouring Belgium. Due to the Schengen agreement, the Belgian borders are unmanned and hence a disproportionate number of drivers from neighbouring countries go into Luxembourg to pay the lower fuel tax. This is facilitated by the central location of Luxembourg as a north-south connection. This type of traffic can make a significant difference in a relatively small country like Luxembourg but would make little economic difference in larger countries such as Germany or France.

Rietveld and Woudenberg (2005) cite many reasons why almost all countries impose a fuel tax. The main reason given is the low cost of collection and control. Fuel tax is a tax that is difficult to avoid. Additionally taxation of fuel is seen as providing a stable revenue base because the demand for fuel does not change significantly with short-term variations in price. In countries such as the US, fuel tax is used as a user fee to finance transport infrastructure. Taxes on motor fuels account for up to 10% of the revenue base of many OECD countries.

In this context, it is important to realise that using public-private financial models is not the equivalent of borrowing money from a different bank. The source of the money is only one aspect and it is the use of entrepreneurship and commercial acumen, coupled with the transfer of risk away from the public sector, that is the key contribution. Consequently it is essential that the public sector is fully supportive of the project and that there is sufficient flexibility to allow the private sector to utilise their skills effectively without disadvantaging the public.

One of the most important issues facing the sustainability of road infrastructure is the question of how we *manage capacity*. This requires a clear understanding of the objective we are trying to achieve and a recognition that the question differs significantly depending upon the economy, the location and the time as well as other parameters. Logically, emerging markets will be radically different to developed markets; urban areas will not be the same as rural networks; and peak times cannot be regarded as typical of the traffic flows at other times. Existing technology indicates that managing the capacity of a road network is practicable and as technological evolution continues the capabilities tend to expand and the costs tend to decrease. Early work by MIT in 2001 validated the concepts of mobile wireless network communications as a means of mitigating urban congestion (S.N. Humbad, MSc Thesis, 2001).

Tolls, particularly time and location variable tolls, do act as an incentive for road infrastructure users. This raises further issues of whether interurban, motorway style routes should be tolled, or alternatively whether the entire road network should be tolled providing the opportunity for cross subsidy for management of the interurban network. It is also important to consider the "Portfolio" or "Bundling" approach where a number of projects can be integrated into a single concession for cross-subsidy and internal risk transfer which has had some success in the UK health and education sectors. Politically, the right to use your own car where and when you choose has been portrayed by some as a metric for individual freedom. Whether or not you accept this view there is likely to be opposition from a proportion of the road infrastructure users to increasing levels of pricing and regulation, despite the demonstrable benefits of the strategy.

Finally, the matter of governance needs to be considered. Whilst it is clear, and has been so for some time, that government must be strongly supportive of each of the business models adopted if they are to be successful in achieving their objectives it is not at all clear what the public sector role should be. There seems to be little argument that the commercial and entrepreneurial expertise of the private sector should be utilised for public benefit; the question is how to best achieve this. Typically, current approaches to this issue have resulted in various PPPs, franchising arrangements, and "independent" hybrid public-private agencies. The question of independent economic regulation, as in other sectors, also needs to be addressed.

4.1. *Public business models*

The public sector has been the prime authority in the provision of road infrastructure, and we believe that this sector will continue to play a vital part in all future developments with all the viable business models. The public sector has a wide range of duties and responsibilities for road infrastructure, and even under the traditional 100% publicly financed model, contracts were awarded to procure private sector expertise in design and construction. Despite the lack of public sector funds and the increasing constraints on investment, the public sector is unlikely to relinquish the power to raise taxation on vehicles and fuel which are key components in the overall strategy for road pricing. Indeed, these strengths confirm the key role of the sector in the future. As Fayard (2003) and others have stated there are only two real sources of revenue, either the public sector pays or the user pays. However, the financing options available to the public sector need to be fully investigated to ascertain the optimum positioning of the interface between public funding and user charging.

In the UK, the responsibility for part of the planning process and the public inquiry for the M6 toll concession scheme were transferred to the private sector. This experiment was not successful. The reactions of individuals and organisations to compulsory purchase orders brought by private sector companies, albeit on behalf of a road project for the benefit of the public, was not the same as the reaction to the state. Long delays in the implementation of the planning process also proved costly and impractical.

There will always be categories of road project for which no other business model will be viable. If politically desirable road projects are not bankable, do not offer value for money, or do not transfer sufficient risk way from the public sector, then these projects must be retained. It is not the function of the public sector to underwrite private sector profits, and sometimes roads for the public benefit are unattractive to the private sector. Privatisation, in whatever form, is not always the optimum solution.

In the US, an example of TIFIA financing is the Central Texas Turnpike, a 196-kilometre (122-mile) toll facility in the Austin-San Antonio corridor designed to relieve congestion, improve safety and enhance freight movement through central Texas. A USD 917 million TIFIA loan will finance nearly one-third of the cost of phase one of the project, and the loan will be repaid using toll revenues.

The use of wholly or partly owned public sector subsidiaries, or of agencies, with or without a public sector golden share presents exciting opportunities for public sector control and for the effective application of private sector finance and expertise. This is an evolving issue and further research is needed.

Box 7.2. **The Austrian motorway system and ASFINAG**

Austria has over 2 000 kilometres of motorways and expressways, of which about 7% are tolled through nationwide charging systems. These are run by a public limited-liability company, ASFINAG, the entirety of whose shares are held by the Austrian state. ASFINAG has wide-ranging responsibilities: financing the primary road network; designing, constructing, upgrading, operating and maintaining the network; and collecting tolls (whereby the Austrian state retains the right to set the tolls). Core services are provided by ASFINAG subsidiaries, of which ASFINAG is either the sole owner or a majority shareholder, with minority shares held by the Austrian state.

The company's income stems entirely from user fees in the form of tolls (an electronic distance-related system for vehicles of over 3.5 tons) and vignettes, and receives no grants from the federal budget. It does however issue bonds in its own name. These enjoy AAA rating since repayment of debts is guaranteed by the Republic of Austria. Over the coming years ASFINAG expects to issue bonds in excess of 1 billion euros annually, and between 2002 and 2015 it plans to invest some 7.5 billion euros in extending the network. (Some new highway projects are likely to involve PPP road concessions.)

A prime aim behind the creation of ASFINAG and the electronic toll system was to set the funding of the motorway and expressway system on a sound footing. But it has also had secondary effects: evidence suggests that, as a result of the system, the freight transport sector has improved its efficiency levels (better logistics, better use of loading capacity, more use of other transport modes). More broadly, the Austrian authorities consider the system to be a significant step towards a more just distribution of costs in the road transport sector.

Source: OECD/ECMT Joint Transport Research Centre/World Bank (2005), Regional Round Table 134, 12-13 May, Thessaloniki, Greece.

4.2. Public-private partnership business models

The PPP business model is not a perfected model but a model, or series of models, which continue to evolve as knowledge, experience and expertise of their purpose and capabilities also increases. This process is likely to continue and we believe it is likely to result in two or three robust sub-business models probably based upon franchising, hybrid public-private agencies, and long-term joint venture organisations associated with land use interests. Nevertheless, it seems unlikely that the claims of PPP as being the total solution to all road problems will be borne out by events.

Interestingly, the issue of project failure is becoming important for many public sector partners. There have been problems on a small number of

Box 7.3. **Hungarian Elmka concession**

In emerging markets, the host government usually does not have financial capacity to finance the construction of the road. In Hungary, Elmka was the first concession company formed, registered in September 1993, and was awarded the contract to finance, build and operate the M1/M15. EBRD provided support for the leading syndicate bank which ensured that foreign debt could be secured. The international debt was based in Deutschmarks and USD while revenues were to be collected in local currency.

The project was completed to budget and time, but soon after opening, traffic volumes fell to below the expected levels which induced the concession company to charge tolls that were considered excessive by the public. In setting the toll rate, the SPV company, Elmka, applied a revenue maximisation policy based on the fact that there would only be one toll barrier between the Austrian/Hungarian border and Budapest.

The Hungarian government did not support the concession which could not be sustained under these circumstances and finally Elmka's debts were transferred into sovereign debt and the company was superseded by a state owned SPV NyuMA. The shareholders of Elmka suffered substantial losses, estimated at about EUR 60 million, and received no compensation. The toll rates were reduced by nearly 50% which resulted in an increase in traffic of 15-20% but an overall reduction in revenue of over 45%. However, the project still continues to be an integral part of the Hungarian motorway system and other toll motorways have been successful. A new generation of toll projects is currently being considered for Hungary.

projects with concession holders walking away from projects, or where principals have had to inject additional debt finance in order to maintain the concession and avoid the public humiliation of an abandoned, part built project. One of the major risks is the willingness to pay and the principal's support in the face of public opposition.

Franchising has attractions as one of the subset of PPP models. Primarily it seems to offer the opportunity to allow both the public and private sectors to maximise their respective strengths by adopting different structures for the capital expenditure and the operational expenditure phases of a road project.

In Norway, three tolled highway projects were selected by the government as part of a pilot study to investigate PPP projects in highways. The first of these, the E 39 Klett – Bårdshaug in Sør-Trøndelag County, was opened to the public in 2005 (two months ahead of schedule). The other two are E 39 Lyngdal – Flekkefjord in Vest-Agder County and the E 18 Grimstad – Kristiansand in Aust-Agder County and are still in the pipeline. The private special purpose vehicle (Orkdalsvegen AS)

Box 7.4. **M6 toll project in the UK**

The M6 toll project was commissioned by Midland Expressway Limited to CAMBBA Construction Group. The scheme was constructed mainly to provide a free flowing alternative to the heavily congested M6 motorway and to provide a distributor to the north and east of the West Midlands region.

Midland Expressway Limited (MEL) is the company jointly owned by Macquarie Infrastructure Group of Australia (75% ownership) and Autostrada SpA of Italy (25% ownership) and has the overall responsibility for the financing, design, construction, operation and maintenance of the M6 Toll until 2054, when it will be handed back to the government.

The company awarded the GBP 485 million design and build contract to CAMBBA, a consortium made up of Carillion, Alfred McAlpine, Balfour Beatty and AMEC.

The secretary of state had to acquire the land for which MEL pays an annual rent, as the only length of toll road in an otherwise non-toll network. The combination of high traffic and revenue risk with unregulated tolls is not the best business model for the public.

Box 7.5. **Public sector funding in France, Italy and Spain**

The basic French, Italian and Spanish model is for the public sector funding of the construction of motorways with private or public-private operating companies collecting tolls and maintaining the asset. Today in Spain, 80% of motorways have been built and are maintained with public funds, while 20% have been built and are maintained with user tolls with little variation in level of road services between tolled and untolled roads.

is responsible for construction, operation and financing of the project. The SPV will receive an annual unitary payment over a period of 25 years, but with the actual level of payment being varied according to performance against a number of pre-defined criteria related to political goals of accessibility, performance and safety on the road network. Funding is from state budget in addition to revenues from tolls. Tolls will be collected by an independent intermunicipal road toll (not for profit) state company over a period of 15 years.

Despite some of the limitations outlined above, the basic business model is robust and within certain operating constraints is sustainable for appropriate road projects in the future. The use of both franchising arrangements and maintenance agencies seems likely to become more popular but these can only function effectively if there is sufficient flexibility to allow the commercial and entrepreneurial skills of the private sector to be employed whilst still offering public accountability and protection.

We consider that this model has many strengths whilst offering some flexibility to the principal. There are many variations on the basic model but its main attraction is in being able to use the expertise of the private sector at the most appropriate points in the project life-cycle. Payment systems can be incentive-based to modify private sector behaviour in a positive manner. This range of options makes the business model robust and potentially viable over a long time period.

4.3. Private operation business model

Roads are viewed as a long-term investment and in terms of relative costing the replacement of the entire road carriageway over a route is normally less than 10% of the capital cost of new construction. The majority of the investment in a road is made in earthworks and major structures. New road construction is likely to be part of plans for economic growth in emerging markets and hence likely to attract investment. Increasingly in the developed markets more use is being made of smart systems and regulation to increase capacity without significant capital investment, most investment is concerned with improving safety and relieving congestion.

Clearly the road infrastructure network is a national asset, possibly one of the most valuable, which requires investment in operation and maintenance in order to continue to deliver the required level of service. A road has long-term investment horizons, flexible pavements are designed for a life before major refurbishment or replacement of about 18 years, concrete pavements 40 years and major structures 120 years. Additionally, the road infrastructure users could be charged to generate investment funds for operation and maintenance work.

Over 60% of UK budget is currently invested in road infrastructure management rather than new build. However, there are also sharp divisions between the management of the highly trafficked interurban motorway networks and the remaining majority of road infrastructure in urban and rural road networks. In the UK, the pressure to maintain the operational service levels of motorways was demonstrated by the use of lane rental contracts. Whilst partially effective, the proposed cost benefits were not easy to evaluate and the method of working required from contractors was not sustainable.

One of the major issues of debate is whether the two infrastructure categories will result in a two-tier standard for road levels of service. As it seems likely that the entire road infrastructure will remain in public ownership, the question has to be asked if it is acceptable to have different standards. Pressure on public sector finances may mean that this model moves towards the TOT

Box 7.6. **Private Finance Initiative (PFI) in Portsmouth, UK**

In July 2004, Portsmouth city council signed the first highways management and street scene project to be procured through the Private Finance Initiative (PFI). The project will put the management and maintenance of all 414 kilometres of Portsmouth roads in the hands of a private company for 25 years. In addition to management and maintenance, the contract also includes road cleansing, repairing pot-holes, bringing street lights up to modern standards bridges, structures, street lighting, maintenance of traffic management equipment, highways-related tree and grounds maintenance, winter maintenance and street cleansing and managing the highways with regards to licences and inspections. Portsmouth city council's requirement reflected a "Highway Asset Maintenance" approach, the essence of which is that the city's road network – substantially failing and suffering from lack of investment – should first be rehabilitated and then sustained at the improved level by planned life cycle maintenance. This offers better value for money than the traditional annual works programme that responds only to immediate and acute need.

The contract includes upgrading, over a core investment period of five years, some 414 kilometres of highway network, including roads, bridges, street lighting and footways.The adoption of whole life costing approach was thought of as a way of achieving value for money. The city council will finance about GBP 300 million of project costs with the rest financed by Department for Transport by a special PFI credits grant. The scheme was awarded to Ensign Highways, a special purpose vehicle (SPV) owned by Colas Ltd. and its parent Colas SA. The contract is based around a core investment period of five years following a mobilisation period to prepare for service commencement. The SPV will fund the core investment through a senior debt facility. Other services will be carried out concurrently to generate revenue streams that are paid by the council as infrastructure starts to meets specified standards. The unitary charge is based principally upon availability and performance, but also includes an element related to usage by heavy goods vehicles.

The main aim was defined as providing the public with safe, attractive, clean and accessible streets. At a strategic level, the contract delivers a long-term strategy capable of halting the decline in highways asset value and restoring the condition of the network to a point where sustainable maintenance is achieved utilising the principles of whole-life costing.

option with the user paying for O&M. Pricing or payment should rationally be based on some form of tariff which reflects accessibility, safety, quality. The gradual implementation of monitoring and regulating technology offers the prospect of moving away from rather simplistic blanket tariffs to a dedicated charging mechanism with transparent links between the toll and the users. This would improve the social "willingness to pay" of users and provide flexibility for the operators to match costs of operation and maintenance to categories of user. Without a clear relationship between charge and service, this business model might be liable to public opposition and could become unworkable.

4.4. *Private business model*

Purely privately financed models are only viable for road infrastructure projects where both the social and political desirability and the financial analysis are positive; and these projects are relatively small in number. These are the projects usually selected by the public sector to encourage the industrial culture change necessary to undertake work with private finance. A number of variants have been used to provide greater flexibility for the private sector; but as the market in both developed and emerging markets matures, these projects tend to disappear. The model is not robust or sustainable.

We are also aware that there are a number of land-use revenue business models, including in the UK where the Highways Agency and its managing agents plus 20 specialist contractors, such as Hanson Construction Projects, came together in August 2002 to form the CMC, a vehicle designed to deliver

Box 7.7. **Private bonds and state infrastructure banks in the US**

In the US, the SAFETEA-LU legislation includes provision for exempt facility bonds which are private bonds issued to finance various types of facilities owned or used by private entities and are municipal securities where more than 10% of the issue proceeds are used by private businesses and the payment of more than 10% principal or interest are secured by private businesses.

State infrastructure banks are continued under SAFETEA-LU. Although such banks or funds can take many different forms, they are generally established at the state level with capitalisation from federal and state funding. These banks can provide financial assistance through loans and credit enhancement/guarantees including bond insurance, loan guarantees, capital reserves, letters and lines of credit.

Consequently, the BOT business model has been used in its differing forms on numerous transport and highway projects. The Republic Act 7718 of 1993 recognizes a range of BOT business models variants including BLT, BOO, BT, and BTO. Additionally, in a move close to a franchise business model, private entities could own toll facilities and states could loan federal aid to private or public agencies to construct the facility.

Table 7.5. **Future trends and business models**

Future trends	Public	PPPs	Private operation	Private
Demand growth	High flexibility to address both congestion problems in developed markets and development projects in emerging markets.	Limited flexibility through re-negotiation but innovative mechanisms continuing to evolve.	Increased pressure on performance in maintaining service levels.	Few projects provide a sufficiently robust cash flow.
Investment	Increasing trend towards investment in road operation, safety and maintenance rather than new build.	Increasing trend towards investment in road operation, safety and maintenance rather than new build.	Business model may distort balance between roads procured by private finance and the remaining road network.	Limited scope most viable projects already "cherry picked", excess profits usually taxed or shared.
Availability of capital	Tight public sector budget constraints in OECD countries.	Access to private finance markets but public sector participation necessary to make projects bankable or operable. Basel II. Innovative land use financing models.	Increasingly based on a user-pays principle. Role for new technology for user charging.	Access to private finance markets but in competition with other risk-based investment opportunities.
Pricing and rationing	Strong position as public sector controls fuel taxes and regulates other transport media. Variable tolls DSCR and GPS based systems.	Tolls used as incentives to reflect users impact on environment and location. DSCR and GPS based systems.	Effectively network charging.	Revert to free use after concession period?
Governance	Clear demonstration of public support. Poor record.	PPP's tending towards hybrid franchising and agencies.	Regulation by public sector but implantation by private sector.	Not an effective long-term model.

GBP 300 million of road and structural maintenance projects over seven years. However, we recognise that this form of business model could equally be regarded as a variant on the PPP franchise business model.

5. Implications for policy

The main dimensions of road policy are:

- Provision of existing networks.
- Pricing and taxation.
- Planning of new investment.
- Pricing of new capacity.
- Funding and financing of new capacity.
- Economic regulation of franchises.

5.1. *Network provision*

We believe that responsibility and ultimate ownership will remain firmly in the hands of government. The public good characteristics of roads as rights of access for traffic of all kinds from pedestrians to heavy goods vehicles and to gas, water and other utilities beneath the road surface make outright privatisation too controversial as a general policy. Even the division of responsibility between national, regional and local road provision is difficult enough without introducing a public-private discussion.

This means, therefore, that the role of the private sector in much of the sector is as a contractor to central, regional or local government. Contracting roles can include everything from planning, consulting and scientific analysis, through to reconstruction, maintenance and operational services, such as snow clearing. In a number of countries, it is at this practical level where organisational change has been greatest – public authorities have changed from being employers of large direct labour organisations to being clients for services delivered by the private sector.

In this area, one of the most interesting questions concerns the organisation of national roads administration itself. There are a number of arguments for an arm's-length agency such as the Highways Agency in the UK. These include depoliticisation of executive responsibilities and separation of responsibility for road scheme promotion from the assessment and decision-making process; this separation is reflected in the arrangements in Sweden also.

5.2. *Pricing and taxation*

Responsibility for taxation of fuel and vehicles will remain with government whatever the organisational arrangements in the road sector. For the reasons given above, we believe that the most likely prospect for network road-user charging will involve tariff reform (*i.e.* changes to vehicle and fuel taxation also), and therefore we see congestion pricing taking place with central or local government as the responsible principal. Of course there will be many private sector agents in the chain contracted to deliver and maintain the street hardware and on-board vehicle units and to perform the back-office contract with the ultimate traffic and revenue risks being taken by the public authorities. Depending on the arrangements, some form of recycling of ring fenced revenues into city infrastructure investment may be a feature of the scheme. Again, depending on the form of organisation, a series of limited interoperable schemes owned by local governments but managed by a single agent and with single billing may be more likely than a single national scheme. However, this is a long way off and it is easier to see the desired end-state than the route from here to there. It is possible that even though the prices are set by public authorities, some form of independent regulator may be needed.

5.3. Planning of new investment

We believe that responsibility for the planning of new capacity will remain with government and its agencies. This will include route location, geometric design and the securing of planning permission and political decision to proceed. Experience suggests that transferring the pre-decision risks to the private sector is inappropriate since there is little or no control over the risk and a correspondingly heavy premium has to be paid. Once the route location and layout decisions have been made the "how" risks associated with construction and operation are potentially transferable under BOT.

5.4. Pricing and provision of new capacity

Here, it is important to decide first what the purpose of tolling is. If a policy decision is taken (as with the M6 toll road in the UK) that a road project may proceed provided it is built "off-balance sheet", then the purpose of tolls is to generate enough revenue to remunerate the capital. However, we believe: *a)* that there are relatively few such fully commercial opportunities; and *b)* that the result can be serious pricing inefficiency and resource misallocation.

The question which needs to be posed at the outset is – from a social point of view – what toll level/structure is it sensible to charge on new capacity? This could vary considerably according to:

- Congestion conditions in the corridor.
- The quality of the all-purpose network and therefore the likely level of diversion.
- The desire and ability to extract a premium for higher quality.
- The feasibility of differentiated tariffs by vehicle type, time of day, etc.
- The shadow price of public funds and the opportunity value of replacing 1 euro of public finance by 1 euro of toll revenue.

We would strongly recommend that a traffic model and economic appraisal which is capable of testing alternative pricing strategies and their effects on traffic volumes and routing should be an integral part of the planning process. The purpose of this is to illuminate the relevant trade-offs between revenues, costs and user benefits. Only then, when an efficient pricing strategy has been found, should consideration be given to how best to administer the strategy. This will depend on the mix of public and private (through tolls) finance that is required and on the assessed desirability of transferring the traffic and revenue risks to a franchisee, and the likely risk premium which will need to be paid.

Once that decision has been reached, then the various organisational options reviewed in this chapter are opened up. In general we favour a significant degree of public control over toll setting, either directly by government as principal, or with the involvement of a regulator. However, circumstances alter cases and where: *a)* a road is socially desirable; and *b)* the only way to get it built is through private debt raised against future toll contributions, then a less "hands-on" regime will be appropriate.

5.5. Concluding thoughts

Overall, we think it is wrong and dangerous to view PPPs as a panacea which can or should relax the financial, political, economic and social constraints on road investment. However, what we think is true is that once there is a public commitment to road investment in a corridor, then especially for international projects with many principals, an overarching delivery agency, operating within a framework on behalf of the principals (member states, EU) may be the best mechanism to achieve what governments have agreed to do. The various models discussed above with their attendant features of risk transfer, the winner's curse, floor and ceiling models, flexible remuneration periods, refinancing rules and so on are then available. Delivery may be of the capital project or of the operation and management or of the pricing regime or a mixture. The crucial task for governments is to work out which part of the total package the private sector can genuinely do better and more cost-effectively.

Bibliography

Bain, R. and J.W. Plantagie (2004), "Smooth Ride for European Tolls in 2004, but Twists and Turns Ahead", *Standard and Poors Infrastructure Finance Note*, London.

Bain, R. and M. Wilkins (2002), "The Evolution of DBFO Payment Mechanisms: One More for the Road", *Standard and Poors Infrastructure Finance Note*, London.

Bellier, M. *et al.* (2003), *Private Participation in Infrastructure in China*, World Bank, Washington DC.

Button, K. (2004), "The Rationale for Road Pricing", *Research in Transportation Economics*, Vol. 9, Elsevier Ltd.

Capka, J.R. (2006), "Financing Megaprojects", *Public Roads*, Vol. 69, No. 4.

De Palma, A. *et al.* (2002), *Overview of policies, markets and institutional and technological issues*, MC-ICAM Task 4.1 Report, *www.its.leeds.ac.uk/projects/mcicam/index.html.*

Edwards, P., J. Shaoul, A. Stafford and L. Arblaster (2004), *Evaluating the Operation of PFI in Roads and Hospitals*, ACCA Research Report No. 84, Certified Accountants Educational Trust, London.

Estache, A., M. Romero and J. Strong (2000), "The Long and Winding Path to Private Financing and the Regulation of Toll Roads", *World Bank Policy Research*, Working Paper No. 2387, World Bank Institute.

European Commission (EC) (1998), Fair Payment for Infrastructure Use: A Phased Approach to a Common Transport Infrastructure Charging Framework in the EU, *White Paper*, COM (98) 466, EC, Brussels.

EC (2001), *European Transport Policy to 2010: Time to Decide*, White Paper, COM (01) 370, EC, Brussels.

Fayard, A. (2003), *Analysis of Highway Concessions in Europe*, Conference on Highways Costing and Regulation in Europe, Bergamo, Italy.

Federal Highway Administration, US Department of Transport (2006), *Federal Register*, Vol. 71, No. 4.

Gannon, M.J. (2004), "A Review of Techniques Used to Assess the Credibility of a Business Case in Public Sector Rail Projects", Proceedings of Computers in Railways IX, 17-19 May, Dresden, Germany.

Hai Yang and Qiang Meng (2000), "Highway Pricing and Capacity Choice in a Road Network under a Build-Operate-Transfer Scheme", *Transportation Research Part A*, Pergamon Press.

Hai, Yang and M.G.H. Bell (1997), "Traffic Restraint, Road Pricing and Network Equilibrium", *Transportation Research*, B31, pp. 257-278.

Heald, D. (1997), Privately Financed Capital in Public Services, *Manchester School*, Vol. 65, Issue 5, pp. 568-598.

Highways Agency Procurement Strategy (2006), *Delivering Best Value Solutions and Services*, *www.highways.gov.uk*.

IASON (undated), *Integrated Appraisal of Spatial, Economic and Network Effects of Transport, Investments and Policies*, *www.inro.tno.nl/iason*.

Irigoyen, J.L. (2006), *Public Private Partnerships in Highways – International Experience and Lessons for Success*, World Bank Transport Learning Week, April, Washington DC.

Levy, S.M. (1996), *Build Operate Transfer – Paving the way for tomorrow's infrastructure*, John Wiley and Sons Inc., New York.

May, A.D. and A. Sumalee A. (2003), "One Step Forward, Two Steps Back? An Overview of Road Pricing Application and Research Outside the US", *International Symposium on Road Pricing*, 19-22 November, Key Biscayne.

Mackie, P.J. and N.J. Smith (2005), "Financing Roads in Great Britain", in Ragazzi, R. and W. Rothengatter (eds.), *Procurement and Financing of Motorways in Europe*, *Research in Transportation Economics*, Vol. 15, Elsevier Ltd.

Merna, A. and N.J. Smith (1996), "Projects Procured by Privately Financed Concession Contracts", *Asia Law and Practice*, Vol. 1 and 2, Hong Kong, China.

Nash, C. and E. Niskanen (2003), *Experiences in Road Pricing in Europe – A Review of Research and Practice*, Institute of Local Government Studies, Denmark.

National Audit Office (1998), *The Private Finance Initiative: The First Four Design, Build, Finance and Operate Roads Contracts*, HC476, Stationery Office, London.

Nickesen, A. and M. Stanfield (2000), "Toll Road Securitization in China", *Roads and Highways*, TopicNoteRH-3, World Bank, Washington DC.

OECD (2006), *Infrastructure to 2030: Telecom, Land Transport, Water and Electricity*, OECD, Paris.

Operations and Products (2006), Foundation (Hanson Ltd.), *www.hansonplc.com/files/pdf/magazine/2006/2006Q1.pdf*.

Øresundsbrokionsortiet Annual report (2005), *http://osb.oeresundsbron.dk*.

Orosz, C.G.S. (2001), "The Effects of Toll Motorway in Hungary", *Proceedings of the AET European Transport Conference*, 10-12 September, Cambridge, PTRC Education and Research Services Ltd., London.

PROFIT jointly with the research team (2001), *Private Operation and Financing of Trans-European Networks – Public Private Partnerships*, Project for the European Commission, DG TREN 5th Framework RTD project ST – 98 – SC.3035.

Queiroz, C. (2005), *Launching Public Private Partnerships for Highways in Transition Economies*, World Bank Transport Paper TP9, Washington DC.

Ramjerdi, F., H. Minken and K. Ostonoe (2004), "Norwegian Urban Tolls", in *Research in Transportation Economics*, Vol. 9, Elsevier Ltd.

Rietveld P., Woudenberg van Stefan (2005), "Why Fuel Prices Differ", *Energy Economics*, Vol. 29, No. 1, pp. 79-92.

Santos, G. (ed.) (2004), "Road Pricing: Theory and Evidence", in *Research in Transportation Economics*, Vol. 9, Elsevier Ltd.

Smith, A.J. (1999), *Privatized Infrastructure – The Role of Government*, Thomas Telford Publishing, London.

Tan, Y. (2006), unpublished PhD thesis, University of Leeds, UK.

Tanczos, K. and G.S. Kong (2001), "Experiences of Using Toll Road and Possibility for Public Private Partnership with Special Respect to Eastern Europe and Some Asian Countries", in *Proceedings of the AET European Transport Conference*, 10-12 September, Cambridge, PTRC Education and Research Services Ltd., London UK.

UK Department for Transport (DfT) (2005), *Transport Appraisal: Wider Economic Benefits and Impacts on GDP*, London, *www.dft.gov.uk/stellent/groups/dft_econappr/documents/page/dft_econappr_038893.pdf*.

Von Hirschhausen, C. and B. Meinhart (2001), "Infrastructure Policies and Liberalisation in East European Transition Countries – Would Less Have Been More?", Annual Congress of the European Economic Association, Université de Lausanne, Switzerland.

World Bank (2005), "China – The National Expressway System: A Retrospective Initiating Memorandum", 20 December, Washington DC.

ISBN 978-92-64-03131-9
Infrastructure to 2030 – Vol. 2
Mapping Policy for Electricity, Water and Transport

Members of the Infrastructure Project Steering Group

The Steering Group

At the beginning of the OECD Futures Project on "Global Infrastructure Needs: Prospects and Implications for Public and Private Actors", a Steering Group was set up to provide overall advice to the OECD Project Team. It was composed of high-ranking experts and decision makers from public and private entities in infrastructure and infrastructure-related sectors that contributed financially to the project. There were four meetings of the Steering Group over the course of the project (June 2005, December 2005, June 2006 and December 2006).

Chairman

Michael OBORNE, Director of the OECD International Futures Programme (IFP), assisted by Barrie STEVENS, Deputy Director of the OECD IFP, and Pierre-Alain SCHIEB, Counsellor and Head of Futures Projects, OECD IFP. The IFP is part of the OECD Advisory Unit on Multidisciplinary Issues to the Secretary-General.

The members

Some members of the Steering Group were replaced during the two years of the Infrastructure Project and/or assisted by other experts from their organisations. The representatives of those organisations are listed below (titles and affiliations are those held during the course of the project).

Andrea de BENEDETTI
Commercial Director
Alstom Transport
France

Daniel BIENVENUE
Secrétaire Associé, Modernisation de l'État
Secrétariat du Conseil du trésor
Gouvernement du Québec
Canada

Karine BIGOT
Chargée d'affaires
Alstom Transport
France

Guy BUJOLD
Senior Assistant Deputy Minister
Policy and Communications
Infrastructure Canada
Canada

Lowri DAVIES
Research and Technology Strategy Division
Department for Transport
United Kingdom

Juan Carlos DELRIEU
Director, Chief Economist
CEMEX
Mexico

Gérard DÉPOND
Stratégie et Prospective
Réseau Ferré de France
France

Thomas EGEBO
Permanent Secretary
Ministry of Transport and Energy
Denmark

Jean FAUSSURIER
Délégué aux affaires européennes et internationales
Réseau Ferré de France
France

Emmanuel FAVRE-BULLE
Chargé de missions, Services économiques et statistiques
Ministère de l'Équipement, des Transports du Logement du Tourisme et de la Mer
France

Paulo Manuel Cadete FERRÃO
Associate Professor
Instituto Superior Técnico
Technical University of Lisbon
representing GRICES
Portugal

Philippe GRATADOUR
Chargé de la sous-direction des actions internationales
Ministère de l'Équipement
France

Sylvie GRONDIN
Secrétaire associée, Sous-secrétariat à la modernisation de l'État
Secrétariat du Conseil du trésor
Gouvernement du Québec
Canada

François GROSSIORD
Analyses Stratégiques
SNCF
France

Gérard HALAUNBRENNER
Analyses Stratégiques
SNCF
France

Per Skrumsager HANSEN
Special Consultant
representing
Thomas EGEBO
Permanent Secretary
Ministry of Transport and Energy
Denmark

Margaret HILL
Director of Research and Analysis
Infrastructure Canada
Canada

Birger HÖÖK
Director
Traffic Registry
Swedish Road Administration
Sweden

John HULTÉN
Analyst
Swedish Road Administration
Sweden

Massimo IEZZONI
Directeur général
Communauté métropolitaine de Montréal
Canada

Casimiro IGLESIAS
Directeur général de Planification
Ministerio de Fomento
Spain

Jean-Christophe LASSERRE
Chargé de missions, Bureau des exportations
Ministère de l'Équipement, des Transports du Logement du Tourisme et de la Mer
France

Richard LAVERGNE
Secrétaire général de l'Observatoire de l'énergie
Ministère Économie, Finances et Industrie
Observatoire énergie
France

Rt Hon Lord MACDONALD of Tradeston
Chairman, Macquarie Investment Banking Group
Europe

Mauricio MORA
World wide Chief Economist
CEMEX
Mexico

José Antonio MORENO
Directeur Technique de la DG de Planification
Ministerio de Fomento
Spain

Alvaro ORTIZ
Chief Economist, Europe
CEMEX
Mexico

Ove PETTERSSON
Senior Analyst
VINNOVA – Swedish Agency for Innovation Systems
Sweden

Stephane PINEAULT
Conseiller
representing
Massimo IEZZONI
Directeur général
Communauté métropolitaine de Montréal
Canada

Grégoire POSTEL-VINAY
Chef de l'Observatoire des stratégies industrielles
Ministère de l'Économie, des Finances et de l'Industrie
France

Michel ROCHEFORT
Conseiller en recherche à la direction générale
Communauté métropolitaine de Montréal
Canada

Kåre SCHJETNE
Deputy
CEO
Statnett SF
Norway

Helga THEIL THOMSEN
Deputy Permanent Secretary
Head of Resource Department
Ministry of Transport and Energy
Denmark

Toon VAN DER HOORN
Director, Strategic Models and Forecasts
AVV Transport Research Centre
Ministry of Transport, Public Works and Water Management
The Netherlands

Jean VERSEILLE
Directeur Développement du Réseau
Réseau de Transport d'Électricité (RTE)
France

Frederik VON DEWALL
General Manager and Chief Economist
ING Group
The Netherlands

Hans WERDER
Secrétaire général
Département fédéral de l'environnement, des transports, de l'énergie
et de la communication
Switzerland

Matthew WHITE
Head of Science Evidence and Expertise Branch, Evidence and Research Strategy
Department for Transport
United Kingdom

Miles YARRINGTON
Project Leader, Intelligent Infrastructure Systems
Foresight Directorate, Office of Science and Technology
Department of Trade and Industry
United Kingdom

Experts Involved in the Infrastructure Project

Contributing experts

Experts were called upon to draft papers and provide comments on the various topics addressed by the project. The list below includes the authors of the papers that were published in the two Infrastructure to 2030 books. (Titles and affiliations are those held during the course of the project.)

Christian ALBRECHT
Head, Transport Policy Section
Federal Office for Spatial Development (ARE), Switzerland

Michel ANDRIEU
Consultant, OECD International Futures Programme, France

Richard ASHLEY
Adrian CASHMAN
Pennine Water Group
Department of Civil and Structural Engineering
University of Sheffield, United Kingdom

Colin BLACKMAN
Editor
Foresight and Shaping Tomorrow, United Kingdom

Erik BOHLIN
Head of Division, Associate Professor
Division of Technology and Society
Department of Technology Management and Economics
Chalmers University of Technology, Sweden

Heather COOLEY, Research Associate
Peter H. GLEICK, President
Meena PALANIAPPAN, Senior Research Associate
Gary WOLFF, Principal Economist and Engineer
Pacific Institute for Studies in Development, Environment and Security, United States

Yves CROZET
Professor, University of Lyon 2
Director, Transport Economics Laboratory
Joint Research Unit (CNRS) No. 5593, France

Simon FORGE
SCF Associates Ltd., United Kingdom

Peter J. MACKIE
Nigel J. SMITH
Professors, Institute for Transport Studies
University of Leeds, United Kingdom

Trevor MORGAN
Menencon Consulting, France

Anil SHARMA
Visiting Professor of Transport
Department of Civil Engineering and Geosciences
University of Newcastle upon Tyne, United Kingdom

David STAMBROOK
Virtuosity Consulting, Canada

Louis S. THOMSPON
Thompson, Galenson and Associates, United States

Rob VAN DER HEIJDEN, Professor of Transport and Spatial Planning
Erwin VAN DER KRABBEN
Bas ZONNENBERG
Institute for Management Research
Nijmigen School of Management
Radboud University, the Netherlands

OECD experts

OECD colleagues were called upon to provide comments on draft papers so as to ensure that the work conducted by the project team fully took into account related work in other parts of the Organisation.

Peter BORKEY
Administrator, Urban Water Sector Reform, GFII
Environment Directorate

Mary CRASS
Principal Administrator, Transport Policy (Urban Travel, Accessibility, Crime and Security)
European Council of Ministers of Transport (ECMT)

Xavier LEFLAIVE
Principal Administrator, Environmental Finance
Environment Directorate

Stephen PERKINS
Principal Administrator, Transport Policy (Railways, Social Costs, Transport and Environment)
Joint OECD/ECMT Transport Research Centre

Paul SCHREYER
Head of Division, Prices and Structural Economics Statistics
Statistics Directorate

Colin STACEY
Administrator
Joint OECD/ECMT Transport Research Centre

John WHITE
Head
Joint OECD/ECMT Transport Research Centre

Dimitri YPSILANTI
Principal Administrator, Communications Policies and Regulatory Reform
Directorate for Science, Technology and Industry

OECD PUBLICATIONS, 2, rue André-Pascal, 75775 PARIS CEDEX 16
PRINTED IN FRANCE
(03 2007 03 1 P) ISBN 978-92-64-03131-9 – No. 55619 2007